The Democratic Soul

The Democratic Soul

A
Wilson Carey McWilliams Reader

Wilson Carey McWilliams

Edited by Patrick J. Deneen
and Susan J. McWilliams

THE UNIVERSITY PRESS OF KENTUCKY

Scholarly publisher for the Commonwealth,
serving Bellarmine University, Berea College, Centre College of Kentucky,
Eastern Kentucky University, The Filson Historical Society, Georgetown
College, Kentucky Historical Society, Kentucky State University, Morehead
State University, Murray State University, Northern Kentucky University,
Transylvania University, University of Kentucky, University of Louisville,
and Western Kentucky University.

Editorial and Sales Offices: The University Press of Kentucky
663 South Limestone Street, Lexington, Kentucky 40508-4008
www.kentuckypress.com

15 14 13 12 11   5 4 3 2 1

Library of Congress Cataloging-in-Publication Data

McWilliams, Wilson C.
    The democratic soul : a Wilson Carey McWilliams reader / Wilson Carey
McWilliams ; edited by Patrick J. Deneen and Susan J. McWilliams.
       p. cm.
    Includes bibliographical references and index.
    ISBN 978-0-8131-3013-2 (hardcover : alk. paper)
    ISBN 978-0-8131-3370-6 (ebook)
    1. Democracy—United States. 2. United States—Politics and government—
Philosophy. I. Deneen, Patrick J., 1964-   II. McWilliams, Susan Jane, 1977-
III. Title.
    JK1764.M394 2011
    320.973—dc22   2011008530

Contents

Acknowledgments   vii

"A Better Sort of Love": An Introduction to the Life and Thought of
Wilson Carey McWilliams   1
  Patrick J. Deneen and Susan J. McWilliams

Part 1. Political Thought in America

Liberty, Equality, and the Problem of Community   21

Religion and the American Founding   44

Civil Religion in the Age of Reason: Thomas Paine on Liberalism,
Redemption, and Revolution   56

The Anti-Federalists   92

Standing at Armageddon: Morality and Religion in Progressive
Thought   98

America's Two Voices in a World of Nations   120

Part 2. Political Thinkers

George Orwell and Ideology   133

Reinhold Niebuhr: New Orthodoxy for Old Liberalism   141

Community and Its Discontents: On Amitai Etzioni and the Future of
Communitarianism   162

Bertrand de Jouvenel on Politics and Political Science in America   178

Leo Strauss and the Dignity of American Political Thought   192

Power After Power: Reflections on Liberalism in Sheldon Wolin's *Politics
and Vision*   207

Part 3. Theory and Practice

On Time and History   229

On Political Illegitimacy   240

Civil Disobedience and Contemporary Constitutionalism:
The American Case   265

The Case for Censorship, Rightly Understood   286

Equality and Citizenship: The Rights of Man and the Rights
of Women   293

Honor in Contemporary American Politics   319

Part 4. Democracy as a Moral Enterprise

Democracy as Means and End   329

The Search for a Public Philosophy   336

Toward Genuine Self-Government   353

Democratic Multiculturalism   361

Critical Rebound: Why America Needs a Catholic Recovery   371

Religion, Morality, and Public Life   380

Index   399

Acknowledgments

Wilson Carey McWilliams—Carey to all his friends—was a prolific author. However, with the exception of his one magisterial book—*The Idea of Fraternity in America*—and several collections of his quadrennial essays, "The Meaning of the Election," Carey preferred to write and publish essays rather than books, and to scatter those publications widely. Also, until the last years of his life, he preferred using his old manual typewriter rather than a computer. These two facts—far-flung publications and few that didn't need to be retyped—made this a particularly daunting project. More than cursory thanks are owed for the many hands that made this collection possible.

First, shortly after Carey's death, several friends at Rutgers University began the process of indexing his considerable writings. Professor Dennis Bathory—longtime friend and colleague as well as student of Carey from his days at Oberlin College—received painstaking and detailed assistance from Alina Vamanu in putting together a comprehensive list of Carey's publications and unpublished pieces. This information was invaluable in helping the editors to track down many difficult-to-find articles.

Second, a note of special thanks is owed in acknowledgment of the extraordinary efforts of Sean Beienburg, who typed nearly all of Carey's writings into electronic format. He also provided valuable counsel to the editors and, it's safe to say, may have the most comprehensive knowledge of Carey's written work of anyone alive. The fortune is his, though it was hard earned, and the editors are extremely grateful for his Herculean efforts. Thanks also go to the Mellon Post-baccalaureate Fellowship Program at Pomona College, which supported Sean during the year he spent working on this volume.

We would also like to thank Rachel Blum Spencer, who worked assiduously toward the conclusion of the project securing permissions from the original publishers of Carey's essays. This involved not a little detective work and extraordinary patience on her part, testimony to Carey's egalitarian efforts to publish with both the great and the obscure.

We are grateful to Dennis Hale and Marc Landy for their friendship and counsel and for their undying allegiance to their and our teacher.

Lastly, the editors would like to thank Nancy Riley McWilliams and the Estate of Wilson Carey McWilliams for permission to republish these writings. It is a blessing for those who knew him and will never have enough of his good companionship. But perhaps even more, this collection is a gift to those who never had the great pleasure of spending time with Carey. Reading these essays, it must be acknowledged, will always prove a poor substitute to Carey's company, but they are a treasure all the same, and undeniably capture the voice, the wit, the brilliance, and the utter decency of Wilson Carey McWilliams.

"A Better Sort of Love"

An Introduction to the Life and Thought of Wilson Carey McWilliams

Patrick J. Deneen and Susan J. McWilliams

Wilson Carey McWilliams was born on September 2, 1933, in Santa Monica, California. His was a pre-freeway, pre-plastic Los Angeles: a city of barely more than a million people still dominated by what he later remembered as a "provincial, boosterish" mind-set, with "its numberless improbabilities always hinting at great possibilities."[1]

It was also a city that McWilliams experienced not as a "city of strangers," but as the home of his large, extended family. By his own account, it was a family of titans. His mother's family, the Hedricks, was a formidable clan of German and Dutch descent that placed great emphasis on education—sending all daughters as well as sons to college, long before doing so was considered fashionable or even appropriate. During McWilliams's childhood, his grandfather Earle Raymond Hedrick, a renowned mathematician and associate of Albert Einstein, served as the provost and vice president of the University of California, Los Angeles, and was well ensconced in the city's intellectual elite. McWilliams's maternal grandmother had received a doctoral degree from the University of Göttingen before she had her ten children, and McWilliams was surrounded by Hedrick aunts and uncles, most of whom were educators and many of whom had advanced degrees. His mother, Dorothy Hedrick McWilliams, was a UCLA graduate with a career as a high school teacher.

If his mother's family members were titans of the academic sort, his father's family produced titans with a decidedly political bent. McWilliams's grandfather, who died before he was born, had been a prominent cattle rancher and Democratic state senator in Colorado. And his father, Carey McWilliams, a California journalist then best known for his writings about migrant farm labor, would go on to edit the *Nation* magazine. Carey McWilliams, a self-proclaimed radical, was from early in his career a prominent public figure, targeted and often threatened for his controversial commitment to racial equality and his attention to the marginal and disenfranchised.

In light of these early familial influences, it seems almost fated that McWilliams would become a political scientist, a relentless intellectual, and a dedicated educator possessed of an unusually keen political insight and committed to seeking the wisdom contained in unpopular or "alternative" points of view.

But the familial closeness of his earliest years was not the only formative influence on McWilliams's life, for, like the provincial Los Angeles of his youth, it was not to last. His parents decided to dissolve their marriage in 1941, necessitating a brief move to Reno, Nevada—the establishment of residency in that state then being the easiest way to acquire a no-fault divorce—and then a series of subsequent moves around California. The transience of those years was a stark contrast to the stability that had characterized his life before, surely underpinning much of McWilliams's later emphasis on the value of rootedness and his attention to the costs of America's culture of mobility.

McWilliams and his mother eventually settled in the Central Valley town of Merced, where in 1951 he graduated from Merced High School. It was here that McWilliams first discovered and refined his skills as a debater—William F. Buckley Jr. would later call McWilliams the most formidable debater in the United States—as a member of his school's forensics team. And the experience of living in Merced, then a railroad town surrounded by farm country, reinforced his appreciation for small communities with strong local ties.

McWilliams graduated from the University of California at Berkeley in 1955, funded in part through a U.S. Army ROTC scholarship, and after graduation he served in the Eleventh Airborne Division of the army for two years, remaining in active reserve service with the Ninety-first Division until 1961. Having considered but ultimately deciding against a lifetime military career, he returned to Berkeley, where he received his master's and doctorate degrees under the tutelage of the eminent political theorists Norman Jacobson, John Schaar, and Sheldon Wolin. Each of these great teachers influenced McWilliams in distinct ways, but together they instilled in him a deep and abiding love of the great texts and arguments of the history of political thought. Words McWilliams spoke about Wolin at the time of his mentor's retirement might summarize his experience of all three teachers: "A secular agora, [their] classrooms were also part sanctuary, places where politics took on a grace and mystery." At Berkeley, McWilliams also helped to found the activist student group SLATE, one of the first formal organizations of the New Left.

In 1961, McWilliams took a position in the government department at Oberlin College, where he involved himself in the ferment of the 1960s and found great success as a classroom teacher. Largely based on his energizing experience at Oberlin, McWilliams would remain a fierce advocate of liberal arts colleges all his life, although he left Oberlin in 1967 to spend most of the rest of his career at larger universities: first at Brooklyn College and then at Rutgers University, where he taught from 1970 until his death in 2005. McWilliams also had visiting and summer appointments at Berkeley, Fordham University, Harvard University, Haverford College, Lafayette College, the State University of New York at Buffalo, UCLA, and Yale University. At all those institutions, McWilliams sought out the company of students, preferring face-to-face mentorship in and out of the classroom to the more impersonal formats of academic publishing.

And yet, as this volume testifies, McWilliams's publication record was substantial in terms of both scope and quality. His most famous work, *The Idea of Fraternity in America,* appeared in 1973 to high acclaim, receiving the National Historical Society Prize in 1974. He became a prolific essayist, his writing appearing regularly in journals such as *Commonweal* and *Newsday* and throughout his career dividing his time equally between high theoretical examination and penetrating contemporary political analysis. He wrote extraordinarily well-regarded essays on the meaning of each American presidential election, essays that were eventually collected in his two later volumes, *The Politics of Disappointment* (1995) and *Beyond the Politics of Disappointment* (2000).

McWilliams was the recipient of numerous professional honors, including the John Witherspoon Award for Distinguished Service to the Humanities. He taught a series of summer seminars for teachers under grants from the National Endowment for the Humanities and served on several editorial boards. He held key positions in the American Political Science Association, including vice president and secretary, and he was active at Rutgers on numerous committees and task forces.

But it is worth noting that for the last thirty years of his life, McWilliams cultivated his community life alongside his professional one. He made a home with his wife, the psychoanalyst and author Nancy Riley

McWilliams, and their two daughters in Flemington, New Jersey. McWilliams became a fixture of the local scene, serving briefly as a town councilman and spending many terms as an elected member of the Hunterdon County Democratic Committee. He was an elder in the Flemington Presbyterian Church and a member of the Hunterdon County Historical Society—living, much as he taught his students to live, a life made valuable through citizenship, association, sacrifice, and friendship.

In one of his last publications, McWilliams described the novelist James Baldwin in words that might easily apply to himself: "He was a fervent critic of the American regime because he was an anguished lover, and nothing is clearer in [his] work than the depth of his concern for American public life and culture."[2] McWilliams too was an "anguished lover" of America, discerning that the nation, born at least partly of the Enlightenment, was worthy of love not *because* of its official philosophy but *in spite* of it. Throughout his writing, McWilliams recommended "a better sort of love": the love between and among citizens, one evoking an older model of citizens as friends—not the self-love that lies at the heart of liberal theory and that at least in part officially undergirded the American founding.

The kernel of McWilliams's thought lies in his insight that the official creed of America—the liberalism of Hobbes and Locke, premised upon the belief that humans are prepolitically individual and whole—is fundamentally a false anthropology, and thus cannot serve as the basis of a viable regime. To the extent that liberalism seems to have proven successful, McWilliams argued, that success is attributable to a preliberal inheritance relying on nonliberal assumptions and relationships—particularly those at the heart of the family and the neighborhood, but also ones that must infuse the schools, the economy, and ultimately the polity itself. "Liberal society is a kind of moral school which must be protected against the logic of liberal theory, walled off and governed according to different precepts," he argued.[3] McWilliams held that America's better and truer pedigree lies in its "unofficial" founding, that "alternative tradition" he plumbed often in the country's religious, literary, and immigrant traditions. The evocative cadences of this, what he called "America's Second Voice," he discerned in such authors and thinkers as the Puritans, the Anti-Federalists, Nathaniel Hawthorne, Herman Melville, Mark Twain, Henry Adams, James Baldwin, Ralph Ellison, and Kurt Vonnegut, and in such political figures as Thomas Jefferson (sometimes), Martin

Van Buren, Andrew Jackson, William Howard Taft, Franklin Roosevelt, and Lyndon Johnson. Above all, McWilliams heard that voice in Alexis de Tocqueville, that great interpreter of America, to whose insights he returned again and again. He found in Tocqueville's analysis of democracy in America the exhortation for America to aspire to be its best self—to pursue that "better sort of love"—and, in eschewing our temptation to credit self-interest as our most fundamental motivation, to cease doing "more honor to our philosophy than to ourselves."[4]

In one of his earliest publications—coauthored with his teacher John Schaar—McWilliams set out a basic premise that would guide his thought thereafter: "The political process is an effort to unite men in the pursuit of a common goal and vision. Politics, then, involves two questions: the question of 'with whom' and the question of 'for what.' Furthermore, it involves these questions in precisely that order."[5] Modern politics stresses "for what"—its view is utilitarian and instrumental, aimed at understanding human relations as a means to achieve particular desired ends of individuals. Modern thought, beginning with Machiavelli, has placed the "for what" question first, viewing the "with whom" question as secondary—subject to convenience and shifting need. According to liberal theory, the public realm exists to serve the private. McWilliams sought to evoke an older tradition in which the private was subordinate to the common weal. In an evocative phrase, he argued that politics is itself a main avenue toward taming the "idolatry of self"; by contrast, modern theory turns this "idolatry" into its main orthodoxy.[6] To the extent that the *ends* of politics become detached from the goal of reinforcing the goods of solidarity in political and community life itself, those ends tend toward destruction of a fundamental human good of our shared human life. The question of "with whom" conditions—even limits—the possible range of answers to the question of "for what." Questions of what politics should seek to achieve will necessarily be conditioned by the question "In what way will our activities support and improve our common life?"

Liberalism, McWilliams consistently argued, was not neutral toward ultimate ends, in spite of some claims of its main proponents. According to McWilliams's analysis of early modern thought in such thinkers as Machiavelli, Hobbes, and Locke, and as distilled in its practical expression in the thought of the founders—especially Madison and Hamilton—politics was to be arranged to increase human power and mastery. According to liberal theory, individuals are understood *by nature* to be "free and independent," and they accede to form and join political community only as a second-best option, preferring in their respective hearts to be unfettered and ungoverned. Law is experienced as an imposition upon natural freedom, a necessary but onerous compromise with the reality of other self-interested humans. A consistent theme in liberal thought is that these inconveniences and compromises are acceptable because of what we ultimately gain in return—namely, the ability to master nature and a resulting increase in human power. As a result, our condition as individuals is apparently improved: while we remain under the impositions of positive law—and, indeed, as the power of the state must increase concomitantly with the growth of power over nature—we appear to escape the rule of nature's law, achieving greater liberation as individuals than would have been possible in a state of nature. Political organization is thus a *means* to achieving the original desired ends of the individual, namely, power and mastery. Liberalism—hardly neutral about ends—contains a deeper teaching, and organizes the polity to achieve the ends of that particular pedagogy.

Ancient conflict within and between communities over ends—the stuff from which politics itself arose and which it sought to contain, yet which is always fraught with the threat of outright violence—was to be replaced by a set of aims and activities that demoted politics to the status of handmaiden to the modern project of mastery. Politics was largely to become subservient to technique, itself becoming a science—"the new science of politics." Modern political thought appears to subordinate concern with *ends* for the promotion of *means,* above all, various techniques based upon that new science. Liberalism's apparent indifference to ends—its vaunted relativism—masks its deeper devotion to *power* and *mastery,* particularly the modern project of nature's conquest along with the aim of material increase through a deeply individualistic economic arrangement. Modern politics contains a teaching that has shaped the human soul over time, transforming all institutions and human aspirations in its image. Among its most effective tutors is the market: McWilliams argued often that it is commerce, more than any other feature of modern life, that has introduced radical relativism and deep instability even into the heart of those parts of life that need to be resistant to its corrosive effects, especially the family, schools, and community. "The great commercial republic, the Framers' creation, is always threatened by the market, its central social institution. . . . The market . . . teaches us to see *all* virtues and goods, all allegiances and loyalties, as so many 'values,' prices set by and shifting with the vacillations of the market and of opinion."[7]

Perhaps what the great liberal project, building on the lessons of the market, above all has taught modern humans is a habituation in *detachment,* and all that follows. Freedom, it is understood, consists in our relative lack of obligations and duties, our capability for—indeed, the inescapable necessity of—mobility and absenteeism. Understanding and tracing the consequences of this inculcated tendency toward detachment is a major theme in McWilliams's work, not only because it constitutes a real psychic loss in our ability to form lasting and stable relations but because of its unintended deleterious social and political consequences, particularly a disposition not to care sufficiently to seek to secure the common weal. The result of the insecurity and instability of our civic domain, McWilliams (following Tocqueville) observed, is that the public realm comes to be seen as "the theater of indignity"; liberal citizens are prone to seek meaning in retreat from this sphere where they are insignificant and weak, shorn of the bonds and connections that Tocqueville praised as arising from a habituation in "the arts of association." They are "disposed to barricade themselves in private life, where they find a measure of significance and control."[8]

For the better part of a century, social scientists have noted the decline in political participation and even interest, but they have tended to address it by considering ways of increasing the convenience of participation—for example, through technology or methods to ease the "hassles" of voting. What McWilliams understood is that this decrease in civic devotions is the *intended* result of liberal theory itself, not a random accident subject to the remediation of technique. A preference for the private over the public was at the heart of liberal intention and design, with the studied aim of producing "timid and cautious" citizens.[9] The very *solution* proposed by liberal theory to the problem of political conflict—to render citizens largely indifferent to politics, instead emphasizing private life by reducing civic attention and devotions, and making the *polis* the servant of the *oikos*—is the main source of the political *problem* that Tocqueville identified and that McWilliams believed had metastasized in our own time. That problem, at base, is the loss of a sense of, or care for, the common good and the attenuation of the learned and practiced capacity of citizens to work in concert to practice the art of self-governance.

In the absence of this kind of civic training, liberty has come to be defined not as a kind of "discipline of freedom" but as the relative lack of constraint upon individuals. The attendant growth in various kinds of human power—scientific, technological, and military, among others—

has obliterated obstacles to the human will and reshaped the world in the image and likeness of the unencumbered individual. A form of *democratic* liberty—what Aristotle defined as "ruling and being ruled in turn"—has been substituted for the aspiration of "living as one likes."[10] What most contemporary people understand to be the very heart of the definition of democracy—freedom as lack of constraint—is, for McWilliams, the polar opposite of democracy. And the pursuit of the theory presents modern democratic human beings with unforeseen privations. The theory that has been developed to advance thoroughgoing human liberty—requiring endless efforts to increase techniques of mastery—leaves humans increasingly subject to the very powers that have been unleashed. Largely incapable of understanding the complexities of modern life, rendered mute and insignificant by a vast and impersonal nation-state, and buffeted by titanic powers that are often "private" and increasingly ungovernable, the modern democratic citizen experiences a radically different outcome than that which had been promised by the modern project. Isolated, voiceless, and civically powerless, they find that a crass materialism and feeble claim to autonomy have replaced the noble calling of citizenship and self-rule. Thus, not only is the practical consequence of this redefinition of liberty an intense violence done to nature in the form of environmental degradation—but a similar violence has also been done to human nature, namely, a profound deformation of the human soul itself.[11]

McWilliams believed that a main impulse to be resisted in considering problems of contemporary politics is that of seeking solutions based on "technique," that is, an approach to politics that resorts to the same motivation from which arises the deepest challenges presented by modern politics. Most policy proposals—even those of a "communitarian bent"—are content to base proposed solutions within the structural framework of the liberal regime, ensuring that they will necessarily be swamped by the regime's deeper individualist assumptions. McWilliams believed that most such endeavors are doomed, if not likely to worsen our condition. Before indulging a reforming impulse that is likely to be born of the same source as the "new science of politics," McWilliams held, deep reflection upon the truth of our condition is necessary. In the first instance, he believed, action should be preceded by a right understanding of our condition—an understanding that needs to be ruthlessly honest about the daunting nature of the modern political challenge. Second—based upon that understanding—thinking about politics needs to be both radical and modest: radical in its aims to change the fundamental assumptions about politics, but modest in its recognition of what can realistically be done in the context of the modern nation-state. McWilliams—borrowing a phrase he once used to describe his onetime teacher Bertrand de Jouvenel—sought to "bring the old gods to a new city," but in a way that understood that any such effort would require "sacrifice and patience more than dazzling exploits."[12]

Above all, he held that any effort to remediate the modern retreat into the private and the individual must begin—as Tocqueville understood—by shoring up those pre- and nonliberal sources that long coexisted alongside America's liberal self-understanding. Ironically, improving civic life would come about largely by sustaining and strengthening largely "private" institutions.

> Many "private" institutions—most notably, families, churches, and local communities—have often taught an older creed which speaks more easily of the public as a whole, appealing to patriotism, duty, and the common good. Of course, these private bodies have been influenced, increasingly, by the liberalism and "modernism" of our public culture, and they articulate the more traditional view only infrequently, incoherently, and apologetically. Nevertheless, the "private" order shaped the American character, in part, in terms of a teaching that human beings are limited creatures, subject to the law of nature, born dependent and—by nature—in need of nurturance and moral education.[13]

McWilliams was a defender of the "traditional" family not out of misplaced traditionalism, but rather because he understood that the family, like church and community, is based on a set of human commitments that rub against the grain of liberal individualist assumptions. This understanding led McWilliams toward what might be called "populist" sympathies, to supporting the sorts of traditional associations and commitments suspected and attacked by a range of historical liberal and "progressive" actors (the sort of "elites" excoriated by a kindred spirit and friend, Christopher Lasch).[14] McWilliams defended not merely groups— in this, he was no trendy supporter of "multiculturalism"—but groups whose basis reflected commitments based in loyalty, memory, and place.[15]

One central institution that McWilliams repeatedly insisted required the concerted efforts of supporters of civic and democratic life was the political party, that irksome splinter in the finger of the constitutional system. Political parties, he argued, function as intermediary links between individuals and a distant government, inviting citizens into the debates of the republic at a local level, fostering the "arts of association" that liberal theory actively seeks to discourage. Political parties are "the best means of narrowing the affective distance between citizens and representatives," a distance that is a design feature of the Constitution. He called the party system—unintended by the framers, and under longstanding assault by a range of thinkers who mistrust its basis in loyalty and affective ties—"a second system of representation based on locality, memory, and conviction."[16] He opposed many modern political "reforms" that were often undertaken with the explicit aim of "opening" the parties—such as the direct primary—but that had the practical effect of weakening party loyalties and attachments. He attacked with consistent ferocity the confusion of speech and money—along with the attendant rise of televised campaigning—insisting that parties function best as local civic associations, linking communities to the national government, and should be based upon speech, persuasion, memory, and loyalty.[17]

It is private or semipublic entities such as the family or political parties that are the training ground of community life within the larger frame of the modern nation-state. While relying upon these preliberal institutions, the modern state also subtly undermines all such inheritances, remaking them in the image of liberal assumptions and thus diluting their affective ties. McWilliams understood that the liberal state was purposefully designed to separate humans, to encourage the assumption that we are at base physical bodies that come temporarily into contact without any natural or teleological relational basis. The vastness and impersonality of the nation-state is part of the intentional design of liberal theory, intended at once to advance the modern project of mastery, while making public life so impersonal and distant as to render modern liberal citizens more likely to favor withdrawal into private life and affairs. While seeming to ensure our dignity—mainly in the form of individual rights—modern arrangements tend instead to undermine the affective basis of every preliberal human institution, rendering us ever more alone and isolated, and bribing us instead by visions of autonomy and a taste of power that distract us from our effective powerlessness.

McWilliams appealed to an older teaching—one he gleaned from ancient Greek philosophy as well as the biblical tradition—that understands community to be the natural home of humans, and political association to be the natural schoolteacher of shared self-government. Politics, according to McWilliams, is a kind of teacher of the human soul—not, as liberal theory holds, a necessary inconvenience to our natural freedom. It is a tutor that makes true human freedom possible, above all the freedom gained in self-government. From Plato and Aristotle, in particular, he absorbed the lesson that political life requires a fundamentally small setting wherein interpersonal relations can be fostered. Drawing particularly on an Aristotelian teleology, McWilliams held that politics is natural to the extent that human flourishing requires formation within well-formed political communities. Liberal theory understands, rightly, that humans tend to experience themselves as separate bodies, but this theory stops short of a fuller comprehension. At best and under good conditions, humans can be drawn out of this individualized existence, coming to see the extent to which the good life rests upon political life. Yet the human capacity to understand and embrace a shared conception of the good life beyond fulfillment of our immediate desires is not infinite and hence needs a bounded and palpable scale. Modern politics rejects this teaching, beginning and ending with our fundamental separation, and concluding that a vast scale is the best setting for the satisfaction of such selves. From the ancients McWilliams learned otherwise.[18]

The biblical tradition echoes this teaching, using different lyrics but the same basic harmonics. Largely relying on Calvinist bearings, McWilliams understood biblical teaching to stress the fact of human fallenness, our partiality, our pride, and our need for stern but loving guidance. Humans strain against limits and law but, properly tutored, can come to embrace those constraints as a self-imposed discipline, thereby achieving a better freedom. Particularly evidenced in God's actions upon Israel, the Bible teaches that politics plays a vital role in this education of the soul. "Political society needs to limit and constrain its citizens, demanding sacrifice and punishing them when needed. In so doing, it imitates—in a small, relatively effective way—God's desolation of pride. At the same time, a good political order nurtures, educates, and improves its citizens: its chastenings are intended to teach the lesson that the whole is a good order."[19] McWilliams was nearly unique among contemporary "communitarian" thinkers in stressing that the communitarian strain in American thought—and, indeed, in the broader Western tradition—if originating with the Greeks, had in many respects been deepened and more fully conveyed through the biblical tradition. Like Tocqueville, he located the American founding not in 1776 or 1789, but with the Puritan settlement of New England. He argued that America's first efforts of self-understanding derived from sources like John Winthrop's sermon aboard the *Arbella*, "A Model of Christian Charity," in which he urged fellow citizens to "delight in each other; make other's conditions our own; rejoice together, mourn together, labor and suffer together, always having before our eyes our commission and community in the work, as members of the same body."[20] In both his writings and his riveting lectures in and beyond the classroom, McWilliams stressed that politics is always fundamentally about *teaching*, instructing us, above all, to seek the excellence of citizenship, a condition aimed at achieving civic equality through the discipline of freedom.[21]

Although McWilliams was largely tentative about suggesting explicit activities for government to undertake in this effort to strengthen local communities and associations, he held that such help is inescapably necessary. He excoriated "conservatives" whose antigovernment animus often veils their willingness to support a market economy that relentlessly undermines the very kinds of associations that undergird the "traditional values" that they claim to support. (Ronald Reagan was a frequent target of McWilliams's withering criticism—among other things, for his fondness for quoting that impious revolutionary Thomas Paine.) Yet McWilliams was also aware of the paradox that our situation presents: support from central government against the corrosive tendencies of the market is inescapable, but too often the government itself is a partner in those activities. His arguments largely sought to clear the way for a new and different understanding of what government ought to aim to achieve—mainly, the ambition to give primary allegiance to "with whom" and then, thus informed, "for what."

> For citizenship, in any case, government is indispensible to any solution, and only incidentally is part of the problem. The school of citizenship is small, personal and local, and in that sphere, "getting government out of the way" does not "empower" citizens: it leaves them nakedly exposed to forces that are titanic, impersonal and international. Citizens need stronger governments to give localities power as well as responsibility and to reduce the extent to which "getting involved" is an exercise in frustration. In fact, government is the target of so much resentment because it is

relatively responsive: citizens can vote against school budgets and elected officials, but not against technological change. Our anger at government is a mark of its humanity, just as democratic citizenship, to the extent that we can preserve and revitalize it, gives us voices against the grey silence of our time.[22]

McWilliams suggested elsewhere that while modern governments are "too clumsy and impersonal to promote friendship directly, they can at least be friendly to friendship."[23]

His understanding of the fundamental need—indeed, the basic dignity—of political life drew him inexorably to the Left. For all of McWilliams's differences with Marx, he was always committed to the left side of the modern political landscape. This was most obviously the case during his active years in the student movement at Berkeley, and is also evident in his lifelong devotion to the Democratic Party. More deeply, McWilliams's critique of the theory of liberalism, and its close social ally, the capitalist market economy, drew him away from the contemporary Right. To the extent that the Right in America tends toward vociferous defenses of liberalism, particularly its economic arrangements—and has often been the font of hostility toward the successive waves of immigrant groups who embody the "second voice" of American thought, including that tragic group of unwilling immigrants, African slaves and their progeny—McWilliams found in the Left and the Democratic Party his natural home.

Yet, McWilliams's relationship to the Left was itself anguished. He broke early with friends who opposed the Vietnam War, and throughout his life was a severe critic of communism and most modern ideologies of progress. His defense of family and other "traditional" arrangements, his criticisms of the idea of a "right to choose" or a "right to privacy," and his defense of the "great books"—among other positions—made him at least as often a critic of modern "liberals" and "progressives," as apt to find a betrayal of fundamental commitments to politics among his political compatriots on the left as he did among those on the right.[24] He admired the arguments advanced by conservatives such as Allan Bloom, and counted him—and many other conservatives—among his friends and allies. Yet, far from experiencing alienation from the Left or the Right, the very source of his discomfort with elements across the contemporary political spectrum was also the basis of at least partial agreement with nearly everyone he encountered: aided by his wit and sense of humor—punctuated by countless anecdotes and a fondness for bourbon—along with his uncanny ability to forge political alliances, he easily made friends and companions across the entire political spectrum. Featured prominently among the speakers at a roundtable organized at the American Political Science Association and dedicated to McWilliams shortly after his death in 2005 was Harvard conservative Harvey C. Mansfield (a lifelong friend) and Princeton leftist Cornel West, and his admirers included people ranging from the liberal columnist E. J. Dionne to the conservative strategist Karl Rove. McWilliams felt equally at home in a gathering of labor union workers and at a reception sponsored by Straussian intellectuals, and would be among the most admired men in either setting.

For McWilliams, politics, as a calling toward the achievement of the common good, is finally ennobling not only for teaching the truth about our human condition—one of dependency and mutual need—but also to the extent that it points us beyond its own limits. McWilliams affirmed again and again that politics teaches us our partiality—points us toward the whole—but that politics itself is finally only partial. It is a *part* that aspires toward the whole; the community itself calls us outside ourselves, but it, too, must ultimately be cognizant of its own partiality, even as it aspires to a kind of partial completeness. "At best, politics encourages us toward philosophy and toward religion, toward a concern for the truth and for the nature of things."[25] Politics is the point of departure toward an understanding of the nature of the created order; at the same time, philosophy and religion alike must be cognizant of the limits—or at least of the need for prudence—that are placed upon that examination of the whole, given the necessity of the human community that encourages and even makes possible their examinations.

McWilliams expressed this tension at the heart of "political philosophy" with simple eloquence on the occasion of his reception of the 1989 John Witherspoon Award from the New Jersey Committee for the Humanities.

> I think that Plato was right: at bottom, human beings are yearning animals, who want more than is simply or narrowly human. They want perfect things, answers to great riddles, beauty that endures, Being that is now and always, justice without fault or error. But if we seek the perfect in things, persons or governments of this world, we will be disappointed—and worse, we will fail to appreciate their decencies and real achievements. We need the critical comparison and argument between high things and

our lower striving, between Socrates who is human and our own incomplete humanity. Even the most successful practice does *not* make perfect though it does make better; but we cannot recognize what is better without some inkling of what is best.[26]

Thus, for McWilliams, politics ultimately points beyond itself. Politics is a means to a further end, the appreciation of the whole and of the truth that we are necessarily always only partly able to grasp. Politics is thus the inescapable condition of human creatures, a sphere of education about our true selves that gives us dignity and meaning. It is to be informed by the goal of seeking the common good of our fellows and compatriots—through the medium of citizenship—but finally it must be aware of its own limits and shortcomings, pointing beyond any of those commitments to a whole that exceeds our earthly grasp. In this, McWilliams was ultimately a partisan of philosophy and religion, but for him these highest pursuits were nevertheless always moderated by the real experience of political life, that condition of being human among humans. He sought to ennoble and chasten, pointing us simultaneously to the high aspirations of the true and eternal things and to the earthy reality of our diurnal political existence. And so—as the essays in this book demonstrate—he was a passionate student of the great thinkers and a lover of the rough-and-tumble, a singular combination of philosopher and politico with a bit of saint and rapscallion mixed in. These essays are a partial testimony to the breadth and scope of his vision, to a deep and profound learning that will awe and humble, and to the wisdom of a lover of political and human things. This book will at least serve as a reminder of that man admired and missed by many, and as an introduction to those who have come too late to enjoy his infectious laughter and embraces.

Notes

1. Wilson Carey McWilliams, preface to *Fool's Paradise: A Carey McWilliams Reader* (Berkeley, Calif.: Clapperstick Institute, 2001), xiii.

2. Wilson Carey McWilliams, "Go Tell It on the Mountain: James Baldwin and the Politics of Faith," in *Democracy's Literature,* ed. Patrick J. Deneen and Joseph Romance (Lanham, Md.: Rowman and Littlefield, 2005), 153.

3. Wilson Carey McWilliams, "In Good Faith: On the Foundations of American Politics," *Humanities in Society* 6 (1983): 34.

4. *Democracy in America,* vol. 2, pt. 2, ch. 8.

5. John Schaar and Wilson C. McWilliams, "Uncle Sam Vanishes," *New University Thought,* Summer 1961, 61.

6. Wilson Carey McWilliams, "The Bible in the American Political Tradition," in *Religion and Politics,* ed. Myron J. Aronoff (New Brunswick, N.J.: Transaction, 1984), 17.

7. Wilson Carey McWilliams, *The Undergraduate Learner: Challenges for the Year 2000* (Trenton: New Jersey Board of Higher Education, 1987), 8.

8. Ibid., 7.

9. James Madison, *The Federalist,* #49. This phrase—not often noted by readers of *The Federalist*—is frequently cited by McWilliams, who regarded it as a key admission by the framers of the sort of citizenry the Constitution intended to foster. See, for instance, "The Anti-Federalists," included in part 1 of this volume.

10. See Wilson Carey McWilliams, "Democracy and the Citizen: Community, Dignity, and the Crisis of Contemporary Politics in America," in *How Democratic Is the Constitution?* ed. Robert A. Goldwin and William A. Schambra (Washington, D.C.: American Enterprise Institute for Public Policy Research, 1980), 80, 81.

11. On the relationship of contemporary definitions of liberty and our crisis of the "environment," see Wilson Carey McWilliams, preface to *Democracy and the Claims of Nature,* ed. Ben A. Minteer and Bob Pepperman Taylor (Lanham, Md.: Rowman and Littlefield, 2002). McWilliams asks, "*Will democratic publics limit themselves in response to environmental crises?*" (vii; his emphasis). And he answers, "The auguries are not promising. Affluent Americans, after all, chafe at suggestions that they sacrifice any of their superfluities. . . . And in the intellectual world . . . a fashionable version of democratic theory argues that democracy resists all constraints, insisting on the public's right to construct its own world" (vii–viii). By contrast, he argues, properly defined, "in a democracy, citizens rule, but also are ruled by laws that they make, of course, but more fundamentally by nature." McWilliams rejected the language of "environment" in favor of that of "nature" (viii).

12. Wilson Carey McWilliams, foreword to *The Nature of Politics: Selected Essays of Bertrand de Jouvenel,* ed. Denis Hale and Marc Landy (New York: Schocken Books, 1987), viii; McWilliams, "Democracy and the Citizen," 100.

13. Wilson Carey McWilliams, "Parties as Civic Associations," in *Party Renewal in America,* ed. Gerald R. Pomper (New York: Praeger, 1980), 52.

14. See Wilson Carey McWilliams, "Back to the Future," review of *The True and Only Heaven,* by Christopher Lasch, *Commonweal,* April 19, 1991, 264.

15. McWilliams provides a valuable contrast between the kinds of groups favored by liberals and those that tend to be demoted. It is the latter sort that McWilliams characteristically favored and believed in need of strengthening.

Notably, the groups that [liberal reformers] recognize are all defined by *biology.* In liberal theory, where our "nature" means our bodies, these are "natural" groups opposed to "artificial" bonds like communities of work and culture. This does not mean that liberalism values these "natural" groups. Quite the contrary: since liberal political society reflects the effort to overcome or master nature, liberalism argues that "merely natural" differences ought not to be held against us. We ought not to be held back by qualities we did not choose and that do not reflect our individual efforts and abilities. [Reformers] recognize women, racial minorities, and the young only in order to free individuals from "suspect classifications."

Class and culture are different. People are part of ethnic communities or the working class because they chose not to pursue individual success and assimilation into the dominant, middle-class culture, or because they were unable to succeed. Liberal theory values individuals who go their own way, and by the same token, it esteems those who succeed in that quest more highly than individuals who do not. Ethnicity and class, consequently, are marks of shame in liberal theory, and whatever discrimination people suffer is, in some sense, their "own fault." We may feel compassion for their failures, but they have no just cause for equal representation, unlike individuals who suffer discrimination for "no fault of their own."

Wilson Carey McWilliams, "Politics," *American Quarterly* 35, nos. 1–2 (1983): 27. See also "Democratic Multiculturalism," in *Multiculturalism and American Democracy,* ed. Arthur M. Melzer, Jerry Weinberger, and M. Richard Zinman (Lawrence: University Press of Kansas, 1998); and "Community and Its Discontents: Amitai Etzioni and the Future of Communitarianism," printed in part 2 of this volume.

16. Wilson Carey McWilliams, "Two-Tier Politics and the Problem of Public Policy," in *The New Politics of Public Policy,* ed. Marc K. Landy and Martin Levin (Baltimore, Md.: Johns Hopkins University Press, 1995), 275. See also "Tocqueville and Responsible Parties: Individualism, Partisanship and Citizenship in America," in *Challenges to Party Government,* ed. John K. White and Jerome M. Mileur (Carbondale: Southern Illinois University Press, 1992).

17. Wilson Carey McWilliams, "A Republic of Couch Potatoes: The Media Shrivel the Electorate," *Commonweal,* March 10, 1989; and "Television and Political Speech: The Medium Exalts Spectacle and Slights Words," *Media Studies Journal,* Winter 2000.

18. McWilliams, "Democracy and the Citizen."

19. McWilliams, "The Bible in the American Political Tradition," 18.

20. John Winthrop, "A Model of Christian Charity," in *The American Puritans: Their Prose and Poetry,* ed. Perry Miller (New York: Columbia University Press, 1982), 83. On the centrality of McWilliams's stress upon the Puritans, see Mac McCorkle and David E. Price, "Wilson Carey McWilliams and Communitarianism," in *Friends and Citizens: Essays in Honor of Wilson Carey McWilliams,* ed. Peter Dennis Bathory and Nancy L. Schwartz (Lanham, Md.: Rowman and Littlefield, 2001), 234–71; Paul Seaton, "Wrestling with Gods and Men: Wilson Carey McWilliams on the Puritans," *Perspectives on Political Science* 34, no. 4 (2006): 195–99; and Peter Augustine Lawler, "McWilliams and the Problem of

Political Education," *Perspectives on Political Science* 34, no. 4 (2006): 213–18. For a critical view of his high regard for the Puritans, see Philip Abbott, "The Tyranny of Fraternity in McWilliams' America," *Political Theory* 2, no. 3 (1974): 304–20 (however, see, McWillliams's riposte in the same source, "Fraternity and Nature: A Response to Philip Abbott," 321–29); and Amitai Etzioni, "Wilson Carey McWilliams's Conservative Communitarianism," *Perspectives on Political Science* 34, no. 4 (2006): 200–204.

21. Wilson Carey McWilliams, "On Equality as the Moral Foundation for Community," in *The Moral Foundations of the American Republic,* 3rd ed., ed. Robert H. Horwitz (Charlottesville: University of Virginia Press, 1986).

22. Wilson Carey McWilliams, "Citizenship and Its Discontents" (lecture, St. John's College, Santa Fe, N.M., April 1, 1995), 6.

23. McWilliams, foreword to *The Nature of Politics,* xi.

24. For a somewhat sympathetic treatment of Progressivism—amid a broader set of criticisms—see "Standing at Armageddon: Morality and Religion in Progressive Thought," included in part 1 of this volume.

25. Wilson Carey McWilliams, "America's Cultural Dilemma," *Worldview* 24, no. 10 (1981), 17, republished as "America's Two Voices in a World of Nations" in part 1 of this volume.

26. Wilson Carey McWilliams, "The Witherspoon Award," *New Jersey Humanities,* Winter 1990, 11. The lecture was delivered in Princeton on November 15, 1989.

Part 1

Political Thought
in America

Liberty, Equality, and the Problem of Community

Created equal and born free, Americans have valued liberty and equality as a child does his inheritance. We have taken them for granted, and we have assumed that because we are familiar with both words, we know what they mean, like a child mistaking received opinion for achieved understanding. Confident that we possessed liberty and equality, Americans have been equally certain that both would be available in abundance.[1]

This is changing. Time out of mind, Americans believed the future would be better; now, most expect it to be worse. Nature no longer seems abundant. We cadge for oil and try, half seriously and all unwontedly, to curb waste and preserve the land. Machines fail us and our fellows disappoint us. The sixties raged because discontented Americans, doubting our goodness, trusted in our power. Now, we are uncertain of both. Americans have begun to suspect that there was a hidden clause in our inheritance.

For all our present doubts, however, we still have not reflected much on the meaning of liberty and equality or the quality of our dedication to them. We have not remembered, for example, Tocqueville's warning that in democratic speech there may be little "sympathy" or likeness between our principles and our feelings.[2] Opponents of conscription, for example, generally see themselves as defenders of equality as well as liberty, and develop arguments, as elaborate as they are meretricious, to make their case. Some of my argument, in fact, tries to show that equality's verbal champions are false friends.

I have a more positive aim. In the Gettysburg Address, reversing the order of the Declaration of Independence, Lincoln urged us to see ourselves as *created* free but *dedicated* to equality.[3] Following Lincoln's example, I want to argue that we love liberty too much and equality too little and to urge that we reverse our priorities. I will be speaking of new situations, but I am appealing to an older understanding of political things.

In both the new and the old aspects of this argument, I have tried to listen to Tocqueville's call for a new science of politics suited to a new world, for the American future is likely to bring us into a strange new world where our accustomed ways of thinking and talking about politics will be inappropriate and we will need to learn the language of the place.[4]

It makes sense to say "I am free," but if I assert that "I am equal," immediately I will be asked "to whom?" Equality describes a relationship between subject and object; liberty is a property of subjects only. Equality looks inward; the statement, "I am equal to you," directs attention to the terms of our connection. In that sense, equality is concerned with domestic affairs. Liberty looks from the subject outward. The statement "I am free to do as I choose" looks from me to my object, the things I may choose, and discerns no obstacle sufficient to prevent me from doing them.

As this suggests, liberty is preoccupied with limits to my ability to do as I choose and with the power needed to overcome them. "Negative liberty," the freedom from restraint, presumes that I already have the power to do what I want if you will let me alone. Hence Hobbes's definition: "A Free-man, is he, that in those things, which by his strength and wit he is able to do, is not hindered to do what he has a will to do."[5] Positive liberty, my claim to have what I need, asserts that left to myself I do *not* have enough power and, implicitly at least, that you are limiting me if you are not helping me.[6] Of the two, positive liberty is the more fundamental idea; negative liberty takes a good deal of positive freedom for granted. I cannot exercise freedom of the press merely because the state will not jail me for what I print; I will also need a press.[7] But both varieties of liberty are engrossed with limits and power. Whether the obstacle to be overcome is your hostility (negative liberty) or your indifference (positive liberty), you stand between me and my freedom.

Even traditional ideas of liberty share this concern with opposition and power. Inner, spiritual liberty is threatened by pride and passion, and such freedom requires that reason or the spirit have the power to rule the soul, even though the most desirable form of that power wears the softening habit of education. Plato, Aristotle, and the great sages of Judaism and Christianity thought it neither possible nor desirable for human beings to go beyond the limits set by nature. This, however, did not necessarily restrict our liberty, since just as human beings are free when they can do what they want to do, they are free when they want to do what they can do. Traditional teaching was concerned to school our desires, reconciling them to humanity's estate. Human beings became free when they no longer desired to do what man was not meant to do. For traditional teaching, nature, not liberty, was sovereign and its spokesmen were devoted to what was naturally right, not to natural rights.[8]

It remained for modern political philosophy to make liberty the highest human end, "the one and all," Schelling called it, of modern philosophy.[9] Locke, Hegel, and Marx all take freedom for the preeminent human goal; even Rousseau, a critic of modernity, felt civil society could be justified only if it made men "as free as they were before."[10] Modernity could give liberty first place only by insisting on a freedom which can overcome all limits and which, consequently, is all-powerful. In the modern view, nature is hostile or indifferent; it means badly or not at all, and its limits deserve no respect. Liberty requires mastering nature, "transforming" it by breaking free from its forms. Human beings are moved by desires more or less infinite: "In the first place, I put for a generall inclination of all mankind a perpetuall and restlesse desire of Power after power, that ceaseth only in Death."[11] We are free, then, only to the extent that our power becomes as infinite as our desires.[12] Locke made seemingly humble self-preservation our ruling principle, but that doctrine sets us at odds with nature, which kills us, and with human nature, which is mortal. Freedom is not in but in spite of nature: it is something made or contrived, a product of the struggle to form nature according to our desire. Work, our striving to master nature, is also a supreme expression of human freedom. Modern idealists and romantics sometimes scorn the utilitarian connotations of work, but they praise "creativity" and "making one's own world":[13] "Modernity means (in intention if not in fact) that men take control over the world and themselves. What was previously experienced as fate now becomes an arena of choices."[14]

Modern liberty aims at my ability to make myself what I want as well as to do what I want. Perfect liberty severs the spirit from "all its relationships," Schelling wrote, for relationships limit us. Alienation—radical separateness—is inherent in modern ideas of liberty.[15]

Many exponents of the modern position have rejected individualism. Nevertheless, their idea of liberty denies that human beings are naturally political and, despite the subtleties in which philosophers seek to entrap it, the modern idea of liberty tends toward individualism and nihilism. Liberty certainly rejects authority, since it tells me to accept what authority decrees, if I do so at all, only after I have questioned authority and chosen to obey. "Autonomy" has been valued by political theorists as a definition of liberty because "self-rule" puts liberty into political terms, but autonomy rejects rule by any external or higher laws (except, again, those I choose). Once it has been made the sovereign end, liberty tends to devour all laws, virtues, and morals, leaving us with only the proposition "Only what (and whatever) I consent to is right." Liberty, Herzen commented, is a "terrible word" which poisons attempts at reconstruction along with the old order.[16]

In fact, since liberty involves "doing as I wish," the regime which most closely approximates liberty is tyranny, so long as I am the tyrant. Hobbes commented that human beings "naturally love Liberty, and Dominion over others" because he recognized that liberty includes doing as I wish *with you.*[17] I am not likely to be a tyrant, of course, and if I were a tyrant my position would be insecure, but those pragmatic objections do not affect the principle that tyranny is the implicit goal of liberty.[18]

As classical philosophy understood monarchy, a king, unlike tyrants, is not "at liberty." *Noblesse oblige,* and a monarch is ruled by the common good. Following Hobbes, modern political thought tends to reject the distinction between monarchy and tyranny because it rejects the idea of the common good. People believe that government "is of one kind, when they like it, and another, when they mislike it,"[19] and names which seek to go behind the form of government are, like the common good itself, only private motives "rationalized in terms of the public interest."[20] This attack on the common good is a measure of modernity's devotion to liberty. If there *is* a public good, then it is shameful to pursue private interests or desires which detract from the good of the whole. But if there is no such good—if politics can be reduced to desires and interests—then it is only clear-sightedness to take care of one's own. The common good restricts us, for it reduces us to parts of a whole. Like all wholes which seek to include humanity, the public good is an enemy to the sway of liberty. In the modern teaching, political society is not prior to the individual in the order of nature. Politics is a product, constructed by human beings who are naturally separate and free.

Equality, in contrast to liberty, is at least uncomfortable in modern dress. I know that this assertion is heterodoxy. Tocqueville told us that the "equality of conditions" was a "providential fact" and assured us that democracies love equality more than liberty, while contemporary social theorists argue the proposition that the "pursuit of equality" is a major force in modern history.[21] But Tocqueville was more precise than his epigones. In the first place, he is at some pains to point out that the rise of the "equality of conditions" cannot necessarily be attributed to equality as an *end*. *Democratie* has been advanced by those who opposed it or served it un-wittingly as well as by those who hoped for it. Very competitive and in-equalitarian passions have contributed to it "the taste for luxury, the love of war, the sway of fashion."[22] Tocqueville recognized, in other words, that it is possible to demand or settle for the "equality of conditions" with-out *valuing* equality at all. For the ambitious and lowly, the demand for equality is a first step on the road to superiority. For others, equality is a second-best alternative to the dominion they dream of, but despair of at-taining. The "equality of conditions," Tocqueville tells us, does engender a love of "that same equality," but the phrase (like the term "equality of conditions" itself) suggests that there are other forms of equality. In fact, Tocqueville lamented the passing, in France, of "the laws of moral analo-gy," the ability to see another's condition as akin to one's own.[23] This inner sense of likeness leads us to see others as our equals and to value them, and their equality, as we value ourselves. This conviction, which made equality a moral law, was not necessarily related to the "equality of condi-tions." As Tocqueville saw it, insisting on equalizing the condition of men was only too likely to destroy the recognition that they *are* equal, whatev-er their condition. Equality as a value, an end of the soul, was threatened by modern doctrines which held the soul to be of little account.

In the first place, equality is relatively indifferent to power. It cares about the ways in which resources are distributed but equality can exist at any level of wealth or power. We can be equally weak, equally humble, or equally poor. Glaucon called the first city of *The Republic* a "city of sows," and modern philosophy is disposed to distrust equality for the same rea-son.[24] Equality is safe, in the modern view, only when it is subordinated to liberty, compelled to make "growth" and mastery the premises of politi-cal life.[25] On its own terms, however, equality is suited to polities which are simple, small, and frugal (something I will be saying more about later on).

Unlike the activistic orientation of liberty, equality is concerned with being more than with doing. We are "free" to do, but we "are" equal. Moreover, equality distrusts works and appearances and is, to that extent, contemplative. Since people differ in skills as they do in appearance, if they are equal something other than work or likeness must make them so. If we declare that people are equal, we are asserting that appearances are deceiving, that the differences between people are accidental and that, in what matters, they are of "one quality."[26]

Aristotle argued that equality is particularly characteristic of friendship. In the friendship of unequal persons, there must be some proportional inequality (i.e., the more virtuous friend ought to receive more affection), but such inequality should aim at making the friends equal. Justice subordinates equality to proportion, distributing rewards and penalties according to merit. Friendship subordinates differences of merit to the goal of equality. This presumes that in this true sort of friendship, the friends share a virtue of soul which is more important than the differences, major or minor, in their attainments.[27]

Equality unites where liberty separates. It asserts that we are of one quality, participants in that quality, parts of a whole. Equality is evidently more social and political than liberty. In everyday speech, equality needs and welcomes politics: "equality before the law" presumes that we are not equal in some respects, but the law makes us so. "Liberty under law," on the other hand, presumes that the law limits liberty.

In fact, equality is the foundation of political virtue. Political society greatly expands the division of labor, combining many skills and crafts. The city gives us liberty because it frees us to do what we do best. But this liberty also threatens the *polis*. The diversity of political society makes its commonality impalpable, unlike the village where most people do similar things in similar ways. Even the common interest of cities is problematic, making appeals to utility uncertain. In the village, a "bad year" means that all of us suffer, each in his own degree, but in political society some people profit while—even because—others suffer. For the health of political society, its citizens need to see their diversities as subordinate to some more fundamental likeness and commonality. Political society, in other words, needs equality precisely because equality tells us that citizens can be both "different" and "the same."

To be sure, Aristotle observed that "political friendship" is essentially second-rate, since any citizenry includes dissimilar persons of dissimilar virtue. The *polis*, unlike friendship in the pure sense, cannot be governed simply by the rule of equal treatment. Political society must, to a far greater extent, consider utility and take different services and contributions into account in distributing rewards. All of this calls proper attention to the diversities of politics. But by calling the civic bond "friendship," even of an inferior sort, Aristotle was also indicating that the relations between citizens must be something more than utilitarian. In fact, Aristotle's denigration of political friendship was only a characteristically prudential qualification to Plato's teaching that friendship, and sharing all things in common, is the standard for political life, the true measure by which all lesser polities may be judged. Citizenship in a *polis* is second-rate friendship at best, but genuine citizenship is more like friendship than it is like the marketplace.[28]

In an army, friends are useful and we need proportional justice, with its attention to unequal skills, in assigning command (and other specialized tasks). But soldiers must also be willing to lay down their lives for the good of the army as a whole. The army needs a sense of commonality, a conviction that its members are "the same" in some respect more important than mere life. An army, in other words, needs equality of spirit. And what is true of the army is even more true of the political society which commands it. Citizens must see themselves as one, parts of a whole which is more important than the individuals it includes.

As I have been arguing, equality need not result in equal treatment. It is quite possible for people to insist that they are equal, yet acknowledge that some people have particular skills. Equality is a higher truth, and does not require people to be blind to lesser facts. John Winthrop argued that since sinful man was disposed to believe in his own sufficiency, God ordained differences so that "every man might have need of other, and from hence they might all be knitt more nearly together in the Bond of brotherly affection." Our unequal skills, and the mutual dependence that results from them, were a step *toward* equality, in Winthrop's view, when tempered by justice and mercy.[29] Equal dignity, the "equality of esteem," is a good deal more important than other sorts of equality. It is not against my dignity to obey orders, but I will be offended if I am treated disrespectfully. A quarterback who begins to act as though he is better than the linemen who protect him is likely to receive a forceful reminder of the equality of teammates, despite the inequality of command.

Equality does suggest one form of equal treatment, majority rule.[30] Even more clearly, equality implies equal deliberation, for my dignity requires that I be heard or, if I am silent, that I listen because I have chosen to do so. Dignity demands that I matter, that I be consulted as a person, not considered as part of some impersonal category. Equality, then, tends to imply "an equal say in what is chosen and for what end."[31]

This equal citizenship was, Aristotle argued, the first principle of democracy, and majority rule derives *from* political equality, "ruling and being ruled in turn.[32] Majority rule, on its own terms, is haunted by the problem of the strong minority. It does not solve the problem for the majority to respect the "rights" of the minority. Why should the minority accept so little if it is strong enough to overawe the majority? Democracies around the world have foundered because they could provide no answer to that question. In fact, majority rule is safe only where the minority accepts the principle—the political equality of all citizens—from which majority rule is drawn. Similarly, equality protects the minority. The principle of equal citizenship requires political liberty, the right to speak on public questions, to be spoken to by those in power, and to present alternative policies to the public at large. In America, we give the minority equal time, which is to say that, in the interests of equal citizenship, we give the minority more freedom than it is entitled to according to the rule of arithmetical equality.

I emphasize that I am speaking of public liberties, the rights that belong to us by virtue of our equality as citizens.[33] The majority will seek to restrain some private liberties; any concern for the public good requires some restraint of private interest and feeling. The majority is especially likely to restrain those forms of private conduct which violate the dignity of citizens. Arrogance, display, "fighting words," and offenses against honor all attack equality by assailing dignity, our sense of commonality, and our capacity to trust. They menace the "good order" of the republic, and the Supreme Court was right to order that a black woman be called "Miss" by a state prosecutor.[34] Civic equality denies us the right to call one another by whatever names we choose; we must use those names and words which comport with civic dignity. Although political friendship is second-rate, democracy aims at a citizenry which is composed of equals. Democracy requires that we behave *like* friends, by constraint of law if not from feeling, and democracy needs genuine friendship and fidelity as a model for the education of its citizens.

By contrast, Aristotle noted that an idea of private, individual liberty, "living as one likes," grows up as a "second form" of democratic freedom. In the terms I have been using, Aristotle is arguing that equality gives rise to liberty. This development is due to the defects of democratic opinion. Democrats, Aristotle observes, "say" that freedom is "living as you like" because slaves do not live as they like. Two problems are evident in this notion. First, it defines "free" as "that which is not slave," a fallacy on many counts, as the experience of America since the Thirteenth Amendment ought to suggest. A freeborn child is no slave, but neither is he free in a democratic sense. Second, no one lives simply as he or she "likes." Slaves are not unique in being ruled but in having no say about that rule. A law-abiding democratic citizen, however, is doing what he "likes" when he obeys the law. A citizen may even "like" to be ruled, since it leaves him freer to pursue his private interests. Such good citizens, however, neglect the fact that they "like" democratic rule because their passions have been schooled and limited by civic education. The principle that they draw from their sense of freedom, that liberty is "doing as you like," may teach their children to become privatistic individualists, not public-spirited citizens.[35] A polity can only tolerate so many such citizens. In the majority, private-regarding citizens tend to make the *polis* partisan and ultimately tyrannical. The wise polity, as Aristotle saw it, kept liberty subordinate to equality.

Equality poses its own dangers to political life. Our equality as citizens hints at and points toward our equality as human beings, and human equality unites us to foreigners as well as to friends at home. It can easily dilute our affection, divide our loyalties, and weaken our willingness to make sacrifices. If we admire Socrates and his city-in-speech, we cannot be unambiguously patriotic Athenians; the greater mysteries can make the lesser seem pale. But a sense of human equality is a humbling doctrine—a knowledge of ignorance, dependence, and imperfection—and in learning those lessons, the equality of the *polis* is invaluable.[36]

Following the classics, Tocqueville praised the small state. The small state was within the emotional compass of the individual and lessened the tension between private feeling and the public good. Especially if such states were stable, citizens could know one another well, which made it more possible that each could be given his due. Most important, the politics of small communities increased participation. Citizens mattered more; each was more likely to see his contribution to the whole and have it seen by others. Citizens were more able to speak, hold office, or preserve a dignified silence. In this parochial world, where each citizen was important and where his fellows were known as individuals, mutual dependence and trust did not seem so threatening. Citizens learned, "first by necessity, afterwards by choice," to be concerned for the public welfare. To some degree, the necessity operates in all states; the choice was a characteristic of small ones, where the citizen learned to see mutual dependence as a lightening of burdens and a source of dignity rather than the reverse. And once learned in small polities, Tocqueville thought, this "art of association" might teach something of the same lesson in a larger one.[37]

The small state was conducive to "warm affections" and it fitted the citizen's dignity. It was not suited to great passions and ambitions which, in Tocqueville's eyes, was an advantage. The ambition of citizens could not express itself in expansion or great endeavors. It would turn inward, cultivating the excellence of citizens, as the community understood them, and their relationships with each other. The small community could be unbearably intrusive, but at its worst, the despotism of small communities is easy to escape or overthrow.[38]

Great states permit great projects. They afford power and, hence, liberty. But each citizen matters very little. His passions are not schooled in the crowd of his fellows; weakness compels and anonymity allows him to be self-concerned. There is far more distance between my senses and the society as a whole, and devotion to the public good, forced to war against the senses, is weaker and more tyrannical than it is in small states where it may more easily claim the feelings for its allies. Hence, the capacity for "great projects" proves to be something of an illusion: it is difficult to assemble a "compact" majority and hence, in a large democracy, great *public* projects are unlikely. Private projects are the arena for ambition, and they take citizens even further from concern for public life.[39]

In Tocqueville's analysis, "tyranny of the majority" resulted from the combination of democracy and the large state. The authority of the majority derives from equality, but so long as I can perceive that majority as only so many individuals, equality tells me that I have a perfect right to disagree with each singly. In the great state, the majority becomes an impersonal abstraction, too massive by far for me to change. As individuals, we are radically unimportant, vulnerable, and dispensable. We fear to be at odds with majority and we tend to see its opinions as "facts" to which we must adapt. Accordingly, we "go along" with the current of ideas as we perceive it. In great democracies, "the body is left free and the soul is enslaved."[40]

In great democracies, the citizen is prone to "individualism," a withdrawal into private life. Faced with his own weakness as part of the public, and his own reasonable competence in private life, the citizen wishes to forget his indignity as part of the public realm and to think of that private world in which he matters. Initially, individualism destroys only public virtue. But, Tocqueville knew, the private life of the individual is dependent on the public order. A world of ambitious, private projects and weak public authority is a world of change, incoherence, and instability. The individual learns to distrust that world: he commits himself to a neighborhood, only to see it decay, or to an idea, only to see it forgotten. He learns to make no commitments in private life, either: in the end, individualism destroys private as well public virtue.[41]

Evidently, Tocqueville did not fear equality as much as its absence. "Tyranny of the majority" and the attendant dangers of mass democracy are products of privatism, individualism, and the failure to learn the "arts of association." In a word, they are caused by liberty, for great states are the product of the preference for grand liberties over the humble equality of the small community.

In the first place, tyrannized by the majority, we are likely to make ourselves the same. Second, since the sources of esteem in a great state are likely to be private, anything less than private equality will tend to seem undignified. (In small states, public dignity makes private inequality acceptable, up to a point.) The more that private life breaks the citizen's ties with past and future and "separates contemporaries," the more he will be reduced to a dignity derived from material well-being. If you are deeply involved with your church, while I have a lot of money, it is easy for you to argue that your dignity is at least as great as mine. If we both have nothing but money, our relative dignities will be quantifiable. Finally, individualism weakens the capacity of government to act for the public good. Majorities are not "compact"; I do not trust my representatives very far and I will not willingly give you much unless I get equal compensation. Still less will I make sacrifices unless you make them too. Liberty, for which great states are created, destroys them, and only the quality of the local community can make them whole.

Obviously, the framers did not share this view. Liberty, for the framers, was "essential to political life," as necessary to politics as the air we breathe and not to be suppressed because it contributed to the "fire" of faction. Liberty is even more, in the framers' view, than a necessary environment for political life. It is the end for which government exists. We are, by nature, without obligation to nature or each other, at liberty to do well. The protection of the "diversity in the faculties of men"—fostering our individual skills and combating any scheme for uniformity—is the "chief object of government." Equality sits below the salt in this view: we have equal rights because we are created equal in that state of nature which precedes all human excellence, but equality is no *end* of political life. Quite the contrary, we invent politics in order to escape from the equality of the state of nature. Even our equality in rights is best understood as a concession without which stubbornly self-interested men will not consent to be governed at all.[42]

The framers' "science of politics" was only one of the voices in American life. Tocqueville thought that American laws were "very subordinate to the manners of the people" in maintaining democracy, and he credited religion and local government with limiting the worst effects of individualism and *democratie*. Political life was especially vital. It was half the existence of the American, and without that citizenship, his life would be unendurable.[43] Similarly, Chesterton was to write that "the theory of equality . . . the pure classic conception that no man must aspire to be anything more than a citizen and no man must endure to be anything less" was unrivaled as the "idealism" of America.[44] Throughout American history, equality—with all its ancient heritage and associations—has rivaled liberty, the gonfalon of modernity. But their political battles have been fought on a modern field and by rules that the framers devised. Gradually, equality has retreated. Even those who are attracted find it an increasingly stern ideal, for equality is distant from our present life, demanding sacrifice, patience, and devotion, and all of these qualities are in short supply in our contemporary life.

Where can one find equality in contemporary America? The inequality of wealth is towering, but differences in wealth may be the least of our problems. Historically, we accepted radical inequalities of income with relatively little opposition. We believed in "equality of opportunity," the sacrifice of equality in favor of an equal liberty to use one's powers to "get ahead." To those at the bottom of the pyramid, the great fortunes were often the romance of opportunity, adding luster to the hope they cherished for themselves or their children. Upward mobility, of course, was never as marked or as prevalent as we believed. The myth drew its strength from economic growth combined with a fervent optimism, a belief in progress which looked past today's ills to their expected remedies tomorrow. Increasingly, however, those supports have been pulled away.[45]

Equality of opportunity is embattled. Growth seems uncertain (and to some, undesirable), and progress, for all kinds of reasons, is questioned where it is not disbelieved. Poverty has declined since the Second World War, but this is due chiefly to Social Security and welfare payments, not to earnings from work.[46] America has become a "contract society" which protects the jobs and position of an increasing number of workers by contract, setting aside the old rules of the market to the disadvantage, in the short term, of the young (and especially, the young and black). Coworkers, in other words, have grown less equal. Moreover, the old, although their pensions suffer from inflation, will have Social Security checks supported by the taxes of relatively fewer young workers. Youth, in general, can expect to work at a disadvantage without the old faith in the promise of American life to make present sacrifices palatable.[47]

Some Americans will struggle to restore the sense of equal opportunity and a boundless future. That effort, I think, accounts for a good deal of the "conservative mood" we hear about. But other Americans may wonder whether the decision to take equal liberty in place of equality was really a wise one.

Inequalities of wealth are, at any rate, relatively tractable. We could equalize wealth if we thought it desirable to do so, just as we could provide employment for everyone. Unequal dignity is a far more stubborn problem, for in a state as large and as complex as contemporary America, only a relatively few people are noticed or matter in shaping the course of things.[48]

More and more, American life is framed by massive organizations, "private governments" that we can hope to control only by a public government more massive still. This is an artifact of the size and intricacy of the regime. If one accepts a gigantic industrial state, whatever its economic system, "the relevant discussion," John Kenneth Galbraith observes, "is how to live with this power."[49] Any organization large enough to have a significant impact on the market or public policy is almost certain to be so large that its members feel weak, insignificant, and slighted. In public life, ordinary citizens find only indignity and, encouraged by the established creed which praises individual liberty, they tend to retreat into private life. The love of one person or a few, if strong enough, may be as much dignity as I need. As the public sphere expands, the private sphere contracts:[50] "The modern individual typically tries to arrange this sphere in such a way that by contrast to his bewildering involvement with the worlds of public institutions, this private world will provide him an order of integrative and sustained meanings. . . . The individual attempts to construct and maintain a 'home world' which will serve as a meaningful center for his life in society."[51]

But all is not well with the private order. The associations to which Americans have turned for identity and meaning—love, the family, and communities of all sorts—are increasingly weak and short-lived. As public institutions have meant less, we have asked private institutions to do more; as public dignity grows weaker, we seek the consolidation of a stronger and more intense private love. But intense relationships are bonds between me and one or a very few other people. The very existence of such relationships, correspondingly, depends on one or a few people.

Intensity is inversely related to security, and the more such relationships mean, the more vulnerable I will be. The intense relationships to which we turn for dignity and meaning heighten our feelings of insecurity and anxiety. We can protect ourselves only by keeping our distance, but this, in turn, deprives us of the love that was to make our public indignity bearable or of no account.[52]

It makes matters worse that, under the sway of liberty, American society is so open and devoted to change. Change is continuous but also "unsteady, irregular and hard to predict."[53] Institutions, laws, and habits seem transient, and yesterday's certainties are today's follies. (The transformation of our assumptions about cars and gasoline should be evidence enough.) Increasingly, it seems dangerous to commit oneself to institutions or to people, for people, like the rules of the game, are all too likely to change. Our relationships, in the family and out of it, are shorter in life. We move more often, just as we change partners, and we learn not to invest ourselves deeply in places or people. Herbert Hendin observes that we are becoming more private, self-concerned, exploitative, and aggrandizing in our relationship with others, and greedy for "experience"— by which we mean a private, short-term sensation, not something learned by long practice or in common. "Harmony, cooperation and affection," Hendin writes, are "more scarce in and out of families." Liberty has mastered private life, making it less and less a haven for dignity or a school for equality.[54]

Politics offers little hope for remedying the defects of the private order. Our public institutions and our political thought are too limited by the individualism and the zeal for liberty which informed the framers.

To be sure, we have come to recognize that in economic life, growing inequalities of power make nonsense of formal equality, and that government may be needed to correct the balance. "The proprietors of these establishments and their operatives," the Supreme Court noted at the turn of the century, "do not stand upon an equality," and after the long, familiar struggle, the partisans of freedom of contract were finally defeated and the Court conceded the government's right to legislate for the general welfare against private inequalities.[55]

In relation to *political* institutions, however, the Court has retained and expanded the abstract, formal equality of individual citizens despite all that it has said and seen about economic life. The reapportionment cases, the "success story" of the Warren Court, turn on the doctrine that "political equality can mean only one thing—one person, one vote."[56]

The Court did not consider that weighted representation might be desirable in order to equalize, in politics, groups which are at a disadvantage economically and socially. Certainly, rural America—widely dispersed, at a distance from media centers and the seats of economic power—is too frequently invisible, neglected, and unnoticed. This is no new discovery: in the eighteenth century, an Anti-Federalist wrote that: "The citizens in the seaport towns are numerous; they live compact, their interests are one; there is a constant connection and intercourse between them; they can, on any occasion, center their votes where they please. This is not the case with the landed interest; they are scattered far and wide; they have but little intercourse and connection with each other."[57] The danger that the "landed interest" would go unrepresented is the basis for the federal principle. But evidently, women, racial minorities, and ethnic groups may suffer from analogous disadvantages, and political equality might demand special, protected representation for them. In fact, despite the logic of *Reynolds v. Sims,* the Court found reason to insist that Hinds County, Mississippi, be districted—rather than electing legislators at large—to allow blacks to elect a representative.[58] But that decision was at odds with the Court's doctrine, for "one person, one vote" is nowhere so strictly observed as in at-large elections. In more recent cases, the Court's principles and not its prudence have prevailed. For example, the Court permitted multimember districts in the Indiana Senate, which radically diluted black voting power.[59]

I am not arguing that the Court should retreat to the doctrine of "political questions." Rather, I am urging that the Court recognize that unequal means (like the income tax) may be needed to pursue civic equality as an end, and that it limit itself to asking if apportionment reflects some rational design related to the goal of civic equality.

In relation to the poor, the Court has demonstrated a genuine concern for the problems of the needy, the uneducated, and the lonely. It has recognized—against classical liberalism—that the isolated individual is not necessarily free and capable of reasoned choice, and that by contrast, freedom may require support and counsel.[60] These decisions, however, have still been defined in relation to individual rights against the state, the ancient liberal concern. In general, the Court has been insensitive to the fact that the poor are at a special disadvantage in the world of associations, communities, and families, and that help in associating might address the problem of keeping the poor out of criminal proceedings.[61] It has ruled, for example, that welfare recipients must be allowed to file for divorce even if they cannot pay ordinary court fees. By contrast, indigent debtors need not be excused from fees in filing for bankruptcy.[62] The Court, then, is in the bizarre position of saying that the poor need the state's help in destabilizing their families, but not in freeing them from an insuperable burden of debt.

In fact, liberty has displaced a more equalitarian wisdom in the Court's view of the family. In *Griswold v. Connecticut,* the Court went out of its way to refer to the citizen's right to association, referring by case citations to religious and ethnic education and proclaiming a "right to privacy" in *such associations,* and especially in the "intimate relations" of marriage. Marriage, Justice Douglas declared, cannot be understood in terms of individual utility. It is enduring, almost sacred, and it "promotes a way of life, not causes; a harmony in living, not political faiths; a bilateral loyalty, not commercial or social projects."[63] But in *Eisenstadt v. Baird,* the Court ruled that Massachusetts could not give contraceptives to married persons and deny them to the unmarried. The Court abandoned its concern for the rights of relationships and associations, dissolving marriage into contract and individual rights: "The marital couple is not an independent entity with a heart and mind of its own, but an association of two individuals. . . . If the right of privacy means anything, it is the right of the individual . . . to be free from unwarranted governmental intrusion."[64] In effect, this individualizing decision ruled that the state may not legitimately prefer the family (at least, in the distribution of contraceptives). It is a doctrine the Court has taken a good deal further.[65] It has had second thoughts, but the basic point remains: the "right to privacy," originally proclaimed in defense of the family, has become an attack *on* it, mounted in the name of liberty. And that bodes little good for the poor, whose families need the state's help against the fragmenting pressures of society.

The poor face an additional problem. The church is the most frequent form of association among the poor. For most of America, the church has been a school for the art of association, and any concern for the civic equality of the poor is bound to consider help for the church in performing that *civic* role. (It is for similar reasons, I think, that the poor of both races—in Lewis Lipsitz's study of Durham—favored prayer in the schools.)[66] The Court, however, has repeatedly barred such aid, clinging—a few exceptions aside—to the "wall of separation" between church and state.

Despite their devotion to liberty, the framers expected public acts supporting religion so long as there was no preference for particular confessions. Very secular men, for the most part, the framers saw no problem in supporting churches when they served secular ends.[67] Justice Brennan, aware of the case for civic education, argued (in 1963) that religious means could not be used so long as secular speeches and documents might serve the same purpose.[68] Justice Brennan did not recall, however, that almost all the documents and speeches he mentioned invoke the Deity. Moreover, if this civil religion does have effects comparable to traditional religious teaching, then it must *be* a religion within the meaning the Court has assigned to that term.

In *U.S. v. Seeger,* the Court held that a "sincere and meaningful belief" which is "parallel" to the place of God in religious views would have to be termed a religion.[69] Faithful to that decision, the Court held that Elliott Welsh, who denied that his convictions were religious, was in fact "religious" because his beliefs were held with the "strength" of traditional views.[70] The Court's decisions, then, suggest that any teaching (Welsh got his ideas, he said, from history and sociology) which imparts beliefs strongly and sincerely is a "religion." That doctrine, in turn, implies that all education, except bad and infective education, is "religious."

The Court recognizes this implication. In *Wisconsin v. Yoder,* it permitted Yoder to withdraw his children from the public schools because to leave them there until age sixteen, as the law required, was offensive to Yoder's Amish beliefs. Following *Yoder,* the Ohio Supreme Court ruled that "freedom of religion" overrides the state's right to set standards for denominational schools.[71] Hence, the courts seem to declare that "freedom of religion" includes the right to refuse to educate one's children at all, and possibly the right to educate them badly. Zealous for liberty, the Court declares that religions have a right to withdraw from public life, but not to receive the public's support or to participate equally in public life. In *Brown v. Board,* Justice Warren declared that education is "the very foundation of good citizenship."[72] Surely this foundation would be safer if the Court allowed aid to religious schools for the support of secular education, but allowed the state to hold those schools strictly accountable to civic standards. Instead, the courts have endangered public schools and the public standards for education, a tendency which threatens all citizens, but especially the disadvantaged.

The failure of political institutions and imagination is serious because the public's condition is desperate. Our work and our lives are increasingly specialized. Friends of individual liberty are cheered by "destandardized" production, "individualized" instruction, and the rise of smaller media aimed at narrow constituencies. These phenomena, however, all point to the fragmentation of life and the shrinking of the common sphere of things. More than ever, we are strangers who do different things and speak different languages.[73]

Local community was once the place where we acquired the foundations of civic equality. Today, the neighborhoods and social circles in which we live are only rarely political bodies, combining all or most of the things needed for the good life. They are highly specialized associations organized on the basis of private wealth and occupation.[74] Even in these tightly fitted circles, we keep a good deal to ourselves. They are too narrow to embrace us and too unstable to be much trusted. Certainly, these neighborhoods are not schools of equality, teaching us the dignity of all crafts and stations. They emphasize our privateness, not our citizenship. (One of the things which moderates my devotion to neighborhood schools is the recognition that, sometimes, such schools are really upper-middle-class private schools funded by public monies. Parochial schools are often more "public" than suburban public schools.)

Once, political parties served the role of civic educators, connecting local places to national leaders.[75] Parties today have been weakened by the decline of local community, but also by a whole tradition of reform legislation which first attacked the party directly and then, in the 1970s, defined party in terms of the relation between individual voters and candidates, leaving out organized, horizontal partisan life. Under that assault, parties are reduced more and more to interest groups rather than vehicles for civic education.[76]

But the hostility to community is even more explicit than that. The Supreme Court has ruled that the "right to travel" is a "fundamental" right which takes precedence over community. In one sense, the right to travel—which sanctifies mobility and instability—is part of a long line of cases asserting to supremacy of commerce over the attempts of states and localities to protect their own citizens by restricting competition and the like.[77] But such cases ordinarily took the form of vindicating the political power of the national government as against the states. In *Shapiro v. Thompson*, by contrast, the Court ruled that a state may not make a residence requirement a condition of welfare even when Congress has authorized it to do so.[78] Even the Court's sympathy for the poor is ambiguous. It agreed that states may set a maximum limit for aid without regard to the number of children in a family. It also ruled that, while local communities may not require a referendum on open housing, they may do so on low-income housing projects; poverty, unlike race, may be a ground for exclusion and, presumably, a badge of shame.[79] A community, then, may be callous toward the poor it includes and may seek to exclude the poor altogether. But it may not prefer its own. Communities may be cruel, but they may not nurture.[80] It damages communities enough to say that localities may not prefer friends to strangers. It makes matters worse to say that such questions are not subject to public policy at all because travel, an individual right, outweighs public claims. The right to travel is yet another instance of the extent to which liberty, in modern America, has been made sovereign over civic equality.

Nothing will make contemporary politics in America anything but difficult and painful. In many ways, we will be forced to learn new patterns of life and—if we are to better the quality of American democracy—we will need to rethink our basic ideas. In my view, we need most of all to restore equality to its place as the highest goal of republics. Civic equality, I have been arguing, does not in the first instance mean equal treatment but rather equal feeling and sympathy, a conviction of equal dignity and common destiny. That sort of equality requires a public policy prepared to strengthen or reconstruct the local places and communities which are the nurseries of civility and citizenship. It also requires that we reduce liberty to the place assigned it by classical political theory—the servant of the *polis* and of nature and the master of neither. Liberty, in an ancient paradox, to be perfected, must be *ruled* by the common good and the good life.

Notes

This essay was originally published as "Liberty, Equality and the Problem of Community," in *Liberty and Equality under the Constitution,* ed. John Agresto (Washington, D.C.: American Historical Association and American Political Science Association, 1983).

1. Hannah Arendt, "Revolution and the Public Happiness," *Commentary* 30 (1960): 413–21.

2. Alexis de Tocqueville, *Democracy in America* (New York: Schocken, 1961), 1:lxxviii.

3. While I do not agree with everything in it, one of the best appreciations of the Gettysburg Address is Leo Paul S. de Alvarez, ed., *Abraham Lincoln, the Gettysburg Address and American Constitutionalism* (Irving: University of Dallas Press, 1976).

4. *Democracy in America,* 1:lxxiii; Plato, Apology, 17D–18A.

5. Thomas Hobbes, *Leviathan,* ed. C. B. Macpherson (Baltimore: Penguin, 1968), 262.

6. Christian Bay, *The Structure of Freedom* (Stanford: Stanford University Press, 1958), 15.

7. Advocates of positive liberty sometimes forget, however, that while liberty requires that I have the power to do as I choose, it does not necessarily mean that there will be no costs. Very powerful people cannot use their power without risking resentment. This may deter them, but they are still "at liberty" to act.

8. Ewart K. Lewis, "The Contribution of Medieval Thought to the American Political Tradition," *American Political Science Review* 50 (1956): 462–74.

9. F. W. J. Schelling, *Inquiry into the Nature of Human Freedom,* in *Sammtliche Werke* (Augsburg: Cotta, 1860), 6:351.

10. Rousseau, *Social Contract,* bk. I, ch. vi.

11. *Leviathan,* 161.

12. Helmuth Plessner, "The Emancipation of Power," *Social Research* 31 (1964): 155–74.

13. Walter Kaufmann, *Existentialism from Dostoevsky to Sartre* (New York: New American Library, 1956), 155–74.

14. Peter L. Berger, *Pyramids of Sacrifice* (New York: Basic Books, 1974), 21.

15. Schelling, *Inquiry into the Nature of Human Freedom;* Arnold Gehlen, *Studien zur Anthropologie und Soziologie* (Neuwied: Luchterhand, 1963), 232ff.

16. Alexander Herzen, *From the Other Shore* (New York: Braziller, 1956), 148–49; Hannah Pitkin, "Obligation and Consent, II," *American Political Science Review* 60 (1966): 39–52.

17. *Leviathan,* 223. Anarchy is only second best; it leaves me free from rule by any other, but I am also likely to be opposed or intruded on by those equally free others, hence the "inconveniences" of the state of nature.

18. Wolfgang Mommsen, "Zum Begriff der Plebiszitaron Führerdemokratie bei Max Weber," *Kölner Zeitschrift fur Soziologie und Socialpsychologie* 15 (1963): 295–322.

19. *Leviathan,* 240.

20. Harold D. Lasswell, *Psychopathology and Politics* (Chicago: University of Chicago Press, 1930); see also David Truman, *The Governmental Process* (New York: Knopf, 1951), 47–52.

21. *Democracy in America,* 1:lxxi, 2:113; J. A. Pole, *The Pursuit of Equality in American History* (Berkeley and Los Angeles: University of California Press, 1978).

22. *Democracy in America,* 1:lxx–lxxi.

23. Ibid., 1:lxxviii; Tocqueville's argument, lamenting the loss of sympathy between the feelings and the ideas of humankind, suggests Aristotle's definition of virtue as a mean between *pathe* and *praxis,* emotion and action (*Ethics,* 1106a–1109b). But the mean (*meson*), in Pythagorean terms, was also called *isomoira,* "just balance," but also an "equal lot" or "equal destiny," a sense that the two extremes "belong together" in a kind of community. Diogenes Laertius, *Lives of the Eminent Philosophers,* trans. R. Hick (London: Heinemann, 1925), 8:26.

24. *Republic,* Bloom trans., bk. II, 372d.

25. See, for example, Henry Kariel, *The Promise of Politics* (Englewood Cliffs: Prentice Hall, 1966), 53.

26. John H. Schaar, "Some Ways of Thinking about Equality," *Journal of Politics* 26 (1964): 876.

27. Aristotle, *Ethics,* 1158b 29–33.

28. Ibid., 1164a 1–30, 1168a 27–1169b 2; Plato, *Laws,* bk. V, 739 b6–c2, 739d9–e3.

29. Edmund S. Morgan, ed., *Puritan Political Ideas* (Indianapolis: Bobbs-Merrill, 1965), 77.

30. Even this is not required by equality: *Democracy in America,* 2:114.

31. Delba Winthrop, "Aristotle on Participatory Democracy," *Polity* 11 (1978): 155. Notably, Plato describes the relationship between the objects of sense and the forms in terms of participation (*méthexis*) in the *eide* (*Phaedo,* 100d).

32. Ernest Barker, trans., *The Politics of Aristotle* (Oxford: Clarendon, 1952), 258.

33. Alexander Meiklejohn, *Political Freedom* (New York: Harper and Row, 1960).

34. Morroe Berger, *Equality by Statute* (Garden City: Doubleday, 1968), 116–17.

35. *Politics of Aristotle,* 258.

36. I have discussed this at greater length in "Equality as the Foundation for Community," in *The Moral Foundations of the American Republic,* ed. Robert Horwitz (Charlottesville: University of Virginia Press, 1977), 195–98.

37. *Democracy in America,* 1:124–27, 176–82.

38. Ibid., 1:62, 176–77.

39. Ibid., 1:177–78.

40. Ibid., 1:299, 311.

41. Ibid., 2:118–20.

42. James Madison, *The Federalist,* #10, ed. Jacob Cooke (Middletown: Wesleyan University Press, 1977). This careful edition indexes sixty-six entries for liberty and none for equality (663, 666). See also Robert Ginsberg, "Equality and Justice in the Declaration of Independence," *Journal of Social Philosophy* 6 (1975): 6–9.

43. *Democracy in America,* 1:383, 293.

44. G. K. Chesterton, *What I Saw in America* (New York: Da Capo, 1968), 16–17.

45. John H. Schaar, "Equality of Opportunity and Beyond," in *Equality,* ed. J. Roland Pennock and John Chapman (New York: Atherton, 1967), 228–49; Bruce Johnson, "The Democratic Mirage: Toward a Theory of American Politics," *Berkeley Journal of Sociology* 13 (1968): 104–43.

46. James Duffy, *Domestic Affairs: American Programs and Priorities* (New York: Simon and Schuster, 1978), 29–30.

47. See Gerald M. Pomper et al., *The Election of 1976* (New York: Longmans, 1977).

48. Bertrand de Jouvenel, "The Chairman's Problem," *American Political Science Review* 55 (1961): 368–72. The recognition of the problem of dignity is the great virtue of Charles Hampden-Turner, *From Poverty to Dignity* (Garden City: Doubleday, 1974).

49. *New York Times Book Review,* June 5, 1977, 24.

50. Grant McConnell, *Private Power and American Democracy* (New York: Knopf, 1966); *Democracy in America,* 2:118–20.

51. Peter Berger, Brigitte Berger, and Hannsfried Kellner, *The Homeless Mind* (New York: Random House, 1973), 65–66.

52. W. J. Goode, "The Theoretical Importance of Love," *American Sociological Review* 24 (1959): 38–47.

53. Alvin Toffler, "Law and Order," *Encounter* 41 (July 1973): 19.

54. Herbert Hendin, "The Ties Don't Bind," *New York Times,* August 26, 1976, C33; see also Hendin's *The Age of Sensation* (New York: Norton, 1975); Christopher Lasch, *The Culture of Narcissism* (New York: Norton, 1979); and Arnold Gehlen, *Moral und Hypermoral* (Frankfurt: Athenäum, 1969).

55. The quotation is from *Holden v. Hardy,* 169 U.S. 366 (1898). See also *West Coast Hotel v. Parrish,* 300 U.S. 379 (1937); and *Lincoln Federal Labor Union v. Northwestern Iron and Metal Co.,* 335 U.S. 525 (1949).

56. The quotation is from Justice Douglas in *Gray v. Sanders,* 372 U.S. 368 (1963). See also *Reynolds v. Sims,* 377 U.S. 533 (1964). Robert McKay, "Reapportionment: Success Story of the Warren Court," *Michigan Law Review* 67 (1968): 223–36.

57. Cited in Cecilia Kenyon, ed., *The Anti-Federalists* (Indianapolis: Bobbs-Merrill, 1966), liv.

58. *Connor v. Johnson,* 402 U.S. 690 (1971).

59. *Whitcomb v. Chavis,* 403 U.S. 124 (1971).

60. *Miranda v. Arizona,* 384 U.S. 436 (1966); *Gideon v. Wainwright,* 372 U.S. 335 (1963).

61. David Price, "Community, 'Mediating Structures,' and Public Policy," *Soundings* 62 (1979): 381–83.

62. *Boddie v. Connecticut,* 401 U.S. 317 (1971); *U.S. v. Kras,* 409 U.S. 434 (1973).

63. *Griswold v. Connecticut,* 381 U.S. 479 (1965).

64. *Eisenstadt v. Baird,* 405 U.S. 438 (1972).

65. *Weber v. Aetna Casualty,* 406 U.S. 164 (1972).

66. Lewis Lipsitz, "Freedom and the Poor," *Western Political Quarterly* 25 (1972): 151–64.

67. Walter Berns, *The First Amendment and the Future of American Democracy* (New York: Basic Books, 1976), 71, 74 .

68. Concurring in *Abington v. Schempp,* 374 U.S. 278, 281 (1963).

69. *U.S. v. Seeger,* 380 U.S. 163 (1965).

70. *Welsh v. U.S.,* 398 U.S. 333 (1970).

71. *Wisconsin v. Yoder,* 406 U.S. 205 (1972); B. Drummond Ayres, "Private Schools Provoking Church-State Conflict," *New York Times,* April 28, 1978, 1, 23.

72. *Brown v. Board of Education,* 347 U.S. 483 (1954).

73. Toffler, "Law and Order," 16–19. Norman Birnbaum, "Is There a Post-industrial Revolution?" *Social Policy* 1 (July/August 1970): 3–13.

74. Schaar, "Equality of Opportunity"; *The Politics of Aristotle,* 4–7, 42, 95, 120, 292, 293, 299.

75. James Ceaser, "Political Parties and Presidential Ambition," *Journal of Politics* 40 (1978): 725, 728.

76. Gerald M. Pomper et al., *Party Renewal in America* (New York: Praeger, 1980).

77. For example, *Hood v. Dumond,* 336 U.S. 525 (1949).

78. *Shapiro v. Thompson,* 394 U.S. 618 (1969).

79. *Dandridge v. Williams,* 397 U.S. 471 (1970); *James v. Valtierra,* 91 S.Ct. 1331 (1971).

80. By contrast, the decision of the New Jersey Supreme Court in *Southern Burlington County NAACP v. Township of Mount Laurel,* 67 N.J. 151 (1975) is almost a model of respect for community in distinguishing a developing municipality, where the state can and must ask for concessions in the direction of equality, and a settled community, valuable in itself, where the claims of equality are weaker.

Religion and
the American Founding

Americans are typically apt to forget that the era of American founding was a time of uneasiness as well as confidence. A political founding demands daring, but entails dread: new laws open new pitfalls as well as new prospects. A political beginning is necessarily a venture into the unfamiliar, and the effort to create a new regime requires a turning from convention to theory, an appeal to first principles rather than second nature. The American framers observed the civil decencies in their speech and writing, but creating a new republic demands, at least, that one be willing to think shamelessly. Custom surrounds ambiguities and guards secrets, but political foundings ask us to envision things unclothed, as they are by nature.[1]

Americans found this sort of thinking uncomfortable because theorizing drew attention to the fundamental discord between biblical religion and secular rationalism, the antiphonies of American culture.[2] Then as now, most Americans felt some attachment to both traditions and preferred a downy equivocation to the discipline of dialectic. Yet willy-nilly, the logic of the founding imposed its own regimen, and Americans were forced to rethink the relation between religion and the new republic.

A great many Americans trusted or hoped that the new regime, while affording freedom of conscience, would be, at least implicitly, a Christian and Protestant commonwealth.[3] Prevailing Christian teaching, moreover, envisages a religious civility, a political order shaped by the principles of redemption and grace.

In that Christian understanding, the doctrine of redemption points toward the reconciliation of human beings with the order of creation—with nature, with their fellow humans, and with their own finite humanity. The Incarnation attests to God's love for the world and proclaims that nature is lovable; Jesus's life reveals that human existence, with all its pains and imperfections, is touched by the divine, worthy of God's Son. For those who have conned its lesson, redemption teaches that we ought to strive to overcome human resentment against nature and its limits, saving life from the fury of human indignation: disciples are the salt of the earth, meant to restore life's savor. The Gospel liberates human beings by teaching them that nature's laws and limits are no bondage; redemption rejects the conquest of nature in favor of mastery of the self.

Political society was understood to play a crucial role in the secular education of the soul, and mainstream Protestant teaching regarded political life as natural and God-intended, necessary for human fulfillment. Indispensable as a restraint on vice, laws are also needed as a help to virtue: "A virtuous society cannot be happy without government," Joseph Lathrop wrote; "A vicious one cannot subsist without it."[4] Civil education should lead human beings out of self-centeredness into a broader sense of self as a part of the whole. And before we can learn to see nature as homelike, we need the experience of home; the effort to reconcile human with human requires laws which nurture and strengthen the bonds of community and the capacity for love. Public spirit, the foundation of secular civic virtue, is a step toward reconciliation with nature and, perhaps, toward Christianity's higher republic.[5]

By nature, Nathaniel Niles contended, there are no private rights. As Aristotle had observed, individuality presupposes the *polis*, a regime under which the division of labor permits each to do what he or she does best. Individual achievements, consequently, depend on the prior existence of political community, and private rights derive from public laws.[6] "Let our pupil be taught," Benjamin Rush argued, "that he does not belong to himself but that he is public property."[7]

Obviously that doctrine wars against the Old Adam, and Christian theory insisted on stern laws to discipline and restrain the passions. At the same time, it held that a good political society will entice the passions and draw the soul into the common life. Rightly governed, material delights and comforts help coax the soul out of the fortress of the self. Even a "Turk's paradise" of luxury, Gilbert Tennent argued, is better than the desire to be "a sort of independent being."[8] At a higher level, human capacities for love and friendship are strengthened by "exercise," just as they are undermined by self-seeking.[9] The best regime, consequently, encourages and honors the practice of civic friendship and public spirit.

Social stability, for example, makes it easier for us to know and trust our fellow citizens. Moreover, human beings will not run the inevitable risks of caring for others without some minimal assurance of *being* cared for: the laws must provide for the "particular care" which affords each child—and adult—the necessary evidence that he or she matters. Similarly, citizens will be more ready to invest themselves in public life when politics grants them dignity. Following ancient theory, Christian doctrine at the time of the founding was inclined to hold that the best political society is necessarily a small one, in which citizens know their rulers and are known by them, and in which individuals can visibly make a difference. In a small state, we can see and experience public benefits at first hand—our children attend new schools and we drive on new roads—but it is even more important that we have the chance to be heard on public questions, or to listen if we prefer. In a large state, most of us are denied the choice between speech and silence, so that we assert our wounded dignity only by refusing to listen, confining our attention to that small private sphere in which we matter.[10] Any "vastly extended republic" can expect only a weak public spirit. Such a regime, consequently, stands in desperate need of the support and sanctions of religion; smaller states are more able to cultivate faith.[11]

Christian ideas of civic education include limits on the wealth as well as the size of political society. The division of labor frees talents and enriches civil life, but it can also divide society into competing interests and factions, each speaking a private argot. Since it is the whole that makes possible the specialization of the parts, in a good regime economics is kept firmly subordinate to politics. Wealth and pursuit of wealth must be ruled by the public good: life must not become so cluttered or so complex that human beings lose sight of their dependence on one another and on the commonweal. "We must be willing to abridge ourselves of our superfluities for the relief of others' necessities," Winthrop told the Puritans, "having always before our eyes our commission and community in the work, . . . as members of the same body."[12] Even in private life, industry must be tempered by frugality, and a republic's citizens, thinking their liberties beyond price, must be willing to sacrifice well-being in favor of self-government. In principle, a good republic is small, simple, and austere, like the Christian Sparta for which Sam Adams hoped.[13]

It is worth emphasizing that Adams dreamed of a *Christian* Sparta: Protestant theorists might admire warrior virtue, but they rejected the closed community. In their view, it was part of the office of religion to remind citizens of their obligations to humanity, freeing public spirit from the reproach of xenophobia. The small republic is a necessary and desirable concession to the "feebleness of human powers"; it must still be ruled by the higher law.[14]

In a similar way, even redemption derives from the ruling principle of grace. God's love is gracious because it is given freely and without consideration, not because of merit but in spite of sin. Love, the royal law, is beyond justice, ignoring or sacrificing what is due the ruler in favor of the good of the ruled, insisting that the exalted must serve the lowly and treating the needs of the weak as obligations of the strong. The principle of grace, in other words, derives authority from the loving qualities of those who rule, not from the "consent of the governed."[15] In a republic this implies that the public spirit of the citizens must rule their private interests and desires. Nathaniel Niles argued, for example, that a social contract founded for the mutual protection of private interests—the Lockean model of the origin of politics—is as much an usurpation as any tyranny, since it seeks to turn public things into private benefits. It changes nothing, in Niles's view, if a majority agree: numbers do not affect the question of right. Moreover, as Niles recognized, public-spirited citizenship often demands personal sacrifice and great courage, as when one defies the many. Even quiet law-abidingness must be willing to bear the burden imposed by the fact that some violate and many minimize their lawful obligations. The principle of grace, as Niles understood, prods citizens to do their duty without regard to reciprocities. In that sense, Christian citizenship ennobles republics by upholding a distinctly aristocratic ideal: "It is good, it is glorious, to espouse a good cause, and it is still more great and glorious to stand alone."[16]

Love must be freely given and reconciliation must be agreed to: Christian teaching at the time of the founding regarded liberty as an indispensable means to what is best in individuals and in polities. At the same time, Christian liberty denied that liberty is the highest—or even a proper—human goal: our natural rights are subordinate to what is naturally right, and the end is dutiful civility in a good regime. Love, after all, chooses to be ruled and to have duties, as Samuel Longfellow's hymn reminds us:

> Holy Spirit, Right Divine,
> King within my conscience reign.
> Be my law, and I will be
> Firmly bound, forever free.

The framers of the United States Constitution, by contrast, were informed by modern philosophies which held that, by nature, human beings are *free,* not political animals. Human nature, in this view, is defined by the body and its motions—human identity, Locke wrote, is "nothing but a participation of the same continued life . . . like that of other Animals, in one fitly organized body"—and our bodies are forever separate. We come into the world as we go out of it, alone: nature imposes no obligations and gives us no claims on one another.[17]

Human beings are naturally moved by their passions, and especially by the desire for self-preservation, a "fundamental, sacred, and unalterable law," Locke argued, prior to revelation or reason and the "first and strongest desire God planted in men."[18] Nature, however, frustrates and ultimately kills us. It does not matter whether nature is hostile, indifferent, or the work of a benign Artificer who intends to inspire us to effort: by nature, human beings are driven to master nature. Humankind, Hobbes had it, is moved by a "perpetual restless desire of power after power that ceaseth only in Death," and that pursuit of dominion is humanity's only truly natural end.[19]

It follows, of course, that the human struggle to triumph over nature precludes any reconciliation with it. Accordingly, when the framers speak of the divine, they often refer to the Creator, but never to the Redeemer. Their modern teachers urged the framers to regard the doctrine of redemption as a prescription for surrender, virtual treason to the human cause.[20]

Modern political science, in the eighteenth century, was no more friendly to the principle of grace. Natural freedom implies that human beings are rightly bound only by their consent. Authority does not derive from or depend on the qualities of the ruler: it is the creature of the ruled, the creation of their agreement and contract.

In the framers' understanding, political society is made or contrived by naturally free individuals in order to further their essentially private purposes—especially the "taste for property," or so Gouverneur Morris told the Convention.[21] In the familiar locutions of social contract theory, we "give up" certain natural rights in order to enjoy more effectively those we retain. The public good is only the aggregation of private goods; political society does not exist to make us all alike, but to preserve our differences. Protecting "diversity in the faculties of men," Madison asserted, is the "first object of government."[22]

This view of politics establishes a prima facie case for a large and affluent state, able to enhance diversity and individual freedom through a more elaborate division of labor and capable of amassing power for the fulfillment of human desire and the conquest of nature. The framers recognized that smaller regimes promote the strong bonds of civic friendship and patriotism, which in turn are apt to promote political daring and human excellence. They conceded that, in a large republic, sentiments of solidarity will be "diffuse" and probably will be outweighed by private loyalties and interests. But remembering the persecutions and disorders of Europe's recent past, the framers held that strong convictions, in politics or religion, are apt to produce turbulence and oppression. The ancient city-states, Hamilton wrote, produced "bright talents and exalted endowments," but these human achievements were "transient and fleeting," tarnished and misdirected by the "vices of government" with which they were associated.[23] Hamilton would have applied his remark to Jerusalem as readily as to Athens; the framers' ideal was a commercial republic, not a sacred city.

Nevertheless, the framers believed, as had Locke, that political society needs the support of religion. Religion inculcates the decencies: a powerful help in the government and moral instruction of children, it is also indispensable in establishing the duties of parents.[24] Moreover, religion is a buttress for law-abidingness among the ruled, for whom the advantages of right conduct are not apt to be immediately evident.

Liberal political philosophy, in the tradition of Hobbes and Locke, had no difficulty in demonstrating that self-interested human beings, exposed to the insecurities of the "state of nature," have every reason to make the promises necessary to make civil society. Once civil order has been established, however, the reasons for keeping one's promises are much less compelling. In fact, self-seeking individuals are bound to conclude that, in theory, it is desirable to be able to break one's promises while one's fellows keep theirs, reclaiming one's natural liberty while enjoying the advantages of civil society.

These calculations, however, are far more plausible in the case of great and prominent persons—who are likely to be noticed and emulated—than they are in the case of private citizens. This is no small problem since, as Hamilton observed, the spirit of enterprise is "unbridled" and strains against all restraints.[25] The liberal response is least persuasive when addressed to those who are obscure and unpropertied, who may calculate their conduct is all too likely to go unnoticed. The framers knew well enough that the poor and the desperate—and in America, the enslaved—may easily come to feel that they have nothing to lose. Locke concludes that "promises, covenants, and oaths," the basis of civil society, stood in need of religious sanction. "The taking away of God, but even in thought, dissolves all."[26] And even Jefferson wondered whether an atheist's testimony could be accepted by a court of law.[27]

Religion was also needed, in the framers' judgment, to support broader interests—the claims of society as a whole or of humanity—against narrowly private concerns. Reason and humanitarian feelings may touch us, but they are unlikely to prevail against bodily desires or the pressures of our immediate, day-to-day relationships. Jefferson did not doubt that slavery was a violation of natural right; he knew, however, that slaveholders would rate their investment in slave property above their more abstract interest in human liberty, unless religion could tip the scale.[28]

"Had every Athenian citizen been a Socrates," Madison wrote, "every Athenian assembly would still have been a mob."[29] He was contending that Socrates took a high moral tone because his public role made him visible and liable to praise and blame. In an assembly of philosophers, however, those in the back rows, feeling themselves less apt to be noticed, would not be able to keep themselves from talking to their neighbors or behaving like rowdies. Madison's precept implies that rulers—caught up in the broader world, honored when public policy succeeds and subjected to opprobrium when it does not—can be expected to give serious attention to the common good. Private citizens, however, naturally must be expected to follow their private interests, defined in more or less parochial and shortsighted terms. And obviously, in a large republic, only a tiny fraction of citizens can participate in ruling in any way other than voting. The framers, consequently, were inclined to seek religion's help in upholding patriotism and enlightened self-interest among the ruled.

In addition, the framers had very special reasons for seeking an accommodation with Christianity. Prudence taught them that it is politically dangerous to combat deeply held beliefs, and most of the framers were convinced that a purely rational religion, like the Deism to which so many of them were attracted, would be inadequate for children, as yet not rational enough to appreciate it, or for those whose rational interests furnished only uncertain support for civil order—preeminently the poor, women, and slaves. And in some ways, the framers approved of Christian teaching. For example, they applauded and appealed to Christianity's proclamation that all human beings are members of one family, regarding Christian universalism as more comportable with reason than narrow national religions like Judaism (in the framers' very distorted understanding).

The framers would not accept a détente with Christianity, however, until they were persuaded of their ability to curb Christian *political* teaching, averting or neutralizing Christianity's tendencies to fanaticism and its desire to elevate the soul. The framers hoped, as Locke had, to discipline Christianity, civilizing it down to a support for a liberal regime.

Forced to deal with an established church, Locke had set down his own theology, a "reasonable" Christianity which deemphasized or denied the doctrines of redemption and grace. Locke's creed proclaims Christ as the Messiah, a triumphant king who overcame death and, hence, an inspiration in the struggle to master nature. He rejects the idea of Jesus as the Son of Man, the suffering servant who assumed, and showed the nobility of, human life and its burdens.[30] Second, Locke's Christianity emphasizes a "good life according to virtue and morality" which, in Locke's view, could be satisfied by observing the secular decencies.[31] In fact, Locke rejects virtually any *political* application of Christian teaching. In the *Letter concerning Toleration,* for example, he denies that charity ought to influence law, asserting that politics should limit itself to safeguarding public peace and protecting "men's rights."[32]

Many of the framers shared Locke's doctrine and more regarded it sympathetically, but they regarded it as unnecessary in America. Lacking an established church, America did not need a civil theology. Civil religion should be embodied in laws and institutions like those Locke had prescribed, denying official standing to any religion, at least at the national level, and relying on the multiplicity of sects to check and confute any particular creed.[33] Thus limited—and even before the First Amendment, the Constitution ruled out any religious test—Christianity and all other religions could be left to their own devices as part of the private sphere.

This familiar solution, however, is less neutral than it may seem to be. Locke's philosophy suggested that the mind naturally follows experience. On that assumption, the laws, by establishing rules of practice, gradually will also establish a variety of civil theology. The framers designed a liberal and commercial republic, opened to the marketplace of ideas as well as of economics. Confronted with competing ways and views, Americans— the framers were confident—would becomes less and less inclined to give their allegiance to any. Over the long term, Americans would insist on their individual right to judge creeds, seeing doctrines and teachings as analogous to commodities for sale. And the framers expected that the accepted standards of value would come to be liberty, the ability to do as one wills, enhanced by an increasing command of nature.[34]

Religion, of course, has proved to be stronger and more durable than many of the framers expected. Biblical political ideas, especially in their Christian articulations, have exerted a powerful force and spell in the life and thought of the republic.[35] In part, this is due to the intrinsic merit of biblical teaching, which knows the soul and speaks to the human condition more profoundly than modern secularity. It is also the result of religion's attention to that shaping of the "first impressions of the mind" which Benjamin Rush prescribed as a protection against indifferent or hostile laws.[36]

Nevertheless, as Robert Bellah and his associates contend, the "habits of the heart" are waning under the influence of the laws. Even where their conduct is influenced by better principles, Americans are more and more apt to speak the language of individualism, whether they appeal to a utilitarian calculus of self-interest or to the expressive individualism of authenticity and "what is right for me."[37] Americans seem to be losing the ability to speak and think in the language of grace and redemption which has been the counterpoint to liberalism in our national composition.

We cannot do without the second voice in our public forums. In its third century, the republic will require more than individualism and self-seeking; constitutional democracy will call for high citizenship and great consecration. Our debts demand financial sacrifice; equal justice and civil order oblige us to curb our passion for individual rights and private liberties; the pursuit of peace binds us to risk both lives and freedom. In these stern duties, there is also a thundering political vocation, and our biblical heritage reminds us that even those who are in the wilderness may have an engagement at Sinai.

Notes

This essay was originally published as "Religion and the American Founding," *Princeton Seminary Bulletin,* n.s., 8, no. 3 (1987).
1. Thomas Pangle, "The Constitution's Human Vision," *Public Interest* 86 (Winter 1987): 78–79; Plato's *Republic* is the classic example of the relation between shamelessness and political founding. It is worth observing that in thought and speech, the sin of Ham is apparently permissible, since Shem and Japheth were not punished for what they heard or imagined (Gen. 8:22–23). But the line is obviously delicate, especially since political founders translate thought into action: a good political founding, in these terms, is necessarily a recovering of what has been laid bare.

2. Michael Kammen, *People of Paradox* (New York: Knopf, 1972).

3. See, for example, the comments of the New Hampshire Anti-Federalist, "A Friend to the Rights of the People," in *The Complete Anti-Federalist*, ed. Herbert J. Storing (Chicago: University of Chicago Press, 1981), 4.23.3, remark 9; or Benjamin Rush, *The Letters of Benjamin Rush*, ed. L. H. Butterfield (Princeton: Princeton University Press, 1951), 1:584, 611–12; and especially, Mercy Otis Warren, *History of the Rise, Progress and Termination of the American Revolution* (Boston: Larkin, 1805), 1:17–18.

4. Charles S. Hyneman and Donald S. Lutz, eds., *American Political Writing during the Founding Era* (Indianapolis: Liberty Press, 1983), 1:659.

5. Samuel Davies, *Religion and the Public Spirit* (New York: Parker, 1761); Gilbert Tennent, *Brotherly Love Recommended by the Argument of the Love of Christ* (Philadelphia: Franklin and Hall, 1748); Isaac Story, *The Love of Our Country Recommended and Enforced* (Boston: John Boyle, 1775).

6. Hyneman and Lutz, *American Political Writing*, 1:260–61; Aristotle, *Politics*, 1253a 19–20.

7. Hyneman and Lutz, *American Political Writing*, 1:684.

8. *A Solemn Warning to the Secure World from the God of Terrible Majesty* (Boston: 1735), 59, cited in Alan Heimert, *Religion and the American Mind* (Cambridge, Mass.: Harvard University Press, 1966), 306.

9. When human beings "neglect" the "exercise" of mutual love, Tennent wrote, they are inevitably "tempted, against the *Law of Nature*, to seek a *single and independent state*" (*Brotherly Love*, 3; his italics).

10. In a large republic where people have only a distant acquaintance with their representatives, the Anti-Federalist "Brutus" argued, "a perpetual jealousy will exist in the minds of the people against them: their conduct will be narrowly watched; their measures scrutinized, and their laws opposed, evaded, or reluctantly obeyed" (*Complete Anti-Federalist*, 2.9.49; see also 2.9.18).

11. Hyneman and Lutz, *American Political Writing*, 2:1252.

12. "A Model of Christian Charity," 1630, in *Puritan Political Ideas*, ed. Edmund Morgan (Indianapolis: Bobbs-Merrill, 1965), 92.

13. *The Writings of Samuel Adams* (New York: Putnam, 1908), 4:238.

14. Hyneman and Lutz, *American Political Writing*, 1:263–64n.

15. For example, rulers must, on the authority of Scripture, be persons who hate covetousness (ibid., 1:299–300, 434, 2:846, 1255).

16. Ibid., 1:274; see also the extended footnote, 1:260–64.

17. *Essay on Human Understanding*, bk. II, ch. 27, sec. 6. "There is no other act of man's mind . . . naturally planted in him," Hobbes maintained," but to be born a man and live with the use of his five Senses" (*Leviathan*, ch. 3).

18. *Treatises of Government*, I, secs. 86, 87; II, sec. 149.

19. *Leviathan*, ch. 11.

20. Catherine Albanese, *Sons of the Fathers: The Civil Theology of the American Revolution* (Philadelphia: Temple University Press, 1976), 112–42.

21. James Madison, *Notes of Debates in the Federal Convention of 1787* (Athens: Ohio University Press, 1966), 244.

22. *The Federalist,* #10.

23. *The Federalist,* #9.

24. Nathan Tarcov, *Locke's Education for Liberty* (Chicago: University of Chicago Press, 1984). While natural reason does indicate some responsibility toward what one has begotten, Locke pointed out, it did not prevent the practice of infanticide among the civilized ancients (*The Reasonableness of Christianity,* ed. I. T. Ramsey [Stanford: Stanford University Press, 1958], sec. 242). Children have even less obligation toward their parents, since they have not consented to parental rule.

25. *The Federalist,* #7.

26. *Letter concerning Toleration* (Indianapolis: Bobbs-Merrill, 1982), 52.

27. *Notes on the State of Virginia* (Chapel Hill: University of North Carolina Press, 1955), 159.

28. *Life and Selected Writings of Jefferson,* ed. Adrienne Koch and William Peden (New York: Modern Library, 1944), 570, 639–40, 703–4.

29. *The Federalist,* #55.

30. For example, discussing Mark 8:35–38, Locke says that the punishment for those who would not follow Jesus was "to lose their souls, i.e., their lives" (*Reasonableness of Christianity,* sec. 15). The passage, of course, suggests that human beings ought to lose their lives, "for my sake and the gospel's," in order to save them. Locke claims that the meaning of the passage is "plain, considering the occasion it was spoken on." But that occasion involves a rebuke to Peter who, like Locke, proclaimed Christ the Messiah and denied that "the Son of Man must suffer many things" (Mk. 8:29–31). Locke implies, however, that Jesus rebuked Peter as part of his "wise and prudent" effort to deceive the authorities about his intent (*Reasonableness,* secs. 59, 61, 139). Locke's argument also points to the conclusion that Jesus eventually bungled this alleged strategy.

31. *Reasonableness of Christianity,* secs. 16, 67, 70–72, 167, 171–72, 179–80.

32. *Letter concerning Toleration,* 30, 42; early in the *Letter,* Locke cited Luke 22:25–26, 2 Timothy 2:19, and Luke 22:32. This amounts to a subtle editing which substitutes 2 Timothy 2:19 for the omitted passages from Luke, the second halves of verses 25, 26, and 32, and all of verses 27–31. These omitted verses suggest a hierarchy of regimes: they assert that among the unfaithful gentiles, *any* lordship is a "benefaction," while the disciples, among whom equality is a rule, have a right to judge the law-abiding Tribes of Israel. Any form of rule is better than lawlessness; law is higher than lordship, equality is the rule for human governance informed by grace. Locke rejects this somewhat radical and very exacting standard in favor of the more limited demands of 2 Timothy 2:19.

33. Hyneman and Lutz, *American Political Writing,* 1:632–33; *Notes on the State of Virginia,* 161; Harvey C. Mansfield Jr., "Thomas Jefferson," in *American Political Thought,* ed. Morton Frisch and Richard Stevens (New York: Scribner's, 1971), 38; *Letter concerning Toleration,* 13, 15, 19, 25, 27–29, 52, 54–55.

34. Sanford Kessler, "Jefferson's Rational Religion," in *The Constitutional Polity,* ed. Sidney Pearson (Washington, D.C.: University Press of America, 1983), 58–78; Thomas Pangle, *Montesquieu's Philosophy of Liberalism* (Chicago: Univer-

sity of Chicago Press, 1973). For a contemporary statement of the same thesis, see Claude Lévi-Strauss, *Totemism* (Boston: Beacon, 1963), 89.

35. See my essay "The Bible in the American Political Tradition," in *Religion and Politics,* ed. Myron Aronoff (New Brunswick: Transaction, 1984), 11–45.

36. Hyneman and Lutz, *American Political Writing,* 1:680, 683; *Letters of Benjamin Rush,* 2:947, 1075.

37. Robert Bellah et al., *Habits of the Heart* (Berkeley and Los Angeles: University of California Press, 1985).

Civil Religion in the Age of Reason

Thomas Paine on Liberalism, Redemption, and Revolution

For all its apparent confidence and optimism, the eighteenth century—in Europe and in America—was also uneasy, Prometheus haunted by Pandora. Celebrating material progress and the advance of science, shrewd observers recognized that these very gains entailed specialization and individuation, the weakening of community and authority, the encouragement of private ambition, and the fragmenting of moral order. As the next century dawned, Jeremiah Atwater, who praised the "spirit of enterprise" and gloried in the extension of commerce, applied the moral to America: "With pain we are forced to acknowledge, that it is the natural tendency of prosperity to corrupt the human heart."[1]

The United States, while free from many of Europe's ills, had its own discomforts. The American Revolution, decorous by later standards, rejected convention and tradition, unsettling civil order and social authority. The gentlemanly code to which the framers adhered was giving way to the "democratization of mind." Engaged in creating a new regime, Americans were necessarily driven to theoretical ground, forced to appeal to first principles and to nature.[2]

Yet theorizing also had its shadows. American culture was antinomic, pulled between the conflicting poles of biblical religion and secular rationalism.[3] Some Americans were single-minded, but the generality gave both doctrines a portion of their allegiance, so that philosophic dialectic was at least a threat to the more comfortable habits of ambiguity.[4]

The Framers' Intent

Religion, of course, was the great voice of popular culture. The Bible was the common text of the new republic, and a great many Americans hoped or confided that the regime they were founding—while affording freedom of conscience—would be, at least implicitly, a Christian and a Protestant commonwealth.[5] These convictions, moreover, were reflected in a widely shared political teaching.

In that Christian view, the secular goal indicated by the doctrine of redemption is the reconciliation of humanity with nature, the order of creation. God's willingness to have His Son undergo human life—with all its silences and sorrows, despair and death—testifies that such a life has high dignity, worthy even of what is divine. The Incarnation shows God's love for the world, thereby attesting that the world is lovable. For those who can read its lessons, redemption overcomes our human resentment against nature and its limits, saving life from the rage of human indignation: "Behold the Lamb of God, which taketh away the sin of the world." The Gospel "sets men free" precisely because they no longer experience nature as bondage; redemption turns human attention inward, toward the soul, rather than outward, toward the mastery of nature.[6]

Politics has a part to play in the education of the soul, helping to lead human beings out of self-centeredness toward a new sense of self as a part of the whole of creation.[7] Public spirit, the foundation of secular civic virtue, is a rung on the ladder to citizenship in the City of God. While the laws must restrain selfishness, their fundamental aim is positive, the development of the individual's capacity to love.[8] An individual will not risk involvement with others if he or she feels totally vulnerable; the soul demands the minimal assurance that it matters, that it is the object of concern. Learning to love others presumes the experience of *being* loved. The laws, while limiting the pursuit of private interest, must also ensure nurturance—"particular care"—and the opportunity for dignity in civil life. Such attentive community, like strong friendship, is necessarily exclusive: to draw close to some is to draw away from others. In secular life, human beings are not suited to universal government, although the church must remind them of their universal obligations. The best regime, in principle, is small, simple, and austere, the Christian Sparta of Sam Adams's vision.[9]

The doctrine of redemption, moreover, is inseparable from the principle of grace. God's redeeming love for humanity is "gracious" because it is unearned, given not because of merit but in spite of sin. At most, God's love may have regard to what human beings may become, overlooking what they are. Love goes beyond justice, insisting that the exalted serve the lowly and treating the needs of the weak as the obligations of the strong.[10] Moreover, love is the free gift of the loving subject, made available without reciprocity. In other words, the principle of grace derives authority from the loving qualities of those who rule, not from the consent of the governed. Applied to a republican regime, the same doctrine requires that the public-spirited qualities of citizens prevail over their servile desires and private interests.[11] Even in that mild, egalitarian form, however, the principle of grace offends modern sensibilities, for it has little respect for individual independence or private liberty.[12] Love cares and feels obligation, and hence is prone to intervene—or interfere—on the side of what it takes to be the best interest of the beloved.

Freedom, in this view, is no fit goal for individuals or for politics. Love cannot be commanded, and reconciliation must be agreed to: Christian political teaching, consequently, valued liberty and consent as indispensable means. The end, however, for the person or the polity, is dutiful civility and "good order." Freely given, loves chooses to be bound.[13]

Widely held Christian doctrine, in sum, envisaged a *religious civility,* a political order shaped and informed by religion.[14] The framers of the American Constitution rejected that teaching, prescribing a secular regime aided by *civil religion,* aiming to discipline religion for the service of political society. Remembering religious wars and persecutions, the framers were also devoted to modern philosophies premised on individual rights and private liberties: principle as well as prudence counseled against meddling with the soul. Convinced that human beings could be reconciled with nature only by mastering it, they spurned the doctrine of redemption, and similarly, they rebuffed the principle of grace in favor of the consent of the governed.[15]

Following Locke, however, the framers did consider that political society requires the support of religion, including the belief in an afterlife. In the first place, religion is needed to inculcate decent civil morals, most fundamentally the responsibility of parents to children.[16] Moreover, in its distinctly political role, religion helps to make good certain practical deficiencies in liberal teaching, especially those inherent in the situation of the ruled, to whom the advantages of right conduct are less immediate and less evident.[17]

For the self-interested and self-preserving human beings of Lockean theory, the state of nature—originally, or soon afterward, a state of war—provided ample reason for making whatever promises were necessary to create civil society. It is much less clear, however, that it is in one's interest to keep those promises once civil society has been established. On the contrary, it would seem that the best life, in theory, is to be able to break one's promises while one's fellows keep theirs, combining the freedom of the state of nature with the advantages of civil life.

Liberal theory responds that, in practice, the risks of promise-breaking are too great: (1) one is likely to be found out and punished; and (2) any successful violations are apt to be imitated, endangering political society and the social contract itself. This argument is plausible in the case of the great and powerful, who are likely to be noticed and emulated. It is less persuasive in the case of private persons, a particular danger in commercial society given the "unbridled" quality of the "spirit of enterprise."[18] The liberal response is least compelling when addressed to persons who are obscure and unpropertied, for they combine a hope of escaping detection and a probability that their conduct will not serve as a socially destructive example with a feeling of having nothing to lose.[19] "Promises, covenants, and oaths," the very foundation of civil society, need the support of religious sanctions.[20]

Religion is also requisite, in the framers' view, as the ally of general interests—the interest of political society as a whole, but also the interest of humanity—against the weight of private interest narrowly defined. These more inclusive interests may appeal to reason and to "diffuse" sentiments, but unaided they cannot hope to overcome the claims of the body and its senses or the demands of immediate relationships and day-to-day life. It is relatively easy for rulers to see the connection between the public interest and their own, since their personal lives are caught up in the broader world and since they themselves are more likely to be moved by the love of fame, "the ruling passion of the noblest minds."[21] For the ruled, however, patriotism—to say nothing of one's duty to humanity—is too weak a sentiment to prevail alone. Especially in republics, religion is an indispensable element of "self-interest rightly understood," the public philosophy of a well-ordered liberal regime.[22]

Given the need for civil religion, the framers saw abundant reasons for seeking an accommodation with Christianity, despite their quarrels with Christian teaching. Prudence alone argued against offending deeply rooted beliefs.[23] In any case, most of the framers seem to have been convinced, as Locke had been, that a strictly rational religion would never command the allegiance of most human beings, among whom reason needed the support of authority and miracle.[24] Upsetting customary beliefs, the products of experience and history, could too easily lead to the overturning of conventional morals and to the breaking out of a purely natural—and hence passionate, narrow, and shortsighted—version of self-interest.[25] Certainly, reason's religion would prove inadequate in indoctrinating children, as yet insufficiently rational to appreciate it, and it would also fall short as a teaching for those whose rational interests afforded too uncertain a support for civil morality—preeminently, the poor and obscure, women and slaves.

In many ways, moreover, Christianity commended itself to the framers. Prevailing Christian doctrine respected personal autonomy, the freedom of conscience, and the consent of the governed, if only as means to very different ends. Less ambiguously, the framers admired Christian universalism, the proclamation that all human beings are members of one family, regarding that credo as more consonant with reason than the beliefs of purely national religions like Judaism (as the framers understood it) or paganism. In this sense, Christianity had value as a civil religion because of its more-than-civil qualities.[26]

For the framers, however, any détente with Christianity presumed that Christian superstitions and tendencies toward fanaticism—and with them, Christian political teaching—could be purged or rendered harmless. Christianity could serve as an acceptable civil religion only if it were civilized, disciplined to serve a rational and liberal regime.

The framers were greatly assisted by Locke's prestige, and especially by Locke's theism, which made his teaching minimally respectable in Christian circles.[27] They stopped short, however, of openly espousing Locke's civil theology.[28]

Locke had prescribed a "reasonable" Christianity which deemphasized or denied the doctrines of redemption and grace. Locke's creed proclaims Christ as the Messiah, a conquering king who overcame death, and hence a suitable inspiration in the struggle to master nature. He rejects the idea of Jesus as the Son of Man, the suffering servant who took on, and showed, the nobility of humanity's life and burden.[29] Second, Locke's Christianity emphasizes a "good life according to virtue and morality," a standard equated with the law of nature and without specifically Christian content.[30] Locke went even further in rejecting any *political* application of Christianity, since he denied that charity ought to influence law.[31]

The leading spirits among the framers shared, or sympathized with, Locke's doctrine, but they considered it unnecessary in the American context. In the United States, civil religion could be sufficiently embodied in and inculcated by the *laws;* it did not require the support of an official, civil *theology* which would, at best, re-create priestly hierarchy in a new form.[32] In America, it would be sufficient to follow Locke's institutional prescriptions, confining religion to a private sphere "wholly exempt" from the cognizance of civil society and relying on the proliferation of sects to check and confute any particular confession.[33] Christianity, and all other religions, could be left untroubled, free to attempt the instruction of the spirit.[34]

Locke's empiricism suggested that the mind, in the natural course of things, will follow its experience, especially if freed from repression and indoctrination. By establishing certain political truths, the laws also, in subtle ways, establish a variety of civil religion. In the framers' design, America would be exposed—through commerce and through argument—to many competing ways and views and would, increasingly, be disinclined to give exclusive credit to any. Gradually and of their own accord, the framers confided, Americans would come to see values and truth as commodities in the marketplace, where the accepted coinage would be human liberty, understood as the ability to do as one wills and entailing the mastery of nature.[35]

The framers' trust in the long-term working of the laws was a vital element in their rapprochement with Christianity. The American regime accorded revealed religion a combination of private freedom and civil respect. In addition, a considerable number of the clergy, especially among the enlightened, were inclined to see history as providential, discerning God's design in natural processes and conceding to human mastery a considerable role in redemption. They shared, in other words, the willingness to leave many questions to the arbitrament of progress.[36] John Witherspoon, for example, trusted that the moral instinct for benevolence, perfected by reason and allied to science, would result in a progressive approximation of Christian truth and virtue.[37] Yet despite this tilt toward natural religion, Witherspoon, like so many of his Christian fellows, upheld the existence of an objective moral order: in principle, natural rights entitle us only to what is right.[38] Similarly, Witherspoon considered it a task of government to develop civil character, and his list of civic virtues contained a number of distinctly religious excellences such as piety and mercy.[39] Civil mannerliness, founded on the appeal to history, shrouded and postponed, but did not resolve, the quarrel between modern philosophy and ancient faith.

The framers were content to have it so, sure that the scientific design of the laws would prove decisive.[40] They were sufficiently assured to allow orthodoxy a certain sway in the private circles of life. In the main, they limited themselves to the sphere of law and institutions, economics and higher education, the stereotypically "man's world." They were disposed to ignore the world of women—the sphere of domesticity and early education—regarding it as a harmless support for civil life. It was just this neglect which alarmed Thomas Paine, for orthodoxy was not so remiss. Paine's old friend Benjamin Rush urged Christians to attend to "the first impressions of the mind" by the "use of the Bible as a school book" and by attending to the education of women, who often regulate the "opinions and conduct of men."[41] Paine mistrusted the framers' reliance on the laws, fearing that the liberal republic might be corrupted by Christian teaching, and his *Age of Reason* is a call to renew the struggle between the Empire of Science and the Kingdom of God.

A Critique of Locke

The Age of Reason is a subtle book with complex intention. As a polemic against revealed religion in general and biblical religion in particular, the book's ostensible purpose, *The Age of Reason* is neither profound nor original, although it is argued with all of the public power of Paine's democratized rhetoric.[42] Paine's forcefulness, however, only emphasizes his abandonment of the stance, adopted in *Common Sense,* of treating Christianity with nominal respect, veiling his criticisms and emendations, and attempting to make Christianity into a "reasonable" support for political order founded on natural rights.[43] Rejecting that earlier position, *The Age of Reason* presumes and involves a critique of Lockean civil religion.

At the same time, the book grew out of Paine's ruminations on the French Revolution. *The Age of Reason* was written in two parts, the first completed shortly before Paine was arrested by French revolutionary authorities and published while he was still in prison, the second composed after he had been released and written largely in response to criticisms of the earlier work. In part II, Paine indicates that his overriding motive for writing was furnished by the departure of the French Revolution from its "just and humane principles," and by his desire to vindicate those tenets by separating them from the revolution's excesses.[44] Since Paine, expecting his arrest, knew that he would have to evade the revolution's censors, it is not surprising that there is no hint of this in part I.[45] There, Paine tells us only that he was moved to write his critique of revealed religion— originally intended for a "more advanced period of life"—by the French abolition of "compulsive systems of religion" and the consequent need to rescue "morality, humanity, and the theology which is true" from the "wreck of superstition."[46] In fact, Paine chose a subject, the critique of religion, and a prescription, Deist theology, in which his views coincided with those of Robespierre. The Committee of the Surety General, which examined the manuscript of part I, returned it with the comment that it would "do much good."[47]

In any case, Paine had no desire to write a work which could be seized and used by the revolution's conservative enemies. Paine was more concerned to defend the revolution's theories than to defend its practices: he spoke of the toleration established by law—the abolition of the "compulsive systems of religion"—but he called no attention to persecution in fact.[48] Where Benjamin Rush argued that the French Revolution proved the insufficiency of reason without Christian revelation, Paine contended that the shortcomings of the revolution stemmed from Christianity itself.[49]

The most important of the "just and humane principles" of the French Revolution, moreover, underline Paine's quarrel with liberal civil religion. Dating the dedication to *The Age of Reason*, Paine—for the only time in the book—uses the revolutionary calendar, referring to "8th Pluvôise, Second Year of the French Republic, one and indivisible," going on to tell his American readers that this is equivalent to January 27, O.S. 1794.[50] The revolutionary calendar, of course, proclaimed openly what the American founding had only hinted at—human sovereignty over time.[51] Paine also chose a date, 8th Pluvôise, almost a month after his arrest, but the day on which the Assembly secularized education in France.[52] Paine's dating calls attention to human supremacy over history and education, indicating the human claim—a just principle in Paine's view—to full mastery over the human world. The revolution's trumpet, as Paine heard it, shattered the silences and challenged the evasion of liberal civil religion in America.

Some of Paine's lamest and most pedestrian arguments point in this direction. The burden of the second part of *The Age of Reason* is devoted to arguing that most of the books of the Old Testament could not have been written by the authors for whom the books are named. If this is so, Paine contends, then "every part of the authority and authenticity of those books is gone at once."[53] His critique leans heavily on anachronistic glosses which refer to times after the death of the supposed author. Yet the fact of later editing does not disprove original authorship, nor does it demonstrate any departure from the original teaching. Paine does refer to the "disorder and ignorance in which the Bible has been put together," but a little later he speaks of the "studied craft of the Scripture-makers."[54] In any case, the Bible on its own terms is immune to Paine's critique, since if God can inspire an author, He can also inspire an editor. Locke, however, relied on the great names associated with the books of the Bible, defining faith as the belief that a proposition comes from God, adopted "on the credit of the proposer."[55]

Of course, Locke also appealed to miracles and "outward signs" as attesting that these proposers held a "commission from heaven."[56] For Locke, however, miracles are fundamentally only means of persuading the credulous many.[57] In Locke's view, no one can tell whether an event is truly miraculous, since to do so one would have to know the whole of the law of nature, to which a purposed miracle claims to be an exception. By reason, we are entitled to say only that a "miracle" is an event whose cause we do not know. The multitude, however, is persuaded by deeds of power, since it is unable to discern or is indifferent to causes.[58]

Locke also maintains that the miracles were witnessed by such numbers as to be indubitable, although the examples he offers cast doubt on this proposition.[59] Paine attacks Locke's ostensible teaching very early in *The Age of Reason,* pointing out that the Immaculate Conception could not have been witnessed and that the Resurrection, though subject to confirmation, was witnessed only by the disciples, and by them ambiguously. The account of the Resurrection, Paine asserts, has "every mark of fraud and imposition." In relation to these two central miracles, Locke's claim of indubitable testimony is false.[60] This, Paine argues, illustrates the general principle that the appeal to miracles "implies a lameness or weakness in the doctrine thus preached."[61] Paine faults the teaching: Locke held that the shortcomings were those of the many. Formally, Locke upheld the Bible's authority, but only by identifying it with—if not subordinating it to—the law of nature. This, Paine implies, amounts to a "pious fraud," adopted in violation of the principle of consent for the supposed good of the many.[62]

Much of Paine's critique of Scripture, in sum, amounts to a democratic critique of Locke, one which calls attention to Locke's pretenses as well as to the Bible's inconsistencies. Stripped of traditional and miraculous sources of authority and revealed as the product of human votes and councils, the Bible, Paine maintains, will be unable to stand comparison with Euclid's *Elements,* a work which rests on "self-evident demonstration entirely independent of its author."[63]

Yet *The Age of Reason* also involves a crucial imposture. Since the text is fundamentally an attack on the Bible, it is curious that Paine insists that in composing part I, he lacked access to a copy of the Scriptures.[64] He explains that in his "precarious situation" he had to write quickly, but he assures us that his quotations from memory have proved to be correct.[65]

In one of these citations, Paine quotes Job 11:7, "Canst thou by searching find out God? Canst thou find out the Almighty to perfection?" Paine goes on to say, "I know not how the printers have pointed this passage, for I keep no Bible."[66] This is a curious reference, one that calls our attention to typesetting by printers, and particularly to *punctuation*. In fact, the King James Bible contains a striking error in punctuation: it does not capitalize the first word in the second question, an error Paine corrects. Paine could hardly have remembered that curiosity; by directing attention to typesetting, Paine gives the lie to his own assertion that he wrote without a Bible at hand. Those who accept Paine's denial, however, are likely to be lulled regarding Paine's use of Scripture, as Paine intended.

Later, Paine finds evidence that the books of Daniel and Ezekiel were written by their supposed authors in the fact that the "manner in which the books are written" agrees with the condition in which the authors found themselves. Commentators, Paine asserts—and by this time, in part II, Paine is responding to commentators on his own work—who lack the "experience of captivity" fail to understand that exile or imprisonment forces a writer to write "in a concealed manner." Daniel and Ezekiel used "obscure and metaphoric terms," dreams and visions, because as "prisoners of war or prisoners of state," they were obliged to devise a "cipher or secret alphabet." They intended to be understood, Paine claims, only by those to whom they wrote, and their intended audience was not composed of "busy commentators and priests."[67]

Paine's own experience, of course, paralleled that of Daniel and Ezekiel: he claimed to understand their "mode of writing" because it was one he had adopted. When Paine wrote these comments, he was free from prison, but he was not, in a fundamental sense, free from exile. About the content of Daniel's prophecy, he said nothing, but he did contend that Ezekiel's writings should be read in relation to "the project . . . of recovering Jerusalem."[68] Paine was also concerned to recover a holy city, the revolutionary ideal.

When he wrote *Common Sense,* Paine recalled, he saw, "or at least thought I saw," a "vast scene opening itself" in America, one which enabled Americans to offer a new system to mankind. At that time, he expected a change in religion to follow from a change in government, still holding—as the framers did—that a change in political and secular principles would, in the long run, shape sacred beliefs, trusting that the principle of consent, enshrined in law, would overcome the principle of grace.[69] Events caused Paine to question his earlier faith: the revolutionary's Jerusalem seemed to demand not new framing, but a new foundation.

Paine's reconstruction involves three interrelated critiques, intended to reveal the weaknesses in revolutionary foundings deriving (1) from Lockean liberal theory, the particular danger in America; (2) from revolutionary practice, as revealed in France; and (3) at the most radical level from the political impact of Christian culture, the common enemy, for Paine, of modern reason and revolutionary hope.

The New Man

Paine offers two prudential reasons for abandoning the Lockean effort to "civilize" Christianity. In the first place, increasing numbers of people have come to recognize or suspect that Christianity is fabulous. Consequently, Christianity is no longer defensible as a "rational" creed; it is now suited to produce only "atheists and fanatics."[70] Second, democratization makes the elitism of liberal civil religion politically unacceptable. A creed professed for the masses made sense when the masses were subjects; the advent of democracy requires educating the many in the principles of rule. Democracy demands a creed which, while suited to the understanding of the many, can be laid "fairly and openly before the world."[71]

Moral and theoretical reasoning, Paine argues, support the same lesson. A variation between inward opinion and outward expression—inauthenticity—is essentially immoral, at least in matters of religion, and tends to prepare human beings "for the commission of any crime."[72] This sort of deception subordinates one's convictions about the highest things to low matters, material interests, and pragmatic considerations, a perversion all too likely to corrupt the soul.[73] Parenthetically, it should be observed that Paine ignores any high motive for restricting what one says, such as the possibility that one might guard one's speech out of love or consideration for another's sensibilities. He accepts the idea of nurturant speech in relation to children, as will become clear, but he fears any extension to the speech of adults. The principle is not inegalitarian—we can limit what we say out of an equal regard for what is best in each other— but it does suggest the doctrine of grace, that love is sovereign over liberty and consent.

In fact, Paine maintains that to be content with inward freedom while acquiescing in a limitation on the expression of one's opinion is essentially slavish. It restricts one's "right of changing" one's opinion about what should be expressed, presuming a kind of permanence to the existing extent of public capacities and to the existing order of things. A "pious fraud" may seem to do more good, but the original deception must be defended, requiring more and more repression—especially against science, which constantly threatens to expose the lie.[74] Like slaves, those who constrain expression voluntarily assume that the external world cannot be transformed or remade but demands an adaptation of the self.

Human freedom, by contrast, consists in doing, acting, and creating, rather than in thinking. The human self must be recognized as essentially a human creation. In the beginning "scarcely distinguishable in appearance and condition from a common animal," humanity has overcome that state only through science and creative action.[75] Nature, still the standard for Lockean liberals, is too restrictive, in matters of right even more than in matters of fact.

In his quarrel with Locke and with the framers, Paine held that both relied excessively on the objective world, overconfiding in the ability of laws and institutions to shape the soul.[76] Writing to the Abbé Raynal in 1782, Paine described commerce—that bulwark of liberal political thought—as a "moral nullity," able to temper the mind's first principles but not to establish them. The object *may* reform the mind, Paine told the Abbé, but the mind may also "corrupt the object," or the two may "separate in disgust."[77]

Paine rejected the last alternative, so similar to the estrangement of church and state prescribed by liberalism, because it deprived civil society of strong and sustaining allegiance. This consideration had special force in America, where "common causes" would not support an "extensive, continued, and determined" union. The American union required a civil religion "capable of reaching the whole soul of man and arming it with perpetual energy."[78] Right laws depend on the support of right principles.

For similar reasons, Paine was skeptical about historicism. Faith in progress, for empirical rationalists, derives from faith in nature, and specifically from trust in the teleological qualities of the passions. Much of human history, Paine conceded, seems to sustain Hume's argument that humanity has been moved toward good ends by the force of human wants. Good consequences have resulted from bad motives as well as good: the motive power of historical advance hitherto has been instinct, not intention.[79]

However, Paine observed, the force of need is no longer an adequate guide. Civilization meets the most pressing and the most obvious needs. Need loses intensity and clarity, weakening the hold of merely natural morality. More complicated and larger-scale societies, moving beyond the range and comprehension of need and feeling, find themselves at odds with natural sensibility. Instinct, sufficient to create nations, is inadequate to lead humanity beyond them.[80]

Hume's reasoning also led to the conclusion that natural morality is limited to "immediate propensity," especially to the bonds created by sexual attraction and by the feeling for one's progeny. All more inclusive moralities are the creations of convention and artifice, increasingly weak as they depart from their natural foundations. Universal morality, Hume held, can never be a ruling standard; in international society, the best that can be hoped for is the moderation imposed by the balance of power.[81]

Paine was unwilling to accept such limits to human creativity. He agreed that the remaining human wants—for example, the desire to be free from war—would be unable to overcome the "curious" and "singular," but universal, force of prejudice. This, however, only led Paine to conclude that any further moral and political progress depends on human intention; it presumes the ascendancy of theory over practice, the mind's triumph over nature.[82]

When he wrote Raynal, Paine still found common ground with the liberals, hoping that commerce—especially in letters and science—would be able to dispel prejudice, leaving the mind "fit for the reception of generous happiness" and able to entertain new and enlightened doctrine.[83] So it had seemed in France, where the "principles of America opened the Bastille." The upshot of the French Revolution, however, taught Paine that prejudice is even more tenacious than he had feared and principles much weaker than he had hoped, conclusions which are the premises of The Age of Reason.[84]

Still committed to revolutionary theory, Paine came to reject a central tenet of revolutionary practice. Revolutionary praxis is informed by the credendum that thought can create rebirth, that new ideas or new consciousness can make new men and women—one source of the perennial tendency of revolutionaries to become obsessed with "correct" ideology. Paine, by contrast, concluded that conscious thoughts and convictions are no more than superstructures in the architecture of the mind.

As part of his argument that biblical prophecy was only poetry set to music, Paine relates that when the Bible tells us of Saul "among the prophets" it does not state what "*they prophesied* nor what *he prophesied*" because there was "nothing to tell." Prophecy was simply a concert. This instance, Paine asserts, by itself "would be sufficient" to prove his thesis.[85]

Prophecy, Paine implies, is pure performance, a making or doing to be judged by its effectiveness and not its content. He goes on to say that Saul "met a company of prophets" and prophesied with them, but it "appears afterward" that Saul "performed his part badly, for it is said that an *evil spirit from God* came upon Saul, and he prophesied."[86] So far, Paine has argued that an "evil spirit from God" can be reduced to a bad performance, a matter of technique and certainly not divine.

But the Bible's reference to an "evil spirit" comes much later than the meeting with the prophets which Paine describes. Telling us that it "appears afterward," Paine conceals the events and the amount of time which intervene between the two incidents.

The meeting with the prophets is itself the fulfillment of a prophecy the content of which we *are* told, part of the proof to Saul that the Lord has chosen him to be king: "Thou shalt meet a company of prophets . . . and they shall prophesy, and the Spirit of the Lord will come upon thee, and thou shalt prophesy with them, and shalt be turned into another man."[87]

Becoming a "new man," with its Christian analogy to Paul (Saul), in this case amounts to a revolution, raising a humble man to supreme power through the exaltation of the spirit.[88]

Yet can such new human beings "perform" well? Later, Paine says of Paul that he "changed his thinking without altering his constitution"; new men are not really transformed because they cannot alter their basic characters.[89] The reference to Saul's evil spirit serves to make Paine's general point. In 1 Samuel 16:14, Saul is troubled by "an evil spirit from the Lord" because he has lost the "Spirit of the Lord." Prophetic ecstasy is not permanent; it creates a transient mood, not a new person.

At the urging of his servants, Saul sends for David, a "man who can play well," and David's playing does, temporarily, drive away the evil spirit. The reference to Saul *himself* prophesying under the influence of the evil spirit comes still later, in 1 Samuel 18:10. That passage does not, however, refer to Saul playing badly at music, although he does "perform his part badly." Rather, Saul's envy and jealousy of David lead him to lose control of himself. Saul's rage is caused by the fact that women have praised David in *their* music.[90] Women, in other words, have a prophetic or poetic power which, in this case, excites jealousy. Saul performs badly because he is not "another man." He is still where all human beings begin, under the influence and power of women.

As this suggests, in *The Age of Reason* Paine turned away from political revolution toward the education of the child and the shaping of those first impressions of the mind which are far more important than later schooling. The education of children, however, is an area of ineradicable inequality, one which can be justified—for an egalitarian like Paine—only if it leads toward eventual equality. Most readers probably construe Paine's title historically, equating the "age of reason" with the Enlightenment, appropriate enough so long as one notices the double entendre: Paine's ultimate concern is the achievement of adulthood, arrival at the "age of reason." The human mind, Paine wrote, progresses by principles one can discern in one's own: psychology, not history, holds the key to the advances which matter.[91]

Paine aims to establish the kind of early education, and the sort of religion, suited to his version of the proper development of the child. The truth of his teaching, consequently, concerns him less than its educational utility.[92] Such doctrine cannot be effective, however, without the transformation of domestic life, a revolution which logically takes priority over the redesigning of the public sphere. Paine's new founding does require a revolution, the overthrow of Christianity and of women, the rulers of the private world.[93]

The Religion of Feeling

Early in *The Age of Reason,* Paine portrays Christianity and Judaism as corrupted creeds, the good aspects of which—monotheism and benevolence—have been fatally marred by pagan accretions and residues. In speaking of Satan, the Bible's stories hint at polytheism; the Virgin Birth is only "the tail of heathen mythology," and so on.[94]

Paine does not attempt to "purify" Christianity. He does, however, attempt to dissociate Jesus from Christian faith, arguing that Jesus—who taught an "excellent sort" of morality, including belief in the equality of man—never meant to found a new religion. Once Jesus's story is cleared of myth, Paine contends, he is revealed as a "virtuous reformer and revolutionist," put to death by Jewish priests and the Roman state.[95]

Jefferson advanced a similar interpretation, but Jefferson held it "justifiable" that Jesus had linked and likened his teachings to traditional doctrines "by evasions, by sophistries, by misconstructions and misapplications of scraps of the prophets."[96] The teaching of Jefferson's Jesus, in other words, was drawn in the image of Locke's (and Jefferson's) attempt to create a "reasonable" Christianity. Paine, however, argued that these accommodations with tradition, whether they originated with Jesus or with his successors, adulterated Jesus's doctrine, reducing it to an "amphibious fraud."[97]

The "amphibious" qualities of Judaism and Christianity, consequently, allow Paine to reveal the peril to new teachings and laws arising from any accommodation with old doctrines and ways. The polytheistic corruptions of Christianity serve Paine as illustrations of the danger *from* Christianity.[98]

Repeatedly, Paine's citations from Scripture point to the problem posed by women—and particularly by women who serve alien gods—exerting their power through children, but also through the vulnerabilities of men. Women imperil the new regime because of their roles as conveyers of tradition and defenders of inner space, the upholders of what is familiar and close in opposition to what is new and distant. Moreover, women's role as mothers and nurturers not only gives them unique power in shaping character; it tends to involve a radical bias in favor of their own offspring.

Discussing the early life of Jesus, Paine relates the story of Jesus at twelve, asking questions in the temple. Going on to speak of the disciples who set this story down, Paine says that "it is most probable that they had this anecdote from his parents."[99] In fact, Luke 2:51 tells us that "his mother kept all these sayings in her heart." Mary's maternal pride is familiar, but it is a sentiment Paine has no desire to reinforce.

Favoring their own, women cater to and foster the child's desire to be the center of the world and the object of loving care. Revealed religion, of course, reifies these infantile yearnings, proclaiming a national or a personal God. Nurtured into narcissistic prejudice, infantilism is the root of nationalism, a failing of the French Revolution which Paine traced to women and to the Old Testament.

Moreover, women's power lies in and through love, and love is a menace to universal benevolence. The number of Solomon's wives, Paine comments, suggests foolishness rather than wisdom; "Divided love is never happy," and Solomon's household was necessarily a place of competition and complot.[100] Paine's aphorism points to a wider rule: love seeks to monopolize the love of its object, so that its corollary is always jealousy, the fear of infidelity. Abstracted into doctrine or principle, love's demand for fidelity translates into inquisition and persecution, the second great flaw of the French Revolution, rooted this time in the New Testament's high teaching.

Christianity, a religion of love, provides a theoretical justification for women's sensibilities; stereotypically "womanish," it deprecates outward mastery in favor of inward freedom and feeling. Moreover, as Paine observed, despite its formally patriarchal imagery, the Bible often portrays God as *maternal*. As part of his argument that prophecy is poetry, Paine adds poetical lines of his own composing to two prophetic sayings in order to show the "poetical measure" of the original.[101] In the first, Isaiah 1:2, Paine substitutes "'Tis God Himself that calls attention forth" for the original "I have nourished and brought forth children, and they have rebelled against me." The God of the Bible gives birth to children and nourishes them; Paine's Deity "calls forth" attention. In the second case, Jeremiah 9:1, Paine adds three lines, making the prophet mourn for the "human race" where the Bible speaks of weeping "for the slain daughter of my people." Paine—who claims to be "carrying out the figure and showing the intention of the poet"—substitutes humanity as a whole for a specific child, the universal city for Jerusalem. Paine's doctrine will admit no womanly Divinity, no "nursing father."[102]

In Paine's eyes, Christianity was also effeminate in being a religion of feelings, founded on the primal desire to be the object of attention and care. The idea of God's self-sacrificial love for humanity, expressed in terms of God's sacrifice of His Son, Paine regarded as "absurd" and "unnatural." He conceded, however, that the doctrine has the power to "enrapture" multitudes by appealing to "gross feelings"—and particularly to the "gloomy pride of man."[103]

The Bible, moreover, frequently depicts heroes as overcome by passion, making strength subject to desire. In its heroines, Paine insinuates, the Bible seems to moralize loose sexual conduct. Ruth Paine dismisses as an "idle, bungling story" of a "strolling country girl, creeping slyly into bed with her cousin."[104] (Although Paine also calls Ruth "one of the best books in the bible, for it is free from murder and rapine": feminine guile, for all its faults, appears to be superior to masculine violence, a point to which I will return.) Similarly, Esther, the only other book named for a woman, inspires Paine to some sly allusions to Esther's sexual availability, and to the verdict that her conduct "is no business of ours; at least, it is none of mine."[105] The Bible, in other words, celebrates what ought to be kept decently private.

The Bible also inculcates the lesson that triumph over the passions can be won only through desolations of one's pride of body and power. In the Bible's teaching, wisdom derives from nature's discipline, not reason's mastery.

Distinguishing the "historical and anecdotal" parts of the Bible, Paine disclaims any interest in "paltry stories" like the tale of Samson—his first specific reference to Scripture in *The Age of Reason*. Whether such stories are true or not, Paine asserts, "we are neither the better nor the wiser for knowing them."[106] Paine goes on to deny that revelation has anything to do with whether Samson made off with the "gate posts of Gaza" (an implicit reference to Judg. 16:3), visited Delilah (16:4), "caught his foxes" (15:4), or "did anything else." Paine thus speaks of Samson's deeds, and of his adult life, omitting any reference to Samson's miraculous conception by a theretofore barren mother (Judg. 13). Even on these terms, he alludes specifically to only two of the three chapters dealing with Samson's adulthood, only hinting at the third. Yet that chapter, Judges 14, *does* contain a revelation: that unknown to Samson or his parents, his desire to wed a Philistine "was of the Lord, that the Lord sought an occasion against the Philistines" (14:4). Paine will not even take notice of the idea that God moves through the sexual passions. Moreover, Samson—force overcome by guile—recovers his powers when, blinded, he is no longer a slave to appearance and, his pride shattered, asks the Lord for strength (an acknowledgement of dependence he did not make before his suffering). In the end, Samson achieves his greatest victory by dying (16:30). In fact, Samson's death shows the true answer to the riddle "Out of the eater came forth meat, and out of the strong came forth sweetness" (14:14). Samson's example gives Israel the *spiritual* strength to resist the Philistines, which they had previously lacked (15:11). Samson's death offers meat and sweetness: the truth that freedom demands inner strength more than physical force. In this sense, Samson is a political redeemer, but for Paine redemption is a repugnant doctrine, best treated as a paltry story.

In Paine's view, the ethic of redemption undermines civil morals. Love, Christianity's foundation stone, is notoriously unjust, leading us to exaggerate the virtues and overlook the vices of those we love. Adding mercy and forgiveness toward those who do evil, Christianity explicitly deprecates justice, and this doctrine is worse—Paine claims—when extended to the principle "Love your enemies." Paine admires the "doctrine of not retaliating," but says it is "better expressed" in Proverbs (a collection he attributes to Gentiles as well as Jews): "If thine enemy be hungry, give him bread to eat, if he be thirsty, give him water to drink" (25:31). However, Paine suppresses the rest of the saying, "For thou shalt heap coals upon his head, and the Lord shall reward thee." As this implies, Paine regards it as prudent to refrain from retaliation in order to break the cycle of violence and bring about civil peace. He also holds that the principle of benevolence, combined with the desire for civil tranquility, requires us to put the "best construction" on the deeds and acts of others. But he prefers Proverbs to the teachings of Jesus because it reserves the right to inner resentment, the desire to see justice done.[107]

In general, Paine rejects any doctrine of forgiveness and reconciliation between human and human as he rejects it between humanity and God. "Love your enemies" for Paine can never be more than a "feigned morality," at best, as in Proverbs, a conscious pretense, at worst a self-deception.[108]

Reconciliation with creation is similarly false because, even putting the "best construction" on what we observe, we experience nature as indifferent, a "vast machinery" which does its work untended by us.[109] Paine praises Job as the work of a Gentile struggling honestly with the human situation. Yet, Paine says, the book shows man as "more disposed to be resigned than he is capable of being." Indeed, Paine goes on (in a footnote) to laud the Prayer of Agur as the "only sensible, well-conceived, and well-expressed prayer in the Bible."[110] Agur, however, asks to be spared contentment as well as poverty.[111] Against that reasoned and moderate irreconcilability, Paine claims, the New Testament's doctrine is "mean and ridiculous," and amounts to "sinking man into a spaniel."[112]

Paine recognizes that the Christian ethic of sacrifice can be regarded as noble beyond the obligations of justice. However, he regards such aristocratic ideals, like Homer's, as appeals to "false glory" reflecting "mischievous notions of honor."[113] Christian nobility is infantilism magnified into a grandiose hope of immortality through love; the coadjutants, women and Christianity, work to perpetuate human frailties.

Nevertheless, those weaknesses—the need for nurturance and the force of passion—are original and durable in human nature. Convinced that the private order must be transformed, Paine recognized that faith, like love, can neither be uprooted by law nor swept away by revolutionary violence.

Paine interrupts his argument that Moses could not have authored the Torah to contend that, in any case, Moses's character is "the most horrid . . . that can be imagined."[114] Paine says he will "state only one instance" to prove his point, referring to Moses's order to slay all the males and all the mature women among the Midianites, sparing only the virgins (Num. 31:13–18). Moses's reason for this savage command is explicit: the women incited Israel to sin "in the matter of Peor"—that is, the Midianite women used their sexual attractions to entice Israelite men to worship false gods (Num. 25:1–3). Moses, in other words, sought to overcome by violence the danger of women allied to alien gods.

Yet even Moses stopped short: he did not kill the Midianite virgins. Paine speaks of the feelings of the Midianite mothers, destined to die, but goes on to inquire into the feelings of the daughters and their inevitable rage and resentment of Moses's cruelty. "It is in vain that we attempt to impose upon nature, for nature will have her course, and the religion that tortures all her social ties is a false religion."[115] Moses shows the horror and the ultimate failure of Jacobinism: even the zealous cannot *obliterate* the world of women, private life, and interest. Sexual desire betrays even very pure revolutionaries, as it did Moses and the Israelites, who kept virgins for their "prey." This compromise, however, introduced embittered alien women into the household of Israel; Moses's policy is futile as well as cruel.

Similarly, in discussing Joshua, Paine makes mention of an anachronistic reference to the capture of Jerusalem, "As for the Jebusites, the children of Judah could not drive them out, but the Jebusites dwell with the children of Judah at Jerusalem unto this day" (Josh. 15:63). He again calls attention to this passage when he is speaking of Judges, going on to maintain that Jerusalem was not taken until David's time and that Judges must have been written during David's reign.[116] The account of David's capture to which Paine refers describes David's ruthless attempt to purify Jerusalem, smiting not only the Jebusites but—monstrously—the lame and blind "that are hated of David's soul" (2 Sam. 5:8). Like the utopian revolutionaries, David yearned for a city free from ugliness as well as free from sin.

Paine proceeds to say that David's taking of the city is "also in I Chron., chap. xiv, ver 4. etc.," but this verse does *not* describe the conquest of the city. Rather, it refers to the children David fathered in Jerusalem, and the preceding verse speaks of the taking, not of the city, but of the alien wives who gave birth to those offspring.[117] Even David, who would not bring the ark into an impure city, succumbs to desire and makes room for alien women.[118]

Yet, conceding the faults of revolutionary violence, Paine still ranked the framers' liberalism among the fatuities. In addition to the defects of its trust in laws and in history, liberalism itself was "amphibious," tainted by its biblical past and rearing. Enlightened thinkers and partisans of science, after all, were founding theories on the "moral sentiments," appealing to the "heart," and speaking kindly of love.[119] Ancient faith and its confraternity of redemption, love, and grace could only be dispelled by a new teaching shaping a new education. To prevail, however, such a doctrine must first win—not conquer—women and the primitive world.

Paine prescribed a new prophecy, a new poetic making, to charm and enchant humanity. Deborah and Barak, Paine wrote, "are called prophets, not because they predicted anything, but because they composed the poem or song that bears their name, in celebration of an act already done."[120] But Deborah *did* predict: she foretold Barak's victory over Sisera, and also that Sisera would fall by a woman's hand (Judg. 4:6–7, 9, 14). Moreover, while the Bible does call Deborah a prophetess, Barak is not called a prophet at all. In fact, Barak is portrayed as a man morally dependent on women, one who will not even go to battle unless Deborah goes with him (Judg. 4:4, 8).

In the same passage, Paine also asserts that "David is ranked among the prophets, for he was a musician."[121] Yet so far as I can discover, the closest biblical connection between David and the prophets is drawn by Paul, who groups Gideon, Barak, Samson, Jephtha, David, Samuel, "and the prophets," praising them not as musicians but as men who have *subdued kingdoms* through faith (Heb. 11:32). Given Paine's claims, it is also noteworthy that Paul mentions Barak, and that he does so without referring to Deborah.

In Paul's list, moreover, the central figure is Jephtha, and Jephtha—a ruthless leader, for whom God's will is made manifest by success in battle—is an important, repeated illustration in Locke's *Treatises*. Jephtha, in fact, is willing to sacrifice his daughter to obtain victory.[122]

Paine elevates Barak and David, the two singers on Paul's list, to the rank of prophets. Unlike Locke, he does not appeal to Jephtha, the man of force. Instead, he praises two men who knew how to fascinate and beguile, masters of womanly arts as well as skilled soldiers. Without appropriate gramarye, Paine was convinced, neither the force of law nor the reason of science would be able to eradicate their old adversaries, and Paine—a great spellbinder—offered his own version of Deist faith in the hope of winning that final victory.

Natural Religion

The articles of Paine's natural religion begin with a Supreme Being who reveals himself only "in the works of creation and by that repugnance we feel in ourselves toward bad actions and the disposition to good ones."

Associated with benevolent morality and with the idea of equality, Paine's Deity appears to be no mere demiurge, especially since Paine asserts his own "hope for happiness beyond this life."[123]

In this spirit, Paine begins his chapter "Of True Theology" by referring to nature as a "fair creation" which "cost us nothing." He proceeds to ask, "Is it we that light up the sun, that pour down the rain, and fill the earth with abundance?"[124] Yet surely the abundance we enjoy is, to a considerable extent, the result of human work, and Paine's reminder that the universe came without *costs* does not speak of any *benefits*. The paragraph ends with Paine observing that the "vast machinery of the universe" goes on "whether we sleep or wake." Nature, that "fair creation," is blindly indifferent to us, "fair" not so much in being beautiful as in being just, no respecter of persons.

In Paine's telling of the story of Bethlehem, nature is revealed as even less generous. Jesus, Paine declares, was the Son of God only in the sense that all human beings are, "for the Creator is the Father of All." He then describes Jesus's family as "extremely poor, as appears from their not being able to pay for a bed when he was born."[125] Of course the text makes no such statement, its familiar words telling us instead that "there was no room for them at the inn" (Luke 2:8). Paine's rendition ties Jesus to the poor and calls attention to social injustice, but it also indicates how inadequately the universal Father provides for his offspring, a point Paine will make more directly later on.

In fact, Paine's subtler teaching is that nature reveals no moral law or meaning. Arguing that human beings can know God only as a first cause, discovered by reason, Paine tells us that "some chapters of Job and the 19th Psalm" are the only parts of the Bible "that convey to us any idea of God." These, Paine says, are "true *deistical* compositions," since they treat God through his works. Paine then quotes, not the text of the Nineteenth Psalm, but Addison's English paraphrase. Addison speaks of discerning a divine hand in the order of the heavens, as the psalm does, but omits the psalm's reference to the Lord's law ("perfect, converting the soul"), to the Lord's testimony ("sure, making the wise simple,"), and to human sin, the result of neglecting law and testimony.[126] Unlike the Psalmist, Paine separates nature from moral truth.

Later, Paine will tell his readers that, while we can observe the working of nature, its "operating cause"—Paine means its first and final cause—is perhaps the only true mystery, unknown and undecipherable. This is for the better, Paine contends, because even if we knew the secret, we could not perform the act of creation. Morality, however, is expected from this argument: "The God in whom we believe is a God of moral truth." The distinction between physical nature and morality, then, lies in the fact that *belief* is the source of truth about moral matters. Moral creation, unlike its physical counterpart, is within our power because morality is essentially a thing of human making.[127]

Paine's exegesis on Job 11:7 maintains that we can, by searching, find out God (in contrast to the rhetorical implication of Job's first question) but that we cannot "find out the Almighty unto perfection" because His attributes cannot be completely known. In this discussion, Paine indicates three times that creation affords some, though ultimately incomplete, manifestation of God's "power and wisdom." In a similar passage, Locke, after speaking of the natural proofs of God's wisdom and power, went on to argue that God's "bounty and goodness" and his "peculiar care of mankind" are made evident only by God's revealed promises.[128] Just so, Paine, who eschews Scripture and revelation, makes no mention of God's goodness.

For that matter, as Paine's argument instructs us, while we can know that we exist "by" God's power, we have no reason to believe that this power is omnipotent. "True Theology," in Paine's treatment, proves to be natural science and mechanics, the means of knowing and moving the universe.[129]

And human beings need to move or master nature. The "munificence" of God in His role as "Almighty Lecturer," of which Paine speaks, appears to consist in not impeding humanity—opening the universe to humanity's discovering, but otherwise leaving humankind to provide for itself.[130] At the end of *The Age of Reason,* as we have already observed, Paine declares that without reason and science, the human being "would be scarcely distinguishable in appearance and condition from a common animal."[131]

God's laissez-faire governance gives special meaning to the principle of benevolence—that we should contribute to the "happiness of our fellow creatures"—since Paine says this is best achieved by acting toward others "as he acts benignly toward all." In these terms, benevolence consists in imposing no unnecessary barriers, and perhaps in providing opportunity, but otherwise in leaving human beings alone. Along with the duty to love our enemies, Paine rejects the obligation to care for strangers, and it might be said that the chilly benevolence of Paine's creed estranges us all.[132]

Just as divine benevolence, in Paine's teaching, eventually resolves itself into indifference, so the afterlife is gradually whittled down to a shadowy possibility. Paine rejects any religious creed that "shocks the mind of a child," having concluded, on the basis of his own experience, that children are naturally shocked by the idea of a father sacrificing his son.[133] Without an afterlife, we would be forced to conclude that the universal Father kills *all* His children. Belief in a future state appears to be a necessary concession to the mind of the child, and perhaps to the child in all of us, but Paine hopes to promote our weaning.

At the end of part I, Paine asserts his "positive conviction" that "the Power that gave me existence is able to continue it . . . with or without this body," adding the very limited assurance that a future state is "more probable" than existence before birth.[134] In part II, however, he rejects the idea of resurrection, holding that immortality is continued "consciousness of existence." Alone among human products, Paine argues, thought is "capable of being immortal." This, in turn, suggests that the consciousness which can produce an immortal thing "can be immortal also."[135] Soon, however, Paine's argument turns utilitarian: since the "Power that called us into being" *can* call us to account, it is rational to believe that he *will*. Probability, "or even a possibility," is enough.[136] Yet if we are rational, a mere possibility will not tempt us to play for high stakes: it may merit a modest investment in faith and decency, but not one that entails a great price. However, the passive benevolence of Paine's creed seems to ask for little more.

Providing children with a religious and moral education suited to their needs, Paine hoped to prepare them for faith in science, his true grail. Just as Paine himself had moved from Quakerism to science, so human beings reared in Paine's "true deism" would be led away from anthropocentrism and prepared for the scientific revelation that the Christian faith—and perhaps this world itself—is "little and ridiculous" when compared with a universe encompassing a plurality of worlds. It was no soft curriculum Paine was outlining: holding it fortunate that he had repressed his "turn . . . for poetry" until he had mastered science, he recommended the same Adeimantus-like censorship of the imagination to others.[137]

Paine hoped for human beings able to assert rational mastery over the feelings and over human relationships. In Benjamin Franklin, Paine found a model: "His mind was ever young, ever serene," Paine wrote; "science that never grows gray was ever his mistress."[138] Those who know

Franklin's reputation may smile, but Paine meant us to think Franklin exemplary because he was not mastered by his mistresses. Paine's deprecation of pleasure as a source of happiness might seem unexceptionable were it not for the fact that he rejected love's dependencies along with the perishing things of this life. In Paine's view, liberty—mastery, or at least independence—shone as the human goal. Paine set out to free human beings from love, regarding that emancipation as the signpost of the age of reason. So understood, however, reason is a little sad and even more callow, lacking Solomon's ancient wisdom and love's high teaching.[139]

Love's Survival

Paine, like his friend Jefferson, appears to have underrated the strength of biblical religion in America. Hoping that the United States had "returned generally to sentiments worthy of former times," Jefferson invited Paine back home in 1801, but Paine met a storm of vituperation. Even old allies like Rush and Sam Adams had critical words. Paine became, as Dixon Wecter wrote, a "hero in reverse."[140] Orthodoxy was only Paine's most visible adversary. Despite Jefferson's theological heterodoxy, for example, his political thinking incorporated Christian ideas and influences in Jefferson's suspicion of commercialism, his opposition to self-love, and his hope of uniting Americans—and humanity—by "love, charity, peace, common wants, and common aids."[141] As Paine suspected, American liberalism was "amphibious," touched by Christian ethics even when it abandoned Christian faith, and unwilling to settle for Paine's bloodless benevolence.

Today, however, most of Paine's anxieties seem exaggerated or misplaced. Liberal civil religion, embodied in the laws, appears to be carrying the day. Evangelism thunders, but in the main the "cosmopolitan, universal theology of the republic" prevails.[142] Ronald Reagan, a paladin for religious conservatives, even quoted Tom Paine; the laws are shaping the "habits of the heart."[143]

Yet even where God is thought to be dead, love is still alive—although, to be sure, love today is too often wordless as well as blind, reduced to hurling itself against the walls of the prison of the self.[144] Still, the fact of love's survival, even in a maimed form, ought to cheer us.

Paine and his allies taught a freedom which too easily becomes servile. Liberal political society cannot survive if it aims only at survival; obsessed with profit and well-being, a commercial society stands to lose everything; having rights is no guarantee against acquiescing in wrongs.

The last half century is document enough. Liberal regimes need more than liberalism, more than individual liberty and self-interest rightly understood.[145] They need that ruler's wisdom to which love holds a key. Love moves human beings beyond the justice of personal claims to the sacrifice that may be demanded by the good of the whole. Anticipating Zarathustra, Paine rejected the camel of faith and the lion of rebellion in favor of the child.[146] Yet human beings are love children even where bereft; it is no small virtue that liberalism lets the camel survive, if only in the desert.

Notes

This essay was originally published as "Civil Religion in the Age of Reason: Thomas Paine on Liberalism, Redemption, and Revolution," *Social Research* 54, no. 3 (1987): 447–90.

1. Jeremiah Atwater, *A Sermon* (Middlebury, Vt., 1801), cited in *American Political Writing during the Founding Era,* ed. Charles S. Hyneman and Donald S. Lutz (Indianapolis: Liberty Press, 1983), 2:1184; see also the comments of Joseph Lathrop (1786), in ibid., 1:659. On the mood in general, see Geoffrey Clive, *The Romantic Enlightenment* (New York: Meridian, 1960).

2. Gordon S. Wood, "The Democratization of Mind in the American Revolution," in *The Moral Foundations of the American Republic,* ed. Robert Horwitz (Charlottesville: University of Virginia Press, 1977), 102–28.

3. Michael Kammen, *People of Paradox* (New York: Knopf, 1972).

4. Perry Miller used the phrase "habit of ambiguity" in referring to the New England clergy of the eighteenth century (*The New England Mind* [Boston: Beacon, 1961], 2:199). Of course, even carefully balanced teachings ultimately rest on first principles. John Wise's assurance that "Revelation is Nature's law in a fairer and brighter edition" implies that, in any apparent conflict, revelation is to be preferred as clearer and more beautiful (*A Vindication of the Government of the New England Churches,* 1717 [Gainesville, Fla.: Scholars' Facsimiles, 1958], 31–32).

5. Donald S. Lutz, "The Relative Influence of European Writers on Late Eighteenth Century American Political Thought," *American Political Science Review* 78 (1984): 192; Benjamin Rush, *The Letters of Benjamin Rush,* ed. L. H. Butterfield (Princeton: Princeton University Press, 1951), 1:584, 611–12; Mercy Otis Warren, *History of the Rise, Progress, and Termination of the American Revolution* (Boston: E. Larkin, 1805), 1:17–18; Benjamin F. Morris, *Christian Life and Character of the Civil Institution of the United States* (Philadelphia: Childs, 1864), 119. Freedom of conscience and the free exercise of religion were upheld even by those who argued for public support for religious instruction or supported religious tests for officeholders. See, for example, Hyneman and Lutz, *American Political Writing,* 1:8, 449–53, 556, 666–69; 2:1255, 1257.

6. John 1:29, 3:16, 10:10; Matthew 5:13 instructs the disciples that they are the "salt of the earth," intended to restore savor to life. See also Hyneman and Lutz, *American Political Writing,* 1:307, 2:850–51, 1249.

7. Hyneman and Lutz, *American Political Writing,* 1:3–4, 13–14, 309, 528–29; 2:848, 1031, 1246–47. As Nathaniel Niles argued, the Christian view necessarily rejects the modern doctrine which gives the individuals priority and legitimates private interest. The logical consequence of this position is that a social contract founded on the aim of protecting rights is a usurpation of what is rightfully public (*Two Discourses on Liberty* [Neburyport: Thomas and Tingers, 1773]). See also Gilbert Tennent, *The Danger of Spiritual Pride Represented* (Philadelphia: William Bradford, 1745).

8. Hyneman and Lutz, *American Political Writing,* 1:5–6, 292, 308–9, 410–11, 414, 432, 529, 552, 561, 659, 668, 1256; Samuel Davies, *Religion and Public Spirit* (New York: Parker, 1761); Gilbert Tennent, *Brotherly Love Recommended by the Argument of the Love of Christ* (Philadelphia: Franklin and Hall, 1748); Isaac Story, *The Love of Our Country Recommended and Enforced* (Boston: John Boyle, 1775). Public spirit is especially vital to republics, since such regimes attempt to minimize coercion; the self-governing soul is the foundation of a self-governing regime. "Let our pupil be taught," Rush wrote, "that he does not belong to himself, but that he is public property" (Hyneman and Lutz, *American Political Writing,* 1:684). See also Rush, *Essays, Literary, Moral, and Philosophical* (Philadelphia: Bradford, 1806), 112–14, 131–34; Hyneman and Lutz, *American Political Writing,* 1:315, 415, 526–28, 659–60; 2:994, 1173–74, 1177, 1250. Abraham Williams (1762) scorned the modern doctrine which attempts to trap and channel private spirit in "artful labyrinths of Machiavellian politicks" as too superficial and weak a remedy (Hyneman and Lutz, *American Political Writing,* 1:14).

9. *The Writings of Samuel Adams* (New York: Putnam, 1908), 4:238; Hyneman and Lutz, *American Political Writing,* 1:264, 419, 525, 659, 677, 685. A "vastly extended republic" like the United States relies heavily on religion and private life to obviate the necessity for a central apparatus of coercion (Hyneman and Lutz, *American Political Writing,* 2:1252). Repeatedly, Christians praise industry because it draws human beings into civil life, but they also insist on frugality, the principle that acquisitiveness must be regulated by a public norm. Warren, *History,* 1:18, 3:336–37; Hyneman and Lutz, *American Political Writing,* 1:267, 554, 661–66; 2:1001–2.

10. Hyneman and Lutz, *American Political Writing,* 1:285; 2:1005, 1247.

11. Religion, Niles observed, teaches citizens to do their civic duty without regard to its probabilities of success. Christian citizenship maintains the distinctly aristocratic proposition that "It its great, it is glorious, to espouse a good cause, and it is still more great and glorious if one stands alone" (*Two Discourses*). Rulers, for example, must—on the authority of Scripture—be persons who hate covetousness (Hyneman and Lutz, *American Political Writing,* 1:299–300, 434; 2:846, 1255). Moreover, since learning to love presumes the experience of love, the yearning love for excellence which elevates the many presumes the love of exemplary figures, condescending in the best sense, who make themselves available as models for emulation (Hyneman and Lutz, *American Political Writing,* 1:302, 556–57; *The Works of John Adams,* ed. C. F. Adams [Boston: Little, Brown: 1856], 6:232, 234; 8:560).

12. Mutual love, Gilbert Tennent wrote, is the "Bond and Cement" of society, but human beings, "by the Neglect of its Exercise, and more by its contrary, will be tempted against the *Law of Nature*, to seek a *single* and independent state" (*Brotherly Love Recommended*, 3; his italics). So defined, the principle of love runs counter to what Rush called the "absurd hypotheses of modern philosophers" (*Essays*, 105).

13. Sidney Mead, *The Nation with the Soul of a Church* (New York: Harper and Row, 1975), 119.

14. Hence John Cotton's reference to the churches as "integral and conservant causes" of political virtue ("The Bloody Tenet Washed (etc.)," 1647, in *The Bloody Tenet of Persecution for Cause of Conscience* [London: Haddon, 1848], 19–20).

15. In their public writings, while the framers were apt to refer to God as the Creator, they avoided the use of the term Redeemer (Catharine Albanese, *Sons of the Fathers: The Civil Theology of the American Revolution* [Philadelphia: Temple University Press, 1976], 112–42; see also Winthrop Hudson, *Religion in America* [New York: Scribner's, 1965], 92).

16. Locke tells us that reason reveals, to all "who would make use of that light," that God is "good and merciful," a kind and compassionate "Author and Father" whose example should inform the relation of fathers with their children (*The Reasonableness of Christianity*, ed. I. T. Ramsey [Stanford: Stanford University Press, 1958], secs. 231–32, p. 55). At the same time, it is clear that natural reason is *not* enough to show this, since it did not teach even the civilized ancients that they must not expose their children. Natural reason has "some light and certainty," but evidently does not create the will to "make use of that light." To this extent, the doctrine of reconciliation is useful to civil society (ibid., sec. 242, p. 64). On the general point, see Nathan Tarcov, *Locke's Education for Liberty* (Chicago: University of Chicago Press, 1984).

17. *Reasonableness of Christianity*, sec. 245, p. 69; see also A. L. Macfie, *The Individual in Society* (London: Allen and Unwin, 1967).

18. *Federalist*, #7.

19. When Madison wrote that "Had every Athenian been a Socrates, every Athenian assembly would still have been a mob" (*Federalist*, #55), he was contending that Socrates was or appeared to be virtuous because his public role made him visible and responsible. But in an assembly of philosophers, presumably, those in the back row would not be able to restrain license with the fear of detection or the hope of honor.

20. John Locke, *A Letter concerning Toleration* (Indianapolis: Bobbs-Merrill, 1982), 52; Jefferson followed Locke in doubting whether an atheist's testimony should be accepted at law (*Notes on the State of Virginia* [Chapel Hill: University of North Carolina Press, 1955], 159). Orthodox teachers concurred with some enthusiasm, of course (Hyneman and Lutz, *American Political Writing*, 1:452; 2:847, 1015–22, 1247).

21. *Federalist*, #72.

22. Alexis de Tocqueville, *Democracy in America* (New York: Schocken, 1961),

2:145–1491; see also Adam Smith, *The Theory of Moral Sentiments* (Indianapolis: Liberty Classics, 1982), 231. Jefferson regarded religion as vital in teaching that slavery is a violation of human rights, especially in offering some counterweight to the immediate interest of slaveholders (*The Life of and Selected Writings of Jefferson,* ed. Adrienne Koch and William Peden [New York: Modern Library, 1944], 639–40, 570, 703–4). Notably, however, Jefferson did not—unlike Benjamin Rush—appeal to biblical sources in condemning slavery (Hyneman and Lutz, *American Political Writing,* 1:217–30).

23. "The office of a reformer of the superstitions of the nation," Jefferson was to write, "is ever dangerous." Jesus "had to walk in the perilous confines of religion and reason, and a step to the right or to the left might place him within the grasp of the priests." Hence, Jefferson argued, Jesus was justified in linking his teachings to traditional doctrine "by evasions, by sophistries, by misconstructions and misapplications of scraps of the prophets" (*Writings of Thomas Jefferson,* ed. Andrew Lipscomb and Albert Bergh [Washington, D.C.: Thomas Jefferson Memorial Assn., 1903–5], 15:260–61; compare Locke, *Reasonableness of Christianity,* secs. 59, 61, 139).

24. *Reasonableness of Christianity,* secs. 1, 143, 237, 238, 252.

25. Ibid., sec. 243. Compare Samuel Kendal's similar, but more orthodox, view, Hyneman and Lutz, *American Political Writing,* 2:1253–54.

26. *Writings of Thomas Jefferson,* 13:377, 15:260–61; *Life and Selected Writings of Jefferson,* 570, 703–4; *Reasonableness of Christianity,* secs. 240, 243. See also Sidney Mead, *The Lively Experiment: The Shaping of Christianity in America* (New York: Harper and Row, 1961), 61.

27. Clinton Rossiter, *Seedtime of the Republic* (New York: Harcourt Brace, 1953), 40, 53; for example, see Hyneman and Lutz, *American Political Writing,* 1:411–13, 416, 419, 422.

28. Most of Jefferson's religious statements, for example, are found in letters, and he did not even complete his *Life and Morals of Jesus of Nazareth* until 1819.

29. In Locke's version, death is the "sole penalty" to which human beings are subject for Original Sin, since—despite "some mistaken places in the New Testament"—God would not place us under the "necessity of sinning continually" (*Reasonableness,* secs. 2, 4). Locke twice cites Romans 5:12, suppressing the second half of the verse, "so that death passed upon all men, for that all have sinned" (ibid., secs. 6, 10). This unorthodox teaching, moreover, obscures the fact that human beings lost "bliss"—i.e., were compelled to work—when driven out of Eden (ibid., sec. 5). Locke rejects the traditional view because it implies that sin is prior to—and worse than—death. Jesus's "peremptory decision," Locke says, puts it "past doubt" that some lives are worse than not having been, but Locke then goes on to doubt it, invoking—against Jesus—our common opinion that mortal life "is better than not being" (ibid., sec. 6). Jesus redeemed man, Locke argues, by saving man from death; Locke has doubts about the resurrection, but he maintains that after Jesus, humanity no longer had to take death as a *given.* He refers repeatedly to what Paul says "concerning the resurrection" (1 Cor. 15:12),

but—aside from the fact that Paul is arguing against doubters, despite what Locke says in secs. 237, 240 about the undeniability of Christ's miracles—Paul maintains the resurrection must *follow* the messianic kingdom: "For he must reign till he hath put all enemies under his feet. The last enemy that shall be destroyed is death" (1 Cor. 15:25–26). This only emphasizes Locke's insistence on Christ the Messiah, as opposed to the Son of Man (ibid., secs. 31, 38). Referring to Philips's preaching "out of Isaiah" to the Ethiopian, Locke cites Acts 8:35, omitting the fact that the prophecy in question speaks of a lamb led to the slaughter (Acts 8:32–33). Similarly, discussing Mark 8:35–38, Locke says that those who would not follow Jesus were punished by being made "to lose their souls, i.e., their lives" (ibid., sec. 15). It is significant enough that Locke equates souls with lives, since the passage in question urges human beings to *lose* their lives in order to save them. Locke claims that that passage's meaning is "plain, considering the occasion it was spoke on." But that occasion involves a rebuke to Peter who—like Locke—denied the teaching that "the Son of Man must suffer many things," proclaiming instead that Christ is the Messiah (Mark 8:29, 31).

30. *Reasonableness*, secs. 16, 67, 70–72, 167, 171–72, 179–80. Consider the fact that Locke's citation of Romans 2:6 (sec. 6) makes no reference to the succeeding verse. By contrast to Locke's doctrine, see Romans 3:20.

31. *Letter concerning Toleration*, 30. "No man ever said," Locke asserts, that "covetousness, uncharitableness, idleness"—among other things which are "sins, by the consent of men"—ought to be "punished by the magistrate." This exaggeration only underscores Locke's determination to limit the political order to the protection of "men's rights" and of "the public peace" (ibid., 42). Early in the *Letter concerning Toleration*, Locke cites three passages from Scripture, Luke 22:25–26, Timothy 2:19, and Luke 22:32. He omits, then, certain passages from Luke 22 (the second halves of verses 25, 26, and 32 as well as all of verses 27–31), substituting a new central teaching which prohibits iniquity. The omitted passages, by contrast, assert a hierarchy of political regimes. Among the unfaithful Gentiles, lordship is a "benefaction"; among the faithful disciples, equality should be the rule and the chiefs are to serve; the disciples are also a kingdom with a right to judge the law-based "Tribes of Israel." Hence, according to the principle of grace, the faithful—who know that loving service among equals is the best form of rules—are entitled to judge, and hence to rule over, even law-abiding Israel, the best regime short of grace. For Gentiles, self-assertive and dominion seeking, almost any rule is a gift. Locke subtly displaces this doctrine in favor of the limited and negative standard of 2 Timothy 2:19.

32. Harvey C. Mansfield Jr., ed., *Thomas Jefferson: Selected Writings* (Arlington: AHM, 1979), xiv–xv; Hyneman and Lutz, *American Political Writing*, 1:635.

33. Hyneman and Lutz, *American Political Writing*, 1:632–33; *Notes on the State of Virginia*, 161; Harvey C. Mansfield Jr., "Thomas Jefferson," in *American Political Thought: The Philosophic Dimensions of American Statesmanship*, ed. Morton J. Frisch and Richard G. Stevens (New York: Scribner's, 1971), 38; *Letter concerning Toleration*, 13, 15, 19, 25, 27–29, 52, 54–55.

34. Consequently, the frequent pagan invocations in the rhetoric of the revolution could be treated, by believers and by rationalists, as only so much hyperbole, not a challenge to Christian orthodoxy (see Albanese, *Sons of the Fathers*, 46–80). For us, of course, this side of civil religion has become second nature; even zealous Christians apparently have no qualms about civil idolatry in relation to the Statue of Liberty.

35. Mansfield, *Thomas Jefferson*, xxv; Sanford Kessler, "Jefferson's Rational Religion," in Sidney A. Pearson Jr., *The Constitutional Polity* (Washington, D.C.: University Press of America, 1983), 58–78; compare Montesquieu, *The Spirit of the Laws*, vol. 1, bk. 20 (New York: Hafner, 1949), 316–17. In our times, Claude Lévi-Strauss speaks of the tendency for ideas of what is "good to think" to follow the processes of exchange (*Totemism* [Boston: Beacon, 1963], 89).

36. R. V. Sampson, *Progress in the Age of Reason* (Cambridge, Mass.: Harvard University Press, 1956); James W. Jones, *The Shattered Synthesis: New England Puritanism before the Great Awakening* (New Haven: Yale University Press, 1973); *Letters of Benjamin Rush*, 1:540–41, 2:1075; and Benjamin Rush, *Six Introductory Lectures* (Philadelphia: Conrad, 1801), 114–19.

37. John Witherspoon, *Lectures on Moral Philosophy*, ed. Jack Scott (Dover: University of Delaware Press, 1981), 67, 78–80, 122–23, 186–87.

38. Ibid., 110; see also 50, 159.

39. Ibid., 109, 112, 159–61.

40. Albanese, *Sons of the Fathers*, 202–4.

41. Hyneman and Lutz, *American Political Writing*, 1:680–83, *Letters of Benjamin Rush*, 2:947, 1075; Rush, *Essays, Literary, Moral, and Philosophical*, 8–9, 81–92, 94–95, 98–101, 105, 112–13.

42. Philip Foner concedes that "every one [of Paine's ideas] had been expressed by Deists before him" (*The Complete Writings of Thomas Paine* [New York: Citadel, 1969], 1:xxxvii).

43. See my essay "The Bible in the American Political Tradition," in *Religion and Politics*, ed. Myron J. Aronoff (New Brunswick: Transaction, 1984), 22–24.

44. *Complete Writings of Thomas Paine*, 1:514; 2:1330, 1335.

45. Almost gratuitously, Paine refers to an essay on Franco-American commerce he had "intended for" the very hostile Committee on Public Safety, one of many indications that Paine wrote with an eye to potential inquisitors (ibid., 1:514).

46. Ibid., 464–65.

47. Ibid., 1:513–14; on Robespierre's views, see Georges Lefebvre, *The French Revolution* (London and New York: Routledge & Kegan Paul and Columbia University Press, 1962), 2:78, 114–15.

48. *Complete Writings of Thomas Paine*, 1:464; compare Lefebvre, *French Revolution*, 2:78.

49. *Complete Writings of Thomas Paine*, 1:514, 516; *Letters of Benjamin Rush*, 2:746, 935.

50. *Complete Writings of Thomas Paine*, 1:463.

51. Americans, of course, asserted the same principle in decorous Latin, while nominally respecting the Christian calendar: *Novus Ordo Seclorum,* 1787.

52. Lefebvre, *French Revolution,* 2:114.

53. *Complete Writings of Thomas Paine,* 1:519.

54. Ibid., 1:544–45, 553; see also 1:574.

55. Locke, *An Essay concerning Human Understanding,* IV:18:2.

56. Ibid., IV:19:5; see also *Reasonableness of Christianity,* sec. 242.

57. *Essay concerning Human Understanding,* IV:18:4; *A Discourse of Miracles,* in Ramsey, *Reasonableness of Christianity,* 86; Paine follows the same line of reasoning in *The Age of Reason* (*Complete Writings of Thomas Paine,* 1:507–8).

58. *A Discourse of Miracles,* 80–81, 86; *Reasonableness of Christianity,* sec. 238. Jesus, by contrast, belittles one of the miracles to which Locke refers repeatedly, rating deeds of mastery as less significant than the suffering of the Son of Man (compare *Reasonableness of Christianity,* secs. 30, 38, 76, commenting on John 1:49, with John 1:50–51).

59. In *The Reasonableness of Christianity,* sec. 240, Locke argues that Julian the Apostate "durst not deny" the evidence of the miracles, "which being granted, the truth of our Savior's doctrine and mission unavoidably follows." Obviously, however, it did not follow in Julian's case.

60. *Complete Writings of Thomas Paine,* 1:467–68; see also the discussion of Locke's argument regarding the undeniability of the miracles in n. 29, above.

61. Ibid., 1:508.

62. Ibid., 1:505; *Reasonableness of Christianity,* secs. 14, 180, 182, 228, 229, 235, 241, 242.

63. *Complete Writings of Thomas Paine,* 1:519; see also 1:472–73, 477, 586, 594. It ought to be clear that Paine is hinting that the truths of the Declaration of Independence, if genuinely self-evident, do not require the Creator.

64. Ibid., 1:484–85. He repeats this disclaimer in 2:514–15 and again on 582. To anyone familiar with Christianity, the fact that Paine repeats his denial three times is bound to raise suspicions (John 13:38, 18:16–27).

65. *Complete Writings of Thomas Paine,* 1:582.

66. Ibid., 1:485.

67. Ibid., 1:564–65.

68. Ibid., 1:565.

69. Ibid., 1:496–97; see also 465.

70. Ibid., 1:464, 472.

71. Ibid., 1:465, 506. For example, during the French Revolution, the urban poor, seeing only immediate benefits, attempted to control the price of commodities, blind to the fact that the long-term effect would be to limit supply (2:1336–37). This suggests a need for discipline and patience as well as economic knowledge. The many need to learn that some things—the laws of the market were apposite, for Paine—are not subject to popular control, and that in some matters the principle of benevolence consists, as it does for Deism's God, in letting things alone.

72. Ibid., 1:465.

73. Paine knew, of course, that this argument would be particularly effective with thinkers who shared Jefferson's conviction that "uprightness" is more important than rightness (*Life and Selected Writings,* 431–33).

74. *Complete Writings of Thomas Paine,* 1:463, 505.

75. Ibid., 1:603; see also 602, 604.

76. Norman Jacobson, "Political Science and Political Education," *American Political Science Review* 57 (1963): 561–69.

77. *Complete Writings of Thomas Paine,* 2:239.

78. Ibid., 2:220. Madison, by contrast, was content to rest the union on the laws and circumspect reason, prosaic substitutes for Paine's "perpetual energy."

79. Ibid., 2:238; David Hume, *A Treatise of Human Nature* (Oxford: Clarendon, 1975), 413–18, and *Essays: Moral, Political and Literary* (London: Longmans Green, 1875), 1:294–95.

80. *Complete Writings of Thomas Paine,* 1:597, 2:240–41. Intellectual progress is even more insecure. Reverence for antiquity, Paine believed, is due to the "interregnum of science" produced by Christian repression, making the ancients tower by contrast to what succeeded. That suppression indicates that religion may, for centuries, prevail over science. In fact, Paine held that the liberation of science in modern times was fundamentally accidental, an unintended consequence of the Reformation (ibid., 1:495).

81. Hume, *Essays: Moral, Political and Literary,* 1:454–55; *Treatise of Human Nature,* 41–46, 477–84; *Natural History of Religion,* in *Hume: Selections,* ed. Charles Hendel (New York: Scribner's, 1927), 253.

82. *Complete Writings of Thomas Paine,* 2:242. Paine regarded it as an advantage that, by the accidents of his early education, his political praxis derived from theory rather than the reverse. Political practice, Paine observes, teaches "Jockeyship," a kind of trivial domination, able to whip people toward victory but unable to ask whether the race is worth running (ibid., 1:496–97).

83. Ibid,. 2:243, 245.

84. Ibid., 2:1303, 1330–31, 1335; 1:514–15.

85. Ibid., 1:475–76; Paine's italics.

86. Ibid., 1:476; Paine's italics.

87. 1 Sam. 10:5–6

88. Acts 9:21; Saul's humility is indicated by 1 Samuel 9:21.

89. *Complete Writings of Thomas Paine,* 1:590; obviously, the comment also refers to the limited ability of a formal constitution to change the organic constitution of a regime.

90. 1 Sam. 18:6–7.

91. *Complete Writings of Thomas Paine,* 1:497. As Paine also indicates, those brought up in the Bible rarely doubt its truth because the ability to evaluate mystery, miracle, and prophecy, separating false claims from true, depends on one's prior principles (ibid., 1:529, 505–11).

92. Ibid., 1:497–98; Paine likens the Bible to Aesop in being composed of sto-

ries which, even when they teach a good moral, are apt to harm a child's "heart" (ibid., 1:543).

93. In the same spirit, John Dewey was to write, "After democratic political institutions were nominally established, beliefs and ways of looking at life . . . that originated when men and women were externally controlled and subjected to arbitrary power persisted in the family, the church, business, and school; and experience shows that as long as they persist there, political democracy is not secure" ("Democracy and Educational Administration," *School and Society,* April 3, 1937, in *Intelligence in the Modern World: John Dewey's Philosophy,* ed. J. Ratner [New York: Modern Library, 1939], 402–3).

94. *Complete Writings of Thomas Paine,* 1:467, 471.

95. Ibid., 1:467, 469, 478.

96. *Writings of Thomas Jefferson,* 15:260–61; see n. 23, above.

97. *Complete Writings of Thomas Paine,* 1:467.

98. In referring to Christianity as "amphibious," Paine meant that it was of a mixed nature. It would be surprising, however, if he overlooked the double meaning, able to survive in water, for Christianity—unlike so many of the Old World's institutions—had been able to cross to the New.

99. *Complete Writings of Thomas Paine,* 1:478.

100. Ibid., 1:550.

101. Ibid., 1:475n.

102. "The Bible suggests that the political leader should be like "a nursing father" who "beareth the sucking child" (Num. 11:12; see also Isa. 49:23). See Aaron B. Wildavsky, *The Nursing Father: Moses as a Political Leader* (Tuscaloosa: University of Alabama Press, 1984). Paul also speaks of apostolic leadership as "gentle . . . as a nurse nourishes her children" (1 Thess. 2:7).

103. *Complete Writings of Thomas Paine,* 1:471–72.

104. Ibid.,1:535. In fact, Paine magnifies Ruth's supposed misconduct, since Boaz is Ruth's cousin by marriage. He also draws no attention to Naomi, Ruth's mother-in-law, who instructs Ruth in the ways of seducing Boaz (Ruth 3:1–4).

105. *Complete Writings of Thomas Paine,* 1:547. In addition to his stated reason, I suspect that Paine also admires Ruth because Naomi, the native woman, not the alien Ruth, becomes nurse to the child, Obed (Ruth 4:16, 17).

106. *Complete Writings of Thomas Paine,* 1:473.

107. Ibid., 1:597–99.

108. Ibid., 1:598.

109. Ibid., 1:472; in *Common Sense,* Paine says that Milton "wisely expresses" the principle that reconciliation is impossible when great injuries have been suffered. In fact, of course, Paine is quoting Satan's rejection of reconciliation with God (ibid., 1:23; Milton, *Paradise Lost,* IV:98–99).

110. *Complete Writings of Thomas Paine,* 1:547–48.

111. Prov. 30:9.

112. *Complete Writings of Thomas Paine,* 1:597–98.

113. Ibid., 1:543.

114. Ibid., 1:528; he acknowledges and calls attention to this digression with an explicit "return to my subject" on p. 529.

115. Ibid., 1:529.

116. Ibid., 1:533–35.

117. Ibid., 1:535; compare 1 Chron. 14:3–4. Later, discussing the errors in Ezra's numbering of Israel, Paine cites Ezra 2:3–60 in arriving at his total, contrasting it with the different figures given in verse 64 (*Complete Writings of Thomas Paine*, 1:546). Paine omits verses 61–63, which may account for the discrepancy; they refer to the children of priests, fathered on captured Gileadite women and regarded as "polluted," but nevertheless protected by David (1 Kings 2:7), who may have hated the lame, but appears to have had softer feelings for children.

118. 1 Chron. 13:13. A third example of Paine's point is found in his treatment of the first book of Samuel (*Complete Writings of Thomas Paine*, 1:535–37). Referring to Samuel's death, Paine first mentions Saul's visit to the Witch of Endor, when Samuel's shade was summoned (1 Sam. 28). Only later does he speak of Samuel's death itself (1 Sam. 25). This inversion of chronological order—and Paine's critique of Scripture has emphasized just such errors—makes Saul's visit central among Paine's three citations from 1 Samuel (the other is 1 Sam. 9). Saul has been zealous to drive out witches and wizards, trying to purge Israel of superstition (1 Sam. 28:9). Yet, beset by fears and anxieties, Saul loses his nerve and turns to a witch's mediation. The woman does not console him, however, and her hostile vision completes the unmanning of Saul. In a moment of uncertainty, Saul needs support; given his record of persecution, he can expect—and gets—only enmity.

119. *Life and Selected Writings of Jefferson*, 395–407; Smith, *Theory of Moral Sentiments*, 85, 113–14, 225.

120. *Complete Writings of Thomas Paine*, 1:476.

121. Ibid.

122. Judg. 11:23–24, 30–40; John Locke, *Two Treatises of Government*, I, sec. 163; II, secs. 21, 109, 241.

123. *Complete Writings of Thomas Paine*, 1:596, 464; however, the proposition that God's "Word" is to be found in things beheld or seen, rather than in things said or heard, assigns a second-class and suspect status to Paine's own words (1:482, 490–91.)

124. Ibid., 1:472.

125. Ibid., 477–78.

126. Ibid., 1:484–85; compare Ps. 19:7–13.

127. *Complete Writings of Thomas Paine*, 1:505–6. Paine is less critical of Genesis 1 than one might expect. He dismisses the account of creation as "traditionary," but Paine also asserts that "every nation of people has been world-makers, and the Israelites had as much right to set up in the trade of world-making as any of the rest" (ibid., 1:474).

128. Ibid., 1:486; Locke, *Reasonableness of Christianity*, sec. 228.

129. *Complete Writings of Thomas Paine*, 1:487–89, 602–3. Paine illustrates his

argument by discussing the triangle—the closest secular approximation of the Trinity's three in one and one in three—in relation to *leverage*. The scientific "trinity," in other words, involves the power to move nature (1:489–90, 493).

130. Ibid., 1:490.

131. Ibid., 1:603.

132. Ibid., 1:506. On the general point, see Michael Ignatieff, *The Needs of Strangers* (New York: Viking, 1984).

133. *Complete Writings of Thomas Paine*, 1:497–98.

134. Ibid., 1:512.

135. Ibid., 1:592. Paine surely recognized that, since thought is "immortal" only to the extent that it is thought by others, the immortality of its authors might rest on the same foundation.

136. Ibid., 1:599.

137. Ibid., 1:496, 498–504.

138. Ibid., 1:551. Franklin's utilitarian—or latitudinarian—approach to sexual matters was well known (*Autobiography of Benjamin Franklin*, ed. Leonard W. Labaree et al. [New Haven: Yale University Press, 1964], 150). Paine's imagery—contrasting gray mistresses with ageless science—is far too evocative not to suggest Franklin's "Old Mistress Apologue" (better known as "Advice to a Young Man on the Choice of His Mistress"). The essay was not published during Paine's lifetime, but it seems likely that Franklin discoursed on the subject, or even read the essay among friends. Long before it was published it had acquired a certain "clandestine fame" (*Papers of Benjamin Franklin*, ed. Leonard W. Labaree et al. [New Haven: Yale University Press, 1959–], 3:27–31).

139. Eccles. 4:7–12; John 16:12–13.

140. Dixon Wecter, "Hero in Reverse," *Virginia Quarterly* 18 (1942): 243–59; G. Adolph Koch, *Republican Religion* (New York: Holt, 1933), 130–46.

141. *Life and Selected Writings of Jefferson*, 570, 639–40; *The Adams-Jefferson Letters*, ed. L. J. Cappon (New York: Simon and Schuster, 1971), 484–85; *Writings of Thomas Jefferson*, 13:377. On Jefferson's theology, see Kessler, "Jefferson's Rational Religion," 58–78.

142. Mead, *Nation with the Soul of a Church*, 22–25, 69.

143. Robert Bellah et al., *Habits of the Heart* (Berkeley and Los Angeles: University of California Press, 1985).

144. *Democracy in America*, 2:120.

145. John P. Diggins, *The Lost Soul of American Politics* (New York: Basic Books, 1984).

146. *Thus Spake Zarathustra*, ch. 1.

The Anti-Federalists

The Anti-Federalists drew strength from ancient wisdom, but they were also eighteenth-century Americans, and—like their countrymen generally—they were "people of paradox," torn between the old and the new. They were also a diverse lot, united mainly by what they opposed, but Anti-Federalism, for all its eddies and currents, followed a mainstream, and Herbert Storing was right to draw our attention to "what the Anti-Federalists were for" in the volume of that name that introduces *The Complete Anti-Federalist.*[1] The Anti-Federalists shaped and defended an ideal of the fraternal republic which is distinctly American. They were the losers in 1787, but their teaching, like a half-remembered song, still tantalizes and enriches our political life and heritage.

The Anti-Federalists began with the conviction, axiomatic in traditional political science, that the measure of a republic is the public spirit of its citizens. The grounds for this view are simple and probably unanswerable: a republic is self-governing only to the extent that laws are enforced by citizens as well as made by them. Self-rule includes rule over the self. Members of a society are not fully autonomous if they are compelled by others to obey the law. Republican excellence, therefore, requires strong assent, a commitment to abide by the law, and submitting one's conduct to a common rule.

When the Anti-Federalists contended that the Constitution would end in despotism, they were predicting, with a tablespoon of hyperbole, that a republic as large and diverse as the United States would depend more and more on enforcement and less and less on assent, coming to lean on a state bureaucracy rather than civic respectability and responsibility. They were right, of course. The American tax code is still remarkably self-enforced, but the IRS is under constant pressure to strengthen its policing mechanism. As the Anti-Federalists worried, in a large republic, the law vacillates between being too weak and growing too strong.

As this suggests, the Anti-Federalists were no libertarians. Their view of politics tended to be stern and exacting, and they were more comfortable with ideas of civic duty than we are apt to be today. Their thinking was deeply influenced by the doctrine of the Covenant. Unlike the Federalists, they held to the older idea that political society is fundamentally a permanent bond between persons, not an alliance created for limited purposes. Political society shapes, and is shaped by, who we are: the cornerstone and proving ground of all politics is the soul.

Although the Anti-Federalists often spoke the fashionable language of the social contract, referring to government as the contrivance of naturally free individuals, their doctrine was more consonant with the view that social and political life is natural for human beings. "A state of society," Agrippa wrote, "is the natural state of man . . . the state of government is as natural to man as a state of society." In other words, although God and nature may leave it to human beings to institute the forms of government, their politicality is not a matter of choice. Aristotle's proposition that the *polis* is prior to the individual in the order of nature—that political society is a precondition for *human* life, just as it is a precondition for human liberty and the pursuit of human happiness—was a familiar doctrine in colonial America. "Individual estates," John Winthrop had remarked at the beginning, "cannot subsist in the ruin of the public." And in 1774, Nathaniel Niles contended that, by nature, there are no private rights: private claims, like individuality itself, derive from the community and are founded in convention. Few Anti-Federalists would have gone so far, but they were willing to concede a moral priority to political community, recognizing that it is political society—as opposed to the village, the family, or the "state of nature"—which, by combining skills and crafts, enables individuals to discover and practice what they do best.

The Anti-Federalists leaned toward the classical view that the best political society is small and stable because such a regime reduces the tension between public reason and private sensibility, and, at its best, can win the affections of the people, as allies for the public good. In the small state, citizens are apt to see and benefit from public goods: they can sit in the new park or attend a meeting at the town hall. In a large state, however, only a small fraction of the government's activities are perceptible in day-to-day life. Reason tells Americans that Justice Holmes was right, that "taxes are what we pay for civilized society," but the taxpayer may not feel that way on April 15th. "The laws of a free government," Richard Henry Lee wrote, "rest on the confidence of the people, and operate gently—and can never extend their influence very far—. . . about the center, where the benefits of the government induce the people to support it voluntarily; yet they must be executed on the principles of fear and force in the extremes."

In any country, civic education involves a discipline strong enough to curb the body and direct the passions. If law and politics are only restraints, however, wholly at odds with private interests and personal feelings, the government will be experienced as a despotism. A large state, distant from the emotional world and daily life of its citizens, can rule only by repression or by "corruption"—a direct appeal to the citizen's private interests. The Anti-Federalists would not have been surprised that totalitarian regimes, with their demand for civic zeal and fervor, depend on state terror. And they might have accused contemporary Americans of a political system that depends, to a dangerous degree, on the lobbying of powerful interest groups, which the Anti-Federalists would see as a civic vice.

The small state can also teach softly because it is more compatible with a citizen's dignity; in such a state, individuals are more likely to feel that they matter. The small country allows one's rulers to hear one's voice and recognize one's uniqueness, so that an individual is not treated simply as a member of some group or statistical class. And, as the Anti-Federalists repeatedly pointed out, government in a small state is easier for citizens to oversee and control. Its activities are likely to be simple and comprehensible, and citizens, as Richard Henry Lee observed, "can unite and act in concert and with vigor" with relative ease, while in large states, those advantages belong only to the few.

As Madison hinted, the daunting scale and complexity of our giant republic makes most of us "timid and cautious," content to have a choice between private governments and to enjoy our private liberties. To the Anti-Federalists, our civic life would have seemed tepid if not sickly; they preferred a good deal of political turbulence to a citizenry grown "languid" or "cool and inattentive."

In a healthy republic, speech and law rule private force and interest, and the Anti-Federalists regarded the right to participate in civic deliberation as indispensable. The force of deliberation, however, turns on willing and attentive listeners, and hence, on public forums that respect the dignity of citizens, where, able to speak if one wishes, one listens from choice. Republican deliberation, the Anti-Federalists would have told us, demands local meetings and forums.

Anti-Federalists also held that, to be a proper school for civic virtue, a state should be stable as well as small. When Roger Sherman told the

Constitutional Convention that the "habits, usages, and manners" of each state "constitute its happiness," he was contending that the customs and attachments of a small regime can help to redefine the passions of an individual, building happiness on common and public foundations. "The good old way" is valuable because it orders and limits, but also because it engenders security and makes it easier for us to trust one another. Stability makes it seem safe to invest oneself in one's fellows and worthwhile to work for the public good: orderliness is the foundation of the arts of association and civic participation. "If it were not for the stability and attachment which time and habit give to forms of government," Samuel Bryan declared, "it would be in the power of the enlightened and aspiring few, if they should combine, at any time to destroy the best establishments, and even to make the people the instruments of their own subjugation."

All of this implies, of course, the propriety of limits to individual liberty and, especially, of restraints on acquisition. Commercial life engenders greed and disunity, the Anti-Federalists observed, because it appeals to passions that are universal and low. The division of labor brightens human life and frees our best talents, but it tends to make common interests subtle and even invisible. Creditor and debtor do not often think of their commonalities. Specialization can destroy the sense of the common life, hence Mercy Otis Warren's alarm at "restless passions" which create a "rage for project, speculation and various artifices to support a factitious dignity."

On the other hand, internal commerce can unite a people—and the Anti-Federalists sometimes spoke as if commerce alone would be a sufficient bond for the Union. External trade, however, can only divide them, because it creates dependence on outsiders. Foreign commerce weakens the civic bond and self-government alike, giving foreign markets and policies power over domestic life. The daily newspaper attests to this, as we listen for the decisions of foreign central banks and OPEC conclaves. Of course, the Anti-Federalists knew that a commercial regime may seek, through imperialism, to reassert political control over economic life, but they recognized that an imperial regime is ruled by its empire and gradually becomes, like ancient Rome, more imperial and less republican.

The Anti-Federalists did not shrink from the conclusion that a republic must be willing, in principle, to accept austerity, sacrificing economic growth for the common good. They regarded frugality as a virtue, but like most of us, they wanted material prosperity, consistent with their higher goals. But they insisted that there *are* higher goals and that, because the allure of money is so great, one must be fully prepared for sacrifice. Sam Adams caught this view in a phrase when he spoke of his hope that Boston might become a "Christian Sparta," an austere republic of heroic spirit.

Yet despite their admiration for the small state and their suspicion of commerce, the Anti-Federalists were not advocates of the classical *polis*. In the first place, the need to survive in what was soon to be a world of nation-states demanded larger political societies. And second, the Anti-Federalists were products of a Christian culture even when they were not, like Patrick Henry, ardent Christians. They believed in human equality and in obligations to humanity as a whole, and they rejected the xenophobia of the closed community. The Articles of Confederation, for example, guaranteed the "free inhabitants" of all states both "free ingress and regress" and the "privileges and immunities of free citizens in the several states." Sam Adams's Boston was to be Spartan in austerity, but Christian in charity, patriotism joined to philanthropy.

The Anti-Federalists relied on representative government, but in a form different from that envisaged by the framers. They wanted a much larger Congress and much smaller districts, so that representatives would feel as though they had been present and given their consent in person. Representatives were to be rotated frequently to safeguard their ties to the home community: "Exactly in the ratio of their removal from the people," Cincinnatus maintained, "do aristocratic principles infect the minds of men." Expert legislators were less important than representatives able to convey strong and genuine assent. And in any case, George Clinton argued, the chance of election should be dispersed widely, so that the "desire of rendering themselves worthy" might encourage civic virtues among the largest number. No legislature practicable for the Union would be large enough, Melancton Smith observed, but we might "approach a great way toward perfection."

The broad side of the Anti-Federal thinking was most evident in the championship of a Bill of Rights, a battle Anti-Federalists both won and lost. They had hoped for a statement of natural rights—probably augmented by those common law rights Americans held almost equally sacred—as a preface to the Constitution. Instead, the Bill of Rights materialized as positive law restrictions, theoretically subject to repeal. In the Anti-Federalist view, the civil liberties to be guaranteed would have been binding on all legitimate governments, including the states. Later, in *Barron v. Baltimore,* Chief Justice Marshall was to argue that the Bill of Rights was intended to restrict and apply only to the federal government. For the most part, however, the Anti-Federalists were concerned to deny to the central government not rights that the states retained, but rights that no government possessed.

The Anti-Federalists envisioned a country made up of deliberative communities in which freedom of speech and assembly would be the rule, linked by internal commerce and "adequate" representative institutions. The sort of republic they hoped for—slow moving, austere, and talky—was suited, as they knew, for the ordinary routines of political life, in which custom is an adequate guide, and for the great crises of politics which demand a public-spirited willingness to make great sacrifices. The framers, by contrast, designed a regime suited to a middle range of political events, those in which change is required but which are not so taxing that speed of decision and expertise may not substitute for strong assent. But in *Federalist, #49*, Madison acknowledged that there *are* "great and extraordinary moments" in which a "recurrence to the people" is necessary. If those moments are likely to be frequent, we would do well to rebuild the local deliberative forums that were the foundations of the Anti-Federalists' America.

Notes

This essay was originally published as "The Anti-Federalists vs. . . . ," *Humanities* 8, no. 2 (1987).

    1. Herbert J. Storing, ed., *The Complete Anti-Federalist*, 7 vols. (Chicago: University of Chicago Press, 1981).

Standing at Armageddon

Morality and Religion in Progressive Thought

Progressivism was more disposition than doctrine, its ideas developed by thinkers who were almost relentlessly idiosyncratic and at least suspicious of the forms, in logic if not in society.[1] Necessarily, the movement was somewhat amorphous, and almost every generalization about it calls to mind an obvious exception, e.g., Progressives, pretty much across the board, were critics of local party organizations and especially of "boss rule," yet no one wrote more appreciatively about ward politics than the remarkable Mary K. Simkhovitch.[2] And Brand Whitlock—successful both as a novelist and a reform mayor of Toledo—came to suspect that the old ward bosses, in their flawed and florid humanity, were "more nearly right after all than the cold and formal and precise gentlemen who denounced their records."[3] It is not surprising, then, that contemporary historians call attention to the Heinz-like varieties of Progressivism, or even deny that the movement had any real coherence.[4]

Still, Progressives saw and spoke of themselves as part of an identifiable movement or tendency, and while I will pay some homage to their diversity later on, I want to begin by focusing on some of their commonalities in life and thought.

In the first place, they were almost all born in the twenty-year period from just before the Civil War (like Ida Tarbell and Woodrow Wilson) to just before the end of Reconstruction (like Charles Merriam, born in 1874). Unlike their parents, they took the war and its aftermath largely for granted. They were the first generation shaped by the problems of late-century America and ready to give them more or less undivided attention.

Second, with few exceptions they were Protestants raised in mainline denominations who had attended similarly denominational colleges (e.g., Oberlin, Amherst, Grinnell) or public universities (Dewey attended the University of Vermont; Charles Herbert Cooley was a graduate of

Michigan). With only slightly less frequency, they had at best a strained relation to churches and organized religion; even the Social Gospel clergy found that relationship heavy going. Nevertheless, they brought to the "search for order"—for Robert Wiebe is right, it was that—a distinctly Protestant and often evangelical tone.[5]

Yet while Progressives drew on that heritage, they were both more troubled and more confident than their teachers. As I will be arguing, they felt caught up in something close to a secular Armageddon, just as Theodore Roosevelt said in 1912, a political battle with supremely high stakes.[6] Beyond mere order, Progressives were engaged in a quest for democracy on the grand scale, informed by the belief that the human spirit or conscience, guided by social science, could eventually create a vast and brotherly republic of public-spirited citizens. That high ambition moved Progressives to humanize American life in any number of ways, but it also led them to endanger the foundations of their own virtues; their legacy deserves to be appreciated, but it is also an occasion for regret.

Progressives, with few exceptions, were trained in a grand moral school, one that sought to address an enduring problem in American culture. Tocqueville had observed that their laws and social condition pushed Americans toward the pursuit of "worldly welfare," distracting them from, and discouraging attention to, the nurturance of the soul. But the wants of the soul—"the taste for the infinite and the love of what is immortal"—inhere in human nature and will make themselves felt, Tocqueville argued, and when they do, the untrained and unformed soul is likely to express itself in a "fanatical and almost wild spiritualism" devoid of "common sense."[7]

Midcentury America, especially in the Protestant mainstream, recognized the danger of materialism and religious excess, and it set out to supplement the laws, producing what D. H. Meyer calls an "instructed conscience" on the basis of a pervasive and remarkably coherent attempt at synthesizing religion and science.[8] Everywhere, this persuasion was broadly pragmatic, more concerned with moral order than philosophic rigor, but it reached a reasonably high intellectual level in the senior-year course in Moral Science (or some similar title) which was a feature of American higher education down to the end of the nineteenth century.[9]

The curriculum of Moral Science tended to draw on Thomas Reid's "common sense" philosophy, but invariably it presumed the moral sovereignty of *conscience,* a term at least ambiguously acceptable to both liberalism and Protestantism, as in Reid's claim that conscience reveals to the individual both the "intention of nature" and the "law of God written in his heart."[10] Note that Reid's nature has intention as well as order: his teaching was attractive, in part, because it provided a stronger natural basis for obligation than its chief rival, utilitarianism. As Meyer indicates, the great teachers of Moral Science were social conservatives who aimed to overcome the anarchic potential of the doctrine of conscience, hoping, through reason, to link *conscience* to *form*—to the Bible, to laws, and to institutions generally.[11] And they hoped to improve and elevate human moral faculties by the discipline and practice of the logic of morals, aiming to instill in their students that inner constraint that Mark Hopkins called the "Law of Limitation."[12]

They saw nature as a moral government, divinely ordained, in which the moral law is roughly equivalent to a "Law of Nature" imposed on moral agents by their "nature or constitution."[13] It is a small step from this to a moralized laissez-faire in which interests—if not naturally harmonic—are believed to work toward good ends, so that self-interest, pursued in a free market, will be at least *socially* redemptive. Thus, James McCosh could argue that "one who pursues an honest and industrious course of life will commonly be successful, by the arrangement of Him who hath appointed all things." Yet McCosh was too honest not to include the fatal word "commonly," acknowledging the exceptions. These were crucial, since Moral Science also characteristically held that government is natural, divinely appointed, and intended to promote virtue.[14] Following an old Puritan line of argument, Joseph Haven held that while human beings are free to vary the form of government according to circumstance, they are naturally constrained to *be* political. In the same way, he insisted that no contract or consent is valid unless it conforms to the moral law, so that one has a duty to struggle against any government or law that endangers either liberty or virtue (Haven was almost certainly thinking of slavery, though not slavery alone).[15] Many, of course, were more moderate: in the years before the Civil War, Francis Wayland argued that the "wickedness" of slavery did not justify abolitionist zealotry.[16] Nevertheless, it is impossible to understand the Progressive impulse without recognizing its foundation in the enduring conviction that government has a moral and magisterial mission.

In Moral Science and for Progressives, the inclination toward the Moral State was reinforced by the familiar argument that advances in human ability—in wealth, skill, or power—are accompanied by a paralleled increase in human responsibility. Consequently, both for individuals and political communities, material or scientific improvements create greater duties.[17] Certainly, most teachers of Moral Science argued that scientific and technological power went hand in hand with moral progress, an unfolding of the spirit that, in practice, virtually identified secular progress with moral law.[18] (The slavery crisis encouraged this view, a point to which I will return later.)[19]

Still, "progress," in this theorizing, was measured in terms of the increasing approximation of standards of right and of excellence that were thought to be rooted in nature, and hence tolerably known. The exponents of Moral Science, well aware of human frailty, were less confident that material progress brings moral achievement than they were that it imposes moral *obligation*. They knew that power in human hands is perennially dangerous, and they regarded moral progress less as a process than as an imperative, as in Lowell's call to battle in the unending struggle between truth and falsehood:

> New occasions teach new duties,
> Time makes ancient good uncouth.
> They must upward still and onward,
> Who would keep abreast of truth.[20]

From their predecessors and teachers, Progressives learned and retained (1) a *pragmatic* temper, concerned with action and synthesis more than philosophic systems; (2) a reliance on *conscience or spirit* as the ruling tribunal of morals; (3) the conviction that material progress imposes an accompanying *duty* to promote *moral progress;* and (4) the belief that government has a broad responsibility for uplifting society.[21] What they did *not* retain, however, was the core of Moral Science, the confidence in the compatibility of science and faith, and the assurance that it is possible to derive morals from nature.

Even in the victorious North, post–Civil War America found itself amid an increasingly perceptible crisis of culture. It may belong to Americans, Alexander Hamilton had written, "to decide by their conduct and example . . . whether societies of men are really capable or not of establishing good government from reflection and choice, or whether they are forever destined to depend, for their political constitutions, on accident and force."[22] The Civil War answered, "On force," a teaching thundered by politics at midcentury.

Reason, experience seemed to indicate, persuades too few, too slowly—or not at all—and cannot *rule* events. It was in response to that perception, after all, that socialism made its decisive turn from an ideal rooted in the Enlightenment to a doctrine of "class struggle," with force and dictatorship harnessed to historical inevitabilities.[23] But the great voice of the zeitgeist was Bismarck's: "The great questions of the time will not be decided by speeches and majority votes—that was the error of 1848 and 1849—but by blood and iron."[24]

So they were, and it underlined the point that the Second Reich was the political success story of the late nineteenth century. A striking number of Progressive intellectuals studied in Germany, and even those who did not were typically influenced by German politics—especially by the example of the state as an agent of economic and social planning and reconstruction—and by German social science, with its appeal to the diversities of history and culture.[25]

In general, in the politics that succeeded the Civil War, more and more Americans came to share at least a part of Henry Adams's dark conviction that the hopes of the eighteenth century had gone a-glimmering and "the system of 1789 had broken down, and with it the eighteenth century fabric of a priori or moral principles. Society hesitated, wavered, oscillated between harshness and laxity, pitilessly sacrificing the weak, and deferentially following the strong. . . . The moral law had expired—like the Constitution."[26]

Nature, in fact, was coming to seem at best indifferent to morality and perhaps to seem its implacable antagonist. In the physical sciences, Darwin and Lyall, increasingly influential among younger Americans, described a nature that is violent, cataclysmic, and wasteful. It is also, as Henry Adams reminded American teachers of history, part of a universe that is slowly dying, according to the laws of thermodynamics.[27] In the new understanding, nature offered no fixed species or qualities, and the status of humanity was contingent, so that toward the end of the Progressive Era, J. Howard Moore wrote confidently that "the earth and its contents were not made for man. . . . Man is not the end; he is but an incident."[28] In the spring of 1864, speaking to the Sanitary Fair in Baltimore, Lincoln had denounced what he described as the wolf's definition of liberty.[29] Now, however, it seemed that human beings were like wolves. At the very least, Darwinism implied, as John Bascom wrote, that the rules and forms of moral conduct necessarily change or vary with the progress of civilization.[30]

Progressives celebrated the moral possibility inherent in the growth of human power over nature, that by transcending old limits, human beings might more closely approach the ideal. History, Richard Ely urged, had been virtually transformed; the expansion of knowledge had taken humanity beyond the limits of purely biological evolution. Society, not the individual, was now the primary unit in the process, one capable of improving on and overcoming the competition for survival of nature's own flawed design.[31]

But at the same time, Progressives were haunted by old doubts about the ability of human beings to master and direct the new energies, especially because the escalating possibilities for destruction and evil made mistakes more or less intolerable. Human beings might be improving over time, but civilization was still only a *second* nature, a veneer of habit built on "natural moral motives"—primarily sympathy and the desire for approbation—but resting on fundamental self-interest and the will to power. Human nature, Howard Moore wrote, is a "product of the jungle, [and human beings are], in some respects, the lowest in the animal kingdom." He hoped that such "vestigial instincts" would waste away—like the appendix and the human tail—until they were next to nothing, but they were still with us, and even Moore's overheated imagination did not envision them disappearing altogether.[32]

Progressives quarreled with William Graham Sumner, but they recognized the force of his case. Civilization, and democratic civilization especially, depends on an abundance that allows for a relaxation of the struggle for survival, but with a closed frontier and an increasing population, maintaining a favorable "Man/Land Ratio" requires increasing capital, a kind of artificial "land."[33] Progressives shared this sense that civilization is a defense against nature, as well as Sumner's belief that civilized life faces an ongoing imperative to grow or perish. What they rejected was Sumner's willingness, in general, to leave the protection of civilization to private initiatives and to the market.

The case was more compelling, in Progressive thinking, than even grim Sumner had allowed. "Common sense," William James noted, had become incapable of keeping pace with force.[34] Hence the familiar Progressive pursuit of social sciences endowed with technical mastery, capable of predicting and harnessing nature and force in the interest of civilized life. The governing of the outer world seemed a more urgent priority than the preoccupation of Moral Science with the government of the self.

That new ranking, however, is an indication of the fact that Progressivism was a search for a new intellectual and moral order as much as for social reconstruction.[35] Henry Adams's wistful yearning for the Virgin was the inner voice of the movement. More or less desperately, Progressives were seeking some way of *comprehending*, as well as *controlling*, the energies in the "power house" of industrial civilization.[36] It is a mark of urgency and the radicalism of the Progressive impulse that Progressive theorists adopted the most transforming elements of the existing alternatives, a liberal *theology* and *philosophy* associated, up to the Progressive Era, with advocates of laissez-faire like Sumner or Henry Ward Beecher, and a *political reformism* hitherto linked to theological conservatives like Joseph Cook, Jesse Henry Jones, or—most famously—William Jennings Bryan.[37]

Relativism, especially of a historical sort, occupied a critical but essentially negative place in Progressive argument. "Reform Darwinism," as Eric Goldman observed, provided a critique that denied existing beliefs and institutions any claim to permanence.[38] It allowed Progressives to treat established authority as only obsolescence in process, a decomposing old waiting to give birth to the new. Even more important, relativism lent itself to the denial that there are fixed or natural *limits* to human aspiration. Human nature, Progressives were fond of arguing, is far more plastic than had been believed, offering in evidence any number of moral gentlings, like the success in curbing duels, once regarded as a necessary outlet for human violence. Progressives, in other words, were inclined to downplay or reject original sin in favor of the kinds of sins that are mitigable or eradicable through education and law.[39] Modern social life, Dewey and Tufts declared, includes "not only what has become institutionalized and more or less fossilized, but also what is still growing (forming and reforming), [so that] not order, but orderly progress represents the social ideal."[40]

The *positive* foundation for the Progressive belief in history, however, was the belief that the spirit—or, in a slightly more secular form, the conscience—guides and sets moral direction amid change, acting as the voice of telos in the soul.[41] In Emersonian philosophy, in Moral Science, or in evangelical religion, Progressives had been trained in a locution that played down forms, sacraments, and laws in favor of being "right in the soul."[42] "Why," Emerson had asked, "should we be such hard pedants and magnify a few forms? . . . Why should we make account of time, or of magnitude, or of form? The soul knows them not."[43] And a variety of the same teaching informs Samuel Longfellow's great hymn:

> Holy Spirit, Right Divine
> Make my conscience wholly thine.
> Be my law, and I shall be
> Firmly bound, forever free.[44]

In this tradition, even—and especially—the Bible was to be read and interpreted under the guidance of the Spirit.[45] Other implications aside, that doctrine may have been crucial to the antislavery movement that, for so many Progressives, typified moral heroism. The letter of the Scripture regards slavery as undesirable, perhaps even unnatural in a high sense, but it *accepts* it as a legitimate secular institution. Trying for the best construction, Francis Wayland had to concede that the Bible teaches the "duty of slaves," while denying that it recognizes the "rights of masters."[46]

In order to argue that slavery was *wicked*—and even Wayland, not inclined to justify abolitionism, went that far—it was necessary to go beyond the text to the testimony of the Spirit, which discerns the meaning and validity of all laws.[47] Hence, in his 1865 amendment to *Moral Science,* Wayland subjected the Bible to a *historical* reading, rejecting the idea that "whatever God allows at one time, he allows for all time." Moses, Wayland contended, made some concessions to the "cherished practices" of a "rude, ignorant, and sensual people," but in a way that would "tend ultimately to abolish them."[48]

But that, of course, referred to the Hebrew Scriptures, which Christians had long regarded as a "preparatory dispensation." It is more striking that Wayland subjected the Christian Testament to the same reading, discerning the "subversive" intention or spirit underlying Jesus's concession to the times.[49] Southern critics, outraged, pointed out that, in addition to disregarding the text, Wayland was claiming that Jesus and the disciples were bowing to expediency.[50] Our more enlightened times, Wayland concluded, called for abolition "without delay," and though he still denied that religion authorized the use of force, his argument left lawful, secular government more room for maneuver.[51]

This appeal from the letter to the spirit, so fundamental to Lincoln's great, resounding cadence at Gettysburg, was even more necessary when

Progressives and other reformers turned to the rights of *women* against the patriarchal and Pauline texts.[52] In the end, it became an unchallenged principle of exegesis: by 1894, for example, G. Stanley Hall—confident in the authority of science—could proclaim a transition from the idea that morality is a *code* revealed by God in Scripture to the assurance that it is a *disposition* founded on "innate intuitions and sentiments."[53] Similarly, Dewey and Tufts traced the evolution of ethics "from custom to conscience," a historical process culminating in the development of the scientific method, so indispensable, especially in the social sciences, for bringing a moral society into being. *Conscientiousness,* Dewey and Tufts argued, differs from the older idea of wisdom as an attainment, something possessed by an elite; the modern principle "rests in the active desire and effort, in pursuit rather than possession." In these terms, the good human being "measures his acts by a standard, but he is concerned to revise his standard. His sense of the ideal, of the undefinable because ever-expanding value of special deeds, forbids his resting satisfied with any formulated standard; for the very formulation gives the standard a technical quality, while the good can be maintained only in enlarging excellence. The highest form of conscientiousness is interest in constant progress." So understood, Dewey and Tufts trusted, "genuine conscientiousness" is the "guarantee of all virtue."[54]

Of course, Progressives were not discarding the moral law; they relied almost "instinctively," as Mark Noll observes, on biblical morality and expected conscience to sustain and enhance it.[55] They did, however, run the risk of taking a complex moral heritage too much for granted, including such far from evident propositions as the duty to sacrifice and the contempt for merely material success.[56]

Progressives certainly followed tradition, however, in believing that the spirit strains toward the universal and the vision of human fraternity. But historic faith had held—as in Mark Hopkins's "law of limitation"—that the Old Adam, life in the flesh, both demands the support of immediate, particular persons and communities *and* indicates that any human devotion to the universal, short of Grace, will be imperfect.[57] Progressives, by contrast, were more apt to credit Emerson's famous vision, "One day all men will be lovers, and every calamity will be dissolved in the universal sunshine."[58] Some Progressives remained more or less orthodox; some listened to new doctrines, like the Comtean "religion of humanity" that influenced Croly; Washington Gladden's hymn, with its appeal to "the future's broadening way," was a song for all choirs.[59] While, of course, there were racist and nationalistic notes in the Progressive anthem, the movement's dominant teaching made the "Great Community" the end in secular history.[60] Dewey and Tufts were emphatic: "The divine kingdom is to come, the divine will to be done *on earth* as it is in heaven."[61]

Progressives saw science, commerce, and education enlarging and extending human sympathy and altruism in a gradual march toward a kind of "species being."[62] Love, Richard Ely argued, has been the unifying principle of earlier, narrow human communities but individualism had shattered old bonds and old boundaries. Strengthening distrust, it had also opened the door to civilization, making it possible to build the material basis for a new, universal solidarity.[63] As yet, Ely contended, modernity had not advanced beyond the externals: European socialism was bound to fail because its doctrine was materialistic, not a new synthesis or a transformation, but the mirror image of the theory of economic man—individualism constrained into an outward equality. The true socialist goal—and the end of history—was a kind of inwardness, an equality of spirit.[64]

Similarly, looking beyond individualism, Charles Herbert Cooley—like Dewey—saw a continuing need for primary groups preserving and nurturing the "instinctive solidarity" of early society in a limited, subordinate sphere. But Cooley's argument included a severe critique of secondary groups—interest groups, but also parties and representative institutions—that pretend to be more than their real, instrumental status: Cooley envisioned the sovereignty of what Dewey called a "fraternally associated public," a national citizenry with the qualities of a primary group, as a way station on the road to the universal.[65] Human beings, Cooley declared, are rightly guided by the spirit of "onwardness," which leads them beyond parochialities toward the realization of the principle that "men live for one another."[66]

Progressives, in other words, inclined toward the view that when technology or trade overcomes material limits, the spirit can extend itself almost indefinitely with little or no effective loss of force. Moral progress, Dewey and Tufts taught, combines an extension in the size and scope of the social group with an intensification of the individual's social interest.[67]

That attitude implies a decisively pre-Freudian slighting of the continuing claims of the body and the erotic. (J. Howard Moore, an extreme case to be sure, suggested that progress pointed in the direction of "sloughing off . . . this inherited animality.")[68] Worse, it can easily slide into a dangerous neglect of the human need for particular attachments and very personal bonds and obligations.[69] And despite the trumpeting about science, at critical points the Progressive faith proves to have been more than a little mystical.[70]

Edward Bellamy's universalism, for example, left him convinced that, in the great administrative collectivity he saw in the future, the feeling of brotherhood en masse would be as "real and vital" as in the family and small communities. That fact, his Dr. Leete tells the time traveler Julian West, is "a key to the mysteries of our civilization."[71] But it is a mystery that Bellamy never explained. The skeptical may note that despite teaching a "merger with nature," Bellamy was at pains to deny that this implied a "commingling" of the races.[72] Dewey wrestled with this problem. He affirmed the permanence of the human need for the local—"as near to an absolute as exists"—and he sometimes indicated that broader, more national allegiances would necessarily be more diffuse: it will be sufficient, he wrote, if "interaction and interdependence" give us "enough similarity of ideas and sentiments to keep the thing going."[73] But keeping the thing going, in Dewey's terms, presumed the sovereignty of public claims akin to the general will.[74] Consequently, Dewey fell back on the hope that locality can be wedded to larger loyalties—and that opinion can be empowered to rule over expert government—by a radically improved "art of communication," hoped for but not described, yet able, as Howard Moore wrote, "to make real and vivid . . . phenomena that are more distant in time and space."[75] It ought to be clear, however, that despite their power, the contemporary mass media—so episodic and so tied to superficial and essentially private sensibilities—are not what Dewey had in mind.

In any case, Progressives had no doubt that history was moving humanity into larger and more complicated social units, and that evolution—pace Darwinian individualism—rewarded the capacity for cooperative action. Bees, so selfless and hardworking, had always had a special charm for Protestant moralists: "Drones," Oberlin College had warned prospective students, "are not welcome in this hive of industry." In the late nineteenth century, however, bees—more attractive than militaristic ants or pestiferous termites—came to be praised for their power. "These," Kipling had Kaa teach Mowgli, "are the real masters of the jungle."[76] And Moore only amplified the argument in claiming that bees manifest "the ideal relations of living beings to each other."[77]

Most Progressives, of course, stopped short of such proto-totalitarian claims, but they were apt to grow more lyrical about patriotism or to cross the line into nationalism or imperialism; and racism had its advocates, although most Progressives were guilty chiefly of indifference.[78] Even Walter Rauschenbusch, who detested war, spoke of the prophets as part of a "national" and "patriotic" movement, and Shailer Matthews, during World War I, proclaimed patriotism "the religion of tomorrow."[79]

Before 1914, the nation-state seemed only a step in humankind's march toward the universal—"Nothing could be more absurd from the historic point of view," Dewey and Tufts contended, "than to regard the conception of an international state of federated humanity as a mere dream"—and Wilson's rhetoric, for a time, fused the state and the dream into a single cause.[80]

It was really only in the aftermath of World War I that Progressives, in general, began to think seriously about the two-sided quality of patriotism, altruistic within the country, but, as Niebuhr was to write, largely "collective egotism" without.[81] And while the critique of nationalism is easily compatible with Progressive universalism, it is also true that the moral problem of patriotism points to a problem for Progressive teaching: the solidarity of large groups—and nations especially—rivals or overrides the claims of erotic and primary groups chiefly in war, and it is not so easy to find the "moral equivalent" of that aspect of war in peaceful civic life, as more than one movement is discovering in contemporary America.[82] Certainly, it is unmistakable that, after World War I, Progressivism lost much of its moral confidence. If older Progressives kept the flame—and many fell away—the younger generation lacked the old trust in the positive, ruling qualities of the spirit, confining themselves more and more to relativism's narrower negations.

Progressivism helped direct American moral impulses into political and social life, and it deserves much of the credit for building a government even remotely adequate to the problems of the twentieth century. As moral theory and in moral education, however, it gets lower marks; as Eisenach argues, crucial aspects of Progressive doctrine disintegrated or self-destructed.[83]

Progressives were moralists with bells on and altogether happy to make judgments—for Dewey, Morton White writes, "a judgment that something is desirable is just as scientific as a judgment that something is desired."[84] But their very confidence that conscience or spirit leads toward the goal encouraged them to substitute training in scientific method for moral education, virtually identifying technique with the end.[85] The "interest in technique," Dewey declared, "is precisely the thing which is most promising in our civilization, the thing which in the end will break down devotion to external standardization and the mass-quantity ideal."[86]

Similarly, Progressives appeared not to notice that their relativism and pragmatism worked in the direction of drift, supporting a tendency to accept prevailing terms and understandings not simply as constraints on action—as surely they are—but as proper limits on thought. In that all-too-familiar persuasion, "adjustment" came to be treated as equivalent to well-being for the soul.[87] It only reinforced this logic that so many Progressives, if not as disdainful of "soul stuff" as Arthur Bentley, were inclined to let appearances and behaviors define reality.[88] The long-term danger of Progressivism, especially if one remembers Progressive enthusiasm for mass communications, points in the direction of the "tyranny of the majority" and the sort of happy nihilism that is apt to be celebrated in our time.

Progressives like Dewey saw the need human beings have for groups smaller than the state as nurturers and protectors against the mass. But they tiptoed around the fact that the mere existence of local or functional groups, the development of citizens—people who extend themselves into public life—presumes relatively *stable* institutions and forms, the bases of civic trust. Progressives seemed surprisingly blind to the tension between democracy and rapid change, and only half aware that their embrace of progress itself threatened their higher, republican hopes.[89]

While Progressives did recognize the need to nurture and develop the emotions and moral faculties in a local sphere, they ignored or slighted the implication: we all begin in a world of particulars, from which the human spirit ascends, on any account, only slowly and with difficulty. The highest, most universal ranges of the spirit, consequently, are not achieved universally at any given time, and very likely, are something most of us can hope to see only in the mirror of the few. Humanity and equality, in that sense, are most broadly discerned in speech and in theory; in political practice, by contrast, the dominating categories are likely to be identity and difference.[90] Still, while the Progressives may have overestimated the reach of the spirit, unlike so many of our contemporaries, they never forgot that its yearning perennially strains against the possibilities.

To this point, I have been emphasizing—and criticizing—general themes and patterns in Progressive thought, and I want to conclude on a different note by giving some attention to two thinkers—Walter Rauschenbusch and W. E. B. DuBois —who (among many) were exceptions, in important respects, to the Progressive rule.

Rauschenbusch was the great theorist of the Social Gospel, and that status carries its own ambivalence. The exponents of the Social Gospel were sometimes mawkishly sentimental and, more often, were tempted to tailor religious teaching to the measure of social utility. But at its best, it offered (and offers) an invaluable witness, and Rauschenbusch is not a bad exemplar.

He does strike many notes that jar our sensibilities. He took virtually no notice of race, for example, and worried that the church might become "feminized."[91] Similarly, he was apt, especially in perorations, to soar into a startlingly Progressive idiom, speaking of human "elasticity and capacity for change," appealing to history and social science and asserting that "the largest and hardest part of Christianizing the social order has been done."[92]

But there was also a strongly orthodox dimension to Rauschenbusch's thought: he believed, for example, in a fixed human nature, with sin included—"History is never antiquated because human nature is always fundamentally the same." Against religious conservatives, in fact, Rauschenbusch argued that it is precisely the ubiquity of sin that demands criticism of the world.[93]

Jesus, Rauschenbusch pointed out, was no modern social reformer, since he worked from the soul outward, beginning with the "sin of the heart" and the soul's need for meaning, aiming at the "inauguration of a new humanity" as the foundation for an attack on the sins of society, themselves rooted in the lust for domination and for "easy and unearned gain."[94]

While Rauschenbusch hoped for moral improvement, his view of history presumed a permanent dialectic between priest and prophet, ceremonial form and righteous life. Consequently, when Rauschenbusch insisted that we understand Jesus in relation to "his times," he meant that Jesus must be freed from later, Hellenizing mysticism, understood as he understood himself, in a tradition that is Hebrew and public.[95]

Even one of his more startling assertions—that ethical conduct, *in principle,* is the "supreme and sufficient religious act"—had Scriptural and even Pauline referents.[96] Rauschenbusch did, however, reject what he took to be Paul's expectation of a spiritually transformed cosmos: human beings, Rauschenbusch maintained, cannot expect to be freed apocalyptically from the limits of sin and bodiliness; the spirit will have to work within the limits of the world. In that sense, Rauschenbusch is less "post-millennial" (a description more easily applied to John Locke) than he is *anti*premillennial.[97]

True to the prophetic tradition, he was at least immediately pessimistic. Progress, he thought, was anything but guaranteed, especially since the new, potentially destructive energies at human command seemed to call for a new humanity as well as new forms of organization. He ruled out the hope for political transformation: revolutions are showy, but superficial; humanly produced change must follow the "law of organic development." But Rauschenbusch allowed himself to hope that it was a crucial moment, a time "at the turning of the ways," when Christianity, by applying moral force to the material world, might hope to turn human beings toward first things. Following the early Christians, he thought in terms of a small beginning and a "Brotherhood of the Kingdom"—a few people, principally young, scattered throughout society and capable, by the "contagion" of speech and example, of creating a new moral discourse, a "new life" set to growing amid the old.[98]

With the ordinary fate of prophets, Rauschenbusch fell well short of achieving his vision, and along with its virtues, his theorizing has shortcomings to spare. But warts and all, Rauschenbusch's teaching reminds reformers that the proper aim and starting point of change is the education of the soul.

On that point, however, W. E. B. DuBois is an even better instructor. Race still muddles us enough that we are apt to forget how thoroughly DuBois fits the Progressive paradigm—raised in Protestant New England culture; educated at Fisk in the Moral Science of James McCosh; trained at Harvard and Berlin in the most advanced social science, and the champion of an educated elite; DuBois was even gulled, for a considerable period, by Woodrow Wilson and the imagined social promise of World War I.[99]

But *The Souls of Black Folk* does not speak of, or even suggest, evolution or historical progress. Quite the contrary, DuBois's chapter "On the Meaning of Progress" describes the decline and the tragedies of the rural Tennessee community where he once taught school. There, change had meant defeat and disappointment and death: "How shall man measure Progress there where the dark-faced Josie lies?" Even the replacement of the old log schoolhouse appeared as loss. "In its place stood Progress, and Progress, I understand, is necessarily ugly."[100] He had come there, walking and lighthearted, in the old time; he left, ten years later, riding the train in the Jim Crow car.

Race pointed DuBois to the failure of any social science that could not pierce appearances. He spoke (and to our time?) of the inadequacy of sociologists who "gleefully count . . . bastards . . . and prostitutes," and his great affirmation—that "the problem of the twentieth century is the problem of the color-line"—indicated that the then-coming century would be measured by its ability to reach beyond the visible to a knowledge of the soul. The "tragedy of the age," DuBois wrote, is "not that men are poor, . . . not that men are wicked, . . . not that men are ignorant, . . . [but] that men know so little of men."[101]

The Souls of Black Folk reaches broadly. It includes some social science and some very personal loss, some stories and some poetry and a grand discussion of the music of the "sorrow songs," and DuBois invoked, too, the centrality of the church and its vision in African American life: "Some day the Awakening will come when the pent up vigor of ten million souls shall sweep irresistibly toward the Goal, out of the Valley of the Shadow of Death."[102]

But beyond evoking the experience and culture of black folk, DuBois called for the education of an elite, one not defined in terms of the mastery of technical skills. DuBois was always an "elitist," even at his most radically democratic (and certainly in his latter-day Marxist-Leninism) because he was convinced of the need for exceptional individuals, the "higher individualism" of those who see beyond the practical and the possible, exerting the *pull* of high culture and theory that DuBois saw— in *The Souls of Black Folk,* at any rate—as the dynamic and meaning of progress.[103]

Liberation, so conceived, requires access to the Great Conversation and its discipline, the "chance to soar in the dim blue air above the smoke" where it is possible to discern the human truth: "I sit with Shakespeare and he winces not. Across the color line I move arm in arm with Balzac and Dumas, where smiling men and welcoming women glide in gilded halls. From out of the caves of evening that swing between the strong-limbed earth and the tracery of the stars, I summon Aristotle and Aurelius and what soul I will, and they come all graciously, with no scorn nor condescension. So, wed with Truth, I dwell above the veil."[104]

If Progressivism has any claim to include that passage in its legacy, and I think it does, then it has left us an inheritance rich enough to excuse many faults.

Notes

This essay was originally published as "Standing at Armageddon: Morality and Religion in Progressive Thought," in *Progressivism and the New Democracy,* ed. Sidney M. Milkis and Jerome M. Mileur (Amherst: University of Massachusetts Press, 1999).

1. Morton White, *Social Thought in America: The Revolt against Formalism* (Boston: Beacon, 1957).

2. Mary K. Simkhovitch, "Friendship and Politics," *Political Science Quarterly* 17 (1902): 189–205.

3. Brand Whitlock, *Forty Years of It* (New York: Appleton, 1925), 204; Whitlock's sympathy for traditional politicos is also evident in his political novel, *Big Matt* (New York: Appleton, 1925).

4. James Kloppenberg, *Uncertain Victory: Social Democracy and Progressivism in European and American Political Thought, 1870–1920* (New York: Oxford University Press, 1986) presents the major variations on the Progressive theme. For the argument that there was no coherent movement, see Peter G. Filene, "An Obituary for the Progressive Movement," *American Quarterly* 20 (1970): 20–34.

5. Robert Wiebe, *The Search for Order, 1877–1920* (New York: Hill and Wang, 1967); John Buenker, *Urban Liberalism and Progressive Reform* (New York: Scribner's, 1973) points to urban and ethnic dimensions of Progressivism, but I am persuaded that Robert Crunden is right in treating leaders like Al Smith or Msgr. John Ryan more as precursors of the New Deal. *Ministers of Reform: The Progressives' Achievement in American Civilization, 1889–1920* (New York: Basic Books, 1982).

6. Roosevelt twice used the trope "We stand at Armageddon and we battle for the Lord," first in a speech given at the time of the Republican convention (June 17, 1912), and then in "Confession of Faith," which he gave at the end of the Progressive convention, August 6, 1912. *The Works of Theodore Roosevelt,* national ed. (New York: Scribner's, 1926), 17:231, 239.

7. Alexis de Tocqueville, *Democracy in America* (New York: Knopf, 1980), 2:134–35.

8. D. H. Meyer, *The Instructed Conscience: The Shaping of the American National Ethic* (Philadelphia: University of Pennsylvania Press, 1972). See, too, Mark A. Noll, *The Scandal of the Evangelical Mind* (Grand Rapids: Eerdmans, 1994); John G. West Jr., *The Politics of Revelation and Reason: Religion and Civic Life in the New Nation* (Lawrence: University Press of Kansas, 1996), 121–22.

9. One of a handful of similar courses in contemporary American colleges is Hadley Arkes's class in Political Obligations at Amherst College, built around the argument in Arkes's *First Things: An Inquiry into the First Principles of Morals and Justice* (Princeton: Princeton University Press, 1986).

10. *Works of Thomas Reid,* edited by Sir William Hamilton (Edinburgh: Maclaclan Stewart, 1863), 2:594–99, 638. See, too, Mark Hopkins, *Lectures on Moral Science* (Boston: Gould and Lincoln, 1862), 205–27; Archibald Alexander, *Outlines of Moral Science* (New York: Scribner's, 1852), 86.

11. Meyer, *Instructed Conscience,* 6–9, 16–17, 28–30, 71; for one example, see

Francis Wayland, *The Elements of Moral Science* (1835), edited by Joseph Blau (Cambridge, Mass.: Harvard University Press, 1963), 100–106.

12. Mark Hopkins, *The Law of Love and Love as Law* (New York: Scribner's, 1869), 129–31; Hopkins, *Lectures on Moral Science,* 59–78.

13. Charles G. Finney, *Lectures on Systematic Theology* (Oberlin: J. M. Fitch, 1846), 1:6; Nathaniel William Taylor, *Lectures on the Moral Government of God* (New York: Clark, Austin and Smith, 1859), 1:7–17, 63–68.

14. James McCosh, *Our Moral Nature: Being a Brief System of Ethics* (New York: Scribner's, 1892), 19, 47. See, too, Hopkins, *The Law of Love,* 268–70; Wayland, *Moral Science,* 311–16, argued along these lines, although he also adhered to a broadly Jeffersonian version of social contract theory. On the general point, see Sydney Ahlstrom, *A Religious History of the American People* (New Haven: Yale University Press, 1972), 787.

15. Joseph Haven, *Moral Philosophy* (New York: Sheldon, 1880), 228–29, 276–77.

16. Edward Madden, "Francis Wayland and the Limits of Moral Responsibility," *Proceedings of the American Philosophical Society* 106 (1962): 352–58; James Murray, *Francis Wayland* (Boston: Houghton Mifflin, 1891), 204–11. Wayland, however, did justify resistance to the Fugitive Slave Law. Murray, *Francis Wayland,* 274.

17. Meyer, *Instructed Conscience,* 82–85; Asa Mahan, *The Scripture Doctrine of Christian Perfection* (Boston: D. S. King, 1839), 9.

18. Emerson Davis, *The Half-Century* (Boston: Tappan and Whittemore, 1851), 222; Francis Wayland, *Occasional Discourses* (Boston: James Loring, 1833), 321–23, 341–43.

19. By 1865 Wayland had strengthened the antislavery argument in his widely used text by reference to the "progressive development" of the moral law from the "rude and ignorant" early Hebrews to the teachings of Jesus. *Moral Science,* 377–78.

20. "Once to Every Man and Nation," *Hymnal for Youth* (Chicago: Pilgrim, 1941), 221.

21. Eldon Eisenach, *The Lost Promise of Progressivism* (Lawrence: University Press of Kansas, 1994), 3.

22. *The Federalist,* #1.

23. Stephen Eric Bronner, *Socialism Unbound* (New York: Routledge, 1990).

24. Speech to the Prussian Diet, September 30, 1862. "Nicht durch Reden und Majoritätsbeschlüsse warden die grossen Fragen der Zeit entschieden—das ist die groose Fehler von 1848 und 1849 gewesen—sondern durch Blut und Eisen," in *Die politischen Reden des Fürsten Bismarck,* edited by Horst Kohl (Stuttgart: Cotta, 1892–1905), 2:29–30.

25. Eisenach, *Lost Promise,* 92–102; David Noble, *The Paradox of Progressive Thought* (Minneapolis: University of Minnesota Press, 1958), 160–61, 166.

26. Henry Adams, *The Education of Henry Adams,* edited by Ernest Samuels (Boston: Houghton Mifflin, 1974), 280–81.

27. Henry Adams, *A Letter to American Teachers of History* (Baltimore: J. H. Furst, 1910).

28. J. Howard Moore, *The Universal Kinship* (Chicago: Kerr, 1916), 317, 319.

29. Abraham Lincoln, *The Complete Works of Abraham Lincoln,* edited by Roy Basler (New Brunswick: Rutgers University Press, 1953), 7:302.

30. John Bascom, *Ethics; or, The Science of Duty* (New York: Putnam, 1879), 354–78; Garry Wills, *Under God: Religion and American Politics* (New York: Simon and Schuster, 1990), 97–106.

31. Richard Ely, *Studies in the Evolution of Industrial Society* (New York: Macmillan, 1913).

32. E. A. Ross, *Social Control* (New York: Macmillan, 1914), 49–50, 59–60, 411–12; Moore, *Universal Kinship,* 245, 239, 132. On the other hand, as part of her feminist utopia, where it was social policy to "breed out" the "lowest types," Charlotte Perkins Gilman did imagine cats bred to kill rodents, but leave birds unharmed. Ross, *Herland* (New York: Pantheon, 1979), 82, 49.

33. William Graham Sumner, *What Social Classes Owe to Each Other* (1883) (Caldwell, Idaho: Caxton, 1978), especially 63–70; Sumner, *Earth Hunger and Other Essays* (New Haven: Yale University Press, 1913).

34. William James, *Pragmatism* (Cleveland and New York: World, 1968), 123.

35. Wiebe, *The Search for Order;* Grant A. Wacker, "The Holy Spirit and the Spirit of the Age in American Protestantism, 1880–1910," *Journal of American History* 72 (1985): 45–62.

36. Adams, *The Education of Henry Adams,* 379–90, 421–22.

37. Ahlstrom, *Religious History,* 787–88; Charles H. Hopkins, *The Rise of the Social Gospel in American Protestantism* (New Haven: Yale University Press, 1940), 39; Henry F. May, *The Protestant Churches and Industrial America* (New York: Harper, 1949), 79.

38. Eric Goldman, *Rendezvous with Destiny* (New York: Knopf, 1953).

39. Ahlstrom, *Religious History,* 779; Charles H. Cooley, *Social Process* (New York: Scribner's, 1920), 103, 418. On dueling, see West, *Revolution and Reason,* 88–97.

40. John Dewey and James H. Tufts, *Ethics* (New York: Henry Holt, 1908), 434, 485.

41. Richard Ely, *Social Aspects of Christianity* (New York: Crowell, 1889).

42. Nathan O. Hatch, *The Democratization of American Christianity* (New Haven: Yale University Press, 1989), 5–9, 17–46, 182.

43. Ralph Waldo Emerson, "History," in *Emerson's Essays,* ed. Sherman Paul (New York: Dutton, 1976), 13.

44. "Holy Spirit, Truth Divine" (1864), in *Presbyterian Hymnal* (Louisville: Westminster/John Knox Press, 1990), #321.

45. Horace Bushnell, *Building Eras in Religion* (New York: Scribner's, 1881), 269–80.

46. Wayland, *Moral Science,* 394.

47. Ibid., 380–81; Finney, *Lectures on Systematic Theology,* 1:20–24.

48. Wayland, *Moral Science,* 394.

49. Ibid., 389, 391–93.

50. Joseph Blau, introduction to Wayland, *Moral Science,* xliv–xlvi.

51. Wayland, *Moral Science,* 394–96; and *Occasional Discourses,* 80–97.

52. Garry Wills, *Lincoln at Gettysburg: The Words That Remade America* (New York: Simon and Schuster, 1992), 37–38.

53. G. Stanley Hall, "On the History of American College Textbooks in Logic, Ethics, Psychology, and Allied Subjects," *Proceedings of the American Antiquarian Society* 9, no. 2 (1894): 152.

54. Dewey and Tufts, *Ethics,* 167–68, 419–20, 422, 419.

55. Noll, *Scandal,* 162.

56. Sigmund Freud, *Civilization and Its Discontents,* in *Complete Psychological Works of Sigmund Freud,* ed. James Strachey (London: Hogarth, 1966), 21:112.

57. Hopkins, *Moral Science,* 59–78; Hopkins, *Law of Love,* 129–31.

58. Ralph Waldo Emerson, "Man the Reformer," in *Selected Essays of Ralph Waldo Emerson,* ed. Larzer Ziff (Harmondsworth: Penguin, 1982), 146.

59. Gladden's hymn, "O Master Let Me Walk with Thee," may be found in the *Presbyterian Hymnal,* #357. On Comte's influence, see Edward Stettner, *Shaping Modern American Liberalism: Herbert Croly and Progressive Thought* (Lawrence: University Press of Kansas, 1993); and Gillis J. Harp, *Positivist Republic: August Comte and the Reconstruction of American Liberalism, 1865–1920* (University Park: Pennsylvania State University Press, 1995).

60. John Dewey, *The Public and Its Problems* (New York: Holt, 1927), 142, 148. Progressive distaste for ethnic communities—like the anti-Semitic and anti-immigrant asides in Gilman's writing—often rested on the belief that such groups were "tribal" or otherwise backward, resisting history's march toward the universal. See Ann J. Lane's introduction to Ross, *Herland,* xvii–xviii.

61. Dewey and Tufts, *Ethics,* 109.

62. John Dewey, *Democracy and Education* (New York: Macmillan, 1916), 73–74; Ely, *Social Aspects of Christianity.*

63. Richard Ely, *The Social Law of Service* (New York: Methodist Book Concern, 1896).

64. Richard Ely, *Socialism and Social Reform* (New York: Crowell, 1894), 50–55.

65. Charles H. Cooley, *Social Process,* 42, 103, 109, 395, 400–401, 418; Cooley, *Social Organization: A Study of the Larger Mind* (New York: Scribner's, 1909), 90, 118; Dewey, *The Public and Its Problems,* 109, 127, 131–34.

66. Charles H. Cooley, *Human Nature and the Social Order* (1902) (New York: Scribner's, 1922), 118–19; Cooley, *Social Process,* 105; see also Cooley, "The Process of Social Change," *Political Science Quarterly* 12 (1897): 63–87.

67. Dewey and Tufts, *Ethics,* 428–30, 435.

68. Moore, *Universal Kinship,* 246. In Gilman's utopia, women reproduce by parthenogenesis, but are attracted by the possibility of "bisexual" reproduction. However, sexual feeling has disappeared, from disuse, and the heroines are

shocked when Gilman's male characters suggest sex without a procreative aim. Even Elladoor, who can see something beautiful in the idea of sexual intimacy, associates sexual passion with men; sexual desire in women, she says, "seems . . . against nature." Ross, *Herland,* 92, 126–29, 138.

69. Wills, *Under God,* 97–106; Christopher Lasch, *The True and Only Heaven: Progress and Its Critics* (New York: Norton, 1991).

70. There are many interesting parallels and connections between Progressivism and the late-century vogue of spiritualism. See Kenneth R. Andrews, *Nook Farm: Mark Twain's Hartford Circle* (Cambridge, Mass.: Harvard University Press, 1950), 53–66.

71. Edward Bellamy, *Looking Backward* (1887) (New York: New American Library, 1960), 99.

72. On the union with nature and similar concepts, see Bellamy, *Looking Backward,* 49, 77, 194; and Bellamy, *Equality* (1897) (New York: Appleton-Century, 1937), 267–69, 341; on the races, see Bellamy, *Equality,* 37, 365.

73. Dewey, *The Public and Its Problems,* 113–14.

74. Ibid., 206–10; Dewey and Tufts, *Ethics,* 435.

75. Dewey, *The Public and Its Problems,* 114, 152–53, 183–84, 206–10; Moore, *Universal Kinship,* 268–69.

76. Rudyard Kipling, *The Jungle Books* (New York: New American Library, 1961), 288.

77. Moore, *Universal Kinship,* 235. Praising *Herland,* Gilman's character Jeff likens that utopian community to bees, who "manage to cooperate and to love." Jeff even has admiring words to say about anthills. Ross, *Herland,* 67. It is useful to compare Hobbes's comments in *Leviathan,* ch. 17.

78. See Dorothea Muller, "The Social Philosophy of Josiah Strong: Social Christianity and American Progressivism," *Church History* 28 (1959): 183–201.

79. Walter Rauschenbusch, *Christianity and the Social Crisis* (New York: Macmillan, 1913), 337, 350; Shailer Matthews, *Patriotism and Religion* (New York: Macmillan, 1918).

80. Dewey and Tufts, *Ethics,* 481–82.

81. Reinhold Niebuhr, *Moral Man and Immoral Society* (New York: Scribner's, 1932).

82. William James, *Memories and Studies* (New York: Longmans Green, 1911), 267–96; present-day conservatives, particularly, feel the loss of the unifying force of the Cold War. E. J. Dionne Jr., *Why Americans Hate Politics* (New York: Simon and Schuster, 1991).

83. Eisenach, *Lost Promise,* 3.

84. White, *Social Thought,* 242–43.

85. Meyer, *Instructed Conscience,* 137.

86. John Dewey, *Individualism Old and New* (New York: Minton Balch, 1930), 30.

87. Ibid., 67–69, 124–27, 130, 143, 148; Dewey, *The Public and Its Problems,* 31–32; Dewey, *Reconstruction in Philosophy* (New York: New American Library,

1950), 62, 65, 102, 141, 147. For a striking example, see Muzafer Sherif, *The Psychology of Social Norms* (New York: Harper, 1936), 15.

88. Arthur F. Bentley, *The Process of Government* (Bloomington: Principia, 1949); for a particularly fine critical response, see Lewis Lipitz, "If, as Verba Says, the State Functions as a Religion, What Are We to Do Then to Save Our Souls?" *American Political Science Review* 62 (1968): 527–35.

89. Jacques Ellul, *The Technological Society* (New York: Vintage, 1964), 208–18.

90. William Connolly, *Identity/Difference: Democratic Negations of Political Paradox* (Ithaca, N.Y.: Cornell University Press, 1991).

91. Rauschenbusch, *Christianity and the Social Crisis,* 367.

92. Rauschenbusch, *Christianizing the Social Order* (New York: Macmillan, 1912), 124; see also 3, 6, 114, 119, 136ff., 209; Rauschenbusch, *Christianity and the Social Crisis,* 209; see also 100–105, 420–22.

93. Rauschenbusch, *Christianity and the Social Crisis,* 1, 17, 349, 39, 213.

94. Ibid., 47, 71; Rauschenbusch, *A Theology for the Social Gospel* (New York: Macmillan, 1917), 4.

95. Rauschenbusch, *Christianity and the Social Crisis,* 5, 8, 55.

96. Ibid., 7.

97. Ibid., 45ff., 104–5; "premillennial" teachings hold that, until the Second Coming, the world is sufficiently lost in sin that secular action offers only pretensions and low possibilities, emphasizing instead a soul that waits expectantly for Christ's return. "Postmillennial" doctrine, by contrast, sees the Kingdom of God as coming into being in and through history. Ahlstrom, *Religious History,* 808–12.

98. Rauschenbusch, *Christianity and the Social Crisis,* 59, 64, 210, 213, 279, 330–31, 353, 356, 363, 400.

99. David Levering Lewis, *W. E. B. Du Bois: Biography of a Race,* vol. 1, *1868–1919* (New York: Holt, 1994).

100. W. E. B. DuBois, *The Souls of Black Folk* (1901) (New York: Everyman's/Knopf, 1993), 62, 60.

101. Ibid., 13, 16, 178–79.

102. Ibid., 163; the church, DuBois observed, "antedates the Negro home" (156). On DuBois's style, see Arnold Rampersad, *The Art and Imagination of W. E. B. Du Bois* (New York: Schocken, 1990).

103. DuBois, *The Souls of Black Folk,* 70–71, 78.

104. Ibid., 88–89.

America's Two Voices
in a World of Nations

Editors' note: This 1981 essay specifically treats the problem at the heart of the relationship between the United States as a liberal democracy and the authoritarian regime of Korea—meaning South Korea. Since the essay was written, South Korea is widely acknowledged to have entered the company of the world's liberal democracies, and thus there is a distinctly outdated quality to these explicit references. However, given that the United States continues to cooperate with and confront authoritarian regimes today (perhaps most notably China), the analysis remains strikingly timely and relevant

It is not surprising that other nations are often puzzled by America. Americans do not understand themselves or their country very well, and in many ways they do not *wish* to. Our leaders often speak of an American "creed" or "way of life," implying that American culture is a unified whole, and periodically a crusade for "Americanism" grips large numbers of citizens, as it seems to be doing today. In fact, however, American culture is profoundly incoherent, composed of elements that are radically incompatible. America descends from Judaism and Christianity, on the one hand, and from Enlightenment rationalism on the other. It praises love *and* individualism, scarcely aware of the contradiction; and Americans scorn "materialism" at the same time that they define an expanding gross national product as an essential element of the common good.

The most familiar definition of the "American creed" points to the Declaration of Independence, the Constitution, and to the liberal political philosophy that underlies them. These doctrines, embodied in our national institutions, have undeniably shaped American public life and thought. Americans learn about "rights" and "checks and balances" even before those doctrines are taught formally in the schools. Philosophic liberalism is presented as if it were the "common sense of the subject," as Jefferson thought, rather than as a controversial and controvertible teaching. Louis Hartz was right to argue that in a great many ways American political thought is governed by an "irrational Lockeanism," a philosophic liberalism planted in the subconscious of the American mind.[1]

The framers began with the familiar proposition that we are "born free." This concern for our birth reflects their idea of human nature as ontological. Human beings are defined by their *origins*. To locate human nature, in this view, it is necessary to strip away the effects of tradition, family, society, and education. "Natural man" is discerned most clearly in the child or in uncivilized settings. Fundamentally, only their biology is natural to human beings.

Two aspects of this doctrine should be noted. First, it asserts that by nature, *human goals are determined by our desires*. Reasons and the higher faculties come into existence to serve the body and the passions. They are instruments only and cannot pretend to rule.

Second, the framers' philosophy is radically individualistic. Human beings are naturally separate, each isolated in his or her own body. We may touch, but we cannot—except by violence—pass the boundary of the flesh, and in that fundamental sense we are always alone. Moreover, *each individual is morally complete* as well as physically separate. Since our innate desires determine the ends we naturally and properly pursue, we need no authority to educate us in goals. The soul of the individual is his or her own business, and no one has the right to intrude on it. We come into the world, the framers taught, owing nothing to anyone and with no obligations to any authority.

Natural right, then, derives from what is most universal about human beings, their bodies and their passions, as opposed to the customs, excellences, and institutions that make us different. The tradition of the framers thus leads to universalistic definitions of human rights—and, in fact, they had an extremely unified view of the human condition.

The ruling desire of human beings, the framers argued, is to be free, by which they meant that human beings, by nature, want to be able to do as they wish and, most especially, to preserve themselves. Consequently we are at odds with all obstacles, especially with nature. Nature, in this view, is an implacable enemy. It does not give us what we want without travail; if it can sometimes be coaxed into relative generosity by arts like farming, in the most important sense nature is unyielding. Nature ordains that we die, frustrating our most basic desire and radically limiting our freedom. Human beings, then, are locked in a struggle with nature, and the aim of *mastering nature by adding to human power* ranks as the overriding goal of human life and politics.

At odds with nature, self-regarding human beings are also naturally in a state of war with their equally self-concerned fellows. Sometimes you refuse to do as I wish; at other times both of us want and compete for the same things. But human beings can be conciliated in a way that nature cannot. We can make agreements—"social contracts"—that create societies and states.

Political society, in the framers' doctrine, is not natural. It is a contrivance, something we make because the "state of war" is unprofitable. In that state every other person is a potential enemy; in Hobbes's famous saying, "The life of man is nasty, mean, poor, brutish, and short." To escape this condition we agree to give up some of our "natural right" to do as we please in order to obtain a more secure and complete enjoyment of the rights we retain.

Hence, *political society is a second-best alternative,* accepted because none of us is strong enough to be a secure tyrant. That practical limitation, however, does not change the fact that, in principle, tyranny—which allows me to do as I wish with myself *and* with you—is the best life. Political society has few claims on our allegiance. It is an instrument and must prove its utility by (1) enhancing the security of lives and properties; and (2) helping people advance in the mastery of nature by adding to their power and, hence, their freedom. The framers rejected the small state, which political philosophy has traditionally regarded as essential for republican government, because such states are too weak. Only a large state has the resources for the war with nature.

As this suggests, "progress," as we have come to understand that term, is an essential measure of the political good. (One of the few positive duties enjoined on Congress by the Constitution is the advancement of science and "useful arts.") Political society must establish *reasonable law and order* and it must *provide material progress.* If it does not, it has ceased to be useful to the ends for which we "entered" society, and such a polity has no claim on our allegiance. Economic growth, in this view, is valued for more than its material benefits: it is a requirement of patriotism, the cement of political society itself.

The Rule of Law

While progress is always desirable in philosophic liberalism, the rule of law is always in danger. In liberal theory, I agree to contracts, the foundation of law, only because I cannot get what I want alone. Since political society is better than the "state of war," I am obliged to keep the promise I made to my fellow citizens when we established our regime. This assumes that if I break my promises, my faithlessness will spread contagiously and society will fall back into the "state of war": but *will* society collapse into anarchy if I violate my commitments? Will my fellows follow my bad example? I have two reasons to doubt this: (1) I may be too unimportant to set a trend; people may simply choose to ignore my peccadilloes; and (2) I may not be detected in breaking the law, in which case I will not have set any example at all. In other words, liberal society cannot rid itself of the tempting possibility that I may be able to break my promises while everyone else keeps his, allowing me to combine the advantages of society with the freedom of the state of nature. This prospect of a socially invisible criminality—the myth of Gyges' ring in Plato's *Republic*—offers me a great many of the advantages of tyranny without the tyrant's damning visibility. In liberal society, law is especially vulnerable to that temptation because our desire to break the law is so easily moralized in terms of "individual freedom" and "natural right." Consequently, a great deal of education in liberal politics is devoted to repressing the temptation to lawlessness, particularly by concealing the relation between the ideal of individual freedom and the tyrannical life.

This is important in the dialogue between America and regimes like South Korea's because it helps explain the strength of America's antipathy to authoritarian regimes. Obviously, an authoritarian or dictatorial government runs counter to philosophic liberalism in that it violates "natural right" and the idea that government originates in agreement. Legitimate government, in this teaching, is limited government and, moreover, government restricted to as narrow a sphere as possible. But Americans also oppose dictatorships *because they find tyranny so tempting*. Dictatorial rule and authoritarian government create anxiety in us because they exert the powerful, threatening attraction of tabooed things. In general, this is all for the good, but it means that authoritarian governments will encounter more than rational suspicion in America.

Military governments find their welcome even more chill. Armies deal with war, and in liberal theory the "state of war" is primitive and prepolitical. War is not "politics conducted by other means." It is outside politics and not subject to rules or laws. All war, in this view, is essentially total war, since war reintroduces the lawless condition of prepolitical life.

The separation between war and peace in liberal theory creates an almost categorical distinction between the "military" and "politics." Since military men are preoccupied with war and violence, they are forever introducing these "prepolitical" concerns into politics. Doubtless we need armed forces, liberal theorists concede, but it is important to keep these more "primitive" organizations and considerations subordinate to civil rule. Moreover, for liberal theory (as well as for its Marxist progeny) violence and the military are characteristic of an early state of society. Progress will gradually replace this "military" stage with an "industrial" one. In these terms military rule may be tolerated in a "backward" society, but at considerable sacrifice to the dignity of the military regime itself.

The Private Order

The liberal tradition in America has always been opposed by an older tradition rooted in ancient Greek political philosophy and in Jewish and Christian religion. The peoples who came to America brought these ideas with them, entangled with their ethnic cultures and customs and embodied in their families, churches, and community institutions. If liberalism shaped and dominated the public order in America, traditional culture retained a powerful foothold in the private order of American life.

In contrast to liberalism, the classical and religious view of human nature is teleological. That is, it defines human beings and institutions by their *ends* rather than their origins. Obviously, a statement like "Human beings are rational animals" does not mean that all humans are rational. Rather, it suggests that human beings are drawn by nature toward rationality and that, given a decent rearing, they will tend to become rational. The statement also implies that human beings who are not rational are incomplete or immature, and that human beings who are not rational cannot enjoy a truly human life. In Aristotle's famous illustration, the nature of the acorn is the oak tree. We cannot possibly understand what the acorn *is* without recognizing what it strives to become. In this understanding, human beings aim at *completeness,* at fulfilling what nature intends. To be complete implies that one has what one needs: one is self-sufficient, capable of self-rule.

But to be self-ruled is to be ruled "by oneself," and that poses the question "Who am I?" Evidently people differ in their minds, and still more in their feelings, about what the "self" is: the classical tradition maintained that genuine self-rule demands that one be ruled by one's true self. To be self-ruled, then, I must be ruled by my nature as a human being. Moreover, since human beings themselves are parts of nature, to be ruled by human nature we must accept the partiality of humanity and its dependence on the whole of which it is a part. In this sense, *to be self-ruled means to be ruled by nature.*

Our ability to be self-ruled is limited by our passion, the ancient tradition argued. Our emotions and feelings are inevitably self-centered. They are parts of a body, and all the senses make the body the center of things rather than a part of a larger whole. Our emotions, left to themselves, do resent limitations, dependence, and mortality. In this liberalism is correct. The classical view differs, however, because it denies that the self can be identified with untaught feeling. Self-rule requires that the passions be educated to accept the real self and the real condition of humanity. This education is never perfect; our senses and passions will always have a strong element of bodily self-centeredness. But the emotions can be schooled. Our feelings lead us out of the self, and the right political and social institutions can encourage us to become emotionally involved and identified with other people and things. We learn to feel that property, family, and country are "our own," so that we are willing to suffer or to die to protect our possessions, friends, and kinsmen.

Force or fear can drive our feelings underground, but it cannot eliminate them. Coerced obedience, the classical tradition observed, is always resisted, and hence obedience to rules is not enough (a proposition central to the Christian insistence on love as opposed to law). Mere obedience leaves us unhappy and angry at even the best rules, and it endangers the rules themselves, for the resentful soul will destroy the laws at the first sign of weakness.

When Aristotle said that human beings are *political animals,* he meant more than the obvious fact that we are born weak and dependent and that we need one another for nurturance, education, and material well-being. He was also arguing that human beings need politics because *participation in political life can teach us to be self-ruled.* Participation is vital because ruling and being ruled in turn affords us the experience of self-rule, and having a role in making a rule lessens our resistance to it.

This does not mean that, given the chance, all human beings will be political activists or even that they will demand democracy. Some may choose merely to be peaceful, obedient citizens but will be resentful unless they feel they can have a say, that they matter; and that it makes a difference whether or not they abide by the law.

Political Society

Plato and Aristotle argued for the small state because (1) its smallness brings the political community within the range of the senses, lessening the tension between private feeling and the public good; and (2) the small state allows us to participate in public life and increases the citizen's sense that he or she matters. The education of human souls, not power, is the measure of a political society in the classical tradition.

It has been a long time since the city-state was practicable, of course. Yet that does not invalidate the ancient argument. It merely proves that we live in a time which does not permit the most excellent sort of regime. The kind of laws appropriate for a country is determined by the character of its citizens and by their political situation. Laws attempt to make human beings better and must start with them as they are. Moral obligations are contingent on circumstances. In this sense, the spirit of the classical tradition is alien to universalistic definitions of human rights.

While political life plays a vital role in schooling the passions, it is not enough. Our love for our country, like our love for our kinsmen, gives it more importance than it is due, given its place in nature. Though more noble than egotism, patriotism is still unjust. To be truly self-ruled is to be ruled by nature, and nature commands that all countries wax and wane, and all regimes rise and fall. Political life may lead us to resist that law of nature, but it also points beyond itself. At least, the ancients observed, politics leads us to see other countries, other ways, and other peoples. The existence of other ways poses the question "What is the best way?" Just so, meeting other people encourages us to ask, "What is like and unlike between us? And what is human?" At best, politics encourages us toward philosophy and toward religion, toward a concern for the truth and for the nature of things.

Political society need not, and probably cannot, make this higher truth a part of the law. Human beings need love of country, for all its shortcomings, because patriotism plays so vital a role in educating the passions. A law designed for the best human beings describes the mark for all lesser law; it cannot be applied to base human beings. Nevertheless, the classical tradition insists that political institutions respect the higher law and that rulers recognize *moral* as well as practical limits to their actions. Power and wealth cannot be goals in themselves, since the legitimate end of political life is a self-ruled humanity. In this case, government is certainly limited, and it cannot be arbitrary, since it is designed for rational creatures. The classical tradition does not reject authoritarian rule, but it suspects dictatorship and it loathes tyranny.

The ancients were also grudging toward military rule. In a good society, military forces are the result of necessity, reflecting the fact that *other* countries are unjust and might become aggressors. Some unjust men, moreover, will yield to persuasion; only the most recalcitrant will give way only to force. Military force, then, is tailored to extreme injustice and its educational role is limited to the control of behavior. Good soldiers are trained to fight, not to decide *whom* to fight. In the *Republic,* Socrates likens the virtue of guardians to the virtue of dogs. Military life places too much emphasis on courage among the virtues, and courage needs to be ruled by wisdom.

Squaring Moral Circles

Much of American political history has been defined by the conflict of these two views, the more modern theory intent on advancing individual liberty, the ancient one struggling to establish a political community which would educate its citizens to use freedom rightly. In America, for example, capitalism has never been *able* to enact or carry out its theories. It was opposed, moderated, and constrained by the heritage embodied in locality, church, and party. Politically, the same forces worked to limit the privatizing individualism of the framers, which is what Tocqueville meant when he said that the customs of the people were more important than laws in determining the character of American democracy.

Tocqueville understood, however, that the liberal Enlightenment tradition—embedded in public institutions endowed with the highest legal authority, and governing economic life—would gradually erode traditional culture. "Individualism," he wrote, "at first only saps the virtues of public life, but in the long run, it attacks and destroys all the others." And so it has. It is easy to see, in contemporary America, the truth of Tocqueville's prophecy: "Not only does democracy make every man forget his ancestors, but it hides his descendants and separates his contemporaries from him; it throws him back forever upon himself alone, and threatens in the end to confine him entirely within the solitude of his own heart."[2] This does not mean that the conflict between America's two traditions has disappeared. The churches and communities that organized the older view and inculcated its teachings have become more and more disordered and fragmented. Fewer and fewer Americans can articulate the classical alternatives as a coherent body of teaching. Nevertheless, that heritage and the values it upholds continue to speak powerfully to Americans. The conflict between ancient and modern culture in America takes place less and less between groups and classes and more and more within the psyche of the individual, schooled in modern individualism but drawn, however confusedly, toward the ideal of political community.

This division in the American soul, more marked today, has been evident for a long time. In *Pragmatism,* William James argued that the advantage of his philosophy lay in enabling one to hold two contradictory beliefs. Americans have sometimes spoken of their "pragmatic" temper as if it reflected a sunny indifference to theory. Actually, it bespeaks their fear of theory, their desire to avoid a choice between God and Mammon. But pragmatism does not solve the problem. Too often the two theories conflict. Consider the Republican Party, for example, caught between its individualism and devotion to economic growth at all costs, on the one hand, and its social conservatism on the other. To be for "morality" may require curtailing individual "freedom," and vice versa. Clever ideologists will try to persuade us that we can square these moral circles, but it is easier to persuade the mind than the soul. At deeper levels, Americans recognize that they face contradictory moral demands and that any decision they make will be painful, and probably wrong. The American psyche exists in a state of chronic tension and nagging guilt.

Americans are thus inclined to become self-righteous whenever their two creeds agree. Freedom from their ordinary ambivalence gives Americans an extraordinary sense of confidence and certainty—and, of course, it makes it much easier to act. Moreover, moral crusading in *one* area of life seems to offer a way of concealing and excusing our sins in other spheres. In fact, given half a chance, Americans will combine the absolutistic elements of both traditions.

Ancient and modern theory *do* agree, for their very different reasons, about certain principles of human rights. Both are hostile to dictatorship. Both insist on limited government and favor the rule of law. Similarly, both regard military rule as, at the very least, undesirable. And both regard consent as a necessary element of any good regime.

I do not think Americans should be reticent in trying to teach what we believe—although civility and understanding would go a long way—and I have no doubt that other regimes have much to learn from us. At the same time, it is equally clear that the United States is often intrusive, self-righteously moralistic, and ignorantly unsympathetic in its dealings with other nations. We are, to put it simply, often very hard to take, and we have to rely on our friends to bear with us. It may help to realize that our worst qualities reflect the conflicts of America's political soul. If the United States is sometimes overeager to heal the ills of others, it is because it suffers from an anguish that may be past healing.

The historic dialectic in our culture may be winding down to a whimpering conclusion. Our religious and classical heritage is waning, and the modern, individualistic side of our culture, already dominant, may win what amounts to a complete victory. But modern political philosophy wins only Pyrrhic victories. The quest for mastery, the great modern project, is a destructive illusion. America and her friends can only hope that we will remember the ancient wisdom that tells us the good life is found in obedience to nature.

Notes

This essay was originally published as "America's Cultural Dilemma," *Worldview* 24, no. 10 (1981).

1. Louis Hartz, *The Liberal Tradition in America: An Interpretation of American Political Thought since the Revolution* (New York: Harcourt, Brace, 1955).

2. Alexis de Tocqueville, *Democracy in America,* trans. George Lawrence (New York: Harper and Row, 1969), 508.

Part 2

Political Thinkers

George Orwell and Ideology

George Orwell is paradoxical in the best sense: he is beyond *doxa,* outside the camps and categories of conventional political discourse. Admiring critics snip and squeeze, but Orwell will not be tailored into an ideology. An anticommunist nonpareil who never doubted that it was necessary to support the United States against the USSR, Orwell in 1948 expressed a preference for Henry Wallace, that scandal to Cold Warriors. In fact, although Orwell called himself a socialist, he scorned both socialism and capitalism as those terms are ordinarily understood, because he rejected the modern political doctrine which is the foundation of both.

Very early, Orwell developed the abiding conviction that modern civilization is shoddy and catabolic. The domination of nature—the goal of modern political philosophy—is neither liberative nor redemptive. In fact, all advances in technology and mechanical power have a dehumanizing dimension since they reduce the significance (and hence, discourage the cultivation) of human arts and powers. In *1984,* Winston Smith is drawn, yearningly, to the products of craft, a leather notebook and a delicate crystal—as alien to industrial capitalism as they are to postindustrial Ingsoc.

Taken as a prediction, *1984* errs about the extent of material poverty, since Orwell portrayed the proles as an overwhelming majority. Orwell's real concern, however, was with quality, not quantity, with the immiseration of the spirit more than the deprivation of the body: "The truly characteristic thing about modern life was . . . its bareness, its dinginess, its listlessness." In those terms *1984* is almost topical. The book begins with an energy crisis in a city where advanced technology is accompanied by urban decay; the underclass proles are demoralized and the lower middle class—the lesser officials of the Party—live wretchedly, eating processed foods and drinking gin; the mass public is diverted by vulgar literature, the lottery, and the telescreen. Only the upper middle class, the Party's elite, enjoys anything like well-being. Change the numbers who belong to each class, and Orwell's depiction is all too descriptive of our times.

In another respect, Orwell seems, at first glance, to have missed the mark. The regime in *1984* is militantly prudish, resembling the censorialism of the Soviet Union more than our own libertine permissiveness. Yet while the Party in *1984* is moralistic in theory, in practice it produces trash—"proletarian literature" filled with astrology, sensationalism, and pornography—and it permits "mere debauchery" provided it is furtive and transient. (Evidently, there is a dreadful similarity between this portrait and the administration's Hollywood Puritanism, Jerry Falwell yoked to Rupert Murdoch.) The Party fears intimacy more than sexuality, and it hates Eros in general because the modern goal, the mastery of nature, cannot be achieved without dominion over human nature. Love, in its lower, instinctive forms as well as the higher yearnings of the soul, resists political control. Since nature is indivisible, human love and freedom are linked to physical nature in a common cause, just as, in *1984*, Julia and Winston Smith retreat to a bower, like Henry and Rosamund. Orwell's indignation at violations of the environment (in *Coming Up for Air,* for example) reflected a basic tenet of his teaching. No forest, no garden: what is humanly and naturally best requires *cultivation,* but it abhors domination and commands a measure of tolerance for the lower side of human nature.

Like Huxley, one of his teachers at Eton, Orwell recognized that sensuality is privatizing, but he did not share Huxley's fear that hedonism would become the ruling principle of a future totalitarianism. In the first place, the pursuit of pleasure ignores the spirited side of human nature, which craves excitement, struggle, and great deeds and which, periodically, is able to enforce its demands on politics. More specifically, sensualism does not comprehend the "abstract, undirected" rage which pervades modern politics, the *ressentiment* that threatens to overwhelm any regime which proves unable to harness it. In *1984,* the technology of law enforcement races—too slowly—to keep pace with crime, and the debaucheries Huxley envisioned are displaced by the two-minute hate.

Complexity, Centralization, and Power

Just as technology discourages craft, the size and complexity of modern economic and social organization dwarf individuals and demand central, bureaucratic institutions capable of producing some sort of order. Where capitalism identifies the danger with the state, Orwell regarded "trustification and Fordification" as processes leading to despotism. But he was equally insistent that socialists are mistaken if they imagine that the problem can be solved by a change in the ownership of property. The evil is in the thing itself, inherent in the most trivial details of modern life. Kipling once imagined a future in which the need to regulate traffic gave rise to a bureaucratic elite armed with tyrannical power, and Orwell admired the insight. He savaged H. G. Wells's vision of a rationalistic world state because such a regime would be hopelessly impersonal and bloodless, an apotheosis of indignity equipped with all the weapons of technology pointing toward an inescapable tyranny.

As this suggests, Orwell was inclined to accept the theoretical superiority of smaller, simpler political societies. In modern regimes, the individual is weak and alone, and totalitarian states accentuate this isolation in order to increase their control. In *1984*, Orwell's description parallels Tocqueville's prophecy: the Party aims to cut its citizens off from one another and from their past, until, in the end, "All you care about is yourself." Liberal capitalism is individualistic from principle; bureaucratic collectivism is individualistic from policy. In the good political society, by contrast, "men are different and do not live alone": genuine individuality presumes a community which knows who I am and cares what I do, warm enough to engage my feelings and small enough so that my work makes a difference. Chesterton's agrarianism attracted Orwell; his first English publication appeared in *G. K.'s Weekly*, and even in the 1930s, he wrote a friend that the policies advocated in Chesterton's paper were the only real solution for Britain.

In practice, of course, that sort of political society is out of the question. Other problems aside, foreign policy demands a more or less centralized, technological state. An agrarian Britain could not have resisted the Nazis, and, given the grim likelihoods of modern politics, as Orwell described them, there will always be evil empires to threaten relatively decent states.

The constraints of practice, in Orwell's view, only make theoretical vision and moral virtue indispensable in political life. The terrible imperatives of modern politics tend to subordinate theory to practice, ends to means, morality to necessity. The competition inherent in the quest for mastery erodes all restraints on the acquisition and use of power. The more horrid our enemies, the more easily will we acquiesce in that logic, producing a fascism "not of course called Fascism." In *1984*, Eurasia really is hateful, and Oceania's own dreadful regime has grown out of the praxis of war more than economic or political doctrine. Totalitarian ideology, in fact, is a kind of pragmatism gone mad, an extreme case of the tendency to identify what prevails historically with what is right.

Orwell's Socialism

Against historicism and relativism, Orwell maintained that human nature provides a standard by which history can be *judged*. Beyond that theoretical proposition, Orwell hoped for a moral force strong enough to direct and govern technological society and able, at least, to minimize the gap between modern politics and human dignity. Hence Orwell's critique, in *The Road to Wigan Pier*, of those socialists who excused the Soviet regime by pointing to its industrial progress, celebrating material power, and turning away from the moral aims and standards which, for Orwell, were the essence of the only socialism worth having. To Orwell, in fact, socialism meant a kind of natural law, human nature governing human creations, industrial and technological power ruled by politically organized morality.

In that sense, Orwell's socialism was never "proletarian." The advantage of the proles—in *1984* or in reality—lies in the fact that they have not yet been assimilated into the established order. This "freedom" of the proletariat, however, is a deficiency, not a virtue. As a class, Orwell's proletariat is essentially demoralized, incapable of self-organization, and easily misled; so long as it lacks more positive defenses against the culture of modernity, it can, potentially, be incorporated into the ethos of the regime at relatively little cost.

So far, Orwell's argument resembles that of Herbert Marcuse, but where Marcuse looked to a youthful counterculture to provide leadership for the underclass, Orwell regarded such bohemian manifestations as part—and probably a proto-totalitarian part—of the dominant culture. As Bernard Crick argues, Orwell envisioned a proletariat led by the lower middle class because, as Orwell saw it, the middle-class code of right and wrong gave that class a limited moral autonomy. Its private virtues, decency and duty, restrain the privatizing emotions, greed and fear, which pervade modern civilization.

Orwell recognized that middle-class morality has a defensive side: decency is a consolation to which, failing more material supports, one can turn for dignity, and in that sense it is terribly vulnerable to corruption. A fragile dignity, however, is better than none at all, and Orwell observed that moral allegiances—patriotism and loyalty to one's family, for example—are part of a positive struggle against isolation. Middle-class morality helps to sustain social relationships and to lay the foundations for Tocqueville's cherished "art of association." The middle class is capable of organization and indignation, and hence possesses at least the rudiments of political leadership and civic virtue.

Orwell's prescription for a socialism manned by workers and led by the lower middle class may, as he believed, offer the best possibility for arresting the drift of postindustrial civilization. Yet as a political strategy, it is gallant but a little wistful, like Orwell's hope during World War II of making the Home Guard into a people's militia, as desperate as Pickett's charge and probably as fated.

In the first place, the raw power of the proletariat seems less and less sufficient to effect radical change. *Animal Farm*, Orwell wrote, originated with the observation that "men exploit animals in much the same way as the rich exploit the proletariat," and that "if only such animals became aware of their strength, we should have no power over them." But the analogy between animal labor and human work is troubling, given the ascendancy of modern civilization over physical nature. Human beings still *devour* animals, but we are less and less dependent on their *work*. In the same way, technology seems to be making proletarian labor redundant; the working class, though not yet ingested by mass society, has received a pretty thorough chewing. In this respect, Kurt Vonnegut's *Player Piano* seems more accurate than *Animal Farm* or *1984*.

Not that the case is any better with the middle class. The middle-class virtues are disappearing along with the old bourgeoisie, yielding to the radical individualism of a *heimlos* meritocracy. Orwell had few illusions: in *1984*, the only surviving representative of the old middle class proves to be a member of the Thought Police, and Orwell's title *Keep the Aspidistra Flying* suggests a besieged fortress with an outmoded banner, brave but already faintly absurd.

Critique of the Intellectuals

The declining social support for moral and political virtue helps account for Orwell's emphasis on the political role—and, especially, on the failings—of modern intellectuals. Higher nature must substitute where lower nature falters; when right opinion can no longer rule, philosophy may be forced into politics. Not that Orwell needed much forcing; he argued that writing is inherently political, since the act of writing presumes an intent to affect some audience. The claim that writers ought to be apolitical, he noted, is itself a political position, and a dangerous one: "art for art's sake" elevates art over morals and politics alike, and the underlying principle that good work is separable from and superior to good ends amounts to the praise of mastery for its own sake.

Orwell's critique of intellectuality was a teaching aimed at intel-

lectuals, intended to fit them for their political role rather than to exclude them from public life. That teaching turns on the proposition that
intellectuals must accept the sovereignty of nature over will, truth over
words, and ends over craft, for, as Orwell insistently argued, the great
peril of the intellectuals is their implicit, though often unconscious, affinity with totalitarianism.

In part, intellectuals are dangerous simply because they have been
trained and become learned in the culture and principles of modern civilization. As the coherent voice of modernity, they accept the idea that
history is a standard to which we must adapt and the even more basic precept that freedom is mastery. Intellectuals, consequently, are likely to be
"supercilious" about morality, relativists and positivists who regard decency as outdated and duty as irrational.

Orwell's criticism, however, does not stop with a particular school or
"new class" of intellectuals. Like Karl Mannheim's "total conception of ideology," Orwell's critique of intellectuality is catholic: it begins with the proposition that intellectuals are dangerous *as such* since they yearn to make their
thought rule the world. Intellectuals are the more to be feared because they
are often more single-minded than any other human beings; they are sometimes indifferent to money and material comfort, and they are adroit at self-
deception, able to spin out justifications of their hope for dominion which
identify the right with the necessary, the noble with the advantageous.

That, after all, is what ideology does, and ideology is tempting because modern politics exaggerates the tension between means and ends
into an enormous disparity between risks and results. Political goals are
always ambiguous; even so villainous an enemy as the Nazis could not
be defeated without increasing the power of the Soviet Union. Political
results must be judged on the balance, and political gains are ordinarily very marginal. But technology and mass organization greatly increase
the risks of political action; just as it may be necessary to risk total war in
order to prevent some limited defeat in foreign policy, in domestic life it
may be necessary to endanger liberty rather gravely if we are to improve
the collection of taxes. More and more, Orwell observed, politics leaves us
only the choice between acting like "a devil or a lunatic." Abstention is not
allowed: those who would not run the demonic risk of war with Hitler
necessarily chose the lunatic risk of attempting to coexist with him. Ideology rationalizes, excuses, and, paradoxically, depoliticizes politics. The
truth about modern politics—that it is mad, evil, and inescapable—is the
strongest political imperative for those who can endure it.

Truth and Freedom

Orwell virtually made a creed out of unwelcome truth. Modern political philosophy argues that liberty exists when people can say and do as they please. Against that view, Orwell argued that "liberty is telling people what they do not want to hear," and I suspect that he was referring to the freedom of the *hearers* as well as that of the speaker. "Freedom is the freedom to say that two plus two makes four. If that is granted, all else follows." Truth, not will or pleasure, is the foundation of freedom. *I* am free only when I act in accordance with my nature. To attempt to overcome one's own nature, as Orwell remarked in relation to Gandhi, is in the most fundamental sense an act of self-denial, possibly saintly but not free. To be oneself is to be limited and mortal and to know loss, but that painful freedom is inseparable from the things that make life worth living: "That one is prepared in the end to be defeated and broken up by life . . . is the inevitable price of fastening one's love upon other human individuals."

The pillars of "Reality Control" in *1984*—newspeak, doublethink, and the mutability of the past—reflect that worst temptation of the intellectuals, the denial of any objective reality, the effort to master nature through thought, sparing human beings the pain and frustration of unwelcome truth. Of course, reality will persist, whatever we think about it: hence doublethink, the Party's combination of *knowing* and *not knowing*, for the Party demands a conscious will not to know capable of directing the apparatus of "not knowing" as part of the systematic effort to escape from the self and anything that might remind one of its nature. There is a grotesque altruism in the Party: it sets out to eliminate our consciousness of finitude and mortality, taking us back to Eden by eliminating knowledge, striving to overcome memory so as to achieve a timeless present in which death is not foreknown and nothing is lost because nothing is remembered.

The modern, radically subjective idea of freedom ends with the Thought Police and Room 101: "For two hundred years we had sawed and sawed and sawed at the branch we were sitting on. And in the end . . . our efforts were rewarded and down we came. But unfortunately, there had been a little mistake. The thing at the bottom was not a bed of roses after all, it was a cesspool full of barbed wire."

Orwell enjoyed celebrity, but he cultivated unfashionability. He hoped to lead a parade, if only a small one, but only if he could march to the beat of his very different drum. And for his teaching and example, he deserves to have his memory kept free from "the smelly little orthodoxies which are now contending for our souls."

Note

This essay was originally published as "George Orwell and Ideology," *Freedom at Issue,* no. 77 (March/April 1984).

Reinhold Niebuhr

New Orthodoxy for Old Liberalism

Reinhold Niebuhr has profoundly affected American thought in theology, on society, and about politics.[1] He has puzzled more than one of his many critics and commentators, especially by the veritable panorama of doctrines which, at one time or another, he has appeared to advocate: several varieties of socialism, liberalism, and what seems to be a sort of mellow conservatism. The confusion engendered by this ideological medley has not been alleviated either by the voluminous extent of his writings or by his Teutonic, yet highly personal style.[2] But Niebuhr's policy suggestions have been shaped in response to changing conditions in the political world. Deeper analysis reveals a remarkably consistent teaching, present in all essential respects at least as early as his *Moral Man and Immoral Society*, which if not a philosophy, is at least a theology of politics. The scope of this paper prevents any examination of the entire intellectual pilgrimage of Reinhold Niebuhr; I shall confine my attention to the main lines of his political teaching.[3]

Most critics and analysts would agree that whatever else he may have been, Niebuhr has been a critic of liberalism, modernity, and American culture. Yet, as so often is the case with Niebuhr, appearances can be misleading. It is true that his characteristic *bêtes noires* have been such comparatively modern thinkers as John Dewey. But this paper will endeavor to demonstrate that Niebuhr's basic political ideas are essentially the same as those of the liberals he seeks to criticize. His criticism is often devastating, but beginning as a critic, he ends with concepts and convictions drawn from the core of the liberal tradition. In this, he is not unique. Niebuhr shares the intellectual tendencies of the generation of which he is a part, which, both attracted and disillusioned by the rhetoric of Woodrow Wilson and the crusade of 1917–1918, was and remains affected by antirationalism, doubtful of human nature, and suspicious of enthusiasms in politics. Yet Louis Hartz has indicated that the most scathing critics of post-Wilson America were unable to escape the "irrational Lockeanism" of the American liberal tradition, and came to terms with it after a period of voluntary expatriation. At the approach of World War II the critics of the 1920s became horrified at the destructive effects of their criticism on the national myth and advocated "responsibility."[4] This pattern is quite descriptive of Reinhold Niebuhr's intellectual history.

But Niebuhr is far too subtle and profound a thinker to be disposed of within the confines of a "generation." Any such effort would do violence to the real character of his contribution to that generation which has so frequently, and frantically, urged America to "come of age." The refurbishing of the liberal creed has not been an easy task. The "truths" which had been so daringly self-evident in the eighteenth century had come to be the "inarticulate major premise," in Holmes's phrase, of American civilization by the early nineteenth century. It is difficult to tell whether the inarticulateness was due to the universal acceptance of these "truths" or to the development of doubts about their self-evident qualities.[5] The original theorists credited the discovery of the "self-evident truths" to reason. Yet they also believed in another, instrumental reason which was the "servant of the passions," so in some ways they were the progenitors of the antirationalism of our times.[6] The discoveries of that instrumental, scientific, and empirical reason have dealt rather roughly with the premises of the old liberal creed. The panoply of beliefs of liberal utopianism, of men "born free and equal," of men forever devoted to increasing individual liberty, and of progress and perfectibility in history, has been radically undermined on a rational level.[7] Niebuhr has often noted that liberalism has become a "holding action."[8] Indeed, his own criticism of reason has not been notably different from that of a number of critics, whether earlier, such as Hume, or more contemporary. In part, it is a criticism of the "pretension" of instrumental rationalism that Niebuhr finds in such theorists as John Dewey. But revealingly, it is not a criticism of instrumental rationalism as such; when reason is reduced to the proportions of a technique, Niebuhr favors employing it instrumentally. His criticism is an effort to reduce it to those proportions, to prevent instrumental reason from "absolutizing" its "finite" perspectives. Niebuhr's quest is for a safer basis than reason on which to rest the great liberal premises. His criticism presents the arguments of a long line of critics to establish the failure of reason to uphold the old creed. But this denial constitutes, in Niebuhr's eyes, a "negative validation" of a faith which comes to embody the articles of the liberal system, especially its central conception of freedom. His argument retains the characteristic argumentative style of early liberalism, what Max Weber called *Wertrationalismus:* the willingness to use means given by reason for ends discerned by "inspiration." But where the early liberals called the inspiration rational, Niebuhr calls it religious or theological. This goes a long way toward explaining the curious fact, which has baffled many critics, that Niebuhr makes a "virtue of incomprehensibility."[9] In fact, the title of Niebuhr's early work *Does Civilization Need Religion?* is incomplete. It is not "civilization" but that civilization of which Niebuhr is a part that is involved; not civilization, but liberalism, "needs religion."

In the analysis which follows I shall attempt to demonstrate that Niebuhr adheres, at least in "this-worldly" and political terms, to four central liberal doctrines: (1) the perfectibility of man; (2) the identification of freedom with the social good; (3) the contractarian conception of the state; and (4) the idea of progress in history. Since he has devoted much of his attention to international affairs, the argument will conclude with the contention that Niebuhr's view of international politics reflects these four doctrines, as well as the equally vital liberal concept of the "brotherhood of man."

Niebuhr has been cited as a "realist" as often as he has been called a critic of liberalism. Of course, "realist" is an appealing term to apply to oneself; every theorist likes to believe himself to be truly "realistic." Yet curiously, "realism" represents only a part of Niebuhr's reality. "Realism" is identified with the comprehension of physical nature, a world governed by an often grim necessity, if unified by an equally deterministic set of "preordained harmonies." But man is more than physical, and more than "realism" is able to realize. Niebuhr's "prophetic" insight reveals to him a radical human freedom, which is "transcendent" and which seeks the absolute and the infinite, beyond any of the limitations imposed by time or nature.[10] But though these elements may be separated analytically, they are never separated in Niebuhrean man. Man forever combines the two and can never escape the resultant tension and ambiguity, an ambiguity productive of anxiety which leads him to the futile effort to escape the demands of nature, on one hand, or of the spirit, on the other. Nature imposes self-seeking passion and egoism on the spirit, and roots the spirit in the finite; the sin of the spirit is to seek to deny that finite or temporal element in man, and hence to be guilty of pretension and pride. Moreover, the spirit breaks the "pre-ordained" harmonies of nature and makes the prudent and limited attributes of "natural man" become infinite and insatiable, leading to conflict, competition, and disorder.[11]

Intermediate between spirit and nature is the area of "human contrivance" or "rational freedom." Though reason is always an instrument of the natural self-seeking of man, it qualifies and restrains it by a kind of prudence and calculation. The purely harmonic world of nature is forever destroyed, yet man, a "creator" as well as a "creature" of history, is able by techniques, institutions, and science to harness nature to his purposes and increasingly to master it.[12] But of course, the more that man masters nature, the more his own natural passions are freed from restraint; the more that men can obtain, the more they will want. Conflict remains eternal, contradictions perpetual.

But this world of conflict and struggle is not the world of nature; it is the product of the spirit and of reason in nature. Consequently, a purely secular "realism," which is typified for Niebuhr by Hobbes and Machiavelli, understands neither the true nature of man nor of conflict in the world. "Realism," it will be seen, represents a doctrine about the world which is developed by empirical and unaided reason; it becomes identified with a curiously old-style brand of naturalism, of the conflict of passions, and of man the acquisitive animal.[13] Nor need "realism" necessarily be secular. St. Augustine represents the "theological realist." Aided by theology and faith, Augustine perceived the radical freedom of the human spirit but he made too sharp a separation between the spirit and nature. While it is by no means true (as Niebuhr seems to imply) that Augustine was prepared to let the world run without ethical restraints, he provided far too small a role for the idealistic element of human nature in this world to satisfy Niebuhr, who regards Augustine as "excessively realistic."[14] Theological realism makes too many concessions to the natural world, and regards Christianity as an essentially otherworldly ethic. Niebuhr, despite his long distrust of the "utopian" effort to apply Christian or other perfectionist teachings directly to the world, will not allow such teachings to be separated from it. He has always contended that the "impossible ethical idea" remains "relevant."[15] He is not a realist on his own terms; he is better regarded as a "realistic" or moderate utopian. Niebuhr has laid stress on the limits which restrict the degree to which any utopia may be attained. But within the ultimate limits, his awareness of the problem of "less and more" has been quite intense, the intensity being especially marked in the years just preceding the outbreak of World War II.[16] In fact, all realists, contemporary or historical, have conceded that given the limits which attach to human endeavor, man should always strive to approach the limits: to become as perfect as his imperfections allow.[17]

Two factors determine the content of such a teaching. The first, and perhaps crucial, question is the nature of the Good toward which human striving should aim. The second question, of importance in "realistic" or pragmatic terms, is the character and scope of the limits that are thought to restrict the attainment of the ultimate and yet impossible standard.

It is quite revealing that, in answer to this second question, Niebuhr is content with the assertion that limits exist; he is adamant in his refusal to specify them more precisely. For to claim to know the limits of human perfection is to claim divine knowledge. If it is prideful to seek to establish goodness in the world, to escape limits altogether, then to seek to define the limits is, in his eyes, no less so. And while the first has at least the merit of overestimating man, the second runs the risk of limiting man to a level of baseness lower than necessary.[18] Niebuhr frequently denounces all theories of "natural law" because they compromise too readily with that nature which man may increasingly "master."[19] His denunciations of these, and other theories, from Catholic rationalism to Marxist-Leninist, center on their supposed identification of a particular political order with the ultimately perfect. It is to be hoped that Niebuhr knows better than that. Almost all the "pretensions" he indicates did not constitute claims that a given state was perfect but that it represented the best attainable state in the conditions and limitations under which men operated.

Niebuhr's attack on the "absolutizing" of such "finite" perspectives has a dual nature. His attack on some theorists is actually a criticism of the good which they defined, *different* from that which Niebuhr holds as a standard. Others perceived the nature of the good, but set the standard at too low a level of attainment, or identified it too much with the preconceptions of an age. Thus democracy, a "perennial necessity," had to be extricated from the "bourgeois" associations of its origin.[20]

Niebuhr's language is apt to delude the reader. Despite his denials, his theory contains an implicit "natural law" or "natural right," that is, a conception of the best state in this world. Despite his "historical relativism," his teaching contains a number of such "perennial necessities" and "constant factors" in politics. To assert that progress is always possible leads to an emphasis on a society which is open to change, as Niebuhr's theory does. But such a state becomes a this-worldly "best state." In fact, such a state is necessary if the "fanatical" effort to establish the ultimately perfect state is to be avoided. For immediate purposes, the significance is that, although Niebuhr denies that man can ever be perfect or that progress is limitless, his theory strives to, and to a large degree does, make the limitations meaningless in political terms; that is, his effort is to salvage as much of the liberal creed as is possible in an age that doubts it.

The content of Niebuhr's "best state" in the world is determined by the nature of the otherworldly best which it strives to imitate, just as his pragmatic opponents, in order to discern policies or states which are "better," must have a standard of the "best" by which to judge them so. Niebuhr's distinctive stance—which often obscures his meaning—is that in a period accustomed to pragmatic evasions, he begins with an ultimate and reasons down to the world. The ultimate standard gives the character to Niebuhr's political teaching as a whole.

There is little doubt as to the "human good" in Niebuhr's teaching: it is contained in the spiritual, in the element of man's nature characterized by "transcendent freedom" and the quest for the ultimate. In fact, this element constitutes the "true" nature of man; without such a teleological conception much of Niebuhr's rhetoric of pathos concerning the human condition would be pointless.[21]

Yet such a good is quite different from classical definitions of virtue, in that it is without content. It is an ability or a way of doing things which does not describe what is done. Niebuhr's terms, used in describing this virtue, are suggestive: man the "creator" as opposed to "creature," transcending his nation, class, or place in history. All suggest an almost romantic individuality, or those conceptions of "creativity" or "autonomy" which have been so fashionable in recent years.[22] One may summarize Niebuhr's idea of the ethical rather simply. It is freedom. The more things of which man becomes free—time, space, passion, class, or nation—the better he becomes. Now it is true that Niebuhr attacks modern theorists for "exaggerating" the degree to which freedom and virtue can be identified.[23] But to suggest an "exaggeration" is to suggest that they can be identified to some degree. And, moreover, the reason modern theorists are said to be in error is that they fail to discern the "natural" element in man. Thus, freedom and virtue cannot be identified completely in this world, not because they are not ultimately identifiable but because *total* freedom is impossible and impracticable. But it remains the standard toward which man ought to strive. Love, of course, is the ultimate value beyond freedom because it cannot be commanded or coerced. And, moreover, love itself is defined in terms of "self-sacrifice" and of overcoming "egoism." Not only is it true that from another point of view this is surely "self-realization" or "fulfillment," but the very existence of "egoism" in Niebuhr's teaching is bound up with the fact that man is in nature.[24]

Much of Niebuhr's discussion and concept of freedom has obvious roots in Kantian idealism; so does his corollary concern that individuals be used as "ends and not means" and with the ethic of "good will."[25] Ultimately, Niebuhr agrees with the idealists as to the nature of virtue. Given his stress on the inevitable corruption of freedom by egoism in the world, it follows that not only can freedom and virtue not be *simply* identified but that greater freedom runs the peril of greater evil as well as greater good. Niebuhr has, in fact, made a point of this. While such a fact demands a certain prudence, Niebuhr's refusal to set limits to perfectibility places him in the idealist camp. Prudential ethics concede too much to "nature." Moreover, they cannot guide men in the extreme case where "heroism" is demanded for the choice between opposite goals: freedom or slavery, tyranny or anarchy.[26] Prudential ethics are valid only if they assume the ultimate importance of freedom. Man's involvement in nature demands that a certain amount of self-interest be "legitimated," particularly in regard to self-preservation. But, not surprisingly, this merely emphasizes that the pursuit of self-interest and freedom should be "enlightened."[27] This enlightenment has two characteristics, a realization of the perils of "natural self-interest" in one's own freedom, and a readiness to pursue self-interest in ways compatible with the freedom of others.

Indeed, Niebuhr's "realism," said to reside in his "recognition of the effects of power," is itself part of that idealistic element of his thought we have discussed. Freedom demands power, the power to free the spirit from nature by "conquering" the natural, a belief which unites Niebuhr with modern theorists from Bacon forward. While the quest will ultimately fail, increasing increments of power will make man freer of the natural. It is for this reason, in fact—that power is never sufficient to free man from nature—that for practical purposes freedom is defined as power.[28] Thus the quest for power (which produces conflict) and historical "progress" (which is ambiguous precisely because power may be used for good or evil) must both be judged good in a relative, "this-worldly" sense. This decisively sets Niebuhr apart from a theorist like Hobbes, who regarded conflict and the quest for power as among the chief evils of man and set his goal instead as the attainment of social peace. It puts Niebuhr in the camp of the liberals, beginning with John Locke, who regarded the state of war as merely an annoyance compared with the loss of "freedom" that would be entailed by accepting the iron peace of Hobbes's *Leviathan*.[29] As Niebuhr has put it, "Self interest may be a source of discord ultimately but it is tentatively necessary to prevent the harmony of the whole from destroying the vitality of the parts."[30]

Niebuhr's concept of the state follows this liberal Lockean model, and although he criticizes the "social contract" theory, his criticism suggests that he accepts that theory in all essential respects. Like Locke, he posits a state of "pre-ordained" harmonies as the "natural" state of man before he "fell." The condition of man after the Fall was, as in liberal theory, a "state of war" which led to the establishment of the state.[31] By placing the "state of nature" in Eden—and outside history—Niebuhr avoids the great dilemma of liberal contractarian theory: the question of how conflict arose among pacific "natural men." Indeed, for practical purposes, Locke and his successors equated the natural state of man with the state of war and may have regarded the idea of a period of harmony as a somewhat deceptive myth.[32] But to both the liberals and to Niebuhr, what follows is that the state is produced only to avoid the state of war; and yet, given the "natural" condition of fallen man, conflict is inevitable. Hence the state, a "human contrivance," exists to channel the conflict into relatively bloodless and law-abiding ways. Niebuhr's attack on the contract theory denies that the contract took place at any definite time; rather, it developed through "organic" and historical processes.[33] (Burke, of course, made the same argument, yet Burke, as we too often forget nowadays, called himself a Whig and not a Tory.)[34] In any case, most contractarian theorists treated the historicity of the social contract as unimportant. It represented a necessary postulate to account for man's escape from the state of war; how long such a development took—or even whether it had taken place—was of little concern.[35] Liberal theorists, who often sought to show that the "original" contract, even granting its existence, had been corrupted and was not yet embodied in government, were even less concerned with the event. Niebuhr's unwillingness to credit the state to an act of speculative or scientific reason is important, but it does not change the concept of the state as such.

For Niebuhr, as for early liberals, the political order is not among the higher ethical achievements of man. Man is not a political animal but an animal "born free." Community is based on "animal gregariousness," and not on human freedom; the goal of harmony within the civil order is "uncivilized" or tribal.[36] The state, since it employs coercion to attain its ends, is perhaps even less desirable than purely natural community. The state is never more than a product of necessity, to which men "give up" freedoms in the effort to escape the state of war. Hence political society is always "ambiguous" and forever "frustrates" the higher impulses of man.[37]

Since the state of war is apparently produced by the action of the spirit in "transmuting" natural harmonies, it might be suggested that the spirit be directed toward the purely spiritual, toward the contemplative life. But here Niebuhr's idealism asserts itself strongly; he is unwilling to allow such a separation even at the cost of conflict. St. Augustine and the medieval theorists committed this fault: they set the standard of human attainment too low. They paid too high a "price in order" and denied sufficient scope for freedom. "Freedom" in this case is notably a freedom to act in and to change the political order, a liberal and not a notably Christian definition of liberty. Medievalism restricted "cultural vanities" in a quest for unity. The synthesis of medievalism was broken up, he asserts, by "creative chaos."[38] Though medievalism may be extreme in this quest for unity, it represents only a part of a general rule: that all political orders are morally mediocre because they "exalt peace over freedom."[39] Given the fact that political orders are, however, necessary due to the presence of evil and the propensity to war, justice consists in that harmony which provides maximum scope for the "unique vitality and freedom of the parts."[40]

One of Niebuhr's "perennial necessities" is the existence of a social balance of power.[41] This "necessity" is "perennial" in precisely the way that the "Rights of Man" were conceived to be inalienable: it is necessary to a just order. The balance prevents just that concentration of power in the hands of a few which limits the freedom of the many precisely because it concentrates the stuff of freedom, power. Hence a state should "institutionalize" conflict to keep power divided. And since "love" is the regulative principle behind justice in absolute ethics, and freedom is the condition of love, the balance should be weighted in the direction of more, rather than less, freedom for the parts.[42] Niebuhr is not unaware that a justice whose principal virtue consists in preventing tyranny is "negative." But he asserts, in "advanced" societies only a "rough justice" or "minimum harmony" is possible.[43] One might ask why such societies are considered "advanced." The answer can only be because they make "freedom" possible. Justice, although a moral norm within the limits of human life, is less desirable than freedom. A "negative" justice which permits freedom, then, is better than a "positive" justice which does not.

Like all of his sometime antagonists, whether Marxist or liberal, Niebuhr sees "chaos" as oftentimes creative, conflict a good, and not merely a mournful necessity. If conflict is the price of freedom, then Niebuhr will accept conflict; and not only accept it, but sanctify it in the name of a higher morality. If Niebuhr chastises "rationalists" for the belief that freedom is always compatible with order, it is not because, as a conservative might, he means that freedom must sometimes be restrained, but rather that one must be prepared to sacrifice order to maintain freedom.[44]

Despite his frequent criticism of that idealism which denies the limits imposed on man by nature, Niebuhr argues for the utility of even these transhistorical perspectives in the attack on political orders from a more perfectionistic stance.[45] Niebuhr's analysis of the limitations of medievalism on "cultural vitalities" suggests Marx's notions of "fetters on the modes of production." But Niebuhr goes beyond this to suggest not only that the "synthesis" became outdated but that it had paid too high a "price in order" from the outset. Both the idea of a transhistorical standard of criticism and the belief in the desirability of historical change suggest a theory of progress. And while Niebuhr regards history as "inconclusive" and progress as a mixture of good and evil, he nonetheless regards the movement of history as a forward one. His emphasis on the mixture of good and evil merely makes progress dialectic, rather than linear.[46] "Like Hegel's new logic," he once conceded, without its "premature finality."[47] Hegel's standard was also set too low. Niebuhr's theory resembles Kant's claim of a "cunning" in war and conflict in history, and progress as virtually limitless.[48] Although they differ in that Niebuhr puts the heavenly city outside of history while Kant puts it inside, the concept of historical progress through conflict is the same for both. And the standard by which progress is measured, the goal of perfect peace in total freedom, is the same whichever side of the history/post-history dividing line it is placed on. Niebuhr strives valiantly to relate this idea of progress to Christian ideals of Providence. Yet orthodox Christianity saw divine Providence as essentially eschatological. God's judgment at the end of history did not guarantee that events in historical time would "lead" to that judgment by a humanly discernible progression.[49]

Yet despite these basically liberal perspectives, Niebuhr has continually asserted a difference between his position and that of liberalism. That he believes this difference to be one of practicability is indicated by his use of the term "realism." Liberals and social scientists, Niebuhr declares, have a "fundamental goal" of anarchy.[50] Yet although anarchy is presumably impractical, Niebuhr is not prone to deny the virtue of freedom or the evil of coercion.[51] His claim to a distinct position rests on the dubious proposition that the presumed anarchist aims of liberals ever constituted the actual goals of their policy, or that they believed that goals of social harmony could be obtained "easily." But of far more significance is the fact that Niebuhr accepts the liberal goal as the valid goal of social policy. Religion, in a rather unusual role, has very little to say about the ends of life and policy which liberalism does not say. It teaches prudence in attempting to achieve them and a safe basis on which to rest them. But the Heavenly City of Reinhold Niebuhr retains a distinctly modern form in which to cast its eternal perfections.

In fact, the best state in this world—as opposed to the heavenly ultimate—seems strikingly to resemble the United States. Niebuhr's best state must be an "open" and a "pluralist" society which, at the same time, must have an "organ of dominion and authority." Democracy, a perennial necessity, is also desirable in that it "obscures" the element of domination in the central organ by making it public, rather than the preserve of a ruling class.[52] Despite the ambiguities of technology, the state should also be technological, so as to maximize freedom over nature.[53] We may pass over the question of how far this picture accurately represents the reality of American politics today; it is apparent that the image suggests the ideal of most traditional American theorists and present-day social scientists.

Niebuhr has less faith in institutional change than many liberals, and is unwilling to credit the "best state" to rational contrivance. We have "stumbled on" the "constant factors" in the human situation. Democracy is not possible for all states at all times.[54] Hamilton and Madison would have disagreed with little of that analysis. They certainly did believe that they had discovered a "science of politics." They were equally aware, however, that what had been "stumbled on" was the opportunity to put this science into practice, and that America represented a unique historical situation in which experiment was possible.[55] Niebuhr's ideal remains, in any case, the same. If his hopes for the realization of that ideal have come to rest more on historical development than on institutional change, he reflects a general tendency among nineteenth-century liberals, once the hopes of the Enlightenment for despots who would establish their program were dissipated. Perhaps even more, he reflects the alienation from a seemingly hostile world and the sudden desperate clinging to institutions which once seemed secure that has characterized the "responsible" liberalism of his generation.

Niebuhr's view of man, the social good, and the best state are directly connected to his conceptions of international politics. Like Kant and the liberals, Niebuhr believes, as we have noted, not only that conflict and the quest for power are inevitable, but that they are beneficial in tendency. Nations are aggregations of individuals (but without the restraints of the individual moral conscience) and must minimally leave men no less free than they were on entering the state. But since a policy based on the goal of stability is impracticable and undesirable, the state must seek to add power, to make its citizens "freer than they were before." Thus Jefferson, whose policy of "protective imperialism" sought only the power needed to preserve his country, is classified as only partially "realistic."[56] A genuine realist, then, must add power in order to increase national freedom. Niebuhr's criticism of the "pretension" of empires does not imply that all imperial aims are equally bad. He regards some empires, such as the British, as clearly preferable to others. The "pretension" of empires consists in the effort to deny that all efforts to add power are equally justifiable and equally good. Differences between empires arise from the effects of their rule on others. As an act of state, however, the addition of power is always morally the same and, in adding freedom to the state concerned, morally defensible. "Universal pretensions," whether religious or ideological, are undesirable because they deny the legitimacy of the freedom of others; the "nationalistic imperialisms" of the seventeenth to nineteenth centuries, Niebuhr argues, avoided this fault.[57] Yet imperial ideologies of that period reveal a number of pretensions, not the least of these being the doctrine of social Darwinism, the claim that imperial states obeyed a "law of nature" and of progress in subjecting the weak. Presumably, Niebuhr does not regard this as a "universalist pretension" because it allows each state an opportunity to subject others, although it is possible that he deems the doctrine unpretentious because he believes it to be true.

But one need not go so far. Niebuhr's picture of international politics regards nations as fundamentally analogous to groups or individuals in the domestic political system, except that nations are somewhat less ethical. Hence, he advocates pluralism among power centers, change and openness, conflict and balance in the international, as well as the domestic, political world. He has always been aware that the balance of power alone could not prevent war.[58] But if the alternative to war is the empire of a single state, or even of a world state based around a single center of power, Niebuhr is quite as hostile as he would be to the rule of an elite in domestic politics. The "current" approval Niebuhr gives the balance of power arises not only from its "necessity" but from the fact that it is inherently more just, morally preferable to either of the alternatives described above.[59] For peace itself is not desirable unless it is compatible with the quest for freedom.[60] Of course, peace is a good and especially so in our day. States should therefore conduct themselves according to the dictates of "enlightened self-interest," seeking to add only so much power as is compatible with the maintenance of international order. To be exact, the policy of states should be a certain moderate variety of imperialism.[61]

This view of international politics is quite characteristic of "realist" theorists; fundamentally it is a kind of nostalgic appeal to the image of nineteenth-century European diplomacy.[62] Such diplomacy not only was permitted the luxury of a large number of centers of power, it was able to look with comparative equanimity on those conflicts which developed into open warfare, and to see such conflict as contributing to historical "progress." That Niebuhr's entire view would be shaken by the development of weapons capable of almost universal destruction is evident. Indeed, he admits that the development of these weapons has upset the traditional balance between "potential good" and "potential evil" in the increase of human power over nature; that balance, of course, is at the core of his concept of historical progress. Men, he concedes, no longer have control of the technology they have created. The power available to man has passed the point where "human contrivance" could harness it to the effort to conquer nature.[63] And Niebuhr is not without a Hobbesian aside to the effect that the peril of universal destruction may cause both the great empires of our time to prefer life to death.[64]

Yet despite these new perceptions, Niebuhr's theory remains unchanged in its identity with older liberalism. While it is presumably desirable that both empires should prefer life, capitulation is undesirable, because it entails the loss of freedom.[65] And—one must presume—it is undesirable whether the United States or the USSR were to be the state capitulating. And, he adds, by far the greater number of states, when confronted with a choice between survival and liberty, have chosen the latter. This is more than an empirical observation. It merely repeats his old argument that any other choice would be "morally perverse."[66] As so frequently in his thought, his argument that a given event must take place, given "human nature" or "history," conceals the optimistic assumption that it ought to take place, a point to which we shall return.

Niebuhr's criticism of liberal attitudes toward foreign affairs is that liberals have seen nothing between the nation-state and the "vague universalism" represented by the idea of a world community. But he is not himself without commitments to just such a "vague universalism." Classical political philosophy and much of modern utopian theory took the small state as ideal. Niebuhr rejects the small state not only because of its lack of power but because it cannot satisfy the limitless demand of humanity for brotherhood, a demand to the realization of which he also refuses to assign limits.[67] In other words, the demand for "brotherhood" is treated in precisely the same terms as is the demand for freedom. But though the terms are fundamentally the same, he offers even less discussion of this presumed human goal. This is not at all unique. Liberal and modern discussions of "fraternity" have been few, especially in comparison to the extensive theoretical discussions of the relationship of liberty and equality.[68] This may not have resulted from any sense that the Brotherhood of Man was an unimportant or secondary goal, to be realized on the attainment of liberty and equality, but rather from the belief that human fraternity was the primary goal, which could only be achieved when men were free and equal. It is likely that just such a concept united the two schools of liberalism, the older school, which demanded "unfraternal" conduct and competitive ethics in the interest of a "long-run" human unity, and the more sentimental and short-term ethics of modern welfare liberalism.[69] Nor is it accidental that Niebuhr, like most of the early liberals, sees an "irresolvable" tension between "planned justice" and "laissez-faire," yet regards both as legitimate values.[70]

The universalism of traditional liberalism sought an expression in which peace and freedom would be compatible through the medium of a world federation, as opposed to a world state or empire. Niebuhr has persistently attacked this as an "illusion."[71] Government, he notes, is founded on community, and men will not be frightened into forming a world regime without a sense of community throughout the world. This seeming despair would appear to make his universalism even vaguer than that of the liberals he attacks. But he does not completely give up the goal. The mistake of his opponents is to believe world government possible immediately, without waiting for "history."[72] Man was terrorized out of the state of war and into society and thence to large political units only by slow historical growth and "accretions" of loyalty and community. Niebuhr is again in agreement with Kant's pre-Darwinian ethic of natural selection, "historical cunning." Implicit in Niebuhr's argument is the conviction that time will bring a world regime into being. Hence his concern with political units between the parliament of man and the nation-state: with regionalism and with empires. These, presumably, men are sufficiently terrorized to form, given the present state of the growth of loyalty and community.

Yet by his own showing, the forces and balances which he has relied on to control nature have broken down; his, and the traditional liberal view of history, are no longer adequate. One cannot be sure that man and civilization will survive long enough for history. Niebuhr is not without hopes that a disaster can be avoided, presumably long enough for history to do its work. We may, he counsels us, hope for more democracy in the government of the USSR. This is assumed to be an "improvement" either because of a belief that democracies are peaceful or because a more democratic regime in the USSR might be more willing to form a world regime. Yet there is little reason to believe either to be the case, within Niebuhr's theory. For the "freer" a government is, the more it will feel obliged to pursue the aim of adding power; and so the more it will come into conflict with others. Niebuhr apparently connects the hope for increased democracy in the Soviet Union with his belief that war will be best avoided if states are "less rigid and righteous" and if they "realize their involvement in a common fate."[73] That is, if they gave any "universalist claims" (but not universalist *beliefs*, such as the belief in the "freedom of all nations"), states would be more inclined to accommodate the claims of others, which would be recognized as quite as legitimate as their own. Moreover, it is presumably true that if states did not make universal claims, they would be less inclined to come into conflict with others in the first place. But even if democratic states are more likely to lack righteous and rigid attitudes, the belief that the absence of such attitudes conduces to peace, however true, is itself a suggestive one. The absence of rigidity, the willingness to compromise, to accept the interests of others as legitimate, comprise once again the traditional liberal belief in "enlightened self-interest" and in the "natural harmony" of the interests of nations. To be sure, Niebuhr stresses the necessity of the sense of a "common fate." But that sense too was part of the liberal creed in the "vague universalism" to which we had have reference, the belief that free, equal, and democratic nations would sense the "brotherhood of nations" just as individuals were to sense human fraternity, and by the same process. That

Niebuhr's theory relies a good deal on this sense of community being produced by terror is no new addition. For terror and the fear of violence have long been involved in the modern hope to realize in practice the vision of human brotherhood, from the Machiavellian belief that necessity and the fear of death make men virtuous though Rousseau's willingness to force men to be free to Wilson's use of war in the service of universal democracy.[74] Reformation through violence has always been close to the center of the liberal-modernist creed, a creed which, in its Jacobin form, was described so brilliantly by Chamfort, "Sois mon frère, ou je te tue."

Niebuhr's dilemma is not his alone. It is the dilemma of modern liberalism, and of those radical ideas based on liberal premises such as orthodox Marxism. For contemporary events have made the faith in historical progress through struggle, the belief that the vital human goal is the conquest of nature, and even that man is born with a desire to be free, seem more and more doubtful, dangerous, or irrelevant. In this light the widespread appeal of Niebuhr's work, even to those Morton White calls the "atheists for Niebuhr," can be made understood.[75] For as a theologian Niebuhr can do what the secular liberal cannot: he can elevate the doubtful basis of liberalism to an area of "prophetic" and revealed insight where it may be safe from discomforting experience in the world and criticism at the hands of reason. If there is a cost for the liberal, that his utopia is placed beyond the possibility of complete attainment, then that cost is small considering the added security of his cherished beliefs. For liberals have come to doubt the possibility of that utopia themselves, and Niebuhr's teaching leaves them the chance to approach ever more closely that undefined set of "limits" which he postulates. To the "vague universalism" of liberalism he has added a "vague utopianism" which is both more vague and more secure by being beyond argument in the sphere of faith. His "realism," his repeated attacks on "utopians," and his rhetoric of "metaphysical pathos" merely enable him to avoid a discussion or clarification of the goals which he believes a man or a state should pursue. Niebuhr notes that the moral issue is persistently raised because men "cannot follow their interest without claiming to do so in obedience to some general scheme of values."[76] But what such a comment overlooks is that men cannot know what their "interest" *is* without reference to some scheme of values. "Interest" is, after all, a term without intrinsic meaning. That Niebuhr, like so many American writers, can use it as though it had such a meaning merely reflects the American "liberal tradition," a connected set of beliefs regarding human nature and moral values which are not discussed at all. He approaches the issues from a curious stance because "realism" is not only a statement of what is practical; when supplemented by a knowledge of man's "free spirit" it is also a statement of what is desirable. The social good is one which "works" for him as for the liberals, because that good is power over nature, the power to "predict and control" the world. The problem of the ends toward which control should strive may be ignored: control is itself the end. For Niebuhr the free man is in essence the good man; virtue follows automatically from freedom. Man's imperfections arise from his involvement in nature—an inevitable involvement, to be sure, but one rooted in lack of power and not of virtue in the classical sense.

Plato and Aristotle, Niebuhr argues, believed the *polis* to be the "final form" of the state. They believed that the small state was the best for man because they distrusted the expansionist urge and its consequent imperialism. They did not claim, as Niebuhr seems to believe, that the *polis* would always endure. His contention that the empires which succeeded the city-state sacrificed order and community for domination would seem to support their view.[77] But the classical theorists were less concerned than Niebuhr with predicting history or with what form of state "works best," preferring to defer such questions until it became clear what form of state *is* best and forms the standard of human aspiration.

Niebuhr, the liberals, and many social scientists have excoriated "utopians." But they did not thereby avoid having a utopia. They simply avoided discussing it. And that lack of discussion conceals the fact that they identify ideality with practicality, and virtue with necessity, what works with what is right. If man in our times feels a "prisoner of forces" outside himself, it is often because he has abdicated to those forces the eternal responsibilities to articulate a vision of what is best. The very bankruptcy of Niebuhr's ideas, his inability to offer a new vision even at a time when, by his showing, the old ideas have proved themselves false, may have a function. That bankruptcy may provide us with the courage, as we already have the opportunity, to resume from history and necessity the old quest to discover by reason the nature of the good life, of virtue, and of Utopia.

Notes

This essay was originally published as "Reinhold Niebuhr: New Orthodoxy for Old Liberalism," *American Political Science Review* 56, no. 4 (1962).

1. In referring to Niebuhr's major works, I have adopted a system of abbreviations. Unless otherwise noted, the publisher is Scribner's, New York. BT =

Beyond Tragedy (1938); CLCD = *The Children of Light and the Children of Darkness* (1944); CPP = *Christianity and Power Politics* (1940); CRPP = *Christian Realism and Political Problems* (1953); DCR = *Does Civilization Need Religion?* (MacMillan, 1944; orig. 1927); FH = *Faith and History* (1949); HD = *The Nature and Destiny of Man*, vol. 2 (1951); HN = *The Nature and Destiny of Man*, vol. 1 (1951); IAH = *The Irony of American History* (1954); ICE = *An Interpretation of Christian Ethics* (Harper, 1935); MMIS = *Moral Man and Immoral Society* (1932); REE = *Reflections on the End of an Era* (1934); SDH = *The Self and the Dramas of History* (1955); SNE = *The Structure of Nations and Empires* (1959); SOT = *Discerning the Signs of the Times* (1946); WCAR = *The World Crisis and American Responsibility*, ed. E. Lefever (New York: Associated Press, 1958).

2. Paul Tillich has suggested that Niebuhr's major stylistic fault is an "overpredilection for paradox." "Niebuhr's Theory of Knowledge," in *Reinhold Niebuhr: His Religious, Social, and Political Thought*, ed. C. Kegley and R. Bretall (New York, 1956).

3. Critical writings about Niebuhr are almost as numerous as his own writings. Among the most useful are Kegley and Bretall, *Reinhold Niebuhr;* Kenneth W. Thompson, "Beyond the National Interest,"*Review of Politics* 17 (April 1955): 167–88 and "Toward a Theory of International Relations," *American Political Science Review* 49 (September 1955): 733–46; Levi Olan, "Reinhold Niebuhr and the Hebraic Spirit," *Judaism* 5 (Spring 1956): 1–15; N. P. Jacobson, "Reinhold Niebuhr's Philosophy of History," *Harvard Theological Review* 37 (October 1944): 237–68; also the sections on Niebuhr in Morton White, *Social Thought in America: The Revolt against Formalism* (Boston, 1956); and Charles Frankel, *The Case for Modern Man* (New York, 1956).

4. Louis Hartz, "The Coming of Age in America," *American Political Science Review* 51 (June 1957): 474–83.

5. Russel B. Nye, "The Search for the Individual, 1750-1850," *Centennial Review* 5 (Winter 1961): 1–20.

6. Geoffrey Clive, *The Romantic Enlightenment: Ambiguity and Paradox in the Western Mind, 1750–1920* (New York: Meridian Books, 1960), 19–38.

7. John H. Schaar, *Loyalty in America* (Berkeley and Los Angeles: University of California Press, 1957), 116–19.

8. SDH, 36, 222; WCAR, 11; IAH, ch. 6.

9. Olan, "Reinhold Niebuhr and the Hebraic Spirit," 2, 7.

10. SNE, 287–90, 298–99, 7; MMIS, 25; HN, 4, 11, 26–27, 48, 68, 125; HD, 95–96, 155, 240, 284, 308; SDH, 13–15, 23, 128; CLCD, 6, 49, 53–55, 187.

11. *Christianity and Crisis* 9 (Spring 1945): 7–8; IAH, 156–58; HN, 178–90, 249–50; BT, ch. 6; SOT, 68; SNE, 107, 287–88.

12. SNE, 40–41, 105–7, 289; thus man is said to be able to "deflect" history without changing its direction. The Baconian roots of the doctrine are evident: FH, 71–94; SOT, 65; CLCD, 154; MMIS, 29; IAH, 407, 71–77.

13. SNE, 133; CPP, 215; SDH, 109–11, 119.

14. SNE, 105–7, 291; CRPP, 127; REE, 205–31.

15. Even so friendly a critic as K. W. Thompson has found the relevance "not clear": "The Political Philosophy of Reinhold Niebuhr," in Kegley and Bretall, *Reinhold Niebuhr*, 169, and "Beyond the National Interest."

16. CPP, passim; IAH, 157; HD, 191–95, 233–34; FH, 27–28; SNE, 28–31, 298–99; "Peace and the Liberal Illusion," *Nation*, January 28, 1939, 117–19.

17. Norman Jacobson, "Political Realism in the Age of Reason: The Anti-rationalist Heritage in America," *Review of Politics* 15 (October 1953): 446–49.

18. FH, 34, 54, 71–83, 91, 123, 174, 180, 238–39; IAH, 130, 158; HD, 47, 85, 95–96, 155, 232; HN, 197, 281; SOT, 265; CRPP, 133; SNE, 291, 298–99; Kegley and Bretall, *Reinhold Niebuhr*, 435.

19. FH, 77, 174; HD, 48, 55, 281; CRPP, 3, 200–201; DCR, 26, 170–75, 218–19; SDH, 109, 229; ICE, 41–46, 114, 188; HN, 178, 281.

20. SNE, 59–61; HD, 249; SOT, 100; CLCD, 48–49, 118; IAH, 96–100.

21. Frankel, *Case for Modern Man*, describes Niebuhr's ethics as "masochism, not wisdom," for much this reason (115); MMIS, 257; CRPP, 159; CPP, 215; FH, 174–85; HN, 16, 48, 249.

22. Kenneth Keniston, "Alienation and the Decline of Utopia," *American Scholar* 29 (Spring 1960): 161–200.

23. SDH, 38–53; HD, 69, 144.

24. HN, 14, 178–90, 249–50, 260, 288–89; HD, 78, 149–51; IAH, 57, 84; SOT, 17, 21; CLCD, 79; SDH, 30–32, 169.

25. SOT, 101–3, 176, 181, 195–201; FH, 77; DCR, 19, 22, 126; MMIS, 170–75; HN, 22, 30–33, 77; SDH, 61; CPP, 139; ICE, 41, 52, 112, 194.

26. CRPP, 110, 132–35; CLCD, 19–21, 61; FH, 119, 134, 174; SDH, 31, 139; ICE, 21, 39, 41, 111, 206, 65; WCAR, 42; DCR, 152–53; HN, 178, 214, 281; BT, 292, 306.

27. SDH, 30–35, 139; SOT, 39; WCAR, 41–42; or "pragmatic" in IAH, passim.

28. HN, 141; FH, 94, 219; IAH, 30; SOT, 48, 65; MMIS, 2; CLCD, 154; Kegley and Betrall, *Reinhold Niebuhr*, 432, even to the shocking and Machiavellian statement "powerless goodness ends on the cross," which is clearly indicated as a stricture; SOT, 143; ICE, 237. For a description of the concept of liberty as power, see Bertrand de Jouvenal, *Sovereignty* (University of Chicago Press, 1957), 248–75.

29. John Locke, *Second Treatise on Civil Government*, ch. vii, 93; HN, 101; SOT, 101–5; CPP, 15, 42–43, 93; SDH, 14–15, 229.

30. "The Moral Issue in International Relations," cited in Thompson, "Toward a Theory of International Relations," 742.

31. SNE, 50–51, 40–41.

32. Richard Cox, *Locke on War and Peace* (Oxford: Clarendon, 1960).

33. SNE, 50–51.

34. I am indebted for the reminder to Harvey Mansfield Jr., Harvard University; for further evidence, see Ralph Barton Perry, *Puritanism and Democracy* (New York, 1944), 14, in which Perry identifies Burke with the "fundamental philosophy of the Declaration of Independence."

35. Thus Hobbes: "It may, peradventure, be thought that there never was such

a time, nor condition of war as this; and I believe it was never generally so. . . . But though there had never been any time . . ." (*Leviathan*, bk. I, ch. 13).

36. CRPP, 91; SOT, 21, 25, 180; SDH, 17, 222; CPP, 63, 119; HN, 270; HD, 79, 310; CLCD, 53.

37. SDH, 10–11, 137, 235; SNE, 33, 50, introduction, 291; MMIS, passim; FH, 77, 96–97, 196, 219; HD, 79, 267–68, 310; SOT, 168.

38. SNE, 135–39, 108–12, 4, 146–63, 44–48, 51–50, 105.

39. SOT, 175–81; FH, 129, 219; SDH, 229; CPP, 104; CRPP, 155–58; HD, 310; HN, 270.

40. "The Moral Issue in International Relations," 742.

41. WCAR, 26; HD, 253–66; SDH, 198; CRPP, 134–35.

42. FH, 34, 128–29, 133, 227; CLCD, 118, 173–74; SDH, 38, 51, 71, 168, 196–98; ICE, 61, 88; 103–6, 117, 155–59, 189–91; REE, 246–47; CRPP, 31, 148–50; CPP, 19, 27, 29; SOT, 46, 68, 81, 134–35; IAH, 2, 84–85; HD, 277; MMIS, 29, 257.

43. BT, 140; HD, 252–58, 266; CPP, 104, 107; ICE, 60; MMIS, 22; IAH, 96–108; SDH, 38, 178, 198, 229.

44. "The Unity and Depth of Our Culture," *Sewanee Review* 3 (1944): 193; CLCD, 66; SOT, 177; SDH, 1; ICE, 122, 171.

45. SNE, 11–13, 105, 59–61, 291.

46. FH, 20–35, 54, 55, 69, 227; SNE, 297–98; HD, 47, 186, 287–92, 315, 320; SDH, 52; MMIS, 60–62; SOT, 48, 65; thus, Niebuhr retains the conviction that "time is on our side"—or at least he did in 1956: "A Qualified Faith," *New Republic*, February 13, 1956, 14–15. Equally illustrative is Niebuhr's conviction that historical "meaning" is a "necessary affirmation": HN, 4, 10, 240; FH, 114; BT, 5, 18.

47. CRPP, 1771; cf. FH, 214–32.

48. Kenneth Waltz, "Kant, Liberalism, and War," *American Political Science Review* 56 (June 1962): 331–40. Niebuhr's continuing belief in the virtue of "rising social forces" is connected to his earlier belief in the utility of catastrophe in advancing progress, and his continuing belief in the role of conflict. REE, passim; FH, 227; SDH, 151, 196; BT, ch. 2; CPP, 198; MMIS, 222; CLCD, 118.

49. N. P. Jacobson, "Reinhold Niebuhr's Philosophy of History," 265–66, 275. See also J. D. Bury, *The Idea of Progress* (New York: Dover, 1955), 21; and the brilliant analyses of Karl Löwith in Kegley and Bretall, *Reinhold Niebuhr*, 282–90, and *Meaning and History* (Chicago: Phoenix Books, 1950), 160–73.

50. CLCD, 66; SDH, 1; MMIS, xvii; ICE, 61, 122, 171; SOT, 177; "The Unity and Depth of Our Culture."

51. CRPP, 148–50; FH, 219; SOT, 81, 145; ICE, 147, 164, 171, 191, 209.

52. SNE, 34–35, 28, 59–65, 234–38, 291–94; CRPP, 91, 96, 148–50; CLCD, 1, 47–49, 118–20; HD, 194–95, 249, 254–58, 266–68; SDH, 38, 51, 178, 196, 198, 229; SOT, 100; IAH, 96–100, 108; ICE, 77–78.

53. FH, 71–94; CLCD, 154; IAH, 71; MMIS, 9; IAH, 18, 30, 95, 54–58; HN, 22, 57, 68.

54. "A Qualified Faith"; SNE, 61–65, 34–35, 294; IAH, passim.

55. For example, *The Federalist*, #1; see also Martin Diamond, "Democracy

and the *Federalist:* A Reconsideration of the Framers' Intent," *American Political Science Review* 53 (March 1959): 52–68.

56. Thus, to Niebuhr all communities are "imperialist" and oriented toward expansion. SDH, 137; SNE, 190–91; FH, 97; CPP, 18; HD, 89, 284–85; REE, 18, 26, 36, 53, 68, 157–58.

57. SNE, 22–27, 146–49, 201–16.

58. CLCD, 173; HD, 258, 266, 285.

59. *Christianity and Crisis,* May 4, 1958; SDH, 202–5, 208; IAH, 2, 18, 40, 77, 91, 97, 129, 133, 140–42; CLCD, 161, 172, 187; CPP, 125, 42, 15; CRPP, 31; WCAR, 85–104, 126; FH, 121, 129.

60. *Christianity and Crisis,* December 20, 1950; CPP, passim; SOT, 194; SDH, 213; CRPP, 136.

61. SNE, 36, 239, 259, 193, 105–7.

62. Michael Oakeshott, "Scientific Politics," *Cambridge Journal* 1 (March 1948): 347–58; Arnold Wolfers, "The Pole of Power and the Pole of Indifference," *World Politics* 4 (October 1951): 39–65.

63. SNE, ch. 16, 190–91, 282–90; MMIS, 2, 142, 176; REE, 91, 99; IAH, 10; SDH, 36, 222.

64. SNE, 31–32.

65. Ibid., 278–79, 25–27.

66. CPP, ch. 1; SNE, ch. 16.

67. HD, 245–46, 85, 95–96; CLCD, 48–49.

68. Kenneth Benne, "The Uses of Fraternity," *Daedalus* 90 (Spring 1961): 233–46.

69. Benjamin Nelson, *The Idea of Usury: From Tribal Brotherhood to Universal Otherhood* (Princeton, 1949).

70. IAH, 108; BT, ch. 3; SDH, 195–200; DCR, 85, 175; "Liberalism: Illusions and Realities," *New Republic,* July 4, 1955, 11–13; "Liberals and the Marxist Heresy," *New Republic,* October 12, 1953, 13–15. For the same problem in early liberalism, see E. Halevy, *The Growth of Philosophic Radicalism* (Boston, 1955).

71. SNE, 28, 66–88, 256, 266, 289; CRPP, ch. 2.

72. SNE, 279.

73. Ibid., 280–83, 236–38, 276–77, 246–55.

74. Hans J. Morgenthau, "Machiavellian Utopia," *Ethics* 55 (January 1945): 145–48; Allan Bloom, "Cosmopolitan Man and the Political Community: An Interpretation of Othello," *American Political Science Review* 54 (March 1960): 130–57; or Michael Polanyi's recently published pamphlet, *Beyond Nihilism.* A brilliant and closely related discussion is John F. R. Taylor's "Politics and the Human Covenant," *Centennial Review* 6 (Winter 1962): 1–18.

75. "Religion, Politics, and the Higher Learning," *Confluence* 3 (1954): 402–12.

76. "The Moral Issue in International Relations," 740.

77. SNE, 42–43, 288.

Community and Its Discontents

On Amitai Etzioni and the Future of Communitarianism

The founder of a significant movement and an important presence in U.S. public life, Amitai Etzioni exemplifies political engagement, but he looks beyond the barricades, seeking first principles and things that endure. It is no surprise, consequently, that his argument for a "community of communities," while thoroughly contemporary, also stands in a grand U.S. tradition, linked to Randolph Bourne's hope for a "trans-national America" and Josiah Royce's precept "Be loyal to loyalty" as well as to that founding mystery, *E pluribus unum*.[1] And as a critic, Etzioni is admirable in recognizing and confronting the shortcomings of intellectual fashion, even among his sometime allies.

The recent political vogue accents America's plurality, with calls for "multiculturalism" echoed, in a somewhat distorted way, by postmodernist suspicions of the universal. But while Aristotle warned against trying to reduce the sounds of political society to a mere unison, he knew that harmony requires an even more complicated discipline.[2] In itself, diversity is often only the occasion for domination, following the old maxim *Divide et impera,* or for civil strife—witness Yugoslavia, where the collapse of communist hegemony has led to competing ethnic cleansings. It is pretty generally recognized that in any political society, some institutions must reliably prevail in cases of conflict, "or else," John Locke noted, "it is impossible it should act or continue one body," *one community*.[3] Yet Locke appealed to the natural rule of majorities—or, more precisely, to their "greater force"—and majorities can repress or tyrannize, just as a political society can include a variety of peoples while maintaining that some are naturally superior to others, or at least entitled to rule.[4] Etzioni goes a step further in realizing that a "community of communities," like a mosaic, must be *framed* and *glued*, that is to say, that it requires both institutions and attachments, norms as well as procedures. His good society is not morally neutral; it depends on a fairly substantial creed.

An inclusive democracy—especially one that, like America in G. K. Chesterton's describing, seeks to make a nation "literally out of any old nation that comes along"—is accepting, paradoxically, because it is judgmental.[5] Democratic inclusiveness, as Abraham Lincoln taught us, is dedicated to equality as a ruling norm, a principle that, while it embraces all communities, denies that any of them is entitled to public rank. Equality, as Etzioni understands, welcomes diversity because, more or less gently, it deprecates all cultures and particularities. In the mirror of equality, all differences are mere varieties and accidents, frequently delightful and ordinarily valuable, but subordinate to what is humanly natural and common. In Etzioni's vision, as in Royce's, the customs and creeds of the communities must, in the last analysis, yield precedence to the hope of the Great Community.[6] Etzioni's prescription is attractive, and he makes his case with force and erudition. Still, I will be arguing that Etzioni understates the elements in American life that work against a "community of communities" and the extent to which, in the United States, politics both contributes to the problem of community and is indispensable to any possible solution. It is hardly a secret, after all, that our political culture, the cornerstone of our commonality, is pervaded by a devotion to individual liberty that views community with suspicion, if not hostility. And to overcome that bias, so deeply planted in our institutions and habits, we will need not only public deliberation—Etzioni's "megalogues"— but also authoritative policy: in Etzioni's metaphor, because the frame of our political mosaic is loose, we need stronger glue.[7] As Alexis de Tocqueville suggested, democratic politics offers the best antidote to the disorders of democratic culture.[8]

To be sure, the U.S. tradition includes a deeply rooted communitarian strain best articulated in biblical religion. In the high versions of that teaching, communities exist to nurture the human capacity for love, coaxing the human soul out of "timid and suspicious privacy" toward a truer understanding of human nature.[9] Human individuals are not independent or separate, but parts of wholes—families, polities, and nature or creation—on whom common goods have rightful claims. In the same spirit, those teachings speak easily of equality, since our commonalities make us all one and all accountable to the same standard; in this version of equality, however, it is much easier to enunciate duties than rights.[10] Those cadences still reverberate in the United States, but the echoes are growing fainter, and for most Americans, the language of strong communitarianism is articulated with difficulty, if at all.[11] In fact, a large part of Etzioni's work, and that of the communitarian movement in general, consists in the effort to bring that old idiom back into civic speech.

At the moment, however, the terms of public debate are defined, with very little challenge, by an individualism premised on our bodily separateness and spiritual uniqueness, and hence on our title to liberty. In this account, we are equal, as Locke taught, chiefly in being free from obligations to others, or from any claim on them beyond the recognition of our own individual rights.[12] Long familiarity, together with new teachers and new times, has exaggerated or amplified the original bases of this persuasion, and great numbers of Americans would agree with Ralph Waldo Emerson's then-startling saying, "Nothing is at last sacred but the integrity of our own mind. . . . Expect me not to shew cause why I seek or why I exclude company. Then again, do not tell me, as a good man did today, of my obligation to put all poor men in good situations. Are they *my* poor? I tell thee, thou foolish philanthropist, that I grudge the dollar, the dime, the cent I give to such men as do not belong to me, and to whom I do not belong."[13]

Political society, in this view, is created as a matter of utility for the better fulfillment of private purposes, chiefly material well-being—"a joint-stock company," Emerson said, "in which the members agree, for the better securing of his bread to each shareholder, to surrender the liberty and culture of the eater."[14] Hence political institutions aim at more bread, more securely guaranteed, at economic growth and the dominion over nature; government is the creation of human beings who themselves seek mastery. The liberty human beings cherish, in this understanding, is the freedom to pursue private ends, unencumbered by limits and duties, liberty *from* community.

Of course, Americans have always thought and felt other, more generous, ideas and impulses, but at least as early as Tocqueville's time, individualist doctrine was regnant in public speech. "Americans . . . are fond of explaining almost all their lives by the principle of self-interest rightly understood. . . . In this respect, I think they frequently fail to do themselves justice; for in the United States as well as elsewhere, people are sometimes seen to give way to those disinterested and spontaneous impulses that are natural to man; but the Americans seldom admit that they yield to emotions of this kind; they are more anxious to do honor to their philosophy than to themselves."[15] As Tocqueville knew, what begins as a somewhat disingenuous habit of rhetoric becomes, across the generations, a basis for self-understanding.

This is especially true because the Constitution—the frame of Etzioni's mosaic—has at best an ambivalent relation to community. It was designed, James Madison tells us, on the principle that government exists not to produce virtue or public spirit but to protect "the diversity in the faculties of men."[16] Traditionally, democracy had been associated with an open politics in a relatively closed and small society, as in Tocqueville's description of America's roots in Puritan New England: "In the moral world everything is classified, systematized, foreseen and decided beforehand; in the political world everything is agitated, disputed and uncertain. In the one is a passive though a voluntary obedience; in the other, an independence scornful of experience and jealous of all authority. These two tendencies, apparently so discrepant, are far from conflicting; they advance together and support each other."[17] Diverse peoples in large states had been thought to require monarchy, with the unity of the state substituting for moral coherence or love for the community as a whole.[18] By contrast, the U.S. founders linked popular government to a radically *open* society within a relatively *closed* politics, multiplying diverse communities in order to subordinate them and to undermine their authority in the interest of republican laws and personal liberty.[19] Hence Madison's celebrated argument, making a desideratum out of the greatest variety of groups and factions possible within the Constitution's forms.[20] That plurality allows for the uniting of government's goal, liberty, with the just basis of its power, majority rule: making rule by any one faction or community difficult or impossible, it also weakens the hold of such groups on the allegiances and affections of individuals.

The framers expected national allegiance to be a relatively "diffuse" sentiment, lacking the strong positive attachments characteristic of more intimate and coherent communities and less able, under ordinary circumstances, to subordinate individual interests to common endeavors.[21] Most of them reckoned this limitation as a virtue: champions of a rather prosaic liberty, they were wary of heroic politics. But they did think that the national regime would be effective *negatively,* by offering rights and opportunities that would detach individuals from state and local loyalties, especially by limiting—potentially, in very severe ways—local power to regulate the commercial economy. The Pennsylvania Anti-Federalist John Smilie had it right when he declared that if the people "find their governments . . . divested of the means to promote their welfare and interests, they will not . . . vainly idolize a shadow."[22] And the existence of federal rights, courts, and authorities, of course, was bound to encourage an appeal by discontented individuals or subgroups from the local community to the national government: as all communitarians know, one cannot speak in favor of community to a contemporary audience without evoking specters of local repression—particularly racial—and reminders of the federal government's role as a defender of individual and civil rights.

In fact, the Constitution today is in crucial ways less favorable to diversity than it was at the time of the founding. Originally, after all, the Constitution accommodated the culture of slavery and it allowed the states to establish churches, while the Bill of Rights did not apply to, or limit the varieties of, state government and politics.

As Etzioni notes, by establishing a national citizenship, the Fourteenth Amendment made states and local communities subject to new restraints, in the spirit of Lincoln's redefinition of the republic as "dedicated" to equality, that high communitarian norm. Of course, for the better part of a century, the Reconstruction amendments were largely ignored or distorted, treated as compatible with Jim Crow and a politics for whites only. But the amendments are also a striking instance of the power of constitutional forms, which—by requiring a deference to principles—affirm standards. If a form "cannot guarantee the result it wants," Harvey Mansfield writes, "it can indicate the direction toward which it wants to go, and thus become the cause of going if not getting there."[23] Gradually, if too slowly, the national norms proclaimed by the amendments have come to govern states and localities and, via civil rights legislation, wide areas of civil society.

Etzioni, in fact, testifies to the success of the framers' design of effacing local authority. His discussion of the ongoing "megalogue" regarding the Bill of Rights is cast in terms of a tension between our "national normative stance" and the rituals and values of "particular communities," in which "the community" refers to religio/ethnic collectivities (the Native American Church, followers of Santería, and hypothetical advocates of female circumcision) but *not* to the local regimes that are attempting to regulate them.[24] Etzioni's analysis seems to presume that states and localities have authority only when they reflect national norms (and not even then, when, as in the case of Santería, the national value—the protection of animals—seems weak when set against the right to practice one's religion). In every other case, Etzioni implicitly discounts state and local claims. Ironically, Etzioni's definition of "constituting communities" within the "community of communities" appears to exclude the only subgroups—the states—that are actually recognized in the Constitution. That stance, John Smilie would surely have argued, is quite consistent with the framers' long-term intent.

Moreover, the Constitution's distrust of subcommunities does not stop with the states. While Etzioni describes the Supreme Court as assessing the place of *community values* within the nation as a whole, the Court itself speaks of *individual rights,* in terms of the claims of persons rather than those of congregations and communities. So it must, since the Constitution acknowledges such rights, but—states aside—speaks of communities not at all, and is virtually silent on the question of any duties beyond the "obligation of contracts."[25] Implicitly, Etzioni attempts to minimize this by contending that the Court's arguments, while "couched in legal terms," are in practice dealing with conflicts between communities, and in a sense he is right. Tocqueville reminds us, however, that the laws—our most authoritative public speech—tend, over the long term, to shape the way we talk about public things and personal duties, just as they exert a powerful influence on the habits of the heart.

The founding generation knew that republics depend on an element of virtue—self-preservation will not move citizens to risk their lives in the country's defense, and self-interest will not lead them to see contracts as sacred and liberties as beyond price—and they expected families and churches to provide the fundamentals of moral education. Consequently, the Constitution leaves considerable room for communities in private life, and even values them, up to a point.[26] But it does so silently and interstitially: in its dominant teaching, the Constitution speaks emphatically in the language of individual rights and liberties.[27]

To borrow Albert Hirschman's terms, in any contest between individuals and a community, if the persons involved are not content simply to be loyal, it is almost always difficult to find a voice—to make a case for change in the community—that has a realistic chance of being effective.[28] Political organization takes time and requires resources; imposing costs and risks, it offers no guarantee of success. Having a personal voice on any but the most local or intimate matters is likely to be impossible: in any reasonably large association or public, only a few of us can speak and most of us will have to content ourselves with being spoken for.[29] That principle surely applies to Etzioni's megalogues and promises to weaken any sense of moral obligation that might grow out of them.

By contrast, U.S. institutions proliferate opportunities to exit—to leave or resign from community, moving oneself or one's resources—with little need to consult others and in ways that get relatively quick results, although not always the results we want. That encouragement to exit, almost inevitably, thins all communities, including the nation as a whole, in the name of liberty. As Lewis Lapham writes, "A man can feel shame before an audience of his peers, within the narrow precincts of neighborhood, profession, army unit, social set, city room, congregation or football team. The scale and dynamism of American democracy grants the ceaselessly renewable option of moving one's conscience into a more congenial street."[30]

Alarm at the rise of the "unencumbered self," combined with the prevailing distrust of the state, defines the enthusiasm for "civil society" that is one of Etzioni's starting points.[31] The strongest voices among U.S. public intellectuals, for all their variety, tend to unite in appreciating the alternative, more communitarian modes and orders preserved in families, churches, localities, and associations.[32] That disposition, too, has found confirmation and encouragement in resistance to Marxist-Leninist totalitarianism in Eastern Europe. But while civil society has its subsidiary autonomy, it remains decisively *civil*, affected by the subtle disciplines of political society. In fact, the subtext of the eulogy for civil society is lament.

In 1927, John Dewey was already writing that, while community had once been relatively autonomous, relying primarily on economic and social sanctions—so that the state was "hardly more than a shadow" on the life of society—its affairs were now "conditioned by remote and invisible organizations."[33] In our times, communities are defending their last bastions: their cultures, relationships, and ways of life are being reshaped, if not shattered, by markets and technologies, mobility and the media.[34]

Everyday experience testifies that communities are pervaded and reformed by an increasingly global economy. Jobs move or disappear; local banks and retailers give way to corporate giants; the homey practice of the family physician is impinged on by the cost-cutting imperatives of the HMO. Businesses, less and less tied to locality, use threats to relocate or downsize as economic blackmail, and local governments, even with the best intentions, seem reduced to hat-in-hand or beggar-my-neighbor politics.[35]

Culturally, communities find outsiders even in their sanctuaries. Socialization in families and neighborhoods once preceded any influence from the media: reading required schooling, even radio largely presumed speech, and for children, access to movies—shown in public settings—was controlled by adults. By contrast, television enters the home as a presence in socialization before reading and even before speech, challenging if not displacing the curricula of communities.[36]

Our local relationships matter less, and our ties to distant others more. These remote connections, however, are too abstract, specialized, and impersonal to constitute anything but the thinnest sort of community. They are more effective than affective, separating us from what is close without binding us to what is far.[37] In our rhetoric and experience, community is increasingly associated with the trapped. The successful "secede," as Robert Reich observes, but they do not reconfederate: their symbol is the modish suburban house without sidewalks, drawn back from the streets, cherishing private spaces, and visibly minimizing any tie to a common life.[38]

Etzioni's insistence on inclusiveness—its philosophic force aside—reflects the extent to which other peoples, institutions, and nations have become part of our *immediate* world, so that parochialism is disabling and supremely impractical. Yet while it makes sense to ask Americans to learn more about other cultures, it has to be recognized that doing so leaves less time to devote to the dominant culture, or to any culture we think of as our own. Human time is limited, and, all things being equal, extending breadth implies a loss of depth. In fact, the ordinary course in "comparative world cultures," when it avoids the excesses of identity politics, is very likely to be a superficial, celebratory travelogue, its language shaped by relativism.[39] In practice, in other words, the danger is that Etzioni's "principle of respect" for the cultures of others—which presumes a knowledge of the things that *deserve* to be respected—will take second place to an exit from any serious engagement with our own.

Community, after all, draws strength from habit and memory, from the expected continuity of past and future.[40] For us, by contrast, virtually exponential transformations have become almost routine, making the past less relevant, the present less comprehensible, and the future less predictable. Aware of the risks, we are apt to be more guarded in our commitments to places, persons, or beliefs.[41]

The great majority of us know that our communities do not have the political resources to govern economic and social life effectively. In the first place, communities suffer from a constitutional disability: the regulation of the commercial economy, like the conduct of foreign affairs, belongs to the federal sphere. Any serious attempt to deal with those shaping forces requires a turn to *national* authority (and these days, more and more Americans fear or are convinced that even federal power, in practice, may prove to be inadequate). Localities depend on grants of power and money from state or federal governments; even "devolution," that conservative nostrum, is tied to federal block grants. And with very few exceptions, communities across the board make pilgrimages to state capitals and to Washington, seeking subsidies or vouchers or laws to enforce moral norms and duties. In crucial areas of policy, local leadership is less engaged in governing than in representing and lobbying for the community at higher levels.[42]

The communities, in other words, need the community. Politics cannot do everything for communities, but it can be a deadly enemy or an invaluable ally. For all their variety, communities are being led, by the logic of U.S. life, to ask government, and particularly the national government, to give their distinctive goods—home, family, culture, and stable relationships generally—status as public goals and interests.

At the moment, public policy leans to the other side. As it should, government accepts a duty to protect outsiders, especially racial minorities, who buy into ethnic neighborhoods. By intervening, however, government does more than protect the rights of individuals: it sides with the market and with change, emphasizing the mutability of relationships and values. Confirming fears that loyalty is futile and that voice is ineffective, it reinforces the impulse to exit, a dynamic evident across the urban United States. Government could balance the scales, giving some support to community stability—for example, by offering property tax reductions to long-term residents. Policies of this sort involve economic costs, of course, but a willingness to pay that piper is a ground of Etzioni's *New Golden Rule:* our first principle ought to be democratic self-government, not economic gain, and to that end, civil order and community are worth a high price.

Of course, some communities are not worth supporting—the Jim Crow South is the inevitable example—and even admirable ones may have indefensible practices. All communities, moreover, constrain individuals, although they regard their discipline as protecting members against temptation and self-betrayal, while pointing them toward the good life.[43] The "French-only" regulations in Quebec are efforts to protect that language—and the culture associated with it—against the greater material rewards of speaking English. For similar reasons, communities may raise the walls of exclusivity, separating insiders from outsiders, as in taboos on intermarriage. But while there is sometimes a good case for such restrictions—and more often, reason for sympathy—it is also true that communities can exaggerate both the extent of their unity and its value. Etzioni is right to observe that the partisans of "identity politics" tend to treat groups as monolithic, underrating their internal differences and the ways in which individual members are linked to people and things outside. It is a major virtue of Etzioni's argument that he recognizes the need for, and does a creditable job of discovering, moral standards by which the claims of community can be judged and limited.[44]

In the contemporary United States, however, repression is a much smaller danger to democratic liberty than fragmentation, privatization, and the conviction that collective action is hopeless. Linked by law—especially given the virtual incorporation of the Bill of Rights into the Fourteenth Amendment—and by the market forces associated with it, local communities are relatively open societies, often to the regret of their members. Meanwhile, the diversity of the nation as a whole is increasing in startling ways: even Madison might be taken aback by the incoherence of present-day majorities. The scale of life and the pace of change, moreover, leave increasing numbers of Americans baffled and feeling powerless, in a situation that is broadly paranoid. The opinion that economics and technology are fundamentally ungovernable is paralleled, among a substantial fraction of the public, by the conviction that our lives are being scripted by hidden powers and conspiracies. And there is something like a common denominator in the wish—reflected in movies like *Independence Day*—for someone to "take charge," even at great cost. Too many Americans "hate politics" because they have lost faith in democratic institutions and forms.[45]

Etzioni is right to urge policies designed to strengthen our sense of national community. As he argues, we need to teach a history that includes all of America's voices, with all their continuing discords, but also develops an ear for commonalities, especially that American leitmotiv, the doctrine of equality.

Similarly, there is a strong case to be made for an extended—ideally, universal—form of national service that, more utilitarian benefits aside, would affirm the proposition that every citizen has the duty and the right to contribute to the common life.

Ultimately, however, any hopes for a "community of communities" depend on organized public support and hence on a revitalized democratic politics, particularly the kind of "megalogues" in which all communities can press their claims through civil speech and majority votes—and which, at the highest level, presume that we know how to be spoken *for*.[46]

In practice, however, Americans are becoming less likely to learn civil speech and the "arts of association."[47] Technological change, particularly, poses a problem for democratic community. It may challenge the position of old elites, but it also creates new ones, drawing a sharp distinction between those who have mastered the latest innovation and those who have not. And by the time the laggards learn the new skills, those skills are likely to have become relatively obsolete.[48] Adding to the difficulty, the local forums that served Tocqueville's America as the common schools of citizenship have been attenuating in favor of national media that speak in sound bites to a passive audience that resists chiefly by inattention.[49] Moreover, as Etzioni notes, despite the hopes of various enthusiasts, the prospects for electronic community are severely limited. John Dewey came very close to the political truth of the matter when he wrote that "the local is the ultimate universal, and as near to an absolute as exists."[50] The body remains stubbornly physical, and the bonds people form in "virtual reality" lack the erotic dimension and the qualities of special place and occasion that Tocqueville associated with the "power of meeting."[51] These shortcomings are most evident in electronic politics, which can enable us to *vote* easily enough, but cannot overcome the time constraints that make it impossible for any more than a tiny fraction of the citizenry to *speak* to any significant part of the electorate. The new media do allow minorities to overcome pluralistic ignorance and find like-minded others. Yet while this heartens some bands of angels, it emboldens at least as many demons, without fundamentally assuaging their feelings of indignity and resentment.[52] In fact, more and more associations dealing with public affairs are centralized, largely self-directed bureaucracies that relate to their supporters almost solely through fundraising, so that "membership" is reduced to the choice of whether to donate and how much. Needing the arts of politics more, communities are less likely to have mastered them.

Education can help: public policy should be urging schools to teach civil speech, particularly the techniques and implicit ethics of deliberation to be found in *Robert's Rules of Order* and the arts of rhetoric and hearing that allowed leaders, at one time, to speak to the larger public and for their own communities. In the end, however, the prospects for a community of communities depend on a rebuilding of local political institutions, where participation can have an effect on the immediate lives of citizens, linking voice to power.

Limiting the weight of money in campaigns, of course, is also an imperative in any attempt to restore confidence in the democratic process. Ordinary citizens, particularly those at the lower end of the income scale, are right to suspect that monumental spending and the corresponding fixation on fund-raising come close to rigging the game against them.[53] Ideally, the Court would reverse its opinion in *Buckley v. Valeo,* which held that donations of money are the equivalent of speech, entitled to the protection of the First Amendment.[54] Yet even within those terms, it may be possible to restrict campaign expenditures on electronic media—by banning paid political advertising on television, for example—and redirecting spending into "retail" campaigns that are more local and face-to-face.

Similarly, among the institutions of democratic civil society, political party organizations have a compelling claim to support. Historically, party organizations, rooted in precincts and wards, linked communities—by a chain of personal relationships, memories, and affections— to higher levels of government.[55] If their concerns, like those of human beings, were often petty or sordid, they developed allegiance and reciprocity, crucial "social capital" for a community of communities.[56] In this century, of course, party organizations have been damaged by a series of "reforms," like the direct primary and the evisceration of patronage, which have had the ironic effect of strengthening the hand of money and organized interests relative to ordinary citizens and communities.[57] And while national party committees have been growing stronger in recent decades, they epitomize the fund-raising bureaucracies of centralized, media-dominated politics. When Congress exempted money used for "party-building activities" from federal contribution and spending limits, it left parties free to use the bulk of such "soft money" in media advertising, and rather ingeniously, the parties have done just that.[58] The scandals associated with the scramble for such funds have inspired a contradictory set of proposals for reform that, promising little, have so far come to nothing. From a communitarian viewpoint, it would make good sense to limit the amount or percentage of such funds that can be spent on the electronic media, pointing such monies toward the rebuilding of party organizations, especially at the local level.

Etzioni is right, however, to recognize that the possibilities for reform or reconstruction rest, finally, on moral foundations. In critical ways, civil society and democratic politics are "inefficient": relying on deliberation, they are ordinarily slower to decide and more amateurish than technicians and elites; they are likely to begin with perspectives that are shortsighted and parochial; most important, they may incline to make stability a rival of productivity in the scales of value. But to the extent that they respect the dignities of their members, such communities are more apt to *be* respected.[59] Formal authority has a stronger basis in personal commitments, so that collective judgments, when arrived at, speak with moral force.[60] Citizenship, a mutuality in governance, is an example of the Golden Rule, not the least admirable, and an excellence essential to Etzioni's high vision.

Notes

This essay was originally published as "Community and Its Discontents: Politics and Etzioni's *The New Golden Rule*," in *Autonomy and Order: A Communitarian Anthology*, ed. Edward Lehman (Lanham, Md.: Rowman and Littlefield, 2000).

1. Randolph Bourne, "Trans-National America," *Atlantic Monthly*, July 1916, 86–97; Josiah Royce, *The Philosophy of Loyalty* (New York: Macmillan, 1908).

2. Aristotle, *Politics*, 1261a18–b17; on the contemporary modes, see Sheldon S. Wolin, "Democracy, Difference and Re-cognition," *Political Theory* 21 (1993): 466, 481.

3. John Locke, *Second Treatise on Civil Government*, sec. 96.

4. The Old South is the obvious U.S. case. For a forceful statement of the problem, see Genesis 26:12–16.

5. G. K. Chesterton, *What I Saw in America* (New York: Dodd, Mead, 1922), 14.

6. Josiah Royce, *The Hope of the Great Community* (New York: Macmillan, 1916); see also John Dewey, "The Search for the Great Community," in John Dewey, *The Public and Its Problems* (New York: Holt, 1927), 143–84. Terry Ball argues that identity politics offers a place to "begin or stand," but not a place to "stay." *Reappraising Political Theory* (New York: Oxford University Press, 1995), 296.

7. On the limits of deliberation, see Amitai Etzioni, *The New Golden Rule: Community and Morality in a Democratic Society* (New York: Basic Books, 1996), 97–101.

8. Alexis de Tocqueville, *Democracy in America* (New York: Knopf, 1980), 2:105, 115.

9. Mark Twain, *A Connecticut Yankee in King Arthur's Court* (Berkeley: University of California Press, 1979), 300.

10. For example, see Galatians 3:28–29.

11. Robert Bellah et al., *Habits of the Heart* (Berkeley: University of California Press, 1985).

12. Locke, *Second Treatise*, sec. 54.

13. Ralph Waldo Emerson, "Self-Reliance," in *Emerson's Essays*, ed. Sherman Paul (New York: Dutton, 1976), 33–34.

14. Emerson, *Emerson's Essays,* 32.

15. Tocqueville, *Democracy in America,* 2:122.

16. James Madison, *The Federalist,* #10.

17. Tocqueville, *Democracy in America,* 1:43–44.

18. Montesquieu, *The Spirit of the Laws,* bk. III, chs. 5 and 6.

19. See my "Democratic Multiculturalism," in *Multiculturalism and American Democracy,* ed. Arthur Melzer et al. (Lawrence: University Press of Kansas, 1998), 120–29.

20. Madison wrote that "notwithstanding the contrary opinions which have been entertained, the larger the society, provided it be within a practicable sphere, the more duly capable it will be of self-government." *The Federalist,* #51.

21. James Madison, *The Federalist,* #17.

22. John Bach McMaster and Frederick Stone, eds., *Pennsylvania and the Federal Constitution, 1787–1788* (Philadelphia: Pennsylvania Historical Society, 1888), 270–71. As David Pearson writes, communities "are necessarily, indeed by definition, coercive as well as moral, threatening their members with the stick of sanctions if they stray, offering them the carrot of certainty and stability if they don't." "Community and Sociology," *Society,* July/August 1995, 47.

23. Harvey C. Mansfield, *America's Constitutional Soul* (Baltimore: Johns Hopkins University Press, 1991), 12.

24. Etzioni, *The New Golden Rule,* 200–202.

25. Art. I, sec. 10.

26. In *Wisconsin v. Yoder,* 406 U.S. 205 (1972), the Court appreciated the private virtues of the Old Order Amish. On the limitations of this principle, however, see *U.S. v. Lee,* 455 U.S. 252 (1982).

27. See my comments in the introduction to *The Constitution of the People,* ed. Robert E. Calvert (Lawrence: University Press of Kansas, 1991), 7–8. This is true even where the framers pretty clearly intended otherwise. The Second Amendment, for example, is concerned with the common defense, asserting that a free state must be defended, primarily, by a popular military. It thus implicitly enunciates an obligation to serve in a militia whose arming and discipline are subject to congressional regulation (art. I, sec. 8). But in public debate, this tends to be reduced to a putative personal "right to keep and bear arms."

28. Here and in what follows, I borrow terms from Albert Hirschman, *Exit, Voice and Loyalty* (Cambridge, Mass.: Harvard University Press, 1970).

29. Bertrand de Jouvenal, "The Chairman's Problem," *American Political Science Review* 55 (1961): 368–72.

30. Lewis Lapham, "Supply-Side Ethics," *Harper's,* May 1985, 11.

31. Michael Sandel, "The Procedural Republic and the Unencumbered Self," in *The Self and the Political Order,* ed. Tracy B. Strong (New York: New York University Press, 1992), 79–94.

32. For example, Robert D. Putnam, *Making Democracy Work: Civic Traditions in Modern Italy* (Princeton: Princeton University Press, 1993); or Jean

Bethke Elshtain, "In Common Together: Unity, Diversity and Civic Virtue," in Calvert, *The Constitution of the People*, 64–82.

33. Dewey, *The Public and Its Problems*, 41, 98.

34. Robert D. Putnam, "Bowling Alone, Revisited," *Responsive Community* 5 (Spring 1995): 18–33.

35. For an anticipation of the contemporary problem, see Charles Beard, *The Open Door at Home* (New York: Macmillan, 1934), 78–79.

36. Robert D. Putnam, "Tuning In, Tuning Out: The Strange Disappearance of Social Capital in America," *PS* 28 (1995): 664–83.

37. See Dewey, *The Public and Its Problems*, 126–27.

38. Robert Reich, "The Secession of the Successful," *New York Times Magazine*, January 20, 1991, 16ff.; see also Richard Thomas, "From Porch to Patio," *Palimpsest*, August 1975, 120–27. This is true even of those forms that attempt to pass as communities. Evan McKenzie, *Privatopia* (New Haven: Yale University Press, 1994).

39. Arthur Metter, "Tolerance 101," *New Republic*, July 1, 1991, 11.

40. Sheldon S. Wolin, *The Presence of the Past* (Baltimore: Johns Hopkins University Press, 1989); Dewey, *The Public and Its Problems*, 140–41.

41. Norval Glenn, "Social Trends in the United States," *Public Opinion Quarterly* 51 (1987): S109–S126.

42. Wolin, *Presence of the Past*, 191.

43. Pearson, "Community and Sociology," n. 22.

44. Ronald Beiner, *What's the Matter with Liberalism?* (Berkeley: University of California Press, 1992), 28–29.

45. E. J. Dionne Jr., *Why Americans Hate Politics* (New York: Simon and Schuster, 1991).

46. Brutus, essay in the *New York Journal* (October 18, 1787), in *The Complete Anti-Federalist*, ed. Herbert Storing (Chicago: University of Chicago Press, 1981), 1:370–71; Stanley Cavell writes that "the alternative to speaking for yourself politically is not speaking for yourself privately. . . . The alternative is having nothing to say. . . . If I am to have my own voice . . . I must be speaking for others and allow others to speak for me." *The Claim of Reason* (Oxford: Oxford University Press, 1979), 28. Tocqueville, *Democracy in America*, 2:110.

47. Tocqueville, *Democracy in America*, 2:110.

48. Jacques Ellul, *The Technological Society* (New York: Vintage, 1964), 208–18.

49. Samuel Popkin, *The Reasoning Voter* (Chicago: University of Chicago Press, 1991), 226–31.

50. Dewey, *The Public and Its Problems*, 215.

51. Tocqueville, *Democracy in America*, 1:192; 2:102–3, 116.

52. Darrell M. West and Richard Francis, "Electronic Advocacy: Interest Groups and Public Policy Making," *PS* 29 (1996): 25–29; see also W. Russell Neuman, *The Future of the Mass Audience* (New York: Cambridge University Press, 1991).

53. Thomas Byrne Edsall, *The New Politics of Inequality* (New York: Norton, 1984).

54. *Buckley v. Valeo,* 424 U.S. 1 (1976). See Scott Turow, "The High Court's 20-Year-Old Mistake," *New York Times,* October 12, 1997, WK 15.

55. Woodrow Wilson, *Constitutional Government in the United States* (New York: Columbia University Press, 1908), 208–10; see my essays "Parties as Civic Associations," in *Party Renewal in America,* ed. Gerald M. Pomper (New York: Praeger, 1980), 51–68; and "Tocqueville and Responsible Parties," in *Challenges to Party Government,* ed. Jerome Mileur and John. K. White (Carbondale: Southern Illinois University Press, 1992), 190–211.

56. It should be noted that the term *social capital* involves a misleading metaphor: see Nancy Tatum Ackerman, *Congregation and Community* (New Brunswick: Rutgers University Press, 1997), 4.

57. Michael McGerr, *The Decline of Popular Politics* (New York: Oxford University Press, 1986).

58. Anthony Corrado, "Financing the 1996 Election," in Gerald M. Pomper et al., *The Election of 1996* (Chatham: Chatham House, 1997), 135–36, 165–66.

59. Donald Wittman, *The Myth of Democratic Failure* (Chicago: University of Chicago Press, 1995).

60. The proposition is illustrated, in a somewhat ironic context, by John McKay, *Foundations of Corporate Success* (New York: Oxford University Press, 1993), 70–72.

Bertrand de Jouvenel on Politics and Political Science in America

References to the United States are relatively infrequent in Bertrand de Jouvenel's major works, but America was never far from his thoughts. He knew America well, at first hand as well as from books, and he united a friend's familiarity with American culture with a profound appreciation of American political institutions.[1]

He admired America as an exceptional regime, the world's chief bulwark against totalitarianism, a liberal polity which survived the Great Depression and total war with its character more or less intact. Recognizing that the power available in American society is so great that the United States can rank as a superpower with a comparatively small fraction of that power made available to the central government, Jouvenel saw the fundamental restraints on American government as political and moral: in *On Power*, he referred to America as a regime in which Power "has no history" and is limited by local authorities, by a stubbornly independent legislature, by a judiciary "with a penchant for a traditional scheme of individual rights," and by the fact that the country is inclined to regard those rights as "sacred."[2]

Yet although the American *imperium* was necessarily "improvised" and bound to be relatively weak for an extended period, Jouvenel did not think it could remain weak *forever:* for all its uniqueness, America was definitely not an exception to Power's "natural history" or the dynamics of its growth. Jouvenel first visited the United States in the 1930s, impressed by the New Deal as a nontotalitarian response to the Depression, yet despite the "complete contrast" between Roosevelt and Hitler, Jouvenel noted that the New Deal involved a prodigious growth in executive authority, an expansion of Power even more "astounding" given the restraints that characterize the American political tradition.[3] Eventually, impelled by the logic of total war, Roosevelt was led to speak of the population of the United States as "human potential" for the war effort, so much fuel for the Powerhouse. Jouvenel was sufficiently struck by the phrase that he quoted it twice in *On Power:* it reflected liberal democracy's bow to the nature of modern war and, with it, modern political life.[4]

Jouvenel, like his Rousseau, was a "pessimistic evolutionist," convinced that while Power's expansion may be *regretted,* it is a basic and pervasive datum of our politics, virtually if not precisely inevitable.[5] Any polity must match or mirror Power anywhere—whether military or economic, in public or private hands—in the interest of minimal self-government if not survival. In our time, Jouvenel recognized, any curbing or taming of Power requires both untimely wisdom and timely prudence, and nowhere more than in the United States, the chief defender of political freedom.[6]

However, in Jouvenel's view, there is a crucial flaw in America's public philosophy and self-understanding. The American tradition is prone to an individualistic view of human nature, one that neglects the fact that human beings are born dependent and that their capacity for liberty, developed in and through political society, naturally requires public authority.[7] American public discourse falls easily into the Lockean idiom of "reserved rights"—the notion that naturally free individuals surrender some portion of their liberty to government but retain the remainder—in which individual rights are conceived as separate from politics and immunities against it.[8] In practice, Jouvenel argued, that Lockean doctrine fails as a restraint on Power. Rousseau's critique of Locke is valid: since, as Locke maintains, individuals cannot be trusted to be judges in their own cases, who will decide the extent of rights and the limits of the private sphere? If individuals are to be judges in some things, they will edge toward becoming judges in all things; to avoid disorder, public authority will have to mark the boundaries of private right.[9] Contra Locke, political authority is a "natural necessity," with a primacy over "social and spiritual authorities."[10] In political society, consequently, individual rights depend on public decision: in practice, *all* rights rest on politics.

In Lockean doctrine, the "higher law" of natural right lacks "concrete sanction" within the laws: its inarticulate premise is the "dominion of religious and moral ideas" in lawmakers, in default of which Locke offers only the extralegal and risky alternative of popular rebellion. In part, Jouvenel wrote in the hope of bringing that moral premise into political speech and political science, but also to point to the dangers entailed by its neglect. In Europe, he observed, Lockeanism had encouraged confiding liberty to the discretion of sovereign parliaments, and hence, given the development of disciplined political parties, to the executive, paving the high road of Power.[11]

By contrast, Jouvenel contended, Montesquieu "demonstrated" that all political authority needs to be restrained within and by law. And since the most natural barrier to power is the desire of others not to relinquish it, it must be arranged so that one authority checks another.[12] The United States, in other words, partly avoided the Lockean pitfall by attention to Montesquieu: the separation of powers is the constitutional foundation of political liberty. And the fact that the American Constitution avoids parliamentary sovereignty, providing for an independent and powerful executive, paradoxically results in a legislature stronger and more autonomous than in parliamentary regimes.[13]

In this, of course, Jouvenel sided with American conservatives and against the liberal-progressive mainstream of political science, which disdained the separation of powers and aspired to an American politics much closer to the parliamentary model of party government.[14] However, Jouvenel defies ideological labels, and in many ways is best understood *as* a liberal-progressive attempting to give his fellows a measure of his own prudential wisdom. Rejecting authority which "fears all change" along with authority which "directs all change"—since both involve radical restraints on freedom—Jouvenel spoke on behalf of an authority which "permits changes to happen," recognizing that this sort of authority is not passive and neutral but active and moral, "filtering and remedying" the insecurities occasioned by change in the interest of the public good.[15]

For example, Jouvenel valued the American development of judicial review for carrying the idea of fundamental law—a "fixed framework" of principles superior to political will—to the logical end of limiting legislation itself, holding "laws to the test of law."[16] But he also observed that the Court is a political institution, at least in large measure. *Judicial* decision, the "rule of law in the specific sense," refers to acts in the past, which are to be assessed in terms of their degree of guilt or culpability. By contrast, *political* decision involves "an endeavor to affect the future state of the world," and as such, it may reject the past as a standard for conduct. When a judiciary attempts to establish a *precedent,* however, it is no longer dealing simply with past events: it is defining a standard meant to guide future conduct. In these terms, the American judiciary is not only a "dam on Power's encroachments" but a striking effort to preserve the link between law and politics, the past and the future, under the authority of the perennial.[17]

In its conflict with the New Deal, Jouvenel argued, the Supreme Court held too rigidly to a narrowly judicial standard, elevating "perishable" principles appropriate to a lost society of independent proprietors into a "monstrously distorted conception of the rights of property." Justly "accused of not moving with the times," the Court fought Power "on a terrain which suited Power well and itself badly," opposing the New Deal's political opportunism with "principles which themselves partook of political opportunism," the pragmatism of time past, and eventually had to retreat after a "Pyrrhic victory" in the Court-packing struggle.[18]

But if the New Deal was right in its critique of the Court, it was wrong in arguing that the "fundamental law should follow the movement of ideas," a position which virtually reduces law to "the flux of interests." There *is* an immutable or natural element in law, first principles which are especially important because the rule of law is desperately embattled in our times.[19]

In the broader political sense (as distinct from the "specific sense" relating to judicial decisions), Jouvenel observed, the rule of law is government by general rule or enactment; law is an expression of the principle of equality. It is most suited to deal with many similar decisions, each of which can cause little harm to the body politic; the more important or damaging a particular decision, the more it will seem necessary to allow discretion for dealing with the case on its own terms. Similarly, the more each case is thought to differ from others—the more political society is or is thought to be characterized by complexity or diversity—the greater the strain against equality and the general rule. And finally, the more the future is expected to differ from the past, the less appropriate it will seem to try to constrain it by rules enacted on past assumptions and calculations (which, to repeat, is precisely the rule of law in the "specific sense"). All of these challenges to the rule of law—the possibility of great harm, political complexity, and the pace of change—are increasingly characteristic of modern times: the tendency of things works against law and in favor of executive and administrative discretion.[20] And this is a matter for deep concern, because the larger and more diverse a political society, the more it depends on law—as opposed to a sense of community—as the guarantor of a "climate of trustfulness."[21]

Among the industrial countries, the United States is notable for the tenacity with which it seeks to preserve the rule of law. Prosperity and full employment evidently cannot be *legislated*, although to a considerable extent these desiderata can be *managed*, but the United States at least attempted to give this management the form of law. Forms matter, as Jouvenel often observed, but the direction of change Jouvenel found "worrying," pointing to the decline of legislative independence and the ascendancy of the executive. Still, while admiring the stubborn dignity of the United States Congress, he acknowledged that it is often "inconvenient," and he sympathized with liberal annoyance at congressional resistance "to such reasonable measures as Medicare." He intended his warning as a caution against zeal, an argument that structural restraints on Power should be cherished and preserved wherever possible, counsel that liberals and progressives came to appreciate by the 1970s.[22]

Nevertheless, the ramparts of liberal constitutionalism—including the framers' Montesquieu-informed contrivances—have "crumbled or been by-passed."[23] For Jouvenel, as for Tocqueville, a new political science is needed for a new world, one in which concern for the source or form of authority (i.e., "the consent of the governed") is supplemented by attention to the quality of political practice.

Toward the end of *Sovereignty,* Jouvenel recites three precepts that he "was taught" but now stand to be corrected. In the first place, the older teaching, reflecting the distinction between state and society, had held that the concern of political science is more or less confined to public authorities.[24] By contrast, Jouvenel says that he has come to believe that political science includes "all agencies tending to establish and develop conditions of fruitful cooperation between men," a definition that points in the direction of Aristotelianism, but is roughly consistent with pluralism's amendment to state-centered political science, then very much the discipline's American mainstream.[25] Yet Jouvenel's position also involves a decisive criticism of the direction of political science in America: his political science, like politics, is emphatically a moral endeavor. If political science deals with efforts to establish "fruitful cooperation" among human beings, it necessarily must attempt some identification of what is fruitful and what not, some evaluation of ideas of the common good.

He had also been instructed, Jouvenel said, that "the rule of law obtained when the men in public office merely executed the laws of the realm and saw to it that these were obeyed by citizens."[26] He had come to think, however, that this teaching was dangerously mechanical and superficial. Government is always at bottom a rule by men who must decide, and—whether we are speaking of citizens or officials—their view of the law is inevitably shaped by moral judgment. In 1950–1951, Jouvenel observed, when President Truman decided to send four divisions to Europe, those who opposed the decision substantively invariably argued that it exceeded the president's authority, whereas none of those who support- ed Truman took this view. Evidently, this was no coincidence: the *what* of policy inevitably colors, and tends to shape, our positions on the *who* of constitutional authority.[27] This tendency is becoming more marked since, "in a society undergoing ceaseless transformation," government by fixed habits or rules of conduct is less and less possible, and depends more and more on decisions by people in positions of responsibility.[28] Political science, accordingly, "cannot . . . evade the responsibility" of teaching human beings how to make better decisions in a world where the best information will always be incomplete and inadequate. And that responsibility for the education of citizens and statesmen inevitably has a moral dimension: since the essence of the rule of law lies in "shared feelings of what is right and proper," constitutionalism increasingly will come down, in the last analysis, to common beliefs that limit and inform decisions.[29]

Political science has a crucial role in this respect because common beliefs and standards—and hence the possibility for genuine popular rule and restraint on Power—are more or less radically threatened by the "freedom of suggestion," the openness to innovation in habit and thought especially characteristic of liberal societies.[30] For Jouvenel, the problem was illustrated by an older example: the original role of the jury as the au- thoritative interpreter of law as fixed standards of custom and propriety, the protector of established rights and expectations, collapsed under the weight of the pressure for change, as law came more and more to be seen as something made or contrived. Yet the jury also furnishes an instruc- tive example: the "most progressive" of countries, the United States, is the most attached to the jury, and the paradox is not resolved by the notion, so often violated in practice, that juries only decide "facts" and not law. The jury is an educational forum, judicial in the *political* sense, suited to afford some balance between initiations and traditional beliefs.[31]

This, in turn, points to Jouvenel's final correction of political science. He was taught, Jouvenel remarks, that the "chief problem" of politics and political science lay in the relation between the individual and the state, but he had come to see that problem in the "dynamic balance between the driving forces and the adjusting forces," and to suggest a political science focused on the Initiator.[32]

The Initiator assembles human forces and power, and his action compels a response, whether of resistance or submission, setting in motion a "global process" on whatever scale.[33] "Globalization," in that sense, is merely an old process, newly recognized and felt with an unshielded immediacy. The state is only one actor in the process; private and social initiations are often more important and are always part of the problem: Power is not confined to government and is often less dangerous in public and broadly accountable hands. And in fact, the freedom of initiation calls for government which is stronger and more active, within the limits of its "essential functions."[34]

For Jouvenel, the great challenge for constitutionalism—and for politics in general—lies in strengthening the balancing and stabilizing forces, for trust and shared belief are necessary *to* Power as well as restraints *on* it. Left to itself, Power erodes "social capital," the commonalities of expectation and conviction, and in so doing it eats at its own foundations: the permanent revolution, undermining moral credit and shattering habit, is increasingly reduced to its *fons et origo* in force, but that, as civilizations and empires unite to instruct us, is the path of self-destruction.[35] Power itself needs Rex, the stabilizer, to balance Dux, the leader.[36]

Especially in modern democratic regimes, the great barrier to Power lies less in government than in politics, in the relatively autonomous intermediate authorities that stand between Dux and public, jealous of their own power. In fact, this principle is as important in nominally private associations as in the state: Jouvenel pointed to the then recently merged AFL-CIO, in which the president was effectively checked by the "barons" who led individual unions.[37]

In any contest with such authorities, the Dux will attempt to win away their followings, particularly by championing equality against hierarchy and individual liberty against social restraint. And as history attests, Power is all but certain to win that competition if the "political set"— rival authorities of whatever description—behave selfishly or resist out of loyalty to outdated ideas and habits. Fought on those terms, even victories against the Dux are likely to be self-defeating: by Jouvenel's account, Theodore Roosevelt, a "man of Power," defined himself as the champion of "the physical independence of the majority of citizens" and their attachment to "libertarian institutions" as against a plutocracy that was in the process of "transforming citizens into salaried dependents." However, T.R. was frustrated by the "blind egoism of men of great place," a setback that argued in favor of a much more radical expansion of state authority.[38] Successful restraint on Power, in other words, demands that intermediate authorities act in a way that is timely and public-spirited. In order to *limit* power, intermediate authorities must know when to *yield* to its claims or, better still, to advance those claims themselves.[39]

This lesson is particularly important for organizations and powers in economic life. The good life has priority over goods; economics is naturally subordinate to politics, and in theory and practice takes for granted a set of institutions and habits that derive from political life.[40] Yet the very successes of capitalist economics contribute to the expansion of Power: the record of growth makes increasing and general well-being into something expected, a matter of right that demands public guarantees and governmental regulations which, given the nature of markets, can scarcely be a rule of law.[41]

Government's extension is also mandated by the fact that economics harshly transforms social life, reshaping social relations and relying on more and newer goods as a substitute for stability, rootedness, and civic dignity.[42] Bourgeois individualism and the laissez-faire economics associated with it tend to ignore the need for restraints on liberty as supports for social security. For those who are "worse placed," the resulting insecurity is "insupportable," but the same uncertainty afflicts the strong, and both look to government to provide some protection against incertitude and anxiety. Social rights, Jouvenel argued, can claim priority as the foundations of individual liberty, and without the supports swept away by economics, the appeal to the state became inevitable.[43]

Thus, the advent of FDR and the New Deal: The second Roosevelt, Jouvenel observed, confronted a world in which individual rights had become the "bulwark of the few" rather than the "shield of each." Unlike Theodore Roosevelt, as Jouvenel understood him, Franklin Roosevelt did not try to combat the economic dependence of the many; he took the concentration of economic power as an "accomplished fact," and built a "structure of Power" in which individual right "had to bow down before social right," a decisive step in transforming the "free citizen" into a "protected subject."[44]

All of this language, of course, suggests Hayek, one of Jouvenel's admirers. It should be noted, however, that although Jouvenel almost certainly regretted FDR's ebullience, he finds little to criticize in his policies: most citizens were already dependent, *unprotected* subjects, made so by economics. The New Deal gave them back a measure of right, and in this sense, FDR deserves some praise as the protector of "the new rights of men," at least as much Rex as Dux. The danger Jouvenel saw in the New Deal was in large measure ironic: the democratic state is an unreliable champion, since the "phantom tenants" of public office, precarious in their tenure, are often "half-hearted" and inclined to accommodate "financial aristocracies," so that Power, erected to curb and edify economics, has a tendency to become its creature.[45] Power's idealism tempts it to undertake too much, accepting tasks that demand unrealistic levels of compliance and support and that lead to a dialectic of coercion and failure.[46] Jouvenel hoped, by contrast, for institutions and teachings able to gentle Power and to preserve it for its indispensable public purposes.

For example, Jouvenel appreciated traditional American political parties at a time when most American political scientists were still caught up in the spirit of reform. He regarded the American development of the mass party as politically "the most important discovery of the nineteenth century" and the source of a "new scheme of politics." Parties need enough doctrine to explain to their followers what they are fighting for, but their allegiances rest on feeling and favor more than ideological elegance or force of argument. Unlike thinkers who overrate the intellectual in human beings (Jefferson and Rousseau were Jouvenel's examples), party and partisanship rest on an understanding of "the real man, who needs warmth, comradeship, the team spirit, and can make noble sacrifices for his side." Amid the anonymities of mass politics, party gives citizens an element of fellowship and dignity.[47]

The most visible dangers of machine politics—graft and a lowering of the quality of political leaders—troubled Jouvenel very little. The greater danger of party lies in the fact that partisan combat is "war in the true sense," and just as war tends to override humanity, party strife and spirit can dampen or extinguish good citizenship. The party is faction, and in that sense, the traditional party machine is the totalitarian party in embryo.[48]

Traditional *American* parties, however, were federal and decentralized, just as machines were essentially local: affording the chief benefits of party, they minimized its risks. But traditional party politics was in the process of being "broken" by the time Jouvenel wrote *On Power*, even though it lingered for a time. Jouvenel was not at all surprised that the decline of traditional party organizations led to the increasing importance of money, the mercantilization of party, and the increasing strength of centralized fund-raising bureaucracies as opposed to local organization: reform replicated the familiar logic by which attacks on intermediate authorities leads to the expansion of Power. Ironically, a major step in this advance of Power has derived from the effort, in *Buckley v. Valeo,* to limit the regulatory power of the state, a decision which only underlined the regulatory power of finance and economics. Even so, Jouvenel noted that American parties, seeking public power, are constrained to do more than express opinions and interests: they are obliged to frame arguments in public terms capable of speaking to and for broad coalitions, so that their contestations have some resemblance to a dialogue between Rex and Dux, more a chorus than an ideological cacophony or unison.[49]

Like the then-emerging pluralist orthodoxy in political science, Jouvenel spoke of interest groups and factions as a "natural phenomenon" and a "corrective" to totalitarianism, and of the liberty to create a group as "the essential freedom." But Jouvenel also observed that since such groups depend on Power's support or tolerance, lacking a "defensive position" from which they can rule autonomously, they must seek to influence Power or to control it. And to the extent that they succeed, they debase authority, tending to reduce it to "nothing better than a stake," devoid of "stability and respect."[50] Every successful group, moreover, is apt to augment Power as an instrument for its purposes, so that the logic of "interest group liberalism" lowers the *standing* and *credit* of an *expanding* public authority. That dynamic, unchecked, points toward political bankruptcy and—since a power vacuum is intolerable—ultimately toward the rule of a tyrant.[51]

Nor is this easily corrected: Jouvenel's essay "The Chairman's Problem" was intended as a reminder of the limits on democratic deliberation and participation, and particularly to indicate the necessity for elites charged with determining who will have access to the rostrum and for how long—"the greater the number of potential participants, the sharper must be the selecting process."[52] He sided with pluralists in holding that these guardian elites are relatively ad hoc, linked into a single coherent elite only "by our innate tendency to mythologize," but his argument also ran counter to pluralist efforts to present an American politics in which access is relatively open and equal. In fact, Jouvenel's position amounted to a warning: rights which cannot feasibly be exercised—like the promise of equal political rights in American practice—make democratic principles seem a lie. And the effort of liberal democratic theorists to define rights, in the interest of realism, as limits on the *abuse* of power rather than claims to a *share* in power, risks promoting a proletarianized citizenry inclined to feel that, politically, it really does have "nothing to lose but its chains."[53]

Jouvenel taught that the *politics* of freedom demands more than liberty, positive or negative: it turns on the recognition that freedom is *a* good, but not the highest good. Lincoln, Jouvenel pointed out, was unwilling to abide by the principle of "self-determination": right sets limits to rights and to self-rule.[54] Politics—and hence political science—aims at understanding and establishing justice.[55]

In the first place, political liberty requires the *formalization* of politics, the restraint and shaping of political acts by the measure of a decent public life, a standard especially notable in the United States and Great Britain.[56] "The words 'overthrow of the government,'" Jouvenel wrote, "fall softly upon the ear" if they evoke "a defeated President driving to the Capitol with his victor and then retiring to enjoy high moral status."[57]

However, government also has a substantive mission. It cannot *solve* the problem of the public good, Jouvenel taught, because attempting to do so destroys liberty, but it can help to create the conditions in which that good can emerge. It can promote trust, which presumes reasonable security of person and station. And it can help to educate desires, to enhance appreciation for beauty and for nature (a goal reflected in Jouvenel's environmentalism), and above all, to strengthen the recognition that what one *wants* is not what is *needful.*[58] A champion of the politics of liberty, Jouvenel hoped to remind liberals and libertarians that government can be limited effectively only when one remembers that it has a moral mission, just as a free spirit is linked to obligation and to honor.[59] Today, when it is all too evident that law and liberty must live in labyrinths and dance with minotaurs, Jouvenel's curriculum is even more urgent for American politics and political science.

Notes

This essay was originally published as "Jouvenel on Politics and Political Science in America," *Political Science Reviewer* 32 (2003).

1. Implicitly, Jouvenel followed Chesterton's advice: often amused by things American, he never refused to be instructed by them. (For Chesterton's comment, see *What I Saw in America* [New York: Dodd, Mead, 1922], 2.)

2. *On Power: The Natural History of Its Growth,* trans. J. F. Huntington (Indianapolis: Liberty Fund, 1993), 4, 276–77.

3. Ibid., 391–92. See also Dennis Hale and Marc Landy's introduction to Bertrand de Jouvenel, *Economics and the Good Life: Essays on Political Economy* (New Brunswick: Transaction, 1999), 3, especially n. 8.

4. *On Power,* 4, 167.

5. *Economics and the Good Life,* 4; "Rousseau, the Pessimistic Evolutionist," *Yale French Studies* 28 (1961–1962): 83–96.

6. For example, see Jouvenel's *The Art of Conjecture,* trans. Nikita Lary (New York: Basic Books, 1967).

7. *Sovereignty: An Inquiry into the Political Good,* trans. J. F. Huntington (Indianapolis: Liberty Fund, 1997), 234–37, 316–17.

8. Ibid., 303–7.

9. *On Power,* 40; *Sovereignty,* 320.

10. *On Power,* 145–46n.

11. Ibid., 265n., 268–69n.; "The Principate," in *The Nature of Politics: Selected Essays of Bertrand de Jouvenel,* ed. Dennis Hale and Marc Landy (New York: Schocken, 1987), 157–90. The Declaration of the Rights of Man, Jouvenel commented, was a "more or less legitimate descendant of divine law" as a check on power, but lacked the kind of sanctions—in faith or in politics—needed to make it effective (ibid., 344). Like many who dreaded the advance of Power, Orwell shared Jouvenel's insistence on the moral foundations of democratic liberty, but Orwell showed no uneasiness about the doctrine of parliamentary sovereignty ("Notes on the Way" (1940), in *The Collected Essays, Journalism and Letters of George Orwell,* ed. Sonia Orwell and Ian Angus [New York: Harcourt, Brace and World, 1968], 2:15).

12. *On Power,* 316; "The Principate," 165–66, where, significantly, Jouvenel illustrated this principle by the example of the AFL-CIO, in which the monarchical power of the president is checked by the baronial presidents of the federation's autonomous unions.

13. "On the Evolution of the Forms of Government," in *The Nature of Politics,* 102–56.

14. Ibid., 155.

15. *Sovereignty,* 66, 364–65.

16. *On Power,* 344, 345, 348.

17. *The Pure Theory of Politics* (New Haven: Yale University Press, 1963), 152–53, 162.

18. *On Power,* 348–49.

19. Ibid., 349.

20. "The Principate"; *Pure Theory of Politics,* 152–53.

21. *Sovereignty,* 158.

22. "On the Evolution of the Forms of Government," 127–28, 155; "The Principate," 169; Jouvenel admired the effort by Congress to develop its own staffs and bodies of expertise, but noted that these were insignificant when compared with executive resources ("On the Evolution of the Forms of Government," 130n39; "The Principate," 178–79). In contemporary politics, Jouvenel would surely have pointed to and been troubled by "fast track" legislation as an indication of things to come. The obvious example of liberal rethinking, of course, is Arthur Schlesinger Jr.'s *The Imperial Presidency* (Boston: Houghton Mifflin, 1973).

23. "On the Evolution of the Forms of Government," 156.

24. John H. Schaar observes that the separation of public and private spheres

is the basic distinction of liberal constitutionalism. "Some Ways of Thinking about Equality," *Journal of Politics* 26 (1964): 884, 886, 888.

25. *Sovereignty,* 359.

26. Ibid., 360.

27. Ibid., 4.

28. Ibid., 360. Jouvenel admired Truman's Farewell Address as a statement of the executive's responsibility to decide (ibid., 360n). If it needs saying, citizens bear their share of this responsibility to decide: see my "Civil Disobedience and Contemporary Constitutionalism," *Comparative Politics* 1 (1969): 211–27.

29. *Sovereignty,* 358, 360, 361.

30. Ibid., 361.

31. Ibid., 231.

32. Ibid., 361.

33. Ibid., 362.

34. Ibid., 365.

35. Force can establish Power, Jouvenel argued in *On Power,* and habit may keep it in being, but to expand, it must have credit (27).

36. *Sovereignty,* 40–41, 65–66.

37. "The Principate," 165–66.

38. *On Power,* 185, 368. Jouvenel's description of T.R. obviously is open to question and seems partly due to his effort to see in the two Roosevelts a parallel to the Gracchi.

39. Ibid., 174n; "The Principate," 165–66. In Jouvenel's view, if white southerners had in fact been interested in the principle of states' rights, they should have seen the need for change in race relations; southern resistance, by contrast, was a perfect example of the sort of conduct that fuels the expansion of power.

40. *Pure Theory of Politics,* 33–34, 199; *Economics and the Good Life,* 2, 21–36, 77–96; economists, Jouvenel comments, are able to assume that the more freedom the better because they rely on a set of restraints associated with the formalization of politics (*Pure Theory of Politics,* 34–35, 35n).

41. *Economics and the Good Life,* 4.

42. This is particularly true because technology, so often the ally of economics, also works frequently at cross-purposes with democracy ("The Political Consequences of the Rise of Science," in *Economics and the Good Life,* 165–77).

43. *On Power,* 388–89.

44. Ibid., 368.

45. Ibid., 185. Of course, the alternative—tenure in office secured by a totalitarian party—is even more perilous.

46. Ibid., 394; significantly, Jouvenel's example is Prohibition.

47. Ibid., 300–301.

48. Ibid., 302–3; *Pure Theory of Politics,* 182. Jouvenel pointed out that graft has political limits: machines were allowed "a few speculations" but only on the condition that they not cause "too great a scandal" (*On Power,* 301).

49. *The Nature of Politics,* 231n7; *Buckley v. Valeo* 424 U.S. 1 (1976). It ought

to be evident that Jouvenel's reasoning stands as a cautionary note for political parties—and third-party advocates—in our time.

50. *On Power*, 291–93; *Sovereignty*, 363.

51. The term "interest group liberalism," of course, is borrowed from Theodore Lowi, *The End of Liberalism* (New York: Norton, 1969).

52. *Pure Theory of Politics*, 44–54.

53. *The Nature of Politics*, 138n52.

54. *Pure Theory of Politics*, 210–11; "Woodrow Wilson," *Confluence* 5 (1957): 320–31. Having appealed to the principle of self-determination in the establishment of Czechoslovakia, Jouvenel commented, Edvard Beneš was properly unwilling to see it applied to the Sudetenland. (This observation has special force because Jouvenel revered Beneš, who had treated him like a son when Jouvenel served as Beneš's personal secretary: *The Nature of Politics*, xv, 106.)

55. *Pure Theory of Politics*, 33.

56. Ibid., 34–35. "Nonfoundational" democrats, Jouvenel would have observed, prove on examination to take for granted a considerable list of democratic norms and forms.

57. Ibid., 185.

58. "The Idea of Welfare" and "Toward a Political Theory of Education," in *Economics and the Good Life*, 21–36, 77–96.

59. *Sovereignty*, 316–17; Sharon Krause, *Liberalism with Honor* (Cambridge, Mass.: Harvard University Press, 2002).

Leo Strauss and the Dignity of American Political Thought

Leo Strauss wrote only rarely about American thought, but he pointed his students and readers toward the "high adventure" of the American political tradition as a serious encounter with the great questions of political philosophy. Strauss saw American theory as a contest—one fought less between Americans than within them—pitting modernity's "first wave," with its appeal to reason and natural right, against the more radical individualism and the historicism of later modern doctrine. Religion and classical rationalism, offering their own standards of a right above opinion, had been historically the allies of "first wave" modernity, but those voices, Strauss recognized, were growing weaker in American life. In recent American teaching and culture, by contrast, Strauss saw that the increasingly dominant ethics of self-interest and success, other political inadequacies aside, were incapable of speaking to the highest aspirations or winning the deepest allegiance of the young. By reviving classical teaching, Strauss also sought to contribute to the rearticulation and reanimation of the American ideal.

Twenty-five years after his death, Leo Strauss still stirs very partisan juices among intellectuals, partly because he is a presence in American public life.[1] His students in their generations—the late Allan Bloom is only the best known—are prominent among the interpreters of American political thought and culture, mostly on the conservative side, and are not much less visible in practical politics, where William Galston is a notable voice among New Democrats and William Kristol a stronger one on the Right. Yet Strauss himself wrote next to nothing about American thinkers or specifically directed to American politics, and even his references to American authors are few and far between. I know of only one published instance in which Strauss addresses an American thinker of the first rank, and that is a review of John Dewey's critique of *German* philosophy.[2]

The explanation of this seeming paradox is not complicated: Strauss began with students who were involved in the dilemmas and controversies of American politics, and—a great teacher even by his critics' accounts— he unsettled their presuppositions and stimulated their wonder, letting them see that their everyday lives were caught up in the quarrels between poetry and philosophy, reason and revelation, ancients and moderns. An exile in America, Strauss called his students home. As I will be arguing, Strauss, explicitly and by intimation, pointed his students to what Allan Bloom called the "high adventure" of the American tradition, the dignity of American political thought and its special, integral relation to the tradition of political philosophy.[3]

At the time when Strauss began to attract the attention of American political science, this was anything but the rule. *The History of Political Philosophy*, which Strauss edited with Joseph Cropsey, contains chapters on *The Federalist* and Paine—as well as Tocqueville, so inseparably linked to things American—and concludes with a chapter on John Dewey. By contrast, the then-established text in the field, George Sabine's *History of Political Theory*, includes no significant discussion of any American thinker. Sabine refers to the *Fabian Essays*, but not to *The Federalist*; he does not discuss Paine, although he treats Burke at length; Tocqueville is omitted altogether, and Dewey rates only a mention, along with Royce, among later liberals who rejected the "metaphysics" of the older liberalism—a comment explained by Sabine's dismissive assertion, in relation to Jefferson, that the doctrine of unalienable natural rights can be defended only by reference to their supposed self-evidence.[4]

By the early 1960s, Progressive history—which, at least implicitly, took the democratic ideal as a universal standard—was no longer ascendant in the specialized study of American thought.[5] The prevailing view was a more radical historicism, a "realism" that discounted ideas when it did not reduce them to reflections of their times or culture. To this persuasion, American political thought was essentially superficial or second-rate, variations affected by time and interest on a "preformation ideal" (Boorstin), "irrational Lockeanism" (Hartz), or liberal capitalism (Hofstadter).[6] American thought was commonly praised for its pragmatism—though sometimes, following the example of Thurman Arnold, condemned for the lack of it—since it was assumed that the virtue of a theory did not lie in its truth, but in seamless adaptation to its times, practice serving both to illumine and to test thought.[7] Recently, the late Judith Shklar attempted to raise the stature of American thought by weaving realism back into the fabric of Progressivism. As Shklar presented it, American political theory, at least after the founding, is a kind of sociology of political science, to be understood first in relation to its times, but second as part of the progressive democratization of values and citizenship. Shklar's hero is Charles Merriam, who united the realism of William Graham Sumner, to whom he "looked back," with the optimism of Dewey, with whom he "looked ahead." In Shklar's terms, American political science, and theory with it, is an instrument of the democratic impulse, devoted to the democratically effectual truth.[8] Strauss, on the other hand, offered American political thought a higher office: he encouraged us to take American thinking, past and present, as a serious attempt to answer enduring questions, possessing a claim to rule practice: not merely a mirror, but a lamp.

Nevertheless, I want to begin by calling attention to two errors of omission or emphasis in what Strauss wrote or implied about American political thought. The first is a paradox: it lies in the fact that Strauss appeared to discourage the application to American thinkers of his most noted contribution, his rediscovery of the art of writing "between the lines." In *Persecution and the Art of Writing*, Strauss argued that the triumph of liberal democracy, making that art seemingly unnecessary, had allowed it to be forgotten. The liberal Enlightenment took philosophy to the people, assuming or looking to a time when there would be no danger in the public expression of any truth—or, for that matter, of any idea. Deception, in these terms, could be justified only by fear of persecution, through an appeal to the author's right of self-preservation, but that excuse vanished with the establishment of liberal rights and laws. The older art of writing is "essentially related to a society which is not liberal," and hence might be assumed to have no place in America.[9] But of course, ancient writers were not simply concerned to avoid persecution: they restrained themselves as much to shelter the public, out of respect for the "opinions on which society rests," and it is as a contribution to an education capable of answering that "political question par excellence"—the reconciling of "order which is not oppression with freedom which is not license"—that Strauss recommended their art to Americans.[10]

Strauss knew that at least some American writers lacked the Enlightenment's confidence in unrestrained expression. Archibald MacLeish, the only American quoted as a primary source in *Persecution and the Art of Writing*, is cited as questioning whether, "in any but the most orderly and settled times," writers should allow themselves to express "the most complete confession, the uttermost despair, the furthest doubt."[11] But by referring to these cautions as having been "raised in our time," Strauss, along with the *correct* impression that MacLeish's doubts, voiced in 1940, were a response to totalitarianism and total war, allows the *erroneous* implication that such thoughts were unknown among earlier generations of American writers.[12]

To the contrary, even at the beginning of the republic, Paine wrote as craftily as his heterodoxy demanded, and Strauss's observation that Burke used the "language of modern natural right" whenever it seemed calculated to win over his "modern audience" begs to be applied to many spokesmen, especially on the Anti-Federalist side.[13] And later American writers, wrestling with mass democratic politics, understood well enough the problem of simultaneously addressing the generally decent public and their more reflective fellows. Consider Thoreau's chapter "Reading" in *Walden:* after urging the study of the classics ("We might as well omit the study of Nature because she is old"), Thoreau notes that reading great books in a "true spirit" is a "noble exercise," for the classics were not written simply in Greek or Latin, but in the "secret language of literature." And Thoreau's appeal to the readers of the Renaissance, while possibly too modern for Strauss's taste, is undeniably shrewd: "What the Roman and Greek multitude could not hear, after the lapse of ages, a few scholars read, and a few scholars only are still reading it."[14] Still, the worst that can be said is that Strauss gave us the key, and left it to us to turn the lock of our own culture.

The second problem lies in an excess. Always intrigued by political foundings, Strauss was taken with the American effort to let theory guide practice, especially in the Declaration and the framing of the Constitution, but also in Lincoln's refounding. That emphasis, however, encouraged Strauss's students to attend to "philosophic statecraft" to the neglect of more purely theoretical American thinkers—Emerson, for example, who might have been expected to be of special interest, given his links to Nietzsche.[15]

Nevertheless, foundings are crucial, and by opening *Natural Right and History* with the most famous passage from the Declaration of Independence, Strauss indicated that the United States and its founding, though seldom mentioned, occupied a central place in his concerns.[16] Thomas Pangle is right when he argues that Strauss saw America pulled between a "less influential classical or civic ideal" and a more modern and individualistic doctrine, participating in the grander tension between "obedient love," the biblical principle, and the philosophic demand for "free inquiry" that Strauss called "the secret vitality of the West."[17] But Strauss treated the American founding as a decisively modern event, using *The Federalist* as an instance of the modern leaning toward Machiavelli's version of "republicanism in the Roman style."[18]

In that passage, *The Federalist* is the only practical document mentioned. Strauss lists a number of theorists (Harrington, Spinoza, Sydney, Montesquieu, and Rousseau), also referring to certain "upper class Frenchmen who favored the French Revolution out of concern for the status of France as a great power." This grouping does more than suggest that the United States was the first attempt to translate Machiavellian republicanism into practice, albeit with the "mitigation" of Hobbes and Locke. It also indicates that in America, theory had a higher standing than in subsequent efforts to realize the "new modes and orders," since the American founding is associated with a text—speech about practice—and with a more principled position: in the United States, unlike the France portrayed in Strauss's example, modern ideas were less simply adopted in the service of power.

The general argument parallels the reference to *The Federalist* at the end of the introduction to Strauss and Cropsey, which observes that *The Federalist* rejects the classical preference for the city along with the belief that large states cannot be republican or free. But, Strauss and Cropsey go on, *The Federalist* retains the classical scorn for "the tribe (or nation)" as incapable of "high civilization"; the framers disdain nationalism in the name of civilization and freedom.[19] Thus, while Strauss and Cropsey present the framers as moderates, partly adopting and partly abandoning classical teachings, their *argument* defines a scale from particular to universal, on which the framers occupy a decisively modern position. The American founding, in Strauss's description, is identified with modernity's "first wave" in its time of confidence, relatively assured in its appeal to reason and natural right, persuaded that intention—armed with science and statecraft—can channel and direct nature, and regarding ideas as something more than reflections of interest and the "Will to Power."[20]

In the same spirit, Strauss associates the framers, on the whole, with Locke's individualism and emancipation of acquisitiveness. In fact, in the only reference to an American founder in *Natural Right and History*, Strauss makes a special point of assimilating Madison to Locke's view, claiming that Madison "perfectly expressed" Locke's dynamic idea of property, one concerned not with protecting inheritance but with forwarding the mastery of nature.[21]

Strauss's quotation from Madison, however, collapses two sentences from *The Federalist,* #10, adding italics to the interpolated portion, so that Madison is made to say that the protection of differing "faculties of acquiring property" is the "first object of government." Actually, Madison's definition of government's primary role refers back ("these faculties") to the previous sentence, which begins, "The diversity in the faculties of men, from which the rights of property originate." Madison, in other words, makes diversity prior to and more inclusive than property, and it is this primal variety that government aims to safeguard.

Implicitly, Madison gives individuality a status higher or more fundamental than property, a position consistent with his later assertions that human beings may be said to have a "property in their rights" and that no right or property may be used to exclude others from their equal rights.[22] Seeming to defer to individual liberty even more than Locke, Madison's doctrine is also—potentially—a good deal more egalitarian and open to modern liberal interpretations.[23] Rather cryptically, Strauss notes Madison's more jealous devotion to liberty by directing his readers—in a footnote that refers, without comment, to an *earlier* footnote in *Natural Right and History*—to the observation that Locke, unlike Madison, does not list "tyranny by the majority" among the types of tyranny.[24] While Madison still regarded the human self as having a pretty definite shape, essentially given by nature, his argument suggests that he had taken a step in the direction of a more radical, Rousseauistic idea of freedom. Strauss's emendation pushes Madison back toward the older understanding, making him more decisively Locke's ally and emphasizing that aspect of Madison's idea of natural right that stresses limits and institutions.[25]

Strauss's discussion of Burke indicates another important aspect of Madison's view of diversity. The American founders agreed with Burke's insistence on the importance of circumstance and experience in "constructing a commonwealth," and with the need to distinguish between theory and practice. Unlike Burke, however, the American founders did not deprecate theory as such: they held that theory can illuminate practice and that constitutions can be made or designed: to that extent, the first wave of modernity accords with classical rationalism.[26] Yet the classical view held that constitutional design, in ordering the variety of human ends, treats one end as the highest. By contrast, Madison's ruling principle, diversity, is all but identical with Burke's insistence—twice quoted by Strauss—on the "greatest variety of ends."[27] But if the American framers accepted that much of Burke's critique of rationalism, they did not follow his road to historicism; believers in progress, the framers did not claim to see—as Burke and his epigones did—a "providential dispensation" in history entitled to rule standards of right. Their lodestar was not history, but nature.[28]

To sum up the argument so far: Strauss's overt teaching identifies America with Locke, and more generally, with the first wave of modernity. His subtler doctrine appears to be that, in America, adherents of that first modern wave at least opened the gates to the second, creating a regime in which the contest of modernities is one of the features of politics. And of course, given that limited choice, Strauss sided with the earlier moderns, especially since constitutional democracy, tied so closely to their teaching, approaches the classical standard—or so Strauss argued—more closely than any available alternative.[29]

However, Strauss also recognized that the choices were not quite so narrow, since in America, all modern teachings have been tempered by older thinking—by elements of classicism, but especially by religion—which makes up the second voice in America's cultural dialogue. Before Strauss's opening quotation from the Declaration of Independence, the epigraph of *Natural Right and History* presents two quotations from the Bible, an invocation that is especially striking since Strauss notes that at least the Hebrew Scriptures contain no idea of "natural right as such."[30] As Strauss implies, however, biblical teaching does offer an intimation of, and a vital precondition for, the "truths we hold to be self-evident."

In the first of Strauss's citations (2 Sam. 12:2–4), Nathan rebukes David for his adultery with Bathsheba and his complicity in the death of Uriah; in the second, Elijah denounces Ahab's role in the despoiling of Naboth (1 Kings 21:1–3). The texts point to the effort of religion to vindicate the rights of families and of inheritance, precisely the "static" sort of property which Madison—according to Strauss—de-emphasized, following Locke, in favor of "dynamic" acquisition.

Religion, through the two prophets, shames (though it does not avoid or undo) the tyranny of desire, leading both kings to repent, so that both stories have a contemporary moral. Modern political teaching, by making mastery or dominion over nature the human goal, at least implies that successful tyranny, were it possible, would be the most desirable human life. Thus, when Strauss commented that "only God knows why" social science—professedly neutral and instrumental—preferred liberal democracy to tyranny, he was indicating, ironically, that in American culture, religious teaching continued to shame and check the darker impulses of ruling doctrine.[31]

Strauss never concealed the enduring quarrel between religion and philosophy, but he certainly was willing to mute it, preferring to emphasize the commonalities of biblical and classical teaching as opposed to modern political philosophy. Thus, he stressed that Max Weber's celebrated interpretation of Protestantism's impact on capitalism relied on a "corruption or degeneration" of Calvin's doctrine; Weber, because of his "fear of value judgments," was led to "identify the essence of Calvinism with its historically most influential aspect." Yet, in a footnote, Strauss pointed to a closer connection between Calvinism—or Puritanism, at any rate—and modern thinking: because of its radical rejection of Aristotelianism, Puritanism was "more open to the new philosophy" and "a very important and perhaps the most important 'carrier' of the new philosophy." In other words, the relation between Puritanism and capitalism *is* partly attributable to the "revolution" in theology, even if Weber "overestimated" its importance in comparison to that of the revolution in secular thought. Like his identification of Madison with Locke, Strauss's invocation of Calvin has the effect of linking somewhat ambiguous Americans to the more coherent teachings of their predecessors.[32]

At the same time, the special contribution of religion to the American regime, and the condition of any alliance between religion and classical rationalism, is a variety of faith that, unlike older orthodoxies, does *not* regard the laws as divinely founded, and hence distinguishes between civil religion and religion per se. Ordinarily the ally of American laws and ways, religion can also be their severe critic. Strauss praised American religion as a "bulwark of diversity" and a protection against tyranny of the majority, presenting it as a champion of variety and dissent rather than a force for uniformity. And it is especially important that, by affirming a City of God distinct from the City of Man, religion supports the separation of theory and practice and countervails the great axiom of Machiavelli's political science, the rejection of "imagined republics and principalities" in favor of the sort of truth that gets results.[33] That quality of religion, in Strauss's view, assigns it a leading role in the high drama of American democratic politics.

The modern democratic ideal, Strauss pointed out, is the elevation of all citizens, aiming at "an aristocracy of everyone."[34] Strauss had no illusions about the possibility of reaching that goal; at most, he may have held, like Nathan Gore—the cultivated man of letters in Henry Adams's

Democracy—that in America, the democratic "experiment" is "the only direction society can take that is worth taking."[35] In any case, this democratic hope depends on an "economy of plenty," the progress of science, and the pursuit of mastery generally.[36] At the same time, given the sovereignty of the many, it presumes a citizenry that takes excellence as an authoritative standard for its own emulation. Yet this sense of responsibility to higher principles cannot be the result of the laws, which are answerable *to* the many: necessarily, it must derive from sources outside, and for the most part older than, democratic laws and politics—in America, from biblical religion and from more or less traditional liberal education.[37]

However, as Strauss observed, these traditions are growing "more and more corroded" in our age, so that the democratic ideal requires something of a new defense. As religion has attenuated, liberal education has been asked (and has often volunteered) to assume greater responsibilities, but in Strauss's familiar critique, liberal education itself is increasingly unreliable, infected by positivism and historicism and needing correction from political philosophy of a better sort.[38] It is less surprising, then, that in the writings in which Strauss deals most directly with American authors and schools, he addresses contemporaries; the greater texts of the American tradition, however, are very much in Strauss's mind.

Strauss's epilogue to *Essays on the Scientific Study of Politics,* like his similar arguments elsewhere, turns on the fact that liberalism, pursuing the mastery of nature, has a tendency to reduce reason to the servant of the passions and to produce a society based on consumerism and allied to technique. Apart from its tastelessness, the technocratic ethos, concerned to fulfill desires, deprecates the disciplines of both decency and aspiration.[39] Accordingly, the then-new political science, concerned to see people only as they are and not as they might be, came to believe that, given the indifference and private spirit of most, no rational case could be made for democracy. Consequently, political scientists, almost all honorable democrats, were more than usually attracted by arguments for the separation of facts and values, hoping to save democratic values by separating them from—and thus making them proof against—disconfirming facts.[40] This inclination was reinforced, of course, by the belief that denying any rational order of rank among values and virtues promotes democratic equality. As Strauss indicated, however, the fact-value distinction relativizes all values *including* equality, and in the same way, it rejects the claim that any end is natural, undermining even the appeal to self-preservation, the foundation of liberal natural right.[41]

Strauss addressed a more profound philosophy of social science in his responses to John Dewey. Conceding Dewey's moral seriousness, Strauss noted that Dewey's rejection of natural law, and of moral universals generally, was rooted in a proper recognition of the dangers of "absolutes" and heroic moralities. Strauss had no quarrel with the proposition that some sort of utilitarianism is a safer basis for civilized life. He observed, however, that Dewey's experimentalism combines a moral individualism with the "method . . . of success," a doctrine which identifies what is effective with what is right.[42] The moral basis of this celebration of technique lay in Dewey's confidence in progress; by contrast, Strauss appealed to Henry Adams ("the best American historian I know") to support the argument that science increases human power without eradicating evil, so that—even conceding that human beings are ordinarily decent—scientific advance offers no guarantee against technology's increasingly terrible possibilities.[43]

Not only is human survival threatened: progress involves an implicit imperialism, a willingness to sweep away "underdeveloped" societies and ways.[44] And as Strauss often commented, the quest for mastery inevitably leads to the view of humanity itself as a barrier, inspiring efforts to overcome human nature in the interest of human dominion. But the rage of nature thwarted, Strauss warned, shadows modern civilization, voicelessly urging the case for natural right.[45]

If Strauss had a political project in the ordinary sense of the term, it lay in the effort to restore the speech and spirit of liberal democracy.[46] But Strauss recognized that for education to reanimate the democratic ideal, it would be necessary to address the defects of modernity, and not always sotto voce.[47] The vitality of American democracy, in other words, presumes the criticism of liberalism, the rearticulation of America's second voice.

Seeking to win the "sympathy of the best . . . of the coming generation," Strauss admitted to ignorance of a good deal of contemporary culture (though I am told he had a fondness for TV Westerns like *Gunsmoke*), but he did know the young, especially the rebelliousness that is bound up with aspiration.[48] Speaking to the young must begin, like America itself, with a turning away from the ancestral and toward nature. Undeniably, Strauss was an "elitist" in being most concerned with those who, finding fewer obstacles in their paths, can achieve what most of us can only admire, affording us a mark to aim at. Yet he also saw that all human beings are drawn by and need a standard higher than material comfort; that im-

perative runs strongly among the young, and it is one that political societies—and political sciences—ignore at their peril.[49] American political
science deserved rebuke because, disdainful of "values," content with a
politics of interest and seemingly unaware of the loneliness of the "sovereign self," it was forfeiting the allegiance of the young.[50]

Strauss cherished his unorthodoxy, and he was only a little playful
when he characterized his position as the "left" of the profession.[51] In fact,
in his reply to my teachers Sheldon Wolin and John Schaar, he suggested
that the *only* relevant debate in political science lay between heterodoxies,
those who "wish to disagree" ranged against those "who are compelled
by reason to disagree"—that is, between those opponents of liberal democracy, who reject liberal practice as well as liberal doctrine, and those
critics of liberal theory, like Strauss himself, who appreciate, without illusions, liberalism's comforts and liberties.[52] Leo Strauss encouraged his
students to be admirers of the cities of speech and faith, aware of the limits of all political practice, and hence exacting critics of liberal democracy,
but also its willing allies.[53]

Strauss helped us to see American political thought as more than a
bland consensus or a series of manuals for practice. In American thinking, Strauss recognized a titanic intellectual struggle, in which the most
obvious combatants were the "first wave" of modernity and its successors,
but one in which older teachings have a crucial and continuing role. No
one was better suited than Strauss, moreover, to discern that if the American agon is elusive, it is because so much of the contest lies *within* Americans rather than *between* them. For American political thought, Strauss's
legacy is a kind of *anamnesis,* the reminder that the stakes of American
politics include great ideas as well as great powers. Strauss's teaching rests
on the truth that there are no souls without longing, only those whose
yearning lacks words and harmonies.[54] Leo Strauss, an Orpheus in the
American Thrace, continues to teach the music of politics.

I thank Harvey C. Mansfield, Steven Lenzner, and Patrick Deneen, who
read and commented on this essay, which derives from a lecture sponsored by the John M. Olin Center at the University of Chicago.

Notes

This essay was originally published as "Leo Strauss and the Dignity of American
Political Thought," *Review of Politics* 60, no. 2 (1998).

    1. Gordon Wood correctly identified my position in these quarrels when
he described me as a self-identified Straussian "fellow-traveler" ("The Funda-

mentalists and the Constitution," *New York Review of Books,* February 18, 1988, 33–40).

2. For those of Strauss's books that I have cited frequently, I use the following abbreviations: LAM = *Liberalism Ancient and Modern* (New York: Basic Books, 1968); NRH = *Natural Right and History* (Chicago: University of Chicago Press, 1953); PAW = *Persecution and the Art of Writing* (Chicago: University of Chicago Press, 1952); RCPR = *The Rebirth of Classical Political Rationalism,* ed. Thomas Pangle (Chicago: University of Chicago Press, 1989); SPP = *Studies in Platonic Political Philosophy,* ed. Thomas Pangle (Chicago: University of Chicago Press, 1983); WPP = *What Is Political Philosophy? And Other Studies* (Glencoe, Ill.: Free Press, 1959).

Strauss reviewed Dewey's *German Philosophy and Politics* (New York: Putnam, 1942) in *Social Research* 10 (1943): 505–7. Strauss did write in response to behavioral political science in *Essays on the Scientific Study of Politics,* ed. Herbert J. Storing (New York: Holt, Rinehart and Winston, 1962), 307–27 (reprinted in LAM, 203–23), but Allan Bloom tells us that Strauss regarded the new social science as intellectually important only for its roots in German philosophy (*Giants and Dwarfs* [New York: Simon and Schuster, 1990], 237).

3. Bloom's comment is taken from his introduction to *Confronting the Constitution* (Washington: AEI Press, 1990), 6; see also *Giants and Dwarfs,* 238.

4. Leo Strauss and Joseph Cropsey, eds., *History of Political Philosophy* (Chicago: Rand McNally, 1963); George H. Sabine, *History of Political Theory* (New York: Holt, Rinehart and Winston, 1961), 529, 670, 725, 789. It is worth noting that, since Strauss and Cropsey refer (vi) to their decision to exclude Dante, More, Bodin, and Harrington, among others, and to include Alfarabi and Maimonides, their *History* is self-consciously less European and Christian than Sabine's.

5. Strauss saw the belief in progress as a middle ground, akin to philosophy in holding to the idea of universal standards, but like historicism in neglecting "eternity" and the transhistoric (WPP, 66; RCPR, 238–39). As far as I know, his only reference to an American historian of the Progressive school—Beard—is generally approving (NRH, 92).

6. Daniel Boorstin, *The Genius of American Politics* (Chicago: University of Chicago Press, 1953); Louis Hartz, *The Liberal Tradition in America* (New York: Harcourt Brace, 1955); Richard Hofstadter, *The American Political Tradition and the Men Who Made It* (New York: Knopf, 1948).

7. Thurman Arnold, *The Folklore of Capitalism* (New Haven: Yale University Press, 1937).

8. Judith Shklar, "Redeeming American Political Theory," *American Political Science Review* 85 (1991): 1–16, especially 14–15.

9. PAW, 36; see also 32, 34, 35; Leo Strauss, *The City and Man* (Chicago: Rand McNally, 1964), 37–38. Harry V. Jaffa's elegant exposition of the political teaching implicit in Lincoln's Lyceum and Temperance addresses pointed to one commonly recognized exception to this rule: Americans know that persuasive political speech is likely to have its subtleties. Jaffa refers to the comment by Roy

Basler, the editor of Lincoln's *Collected Works,* that in the Lyceum speech, Lincoln was not simply avoiding direct reference to the lynching of Elijah Lovejoy, but seeking an indirect, less defended route to his audience's conscience. *Crisis of the House Divided,* 3rd. ed. (Chicago: University of Chicago Press, 1982, orig. 1959), 183–272, especially 196; *Collected Works of Abraham Lincoln,* ed. Roy P. Basler (New Brunswick: Rutgers University Press, 1953), 1:111n3.

10. PAW, 34, 37; WPP, 222. Catherine H. Zuckert, *Postmodern Platos* (Chicago: University of Chicago Press, 1996), 164.

11. PAW, 34n14. As examples of the sort of interpretation he seeks to correct, Strauss also refers to two American scholars, James T. Shotwell on Gibbon and George Sabine on *The Spirit of the Laws* (which Sabine found to be studded with irrelevancies and without coherent arrangement). More favorably, Strauss praises Harry Austryn Wolfson's "judicious remarks" on Halevi and cites him as an authority on Spinoza, and he quotes a few words of Salo Baron's on the Torah. Works by several American authors are also noted, without quotation, as secondary sources (PAW, 28, 29, 108n14, 188–89, 50).

12. Eric Goldman discusses MacLeish's discontent with intellectual "irresponsibles" in the thirties as part of his broader argument that Progressive appeal to the relativism of "reform Darwinism" undermined its own democratic faith (*Rendezvous with Destiny* [New York: Knopf, 1953], 383).

13. NRH, 296; see my essays "The Bible in the American Political Tradition," in *Religion and Politics,* ed. Myron Aronoff (New Brunswick: Transaction, 1984), 22–24 and "The Anti-Federalists, Representation and Party," *Northwestern University Law Review* 84 (1989): 19–20.

14. Henry David Thoreau, *Walden,* ed. J. Lydon Shanley (Princeton: Princeton University Press, 1971), 100–101.

15. Stanley Hubbard, *Nietzsche und Emerson* (Basel: Verlag fur Rechts und Gesellschaft, 1958); Strauss's students have also tended to slight Puritan and colonial thinking (see Oscar Handlin's review of Lorraine Smith Pangle and Thomas L. Pangle, *The Learning of Liberty: Educational Ideas of the American Founders* [Lawrence: University Press of Kansas, 1993], in *Washington Times,* June 6, 1993, B1).

16. NRH, 1.

17. RCPR, xxiv, 72, 270; see also NRH, 74–75; SPP, 147–73.

18. WPP, 47.

19. *History of Political Philosophy,* 6; WPP, 65.

20. WPP, 51, 54; as Strauss noted, although the term *philosophy of history* was known among the framers, the establishment of the United States antedates the advent of historicism (WPP, 58).

21. NRH, 245; on Locke's teaching, see NRH, 216–19, 226–30, 249; see also, on Lincoln, NRH, 70n29.

22. "Property," *National Gazette,* March 29, 1792, reprinted in *The Mind of the Founder,* ed. Marvin Meyers (Hanover: University Press of New England, 1981), 186. Madison's comment involves a not very oblique hint in the direction of slavery.

23. For example, see Ralph Ketcham, *Framed for Posterity: The Enduring Philosophy of the Constitution* (Lawrence: University Press of Kansas, 1993).

24. NRH, 233n104, referred to in NRH, 245n122.

25. On Rousseau's view, see NRH, 277, 281. Strauss, Thomas G. West writes, "was persuaded that Rousseau's critique of Lockean natural right on Locke's own premise was sound" ("Leo Strauss and the American Founding," *Review of Politics* 53 [1991]: 171). In that sense, Madison was following the logic of modernity: Strauss refers to the status of "individuality" as the omega and possibly the alpha of the "quarrel between ancients and moderns." NRH, 323. For a similar argument, see John H. Schaar, "And the Pursuit of Happiness," *Virginia Quarterly* 46 (1970): 1–27.

26. For Burke's position, see NRH, 311–13.

27. Ibid., 314, 322.

28. Ibid., 318. Michael Kammen describes the framers' doctrine as a "blend of cultural relativism . . . with theoretical universalism" (*A Machine That Would Go of Itself* [New York: Knopf, 1986], 65).

29. WPP, 113.

30. NRH, 81; for the idea of natural right in the Christian Scriptures, see Romans 2:14–15, 11:21, 24; and Galatians 4:8.

31. NRH, 4; this despite the fact that, methodologically if not by personal conviction, social science seemed to reflect a "dogmatic atheism" (LAM, 218).

32. NRH, 60–62. See also Nathan Tarcov, "On a Certain Critique of 'Straussianism,'" *Review of Politics* 53 (1991): 11. In at least one instance, Strauss made an argument strikingly similar to Weber's: in *Robinson Crusoe*, faith in Providence is crucial in enabling Crusoe to overcome despair and in moving him to "bestir" himself to make use of his talent, but Strauss argued that Defoe's story—in contrast to the work by Ibn Tufayl which was Defoe's model—is best read as depicting a "modern man" using his "natural powers" to lay the basis of a "technical civilization," implicitly relegating Crusoe's religiosity to the role of an inward foundation for outward achievements (RCPR, 218).

33. RCPR, 233; LAM, 264–66. In a similar spirit, Strauss suggested learning from Judaism the lesson of "fortitude in suffering," an ability to endure grounded in inner emancipation (LAM, 268). Of course, Strauss's argument implicitly assumes that religion, in America as elsewhere, has another side and darker possibilities. My reference to Machiavelli, of course, is to *The Prince*, ch. 15.

34. LAM, 4–5; "On a New Interpretation of Plato's Political Philosophy," *Social Research* 13 (1946): 357. This democratic ideal seems indebted to Spinoza's emphasis on human dignity, and hence stands as a nobler but riskier alternative to other democratic possibilities (LAM, 241). The phrase "an aristocracy of everyone" is from Benjamin R. Barber, *An Aristocracy of Everyone: The Politics of Education and the Future of America* (New York: Ballantine, 1992).

35. Henry Adams, *Democracy and Esther: Two Novels*, ed. Ernest Samuels (Cambridge, Mass.: Harvard University Press, 1961), 44ff.

36. WPP, 37; LAM, 15–16.

37. LAM, 11, 14–16, 245; *An Introduction to Political Philosophy*, ed. Hilail Gilden (Detroit: Wayne State University Press, 1989), 98.

38. LAM, 23–24.

39. Ibid., 20–22, 210–12, 264; WPP, 38.

40. LAM, 5, 223.

41. Ibid., 221. Similarly, radical relativism points toward perspectivism, and hence threatens the science which behavioralism champions.

42. WPP, 279–81; RCPR, 22.

43. RCPR, 32, 76; *City and Man*, 3–7. While praising Adams, Strauss observed that, like all modern historians, Adams differed from Thucydides in feeling compelled to go beyond the specifically political to a discussion of social, economic, and cultural life. Strauss comments that Thucydides offered no explanation for the limitation of his work; Strauss does not explain the inclusiveness of modern history. It seems clear, however, that the reason lies in the moral plurality of modern regimes, as contrasted with the relative unity of the *polis* (RCPR, 76; NRH, 245, 314, 322).

44. RCPR, 22, 23.

45. *City and Man*, 7; NRH, 201.

46. Nathan Tarcov, "Philosophy and History: Tradition and Interpretation in the Work of Leo Strauss," *Polity* 16 (1983): 9.

47. Strauss's letters to Karl Löwith indicate a strategy of undoing modernity *privatissime*, but that caution is balanced by his conviction that modern states, in critical respects, run contrary to nature ("Correspondence concerning Modernity," *International Journal of Philosophy* 4 [1983]: 114, 108).

48. LAM, 204, 261. I have elided Strauss's reference to "the best men" because that language would be apt to jar contemporary sensibilities in a way that distracts from his argument.

49. Ibid., 24; Kenneth Deutsch and Walter Sofer, eds., *The Crisis of Liberal Democracy* (Albany: State University of New York Press, 1987), 3.

50. LAM, 262.

51. Ibid., 204. This stance has occasioned comment from Strauss's most bitter critics (i.e., Stephen Holmes, "Aristippus in and out of Athens," *American Political Science Review* 73 [1979]: 113) as well as much shrewder ones (Wood, "Fundamentalists and the Constitution," 36).

52. "Replies to Wolin and Schaar," *American Political Science Review* 57 (1963): 152.

53. Harvey C. Mansfield Jr., *The Spirit of Liberalism* (Cambridge, Mass.: Harvard University Press, 1978). Ultimately, Allan Bloom wrote, Strauss's politics "were the politics of philosophy and not the politics of a particular regime" (*Giants and Dwarfs*, 240).

54. "All of us contain Music and Truth," Mark Twain once noted, "but most of us can't get it out" (Notebook 42 [June 1897–March 1900], 68, Mark Twain Papers, Bancroft Library, University of California, Berkeley). The phrase "souls without longing" comes from the original title of Allan Bloom's *The Closing of the American Mind* (New York: Simon and Schuster, 1987).

Power After Power

Reflections on Liberalism in *Sheldon Wolin's* Politics and Vision

In *Politics and Vision*,[1] liberalism—and specifically, Anglo-American liberalism—is nemesis, framing modern political thought as alpha and dark omega.[2] Already in part 1 (chapter 9), liberalism is identified with the "decline of political philosophy," and in part 2, liberalism—its great antagonists destroyed or self-destructed—is the official doctrine of "Superpower," being promoted as the basis of a world system, a *pax liberalis*.[3]

Liberalism has had its conquests, but its characteristic triumphs have been won by insinuation and temptation, its happy accommodation to human frailty. One of Sheldon Wolin's great contributions, in fact, has been to correct the notion that liberalism was rooted in rationalism and naïve confidence in human goodness,[4] in favor of a truer account of liberalism's genealogy: "born in fear, nourished by disenchantment and prone to believe that the human condition was, and was likely to remain, one of pain and anxiety" (298). And, masterful in his account of liberalism's past, Wolin is indispensable as a guide to its present and probable future.

Of course, I am not objective where Sheldon Wolin is concerned. Wolin was my first teacher of political theory, and there is no way to disentangle my thinking from his; at every reading of Wolin's work, I am shocked to discover how many of my best ideas have made their way into his writing. I do have some questions about his analysis: Wolin may understate both liberalism's genuine charms and its tendency to self-contempt, and I worry that Wolin's contemporary reflections may underrate the dependence of democracy—even "fugitive" democracy—on institutions and forms. But these are at most minor quarrels, and what follows amounts to a set of reflections on an argument that, in the main, I regard as unanswerable.

In an age of spin and cant, in the academy as well as outside it, Wolin is a compelling voice for democracy and for politics, unsparing in his diagnosis of democracy's bleak prospects and hence more credible in his whisper of hope. Most important, Wolin is a living rule, a constant exemplar of political theory as a vocation.

Past: Natural Freedom and Liberal Politics

Philosophically, if not anthropologically, liberalism begins with the individual.[5] Human beings are bodies, naturally separate, who become conscious of others only when they "collide." The other is she who resists my will and desire, and since human beings strive to overcome such resistances to their natural freedom, "conflict and friction are thus the sources of man's awareness of man" (305).[6]

Liberty, rooted in nature, needs only more or less passive protection; order requires active construction. Yet liberal politics, a creative human achievement, is also "derivative" (259). Aristotle held that while human beings are partly moved toward politics by the goals of prepolitical or subpolitical relationships—by the desire for safety or gain—they are also drawn by their own political nature. The efficient causes of political life, in other words, are subordinate to its final cause; private goods constrain politics in practice, but the political good is naturally entitled to rule. Liberalism, by contrast, regards politics as naturally the servant of private ends. This does not at all entail a limitation on political *power*. Rather, as Wolin argues, liberal argument diminishes the *status* of the political, implicitly reducing it, in Thoreau's dismissive description of government, to "an expedient by which men would fain succeed in letting one another alone."[7]

The ideal of liberal politics, as Wolin argues, is a "rediscovery" of Locke's state of nature, in which human beings, informed by the law of nature, largely leave one another alone. Separating nature and war, Locke made the political a less "dramatic" achievement—hence less impelled toward absolutism—than Hobbes's Leviathan, but Wolin aside, it is hard to call Locke's imagined nature "political" (274).[8] At bottom, Locke seems to be describing a kind of companionable indifference, rather like the "parallel play" of children, interrupted only by an occasional squabble.

In any case, Locke's nature slides into war by way of what Wolin calls a "fallen state of nature" (275), an exceptionally apt formulation, both because it captures Locke's argument and because the biblical metaphor articulates part of the appeal of Locke's theorizing to more or less orthodox Christians alarmed by Hobbes's irreverence. The force of Wolin's argument is strengthened, I think, by recognizing that Hobbes's teaching contains its own, prior version of the Fall, one tacitly assumed by subsequent liberal theorizing.

Seeking empirical examples, which he concedes are hard to come by, Hobbes asserts that "among savage people in many places of America," the "government of small families" rests on a "concord" that "dependeth on natural lust," while outside these families, there is "no government at all" and the "brutish" condition of the state of war prevails.[9] This argument suggests that there is a natural sociability of sorts, but one that is limited by the narrow compass of erotic attachment. The government of children, moreover, includes a special affective bond: the parental decision to preserve the lives of children—a choice Hobbes strongly associates with the natural authority of mothers—creates a permanent obligation in the child.[10] The implicit children's covenant that makes the "law of gratitude" thus applicable, however, cannot be based on reason; necessarily, it rests on the affections.[11]

In these terms, "sin" is not concupiscence, but expansion beyond the constricted boundaries of lust and obligating affection. Hobbes's argument at least implied that human families might have remained peaceable so long as they could be separate: peopling and crowding, the need and ability to extend the family's sphere of dominion, made war between the heads of families more or less inevitable.[12] Correspondingly, later social science inclined to rank the family as a uniquely natural association—"the only case of sacrifice in Nature," William Graham Sumner wrote—while other relationships (possibly excepting intimate friendship) were classed as artifacts, linked to calculations of interest.[13]

Locke, however, modifies this account. As the *First Treatise* indicates, he aimed to rule out the family, an institution that appears to include natural hierarchy, as a model for politics (although he concedes that the transition from paternal to political power is "easy" and even "natural.")[14] The *Second Treatise* lacks even Hobbes's passing reference to erotic bonds, and more importantly, Locke aims to lessen the confining power of affective attachment in favor of an "education for liberty" which emphasizes independence and interest.[15] Bertrand de Jouvenel's assertion that social contract theory is "the view of childless men who seem to have forgotten their childhood," in part evidently unfair, is defensible on the understanding that this seeming forgetfulness is willful.[16] The liberal project took it as a goal to limit the encumbrances of the self, helping to give the name of liberation to the isolating logic of individualism.[17]

Similarly, Locke intended his state of nature to be a standard for civil society rather than a historical construct (274–75).[18] In fact, I think the evidence suggests that Locke thought that the original condition of humanity was closer to Hobbes's description, and that the first societies were a common subordination imposed by leaders preeminent in force and will—consider only Locke's repeated appeals to the example of Jephtha (Judg. 11, 12), which suggests that the real law of nature's God and natural reason is force and the determination to prevail whatever the cost.[19]

Locke lays it down as a law of nature that a human being has an affirmative duty to preserve humankind, and not to "take away or impair . . . what tends to the preservation of the life, the liberty, the health, limb or goods of another," but only "when his own preservation comes not in competition." In any case of uncertainty, an individual is to assess by "calm reason and conscience" whether there is in truth a threat to his own preservation, or that of humankind in general, that would justify restraining or punishing another.[20] Yet Locke knows, as surely we do, that reason and conscience are not reliable: the American intervention in Iraq was justified precisely in terms of a threat to our preservation and that of humanity. The unreliability of reason is increased, moreover, if liberty and estate—the freedom and respect to which one feels entitled—are included in the things of one's own that one is entitled to preserve.[21] Liberal reason, as Wolin emphasizes, is at bottom the servant of the passions; as Franklin famously observed, "So convenient a thing it is to be a reasonable Creature, since it enables one to find or make a Reason for everything one has a mind to do."[22] It is hardly surprising, then, that the "greater part" of humankind are "no strict observers of equity and justice," so that "full of fears and continual dangers," human beings are "quickly driven into society" from the "ill condition" of nature.[23]

Locke minimizes or denies conflict in nature—at one point, he seems to suggest that there was "no doubt of right, no room for quarrel"—but his examples suggest that the harshness of nature leaves human beings with little time for debates about right or energies for quarrel.[24] (Originally, Locke writes that nature provides 1/10 of what is needed for life, which he quickly modifies to 1/100, and eventually to 1/1,000).[25] Nature's severity, in fact, drives human beings together—Paine, a democrat but emphatically a liberal, saw it that way—linking human beings by a combination of natural sympathy and overriding necessity.[26]

As human beings push back the boundary of nature, they may be able to avoid conflict by separating, for despite—or because of—the penury of nature, land is abundant (hence Locke's appeal to the separations of

Abraham and Lot and Jacob and Esau.)[27] But open space, though it *permits* such separations, does not guarantee peace: witness Locke's wonderfully devious observation that "at the beginning, Cain might take as much ground as he could till and yet leave enough to Abel's sheep to feed on."[28] The subtext is obvious: the existence of enough abundance to permit the offering of sacrifices signals the end of crushing necessity, but it also opens the question of respect and recognition, issues which in the Bible's account result in fratricide—"inconveniences" serious enough, though still on the small scale of "polecats" and "foxes," to move human beings to create political authority.[29]

Yet Wolin indicates that the contract creating political society only reframes liberal anxieties. As soon as the memory of nature's "ill condition" begins to fade, human beings will regret their self-limiting promises, and will be tempted by the possibility of crimes great and small, the hope of enjoying the freedom of the state of nature within the advantages of political society. They may be deterred by the threat of detection and punishment and—more distantly—by the risk that their example, imitated, might lead to social disintegration, but those cautions can be overridden—in the powerful, by pride and the hope of great gain, and among the poor and excluded, by desperation and the sense of having nothing to lose.

Convinced of the unreliability of reason, yet devoted to personal liberty, liberalism developed a preoccupation with the nonrational foundations of order. Projects for the direct socialization of citizens—Locke's ideas about early childhood education, for example, or his insistence on "reasonable" religion for an imperfectly rational majority—were, to the developing liberal taste, improper objects for state authority and better left to indirectly managed opinion (as in the later liberal exchange of Locke's limited religious toleration for the "marketplace of ideas").[30] Liberalism preferred to rely on science, trusting that its understanding of the subrational (motion, force, refraction, and the like), applied to human affairs, would permit the construction of regimes able to minimize reliance on both compulsion and civic virtue.[31] For Americans, of course, this is civic catechism. "The reason of man, like man himself," Madison wrote, "is timid and cautious when left alone, and acquires firmness and confidence in proportion to the number with which it is associated."[32] In the large state, characterized by complex fragmentations of power—the grand design of *The Federalist*[33]—individuals would be "circumspect," aware of their comparative impotence and vulnerability, at the same time deriving at least relative confidence from their status as members of the great, anonymous public. As shrewdly channeled interests and desires substitute for public speech and spirit, governmental power may grow, but—as Wolin teaches us—politics withers away,[34] and while citizens might, on some definitions, be called "free," it is hard to see them as self-governing.

Present: The Natural History of Superpower

Wolin is also right to observe that the liberal project involves a totalitarian logic. The association of liberty with the desire for self-preservation and gratification links human freedom to limitless will and the perennial effort to extend human power, especially through the pursuit of all discoveries and inventions that "let light into the Nature of Things, tend to increase the Power of Man over Matter and multiply the Conveniences or Pleasures of Life."[35] And necessarily, increasing human mastery over nature increases human mastery over humanity as a part of nature, although liberals have sometimes displayed a chilling innocence in relation to that corollary, as in Dewey's cheerful comment that experimental science "must force the apparent facts of nature into forms different to those in which they familiarly present themselves; and thus make them tell the truth about themselves, as torture may compel an unwilling witness to reveal what he has been concealing."[36]

Power must expand to answer power.[37] In our time, political society requires that, somewhere, there be power sufficient to afford minimal security, not only against the threat of the terrible weaponry made available by the modern arsenal, but against the dreadful vulnerability of a specialized and intricately interdependent society, in which minor errors or relatively small applications of force at crucial points can do such disproportionate damage. (Wolin [395] reminds us of the fortunately misplaced anxiety about "glitches" at the millennium, anticipating by less than two years the political glitches of 9/11.) And the greater the risk of error or failure, the greater the need to amplify and multiply countervailing powers, even at the cost of redundancy and including the expansion of morally permissible conduct.

The same dynamic involves an imperative to assimilate or overcome those who resent exclusion *and* those (most often local elites and traditional peoples) who resist the intrusions of a pursuit of mastery that is inherently "law-breaking, transgressive, and boundary-defiant" (493). This may involve the use of force, but—as noted earlier—it is more likely to involve an undermining of alternative authorities through the temptations of consumerism and individual rights. "Low prices," Marx and Engels wrote in the *Manifesto*, "are the heavy artillery with which the bourgeoisie levels all Chinese walls," and not only in China, as Wal-Mart testifies. All political societies, whatever their nominal boundaries, are part of a regime of expanding scale and extent: "Superpower," liberalism's ruling political form, transcends all boundaries, even its own (404–5, 559).

The growth of power's threats and benefits fuels demand for the state's protection and advocacy, and citizens—especially when they are thinking about besetting dangers—worry that government has too little power to control outsiders, economics, and the whole, shadowy array of "alien" forces. At the same time, when they are thinking about government in relation to themselves, citizens experience the state as overwhelming and baffling, and its power as something to be distrusted and evaded. Political authority, confronting "deauthorization" and "disaffiliation" (491–92, 551–56, 601) learns not to trust its citizens, and the result is a state of "highly concentrated powers" that relies on technique and covert politics—including a renewed reliance on the ancient liberal mode of indirect control via the market and privatization—to avoid making any demands on its citizens (459–60).

The regime offers its citizens "protean, premeditated, manufactured" (582) opportunities to "redesign" or "construct" the self, Dewey's experimentalism with the self as object. We are presented with dazzling chances for cosmetic transformation and for changes in fashion and style (580), paralleled by the fascination with "virtual reality" and "reality television," both forms in which "reality" is the product of artifice and contrivance. Yet this heightened "oblivion of the past" (394) is in large measure the oblivion of oblivion, an attempt to forget not simply our mortality but the broader and startling transience of almost everything human, like the cacophonies that are so transparently intended to drown out our silence (567, 587).

With "Superpower" titanic but uncertain in its foundations, it is not surprising that contemporary liberal theorizing relies so heavily on what Patrick Deneen calls "democratic faith."[38] John Dewey, for example, sought to redefine liberalism in terms of a faith in science, its old quest for power and effectiveness dressed up in the language of "growth" and "potentiality," its confidence in history expressed in terms of an experimentalism (the "method of democracy") that made democracy itself contingent on effectiveness and results. And Dewey trusted that publics capable of controlling large-scale organizations and governments would be created by a new "art of communication," with no apparent worries that such an art might make the media—or now, the Internet—into even more effective instruments of control and the "totalization of democracy" (506, 508, 511, 513, 519). All that suggests, of course, that Dewey was an essentially pre-totalitarian writer, still comfortable with a version of his early confidence that history was marked by an ethical advance from "code" to "conscience."[39]

Karl Popper barely merits Wolin's attention, but he was clearly a post-totalitarian thinker who, having learned to distrust "utopianism," argued that just as it is impossible to predict the future well enough to lay utopian plans, it is impossible to know that future well enough to set *limits*. The faith in progress yields, consequently, to a faith in drift, incremental "solutions" sufficient to keep the ship afloat in a current whose direction is power, like Huck and Jim going down the river. Popper, as Wolin observes, is akin to the neo-pragmatists who have "faith in the ultimate good nature of liberal society" (583) or, Wolin might have added, to the pluralists who trust in the application of the market metaphor to interest group politics.[40]

As we are often reminded, however, John Rawls is the preeminent political theorist of our day, especially since in so many ways, Rawls seems like Locke revivified, purged of his ambiguous anthropology. His theory of justice, Rawls wrote, "generalizes and carries to a higher degree of abstraction the familiar theory of the social contract."[41] Like classical liberalism, Rawls begins with human beings who are not naturally political animals, and whose rights are prior to and the condition of any agreement about the good. And like Locke, Rawls makes an essentially utilitarian case for equality, arguing for only as much equality as will permit the development of inequalities.[42]

For Locke, however, no "veil of ignorance" shielded human beings in the state of nature from an informed estimate of their prospective advantages in civil society. In fact, Locke assumed that it was the expectation of secure advantages, including the protection of property and the recognition of status, that would induce the strong to accept a political sphere based on equal rights, just as the "less advantaged" would be happy (at least in the short term) to accept relief from arbitrary rule, an exchange that is entirely plausible.

On its own terms, by contrast, Rawls's veil is not plausible; as Wolin remarks, it presumes human beings "deprived of essential human attributes" (538), unable or unwilling to see or imagine their own prospective positions. To make it plausible, even as an abstraction, Rawls must assume a change in the *terms* of exchange, reflecting what is not an "original" position but something very much like contemporary liberal society.[43] In such a set of conditions, advantaged elites might find the benefits of social order (and the corresponding fear of disorder) so great that they are willing to pay a greater price to get it, while the disadvantaged are relatively less fearful of arbitrary rule and repression and are willing to insist on more favorable terms.

The implicit sense of an order that is both more fragile and more desperately necessary for the established classes is evident in Rawls's *Political Liberalism*.[44] At first glance, Rawls's "modern democratic society" appears more "open" than Locke, whose toleration excluded atheists and Catholics. As Wolin indicates, however, Rawls himself imposes what amounts to a "political loyalty test," excluding "comprehensive doctrines" and "unreasonable" speech from public forums (539). Rawls presumes that the adherents of such "comprehensive doctrines" will accept these terms based on an "overlapping consensus," an area of agreement that constitutes a public culture. This "overlapping consensus," however, would be experienced as a *truncated* form of justice by the adherents of the excluded "comprehensive doctrines" and a *complete* form of justice by the liberals whose position it is. There is, in other words, a tension and an imbalance of advantages in Rawls's public culture: the pretensions of *Political Liberalism* aside, laws are never neutral: as Wolin observes, in the United States (and even more, in Rawls's theorizing), the laws deny the public claims of religion, but not those of economics (403). Rawls's position would seem calculated to infuriate any number of religious groups in the United States, groups that already seem resentful enough (541–42). Fearful of just that sort of resentment, Rawls appears to hope for a *will to peace* that, more than a mechanical overlapping of interests, amounts to a first principle capable of overriding old discords or newly discovered ones, a position that points not to Locke, but to Hobbes. It is one measure of liberal uneasiness in the age of Superpower.[45]

Contradictions: Liberal Spirits, Liberal Politics

Wolin touches only lightly, however, on the ironic resonances between his Superpower and liberalism's chronic self-disgust, the contradiction between liberal spirits and liberal politics.

Begin with the proposition that liberal politics derives from fearfulness, the impulse to preserve life and avoid pain and the corresponding desire for security and comfort. Human beings enter society precisely as part of an "escape from freedom," as Gouverneur Morris told the Convention: "The savage State was more favorable to liberty than the Civilized.... It was preferred by all men who had not acquired a taste for property."[46] Liberty, for model liberal citizens, is in part burdensome and inconvenient; they prefer caution to daring and their conduct is "modest and unheroic" (296). Politically "desensitized" (429), they agree with Hamilton's assertion that the "bright talents and exalted endowments" associated with ancient cities are not worth the price of the turbulent politics of the *polis*.[47] They are hesitant even to defend their rights, as Locke was at some pains to indicate, hard to move toward change, more disposed to suffer than to run the risk of resistance, and likely to act only after "a long train of abuses."[48]

Leaving the state of nature, in other words, involves a measure of slavishness, a barter of liberty for safety and support that is partly disguised and made tolerable for liberals to the extent that it is not—as Leviathan is—a submission to some *one:* it is slavishness without a master.[49] Political society is always a questionable bargain, a matter of "selling out" in which the price is always open to question, and nowhere more than in liberal souls.

Liberals cherish liberty as a defining human value: "Liberty is to faction as air is to fire," Madison said,[50] the comparison suggesting that freedom is the moral equivalent of breath, essential to any genuinely human life. They admire the free spirit, one disinclined to revere authority and zealous to defend the rights and liberties of person or country, as in the traditional celebrations of Cato, Brutus, or William Tell. And since those who give the law are free in a higher sense than those who obey, liberal spirits are apt to take as models those who carve out new orders by force of mind or will—Locke's repeated appeals to the example of Jephtha, for instance, or Jefferson's reverence for Newton, Locke, and Bacon[51]—and to be at least somewhat tempted by those moments of crisis that open the possibility of political founding.[52] The "impulse to mastery" in liberal theory, as Wolin observes, runs counter to bourgeois "timidity" (263–64).

Liberal society and the rule of law are possible only within defended space, and they presume and rely on those truly free persons—Harvey Mansfield would want us to call them "manly"[53]—who are willing to risk life and liberty and estate for the freedom of others. Patrick Henry, an evangelical Christian, was an uncertain liberal, but his rhetoric has spoken to and for generations of liberal spirits, just as John Adams did when he said that the principle of self-preservation, that liberal cornerstone, was "a point I would not give up for my right hand, nay for my life."[54] In fact, liberalism teaches a not very secret contempt for the bourgeois "half men" who, beset by fear for life or respectability, cannot play for liberty's high stakes.[55]

Wolin associates this disdain for bourgeois prudence with the enterprise of the "restless, aggressive, buccaneering entrepreneur" (296), a connection often cultivated in business circles. But commercial daring risks estate, not life and liberty: it operates largely within the protection of law, sometimes stretching its limits or unsettling order, but always relying on civil society. Theodore Roosevelt expressed appreciation for the contribution made by material prosperity to civic life, but argued that "a scrambling commercialism, heedless of the higher life . . . busying ourselves only with the wants of our bodies" is unsuited to rule: "Far better it is to dare mighty things, to win glorious triumphs, even though checkered by failure, than to take rank with those poor spirits who neither enjoy much nor suffer much, because they live in the gray twilight that knows not victory or defeat."[56]

Even those who do not share T.R.'s admiration for the martial virtues will find it hard to fault either his observation that America could have avoided the suffering, slaughter, and cost of the Civil War by letting the South go its way, or his moral, that there is reason to be thankful for the courage of those who took up that struggle. In fact, change the specifics of Roosevelt's prescription and keep his moral teaching and you have a doctrine that applies to Dr. King and the SCLC, but certainly not to bourgeois prudence.

In greater or lesser degree, liberalism offers, if it does not positively encourage, rebellion in *style*, the sort of "artistic" freedom that delights in scandalizing, a pleasure that is possible only to the extent that the established order remains capable of shock. But at least periodically, liberalism's self-disgust at liberal politics seeks a grander, less peripheral role.

Both elements are present, I think, in what Wolin calls the "vogue of Nietzscheolatry" (457), the effort to adapt Nietzsche to liberalism, burying the "older, less presentable Nietzsche" and embracing Nietzsche's admiration for creativity and singularity (460, 462), as in Richard Rorty's admiration for the "strong poet" or the "revolutionary" artist or scientist.[57]

That attraction leads some intellectuals—among political scientists, most notably George Kateb[58]—to Emerson, whose belittling of institutions and concrete relationships was on a par with Nietzsche's, but Emerson—although he deprecated forms and spoke of Good and Bad as mere "names"—was a moralist, albeit of a cosmic sort, and his version of individualism asks us to throw ourselves into our times, confiding ourselves to the "genius" of the age.[59] Nietzsche is better suited to the role of liberalism's guilty conscience, "more prescient" than Marx, Wolin says (490), about the crisis of the liberal state and better able to speak to the individual who cherishes liberty in the most radical sense—the liberal who yearns for the freedom of nature within political society, and even beyond that, itches to be free of Locke's natural law or Hobbes's rules *in foro interno.* "The highest men live beyond the rules, free from all bonds," Nietzsche wrote,[60] and in those terms, the freedom of the highest man (as Wolin shows) is tyranny, if only in private life, the fantasy liberal politics was designed to suppress.

Since Socrates, it has been part of the calling of political theory to attempt the seduction of would-be tyrants, offering—as Wolin does—the vision of an even higher freedom. And in that sense, Wolin's democratic alternative should, for liberal political society, be considered as an attempt at the soft impeachment of a friend.

Fugitive Democracy and the Politics of Limits

Wolin is surely right that democracy is "beleaguered" and "discordant" in modern politics and "permanently in opposition to structures it cannot command." An ideal whose standard is rough political equality and that aims to extend the citizen's "measure of control" in framing choices is necessarily at odds with a regime that involves large-scale, specialized, inevitably hierarchical institutions and organizations "structured to produce differentials" (601, 604).[61]

In modern politics, then, democracy is essentially a critical standard. That, it needs to be said, is not the worst thing: political theory is primarily concerned with the way we *think* about politics. It may hope for more, but even a theory as activistic as Dewey's engages in politics, in the first instance, by addressing minds and speech.

But is it possible to go beyond criticism to reduce democracy's ephemerality in political practice? If the totalitarian logic of politics is inescapable, it might be necessary to conclude—as the majority of contemporary political theorists have concluded—that liberal totalitarianism, at least disposed to avoid cruelty and to afford private liberties, is the best available alternative.[62] Wolin concedes the "urgency" of the question, at the same time as he acknowledges the difficulty of giving a democratic answer (389).

The most obvious democratic remedy involves decentralization, reducing the scale of political life, and especially, the size of public forums, but that would at best be a matter for inchworm incrementalism. As noted earlier, there is a need for political power, somewhere, that is strong enough to address the threat of weapons of mass destruction. If Superpower did not exist, would it be necessary to invent it? Second, it would be necessary to face the "political meaning" of the economy (527), and with it, the possibility that a democratic economy would almost certainly be incompatible with an economy of global scale,[63] and would also very likely prove to be inconsistent with an economy of unlimited abundance and inclusion. Third, we would need to find a means of controlling the intrusions of technology, that vanguard of the project of mastery, an objective made more difficult by the fact that technical advances (e.g., stem cell research) are linked to so many human hopes.

Finally, it would be necessary to wean citizens away from the tendency to look to national institutions as a means of overcoming local resistances (as, in their different ways, both sides of the abortion debate are wont to do), a goal that requires the development of very refined public judgment, since many local variations (most obviously, racial segregation) are unacceptable in democratic life. Wolin does see some reason for hope, arguing that citizens are parts of neighborhoods, localities, and states "with institutional roots and participatory traditions older than the constitution" (603). Unfortunately, this is hyperbole: thirty-seven states and the District of Columbia are the creations of government under the Constitution, and the neighborhoods in which more and more Americans live are transient and formless, without roots or participatory traditions of any kind. Still, up to a point Wolin is right: there are local traditions and habits, and even the most amorphous localities are at least places, political space occupied by bodies and possible starting points for democratic politics.

As Wolin recognizes, any effort to bring democracy into political practice is a task for political art (389), and in the aesthetics of politics, there are tremendous advantages on the side of the totalitarians. Wolin's own outline of political artistry, moreover, may concede too much—despite Wolin's own trenchant criticism—to postmodernism's distaste for institutions and forms.

In a sense, it is correct to observe that democracy, like any regime, strains against "stable forms" in the name of its ruling principle (602). But that principle—in the case of democracy, the equality of citizens— is necessary as an unchanging standard for dedication: the combination of localism and "centrifugalism" which is Wolin's desideratum (604) assumes that *both* are subject to equality and the common good.

Moreover, "continuous destabilization" and "accelerated rates of change" disconnect the present from the past, "leave opposition outdated before its case is mustered," and disempower citizens as "carriers of everyday cultural traditions" (567, 581, 604). And just as habit is some protection against manipulation, forms make it easier for a public to organize its energies. Wolin is right that the destabilizing elements of the culture are mirrored in postmodernism's "postures" of revolt, its "appetite for theoretical novelty," and its "antipathies to centered discourse," all of which parallel, and even reinforce, the ideologies of the market (566–67).[64]

While it is true that democracy is "fugitive," "necessarily occasional," and a "moment of experience" (602–3), the extent of its ephemerality is defined, at least in large part, by forms and institutions. Democracy today is surely more fugitive and momentary than it was, say, in a New England town.[65] Liberal institutions, after all, were designed to accentuate the "fugitive" qualities of democracy. Presuming the will to form a political community, Locke taught, political society must go "whither the greater force carries it, which is the consent of the majority."[66] The operative principle, however, is not majority rule but "the greater force," something associated with majorities only in the state of nature[67] or those rare instances in which differences in craft, position, or military force are more or less leveled out—as they were in the eighteenth century, for example, when the musket was a genuine equalizer, since differences in skill counted for relatively little.[68]

In civil society, by contrast, democracy is profoundly unnatural, possible only through conventions and only to the extent that it accommodates itself to the normal inequalities of power. Natural democracy can reassert itself only in moments of political collapse and reversion to something like the state of nature.[69] While these fugitive democratic moments are endowed with remedial authority, liberalism regarded them with something between uneasiness and dread.[70] Jefferson sometimes spoke welcomingly about democratic moments, but only on the assumption of social conditions neither "crowded" nor "overcharged," like those he saw in America.[71] And Madison congratulated America on constitutions premised on the "total exclusion of the people in their collective capacity" from any share in the government—wholly representative regimes, in which democracy is *defined* as "fugitive," confined to the moment of voting that Madison's successors have helped to make increasingly private and solitary.[72]

Tocqueville embraced but went beyond locality and decentralization to discuss forms of press, party, and association by which popular government could be made more or less substantial, even in a large republic. The democratic political art that Wolin champions—evidently close to Tocqueville's "art of association"—needs to envision institutions by which democracy can be made less fleeting, even within the titan state and the constraining possibilities of our times. Most urgently, however, Wolin reminds his readers of political philosophy's most specific vocation, the need to articulate a democratic voice, a political vision, critical of liberalism's modern project, that, "rooted in the ordinary, affirms the value of limits" (606).[73] Chesterton put it with characteristic eloquence: "It is the experience of men that always returns to the equality of men; it is the average that ultimately justifies average man. It is when men have seen and suffered much and come to the end of more elaborate experiments that they see men as . . . under an equal light of death and daily laughter; and none the less mysterious for being many."[74]

Notes

This essay was originally published as "Power After Power: Reflections on Liberalism in *Politics and Vision*," *Theory & Event* 10, no. 1 (2007), http://muse.jhu .edu/journals/theory_and_event/toc/tae10.1.html.

1. Sheldon S. Wolin, *Politics and Vision: Continuity and Innovation in Western Political Thought* (Princeton: Princeton University Press, 2004), hereafter cited in the text by page number, without further identification.

2. Wolin's focus on Anglo-American liberalism is especially clear in part 1, where—following Wolin in setting Hobbes aside—Locke merits most of a chapter, while Bentham and Mill are each mentioned at least two dozen times, and Smith three dozen. In part 2, Dewey, Popper, and Rawls get extended treatment. By contrast, there are only two references to Montesquieu; Kant is mentioned only three times (as is Benjamin Constant); Hegel gets ten mentions, but eight are in relation to Marx; even Tocqueville merits only eight references. In general, continental liberals past and present seem more appreciative of the role of "social authorities," and perhaps, of political life (Aurelian Craiutu, *Liberalism under Siege* [Lanham: Lexington Books, 2003]).

3. Francis Fukuyama, *The End of History and the Last Man* (New York: Avon, 1992), xi, 203–4.

4. Russell Kirk was not atypical in writing that "liberals postulate the su-

premacy of human reason . . . they believe fatuously in the natural goodness and infinite improvability of man." *The Conservative Mind* (Chicago: Regnery, 1953), 251.

5. The claim that human beings are "born free," Ruth Grant observes, is "moral" rather than "sociological." "Locke's Political Anthropology and Lockean Individualism," *Journal of Politics,* 50 (1988): 43.

6. See also John Locke, *Essay concerning Human Understanding,* bk. II, ch. xxvii, sec. 6, ed. Peter Nidditch (Oxford: Clarendon, 1975), 331–32.

7. Henry David Thoreau, "Resistance to Civil Government," in *Reform Papers,* ed. Wendell Glick (Princeton: Princeton University Press, 1973), 64.

8. See also Grant, "Locke's Political Anthropology and Lockean Individualism," 55; and Norman Jacobson, "Behold Leviathan! The Systematic Solace of Thomas Hobbes," in *Pride and Solace* (Berkeley: University of California Press, 1978), 51–92.

9. Thomas Hobbes, *Leviathan,* ch. 13.

10. Thomas Hobbes, *The Elements of Law,* ed. Ferdinand Tönnies (New York: Barnes and Noble, 1969), II.4.3, p. 132 and II.3.2, p. 127; see also *Leviathan,* ch. 20; hence sons, and presumably daughters, are never in the state of nature (*De Cive,* ed. Stuart Lamprecht [New York: Appleton Century Crofts, 1947], I, 10n, p. 28).

11. *Leviathan,* chs. 15, 16, 26.

12. Gordon J. Schochet, *Patriarchalism in Political Thought* (New York: Basic Books, 1975), 238.

13. William Graham Sumner, *What Social Classes Owe to Each Other* (Caldwell, Idaho: Caxton, 1978), 64.

14. John Locke, *First Treatise of Civil Government,* secs. 75, 76, 105.

15. John Locke, *Some Thoughts concerning Education and of the Conduct of the Understanding,* ed. Ruth Grant and Nathan Tarcov (Indianapolis: Hackett, 1996), secs. 32, 33; Nathan Tarcov, *Locke's Education for Liberty* (Chicago: University of Chicago Press, 1984).

16. Bertrand de Jouvenel, *The Pure Theory of Politics* (New Haven: Yale University Press, 1963), 45.

17. Alexis de Tocqueville, *Democracy in America* (New York: Knopf, 1980), 2:98–99; I adopt the term "encumbrance," of course, from Michael Sandel, "The Procedural Republic and the Unencumbered Self," *Political Theory* 12 (1984): 81–96.

18. Grant, "Locke's Political Anthropology," 49–50.

19. *Second Treatise,* secs. 109, 176, 241; see also Locke's *Essays on the Law of Nature,* ed. W. von Leyden (Oxford: Clarendon, 1954), 141. Benjamin Franklin, at any rate, gave it as his opinion that Hobbes was "closer to the truth" than the idea that the original condition was a "State of Love." *Benjamin Franklin: Writings,* ed. J. A. Le May (New York: Library of America, 1987), 425.

20. *Second Treatise,* secs. 6, 8.

21. Reason allows us to rise above instinct, Locke observed, but also to fall below it. *First Treatise of Civil Government,* sec. 58.

22. Benjamin Franklin, *Autobiography and Other Writings,* ed. Kenneth Silverman (New York: Penguin, 1986), 39.

23. *Second Treatise,* secs. 123–24, 127.

24. Locke quotes 1 Timothy 6:12, "God has given us all things richly" (*Second Treatise,* sec. 31), but he cites the passage only to question it. God's gift presumes our labor; moreover, in nature, there is a limit to these "riches" because they cannot be stored. The riches of God's gift appears to lie in the fact that there is no natural *limit* to what can be accumulated, if it can be used to "any advantage in life," so that when human beings acquire a means of storing and saving, especially money, God licenses accumulation. But in nature, since accumulation is limited to what can immediately be used, there are fewer possibilities for inequality and rank, hence fewer grounds for quarrel.

25. *Second Treatise,* secs. 39, 40.

26. *Common Sense,* in *The Complete Writings of Thomas Paine,* ed. Philip Foner (New York: Citadel, 1969), 1:5.

27. *Second Treatise,* sec. 38; Genesis 13, 36.

28. *Second Treatise,* sec. 38.

29. Ibid., sec. 93.

30. *Some Thoughts concerning Education,* secs. 32–33, 38, 48, 53, 56–62; *The Reasonableness of Christianity,* ed. I. T. Ramsey (Stanford: Stanford University Press, 1958), secs. 241–43, 252; especially notable is Locke's concern for opinions planted in children "before their memory began to keep a Register," *Essay concerning Human Understanding,* I.3.23; see also IV.14.4 and IV.20.23. Locke's most striking utterance on religion, of course, is the claim that "the taking away of God, though but only in thought, dissolves all." *Letter concerning Toleration* (Indianapolis: Bobbs-Merrill, 1955), 52; Jefferson flirted with the idea that an atheist's testimony might be unacceptable at law (*Notes on the State of Virginia,* ed. William Peden [Chapel Hill: University of North Carolina Press, 1955], 159).

31. "On the basis of sensation, of matter and motion," Jefferson wrote Adams, "we may erect . . . all . . . certainties," *Adams-Jefferson Letters,* ed. Lester Cappon (Chapel Hill: University of North Carolina Press, 1959), 568–69; see also Hamilton's reference to directing the "channels and currents in which the passions of mankind naturally flow" (*The Federalist,* #27), employing the hydraulic metaphor that the American framers regularly borrow from *The Prince,* ch. 25.

32. *The Federalist,* #49.

33. Madison indicates the design in his reliance on the "silent operation of the laws" (*Writings of James Madison,* ed. Gaillard Hunt [New York: Putnam, 1900–1910], 6:86), a phrase which highlights the displacement of speech by subrational process.

34. Consider, for example, Hamilton's appeal to the "irresistible and unchangeable course of nature" against the "little arts of little politicians." *The Federalist,* #11.

35. Benjamin Franklin, *A Proposal for Promoting Useful Knowledge among the British Plantations in America* (1743), in *Benjamin Franklin: Writings,* 296; see

also Locke, *First Treatise,* secs. 86, 87; *Second Treatise,* sec. 149; and Hobbes, *Leviathan,* ch. 11.

36. John Dewey, *Reconstruction in Philosophy* (New York: New American Library, 1950), 48.

37. I take the idea that power has a "natural history" from Bertrand de Jouvenel, *On Power: Its Natural History and Growth,* trans. J. L. Huntington (New York: Viking, 1948).

38. Patrick Deneen, *Democratic Faith* (Princeton: Princeton University Press, 2005).

39. John Dewey and James Tufts, *Ethics* (New York: Holt, 1908).

40. Theodore J. Lowi, *The End of Liberalism* (New York: Norton, 1969).

41. John Rawls, *A Theory of Justice* (Cambridge, Mass.: Harvard University Press, 1971), 3, 11.

42. Ibid., 225–26.

43. Richard Rorty rather admiringly concedes this in *Objectivity, Relativism and Truth: Philosophical Papers* (Cambridge: Cambridge University Press, 1991), 1:30n.

44. John Rawls, *Political Liberalism* (New York: Columbia University Press, 1993).

45. *Leviathan,* ch. 18. David Truman, from whom Rawls may have derived the idea of "overlapping consensus," held that groups in a pluralist democracy must obey the "rules of the game," a position similar to Rawls's but rhetorically more lighthearted, possibly reflecting a dangerous but less anxious time (*The Governmental Process* [New York: Knopf, 1951]).

46. James Madison, *Notes of Debates in the Federal Convention of 1787* (Athens: Ohio University Press, 1966), 244. Morris was echoing Locke, *Second Treatise,* sec. 222. In the *Letter concerning Toleration,* Locke spoke of the aims that led men into society as "life, liberty, health, indolency of body and the possession of outward things," but the mark of liberty in question, as Morris surely would have insisted, is that it is secure.

47. *The Federalist,* #9.

48. *Second Treatise,* secs. 223, 225.

49. For D. H. Lawrence, that made it worse (*Studies in Classical American Literature* [New York: Anchor, 1953]), as, in a sense, it had for Tocqueville (*Democracy in America,* 1:264).

50. *The Federalist,* #10.

51. See Jefferson's letter to Benjamin Rush, January 16, 1811, contrasting his hardly humble heroes to Hamilton's admiration for Caesar. *The Life and Selected Writings of Thomas Jefferson,* ed. Adrienne Koch and William Peden (New York: Modern Library, 1944), 609.

52. In *Common Sense,* Paine celebrated the "happy something" in the "quiet and rural lives of the first patriarchs"—lives that, according to Scripture, had in fact been full of conflict and not a little florid. Paine, after all, was trying to coax Americans out of "quiet and rural lives" in favor of the "happy something"

that, for Paine, was precisely the patriarchs' sturdy devotion to independence and their resistance to any secular authority (*Complete Writings*, 1:10–11).

53. Harvey C. Mansfield Jr., *Manliness* (New Haven: Yale University Press, 2006).

54. *The Legal Papers of John Adams*, ed. L. Kinvin Wroth and Hillel B. Zobel (Cambridge, Mass.: Harvard University Press, 1965), 3:254; see also Sharon Krause, *Liberalism with Honor* (Cambridge, Mass.: Harvard University Press, 2002).

55. The phrase "half men" is Colonel Sherburn's, defying a lynch mob in *The Adventures of Huckleberry Finn.*

56. Theodore Roosevelt, *The Strenuous Life* (New York: Century, 1902), 4, 6.

57. Richard Rorty, *Contingency, Irony and Solidarity* (Cambridge: Cambridge University Press, 1989), 28–29, 37–43, 60–61.

58. George Kateb, *The Inner Ocean* (Ithaca: Cornell University Press, 1992).

59. Ralph Waldo Emerson, "History" and "Self-Reliance," in *Emerson's Essays* (New York: Hurst, n.d.), 1:9, 28, 30.

60. Friedrich Nietzsche, *The Will to Power*, trans. Walter Kaufmann and R. J. Hollingdale (New York: Random House, 1967), 519.

61. The problem is at bottom an inequality of power, although that difficulty cannot be separated from inequalities of wealth (*Politics and Vision*, 602). William Graham Sumner, who tried to make the distinction, was at least close to the mark in calling plutocracy "the most sordid and debasing form of political energy known to us" ("Democracy and Plutocracy," in *On Liberty, Society and Politics; The Essential Essays of William Graham Sumner*, ed. Robert Bannister [Indianapolis: Liberty Fund, 1992], 144).

62. Judith Shklar, "The Liberalism of Fear," in *Liberalism and the Moral Life*, ed. Nancy Rosenblum (Cambridge, Mass.: Harvard University Press, 1989), 21–38. After all, radical students, two generations back, generally trumpeted their rights and emphasized individual freedom of "expression" even before, but especially after, political setbacks (*Politics and Vision*, 723n137).

63. Theodore J. Lowi, "Think Globally, Lose Locally," *Boston Review*, April/May 1998, 4–10.

64. Similarly, I have described postmodernism as suited to be "the ideology of the administrative state" ("Two-Tier Politics Revisited," in *Seeking the Center: Politics and Policymaking in the New Century*, ed. Martin Levin, Marc Landy, and Martin Shapiro (Washington, D.C.: Georgetown University Press, 2001), 384.

65. Joshua Miller, *The Rise and Fall of Democracy in Early America, 1630–1789* (University Park: Pennsylvania State University Press, 1991).

66. *Second Treatise*, sec. 96.

67. Ibid., sec. 95.

68. S. B. McKinley, *Democracy and Military Power* (New York: Vanguard, 1934); Jefferson wrote Adams that "the invention of gun powder has armed the weak as well as the strong with missile death." Letter of October 28, 1813, in *Life and Selected Writings*, 633.

69. It should be noted that not all revolutionary moments bring this result.

70. *The Federalist,* #49.

71. Letter to Adams, October 28, 1813, in *Life and Selected Writings,* 633–34; Richard K. Mathews, *The Radical Politics of Thomas Jefferson* (Lawrence: University Press of Kansas, 1984).

72. *The Federalist,* #63; see also Michael E. McGerr, *The Decline of Popular Politics* (New York: Oxford University Press, 1986).

73. See also Christopher Lasch, "The Age of Limits," in *History and the Idea of Progress,* ed. Arthur Melzer, Jerry Weinberger, and M. Richard Zinman (Ithaca: Cornell University Press, 1995), 227–40; and Michael Sandel, "The Case against Perfection," *Atlantic Monthly,* April 2004, 51–62.

74. G. K. Chesterton, *What I Saw in America* (New York: Dodd, Mead, 1922), 18.

Part 3

Theory and Practice

On Time and History

Men have times; mankind has history. Times are close and personal things: "having a good time" is possible only for small groups of men, in comparatively intimate settings. Our most generous feelings toward those who are not present can be expressed only as a "wish" that they were; times are things of narrow boundaries and exclusive limits. History is comparatively open and indiscriminate. It refers to a stream of related events, made up of myriad individual lives and times.

No profundity is required to make the distinction between times and history, and it requires only a little more insight to recognize that the separation between the two temporalities of man is one of the roots of human discontent. In his times, a man has significance, meaning, and dignity; in history, the individual is only too accurate in seeing himself a finite and almost entirely dispensable unit of a great process which began before his birth and will continue after his death.

Much of modern political thought is concerned with the effort to unite the two aspects of temporality. Men have always sought to control their times, endeavored so to manage events and environments that the times would be good. So, too, they have sought to predict history in order that, when the prediction enters the immediate world of "the times," it *may* be controlled. Yet prediction and control are logically separable, and the arts of the seer exist only to serve the architects of good times. Early modern political thinkers preserved that sense of the order of things. Yet, with Bacon and Machiavelli, many affirmed that by "obeying" nature man might "master" it: by discerning and using the laws of movement and process in history, man might conquer it for his own purposes. In other words, the early modern theorist, preserving the sense that control is the purpose of prediction, nonetheless set up an inseparable relation between prediction and control. Man's hopes for his times became almost indissolubly related to his hopes for history.

The political arguments of the thirties reflected the embattled moment of that modern creed. In an age of enormity and horror, of arguments as to which creed in fact represented the "wave of the future," what was at stake was nothing less than the modern creed of history itself: the belief that one's times must yield in the interest of our history. Yet whose was history? In a marvelous distortion of Christian teaching, the answer read, "Those who have the most impoverished times inherit history."

> And the poor in their fireless lodgings, dropping the sheets
> Of the evening paper: "Our day is our loss, O show us
> 　　History the operator, the
> Organizer, Time the refreshing river."

In the war of faiths, it became a test of devotion and conviction to impoverish one's times by will to demonstrate one's certainty of triumph. Stalin's men began with the advantage of identification with poverty; Hitler's overcame that advantage by the application of scientific inhumanity. The absurdity of the ideological conflict of the thirties is only a comment on the disintegration of the modern creed of time and history.

The early prophets of modernity still had faith in the power of ideas, the belief that political imagination and creativity could "master" history if guided by prediction. That belief provided a link with the classical tradition, and its decay has been one of the characteristic processes of modern history. It became clear, and has become more clear as the processes of social and political change speeded up, that ideas are at best slow in influencing the actions of men. The most successful of ideologists could gain a following only after a generation, and after a generation of change his ideas were likely to have an archaic ring. Technological, and especially military, innovations might transform the life of nations and men with far greater speed and thoroughness than any idea. The advent of a mass public, itself the result of social and political change, complicated the problem of the ideologist by requiring him to reach more minds. Yet those minds were not such as to be inspired by a utopian vision. The world of mass and change produced men confronted with a universe of numberless unknown others; by a process only too familiar, it encouraged a sense of insignificance, and with that sense, a desire for protection. The case of the intellectual or ideologist was made only worse by the fact that he was less able to remain unconscious of the state of things; instead, he was more prone to see himself as swept by great forces certainly beyond the control of his ideas and only doubtfully subject to control by masses of men acting in concert. The times of men, and especially the intellectual, had been swallowed up in history.

Prediction remained vital, but no longer as the servant of control and political imagination. Rather, prediction became the prerequisite of security, the indispensable ability to determine the winning side and the prevailing direction, which made it possible for the individual to guard himself against defeat. Ideologists exerted themselves to prove that men might realize their most exalted dreams by obeying history, but at times the pretense was thin. Hegel never adequately explained, Bertrand Russell noted, precisely why history should repeat the dynamic psychology of the dialectic. Implicitly, ideology was a gospel of defeat and desperate faith, which argued that men *must* in any case "adapt themselves" to history, allow history to command their times, and let prediction order control. Beyond that necessity, and out of despair of any alternative, men might have faith in the benevolence of the process itself. It was against that tendency of ideology that the humanist Marx protested: "The real task is to change it." Yet Marx fell subject to the malaise of seeking inevitabilities as a source of security. Security is a relative term. The intellectual and the mass joined forces, the one seeking security for his ideas, the other, for his life and well-being, but there was a unity, however artificial, to the common quest.

Yet change and process ultimately seemed to destroy the efforts of the great ideologists to pen change safely within the walls of doctrine. Karl Mannheim's *Ideology and Utopia* heralded a new consistency in devotion to history by pronouncing that all thought is itself historical, that men lack the intellectual capacity to understand history, much less the physical ability to control it. The intellectual was no longer the prophet, for his predictions reflected only the "spirit of the times." He could at best "unmask" the pretensions of those who still clung to the older claims of transhistorical thought, and having demonstrated the importance of thought, arrange some minimal accommodation between "worldviews" that would enable men to adjust themselves to history and to one another. The modish social theorist of our times takes Mannheim for his model. The vocabulary of concerns is almost identical: concern for "balance" and "adjustment," a pragmatic pluralism, and the proclamation of an "end to ideology."

In the most important sense, however, those who proclaim an "end to ideology" represent the apotheosis of ideology. The nineteenth-century ideologist was tempted to surrender the idea of control to that of prediction. The twentieth-century social theorist surrenders both to the process of history itself. The great doctrinaires tempered their faith in history by seeking to give it laws, and the early theorists like Machiavelli sought laws only for their utility to the political artist. Current social theory, by contrast, speaks of an "equilibrium," but insists that such a balance must be "dynamic," open to the forces of change and history: the counsel of such theory at any time, however, is merely that of attaining an acceptable compromise within times to which the individual is "adjusted." In other words, it has no language for guiding, directing, or even for predicting the "course" of history; it speaks a language of drift, while counseling that we remain open to that drift and process. The advocacy of drift is possible only on the basis of an unqualified and unconditional faith in the laws of movement as such, one which requires neither long-term prediction nor the minimal directive role such as orthodox materialism still envisioned for a Marxist party. Those who announce the "end of ideology" do so with a sanguine tone which suggests that men have "learned better" than to pit their ideas against history. Their real proposition is simply that ideology has ended because it is unnecessary: one need only have faith in the laws of movement themselves. That teaching is the final inversion of the vision of Machiavelli: history triumphs over control, process over events, without even the minimal intervention of mind implied by prediction.

Yet there was once a different variety of history, a history which was built up out of the times of men, rather than the reverse. Traditional history took the form of the tale, the relation of notable events and unusual occurrences. The chronicles do not provide an account of detail: they describe the character of kings and the meaning of their reigns. The tale treats of nobility or vice, the excellent and the base. The "example" employed by traditional history is not the typical, but the exemplary. It is, in other words, history designed to serve to educate man, and not to stand either as a tool or as a master.

Traditional history could easily degenerate from "the tale" into "the story," an anecdote related for its capacity to please the historian's audience, whether by charm or by appeal to amour propre. To tell the tale required both a firm sense of "the ordinary," the everyday process of life and decision, and a realization that the ordinary is not enough: that it limits, frustrates, or even distorts man, whose yearning is for "the extraordinary." Obviously, that structure made traditional history vulnerable to the charlatan, who could capitalize on the tendency of men to confuse the unusual for the extraordinary, a release from the limitations of the ordinary for liberation from ordinariness. Gyges and his ring could become the equals of Oedipus or Orpheus.

To protect traditional history against degeneration, the historian was compelled to transform it into sacred history. Sacred history provides an analysis of the "course" of events, the iron logic of processes and developments which bind man so long as he remains within the sphere of the ordinary, the quest for life, for pleasure, procreation, and continuity. To be sure, sacred history recalls the penalties for striving beyond the ordinary, but in truly sacred history, it is not "the gods" but the pettiness of ordinary men which brings the extraordinary man low. The central point of sacred history is that the ordinary is itself destined for disaster. At best, the ordinary results in a meaningless cycle of events, permanent and unchanging. Ordinariness escapes from cycles only by winning victories, but the victories of ordinariness consist in expanding the sphere in which the world yields to the will of ordinary men: the desires for self-gratification and escape from death. Yet each expansion merely confronts the ordinary man with new frustrations: the world will not be mastered so easily. Indeed, even at the moment of his success, the "world master" finds himself deprived of the good which, at the base of his psyche, moved his quest. He is denied love and affection, trapped in an inescapable loneliness in which no other will exists but his own. The logic of ordinariness is *hubris* in the true sense and only the extraordinary man escapes from it.

For St. Augustine history never lost its connection with individuals. It remained traditional history, telling tales of what individual men did and do. "It is in thee, my mind, that I measure my times. . . . The impression which things passing by cause in thee and which remains when the things are gone is that by which I measure time, rather than the things which passed by and thus produced the impression." Thucydides might find *nemesis* in history, but the source of the nemesis was not in forces around man but in man himself. History is testimony to the meaningless nature of the ordinary, and to the weakness and folly of men. Yet some lives of some men had meaning and dignity, and it was the purpose of sacred history to tell the tale of such lives that men might have a chance to learn the lesson in them. The record of the ordinary existed to provide a contrast to the life of a Pericles, a Socrates, or a Jesus, for to the sacred historian, "the extraordinary" was the natural, the "great man," Man in his true form: hence the medieval reference to Jesus as *humanitas*.

Karl Marx's history recaptured, in part, the perspective of sacred history, restored it against the modern notion of history and time. In its most basic structure, Marxist history is a record of historical process, the march and logic of man's struggle for material gain. Yet what makes

Marxist history "Marxist," and not a reaffirmation of Condorcet, is that it is also the record of human *resistance* to the process, of man's demand for something more than acquisition as the law of history, his yearning for "times" which are his own. Surely no note sounds louder in Marx than his own rejection of a time measured by the movements of matter in motion rather than by the experience and consciousness of men. Dehumanization begins, Marx would have assented to Lewis Mumford, when the clock and not the mind becomes the standard of time.

Yet Marx committed two errors, both of which can, for his admirers, be blamed on his intellectual ancestry: (1) he was unable to separate himself from the belief that the process of secular history is somehow "good," a law of progress; and (2) he was unwilling to surrender the "historical" view which accompanied this belief, that man and his thought are radically historical, no more than reflections of the "spirit of their times." Hence, Marx was driven as Hegel had been to try to discover a "synthesis" of the two times and histories, a "moment" at which Marx, the humanist and sacred historian, might be one with Marx, the theorist of progress and historical relativism.

The "revolution" symbolized that moment for men at large. Marx's contention was an accurate one: that the antipathy of men to clock-time, to the process of secular history, is so great that (unless they have some material interest in the established order which binds their hands and blinds their eyes) resistance will break out in rebellion whenever that process appears weak. Hence, for Marx, the skill of the historian consisted in calculating the moment at which the established order is so weak that rebellion can become revolution, and especially, the "absolute moment" of "absolute revolution" in which, with the advent of the proletariat to power, man is enabled to escape from secular history altogether and "leap from necessity into freedom." Yet Marx's assumption that the two times were integrally related blinded him to the fact that a moment is never absolute in secular time; it is merely one of a chain of moments in an endless procession. However true it may be that in the moment of revolution man escapes from secular time, the subsequent moments will reestablish it: now I am unconcerned for my stomach, my progeny, or my life, but soon I will be again. The perennial disappointment of revolution to its own instigators is witness: the two times may become tangent, but never united.

Marx's "moment," moreover, errs in a less fundamental but equally important sense. For Marx, the proletariat pursued the truth, the liberation of man, but only because that truth coincided with its interest. Led by that interest to seek self-protection or self-aggrandizement, the proletariat would strive to seize control of the process of secular history; yet, Marx argued, it would logically be unable to do so without ending secular history. This thesis may reveal the underlying reason why Marx, the humanist and psychologist, became Marx the philosophic materialist. He was, in other words, aware that the *motives* of almost all men, and certainly the proletariat, were imperfect: hope for liberation from secular history required that from imperfect motives, perfect things may arise. That too was always a theme of sacred history, but sacred history assigned to God or Fortuna the task of weaving what seemed illogical into a pattern of events.

Marx began with the illogical proposition "From the imperfect, perfection," yet he assumed that the proletariat, not God, would find the logic which connected the two. Not that Marx expected the proletariat to do so without help: the intellectual was to serve as a guide for the path which led from the "dictatorship of the proletariat" to freedom. Eventually, the new order of society would, Marx was confident, transform the motives of the proletariat, and with the proletariat, mankind. Yet at the beginning, the proletarians were to be men with very material aims, men not devoted to the very nonmaterial ideal of freedom which informed the intellectual. Would the materially minded proletarian listen to his would-be guide with his nonmaterial ideals? Almost certainly not: hence, the intellectual must, as Marx himself did, speak of material goals whatever his own nonmaterial motives. The intellectual, in other words, would be compelled by political necessity to reverse the proletarian order of things. He must seem to be what he is not in order to convince the proletarian to act in ways which reflected what, in a "real," historical sense, the proletarian *is:* the liberator of mankind. Yet if Marx is right, that the proletariat is what it does and not what it thinks, what becomes of the intellectual who does what he does not think in order to influence the proletariat? How are his ideals to be retained if action is more real than thought?

These questions only call attention to the fact that the Marxist synthesis collapses the moment following the revolution. The two times will not stay joined. Marx's assertion amounts to this: that the proletariat, *as a part of secular history,* is what it does, while the intellectual, *as a part of sacred history,* is what he thinks.

That conflict is only illustrated by the problem of the "historical-materialist" thesis that "all thought is historical," a reflection of the zeitgeist. This thesis is involved in the contradiction of all relativist doctrine: that it excludes or exempts those who assert it. To be sure, there is an escape via the "absolute moment" of the intellectual: that history has developed so as to "reveal itself" to a particular time. Since all men in Marx's time did not accept his idea of history, they must be explained away. Nor was Marx hesitant to do so: they were misled by interest or by cowardice, by some defect of character which caused them to reject what "the times" made it possible to see. That is, the peculiar life circumstances and the moral will of Marx himself, and of his disciples, enabled them to perceive the one truth not historical: the nature of history itself. Yet at this point, relativism loses its seeming humility: it becomes a claim to *revelation,* not relativity. Indeed, almost in spite of himself, Marx, like other historical relativists, is made to reassert the central proposition of sacred history that "historical materialism" had set out to deny.

That proposition is a simple one: that there is no "meaning in history" which gives purpose to humanity. Rather, history acquires meaning in relation to man. Men are born enslaved, just as Marx would have had it, to material desires and the futile quest for a triumph over nature—a quest which inevitably involves them in a conflict with other men as a part of nature. Yet sacred history added two facts which Marx ignored: (1) that man is *always* born enslaved, that each generation begins in the caves; and that (2) the defect of man is a defect in the emotions which will not be cured by material prosperity. That defect is the will not to be dependent or obstructed, which meets its greatest antagonist not in physical nature but in man. Yet at times, the sacred historian recorded, men have become liberated from the logic of secularity, have pierced through the camouflage of events and happenings as most men perceive them to an insight into human reality. That reality is not "historical," and, consequently, the perception of it is not historical: it is a perennial possibility, attained once and again many times in history. Finally, the sacred historian contended, it is in that perception that human life acquires its justification and its meaning: indeed, the ordinary "course of events" is justified only insofar as it contributes to "times" in which some may gain a glimpse of things "as they are" and man as he is.

The argument of sacred history has become more contemporary than antiquarian. The modern idea of history rings false in our times; indeed, the times that we live in are more at odds with history, perhaps, than has ever before been the case. Change and transformation in life and society have become so rapid as to accelerate "the times" as men perceive them.

The past, as Kenneth Keniston has observed, becomes more distant: custom no longer serves as a useful guide; the past itself comes to include events and times more and more recent (half a century back, we were in the "pre–atomic age"). The future becomes harder to predict—save in the sense that it will be unlike what we have known—and more immediate, harder both to anticipate and control. Men no longer can afford *faith* in time: they *need* time in which to master the engines of destruction with which we intended to master nature and now threaten to master us.

C. P. Snow has made valiant efforts to argue the thesis of modern ideas of time: that we must "speed up" to adjust ourselves to the process of technological change, that humanistic culture must "adjust itself" to scientific culture. Yet there is another chorus, one which asserts that we must control and slow down the processes of technological change itself. That, I take it, is the basic argument of the advocates of disarmament and arms control. Their propositions have far more general applicability, however. As Ernst Haas has suggested, the evidence suggests that there may be limits to how much men *can* "speed up"; there is no inherent quality of technological change that prevents it from being "slowed down" or subjected to control.

The most urgent necessity of contemporary life lies in breaking down the connection, established by early modern theorists, between *prediction* and *control*. We do not need to know how history is going in order to know how or for what purpose we might seek to control it. Prediction becomes relevant only as a second-order question: once we know what sort of controls we desire, predication may be essential to establishing them. The two questions, however, form a hierarchy and not a unity: the ethical question, implicit in the idea of control, ranks higher in the order of priorities. Unless the two are separated, we run the peril which modern theorists always ran: that of allowing prediction to command control, of allowing "what works" to determine what is right, of asserting with Hegel that *Weltgeschichte* is *Weltgericht*.

The collapse of the modern conception of time leaves us, as many commentators have observed, in a "present" isolated from past and future. Yet the "present" is not without its dimension in time and history, though a different time and history from that of modernity. The present is not simply a moment, the "existential fact": the human present is always part of the continuum, which stretches back to birth and forward to death. To capture the existential moment is to lose the essential reality of man and his times. Modern historical theorists have argued that the

Greeks and others "lacked a historical sense." Yet, as Leo Strauss notes, this is absurd given their concern for how things "came to be." The older view, one shared by traditional and sacred history, is that human history is the history of how a man comes to be. The "ages" are not epochs, but periods in the life of a man, each of which may contribute to or detract from his development toward humanity. When men come to feel themselves too small to be of worth, they often sacrifice that history for a surrogate grandeur in the great unities which do not die: the nation, the empire, ultimately "the human race." The development of given men yields to the "development of mankind" as a principle of time. Yet, as Augustine or Thucydides would remind us, the sacrifice was vain and offered to false gods. The nations fall; the empires perish. Mankind may have survived, but a mankind which sacrifices the development of individual men to the "development of humanity" builds a rage in individuals which Marx felt and expressed—a rage which threatens, in our times, to add another and final empirical confirmation to the thesis of sacred history.

The safer and possibly truer perception of time and history is that older notion that we should devote ourselves to the study of how given men have reached a humanity more fulfilling and more genuine than that of "the ordinary," reached that state of extraordinariness which completes the unfulfilled thing that most men are. The mystique of "genius" only diverts our attention from the historical task of discovering how given systems of education, social, and political organization contributed to or detracted from the development of men.

This argument may seem "elitist": indeed, it has been the stock-in-trade of modern elitism. Yet democracy is not a "modern" doctrine. It asserts that very ancient thesis that certain kinds of relations between citizens are essential to the best development of the man: it denies that the relations between individuals should be judged "efficient" in terms of their contribution to the quest for power over nature, or to the "dialectic process of history." Democratic theory presumes that it is pointless to dispute whether "a man" is a higher social goal than "most men." We average men are limited ourselves by the best men that we have as models for emulation. We can study what they did, or even what factors seem to have assisted them to do it: insofar as we cannot and others do not excel them, they form the boundaries for our aspiration. Since the genuine democratic ideal is the elevation of the many, democracy presupposes the elevation of the few. Democracy as a system of ideals may be different from democracy as a set of devices, a fact we are being forced to learn in the politics of the non-Western world. Democratic *ideals* are equalitarian because they assert that all men should, so far as is possible, be elevated to the highest level men can attain; the democratic ideal presupposes a perception of the inequalitarian facts with which any society must begin. In short, democracy is less equalitarian than aspirational.

Aspiration is a deeply personal act, one which involves the individual, that circle of comrades who encourage and rebuke him, and those ideas or figures that inspire him. Men act in history; they aspire in time. Hence, an aspirational political order is committed to the effort to make time sovereign over history insofar as possible. Modern historical faiths deny the fundamental premise which democracy shares with aspiration: that the education and relationships of men *determine* "what is needful." Rather, the modern creeds suggest that man and his relationships should be harnessed to the chariot of history, conceived as man's march to "power over nature."

More than the aspirations of men and of democracies is at stake, of course, in reversing the order of priorities fixed by modernity for the relations of time and history. History itself may depend upon the reduction of history to a subordinate role, for in our times it is not at all clear that the future will come to be. It is not always a pleasant world, and men often find it more comfortable to face the warm fire of the ordinary and to turn their back to the surrounding circle of night. Yet around the old tribal fires, men told one another tales of the times in which others had faced darkness. To lose faith in history is to rediscover time, and if a loss of faith is painful, the loss of a false faith results in a pain which is beneficial. In the effort to restore the supremacy of time to history may lie the seeds of a better faith, and certainly of a life more appropriate to the nature of humanity.

Note

This essay was originally published as "On Time and History," *Yale Review,* Fall 1966.

On Political Illegitimacy

Ours is a "crisis of illegitimacy," a decline in the conviction that some actions are impermissible, for one's self as well as for others. Lacking the secure expectation that their political opponents will feel morally restricted in their choice of means, men are forced and permitted to reject such limitations on themselves. And as Hobbes knew, a condition in which "nothing can be Unjust" is one in which "Force and Fraud are . . . the two Cardinall vertues" and the rule of right comes to be that it is "every mans that he can get; and for so long as he can keep it."[1] If we are still far from that "ill condition," there are grounds to fear that it may pass from Hobbes's imagination into the life of modern America.

"Legitimacy" is itself a new masterword in political science,[2] but unlike so many of the terms introduced in recent years, it cannot claim to have added "precision" to our discourse. The most familiar definition is probably Lipset's description of political legitimacy as "the belief that the existing institutions are the most appropriate ones for the society."[3] This formulation is impossibly inclusive. It enfolds: the passionate patriot who believes the established order to be the ordinance of God; a thoroughly alienated man who believes that existing institutions are contemptible but the best that his debased fellow citizens can hope for; the revolutionary who, aiming at the eventual overthrow of the system, believes it to be "appropriate" for this "stage"; a homogenous community and a police state accepted because it "divides us least"; any society characterized by minimal stability and orderliness—most societies, probably, at most times.

Even without social scientists, however, "legitimacy" would have an indefinite quality. In our usage, "legitimate" is an intermediate moral term applied to a relationship between what is right simply, the abstract rule for the best case, and present conditions.[4] Actions are legitimate when, given existing possibilities and alternatives, there is some reasonable relation between them and what is "right." Legitimacy is always relative to circumstance; there is, John Schaar writes, "a certain pragmatic or expediential element in all theories of legitimacy."[5]

Moreover, an action or a regime can be legitimate without being the "best possible," even given existing limitations. There can, at any time, be many legitimate systems or modes of conduct. In this sense, even Lipset's definition claims too much; a legitimate action or regime is "appropriate," not necessarily "most appropriate." The moral content of legitimacy is established when action is "defensible," when it is not demonstrably wrongful, when it avoids some illegitimate alternative.

To call something a "legitimate practice" concedes that it is ethically suspect, and every intellectual knows that the statement "Your argument is legitimate," is almost invariably followed by some assertion like "but not conclusive," and probably means only "I cannot refute it—yet."[6] We would prefer to call our arguments "accurate" and our conduct "righteous." We appeal to the standard of legitimacy only when we know or suspect that our performance is less than ideal, that it requires defending. The claim that my conduct was legitimate is always an answer to an accusation made or anticipated, an attempt to shift the burden of responsibility. And like pleas in a court of law, I answer that I am "not guilty" rather than that I am innocent.

The most familiar line of defense blames existing conditions for whatever defects appear in my conduct. ("We'd all be glad to live in peace forever," the sententious Peachum declares in Blitzstein's translation of Brecht; "it seems that *circumstance* won't have it so.") Confessing that I lacked the power, skill, or status (which I prefer to subsume under the term "significance") to create better alternatives, I assert that given the choices which did exist, my decision was not illegitimate.

I may also contend that the situation was so fundamentally incomprehensible that my decisions were legitimate even if they prove to have bad consequences or if hindsight suggests a better course. President Nixon presumably would feel that his policies had been legitimate even if they were "proved wrong," as he conceded they might be. In making this argument, I do not claim that I acted "reasonably"; acting without adequate information is *not* reasonable. Rather, I am stating that in the irrational situation I faced, a "reasonable man" might have acted as I did. My decision, then, was "not irrational," not illegitimate, given my lack of knowledge.

Finally, I can defend my conduct by limiting the claims which morality can make on me. That, after all, is the meaning of the doctrine that the exalted end hallows any means, a notion quite adequately discussed in political science. I can also argue that what I have done is "my right" or "my business" and no legitimate concern of yours. But I can also contend that it is not my business to worry about your conduct or, for that matter, the moral character of my own, as when a soldier appeals to the principle of "superior orders." Most inclusively, I can adopt the theory that morality is unknown or unknowable, that it is variable or a matter of personal preference. None of these arguments makes any claim to moral excellence; like those legitimations which point to my lack of significance or knowledge, the contention that it was "my right" to do as I have done or not "my right" to question others turns on the proposition that what I did was "not illegitimate."

Since the claim to legitimacy is partly a defense, it is also in part a request for reassurance, an attempt to eliminate self-doubt. Almost certainly, protestations of legitimateness always involve an element of rationalization. But that psychological truth should not blind us to the fact that some claims are reasonable whatever the state of mind of those who make them, while others are not. It is an obligation of social science to separate reason from simple rationalization, legitimate from illegitimate pretensions to legitimacy.

That separation, however, is one which too few social scientists have been willing to make.[7] Radical critics have explained this as a self-serving attempt to justify the established order and the position of social scientists within it, but I think they miss the point. As or more important in overexpanding the meaning of legitimacy has been a generous and compassionate desire to understand others and to avoid self-righteousness. Social scientists have, in effect, been filing a kind of "Darrow brief" for men and regimes which pleads that "society" or "circumstance" is the real criminal.

So it often is, but making legitimacy an almost universally inclusive term destroys the moral quality which leads men to appeal to it at all. Being told why men committed an offense may make us understand or even pardon it, but we do not give them an acquittal. Yet men assert that they acted legitimately in order to be acquitted; they aim at removing the stigma of wrongdoing from their conduct. The moral force of the statement "My action was legitimate" lies in the contention that although I have acted in less than ideal ways and may have chosen a less than optimal course, I have at least avoided some worse alternative. I do not ask you to understand why I did wrong; I demand that you acknowledge that I have *averted* wrong.

This aspect of legitimacy is even stronger if, beyond defending my own conduct, I seek to make claims on yours. If I believe that the Nixon administration is the "legitimate government" of the United States and that its policies are legitimate, I may still oppose it and them, even very strongly. If the administration asks for more than my acquiescence by taxing or conscripting me, it is asking that I identify with it to a degree. Obviously, it will first attempt to persuade me to *share*, rather than merely accept, its judgments of legitimacy. Hence the president's argument that in Vietnam there are three alternatives, of which two are illegitimate; his own policy, if we accept his case, is legitimate for want of a better one. Failing that, a regime may argue that however strongly I disagree with it or its policies, my failure to give support will involve some other, still *more* illegitimate consequence. It may argue, for example, that my resistance to the draft will undermine respect for law; if I think that result both likely and illegitimate, I may feel an obligation to accept induction.[8]

Illegitimacy becomes central in times of uncertainty because men can agree about things they believe to be wrong even when they cannot agree or are unsure about what is right. Many moral theories can account for the same prohibition; we can agree that stealing is wrong without accepting a "right of property." Similarly, we can agree to reject theories which do not account for the phenomena without in the least deciding between those which do. It is arguable that most moral theories originate in the search for some norm which is common to and unites various prohibitions. In the *Republic*, for example, Cephalus's original definition of justice as "paying your debts" is rejected because it is agreed that it is illegitimate to return a borrowed weapon to a madman.

Common ideas of illegitimacy are a basis for unity among men who do not otherwise agree. We appeal to "legitimacy" when reason and morals seem uncertain and conduct is ambiguous because the real content of the term is negative and refers to that last hope of communality. And social scientists have adopted the term because of the feeling that lowering the moral language of politics to its relatively inclusive and unexacting terms offers what may be the only possibility for peace, stability, and the loose toleration which may be the closest approach to comity possible in our age.

Given the perils of the time, such convictions and arguments are comprehensible. But social scientists have been betrayed by their own zeal. Their theories credit so many actions and regimes with legitimacy that the idea of illegitimacy almost vanishes, a result which eviscerates the idea of legitimacy itself. Avoiding self-righteousness to a considerable degree, they also undermine the idea that there are self-wrongful forms of political conduct. In this, social science merely reflects and reinforces tendencies which are visible in political life. But in an important sense, social science goes further; it legitimates where men in practice—including social scientists—still discern illegitimacy.

If applied to individuals, Lipset's definition, by reducing legitimacy to belief, makes it impermeably subjective. My beliefs about the appropriateness of existing institutions define their legitimacy and logically, the same standards apply to my own conduct. I cannot, then, be said to act illegitimately unless I was "insincere." If I am consistent, I can claim that another acted illegitimately only if I charge him with insincerity or with "false consciousness."

Yet Professor Lipset, to take only the most salient example, has been a frequent and articulate critic of the New Left. Now, whatever else may be said of that diverse movement, most of its elements are impeccably, even intolerably, sincere. If belief is all that matters, their conduct is legitimate prima facie. Critics argue, however, that sincere or not, the movement is wrong in some important respects; New Leftists, in their turn, do not concede that the vice president's evident sincerity legitimates his public policies.

Of course, Lipset's definition was directed to social rather than individual beliefs, and can be interpreted to mean that institutions and actions are legitimate only if a great majority in any society concedes them that status. If so, then dissent alone can be stigmatized as illegitimate; for the romanticism of individual belief, this formulation substitutes a romanticization of the many. (And, as an odd consequence, involves the doctrine that Galileo's belief that the earth moved was, "for the times," illegitimate.) Needless to say, this doctrine was precisely that which Tocqueville feared that democratic man might internalize, with consequences which he presented far too eloquently to need replication here.

It is useful, however, to point out that the vast majority of Americans—and social scientists—reject this definition in practice. We may agree about little else, but we do consider that Nazism was and remains illegitimate—so much so that "pinning the Swastika on the Fascist" is a favored device of political rhetoric, with advocates on the right and left trading specious arguments "proving" that the other is acting like a Nazi if he is not charged with being one. But according to the established theories of social science, the Third Reich was a legitimate regime. It came to power constitutionally; its devotees were noxiously sincere; the great majority of Germans felt that it was "most appropriate for the society." Theory in social science is at odds with the most widely accepted proposition in contemporary political morality, one with which almost every social scientist agrees.

That need not mean that established theory is wrong, but it ought to give us pause. Having neglected the idea of illegitimacy, conventional theory in social science has explored no more than the surface and remains uncertain what quicksands may lie beneath. Practice is in no better condition and offers no safe path. Trembling theory and troubled practice, in fact, have common roots and blind spots; neither is suited to judge the other. Even those who would defend either or both need to dig up the tangle of premises and convictions that bind them together.

I

Legitimacy is always partly the fruit of distrust. The very idea of "legitimate authority" presumes the existence of illegitimate authority and insists that authority be judged. But legitimacy can also be part of the flower of faith.[9] "Legitimate authority" also appeals to a standard of right which is above authority, which men and rulers do not and probably cannot embody.[10]

That idea of rightness was fundamental to the theories which were the beginning of our tradition. Informed by classical antiquity as well as theology, those theories argued that man was a political animal and that the common good was an essential element of the good life. Government, to be legitimate, had to aim at this good, using "right reason" to design measures which would enable the closest approach to the good life that circumstances would allow. Conditions might make it legitimate for government to depart from an otherwise desirable rule of law. ("Necessity," the medieval maxim declared, "knows no law.") But law and the public order were common properties because the good they aimed at was common and shared. Change could not be made lightly or by fiat; in one form or another, almost every medieval theory insisted that "what touches all must be approved by all," that the community had a right to judge whether "necessity" really existed and if so, whether the measures proposed were in fact appropriate to the case.

That judgment was, however, not a consent which could be given or withheld on the basis of personal will. Authority had to "make its case," and if it could not its measures were illegitimate. If it could prove its point, however, men were *bound* to give their consent. Authority was on trial before the event, and the decision to give or withhold consent was no more a matter of preference than a verdict of guilty or not guilty. Failure to agree to a rational case was quite as illegitimate as an ill-founded measure.[11]

In those traditional theories, a policy is made legitimate by its "right rationality," not by the fact that men consent to it. Approval was necessary for two reasons: (1) it was due to man as a rational animal that he be given reasons and that his own reasons be consulted; and (2) no man and no ruler is infallible; requiring both to give reasons helps free them from private passions and perspectives, since reasoning involves speaking to others in what is necessarily a common and shared order. Approval was essential to legitimacy because it was necessary to the highest rationality.

Liberalism, and with it most modern political theory, regarded man as by nature a private and apolitical (or antipolitical) being. Government, necessarily a violation of the natural rights of the individual, was legitimated by reference to a common *evil*, being justified by lessening or averting the "state of war" which was either identical with or grew out of the "state of nature." Even Rousseau, no liberal and possessed by a vision of the positive role of political community, felt it necessary to "make legitimate" the bonds which government placed on men to refer to the less-than-human illegitimacy of the state of nature.

But in liberal theory, illegitimacy was something external to the individual. Liberal doctrines spoke of things which should not be endured—oppression, and in the case of the state, defeat—rather than of things which should not be done. Rights were given up grudgingly, in order to prevent the evils men feared they might suffer, not those which they feared they might do. Given its theory of human nature, liberalism could hardly develop any but the most limited idea of internal illegitimacy. Either the liberal theorist boldly affirmed that man had a right by nature to desire whatever he would or he asserted that "natural man" desired only the good. In either case, it was external circumstances—scarcity, the corruptions of society, or both—which were the source of evil and the basis of illegitimacy. And the moral basis of political legitimacy was the sweeping away of such impediments as rapidly as circumstances would permit.

Since man was by nature morally complete, his natural will being identical with natural right, he could be bound only by his consent. Consent ceased to be an aid to reason in seeking the common good; it *defined* that good, insofar as the concept had any standing at all. As Bertrand de Jouvenel put it, liberalism located the moral basis of legitimacy in the origin rather than the ends of power. Logically, this doctrine tends to undermine any limitation on what the people may will legitimately.[12] In that sense, it is the antecedent of that romanticism of men and majorities which is the closest approach to a theory of legitimacy in contemporary social science.

Liberal theorists themselves, of course, did not go so far. They developed three basic limitations which defined an internal standard of illegitimacy. But all of these have been shaken if not shattered with the passing of time, and their loss, in a country so dominated by the "liberal tradition," is a major element in the contemporary crisis of illegitimacy.

Reason

Consent which is not reasoned, liberal theorists argued, is not consent at all; a man who does not know what he agrees to and who has little or no knowledge of the consequences of his agreement has not "consented" to either. Consent won by fraud was illegitimate, and some categories of persons were unable to give rational consent (a concept which more than one young man has discovered in relation to the "age of consent"). Some regimes were illegitimate ipso facto, even if their subjects appeared to accept them, because there some rights which no man could rationally abandon and which were "inalienable" morally if not in fact. To suppose otherwise, Locke wrote, is "to think that men are so foolish that they take care to avoid what mischiefs may be done them by polecats or foxes, but are content, nay, think it safety, to be devoured by lions." Of course, Locke knew that in the human, as contrasted with the animal, world, men were often that foolish; their folly, however, was illegitimate because "no rational creature can be supposed to change his condition with an intention to be worse."[13]

The great liberal doctrinaires saw unreason as far less pervasive than we do. That difference is due only in part to intellectual changes like the "Freudian revolution"; in equally important ways, our belief in "substantive reason" has declined because the world has become so baffling that knowledge of the consequences of action, beyond the narrowest compass, seems unattainable. The decisions of men, leaving hidden motives and anxieties aside, are little more than desperate guesses and stabs in the dark.

Public policy has retained the liberal premise and that shadowy figure, "the reasonable man," still stalks the opinions of the Supreme Court. Given the recognition of the difficulties of reasoning in our times as well as the newer doubt of man's rational capacity, the Court has responded logically by *narrowing* the category of legitimate consent. This, evidently, is the meaning of the rule that "voluntary" statements made to law enforcers are illegitimate unless the individual was explicitly informed of his rights and of the consequences of breaking silence, as well as the presumption that an individual cannot legitimately waive his right to counsel in certain cases.

Social science, however, has responded to the declining faith in reason by abandoning the requirement that consent be rational in order to be legitimate. "Belief" or "opinion" will do as well—possibly better, for, as Burke observed, "prejudice" is a more certain foundation than is reason. But prejudice, of course, is an excellent foundation for lawlessness as well as for law. If social science stops short of the nihilistic consequence, it is partly due to the conviction that "systems" possess a "functional rationality" and hence a presumptive legitimacy, a dogma no more demonstrable or rational than Sir Leicester Dedlock's conviction that the Court of Chauncery was "a something devised in conjunction with a variety of other somethings, by the perfection of human wisdom, for the eternal settlement (humanly speaking) of everything."[14] And it is no surprise that some of our citizens, doubting that comforting creed, go no further than the premise that any belief they happen to entertain is legitimate.

Constitutional Procedure

The most optimistic of liberal theorists knew that the people were not always watchful, nor did they always look further than their own immediate interests: hence the whole panoply of devices which liberals devised in order to render governmental legitimacy proof against the possible base motives of rulers and the inattention of citizens, like individual rights and the separation of powers. But although such procedural norms often became closely identified with ends, liberal theorists knew that procedures which fail to obtain the substantive results they are designed to achieve may be illegitimate. And they were also aware that procedures constructed to deal with one environment may be maladapted or destructive in another.

The rights and procedures which liberal theory delineated were, consequently, always subject to violation if doing so was necessary to defend the state or the ends for which it was created. Men had a right of property, but they could be taxed if the majority so willed. They had a right to life, but they could be required to fight in defense of the state. (In the course of his defense of the right of property, Locke observed that in war, where the end required it, a soldier could legitimately be ordered to "march up to the cannon's mouth" and that he was bound to obey "the most dangerous and unreasonable" of orders.) Similarly, because changed and unforeseen situations occur in which the legislature is too slow and too rigid, Locke accorded the executive the prerogative of acting "for the public good, without the prescription of law and sometimes even against it" when the case required.[15] It was such "legitimate exceptions" that Holmes attempted to summarize in the "clear and present danger" test in *Schenck v. U.S.*[16]

That "test," never very precise, can now be used to legitimate almost any action. All times are "abnormal," and with the acceleration of change the distant future becomes "present" if not "clear." Far-removed places become close; risk increases; the time in which error can be rectified shrinks to the vanishing point and commands action long before the event, while political orders grow in complexity and inertia, becoming so slow to change that something close to prophetic power is required to keep them from rumbling toward some unforeseen and disastrous end.

Governments will insist that more and more problems become their "legitimate concern." If they do not, they will have such responsibilities thrust on them, which is one of the lessons to be learned from the relatively passive and acquiescent citizenries in the great industrial states. But governments, surrounded by threat and change, feel themselves weak and insignificant in important respects. The willingness to accept procedural limitations has declined sharply. Officials repeatedly declaim against "inflexible rules" which "tie their hands," and as Theodore Lowi has pointed out, the whole category of "unconstitutional delegation" has virtually disappeared from the law.[17] It is curious for the president to insist that the United States keep its commitments while demanding that Congress leave his own hands free.

But if citizens have been generally willing to allow this expansion of governmental legitimacy, that willingness is a two-edged sword. If the range of actions which are legitimate is expanded for the state, I will insist that it be expanded for me; if the state cannot be asked to make procedural commitments to me, I will make none to the state. An increase in the range of actions thought to be legitimately self-protective is inseparable from a similar growth in actions thought to be legitimately state-protective.[18]

Private citizens excuse themselves much on the grounds that their conduct does not matter to anyone but themselves or, if it does matter in some remote sense, they feel themselves so insignificant as individuals as to be free from moral claims on their conduct. Nor is this simply a matter of private and passive actions. Members of politically committed groups appeal to weakness as a justification for extreme tactics. Officials, meeting active or passive obstruction, are reinforced in the conviction that still more extreme measures are legitimate for them. The spiral escalates; the shots at Kent State and bombs in research centers are echoes, and preventive detention will probably be answered by abduction, with all parties denying that their acts have been illegitimate. The old procedural restraints have lost both the prestige of science, which liberalism once claimed for them, and the majesty of law.

Progress

The mastering of nature, removing the obstacles it placed in the way of human desire, was a central element in liberal ideas of liberty and the major goal of human endeavor. Progress toward that end was related— especially by the historical theorists of the last century—to virtually every other aim, reason, the rule of law, and peace within and between nations. It followed that any regime and any form of human conduct which failed to further man's cause in the war against nature was illegitimate.

The "penury" of the human condition, Locke wrote, required man to labor and made it clear that the earth rightfully belonged to "the industrious and rational" alone.[19] Those who wastefully allowed the earth to go untilled, like the American Indian, had no legitimate title. The language of liberalism changed and rival schools challenged it, but that norm remained at the center of modern political thought. John Stuart Mill found an exception to the "principle of non-intervention" in backward, "uncivilized" societies that needed tutelage. Radicals, like Marx, argued that a regime becomes illegitimate when it loses the capacity to progress, when its social relations become "fetters on the modes of production," but liberals were only more moderate in denying the legitimacy of "reactionary regimes" while Marx and Engels—with some regret—saw colonialism as progressive and legitimate.[20]

It makes quaint reading to peruse those nineteenth-century treatises which identified progress with the cause of peace. Transforming rather than eliminating war, technological and material progress have destroyed more than one standard of illegitimacy. In our own Constitution, the war power has become voracious, devouring one procedural restraint after another. In war itself, the category of legitimate "military necessity" has expanded as war became total; even limited wars are total within their own boundaries, partisan war more than most because it eliminates the "rear areas" where normal restraints were relatively applicable.[21]

But there is an even more integral relation between war and the "struggle with nature." Implicit in all contractarian theory was the notion that, amid the comforts of peace, men would forget the necessity which legitimated the state. The dangers of war, Madison wrote, "repressed the passions most unfriendly to order and concord" and made the democracy of the early American constitutions workable. With the advent of peace, those passions reappeared, Madison argued, making it necessary to win prejudice as a less rational but more pacific support for legitimacy.[22]

Other theorists have not always been so complaisant. Some have argued that war and threat are needed to remind men of the insecurity of their condition and the need to "give up" some of their rights. Many have seen war as a means of *removing* "prejudice," the internal standards of illegitimacy that stand as effective barriers to progress. Frantz Fanon is only a recent example of those who have urged that combat is partly legitimated by the transformation it works in a traditional society.[23]

There is something to be said for that case. But war has a way of ceasing to be a device and becoming a necessity.[24] If moral and political changes undermine security, especially if they destroy the confidence that there are things which one's government and fellow citizens will not do, then the enemy may be needed to give the political community a measure of solidarity and legitimacy. The decline of internal standards of illegitimacy is directly related to the need for external standards of illegitimacy. In that sense, the war with nature leads toward, rather than away from, a "state of war."

Progress is no longer coherent enough to provide a test of illegitimacy. Its meaning is uncertain, its moral consequences ambivalent. So many enormities have been committed in the name of progress, so much human wreckage is left by each "wave of the future," that more and more of us begin to suspect, as Hawthorne did, that "the Celestial Railroad" leads to the pit. Man as master of nature proves rapacious, and the chains which bind nature are too well suited for the enslaving of men.[25]

The liberal standards of illegitimacy are in ruins or have become evanescent. Social science, which grew up in the shelter of liberalism, shares in the decay. Partly creators, partly creatures of the modern world, neither can provide it with a "moral center." Many, especially the young, reject the old restraints out of a growing suspicion—once only a shadow on a radiant canvas—that political illegitimacy is a characteristic of the modern world itself.

II

Our situation is ambiguous enough that for some time we will probably continue to shamble in whatever way we are pushed by events. I do not propose here to set us on some new and straight path. I intend only to discuss four interrelated criteria of political illegitimacy and to suggest, finally, that illegitimacy cannot be treated simply as a matter of belief. It will be enough if this paper makes some beginning in the search for a theory of illegitimacy.

Impersonality

If the established order does not know or care about me, it can serve my purposes only by accident and it is almost impossible for it to treat me justly. It is even worse if the regime is "alien" in the sense that it neither knows nor cares about my kinsmen or my people, for then it cannot even treat me as a part of a category. (Rule by foreigners can be and often is legitimate, but only when the foreigner is thought to have some measure of understanding and concern.) Illegitimacy is easier to avoid when men identify themselves with groups and categories, for the regime is then not required to have knowledge of each individual; privatization and illegitimacy go hand in hand.

I am aware that liberal rationalists insisted on a justice which would be "impersonal." By that, however, they meant a justice which would be fair because it would weigh their virtues accurately—in liberal terms. It would, in other words, inquire no further than the "objective" facts of overt action and measurable "achievement."

Justice can, in fact, never be impersonal; a blind goddess, she must not be deaf. Over and over in American history, liberal ideas of justice were opposed by traditionalistic and immigrant groups which thought that liberalism radically misunderstood the nature of man, insisting that virtues like loyalty and concern were "merits" in their own right. John Schaar questions whether the partisans of the old machines thought of the "indifferent formal institutions" of American politics as legitimate. Indeed they did not; witness the famous comment attributed to Tim Campbell, "What's the Constitution between friends?"[26] The established institutions and procedures were at best a harmless bother or a nuisance to be ignored. They became legitimate only to the extent that those who held office saw to it that the "output" of such institutions was not impersonal, whatever nominal norms were broken in the process.

As a device to lessen or eliminate impersonality, representative government is not always necessary and not always adequate. I may believe that a regime understands and cares for me without such a device, though such faith is rare in the modern world; I may be convinced that the representative mechanism is inadequate, either fundamentally or in the details of its design. I will insist on being "consulted" to the extent that I think it essential to being "considered." In this, I must be considered as a whole personality; I have not been considered if "my dignity" is ignored or misunderstood. (We know this in practice; if Lyndon Johnson desired to be heard on a matter of foreign policy, a secretary of state would not tell him to "take it up with your congressman." But dignity does not always have the power to make its claims good.)

The more aspects of my personality that the regime considers, the more legitimate it will be; if it ignores any, it will be to that extent illegitimate. It was this which led so many classical theorists to argue that the best state must be small and a good one at least limited in size. Equally, it led to the liberal attempt to separate state and society, denying the state access to those areas of life in which it was thought impossible for any government to act legitimately. That effort was futile in many ways, not the least that "society" can also be an illegitimate force in the lives of men. But in the mass states of today, some "right of privacy" is made essential by the fact that the best-informed and best-intentioned government cannot hope to understand me as a unique personality. A truly totalitarian state would be necessarily illegitimate.

But our own institutions are more than suspect. Repeatedly, political movements have made clear—whatever one thinks of their programs or lack of them—that some important aspect of the personalities of those they represent has been misunderstood, ignored, or treated with contempt.[27] With blacks and racial and ethnic minorities generally, I take it that this is obvious; with students and women it is only slightly less so, and the list could be prolonged.

It is not simply discrimination that is protested. Sometimes, the charge is that we ignore the distributive aspect of justice by treating different things alike. Often, the accusation is that we destroy community or deprive men of it, that the implicit individualism of our institutions misunderstands man as a political animal and his need for community.

Inheriting community from a preindustrial and immigrant past, we have tended to think of it as something to be escaped or taken for granted, a kind of perennially spontaneous growth. But in industrial society, community is a delicate plant in a hostile environment, needing the support and encouragement of law.[28]

We need new, explicit ways in which communities can be given legal status and effective power. That, I think, is part of the contemporary meaning of the right of men to be tried by juries of their peers. And such a departure is necessary not only because without it, men will feel the state to be distant, impersonal, and illegitimate; it is needed because a world of one's peers is necessary if one is to have a standard of what is illegitimate for himself.[29]

Political Bankruptcy

Expectation, by creating possession before the event, generally legitimates the consequences it foresees. The mere belief that a regime will endure helps greatly to make it seem legitimate. A belief in process, similarly, makes us see events in relation to their consequences, not simply in themselves, a fact which may change their moral character in our eyes ("You can't make an omelet . . .").

The conviction that a regime or condition is changing for the better may help legitimate it now in view of its presumed "good tendency." In that case, the sense that there are "better alternatives" does not deprive the regime of legitimacy. We must always consider the cost of imposing those alternatives, a measure which involves more than their rightness. If I can persuade the president to change a policy of which I disapprove, I will probably do so; if I can change his course only by violence, the costs rise and the legitimacy of his policies rises with them. Belief in the possibility of changing the existing order legitimates it even if I am not at all hopeful about the chances of enlightening its present personnel. But we often forget that such hopes, the core of proceduralist theories of legitimacy, are effective only in the short term. The belief in change legitimates only by becoming an expectation, and expectancy deferred is a source of tension, eventually of the conviction that one has been cheated.

When a regime is legitimated by expectation, it *borrows* legitimacy based on what de Jouvenel calls its "political credit," offering as collateral its past successes and those hopes to which it can appeal.[30] At some point, however, a regime must "pay off" or it becomes a bad risk, facing political foreclosure and eventual bankruptcy.[31] A government which encourages unrealistic expectations, consequently, acts as illegitimately as a promoter who deals in fraudulent stocks.

Citizens tend to be forgiving and seem willing to excuse a government on the ground that "circumstances" prevented it from producing the hoped-for results. We do not always blame management if a corporation fails to show a profit during a depression, nor do baseball fans hold a manager responsible if a team is obviously inept. (Consider only Casey Stengel and the Mets.) If, on the other hand, failure is thought to result from perverse *ends,* we will hardly be forgiving. In this sense, rationalism's belief in the "logic of events" and systemic rationality may injure legitimacy. The belief that the regime has its reasons may win our support, but the same conviction, confronted with failure, may lead us to *discern* perversity, to see the result as "part of the system" and the reflection of a moral gap which may not exist at all.

Pessimism may legitimate a political regime by encouraging us to cling to the "devil we know." But pessimism can lead to the conviction of illegitimacy in at least two cases. First, if we believe that there is "no worse alternative" than the present regime, the government cannot even point to enemies it fends off without our answering something like "Better Hitler than Blum." The regime, in other words, has become so odious that all the existing alternatives which we perceive seem more acceptable. (That we may be wrong in believing that nothing could be worse is, for the moment, beside the point.)

Second, if the measures of a government are thought to have a "bad tendency" they may be regarded as illegitimate even if, at the moment, they seem innocuous or beneficent. Like all the categories discussed here, this view may be applied to individual as well as governmental acts, as it was, unfortunately, in *Gitlow v. N.Y.*[32] C. Wright Mills, for example, conceded that American policymakers were within the bounds of reason at the moment, but charged that they were "crackpot realists" because their policies tended toward disaster.[33] And more than one revolutionary has opposed some measure to relieve the oppressed, fearing that it would delay political transformation. (Though I agree with Michael Walzer that such an attitude is illegitimate if defended in terms of commitment to the oppressed themselves.)[34]

No regime is politically bankrupt, however, if it can still arouse shock. Shock, the result of a dramatic violation of one's expectations, certainly unsettles a regime and is likely to lead to militant protest. But it need not result in the revolutionary destruction of a regime unless the regime itself shows willful perversity and intransigence.

Modern man has become subject to what Allard Lowenstein once called (in relation to South Africa) "the insulation effect." Successively greater crimes temper the impact of those which preceded; enormity becomes an expectation and destroys the capacity to be shocked. For too many of us, only a gesture of humanity would be shocking if, in fact, we did not interpret it as part of some devious design.

Younger Americans have been part of a world relatively shielded from such "lessons." Exposed to a world of betrayal, they still have the capacity to be made indignant. Something similar, too, is notable among blacks. Decisions like *Brown v. Board*, legislative enactments, and political promises created expectancy because they were believed. The resulting outrage was a mark of faith and of political loyalty. The danger, obviously, is not that these and others like them will be shocked, but that they will develop a radical cynicism which is the true rejection of the legitimacy of the political order. Outrage when the government behaves badly reflects the expectation that it will behave well. Those who are unable to become indignant deny the government any moral status at all, and their alienation is no less revolutionary because it does not, for the moment, disturb the appearance of political calm.

Bad Faith

When a regime promises to do what it does not intend to do, or when it gives reasons which are not the real bases of its action, it acts illegitimately. Restoring the political credit of a government, if it remains in power, may be fairly easy; restoring its credibility is difficult in the extreme. The government, for example, promises to protect us, and if it does not we may acquire guns. But where the conservative weapon-buyer may doubt its will or ability, the radical may doubt whether it intends to protect him at all. Disarming the first only requires that the government grow stronger or more firm, but such conduct will only strengthen the conviction of the second that he needs the tools of self-defense.[35]

Distrust generalizes. In a mass state, most of our pledges and understandings are made with strangers, men beyond our circle of effective knowledge and control, and the credibility of the government is a vital element in our confidence that such promises will be carried out. Distrusting it can easily lead to distrust for our fellows; mistrust is a form of insecurity, more able than most to make us sure that we act legitimately in doing whatever is needed to protect ourselves.[36]

It only makes matters worse that bad faith can be unconscious, as when we deceive ourselves at the same time that we deceive another. We can, at least, admire the cunning of a confidence man, but the self-deceptive are likely to act most illegitimately when moved by what they take for pure-heartedness. It is they who are most likely to be guilty of vindictiveness, for reasons that need no explanation in a post-Freudian age; the man of cunning will at least economize his cruelties.[37]

Quite often, bad faith reflects the self-distrust of men and regimes, their doubt of the legitimacy of their own aims and conduct. It is frequent for a government to be convinced that its people are so misinformed and irrational that the administration cannot make them see the legitimacy of its policies. But in a legitimate autocracy, the government might simply say as much, relying on the people to accept its estimate of themselves. "The king has lost a battle," the Prussians were told after Jena. "Silence is the first duty of the citizen." But in a democracy, a regime which is convinced that the people cannot even be persuaded of their stupidity in critical matters of policy holds its title to rule by a species of bad faith. The illegitimacy of title compels illegitimate means, for it denies both the great defenses of democracy, the liberal belief that the people are the fountain of legitimacy and the classical creed that deliberation and participation are essential to that improvement of the citizen which is the chief end of the state.

None of this means that a regime or a man must always "act honestly." It is impossible to do so and probably often wrong in the bargain. Some of our noblest actions result from suppressing rather deep feelings; if a regime or a man acts better than either "really is," we are gratified rather than angry. The test of permissible or noble lies is that they are legitimated by reference to common standards and are, hence, a means of keeping rather than breaking faith. We can imagine—and probably have watched—a public man who, harboring the belief that we are not rational, manfully but dishonestly treats us as though we were. A democratic regime may withhold information, may deceive or even lie outright provided that it has convinced us beforehand of the necessity of its doing so. Few objected, for example, to the wild manipulation of news which took place during World War II. Since the war, the government has made its case for classification, but it is evident that secrets have been kept outside the bounds of our agreement that we are not to be trusted with certain kinds of information, and the conviction that it has acted illegitimately follows as a matter of course.[38]

Arbitrariness

The prohibition of arbitrary conduct is perhaps the oldest and most inclusive standard of illegitimacy. Arbitrary conduct is the product of caprice and follows no rule but the private will of him who engages in it. Often, arbitrariness is called illegitimate because it is capricious in the choice of means and bears no reasonable relation to ends, as when we distinguish between cruelty and punishment.

We may also mean, however, that the ends of action are themselves arbitrary. In some spheres of life this is no reproach; *de gustibus, non est disputandum.* That exception, however, presumes that the matter in question is truly a matter of private concern which does not involve others. It is legitimate for me to detest pickled pigs' feet, but it will probably seem illegitimate for me to assert this truth in the presence of a maiden aunt who has lovingly prepared that dish for my delectation.

Arbitrary choice of ends in a man or regime is illegitimate when it takes place in a sphere which is common. It is "contrary to nature," treating as private what is in fact not private at all. Arbitrariness is illegitimate, in other words, when it is unreasonable.

The state acts illegitimately when its rewards and punishments have no relation to merits or offenses, and when it excuses some for what it punishes in others unless there is some clear reason for doing so. Punishing men for violating the Volstead Act had come to seem arbitrary before the Eighteenth Amendment had become very old; the same attitude may develop in relation to marijuana, as it already has in a wide circle. And, in my view, it would be arbitrary if the regime gave an amnesty to those who have deserted the armed forces or who have emigrated to avoid service. Such an amnesty would be arbitrary because it ignores the merits of those who "did their duty" to the community either by serving or by going to prison in protest, hoping to awaken their fellows and giving them proof of personal sincerity. And second, to demand sacrifice of some and not of others is arbitrary on its face and would require a better justification than any I have seen yet. (The Selective Service System, clearly, is almost as reproachable.)

It is also arbitrary to hold men and regimes responsible for results they cannot effect, and this results in a serious problem. Regimes must be excused much on the grounds that they are dependent on the actions of others; even the United States does not completely control even so small a state as Israel, nor can the Soviet Union simply dictate to the United Arab Republic. But the case is even more marked in relation to individuals; men are sufficiently unimportant and weak that it comes to seem arbitrary to hold them responsible for a wide range of acts and consequences.

But the conviction that individuals are unimportant can also encourage an extreme form of arbitrariness. We may, for example, come to believe that *individual* guilt or innocence is as "unimportant" as the individual himself is thought to be. If so, it may seem legitimate for us to select any individual or individuals for punishment so long as they belong to certain "categories" whose conduct we desire to influence. No one, at Jackson or Kent State, seems to have worried much about his aim; bombs left in buildings do not discriminate between the lamblike and the porcine. In the extreme case, such attitudes approximate the doctrine that some men are "objectively criminal," one of the horrors of totalitarianism, illegitimate in its arbitrariness and impersonality alike.[39]

It is an offense in many ways, whether we forgive or convict, to see a man as no more than the reflection of something else; even in setting him free, we have defined him as a prisoner.[40] Men need to be held responsible, for excellence unrealized no less than for sins committed. Self-betrayal is illegitimate, but among the most frequent of offenses. And it is arbitrary because contrary to nature if we deny others and ourselves the support of encouragement and sanction; as Rousseau knew, man often needs to be forced to be free.

Illegitimacy Is More Than Belief

I have selected my criteria of illegitimacy with some license, for each of them is essentially a question of fact, not merely of opinion. That officials in Mississippi and whites in general misunderstand blacks has been eminently verified, and it is proverbial that women are mysteries to men. My expectations about the tendencies of a given regime, or the likelihood that there exists any alternative to it that I would prefer, are predictions subject to scientific treatment if normally tested in the harder school of experience. Similarly, my belief that the regime is acting arbitrarily or in bad faith is either correct, incorrect, or a bit of both.

Of course, the questions involved are difficult, especially at the highest levels of meaning, but that does not change their character. Belief is a conviction about fact, and in this sense, some beliefs and opinions are better than others. I can, of course, believe that it is illegitimate to teach that the earth goes around the sun out of my stubborn adherence to Ptolemaicism, and social science should take note of my quaint conviction.

But that does not in the least affect our theory of the legitimacy of Copernican premises; no more should it do so in relation to states and men.

This helps us to avoid the gap between theory and practice discussed earlier. Nazism, to take the extreme example, was illegitimate on every count: (1) it radically misunderstood man, as every racism must; (2) it aroused unreal expectations, almost destroyed the capacity to be shocked, and even on its own terms had a "bad tendency"; (3) it was frequently and sometimes explicitly arbitrary; and (4) it acted in bad faith, for despite the sincerity of the regime, our evidence indicates that leaders were so self-deluded that they could not help deceiving others.

The question can be put another way. In a purely rational sense, I owe the least obligations if I am a slave. I can, of course, legitimately obey if resistance is pointless or if my significance is great enough that my resistance would cause suffering but only that. To resist, I must have what George Wada and James Davies call a "freedom to react."[41] Illegitimacy and resistance are not necessarily found together.

In the extreme case, I may be so weak and so threatened that even resentment against enslavement is a danger, constituting a constant temptation to resist. I may seek to destroy it in myself; I am even more likely to try to destroy it in my children, who cannot be expected to be masters of deceit. I and my progeny may, then, come to internalize the standards of the enslaver, turning our resentments onto ourselves or our fellows among the oppressed. This has become a truism in the analysis of race relations in America. It is no less applicable to those who, terrorized by insecurity, turn to the weak defense of believing that only the guilty are punished in order to make themselves feel safe. Men in such situations will "believe" that the existing order is legitimate, but the belief is spurious.[42]

Our power to shape alternatives and our beliefs about that power affect our sense of what is rightfully ours; what I think myself able to do influences what I believe that I ought to do. As my sense of significance rises, so does my sense of right and with it, the likelihood that I will perceive the existing order as illegitimate. The more thoroughly oppressive and illegitimate the regime, the less it is likely that I will see it as being so. And, with that peculiarity of perception which is all too human, I am more likely to believe in the illegitimacy of the regime as it becomes less oppressive, whether because it is earnestly striving to reform or because it has become weaker and more ineffective.[43]

We may draw some comfort from this. The increasingly strident assertion that the political order is illegitimate may mean that we are on the verge of a legitimate one, free from long-hidden injustice. Conflict and violence will certainly be with us, especially because a rise in your significance is likely to make me sense a fall in mine; security for you, illogically, seems a threat to me. And if I respond by lowering the standard of what I think illegitimate in my own conduct, you may be forced to answer in kind.[44] All of this is distinct from the fact that in a culture which has taught men to think of will as "right," and in a world which makes all men feel relatively insignificant, standards of illegitimacy will never be very exacting. It is not a prospect which promotes confidence.

We could try to make those who now protest feel weaker and more threatened until they lapse into quiescence. But when man's sense of right is aroused, the battle is likely to be hard and the costs unacceptable. Even victory would involve an intolerable moral cost, for the protesters are fundamentally right if often wrong in detail. We can also attempt to raise the sense of significance of all our citizens, which involves more than the classical American device of increasing their possessions. Success would require something of a revolution, but in the sense of "turning back," a reconstruction of communities and institutions which give men dignity.[45] Lest I am sanguine, that task is difficult at best in the present day and with men as they have become; it may be necessary nonetheless.

Finally, we can and probably must face the substantive issue, the possibility of redefining what men think of as their "right." Defining right as will, in the liberal mode, is illegitimate because it makes right arbitrary, and surely we have learned enough to suspect that such a definition is contrary to the human condition. Modern America, with its liberal heritage, has thought of man's estate as a matter of property, something he comes into only when he makes things and others his own. But a man's debts are as much a part of him as the things he controls; his owing is a stronger and truer source of dignity than owning. Most of all, the knowledge that one owes much is more likely to lead men toward forgiveness of others and standards of illegitimacy for themselves.

Notes

This essay was originally published in longer form as "On Political Illegitimacy," *Public Policy* 19, no. 3 (1971).

1. *Leviathan,* ed. C. B. Macpherson (Baltimore: Penguin Books, 1968), 188. Hobbes's sense of the importance of illegitimacy is also indicated by his negative formulation of the Golden Rule, "Do not that to another, which thou wouldest not have done to thy selfe" (ibid., 214).

2. A glance at a few older texts will confirm this; if they use the word at all, such works generally refer to monarchical theories of legitimism.

3. Seymour M. Lipset, *Political Man* (Garden City: Doubleday, 1960), 77.

4. Legitimation, in Talcott Parsons's definition, is the "appraisal of action in terms of shared or common values in the context of the involvement of the action in the social system." See C. J. Friedrich, ed., *Authority* (Cambridge, Mass.: Harvard University Press, 1958), 201.

5. John H. Schaar, "Rationality and Legitimacy in the Modern State," in *Power and Community*, ed. Sanford Levinson and Philip Green (New York: Pantheon, 1970).

6. I have made a similar argument in "On Violence and Legitimacy," *Yale Law Journal* 79 (1970): 623–46. Alan Wertheimer has objected to this argument ("Political Legitimacy, Political Obligation and Political Size," paper presented to the American Political Science Association, September 11, 1970), arguing that we have a stronger moral meaning in mind when we refer to *political* legitimacy and protesting against my "*use* of analogies" which he compares, rather flatteringly, to Plato's. This paper has many virtues, but Wertheimer should note that the statement "X *is* the legitimate government of Y" implies some *defect* of title, whether of power or of moral standing. We do not call the British regime the "legitimate government"; we call it either "the British government" or simply "Britain" because its title is unchallenged in right or fact.

7. See A. M. Lee, "The Concept of System," *Social Research* 32 (1965): 229–38; and Bertrand de Jouvenel, *Sovereignty* (Chicago: University of Chicago Press, 1957), 3–8.

8. The government may, if appeals to common standards of illegitimacy fail, appeal to private ones. It may tell me, "If you do not obey, you will go to jail," which will succeed if I think it illegitimate for me to be in prison. But this alternative is risky as well as weak, for if I think that my example will inspire my fellow citizens to oppose the government, it may seem illegitimate *not* to go to jail. And I may think that going to jail is something which I owe to God, my friends, or myself.

9. Without the qualification, authority defines its own legitimacy. (See Jerome Hall, "Authority and the Law," in Friedrich, *Authority*, 63.)

10. Hannah Arendt, "What Was Authority?" in Friedrich, *Authority*, 83.

11. Ewart K. Lewis, "The Contribution of Medieval Thought to the American Political Tradition," *American Political Science Review* 50 (1956): 462–74.

12. *On Power* (Boston: Beacon, 1962), 33–43.

13. John Locke, *Two Treatises of Government*, ed. T. Cook (New York: Hafner, 1947), 167, 186.

14. Charles Dickens, *Bleak House* (New York: Appleton, 1868), 8.

15. *Two Treatises of Government*, 193, 204.

16. 249 U.S. 47 (1918).

17. Theodore Lowi, *The End of Liberalism* (New York: Norton, 1969).

18. On this point and on the decline of procedural limits generally, see my

"Civil Disobedience and Contemporary Constitutionalism," *Comparative Politics* 1 (1969): 2111f.

19. *Two Treatises of Government,* 136–37.

20. See John Stuart Mill, "On Non-intervention," *Fraser's Magazine* (1859); and Karl Marx in *Karl Marx on Colonialism and Modernization,* ed. Shlome Avineri (Garden City: Doubleday, 1969), 88–95.

21. Ernst Fraenkel, *Military Occupation and the Rule of Law* (New York: Oxford University Press, 1944), 189; and L. H. Miller, "The Contemporary Significance of the Doctrines of Just War," *World Politics* 16 (1964): 254–86.

22. *The Federalist,* ed. Max Boloff (Oxford: Blackwell, 1948), 258–59.

23. Frantz Fanon, *Studies in a Dying Colonialism* (New York: Monthly Review Press, 1959).

24. Hannah Arendt, *On Violence* (New York: Harcourt Brace, 1970).

25. For those not yet convinced, I recommend Matthew P. Dumont's delightful "Urban Life and the Banality of Good Will," *Psychiatry and Social Science Review,* July 14, 1970, 9–11.

26. Schaar, "Rationality and Legitimacy in the Modern State"; William Riordan, *Plunkitt of Tammany Hall* (New York: Dutton, 1963), 13.

27. For a foreign example, see J. P. Mackintosh, "Scottish Nationalism," *Political Quarterly* 38 (1967): 389–402.

28. Henry Kariel, *The Decline of American Pluralism* (Stanford, Calif.: Stanford University Press, 1961).

29. Wertheimer, "Political Legitimacy, Political Obligation and Political Size," makes this point very well in relation to the size of societies.

30. *On Power,* 25.

31. James Gusfield, "Mass Society and Extremist Politics," *American Sociological Review* 27 (1962): 19–30.

32. 268 U.S. 652 (1925). The Supreme Court held that a state did not infringe freedom of speech or of the press by prohibiting the advocacy (in this case, by communists) of the violent overthrow of government, even if there were no indication that the advocacy had had, might have, or was likely to have any such effect. Holmes and Brandeis dissented, citing the "clear and present danger" criterion of the *Schenck* case (see n. 16).

33. C. Wright Mills, *The Causes of World War III* (New York: Simon and Schuster, 1958), 81–89.

34. Michael Walzer, *Obligations* (Cambridge, Mass.: Harvard University Press, 1970), 52–70.

35. For an excellent discussion of bad faith, see Gordon J. Schochet, "Disobedience and Beyond," paper presented to the Canadian Political Science Association, June 1–4, 1970.

36. For a powerful description, see *Collected Essays, Journalism and Letters of George Orwell* (New York: Harcourt Brace, 1968), 3:200.

37. S. Wolin, *Politics and Vision* (Boston: Little, Brown, 1960), 220–24.

38. William Barnds et al., *The Right to Know, to Withhold and to Lie* (New York: Council on Religion and International Affairs, 1970).

39. Hannah Arendt, *The Origins of Totalitarianism* (New York: Harcourt Brace, 1951).

40. Ralph Ellison, *Shadow and Act* (New York: New American Library, 1966), 128.

41. George Wada and James C. Davies, "Riots and Rioters," *Western Political Quarterly* 10 (1957): 864–74.

42. Edward Sapir, "Culture, Genuine and Spurious," *American Journal of Sociology* 29 (1924): 401–29, is to be thanked for introducing the notion of spurious culture.

43. For a similar analysis, see my "On Violence and Legitimacy."

44. Hans Speier, *Social Order and the Risks of War* (Cambridge, Mass.: MIT Press, 1969), 27–35.

45. Hannah Arendt, *On Revolution* (New York: Viking, 1963).

Civil Disobedience and Contemporary Constitutionalism

The American Case

The idea of civil disobedience is coeval with political philosophy but, until events of the 1960s catapulted it into the headlines, it was given little attention by modern political thought. The "serene stream" of constitutionalism[1] had sought to lower the risks of political life by substituting the rule of laws for that of men; constitutionalist thought tended to reduce the great human choices to the single standard of legality. Seeking to minimize dependence on the statesman, it also tried to minimize dependence on the citizen.[2]

From Birmingham to Chicago—to take events of that time—political life in the modern world has disturbed the constitutionalist's serenity, if not his adherence to the faith. The laws seem to have lost their power. Justice Whittaker apparently spoke for a majority of Americans in asserting that "our nation is in the grip of a rash of rapidly spreading mass lawlessness and violence which, in large part, is planned and willful." Whittaker, like many of his fellow citizens, attributed this crisis to ideas of civil disobedience and advocated a stern reverence for laws: "The Bible does say that thou shalt obey the civil authorities. . . . It seems a pretty plain statement to me. And for myself I see no reason to depart [from] a literal construction of it." Even the phrase "civil disobedience" seemed dangerous to Whittaker: "Violations of our criminal laws are criminal violations, not civil disobedience."[3]

To those who share this view, it does not occur that civil disobedience might be a means of remedying critical defects in the constitutional system which otherwise might encourage more serious forms of disorder. Established means, Whittaker stated, "are fully adequate to all ends that are loyal to our form of government."[4]

This article is a challenge to that thesis. It will attempt (1) to restate some general principles of traditional constitutionalism; (2) to argue that the contemporary constitutional crisis is a result of a breakdown of those principles; and (3) to suggest that civil disobedience may have a vital role in any contemporary constitutional order.

Constitutionalism seeks to transform a given political environment in the direction of valued ends by means of institutions designed, more or less rationally, for that purpose. Even presuming a perfect knowledge of human nature, a scheme of unchanging values, and a precise science of institutions, changes in the environment will affect, when they do not wholly undermine, the basic design.[5] Plato's Eleatic Stranger said of the law that "it is like a self-willed, ignorant man who lets no one do anything but what he has ordered and forbids all subsequent questioning of his orders even if the legislation has shown some marked improvement on the one for which he first legislated."[6]

A perfect constitutional system would demand a perfect philosophy of history which would enable the exact prediction of environmental change. Lacking that, William Sloane Coffin's comment on the tendency of institutions in times of change is to the point: "Instruments of order, instead of serving, begin to dominate. Servant structures become semigods claiming men's allegiance. . . . Men become more loyal to the law than to the people law was designed to serve."[7] The wisest of constitutionalists, however, knew this danger and sought to avoid being trapped between the poles of a ritualistic assertion—like Whittaker's—of the validity of existing institutions and an anomic disregard for stability of procedure resting on ad hoc judgment of individual cases.

Some of the oldest forms of constitutionalism recognized that procedures can be designed for, and applied to, only the "normal" cases and that political wisdom requires the making of exceptions.[8] If the Supreme Court appeals less frequently to "natural justice" than it did in the past, it has recourse to the "rule of reason," which was the substance of that appeal.[9] The Court is forced to realize that even if Justice Fortas is right to declare that "procedure is the bone structure of a democratic society,"[10] procedure is not necessarily the flesh of society and certainly not its soul. This is only to recognize, as did the great constitutionalists of the past, that government must be restrained *substantively* as well as procedurally. What is done with power is at least as important as the title by which power is acquired, and limited government requires both constraints.[11]

Locke, well aware of the unforeseen (especially in foreign policy), laid down the maxim that substantive norms override procedural limitations. A "strict and rigid" adherence to law, he wrote, is not always possible; governments need, at times, to act against the law in the interest of those ends for which men "entered" the state. When government thus escapes from institutional constraint, Locke argued, substantive limitation of its actions rests with the citizenry, with that "right of resistance" which is the ultimate restraint of the political order. Indeed, Locke wrote, the people must be enabled to act *before* any usurpation occurs, for once established, it may be impossible to remove.[12]

To achieve this result, Lockeans insisted on the "separation of state and society" which formed the "basic distinction of constitutionalist thought."[13] The exclusion of the state from a reserved, private sphere ("society") was designed to protect an area in which the public could form values, evaluate policies, organize freely, and from which it could emerge in public acts to control the state.[14] The framers parted company on the question of how easily and how often that shadowy abstraction, "the people," should become concrete, but they agreed that in the "ultimate" sense any constitutional order depended on public character and virtue. Political education was to be left almost entirely to the people themselves.[15]

Thus the habit of stating laws negatively, prohibiting overt acts: the practice prevents the state from inquiring into the values and motives of those who refrain from disobedience. It bars the government from distinguishing between "good citizens" and others; the public alone determines the hierarchy of civic virtues. The great social institutions—family, church, and school—are, and were intended to be, in a broader sense, *constitutional* agencies concerned with substantive restraint. (This indicates the fragility of the public-private distinction and of the theory of man on which it was based, for the state affects these institutions when it makes any policy at all.)

Much of the doctrine of "separation of powers" derived from the premise of a noncreative state that should follow the substantive decisions of the public. From this doctrine followed the constitutionalist's emphasis on the legislature.[16] The formation of values and policies demanded deliberation, and the limitations of man restricted that deliberation to small and (then) territorial groups in which the individual would feel a sense of participation and collective responsibility. Only such groups could be legitimately "represented," and only the deliberation of their representatives could be regarded as reflecting the public as a whole.[17] The judiciary and the executive were little more than qualifications on what, but for the frailty of men, might have been a plenary legislative power.

Even to state that creed is to emphasize how little it is reflected in present-day reality. The floodwaters of change have caused politics to spill out of the institutional channels designed by men in the past. Older political science could be institutional because it assumed that institutions *described political reality.* Recent analysis stressing "process" has presumed that institutions are, for the most part, reflections of forces located somewhere else.[18] Even by the end of the last century such a conservative as John W. Burgess could write that the "organization of the sovereign power" within the Constitution had failed and that political forces were compelled to act outside it.[19]

International politics was always a threat to constitutional design, standing outside the control of the laws. Today, of course, foreign politics are close, supremely perilous, and not regulated to any great extent by international law. "Constitutional dictatorship," once a temporary expedient, has become an almost permanent necessity as war and peace cease to be sharply distinct. Those who yearn for a declaration of war in Vietnam show more nostalgia for the age of tidy constitutionalism than understanding of world politics. The most vital decisions have escaped the government of laws and depend on the judgment of men.[20]

The pace of change and the degree of political complexity, which have eroded the role of the legislature in foreign policy, have also weakened it in general. Statute law, general in statement, slow in enactment and revision, cannot deal with shifting environments and unpredictable detail. Legislative enactments have become increasingly dependent on administrative interpretation, and the category of "unconstitutional delegation of power" has almost disappeared.[21]

Legislators have been ingenious in devising techniques for intervening in administrative decisions, yet these techniques tend either to restrict dangerously the capacity of administrators to respond to changing situations or to be no more than after-the-fact responses to administrative actions, a stage behind events. Frustration may lead legislators to resistance and harassment in areas still subject to their control, but this only adds an irrationality to the decline of the separation of power without changing the fact.[22]

"Confidence"—or the lack of it—in the personnel of particular agencies is coming to represent the major "oversight" of the legislature.[23] That alone is a major departure in the direction of a "government of men." Confidence, moreover, is not infinitely extensible; each intermediary attenuates it. Even citizen and representative are connected, in fact, by so long a chain of intermediaries that their relations tend toward impersonality. With small enough resources of citizen confidence, the representative has less ability to transfer them to administrators.[24]

In any event, contact between citizen and administrator normally takes place only at the end of still another lengthy chain of communication. The application of a general rule to the citizen's case is made not by someone who stands close enough to the citizen to know his personality and needs—as might have been the case with older, semivoluntary forms of administration—but by an official who is outside his circle of acquaintance, an "alien" whose decisions often appear unfathomable and arbitrary. Such a relation produces hostility toward officials, who respond in kind. Even if initially unjustified, distrust becomes self-fulfilling.[25]

Though courts devote more and more time to complaints against administration, they cannot hear all cases, and legal victories are often isolated, without effect on normal administrative routine. Even the abundance of statutory and procedural limitations on administration may, as Walter Gellhorn argues, serve to baffle rather than to assist the citizen.[26]

Generally, in fact, the generic limitations of the courts make them unable to do more than qualify governmental policies; they are no long-term substitute for public action and were never intended to be such, a problem that has only grown more severe with the increasing speed and proliferation of governmental decision. Justice Jackson wrote of the war power, in terms more generally applicable, that the Court could not exert control, which would depend on the "political judgment of the times and the moral judgment of history."[27]

The historic role of the Court—and of courts—has been to guard the people in their inattention to daily political life, keeping open the channels of public control for times when the public finds them needful.[28] Yet even this task depends, in part, on public action. Court intervention against usurpation depends on a public response which not only will refrain from opposing but will take action to insist on the application of court rulings; otherwise, decisions may become dead letters in dusty volumes of law. The Court acts, in fact, to *authorize disobedience* to otherwise legitimate authority, and it depends on citizens who will take advantage of its authorization.[29]

Defects in the system of separation of powers may be corrected—or deemed unimportant—where there exists a virtuous citizenry. If such a thing ever existed, however, it has passed from the scene. The most serious element of the constitutional crisis of our times is the breakdown of traditional assumptions regarding the nature and structure of civic life.

The distinction between public and private spheres, always tenuous empirically, has lost almost all reality with the growing integration of economic life.[30] The language of *Lochner v. New York* was archaic when it was pronounced,[31] and the right to form "voluntary associations," itself a form of freedom of contract, is only slightly less so. Organized groups require more than "shared attitudes"; they demand communication of those attitudes and the skills and resources necessary to give such attitudes effective organization. In wide areas of economic and social life, the citizen must submit to "private governments" that he did not create and to which he can create no alternative. Citizens may, and this less frequently than imagined, have some choice between alternative "governments," but this choice affects their dependence in only marginal ways.[32]

Private governments, at best, are only a limited constraint on governmental action. Often able to capture a sphere of governmental authority, they may countervail one another but rarely compete for allegiance, more often establishing spheres of influence with competition occurring at the borders, if at all. Based on narrower constituencies and concerns, private government tends to be too parochial to stake much on the widely shared values that McConnell identifies with the public interest or even to sense very clearly its interest in the procedural rules of the game. As Michael Paul Rogin has demonstrated, the success of Senator Joseph McCarthy depended on both the absence of group opposition and the support he received from public and private governmental elites.[33]

The mass media, among private governments, have long been a matter of special concern. The only means of access to a sizable proportion of the public, they must decide—given the limited time the public will devote to political affairs—who will have access and for how long. Charges of "slanting" aside, the "chairman's problem" is a measure of power.[34] Ability to command media attention was the true success of the series of demonstrations at Chicago. That the media attempt to evade the decision, devoting more time and space to politics than the public desires of its own accord, does not change the fact; not all men can gain access, and the desire to avoid criticism leads—at best—only to a surrender of leadership.[35]

Confused by events, suspicious of dependence on the media, the public seems to demonstrate a marked short-term resistance to persuasion, but when this resistance does not result in avoiding information altogether, it takes the form of clinging to older and accepted ideas through which information is filtered. This is hardly new; the traditional beliefs of men have always been defenses, functional when they prevented premature change. As the pace of change increases, however, resistance results in a gap between men's ideas and expectations and the world of action. This is the fundamental "credibility gap" of our times; the world becomes incredible to those who gaze at it.[36] That experience increases suspicion, and suspicion, resistance. Even the technicians of mass persuasion may be pressed to keep up with the cycle. Even a passive public deprives political leaders of the support needed to introduce new departures in policy that change may require. Resistance—passive or active—tempts public men to build short-term coalitions by appealing to traditional attitudes and values, but that effort only increases the long-term problem of the credibility gap.[37]

Traditionally, political parties have been assigned the task of mobilizing public support for governmental policies. Parties, however, are also private governments. They are, of course, a special case, so clearly tied to public government that the latter has often intervened in their internal affairs.[38] Yet although parties are different from other private governments in that they appeal to their constituents, in part, directly on the basis of public values,[39] they retain some of the characteristics of private government.

Certainly, the local elites who are the basis of party organization are often unrepresentative, especially as judged by voter commitments on general issues of public policy. Herbert McClosky has demonstrated that even national political parties present alternatives that do not correspond to voter opinion, and any such distortion weakens the base of support for the party system, leaving it with shallow roots that can be assaulted, from inside the system or without, by demagogic appeals. Surely this proposition requires less argument today than when Jack Dennis originally presented it.[40] Even the established argument that the party system penalizes "irrationality" has two serious defects: (1) the system tends to pivot on the uncommitted, apathetic, and ill-informed voter, not on "rational men"; and (2) the excluded "extremes," even if irrational, do not become more reasonable by exclusion. Signs of weak commitment to parties—from whatever sources—could be seen in the data long before recent political crises.[41] The task of forming a new party, even for bargaining purposes, is formidable for citizens and not necessarily a welcome development for constitutional government even should it occur.[42]

All of these developments undermine traditional constitutionalism. They effectively breach the wall between public and private spheres and render the public less autonomous, less capable of self-organization. The willingness of political scientists to slight or ignore them is due in part— as critics have hastened to point out—to a fear of the public itself, an identification of widespread politicization with unreason or even with totalitarianism. If the fear has been exaggerated, it is not groundless; V. O. Key's posthumous defense of public competence makes little dent in the established wall of doubt.[43]

Traditional democratic theory assumed that, given alternative programs, the citizen could make a moral choice between them by comparing both to norms of public policy; the more optimistic even hoped that the citizen would see a connection between such general norms and his private interests. Today, complexity and technicality—not to mention the scale of the political universe—have undermined both hopes. Citizens are often unable to see how—or that—particular alternatives affect them or to map out the indirect—sometimes convoluted—relations between particular policies and the fulfillment of public values.

The problem is not that citizens have become anomic or alienated (though these murky terms may be involved). Rather, citizens seek to avoid the kind of moral crisis that might result in anomie or alienation, and since that crisis is a necessary by-product of the tension between inherited ideas and the problems of the time, citizens seek to render the latter invisible. In a fairly comfortable, familistic isolation, citizens find a justification for lack of active concern—and a measure of security against reminders of peril—in viewing the state with passive reverence.[44]

This social quiescence, however, is only tenuously stable. Men do not relish dependence, and resentment against indignity is at least a constant undertow in even the calmest of states. Moreover, the indignity of dependence is not to be endured unless it pays the desired reward of security and an ability to enjoy private goods untroubled; the state, unlike the Lord, must make good its claims to reverence in this world. Citizen devotion and sacrifice cannot be relied on in the crises associated with the radical changes of the times.[45]

Classical liberal constitutionalism founded the doctrine of public-private separation on the belief that men possessed whatever resources and group relations were necessary for personal development. All that was needed was to free men from repression by involuntary "communities of orientation" and to guarantee individual liberty. Yet, as Sheldon Wolin points out, liberalism had its fears, and these grew with time. An element of the doctrine saw man as nearly anarchic by nature and feared that once freed from superstition, force, and habit, he would be turbulent and difficult to control. Thus Madison's order of priorities: "You must first enable the government to control the governed." Such felt danger led to comparative inattention to the means by which citizen initiative might be developed; it was only too likely to take care of itself.[46]

These older liberal fears, part of the effort to wall off a secure private space for men, have multiplied as men have acquired more to protect while losing almost all effective power to defend it against environing peril and insecurity. As we have observed more than once (and as we may again), the fear *for* order can be more dangerous to a constitutional polity than active hostility *to* order. Once again, the reaction against the troubling disorders of the times may wreak more havoc than the disorders themselves with the system of limited government.

Earlier constitutionalists were wiser and less fearful. Locke was aware that his "right of resistance" might be appealed to against lawful as well as against usurping government. This possibility he felt less serious than the tendency of most men to seek immediate security and personal well-being, which led them to be "more disposed to suffer than to right themselves." This danger was emphasized by the fact that men were "rarely nice and scrupulous" in cases involving the rights of others.[47]

Rousseau added that in large states, where the individual loses the sense of identity with the public and comes to feel himself alone, he is reduced to a choice between worshiping authority and cursing it. The former is likely to predominate, but should never be confused with citizenship. The problem, as Rousseau saw it, is to break the cycle before those who would deify the state and those who would destroy it monopolize political dialogue. "Some small amount of disturbance," he wrote, would give "wings to the soul" of republican government.[48]

There is a danger in applying such comments to our own times, but the threat lies principally in the possibility that political decay may already have gone too far—that the political alternatives are reduced to the fearfully reverential and the fearfully hostile. If so, the prospects could scarcely be grimmer. If not, there is a need to reverse Madison's order of priorities: the first task in our times is to break the cycle of fear and resentment, to give men a sense of controlling the government, that government may be able to ask for the commitment and the sacrifice needed to meet the gathering problems of the age.[49]

In our time as in any other, constitutionalism must begin with the aims of the political order, the substantive restraints that procedural guarantees are designed to support.[50] Merely negative goals—avoiding totalitarianism, violence, or instability—are important, but they might be shared by all constitutional states, a feudal monarchy as well as a democratic republic. The principle of substantive restraint in a democracy is that the public interest and policies to further it must, so far as possible, be decided by the public's deliberations, using some form of majority rule. Restrictions on the majority are derived from the ideal of a citizenry able to discuss and weigh, free from constraint, the values worthy of its devotion.[51]

The constitutional crisis of the times is due not to any rejection of that ideal but to a process of change that makes almost any institutional system inadequate for the organization of political life. Hence, the traditional alternatives for change—amendment or revolution—are not enough. The current need is not for ways to overthrow the constitutional order, but for means to preserve its virtues now that environmental change has become a continuing, informal amendment of the meaning of institutions which the formal process of amendment is too slow to overtake. (Nor would wisdom dispense with the Constitution: in addition to the restraints it still provides, it is an indispensable instrument for political education, given the reverence with which it is regarded.) The demand of the times is for "political forces maintaining an existing constitutional order," which Friedrich accurately defines as the political meaning of constitutional government.[52]

The present context makes it difficult, too, to draw analogies from historical discussions of civil disobedience, many of which center on tyrannicide, a violent resistance to the extreme case of unlawful rule.[53] There are useful parallels, however, in the description of the tyrannical *situation,* the political environment produced by tyranny, which justified acts of resistance to it.

Tyrants, aware of their fragile position, seek to make it impossible for citizens to meet, discuss, or organize. The essence of tyranny lies in the exclusion of the public forum from the political, in the effort to perpetuate a sense of individual isolation and weakness that creates a felt need for and a willingness to endure the rule of the strong. Given the inability of the public to act for itself and the vulnerable dependence of tyranny on a single life, an individual given the opportunity might strike the blow the community could not strike itself.[54]

Our political environment has much in common with the tyrannical situation, though the *cause* is radically different: it lies in the environment of life, not in the corrupt will of a tyrant.[55] Since the channels of public action remain open, moreover, there is at least the possibility of public action.

A defensible concept of civil disobedience in our times is based on a claim to act not for the public, but for *access* to it. The dramatic quality of disobedience has the ability to focus public attention on issues in ways that stir action despite the ubiquitous pressures for political passivity. In Joseph Tussman's phrase, civil disobedience is based on the belief that the community requires a "self-appointed test case."[56]

This is taking the law into one's own hands, yet the law must be taken into someone's hands before it becomes a political fact. Institutional crisis has made the someone who occupies official positions bulk very large. These magistrates and officials have primary responsibility for the law, yet every citizen of a democracy is in one sense a magistrate, with duties to his fellows, to those excluded from political participation, and to the system as a whole. Even Justice Fortas, though critical of the idea of civil disobedience, comments that "laws that are basically offensive to fundamental values of life or the Constitution" provide a "moral (though not a legal) defense of law violation." No citizen can wholly evade the obligation imposed by the example of Socrates in the greatest democracy of his times.[57]

In fact, all the arrangements of a democratic republic point to the belief that citizenship is an essential element of the good life; the citizen is, in that sense, a major goal of public policy. Lewis Lipsitz has written, "If we regard a democracy as, in part, a problem of developing the self, then a passive, reverent citizenry is undesirable no matter how much stability it may generate. We need to think of measuring democracy, not by defining it blithely as whatever exists in so-called democracies, but in terms of the creation of citizens."[58]

The task of developing the citizen was assigned, traditionally, to the private sphere. The image of the citizen as a participating magistrate of the republic clashes sharply with the legal usage, by which a citizen is any resident not an alien. This only emphasizes that government is forbidden to evaluate citizen virtue (that it may do so in naturalization suggests why this is a sensitive area of constitutional law). Nor has that prohibition lost its importance with time. The erosion of older social and legal barriers to power and the growing dependence of the individual have made the legal status of citizenship an essential "right to have rights." To be excluded from citizenship is to be Cain without the protection of the mark.[59] The citizen in the ideal sense remains a democratic *goal;* citizenship as a legal status is a necessary *means* to that end.

There is a hierarchy between status and ideal:

1. *The Good Citizen:* One who has internalized the goals and values of democracy and who is able to discern and act on connections and comparisons between those values and his own practices.
2. *The Ordinary Citizen:* One less interested or informed in political life, but who has internalized democratic values, at least at a high level of abstraction. He sees few or none of the connections between these values and action.
3. *The Noncriminal Citizen:* One who either does not yet accept or actively rejects democratic values, but who obeys law for reasons of prudence, habit, or indifference.

These categories are derived from empirical research as well as from abstract ideas. The first category is a small minority in the United States; the second, the great majority. The third category includes persons of low education and social mobilization (older foreign-born persons, marginal rural groups, children, and so on) as well as ideological groups that adhere to law only tactically.[60]

It is the good citizen who must carry the conscience of the community, especially since he is likely to be a leader in formal and informal groups. Such leaders have rightly been likened to gatekeepers and guardians: like the Court, they must protect the public in its inattention to the relation between democratic values and daily life.[61] In difficult situations, however, few such citizens will perform the role. Good citizens tend to high status and income, powerful motives for avoiding an onerous duty.[62] Their generally higher education may provide only greater ease in explaining away acts of civil cowardice. Higher motives conspire to the same end: a lover of his country, the good citizen is ever ready to believe the actions of his government to be defensible. "I seek . . . an excuse for conforming to the laws of the land," Thoreau wrote of his own civil disobedience. "I am but too ready to conform to them."[63]

Half a century ago, Bryce spoke of the good citizen's need for "the spectacle of courage and independence taking its own path" to move him to perform his civic duty.[64] Civil disobedience hopes to provide the spectacle: ultimately an appeal to the public, civil disobedience is, in more proximate terms, an effort to activate the conscience of the good citizen.

It may be too much to ask polities to cherish the minorities that serve them with conscience as well as body, but the dangers of anarchic disobedience are smaller than the danger that the duty will be evaded in an age when many seek to escape not only duty, but politics itself. Nor should we forget that the most violent disobedience of those years, the ghetto riot, results from prolonged civic indifference, from the failure to translate public values into empirical fact. Tocqueville wrote, "I am convinced . . . that anarchy is not the principal evil that democratic ages have to fear, but the least. For the principle of equality begets two tendencies: the one leads men straight into independence and may suddenly drive them into anarchy; the other conducts them by a longer, more secret . . . road to servitude. Nations readily discern the former tendency and are prepared to resist it: they are led away by the latter without perceiving its drift, hence it is particularly important to point it out."[65] There are many reasons for encouraging those citizens who accept the burden of "pointing out" that quiet danger now that the old laws have lost some of their former power.

Encouraging men to perform the citizen's duty—which potentially includes the duty to disobey—may involve (1) lessening the penalties that performance entails; and (2) strengthening the penalties for failure to perform it, principally by giving the sense of duty greater sway in the individual psyche.

It has been acknowledged that disobedience to a rule is legitimate in order to create a case or controversy that will enable the rule to be adjudicated (including cases where the court has not yet ruled or where there is reason to believe it will revise or reverse a past ruling). Yet despite this acceptance, he who disobeys runs the risk, if his challenge fails, of suffering all the penalties the rule prescribes. Justice Fortas concedes that this "may seem harsh," but argues emphatically that "*this is what we mean by the rule of law.*" Italics cannot conceal the fact that this argument by assertion is nonsense. The "rule of law" does not exclude advisory opinions; that is only a custom—with strong prudential basis—which had developed in America. In the absence of advisory opinions, however, the public has a clear interest in having some ruling on difficult points of interpretation and on the constitutionality of statutes. It would seem little threat to give legal protection to an effort to create a test case where reasonable grounds existed for bringing such a case to the courts.[66]

Disobedience to private governments may only be a specific form of test case. It may also be an appeal to the public in cases in which private decisions violate the norms of public policy but legal constraints are lacking. The "restrictive covenant," though unenforceable, cannot be judicially prohibited because it falls into the private sphere in which sanctions derive not from the Constitution but from the public and such statutes as it may enact.[67] The right to call the public's attention to such a violation of public norms follows necessarily: hence the broad protection extended to picketing and sit-ins, and, more recently, to rent strikes.

This principle might be extended to economic decisions by private governments which have marked impacts on public policy. In 1965, the Hammermill Paper Corporation was attacked for its contract to build a new plant in Alabama at a time when the state's government was vigorously obstructing public policy. Dramatizing the protest, demonstrators blocked entrances to Hammermill's plant in Erie, Pennsylvania, defied an injunction that Hammermill obtained, and subsequently were arrested. Hammermill spokesmen had conceded that the contract might be regrettable but insisted that it was binding; a limited extension of the rule in *Shelley* might have voided that objection, but however reasonable, the courts could not have made such a ruling. The demonstrations at least produced some concessions regarding future conduct. Moreover, Hammermill and local authorities declined to press for criminal penalties. These developments suggest that the dispute was a successful appeal to public norms against private power; at bottom, the dispute was a disagreement between citizens regarding the relevant norms of public policy. Though the corporation might have had a claim for damages, the dispute was in no sense "criminal" and criminal penalties were thought inappropriate by all parties. Justice Whittaker's dictum "Violations of our criminal laws are criminal violations" is all too simple; it would be reasonable to regard disputes in cases like that discussed above as exempt from other than civil remedies.

Resistance to unconstitutional orders of otherwise legitimate authority is the most familiar effort to make public policy justiciable. However, it is possible to claim that procedurally *lawful* acts violate substantive norms of public policy; it has been effectively argued—if not demonstrated—that it is illegitimate to deprive public employees of the right to strike in the absence of other, adequate means of protecting the substantive right involved. Obviously this form of disobedience is the most difficult to protect. Procedurally legitimate actions must be presumed to have public support; the burden of proof lies with the demonstrator.

This is especially clear in areas that require rapid decisions and action, where obstruction may impair seriously the government's ability to act (i.e., obstructing troop movements or refusing to obey military orders). Yet the dangers of disobedience are directly proportional to the importance of the issue and to the public's interest in preventing illegitimate acts.[68]

Security classification and wide discretion in imposing it are necessities of modern diplomatic and military policy and are obviously of vital public concern. Classification guarantees, however, the existence of a credibility gap by denying information to the public (leaving aside the possibility of abuse). Powerful public protection may exist for the disobedient regardless of the formal legal situation. The government's decision to refrain from prosecuting those who revealed information regarding the link between the CIA and several private associations reflects a public decision (or, at least, the decision of enough "good citizens") to sustain the violators' decision to disobey. The information was felt to be of a type that the government had no right to conceal, and the otherwise legitimate use of security regulations was considered to violate substantive restraints on power.

Even in those cases in which disobedience cannot be exempted from prosecution, it is certainly legitimate that in assessing penalties, courts give favorable consideration to the disobedient's motives (not—as is sometimes threatened—particularly unfavorable consideration). All the modifications suggested in current practice require courts to distinguish between those who act from civil as opposed to other motives, and this involves the courts beyond the traditional boundary of "overt acts." Yet such decisions are required by the decay of the public-private distinction that that boundary was designed to protect. It will not do to assert that the "motive of civil disobedience . . . does not confer immunity" in all cases; it is not more difficult or less relevant to determine whether disobedience was civil than to discover whether a membership was "meaningful" or adherence to a doctrine "abstract"—duties courts have already assumed.

Yet whatever concessions may be made to civil disobedience, on the most vital of issues it cannot be protected from the threat of punishment. In fact, precisely because civil disobedience may be a vital part of constitutional order in our times, there are limits to how much it may be shielded from penalty. Punishment is often essential to the disobedient himself: it provides a dramatization of his concerns, an instance of his sincerity, and a challenge to complacency which may be essential if he is to command the attention of those "good citizens" who may be moved by the "spectacle of courage . . . taking its own path."

Here as elsewhere, civil disobedience requires a measure of political prudence. (Another instance lies in the fact that the appeal to the public is a risk; arousing conscience may produce results the opposite of one's hopes.) This only indicates that however ingenious a scheme of institutions, in the great crises constitutional government depends on the wisdom and devotion of statesmen and citizens. Protection in these crises lies not in eliminating legal penalties, but in informing and strengthening the sense of civic duty. Once that task could be entrusted to the great social institutions whose early sovereignty enabled them to take a firm hold on the emotions and minds of men. Yet when social and civic life decays, such trust is insufficient or impossible. If only by default, greater responsibility falls to schools and universities as agencies of constitutional restraint (a fact that suggests, first, the vital importance of preserving academic autonomy amid the ubiquitous pressures of public and private governmental power and, second, the continuing need for faculties to consider their civic role as well as the private demands of their professions).

Much of this analysis must inspire foreboding. When institutions fail, political society depends on men, and men are feeble reeds, prone to acquiesce in—if not to commit—iniquity. Yet because man is unreliable, when political order must depend on men, the good citizen's duty becomes only greater. Tocqueville touched a relevant, if more general, point: "Far from thinking that humility should be preached to our contemporaries, I would have endeavors made to give them a more enlarged idea of themselves and their kind. Humility is unwholesome to them; what they most want is . . . pride. I would willingly trade several of our small virtues for this one vice."[69]

Notes

This essay was originally published as "Civil Disobedience and Contemporary Constitutionalism: The American Case," *Comparative Politics* 1, no. 2 (1969).

1. The phrase is from Oscar Jaszi and John D. Lewis, *Against the Tyrant: The Tradition and Theory of Tyrannicide* (Glencoe, 1957), vi.

2. John H. Schaar, "Some Ways of Thinking about Equality," *Journal of Politics* 26 (November 1964): 885.

3. Charles E. Whittaker, William Sloane Coffin, Jr., et al., *Law, Order, and Civil Disobedience* (Washington, D.C., 1967), 3, 52, 2. So pervasive is Whittaker's view of disorder that he sees it being incited by Dean Rusk, Hubert Humphrey, and President Johnson (17–18).

4. Ibid., 4.

5. Karl Loewentstein, in "Reflections on the Value of Constitutions in Our Revolutionary Age," in *Comparative Politics*, ed. Harry Eckstein and David Apter (New York: Macmillan, 1963).

6. *The Statesman (Politicus)*.

7. Whittaker, et al., *Law, Order, and Civil Disobedience*, 31.

8. See the argument in Christopher St. Germain, *The Doctor and the Student; or, Dialogue between a Doctor of Divinity and a Student of the Law of England* (1518) (Cincinnati, 1874).

9. Compare Harlan in *Monongahela Co. v. U.S.*, 216 U.S. 177 (1910) and Green in *Bank v. Cooper*, 2 Yerg. 599 (1831), with more recent "rule of reason" cases.

10. Justice Abe Fortas, *Concerning Dissent and Civil Disobedience* (New York, 1968), 60.

11. Carl J. Friedrich, *Constitutional Government and Democracy* (New York, 1937), 101, 102, 133. Early constitutionalism embodied the two restraints in separate covenants. See Harold J. Laski, *A Defense of Liberty against Tyrants: A Translation of the "Vindicia Contra Tyrannos"* (New York, 1924). Burke wrote that "the forms of a free and the ends of an arbitrary government are not things altogether incompatible." *Burke's Politics,* ed. Ross Hoffman and Paul Levack (New York, 1949), 8. For other traditional statements of the problem, see Rousseau, *The Social Contract*, bk. III, ch. 1; and James Bryce, *The American Commonwealth* (New York, 1913), 2:338. I find the same distinction in the works of many theorists of administration. See Herbert Simon, *Administrative Behavior* (New York, 1958), 118; and Phillip Selznick, *Leadership in Administration* (Evanston, 1957), for the distinction between "institution" and "organization."

12. John Locke, *Second Treatise on Civil Government,* secs. 159, 160, 220, 240, 242. Algernon Sidney wrote, similarly, of the need for "extra-judicial proceedings" taking place "by tumult" when "the persons concerned are of such power that they cannot be brought under the judiciary." *Discourses on Government* (New York, 1805), 1:205, 410.

13. Schaar, "Some Ways," 884, 886, 888.

14. Ibid.; see also Woodrow Wilson, *The State* (New York, 1889), 626, 645.

15. Norman Jacobson, "Political Science and Political Education," *American Political Science Review* 57 (September 1963): 561–69; and Adrienne Koch, "Power and Morals and the Founding Fathers," *Review of Politics* 15 (October 1953): 483. See also *The Federalist*, #44.

16. Wilson wrote that the legislature should be the "originator of policies"

and should "adjust every weighty plan, preside over every reform, provide for every passing need of the state" (*The State,* 581–83). Yet in his later *Constitutional Government in the United States* (New York, 1908), 73, he referred to the executive as the "vital place of action." This typical shift suggests how early it became clear that there was a need to revise the separation of powers to fit "the needs of an industrial society." Friedrich, *Constitutional Government,* 159.

17. Wilson, *The State,* 109.

18. Nelson Polsby writes that "in this day and age, the Constitution is a fallible and incomplete guide to national policy-making," surely a moderate statement. *Congress and the Presidency* (Englewood Cliffs, 1964), 4.

19. *Political Science and Comparative Constitutional Law* (New York, 1890), 1:150ff. For a progressive's view, see Roscoe Pound, *The Spirit of the Common Law* (Boston, 1921), 185–89.

20. Stanley Hoffman, "International Systems and International Law," *World Politics* 14 (October 1961): 205–37; Clinton Rossiter, *Constitutional Dictatorship* (Ithaca, 1958); and Justice Wiley Rutledge, "Civil Rights in Wartime," *Iowa Law Review* 29 (1944): 379. Compare Rousseau, *Social Contract,* bk. II, ch. 9 and bk. IV, ch. 9.

21. Bertrand de Jouvenel, "The Principate," *Political Quarterly* 36 (January 1965): 20–51. See also *Opp Cotton Mills v. Administrator,* 312 U.S. 126 (1941); and *Yakus v. U.S.,* 321 U.S. 414 (1944).

22. Edward A. Shils, "The Legislator and His Environment," *University of Chicago Law Review* 18 (1950–1951): 571–84; Robert A. Dahl, *Congress and Foreign Policy* (New York: 1950), and *Pluralist Democracy in the United States* (Chicago, 1967), 297; Jean Meynaud, "Le peril technocratique," *Revue de l'Institut de Sociologie* 1 (1961): 189–202. For some of the ingenuities, see Raymond H. Dawson, "Congressional Innovation and Intervention in Defense Policy," *American Political Science Review* 56 (March 1962): 42–57.

23. Aaron B. Wildavsky, *The Politics of the Budgetary Process* (Boston, 1964), 78–84.

24. Warren Miller and Donald Stokes, "Constituency and Influence in Congress," *American Political Science Review* 57 (March 1963): 45–56; Lewis Dexter, "The Representative and His District," and "What Do Congressmen Hear?" in Nelson Polsby et al., *Politics and Social Life* (Boston, 1963), 485–512. See also the unpublished evidence from Almond and Verba's research cited in Dahl, *Pluralist Democracy,* 199–202. Compare Kurt Lewin, "Studies in Group Decision," in Dorwin Cartwright and Alvin Zander, *Group Dynamics* (Evanston, 1953), 287–301.

25. Grant McConnell, *Private Power and American Democracy* (New York, 1966), 91–118, 164, 296–97, 349; Charles Wiltse, "The Representative Functions of Bureaucracy," *American Political Science Review* 35 (June 1941): 510–16; Joseph Lyford, *The Airtight Cage* (New York, 1966). Compare Francis Lieber, *Civil Liberty and Self-Government* (Philadelphia, 1874), 310–23.

26. Felix Frankfurter, "The Supreme Court in the Mirror of Justices," *University of Pennsylvania Law Review* 105 (1957): 793; Walter Gellhorn, *When Americans Complain* (Cambridge, Mass., 1966).

27. *Korematsu v. U.S.,* 323 U.S. 214 (1944). See also Clinton Rossiter, *The Supreme Court and the Commander-in-Chief* (Ithaca, 1951); Glendon Schubert, *The Presidency in the Courts* (Minneapolis, 1957); and Robert A. Dahl, "Decision-making in a Democracy: The Role of the Supreme Court as a National Policy Maker," *Journal of Public Law* 6, no. 2 (1958): 279–95.

28. C. Herman Pritchett, *The Political Offender and the Warren Court* (Boston, 1959); among relevant cases, see *Baker v. Carr,* 369 U.S. 186 (1962); and *Reynolds v. Sims,* 377 U.S. 533 (1964).

29. Wilson C. McWilliams, "The Constitutional Doctrine of Mr. Justice Frankfurter," *Political Science* (Wellington, New Zealand) 15 (June 1963): 34–44. A possible and certainly interesting illustration is *Chaunt v. U.S.,* 364 U.S. 350 (1960). Justice Clark, dissenting, called the opinion an "open invitation to false-swearing." The majority seems to have developed the doctrine of "let the administrator beware," authorizing the use of techniques—at least in naturalization cases—not very different from those used to cheat on personality tests.

30. See *Wickard v. Filburn,* 317 U.S. 111 (1942).

31. 198 U.S. 45 (1905).

32. McConnell, *Private Power,* 108–9, 113–15, 146–50, 245, 296–97, 349; Richard Eels, *The Government of Corporations* (New York, 1962); John C. Scott, "Membership and Participation in Voluntary Associations," *American Sociological Review* 22 (June 1957): 315–26.

33. McConnell, *Private Power,* 164, 349, 358, 366, 367; Rogin, *The Intellectuals and McCarthy: The Radical Specter* (Cambridge, Mass., 1967), especially 261–82; Philip Selznick, *TVA and the Grass Roots* (Berkeley and Los Angeles, 1953); and Robert A. Dahl, *Who Governs?* (New Haven, 1963), 190–99.

34. The concept is from Bertrand de Jouvenel, *The Pure Theory of Politics* (New Haven, 1965), 99–117, 131–41.

35. V. O. Key, *Public Opinion and American Democracy* (New York, 1961), 344–410.

36. Ibid.; Dorwin Cartwright, "Some Principles of Mass Persuasion," *Human Relations* 2 (July 1949): 253–67; Paul Meadows, "An Age of Mass Communications," *Psychiatry* 10 (September 1947): 405–11; Arthur Kornhauser et al., *When Labor Votes* (New York, 1956), 88–91, 155; John H. Kessel, *The Goldwater Coalition* (New York, 1968).

37. Robert E. Lane, *Political Life* (Glencoe, 1959), 282.

38. *Smith v. Allwright,* 321 U.S. 649 (1944).

39. Bernard Berelson et al., *Voting* (Chicago, 1954).

40. Herbert McClosky et al., "Issue Conflict and Consensus among Party Leaders and Followers," *American Political Science Review* 54 (June 1960): 406–27; V. O. Key, *Southern Politics in State and Nation* (New York, 1949), 299, 304–7; E. E. Schattschneider, *The Semi-sovereign People* (New York, 1960); Jack Dennis, "Support for the Party System by the Mass Public," *American Political Science Review* 60 (September 1966): 614.

41. Samuel Lubell, *The Revolt of the Moderates* (New York, 1956). In Angus

Campbell et al., *The American Voter* (New York, 1960), chs. 6, 7, only 13 percent of the public gave no party identification at all, but an additional 11 percent identified themselves as "independent" members of the party and 40 percent called themselves "weak" partisans—a total of 74 percent unable to make strong commitments.

42. One of the few exceptions—though not the happiest—is discussed in J. Daniel Mahoney, *Actions Speak Louder: The Five Year Miracle of the Conservative Party of New York State* (New York, 1968). Needless to say, leftist groups find fewer resources at their disposal than does the Right.

43. V. O. Key Jr., with the assistance of Milton Cummings, *The Responsible Electorate* (Cambridge, Mass., 1966). For a critique of many fashionable views, see Rogin, *The Intellectuals and McCarthy;* and Peter Bachrach, *The Theory of Democratic Elitism* (Boston, 1967).

44. Sidney Verba, "The Kennedy Assassination and the Nature of Political Commitment," in *The Kennedy Assassination and the American Public,* ed. Bradley S. Greenberg and E. B. Parker (Stanford, 1965); Joseph R. Gusfield, "Mass Society and Extremist Politics," *American Sociological Review* 27 (February 1962): 19–30; Scott Greer, *The Emerging City* (New York, 1962).

45. Alexis de Tocqueville, *Democracy in America* (New York, 1959), 2:277; Karen Horney, *The Neurotic Personality of Our Time* (New York, 1937); Herbert McClosky and J. H. Schaar, "Psychological Dimensions of Anomy," *American Sociological Review* 30 (February 1965): 14–40.

46. Sheldon S. Wolin, *Politics and Vision* (Boston, 1960), 286–381; John H. Schaar, *Loyalty in America* (Berkeley and Los Angeles, 1957); Roscoe Pound, "A Survey of Social Interests," *Harvard Law Review* 57 (1943): 33.

47. *Second Treatise,* secs. 161, 163, 165, 168, 198, 200–204, 223–25, 230, 242.

48. *Social Contract,* bk. IV, ch. 2; bk. III, ch. 9, n. 1.

49. Senator Fulbright writes: "It is only when Congress fails to challenge the executive . . . when politicians join in a spurious consensus, and when institutions of learning sacrifice traditional functions . . . to associations with the government in power the campuses and the streets . . . are likely to become the forums of a direct and turbulent democracy." *The Arrogance of Power* (New York, 1966), 39–40.

50. Bertrand de Jouvenel, "The Technocratic Age," *Bulletin of the Atomic Scientists* 20 (October 1964): 27–29. Friedrich has recently emphasized the substantive element of traditional constitutionalism in *Transcendent Justice* (Durham, N.C., 1964).

51. Joseph Tussman, *Obligation and the Body Politic* (New York, 1960); Henry S. Commager, *Majority Rule and Minority Rights* (New York, 1943).

52. *Constitutional Government,* 112.

53. Jaszi and Lewis, *Against the Tyrant.*

54. Ibid., 33, 91–93.

55. Tocqueville was prescient: "I seek in vain for an expression that will convey the whole of the idea I have formed of it; the old words despotism

and tyranny are inappropriate; the thing itself is new" (*Democracy in America,* 2:336ff.).

56. Tussman, *Obligation,* 43–46. S. M. Lipset has used this idea to justify civil disobedience in the South but has insisted—almost obtusely, in my judgment—that "access" exists in northern states.

57. Tussman, *Obligation,* 104–21. Fortas, *Concerning Dissent,* 63. Attention to the idea of the philosopher-king may make us forget that the philosopher is an ideal king because he is an ideal citizen; since philosophers are rarely kings, it is in the role of citizen that they are most often seen. For an excellent discussion, see Nathan Greenberg, "Socrates' Choice in the *Crito,*" *Harvard Studies in Classical Philology* 70, no. 1 (1965): 45–82.

58. "If, as Verba Says, the State Functions as a Religion, What Are We to Do Then to Save Our Souls?" *American Political Science Review* 62 (June 1968): 527–35.

59. Hannah Arendt, *The Origins of Totalitarianism* (New York, 1951); *Trop v. Dulles,* 356 U.S. 86 (1958).

60. Herbert McClosky, "Consensus and Ideology in American Politics," *American Political Science Review* 58 (June 1964): 361–82; Robert E. Lane, "Political Personality and Electoral Choice," *Political Science Review* 49 (March 1955): 173–90; Bernard Kutner, "Elements and Problems of Democratic Leadership," in Alvin Gouldner, *Studies in Leadership* (New York, 1950), 459–67; Samuel Stouffer, *Communism, Conformity, and Civil Liberties* (Garden City, 1955); Gerhart H. Saenger, "Social Status and Political Behavior," *American Journal of Sociology* 51 (September 1945): 103–13.

61. V. O. Key, "Public Opinion and the Decay of Democracy," *Virginia Quarterly* 37 (Fall 1961): 481–94; Elihu Katz and Paul M. Lazarsfeld, *Personal Influence* (Glencoe, 1955).

62. Locke, *Second Treatise,* secs. 168, 208, 209. Students have had a unique role because they possess the other leadership skills, without the responsibilities, of good citizens.

63. Henry David Thoreau, *Writings* (Boston, 1906), 4:367.

64. Bryce, *American Commonwealth,* 2:641 (see also 256–58, 364); G. D. Wiebe, "The Army-McCarthy Hearings and the Public Conscience," *Public Opinion Quarterly* 22 (Winter 1959): 490–502.

65. *Democracy in America,* 2:304–5. Coffin, in Whittaker et al., *Law, Order, and Civil Disobedience,* 35, 113, makes some of the same points.

66. Fortas, *Concerning Dissent,* 30. Anthony Lewis's comment is no favorable assessment of the American system: "Gideon's maniacal distrust and suspicion led him to the very borders of insanity. Upon the shoulders of such persons are our great rights carried." *Gideon's Trumpet* (New York, 1966). It would seem more prudent to make it easier for safer shoulders to carry some of the burden.

67. *Shelley v. Kraemer,* 334 U.S. 1 (1948).

68. Rousseau, *Social Contract,* bk. IV, ch. 2.

69. *Democracy in America,* 2:262.

The Case for Censorship, Rightly Understood

The arts and sciences are forces to conjure with, magical powers that speak to the deepest desires and hopes of men. They puzzle, tempt, and beguile the rudest barbarian; the city without art and science will not endure, whatever its theoretical virtues, because it is less than human.[1] The power of the arts and sciences necessarily makes them a political problem, for magic is black as well as white.

All political societies short of the ideal are founded on opinion, and opinion is an uncertain ground. The charlatan can mislead "true opinion," and base art and science can corrupt a good society. To that extent, Walter Berns's case for prudent forms of censorship cannot be refuted. But it is equally true that a corrupt society generates degraded arts and sciences. That sad result is, in fact, more certain than the possible evils that ignoble art and science may inflict on a good state, for man is a political animal before he is an artist, a scientist, or a philosopher. At best, censorship corrects exceptions; it cannot create the rule. In a corrupt society, the censor himself is likely to reflect the general degeneracy and will make matters worse rather than better.

The core of my disagreement with Berns is that he understates the problem. Perhaps this is due to the limitations of the dialogue between Berns and the liberal ideologues whom he chooses for antagonists, but Berns does seem to contend that America has a sound civic morality to which our permissive attitude toward obscenity is an exception. This, I think, is nonsense. In fact, Berns's argument, as stated, partially supports those who regard censorship of the obscene as no more than a neurotic fixation, a hypocritical, secretly leering fascination with sexuality devoid of genuine moral judgment.

It is significant, after all, that Berns states his case in terms of the relationship between censorship and republican virtues, but limits its application to the single instance of obscenity. Why should obscenity be singled out? The censorship of antiquity dealt with the "whole range of our social proprieties,"[2] with all offenses against republican morals and good order. And by any reasonable standard, there are offenses against civic virtue in America which are both more serious and more worthy of censorship than is obscenity.

The ancients asked their censors to punish pride, arrogance, display, and contempt for one's fellow citizens, recognizing all of these as violations of the principle of the equality and dignity of citizens and a danger to the harmony—the "good order"—of the republic. By that standard, racist oratory and ethnic slurs merit censorship, and it would not be hard to argue that Jensen's theories—their dubious scientificity aside—should have been denied circulation. It is no small defect in the case against violence made by "law and order" fanatics that they neglect the provocations offered by contempt, bad faith, and luxury;[3] the East Side socialite in Manhattan, the "limousine liberal," offends against good order as much as or more than the ghetto rioter or the middle-class vigilante, for his life is an affront and a provocation to both. Here, too, certainly is a case worthy of censorship. Finally, one offense punished by the ancient censors was negligent cultivation of land (because misuse of the land is, in an almost literal sense, unpatriotic);[4] therefore a contemporary censor might punish the polluters of air and water. Given all of these crimes against the polity, why does obscenity, in Berns's case, occupy not merely the center, but the *whole* of the stage?

The question is far from captious, for it raises the issue of the status of the United States as a political community. Civic virtue was never universal in America and our common moral standards were always limited in extent. The mechanistic liberals who shaped our institutions set out to make civic virtue unnecessary to the realization of what they took to be the common good, faithful to the doctrine that private mischiefs may be public benefits if rightly channeled. And mass, industrial society makes that virtue difficult at best. Ruled by great abstractions, men develop the morality of serfs; the artists and scientists are guilty only of being no better than their fellow citizens—fawning, secretly resentful, fearfully ambitious, and irresponsible.

That is not the whole story, of course; there is another, better side to Americans and American life. It is true enough, however, to justify the fear that whatever "laws of common decency" we may have had have been slipping into oblivion. This is nothing new; it is as old as the historical pattern which is the source of the fear. There have been battles to defend each "line" of morality; the censorialism of Prohibition is only the most obvious example. And naturally, each defeat made subsequent defenses more desperate. The sexual code seems, to many, to be the last bastion. (It is suggestive that lewdness and obscenity were the last of the crimes which Blackstone classified as "offenses against God and religion.")[5] It is hardly to be wondered at, then, if the sexual code acquires a disproportionate standing in the moral concerns of many.[6]

The very general decay that is complained of, however, makes censorship an inappropriate remedy. It is a frequent defect of censorship, in fact, that men resort to it too late, and that shortcoming is especially likely in a society devoted to individualistic principles. Degeneracy becomes socially visible, emerging from underground, only when it has reason to expect a welcome. Certainly this is the case in relation to sexuality.

Our verbal sexual morals had become nothing more than cant some time ago for most Americans. Worse, they were a form of hypocrisy which discouraged respect for law. Students were told by college officials that dormitory regulations were necessary for the "image" of the institution, but that numerous ways existed by which sexual desire could be gratified without attacking those rules openly. Parents, whose conduct meshed badly with their admonitions, welcomed the second family automobile because it allowed them to overlook what they hesitated to condone. Our sexual morals were like the proverbial Mississippi voter who drank wet and voted dry, and with the same results in relation to the law.

I am not arguing the familiar and foolish liberal proposition that "unmasking" hypocrisy is a form of moral progress, nor am I denying Berns's contention that much of "liberated" arts and literature is shameful. I am contending that the mask, once off, is difficult to replace, especially because the "laws of common decency" collapsed long *before* the "legislation that constituted their foundation." The statutes were not the foundation of anything; they were the means of penalizing exceptions to the "common law," the beliefs of the many. When that law lost its standing, the statutes could exist only so long as they were no more than a nuisance; on that basis, they could be restored, but that would not solve or even address Berns's problem. A verbal reaffirmation of the old code would bear no more relation to reality than Vichy did to France.

Moreover, censorship is a danger in the context of modern politics. The problem of guarding the guardians is not only perennial; it has become progressively more insoluble. Berns hardly helps matters by discussing the permissiveness of ancient tyranny in the text and relegating the censoriousness of modern totalitarianism to a footnote. The bureaucratic industrial state is not a *polis,* and though I would argue we should move toward the latter to the extent we can—that we should in a literal sense seek to recover politics—it is necessary to realize how different our current environment is. Modern liberal industrialism *has* become the analogue of ancient tyranny, by accident or design. The fact that most men are denied any genuine political or even public life creates a demand for, and requires society to provide, abundant private gratifications. But man is a political animal, and his apolitical existence leaves him with a gnawing sense of something missing, while modern society multiplies threats around him. Gratifications prove inadequate and lose their savor; and new, more elaborate or grosser pleasures are sought in turn; what else is to be expected in a society which dominantly thinks of freedom as the "absence of restraint" except a progression toward shamefulness? "Repressive desublimation," whether one accepts Marcuse's formulation or not, is part of our political reality.[7]

At the same time, however, those modern states which have set out to establish the empire of virtue inspire even less confidence. Even when there are "common values" there is great personal distance between rulers and ruled. The high justice, and with it, the high civic virtue of small states, is impossible in great ones. Rulers cannot give me my due if they do not know me, and it is absurd to ask men to trust their rulers today with the extensive powers they once gave readily to men they knew.[8] Modern man is already asked, in clearly public matters, to accord government a trust that borders on credulity; it is too much and too dangerous to ask him to extend the same trust over any extensive areas of private life. And it is more dangerous still to allow any power which touches the freedom of speech of the press. The *suspicious* aspect of the liberal creed, which feared and sought to limit power, is only made more necessary by the evident folly and failure of its positive faith.

In fact, the change from the censor to the critic reflects the change of our political world. The critic speaks to the social circle, where men are confident that their values are shared, in which they feel some element of personal importance and acquaintance with their fellows. The critic is, simply, the appointed guardian of the standards of the circle. Berns is right and the *Times* is wrong; at least in the short term, the critic cannot prevail because his power is limited by the circle to which he speaks. But that limitation reflects the fact that modern men, prudently, limit their allegiance and their trust.

I am not attempting to minimize the problem of which Berns speaks. Quite the contrary; the problem is real because it is part of the generally grim and decadent character of modern politics. But precisely because those politics are as base and as threatening as they are, it is necessary to beware of cures that may be worse than the disease. Moral standards are needed; civic virtue is required. Both, however, require construction as much or more than they do maintenance, and either may demand the re-making of modern society, not the tinkering of the censor.

In one area, however, censorship would be both safe and possibly helpful: the censorship of one's self. Artists, scientists, philosophers, and intellec-tuals generally owe themselves and their fellow citizens the duty of gaug-ing their utterances, works, and writing in terms of their likely impact on the life of man. There is no requirement that "all things be revealed" directly; as the greatest of teachers knew, parable and allusion will suf-fice for those "who have ears to hear." Oliver Wendell Holmes Sr., to take only one of many American examples, found it possible to say "shocking" things in an idiom which did not affront respectability (or at least, not often; audiences read more carefully in those days, and at least one critic discerned "obscenity" in *Elsie Venner*). And Twain was even more a mas-ter of the art.[9]

There are, moreover, things which one should not say at all and re-search which one should not reveal in even the most guarded ways. The path of evil crosses the human high road too often for some tools to be put into man's possession. Scientists need that admonition, for their re-cord contains crimes greater than any that may be charged to obscenity (nor are the sins of philosophy due to salaciousness). There have been many who knew the necessity of that restraint. John Napier, the inventor of logarithms, fearful of the Spanish Armada, developed (then) terrible engines of war, but he suppressed his discoveries for reasons he summed up on his deathbed: "For the ruin and overthrow of man there were too many devices already framed, which if he could make it fewer he would with all his might endeavor to do. . . . By any new conceit of his the num-ber of them should never be increased."[10]

Liberalism's sunny faith that progress would make any invention safe and profitable helped destroy that attitude and that wisdom. And when darkness gathered on the horizon and progress became suspect, scien-tists—social and natural alike—contented themselves with the asser-tion that the "process" of discovery would guarantee that, sooner or later, someone would make the discovery anyway. This is a dubious proposition and the more suspect because this "delusion of impotence" masks self-assertion; it justifies me in my desire to "get the credit," to win fame and eminence associated with the discovery of a new tool, a new weapon for man to turn against man. Even if true, however, it matters a good deal whether inventions are made sooner or later, and if the probable or likely impact is destructive, a moral man will hope that the event is delayed.

None of this, of course, solves the problem of an Einstein who finds himself faced with Nazism. But it is important to emphasize that, even in such a case, the decision to labor on weapons of destruction is a moral and political decision. The decision to write or not to write, to speak or to remain silent, to portray or to leave hidden, is always a political decision to be judged by its impact on men. If truth is a "good in itself" and art is truly for "art's sake," neither needs a public revelation. That public expression is necessarily political, and sometimes of greater import for good or ill. Art and science have dignity because they matter, and artists and scientists acquire dignity from that fact. But dignity, like liberty, involves discipline and constraint. Surely that is the vital lesson we owe our fellow citizens and each other in our shadowed times.

Notes

This essay was originally published as "Concurring and Dissenting Opinions," *Public Interest*, no. 22 (Winter 1971). It was written in response to Walter Berns's lead essay in the same issue, "Pornography vs. Democracy: The Case for Censorship." Addressing a series of contemporary judicial and cultural developments, Berns urged a reconsideration of the classical and early modern case for censorship, arguing at one point that democracy, above all, required the legal inculcation of modesty and self-governance: "Such, indeed, was the argument made by political philosophers prior to the 20th century, when it was generally understood that democracy, more than any other form of government, required self restraint, which it would inculcate through moral education and impose on itself through laws, including laws governing the manner of public amusements" (13). As McWilliams's response makes clear, the main emphasis of Berns's argument concerns sexual proprieties.

1. Plato, *Republic*, bk. II, 372–73.

2. Livy, *The Early History of Rome*, trans. Aubrey de Selincourt (Baltimore: Penguin Books, 1960), 262.

3. See my essay "On Violence and Legitimacy," *Yale Law Journal* 79 (1970): 623–46.

4. Theodor Mommsen, *History of Rome* (Glencoe: Free Press, n.d.), 2:64.

5. William Blackstone, *Commentaries on the Laws of England: Of Public Wrongs*, ed. Robert Malcolm Kerr (Boston: Beacon, 1962), 60–61.

6. When I was active in SLATE, one of the predecessors of the New Left at Berkeley, many of us were shocked when we found out that our statement that a female opponent was "immoral"—because she had broken a promise to us— was taken to mean that she was sexually promiscuous. That was years ago, and American moral sensitivity, despite the stridency of the times, has not grown much greater.

7. Herbert Marcuse, *One Dimensional Man* (Boston: Beacon, 1968).

8. There were problems even in antiquity, despite a more favorable environment. Livy tells us that when Mamercus had a law passed limiting the term of the censors, saying that "it was not an acceptable thing to have the same people in control for so long over so many aspects of one's life," the censors octupled his tax and disfranchised him. Perhaps that is what gave pause to the patricians, who had originally opposed the law, for Livy tells us that they came to be "aware . . . that individually they would all have to suffer the jurisdiction of the censors much more often . . . than they would have a chance of exercising it." *Early History of Rome*, 279.

9. For a striking example, see "A Double-Barrelled Detective Story," in *The Complete Short Stories of Mark Twain*, ed. Charles Neider (Garden City: Doubleday, 1957), 423–69.

10. John Napier's views are cited from John U. Nef, *War and Human Progress* (Cambridge, Mass.: Harvard University Press, 1952), 122.

Equality and Citizenship

The Rights of Man and the Rights of Women

The Equal Rights Amendment has been defeated, but this blow to the advocates of women's rights may be a blessing in disguise. Constitutional provisions can be slippery footing. For a century, the Fourteenth Amendment failed to fulfill the racially egalitarian aims of its framers because there was insufficient political will to carry them out; the Eighteenth Amendment is another case in point. Law is a kind of speech, and its effect depends on the audience to which it is addressed. The most eloquent words are mute when they fall on deaf ears, and a hostile public can turn legal harmonies into cacophonies. Law can shape a political society, but law itself is limited and defined by the political foundations on which it rests.[1]

In relation to women's rights, this is crucial. The failure of the ERA is likely to lead feminists to a renewed emphasis on "politics"—organizing, building coalitions, and supporting candidates.[2] This is appropriate and desirable. Nevertheless, this narrow understanding of the meaning of politics and political things limits the goals of the movement, encouraging the surrender of broader claims which women cannot afford to abandon.[3] I will be arguing that equal rights for women—a goal which necessarily raises the question of woman's status in American life—requires a much more fundamental, more genuinely political solution. The demand for the rights of woman poses a challenge to our traditional understanding of the "rights of man"; it suggests that there may be cracks which require reparation in the foundations of the republic.

In the first place, the claim that women are entitled to be treated as equals forces us to ask what equality means. When we say that two things are equal, we are stating that they are "the same," but we are not necessarily declaring that they are identical. We can be equal with respect to one quality or characteristic and unequal with respect to others: all Americans are the same in being American, but different in being Democrats or Republicans. When we say that human beings are "equal" in spite of the obvious differences between them, we ordinarily mean that the quality in which they are alike—their human nature—is important and essential and that the differences between them are trivial and accidental.[4] Similarly, if we say that citizens ought to be equal regardless of gender, we are contending that all citizens are alike in being citizens and that gender is irrelevant or unessential with respect to citizenship.

In these terms, we cannot discriminate between citizens on the basis of sex in what *pertains* to citizenship. Since voting is evidently an important prerogative of citizenship, the logic of the Nineteenth Amendment is overwhelming: both men and women must be granted the right to vote. Yet government is allowed to recognize, in laws relating to child-bearing, that women can bear children and men cannot. This discrimination is justified because the capacity to bear children does not pertain to citizenship: it is neither a prerequisite of citizenship nor a citizen's right.[5]

In general, two kinds of discrimination are compatible with the idea of civic equality. First, we can be said to have been treated equally if we have been held to the same standards as our peers. If you fail to live up to those standards, it is appropriate that you should suffer relative to those who satisfy them. The slayer and the slain are different, the mystic unity of Emerson's vision notwithstanding, and political societies must treat the two differently. Equality does not forbid us to distinguish between vice and virtue. Since it suggests that we are alike in our capacities for virtue and our liabilities to vice, equality implies that we have an equal right to expect that political society will encourage the former and discourage the latter.[6]

Second, it follows that we are allowed to discriminate between citizens in relation to common ends and public purposes. The equality of citizens, moreover, is itself a goal of policy, and we may be required to treat citizens differently in the interests of making them equal.

In America, this is sometimes obscured by the low status of equality in the liberal tradition. Liberalism asserts that we are "born" or "created" equal, but this original equality means chiefly that we are equally free. By nature, individuals have no obligations except by their own consent. As the price of authority, law and politics are constrained to recognize this equal freedom to give or to withhold consent, but the "first object of government" in liberal theory is to secure rights which will lead to private inequalities.[7] Public equality, in other words, is valuable only if it contributes to private freedom. However, even in these limited terms, equality is a value—if only an instrumental one—and citizens are entitled to policies which aim at "equality of opportunity."

Other schools give equality a good deal higher rank among political goals. Aristotle, for example, argued that political society aims to make its citizens as excellent as possible. To the extent that circumstances permit, a polity seeks to raise the many to the level of the few. No regime can achieve that goal and few can even begin to approximate it, but equality with what is best remains the ultimate measure of policy.[8]

In any case, equality as an end may require inequality in means. Children are citizens and are entitled to "equal protection of the law," but children are and ought to be treated differently from adults. We justify this discrimination only when it is educational, calculated to help children develop into adults and citizens. Special treatment of children is the means; equality is the end.

Similarly, the graduated income tax discriminates between rich and poor with a view to equalizing the burden of taxation. Special programs for the disadvantaged and policies like affirmative action, which try to compensate for undeserved inequalities, are also unequal treatments which aim at equality as an end.

To summarize: our equality as citizens means that discrimination must be justified. Such justification is possible (1) when the discrimination deals with matters that do not pertain to citizenship; (2) when different treatment results from the application of an equal rule or standard; and (3) when discrimination serves an overriding public purpose, especially the goal of civic equality. Public purpose, in fact, measures the sphere of citizenship; it determines the standards we set for behavior; it is coterminous with the ends which can justify unequal means. The argument, then, comes down to this: we can justify discrimination only when it is related to a public goal which outweighs the norm of equal treatment.

But how close and how clear must that relationship be? For many years, the Supreme Court held that discrimination is permissible when it has a *reasonable* relation to a public purpose. The Warren Court modified that rule in two ways, both of which turn on a broader understanding of what it means to be a citizen. First, in the new interpretation, certain rights are *fundamental,* so essential to citizenship that they override all other purposes.[9] Primarily, the Court made reference to the right to vote and the right to seek and hold public office, the rights essential to a share in rule and being ruled.[10] The Court also held that citizens have a right to be secure in their citizenship, once it has been granted to them.[11]

Second, the Warren Court argued that certain categories by which people may be grouped and judged—the Court was thinking primarily of race and ethnicity—are inherently "suspect." Any discrimination based on such categories is *presumed* to be invalid: suspect categories bear the burden of proving their appropriateness. A "reasonable" relation to a public purpose is not enough. Suspect categories like race and ethnicity cannot be used by public authority unless they have a *compelling* relationship to some equally compelling state interest.[12]

There is no way, for example, by which the regime can compensate racial minorities for racial discrimination in the past which does not involve the use of racial categories in the present. Such affirmative action programs are, however, almost the only cases in which a suspect category can be used. And even the effort to compensate for past injustice, the Court has held, is not enough to justify the use of racial quotas.[13]

The idea of "suspect categories," like the doctrine of fundamental rights, is meant to protect the heart of citizenship. Voting, seeking office, and the like—our "fundamental rights"—are the formal essentials of citizenship. But the Court recognized that categories like race and ethnicity have a vital relationship to personal dignity, and hence to the equal respect which is the psychological foundation of citizenship.[14] In fact, since equal respect is necessary to the citizen's soul, it is more fundamental than the behaviors which are citizenship's exterior signs.[15] Dignity is the first principle of citizenship, made even more compelling by the fact that, in the United States, the political power of the citizen is diluted by numbers to the point of insignificance.[16]

Categories like race and ethnicity are suspect, as the Court held, because they imply a hierarchy of *persons* as opposed to a hierarchy of attainments.[17] Discrimination on the basis of achievement is permissible or even mandatory: it is our duty to revere excellence and deplore vice, just as it is our prerogative to tax the wealthy and give aid to the poor. What we cannot do is to imply, in law or by public authority, that some citizens are better than others in a fundamental, moral sense. Especially in what pertains to ruling and being ruled, citizens must be treated as morally equal persons who have equal dignity and are entitled to equal respect.[18]

Even the Warren Court, liberal as it was, allowed a whole set of economic discriminations.[19] The Burger Court has gone further, holding that while it is unacceptable to discriminate on the basis of race, it is relatively acceptable to discriminate on the basis of poverty: a community can, within certain limits, exclude lower-income housing.[20] The reasoning in such rulings is clear to me even when I find it offensive. The Court is arguing that economic discriminations are permissible because they involve judgments about your material success but not about your moral worth. To say that you have not made much money is not to say that you are a worse person. As a matter of fact, there is probably a rebuttable presumption that people who *have* made a great deal of money are worse than those who have not.

In any case, the Court's doctrine certainly seemed to make gender into a suspect category. Our sense of gender identity is one of the earliest foundations of a sense of self, preceding any racial or ethnic identity. Discriminations based on gender, consequently, attack equal dignity and respect at a fundamental level, especially when almost all such distinctions between the sexes imply—as they have in the United States—the inferiority of women to men.

In the case of *Frontiero v. Richardson,* four justices of the Supreme Court did declare that gender was a suspect category. But although they were on the winning side of the case, they fell one short of a majority. Their side, but not their reasoning, prevailed. The Court stopped just short of accepting the view that gender is a suspect category, and there the Court has remained.[21]

Even the relatively more conservative Court has taken some steps in the direction of sexual equality. In 1976, the Court declared gender to be a "semi-suspect" category.[22] The idea that something can be "semi-suspect" has wonderful possibilities for those of us who had assumed that any amount of suspicion is enough to make a suspect. Could Caesar's wife have pleaded that her virtue was only "semi-suspect"? Nevertheless, the Court meant to indicate that gender, while not a "suspect category," demands a clearer and more compelling relation to a public purpose than other discriminations. Distinctions based on gender, the Court argues, can only be justified by "important" interests to which the law is "substantially" related, as opposed to the "fundamental" interests and "compelling" relationship necessary to legitimate the use of a suspect category.

In practice, it is hard to discover what the Court means. For example, the Court has held that alimony cannot be limited to men; women may have to pay too.[23] It has held that women cannot be excluded as trustees for their children, nor can they be given automatic preference in custody hearings.[24] The Court has even held that women cannot be said to mature at an earlier age than men.[25] In fact, the evidence of many cultures and many times attests that women *do* reach maturity earlier than men. Since the age of maturity is chiefly an "important" interest and the evidence is strong enough to indicate a "substantial" relationship to gender, the criteria for using a "semi-suspect" category would seem to be satisfied. However, the Court rejected the idea of differing rates of maturity as old and "out-dated," an argument which—historicist at best—outruns both the evidence and the claims of all but the most lunatic advocates of sexual equality. The Court, in other words, has chipped away at the structures of inequality, but it has been unwilling to proclaim that distinctions of gender are suspect on principle, probative violations of civic equality, even when the logic of its opinions points in that direction.

The Court's position, in fact, is similar to the opinions of most Americans. The public is generally sympathetic to women's claims; a considerable majority appeared to favor the ERA or something like it.[26] At the same time, a great many people suspect the women's movement and its leaders, regarding them as an "elite," out of touch with ordinary women.[27] Even more Americans worry that feminism has gone or will go too far, especially in extending the principle of equality into the sphere of private life.[28]

A great many of the anxieties that contribute to this mood are excessive. Equal rights would not—as the opponents of ERA implied—forbid all discriminations based on gender. Equality, in this context, would mean that gender cannot be used where other categories can achieve public goals. For example, if a legislature wants to limit certain dangerous jobs to those who have the physical strength to perform them, it makes a kind of sense to exclude women from such employment. In general, women are not as strong as men. But this argument, often invoked in the past, does not make *enough* sense to overrule the claims of equality. Some women are stronger than some men, and if the legislature aims to protect the weak, it needs a test of *strength*, not a test of *gender*. Any other reasoning opens the possibility that weaker men will be asked to do jobs that strong women can do better and more safely.[29]

On the other hand, there are certain exceptional areas in which gender would be an appropriate category. Equal rights does not imply that we must all use the same washroom or that women soldiers must sleep in the same barracks with men. The law is allowed to notice that American society is predominantly heterosexual and that certain demands for personal privacy derive from that fact. Similarly, the Court has already ruled that there seems to be adequate reason for rejecting women as guards in a maximum-security prison for men.[30]

Despite these reassurances, the opponents of the equal rights movement are correct in arguing that intrusion into private life is inevitable if we are to treat women as anything like equals. The dignity and respect which citizens owe to each other inherently involve our social relationships.

In speech, for example, civic good manners require us to address our fellow citizens in respectful ways. Very early in American history, terms like "Goodman" and "Goodwife" fell into disuse.[31] The two terms reflected the contempt of the gentle and refined for the merely "good," and democratic America preferred to make us all into gentlemen and ladies. But the terms "lady" and "gentleman" have aristocratic roots, although America democratized them in practice, and contemporary usage, referring to us as men and women, is more thoroughly egalitarian. In any case, respect for other citizens demands that we refer to them by the terms they prefer.

One cannot call black men "boys" in a court of law, nor can one call black women by their first names if they object to the practice.[32] It is necessary to use words which the person addressed finds acceptable and undemeaning. Demeaning jokes and epithets are at least in bad taste, and there is good reason for thinking that the law may have some obligation to forbid them. The Supreme Court recognized long ago that certain kinds of demeaning language constitute "fighting words," so offensive that government has a duty to prevent them in the interests of public order.[33]

A woman who is addressed as "honey" by a man she has met only a few minutes before may be excused if she thinks of the term as a fighting word. Yet that is by no means the most offensive locution women are likely to encounter. If our private manners are unequal to the task, we may very well need public sanctions to discourage sexist incivilities.

In the neglected case of *Beauharnais v. Illinois*, the Court held that some forms of speech constitute *group* libel.[34] Speech can damage me, the Court held, if it libels a group with which I identify so deeply that my person and the group are fundamentally inseparable. My honor and dignity may be bound up with that of the group to which I belong. This is especially true in mass society, since individuals are dwarfed and the group takes on even greater significance as a source of strength, identity, and personal freedom.[35] In the case of racial and ethnic groups, it is obvious that a slur on the group involves an offense to its members.[36] Yet this is at least equally true in relation to the sexes, since our perception of gender identity is so basic a cornerstone of personality. Civic equality, consequently, requires that we rule out language disrespectful to either of the sexes, certainly as a matter of good manners and possibly as a matter of law entitling the injured party to civil damages.

Similarly, the attempt to prevent sexual harassment entails an intrusion into private life. Sanctions against sexual harassment turn on the argument that it is impermissible to use one's power or one's wealth to extract sexual favors from a person who is otherwise unwilling to grant them. The offense is extremely difficult to delineate, not the least because power and wealth often make their possessors sexually attractive. It is hard to determine whether a powerful person is attempting to coerce another into compliance because the threat of power need not be overt. The presence of power and its potential to do harm are often enough, just as the bribe of wealth may be temptation enough whether or not money is explicitly offered. Slave masters did not openly threaten their female slaves, as a rule; they did not need to do so.

Despite these difficulties, it is not impossible to determine whether someone is being sexually harassed. Juries can do a passable job of deciding whether a woman was being exploited by her employer or, whatever she claims now, was simply drawn by his wisdom and social position. Yet making such judgments does presume an evaluation of our motives and implicit meanings. If an employer tells an employee, "I could make things wonderful for you," is he a would-be lover pleading his suit? Or is he implicitly threatening the employee with the terrible things he could also do? The law cannot forbid sexual harassment without becoming, to some extent, the censor of our relationships and the judge of our souls.

Liberal individualism, the foundation of the framers' theory of politics, aimed to protect private life against public prying and, as we have observed, put up with public equality in the interest of private freedom and inequality. American institutions permit and encourage private acquisition, and it is always difficult to forbid Americans to use their private resources as they choose. As Justice Holmes remarked about the Sherman Anti-Trust Act, if you permit people to compete, it is hard to forbid anyone to win the competition.[37] Liberal political thought and the Constitution of the United States put the burden of proof on any claim to intrude on or regulate the private use of private power.

Yet even if we grant this narrow definition of the public sphere, there are overriding reasons for prohibiting sexual harassment. Sex is a uniquely powerful and personal area of life, one closely related to one's dignity and identity. When we referred, beforetime, to a woman "defending her honor," that language spoke to a psychological truth, the intimate connection between sexuality and self. It defames Eros to say anything less.

All societies have recognized that erotic relationships have a singular importance, involving strong passions and exerting a powerful influence on our view of ourselves and others.[38] Any political society—and especially, any polity based on civic equality—has the right to provide that sexual exploitation will not result from the inequalities it permits. That, after all, is the root of the historic power of the state to forbid or regulate prostitution. The logic behind such legislation is the conviction that the market, and the inequalities which stem from it, should not extend to sexual relations. The argument against sexual harassment, in other words, speaks to traditions older than the American republic and wise enough to command its law.

But the most serious opponents of the equal rights movement might concede the arguments against demeaning language and sexual harassment. Their concern is with the family and with the changes in family life implied by equal rights for men and women. The argument of these opponents goes something like this: the family in the United States is invaluable and embattled, so threatened that any change in family life may very well shatter it and so invaluable that we cannot afford to lose it, whatever injustices are embodied in the contemporary family.[39] Women must put up with the conventional family, the argument goes, because the consequences of interference would be worse than the injuries of domesticity. The shrewdest opponents of the equal rights movement do not believe that, by nature, woman's place is in the home. Instead, they believe that *someone's* place is in the home, and they fear that no one will fill that place if woman does not. In this view, the real issue is not the rights of women but the survival of the home.

I will argue, by contrast, (1) that the home is even more troubled than this somber assessment suggests; (2) that the crisis of the home is part of a broader political crisis affecting the whole of the private order; and (3) that recognizing the equality of the sexes can contribute to the strength of the home as well as to the justice of political life.

The home and the family, even if we refer to them as parts of "private life," are crucial elements of political society. The early life of children shapes their basic images of the world, forming perceptions and presumptions which precede words and values and decisively affect both. Childhood gives us our postulates about the nature of authority and the safety of trusting others, and what we learn later in life is ordinarily interpreted in the light of the axioms we learned at home. Moreover, the power of home and family is not confined to children. Apart from the love adults may feel for each other, the family appeals to the primordial desire to leave behind something of oneself.[40]

All this is to say the obvious, that the family speaks to our earliest and most enduring passions. When home and family do their job well, they coax the emotions out of the body, leading us into involvement with others. Home and family teach us to see ourselves as parts of a whole, albeit a small one; it is at home that we take our first steps toward the recognition that we are social and political animals. Evidently, this is the basis of patriotism and public spirit; good politics requires good homes.[41]

At the same time, the family is dangerous to political society in two distinct ways. Inherently, the strength of the bonds between family members ordinarily means that they will prefer one another to the law or the public good. Parents notoriously seek to bend the law for their children: conservatives pay for the best attorneys to defend children who break drug laws and liberals send their children to private schools. We regard it as monstrous that totalitarian regimes encourage children to inform on their parents because we think it unnatural for a child to do so, even when a parent has violated the law.[42] In the interest of justice, the rulers in Plato's best regime are denied private families altogether; all regimes less excellent than the Republic must endure a tension between the family and political society as a whole.[43]

Contingently, the family may pose a political problem by teaching—knowingly or unknowingly—values and beliefs at odds with those of the regime. The ancient Greek family is an excellent example.[44] By nature, Aristotle argues, the relation between man and woman is shaped by the fact that men are stronger (*kreitton*), which makes them rulers.[45] But, as any reader of Plato's *Republic* knows, the rule of the strong is not necessarily just. In fact, Aristotle goes on, there is a natural distinction between the relation of master and slave, that of husband and wife, and that of parent and child. Yet while the ancient Greeks had a term—*despotike*—to describe and apply to the relation of masters and slaves, they lacked any special terms for the relationships of marriage and parentage.[46] Implicitly, Aristotle is arguing that the Greeks lacked these terms because they confounded the relationships of marriage and parentage with despotism and slavery. While despotism is the relationship natural to masters and slaves, however, the relationship of husband and wife is naturally *political*, analogous to the terms on which two citizens of different talents would conduct their dealings.[47]

The ancient Greek family, then, reduced all the forms of government to one—despotism—and it thereby taught that all who do not rule are enslaved. Since the worst condition for a human being is to be enslaved contrary to nature, the Greek family also taught children to despise the very virtues of women. (Even slaves might be held in less contempt, since their enslavement was ordinarily due to bad fortune—most often, capture in war—rather than any defect of nature.) Woman's qualities and skills, insufficient to win her genuine freedom, were presumably not worth cultivating. Womanly values—gentleness, nurturance, and the concern for domestic harmony—were disdained or feared by male citizens.[48] Yet this meant, paradoxically, that the early education of citizens was entrusted to women and slaves, those with the greatest grievance against the political regime. The future of the city, consequently, depended on those who had reason to hate it: Troy was no more foolish when it opened its walls.[49]

Subtly and openly, a child reared in such a family is taught to equate freedom with despotism and to regard it as shameful to be ruled. Yet the public life of the *polis*—especially in democracies—depended on and sought to instill the proposition that citizens should rule and be ruled in turn and the collateral doctrine that the equality enjoyed by friends is essential to the good life.[50] In ancient Greece, private and public teachings warred, to the great detriment of both. Even under the best circumstances, however, kinship and citizenship are no more than uneasy allies, and one test of statecraft is its ability to harness the family to the law.

The framers of the American republic made no explicit effort to legislate for the family, but their nomography nonetheless comprehends the family and its importance in political life. The framers relied on a political theory—Locke's—which begins by rejecting patriarchalism, the doctrine that political society must be shaped in the image of the family.[51] The framers' silence about the family is explained, in part, by the fact that they constructed the American regime on antifamilial principles.

Free, independent, and self-seeking human beings—in the framers' view—create social groups by convention and are bound only by their consent. But the family does not have the child's consent. The authority of parents rests on the fact that physical weakness and dependence prevent the child from realizing his or her moral freedom. Parental authority derives from superior power more than the consent of the governed. When we yield to a tyrant in order to protect our lives, the tyrant's right to command lasts only so long as his power. Similarly, the framers believed, parents have no authority over their grown children.

In this theory, the family's power over the emotions only makes it more suspect. The family creates bonds of affection between its members strong enough to make them think of themselves as parts of a whole, counterpoising the claims of individual freedom. Our love for our homes and families moves us to stay near them, a tender captivation which tries to hold us even when self-interest, rationally calculated, pulls us away.

We feel affection, the framers reasoned, because we associate certain persons and things with the gratifications we experienced in the past. Sentimentality is only the wraith of old interests which may or may not survive in the present. Affection ties us to bygone things. It is also parochial, because we feel it more strongly—other things being equal—for what is close at hand. Finally, affection is linked to complacency, especially in the family. Home is safe; one can relax "in the bosom of one's family." But the human condition, as the framers understood it, is cold and compelling, not warm and comfortable. Human beings are at war with nature, which thwarts us and eventually kills us. Homes are only oases of relief in the desert of struggle, not the first principles of human life.

At the same time, the framers believed that the family—and the traditional and religious doctrines they expected families to teach—had an essential role in the moral education of citizens.[52] Building on the individualistic precepts of natural right, the framers had great confidence in the capacity of the "science of politics" to produce public peace out of private impulse. Nevertheless, they knew that human passions are liable to foil the designs of science and law. Even rational individuals, who see the need for law and government, are tempted by the hope that they can break the rules and go undetected. Civilized life depends on certain moral foundations—such as the principle that one ought to keep one's promises—which make liberal *politics* possible, but which are at odds with the individualism of liberal *theory*.[53] The framers realized that the republic they proposed depended, in practice, on a "moral and religious people," prepared in private life for public liberty.[54]

In the framers' design, the family is invaluable as a moral educator because, while it is a small group which creates and appeals to the strongest human affections, the family is too small to pose any serious challenge to public life and institutions. The familiar logic of *The Federalist* tells us that the plurality of factions in a large state makes it difficult for any group of factions to "concert and execute their plans of oppression."[55] Strong factions are dangerous nevertheless. Large groups find it relatively easy to form alliances: eleven states were almost enough to disrupt the Union, and a handful of giant organizations, in our time, can be decisive in the political balance. Strong factions, consequently, need to be watched suspiciously when they are not explicitly limited by law.[56]

Families, however, are not strong factions. Very few families have wealth or political influence enough to imagine that they can affect the life of the republic. Outside the domicile, the family is too weak to make us complacent. Consequently, liberal political theory feels safe in assigning to the family all the tasks which the public order disclaims but which are vital to political life.

Very early in the history of the republic, Americans came to believe that the family has the primary responsibility for educating the soul and for developing virtue and moral character.[57] The emotional foundations of good citizenship, moreover, were conceived to be the family's all but exclusive province.

Similarly, the family plays an important role in the life of adults. The family is small, intimate, and personal; in the family, individuals *matter*. The family consoles us for our lack of importance in the mass society which is the logical outcome of the framers' case for a large republic.[58] In the family, we mean enough to be missed, and there are no longer many places where that can be said. The family is the major exception to the American rule that the individual is dispensable, and that alone makes it desperately important to most Americans.[59]

In providing moral education and solace, families play a useful, intended role in the framers' scheme. But families have done something more than that: they have been bearers of values and traditions *at odds* with liberal secularity and individualism, and in so doing have inspired resistance to liberal politics.[60] Consider the following exchange between Ann Landers and one of her correspondents:

Dear Ann Landers:
My little sis is 14. We both baby sit for extra money. Sis sits weekend afternoons. I sit evenings. Of course, I make a lot more than she does. Mom makes us pool our money and divide it every

month. I don't think this is fair. She says sharing is more important than money. Please print your answer.
Hillsdale, Mich. Complaint

Dear Hilly:
I'm all for sisterly love, but your mom is advocating Marxism. I favor the free enterprise system myself. People should not be forced to share what they earn with others who earn less for whatever reason.[61]

Miss Landers's spirited response speaks to the conflict between the family and the public doctrines of the liberal regime. In fact, even when the American family has taught liberal precepts, it has helped to make those ideas ego-alien, rules with which we must comply rather than values with which we identify.[62]

Let me relate an American folk story. A child is taught, in the family, that one ought to love and share with one's fellows. Eventually, the child matures enough to be allowed to play alone and goes outside, pulling a little red wagon. He or she meets the child next door, who says, "Let me play with your little red wagon," whereupon our child, having been trained to love and share, hands it over. After a while, our child says, "It is my turn now. Give me back the wagon," and the child from next door answers, "Possession is nine-tenths of the law. It is now *my* little red wagon." Our child goes home and complains to his mother. Since this is a folk story, she isn't working, and the family believes in conventional sex roles. True to her role, the mother replies, "Wait until your father comes home." On his return, Father may rush out to avenge a daughter, but he is likely to ask a son, "Did you fight back?" The burden of the boy's answer will be, "How could I? All you people ever taught me was sharing and loving." Then, according to the story, the father buys him boxing gloves or karate lessons. Whatever the sex of his child, moreover, Father will give a lecture about the "real world," almost certainly remarking that "it's a jungle out there."

Such a reference to the "real world" seems to suggest that the world of the family is an illusion, an excessive notion by any standard. Even the framers, who might have contrasted the family's "conventions" with the "state of nature," would not have argued that convention is unreal. The hyperbole of terms like "the real world" is intended to balance our emotional conviction that it is the *public* world which is unnatural or unreal.

To our feelings, the real world is the home. (This is true, incidentally, if the public world—unlike that in our story—is more benign than that of the home.) In fact, the trite saying that the public world is a "jungle" only emphasizes its alienness: a jungle is a place fit for beasts, not an environment suited for human beings. The family, in other words, teaches that the public world is powerful but subhuman, an environment against which we need defenses in spirit as well as in body. The public world imposes itself on us, but we do not consent to it or acknowledge its authority. Left to itself, the family denies that liberal institutions are rightful; it poses a standing, though often silent, challenge to the framers' design.[63]

The position of the family, as Christopher Lasch observes, was "precarious from the beginning."[64] The culture of liberalism has intruded on and modified the teachings of the family, over the years, as public institutions have sought to enlist the family in support of the regime. Tocqueville observed that there cannot, over the long term, be a difference in the principles which rule public and private life. The two spheres overlap, especially since both teachings lay claim to the individual's highest allegiance. Any democratic regime is torn between political freedom, the genuinely democratic principle of shared rule, and the claim to individual freedom, the implicitly lawless desire to do as one pleases.[65] In America, Tocqueville knew, the privatistic principle was sanctioned by the highest *public* authority. Supported by the law *and* by the lowest side of human nature, the framers' theory was almost certain to prevail.

> Egotism is a passionate and exaggerated love of self, which leads a man to connect everything with his own person, and to prefer himself to everything in the world. Individualism is a mature and calm feeling, which disposes each member of the community to sever himself from the mass of his fellow creatures and to draw apart with his family and his friends. . . . Egotism blights the germ of all virtue: individualism, at first, only saps the virtues of public life; but, in the long run, it attacks and destroys all others, and is at length absorbed in downright egotism. Egotism is a vice as old as the world, which does not belong to one form of society more than to another: individualism is of democratic origin, and it threatens to spread in the same ratio as the equality of conditions.[66]

Since individualism corrupts the mind in modern democracies, the only hope for avoiding this denouement lies in feelings and in personal character strong enough to resist its base teachings. Democratic regimes, in other words, have become radically dependent on the family, but the family is everywhere endangered: "Amongst democratic nations new families are constantly springing up, others are constantly falling away, and all that remain change their condition; the woof of time is every instant broken, and the track of the generations effaced. Those who went before are soon forgotten; of those who will come after, no one has any idea: the interest of man is confined to those in close propinquity with himself."[67]

In these terms, it is fatuous to argue, as conservatives often do, that government is the sole or the chief enemy of the family. The individualism of the framers pervades our institutions. Government, in fact, is sufficiently responsive to opinions shaped in and by the family that it has often tried to champion the home. The competitive market economy has been the most relentless enemy of family life in America.

The evidence for this is everywhere around us. The family is increasingly specialized and socially isolated. Family life is more and more distant from work: we are likely to travel greater *distances* to get to our jobs and the *quality* of our work on the job diverges from the work of the home. Our work is specialized and esoteric, difficult for family members to observe or understand, unlike the tasks of farmers and townspeople beforetime. Moreover, a growing number of women work outside the home, and in general a smaller portion of our time is spent in the home and in family life. The home is more and more reduced to the care of our bodies, our senses, and our feelings, and an expanding section of the public has come to suspect that—cost aside—these specialized therapies may be provided best by "experts" outside the family.[68]

In fact, it is no surprise that so many women have moved to escape from home so defined. The specialized home which women were supposed to "make" was both too narrow to be satisfying and too burdensome to be tolerable.[69] Domesticity, conventionally defined, limits the scope of woman's life and, at the same time, asks her to accept almost total responsibility for the emotional and spiritual needs of her family. Wives and mothers are expected to solve problems which are not of their making and which are insoluble within their sphere. If a man lacks self-esteem because he is convinced that his work is unimportant, how is his wife to reassure him? It may help to remind him that he matters to her and to the children (if he does), to feed him well, or to commend his sexual prowess. None of these things, however, will address the man's feeling about his *work,* and in the conventional family, the man's work is far and away his most defining activity and his most significant contribution to family life. A wife relieves her husband's anxieties about work or life outside the home only by creating a sort of illusion, and if this deception fails to work, she has failed in her role as a wife. Either horn of the dilemma, obviously, involves its guilts. Problems like these, incidentally, are likely to grow more severe, since an increasing number of us work at jobs which are insignificant and in which we are personally dispensable.[70]

Moreover, the market demands that our attachments to locality, friends, and kindred must yield to the currents of economic change. The framers hoped to free individuals from the parochial ties of affection; the national market works to fulfill their design: "The national labor market has become so efficient that, for example, if the demand for spot welders declines in Cleveland and rises in Houston, a man trained in that trade is expected to respond to this market cue by moving from Ohio to Texas. The market cannot take into account the fact that this spot welder also happens to be an uncle, a church deacon and a Republican ward committeeman. These other roles do not comprise part of his commodity value."[71]

Accustomed to the transformations that technology works in our lives, we are coming to take geographic mobility for granted as well. Something like one in five Americans will move this year; AT&T tells us that "long distance is the next best thing to being there," assuming—as we do—that we will not be near our relatives and old friends. Managing the "relocation" of corporate employees, which includes attending to their "emotional needs," is a profitable and growing business.[72] The primary aim of such services is to overcome resistance to moving with one consolation or another. We "adjust" to these "relocations," however, only at considerable personal cost. Through the pain of being uprooted, we learn, often very early in life, to be hesitant and superficial in our commitments to people and places. Matters are even worse for those who are left behind, since they are made so terribly aware of their vulnerability to the choices of others. That helplessness is especially visible in neighborhoods where the old have been deserted by the young. Witnessing such abandonment is ordinarily enough, without any closer experience, to make Americans determine to avoid a like fate by being among the first to go.

The women's movement has helped to create a counterweight to mobility. When it is proposed that the family move, equality demands that both husband and wife should have a say. This case for an equal voice is reinforced by the growing likelihood that women will have independent careers and make a significant contribution to family income. Persuading two people to "relocate," especially if it is necessary to find two jobs, is probably more than twice as difficult as reassigning one employee. Local attachments count for more, and a reluctant employee can always plead a recalcitrant spouse.

This resistance to mobility has led to a new tension between capitalism and the family. Traditionally, businesses preferred "family men" on the grounds that families created motives for success and that a stable family testified to personal reliability. Increasingly, however, corporations welcome single executives because they are mobile, free from the impediments and complications of family life.[73] Capitalism is not the friend of the family: it tolerates the family so long as the home is subordinate to the market. The more equal the family, the less reliable is its subordination and the greater the implicit hostility of our economic system. The market does not worry that feminism will lead women to scorn the home; it fears that the movement for equality will lead men *and* women to hold the home too dear.[74]

The threat to the family from such external forces, however, only amplifies its internal crisis. Divorce has become one of the routine possibilities of married life, so familiar and so likely that we feel almost compelled to overlook the damage. For children, so much in need of reliabilities, divorce introduces a sense of helpless vulnerability in relation to the most basic of human relationships. The frequency of divorce means that even the children of stable marriages must feel a tinge of worry. The injury is reparable, but divorce ordinarily produces people who are less trusting.[75] Adults, moreover, are bound to be affected by the realization that, in our closest relationships, stability is becoming the exception to the rule. The safe assumption, we are learning, is that no human bond lasts for very long.[76]

There is no denying that the women's movement has often encouraged or led to divorce. The claim that women are entitled to "self-realization" has an undoubtedly individualistic tone (by contrast, the proposition that women are entitled to equality makes sense only in relationships with others). Some feminists virtually identify the family with oppression. More commonly, marriages in which both spouses originally held the traditional view of the roles of men and women prove unable to survive the woman's new sense of herself. Recognition of the rights of women *does* demand change in the family, but the passing of the old order of family life implies a redefinition of the family, not its destruction. The movement for equal rights may be the family's best friend, for it is certain that the ancien regime in the family would not survive even if it were possible to silence the women's movement.

Divorce has become acceptable in America. That conservatives chose to nominate the first divorced person for the presidency (and that voters chose to elect him) indicates the new respectability of divorce. Mr. Reagan's speeches in favor of "family values" cannot overcome the symbolic significance of his marital history. In both his speech and his past conduct, Mr. Reagan mirrors the dominant pattern of contemporary American opinion. Americans are disturbed by the radical instability of personal life, but that very uncertainty counsels them to make and take their commitments ever more lightly. This is especially true since we are no longer tied to any locale or set of relationships. Without those constraints, the individualist principle, that I have a right to do as I please so long as I do no physical injury, tends to prevail. Even those who reject that doctrine are nudged toward it, in practice, in self-defense.

Individualistic doctrine speaks with the authority of law. In *Griswold v. Connecticut,* Justice Douglas spoke of marriage as a relationship with a "noble purpose," deserving special protection from the law.[77] Yet in *Eisenstadt v. Baird,* a more conservative Court proclaimed that marriage is nothing more than a contractual relationship between two *individuals.*[78] The rights of a family, in these terms, are only the rights of the individuals who happen to make it up. Increasingly, the courts treat marriage as a contract between essentially separate individuals rather than an enduring bond with rights of its own. In this view, government has no legitimate interest in protecting marriage. Its role is confined to making it easier for people to enter into marriage and to dissolve it. In the law, as Mary Ann Glendon writes, marriage seems to be "withering away."[79]

Under attack from so many directions, the family needs all the help it can enlist. It is certainly not enough for government to leave the family alone; the family needs the *support* of active government against the fragmenting pressures in society. For government to uphold the home, however, it must consider that security in affective relations has a claim to compete with individual freedom and that social stability can rival the pretensions of economic growth. Public policy (and American culture in general) will sustain the home and the family only when it values community, as the framers did not.

So profound a change in our political culture presumes the recognition that human beings are born dependent and live as political animals in need of the nurturance and encouragement of their fellows. To appreciate the family is to cherish closeness, harmony, and solace. The home, in other words, cannot claim an honored station without asserting the rights of what is womanly, the dignity of the soft and domestic virtues which the framers—and modern thought generally—have held in slight esteem.

Of course, there is only a loose association between these traditionally feminine values and women as individuals. Yet it is really impossible to give just recognition to womanly values without acknowledging the rights of women, and vice versa. In the first place, the biological fact that women bear children and men cannot means that there is an almost necessary link, in the infant's crucial first bonding, between nurturance and woman. Second, our traditional sex roles, even when they give women great authority within the family, deny that "women's values" have an equal claim on *public* life. To say that "woman's place is in the home" segregates the *home* and what is homely as much as it does women. To end the inferior status of the home, it is necessary to make the home the place and concern of every family member, and the home and those who care for it must have an honored place in public life.[80]

In fact, lacking equality, woman's power in domestic life and in moral education involves a danger to "family values" and to the republic. If the political society is contemptuous of "womanly" things and treats the soft virtues as inferior, it teaches women (as well as the rest of us) to despise what is feminine. Obviously, this damages women's sense of their own worth. It is also important, however, that the deprecation of womanly things affects what mothers teach their children. Since mothers want the best for their children, a polity which rewards and honors the "masculine" virtues proclaims that the second-rate, "feminine" qualities are to be adopted only in cases of necessity. Implicitly, in this view, while women are compelled by the body to play feminine *roles,* they should be devoted in spirit to masculine *values.* If women are constrained to live a domestic life, they should scorn domesticity. A political society which denies equal dignity to women and to womanliness promotes a secret treason against the home within the family itself.

As Tocqueville recognized, this is especially true in America. Very early, Americans felt it necessary to give women a "masculine" education.

They have found out that in a democracy, the independence of individuals cannot fail to be very great, youth premature, tastes ill-restrained, customs fleeting, public opinion often unsettled and powerless, paternal authority weak and marital authority contested. Under these circumstances, believing that they had little chance of repressing in woman the most vehement passions of the human heart, they held that the surer way was to teach her the art of combating those passions for herself. . . . As it is neither possible nor desirable to keep a young woman in perpetual and complete ignorance, they hasten to give her a precocious knowledge on all subjects. Far from hiding the corruptions of the world from her, they prefer that she should see them at once and train herself to shun them; and they hold it of more importance to protect her conduct than to be over-scrupulous of her innocence.[81]

Women, consequently, were initiated into the public world and given a knowledge of men and of men's activities. Educated in that life, they were not permitted to enter it. It is scarcely surprising, then, that while the American women of Tocqueville's time displayed "great delicacy of personal appearance" and retained the "manners of women," they sometimes revealed that they had "the hearts and minds of men."[82]

This covert devotion to "manly" values involved a special danger to civic life. Aristocratic and patriarchal regimes gave formal authority to the father; families in such regimes were hierarchic on principle, and interest and law were important supports for rule and solidarity within the family. In America, Tocqueville remarked, these supports were undermined where they had not already fallen. Necessarily, the American family rests on the "natural bond" of affection. Relations between family members are warmer and less formal; the family is less hierarchic and hence less competitive; there is more trust and less calculation among kindred. The democratic family, at its best, prepares children for equal citizenship: it makes brothers equals and "allows their minds and hearts to unite."[83]

This result, however, is far from inevitable. Tocqueville knew very well that intimacy and strong feeling do not always produce affectionate union. At least as often, they lead to jealousy, envy, and contention. Families based on strong feelings are a necessity for American democracy. They are also a stupendous gamble which turns on the hope that families, as a rule, will lay the foundations for fraternal citizenship rather than fratricidal competition. Since moral education, in Tocqueville's view as in American conventionality, lies in woman's sphere, it follows that the character of women is the crucial fact of American political life.[84]

If women regard domesticity as an inferior life and hold its warm harmonies in lower esteem than individual self-assertion, democratic hopes for the family are certain to be dashed. Yet American women are too shrewd and too worldly to be deceived by flattering insincerities about the value of the home. If America expects women to honor the home, it must demonstrate its own regard for domestic life. To that end, women must be assured of equality outside the home so that family life will be a choice, perhaps an honor, and certainly not a bleak necessity. It is at least as important to make men free to play an equal role inside the family.

Politics and family life have at least one principle in common. Plato pointed to the likeness between ruling and weaving, the most womanly of the arts in ancient Greece; weaving, like statecraft, involves making a whole fabric out of individual threads. Weaving, a domestic craft, rests on an art of solidarity, the making of parts into wholes.[85] Similarly, true statecraft recognizes that domestic order and justice have priority over foreign policy; a polity engages in foreign affairs for the sake of domestic well-being. Soldiers and diplomats are always inclined to urge that domestic life be ordered in the interest of victory or success abroad. Too much of their time and attention is given to the external world, too little to internal life. Political rulers need always to be reminded of the natural sovereignty of domestic things. So too, America needs to free women for public life and to bring fathers home from their place of exile.

Notes

This essay was originally published as "Equality and Citizenship: The Rights of Man and the Rights of Women," *Discourses*, April 1983.

1. Woodrow Wilson, *Constitutional Government in the United States* (New York: Columbia University Press, 1908), 22–23; see also Raymond Tatalovich and Byron Daynes, "The Limits of Judicial Intervention in Abortion Politics," *Christian Century*, January 6, 1982, 18–20.

2. Enid Nemy, "Feminist Cause Looks Back to Grass Roots," *New York Times*, November 8, 1982, B10.

3. For example, see Marian Leif Palley, "Beyond the Deadline," *PS* 15 (1982): 588–91.

4. G. K. Chesterton, *What I Saw in America* (New York: Dodd, Mead, 1922), 17.

5. Plato, *Republic*, 454e.

6. Joseph Tussman and Jacobus Ten Broek, "The Equal Protection of the

Laws," *California Law Review* 37 (1949): 341ff; the comment on Emerson refers to his poem "Brahma."

7. *The Federalist*, #10.

8. Aristotle, *Nichomachean Ethics*, 1158b 25–33; this is even more true if, like Thomas Aquinas, one regards the subjection of one human being to another as a "penalty for sin" (*Summa Theologica*, I, q. 96, article 4).

9. The concept of "fundamental rights" is itself an old one (*U.S. v. Cruikshank*, 92 U.S. 542 [1876]). The Warren Court, however, gave a rather new turn to the idea, although it was also following Justice Stone's doctrine of "preferred position" (*U.S. v. Carolene Products*, 304 U.S. 144, 152–53 [1938] and *Jones v. Opelika*, 316 U.S. 584 [1942]). In making citizenship the ruling purpose and defining characteristic of political life, the Warren Court was following Aristotle, probably without knowing it (*Politics*, 1274b39–1275a4).

10. *Harper v. Board of Elections*, 383 U.S. 663 (1966); *Bullock v. Carter*, 405 U.S. 134 (1972); *Dunn v. Blumstein*, 405 U.S. 134 (1972); *Carter v. Jury Commissioners*, 439 U.S. 357 (1979).

11. *Afroyim v. Rusk*, 387 U.S. 253 (1967).

12. *Brown v. Board of Education*, 347 U.S. 483 (1954); *Graham v. Richardson*, 403 U.S. 365 (1971).

13. *Regents v. Bakke*, 438 U.S. 265 (1978).

14. J. R. Pole, *The Pursuit of Equality in American History* (Berkeley and Los Angeles: University of California Press, 1978), xii–xiii, 302, 322.

15. Compare Aristotle, *Politics*, 1266b29–32.

16. Alexis de Tocqueville, *Democracy in America* (New York: Schocken, 1961), 2:296–97.

17. Hence, among other things, the Court's sanctions against penalties for illegitimate birth: *Weber v. Aetna Casualty & Surety*, 406 U.S. 164 (1972).

18. James Bryce, "Equality," in *The American Commonwealth* (New York: Commonwealth, 1908), 2:692–704. The qualification "morally" is necessary because, other problems aside, children—while citizens—are not yet entitled to rule; incarcerated criminals are also denied a share of rule, but they are so deprived *because* they are morally equal and accountable.

19. *Baltimore and Ohio Railroad v. U.S.*, 386 U.S. 372, 478 (1967); see also *San Antonio v. Rodriguez*, 411 U.S. 1 (1973) and *Lindsey v. Normet*, 405 U.S. 56 (1972).

20. *James v. Valtierra*, 402 U.S. 137 (1971) and *Arlington Heights v. Metropolitan Housing*, 429 U.S. 252 (1977), although see also *Hills v. Gautreaux*, 425 U.S. 284 (1976).

21. *Frontiero v. Richardson*, 411 U.S. 677 (1973).

22. *Craig v. Boren*, 429 U.S. 190 (1976).

23. *Orr v. Orr*, 440 U.S. 268 (1979).

24. *Stanley v. Illinois*, 405 U.S. 645 (1972); *Reed v. Reed*, 404 U.S. 71 (1971); *Weinberger v. Wiesenfeld*, 420 U.S. 636 (1975).

25. *Stanton v. Stanton*, 421 U.S. 7 (1975).

26. Mark R. Daniels et al., "The E.R.A. Won—At Least in the Opinion Polls," *PS* 15 (1982): 578–84.

27. Peter Sherry, "The Class Conflict over Abortion," *Public Interest* 1, no. 12 (1978): 69–84; compare the parallel view of "reformism" in Gerda Lerner, "Women's Rights and American Feminism," *American Scholar* 40 (1971): 35–248.

28. Palley, "Beyond the Deadline."

29. *Albemarle Paper v. Moody,* 442 U.S. 405 (1975); *N.E.A. v. No. Carolina,* 434 U.S. 1026 (1978).

30. *Dothard v. Rawlinson,* 433 U.S. 321 (1977).

31. Hawthorne used the term, for example, to enhance the archaic tone of his famous story "Young Goodman Brown."

32. Monroe Berger, *Equality by Statute* (Garden City: Doubleday, 1968), 116–17.

33. *Chaplinsky v. New Hampshire,* 315 U.S. 568 (1942).

34. *Beauharnais v. Illinois,* 343 U.S. 250 (1952).

35. Hadley Arkes, *The Philosopher and the City* (Princeton: Princeton University Press, 1981), 23–91.

36. Harry Kalven, *The Negro and the First Amendment* (Chicago: University of Chicago Press, 1965).

37. Compare Holmes's dissent in *Northern Securities Co. v. U.S.,* 193 U.S. 197 (1904).

38. W. J. Goode, "The Theoretical Importance of Love," *American Sociological Review* 24 (1959): 38–47; Aristotle, *Rhetoric,* 1371a18–22.

39. Joyce Gelb and Marion Leif Palley, *Women and Public Policies* (Princeton: Princeton University Press, 1982), 7–8.

40. Aristotle, *Politics,* 1252a26–29; Plato, *Laws,* 721b.

41. See the demand in Plato's *Laws* that citizens beget children, and the corresponding provisions for stabilizing the family (*Laws,* 740b, 774 b–c, 784 a–e). The *Republic* abolishes the family among the guardians, but its regime claims to provide the guardians with the best of homes.

42. Plato, *Euthyphro.* The average Athenian would have been as shocked by Euthyphro's prosecution of his father as Socrates is in his own way.

43. *Republic,* 457d–464e.

44. For a general discussion of the ancient Greek family, see Marilyn Arthur, "Women and the Family in Ancient Greece," *Yale Review* 71 (1982): 532–47.

45. *Politics,* 1254b14; I am indebted to Ken Masugi, "Another Peek at Aristotle and Phyllis: The Place of Women in Aristotle's Argument for Human Equality," presented to the Pacific Northwest Political Science Association, April 30–May 2, 1981.

46. *Politics,* 1253b5–12.

47. Ibid., 1259b1–2. Aristotle goes even further, since he suggests that there is a distinction between the rule of a household, which must be monarchic, and political rule, which is exerted over persons who are free and equal (1255b18–21). Implicitly, a household must be ruled in the terms appropriate for the rule of children, since the education of the young is its regulative task. Parental authority is exercised monarchically in the public life of the household, but privately—and by nature—parental decisions are made politically, by persuasion and

deliberation among equals. This position, I think, explains the argument and the allusions of *Politics*, 1259b4–18.

48. By contrast, in the *Republic*, feminine roles like nursing are shared by men (460b–c). When Aristotle denies that all the forms of rule are the same, "as some assert," he is arguing against the implicit teaching of the household—the context of his remark—as well as the common public teaching that all forms of government come down to the rule of the strong (*Politics*, 1255b16–20).

49. The danger of conflict between father and son, often explicitly encouraged by the mother, pervades ancient Greek culture, especially through the "tales told by nurses and mothers" which are ruled out of the best city (*Republic*, 377a–378e). Plato likens women to a tyrant who cannot travel. Her politicality is confined to the household, and she raises, in her child, the image of the despotic authority she envies (*Republic*, 549e, 579b; *Laws*, 694c; compare *Alcibiades*, I).

50. *Politics*, 1275b6–8, 1280b39–a2, 1295b24–29.

51. Gordon J. Schochet, *Patriarchalism in Political Thought* (New York: Basic Books, 1975).

52. Max Horkheimer, "Authority and the Family," in *Critical Theory: Selected Essays*, trans. M. O'Connell et al. (New York: Seabury, 1972), 59, makes this point in relation to the current of theory of which the framers were a part.

53. Marc K. Landy and Henry A. Plotkin, "Limits of the Market Metaphor," *Society* 19 (May/June 1982): 8–17.

54. John Howe, *The Changing Political Thought of John Adams* (Princeton: Princeton University Press, 1966), 185.

55. *The Federalist*, #10.

56. As religion, for example, is limited by the First Amendment.

57. John Demos, "The American Family in Past Time," *American Scholar* 43 (1973): 432, 441.

58. The family, Otto Pollak writes, is "a place of intimacy within a world of loose, depersonalized relationships" ("The Outlook for the American Family," *Journal of Marriage and the Family* 29 [1967]: 198–99).

59. Karen Horney, *The Neurotic Personality of Our Time* (New York: Norton, 1937), 286.

60. Demos, "The American Family in Past Time," 432–33; Horkheimer, "Authority and the Family," 58ff.

61. I cite Ann Landers's column from the New Brunswick, N.J., *Home News*, July 15, 1981.

62. John Seeley et al., *Crestwood Heights* (New York: Basic Books, 1956).

63. As Mark Gerzon writes, in modern America, "the very idea of a home is radical." *A Childhood for Every Child: The Politics of Parenthood* (New York: Dutton, 1973), 137.

64. Christopher Lasch, *Haven in a Heartless World: The Family Besieged* (New York: Basic Books, 1977), 168.

65. *Politics*, 1317a40–b16.

66. *Democracy in America,* 2:118–19.

67. Ibid., 2:119–20.

68. Lasch, *Haven in a Heartless World.*

69. Other problems aside, the term "homemaker" denies men any role in "making" the home.

70. Kenneth Keniston, *The Uncommitted* (New York: Harcourt, Brace and World, 1965), 277–81, 293–99.

71. Landy and Plotkin, "Limits of the Market Metaphor," 14.

72. Elizabeth Fowler, "Relocating Corporate Employees," *New York Times,* July 22, 1981, D20. It is more than a little suggestive that "relocation" was also the euphemism for the internment of Japanese Americans.

73. Jacques Donzelot, *The Policing of Families* (New York: Pantheon, 1980).

74. I do not deny, of course, that there are feminists who scorn home life or who take radically individualistic positions. This affects neither the social impact of equality discussed here nor the more hopeful political possibilities of the movement. (See, for example, Nancy R. McWilliams, "Contemporary Feminism, Consciousness Raising, and Changing Views of the Political," in *Women in Politics,* ed. Jane S. Jaquette [New York: Wiley, 1974], 157–70.)

75. Judith Wallerstein, "The Impact of Divorce on Children," *Child Psychiatry* 3 (1960): 459, 461–62.

76. Selma Fraiberg's warning about day-care centers, it seems to me, applies to all of us, adults and children alike: "Young children who get to know . . . a person then lose that person show anxiety, agitation, tearfulness. When those children keep meeting someone, then losing someone, and meeting someone and losing someone . . . there are going to be emotional consequences: lack of confidence in the future, a degree of withdrawal" (interview in the *New York Times,* December 11, 1977, cited in Brigitte Berger, "The Family as a Mediating Structure," in *Democracy and Mediating Structures,* ed. Michael Novak [Washington, D.C.: American Enterprise Institute, 1980], 155).

77. *Griswold v. Connecticut,* 381 U.S. 479 (1965).

78. *Eisenstadt v. Baird,* 405 U.S. 438 (1972).

79. Mary Ann Glendon, "Marriage and the State: The Withering Away of Marriage," *Virginia Law Review* 62 (1976): 663–720.

80. See, for example, Jean Bethke Elshtain, "Family Reconstruction," *Commonweal,* August 1, 1980, 430–31, and "A Feminist's Journey," *Commonweal,* June 5, 1981, 331–33.

81. *Democracy in America,* 2:238–39.

82. Ibid., 2:252.

83. Ibid., 2:233–35.

84. Ibid., 2:255.

85. Plato, *Politicus,* 279a–283a, 285d–286b, 308d–311a. I am indebted to Laura Greyson's paper, "Kinship and Citizenship: Plato on the 'Family and Civic Education,'" presented to the Northeast Political Science Association, November 1, 1982, for many of these comments.

Honor in Contemporary American Politics

Honor is associated with rank and inequality, so that it is somewhat paradoxical to speak of democratic honor at all. A democracy can aspire to "an aristocracy of everyone" in the sense of making excellent things available to all its citizens.[1] But inevitably, increasing the number of those honored decreases the value and significance of honor.[2] As Gilbert had the Inquisitor sing in *The Gondoliers,* "When everyone is somebodee / Then no one's anybody." Honor demands an audience who observe and admire.[3] But inequality of honor, as Tocqueville recognized, creates its own paradoxes. Tocqueville presented honor in the Old Regime as the epitome of convention and particularity, sometimes admirable, but often "fantastic" and not a little absurd, preferring war or gambling to work and "great crimes to small earnings." Inequality tends to "invert the natural order of conscience," so that in the United States, "to debauch a woman of color scarcely injures the reputation of an American; to marry her dishonors him."[4] Tocqueville was suggesting that *in principle* the standard of what is honorable is universal, an equal measure, even though *in practice,* honor can be awarded only to the few.

In these terms, democratic honor at its best is an appeal from convention to nature, as in the Declaration of Independence, holding up to a community the model or ideal of what is humanly best or true. Always suspicious of forms, it requires a people to set its own marks to aim at: democracy, seen in the mirror of honor, is characterized by equality in defining the inequalities that are worth pursuing.

There is more than one problem with this notion of giving the power to bestow honor to those who are to be edified by it, a point to which I will return. For the moment, it is sufficient to note that Americans, in an earlier time, gave high honors to public life. *Tom Sawyer,* for example, portrays a people obsessed with rank and standing. It begins by telling us that Aunt Polly wore spectacles "for style," not because of any defect of vision; "they were her state pair, the pride of her heart."[5] And throughout the book, eminence is almost invariably identified with public office—Judge Thatcher, Senator Thomas Hart Benton, or praising Tom by predicting that he might be president someday, "if he escaped hanging."[6] Tom does indicate that he would rather be Robin Hood than president, but as everyone with memory knows, the comparison itself honors the presidency.[7]

By contrast, as all the surveys tell us, contemporary Americans have few heroes, and those almost entirely in private pursuits. Even sports, still a place for titans, have been tainted by association with commerce. And public life seems too ambiguous, too involved with conciliation and compromise to deserve any laurels. Far from being a source of honor, public office seems to constitute a reason for suspicion.

But this is a recent chapter in an old story. As Tocqueville indicated, practice—and democratic practice especially—works to erode and undermine honor. In one sense, honor is a *code* or *standard* by reference to which we can be said to deserve respect or acclaim. In principle, such a rule asks us to uphold, for the edification of others, something truly fine or admirable, as Socrates does in *Crito* when he expresses concern for the honor of philosophy.[8] So understood, honor is largely indifferent to opinion. However, the term honor also refers to *esteem*, a measure that is resolutely social and subjective, and to that extent, concerned not with what is, but with what is seen.

To desire honor—to want to be noticed and admired—puts one into the hands of those whose good opinion he or she covets. And obviously, in the ordinary course of democratic politics, those who *desire* honor have an advantage over those who *deserve it*. Brutus told the crowd to "believe me for mine honor, and have respect unto mine honor that you may believe,"[9] presenting his honorability as a fact entitled to deference. Well, that is no way to run for alderman, and no one who knows democratic politics is surprised at the way Antony beats up all those "honorable men." In democratic politics, Tocqueville wrote, the public is "the natural and supreme arbiter of the laws of honor."[10] And since democratic politicians are characteristically eager for the public's love and esteem, they slide easily into shamelessness. Even those who are nominally forceful, like Callicles, are tempted to play to Demos.[11]

This is especially true in a republic like the United States, with a public whose size and complexity make it difficult to persuade, difficult to understand, and given to maddening variability. Mass democracy encourages political leaders to minimize their commitments, seeking room to adjust to opinion and to the current of the times. The hope of being elected, after all, is prominent among Tocqueville's examples of motives that bend Americans to the "tyranny of the majority."[12]

To come at the question in a slightly different way: in any regime, those who bestow honor are not identical to—though they may be included in—the audience intended to be uplifted by honor's example. The Baseball Writers or the Veterans Committee select the inductees at Cooperstown, not the players and not the fans; even in democracies, those who vote make decisions for those who do not, and for those, like children, who are not entitled to. But in democracies, the distinction is more or less accidental and frictional. Democracies tend to collapse the distinction between bestower and observer, and that tendency is always a factor in democratic politics. (Even in baseball, for example, fans now select the eight starting position players on each All-Star team; the managers, selected by rule, still choose the pitchers and other team members.)

Historically, however, the United States has benefited from at least three sources of honor—three kinds of bestowers—distinct from mass opinion, which have worked to limit that opinion and to elevate it. In the first place, some predemocratic ideas of honor, especially what Tocqueville called "the spirit of religion," have been embedded in families, churches, and local communities.[13] Second, American institutions were framed to provide distance, psychological and physical, between representatives and mass opinion, that "total exclusion of the people in their collective capacity" celebrated by Madison.[14] And that separation provided space for the development of standards of honor and esteem among representatives, the judgment of peers and friends, quite distinct from popular perceptions. Third, democratic politics itself taught Americans forms and civilities, and party provided a bond of political friendship, filtered choices, and held candidates to some standard of fidelity. A popular institution, party checked the pursuit of popularity, if for no other reason, because standing well with one's fellow partisans was a condition of standing before the public.

These days, admiring Harry Truman is much in vogue, and it would be hard to find a better example of democratic honor. But it is important to note that Truman was a man rooted in institutions: in place and personal relations; in the Senate, where he was a consummate insider; and, above all else, in party, a loyal friend of the Pendergasts and all his life a fierce and unwavering Democrat.

Today, however, as we all know, technology, the increasingly international scale of life, and our relentless mobility work to embattle families and to weaken and fragment localities. The media—television, polling, or the newer "interactive" networks—are eliminating the distance between the public and its representatives, intruding on deliberative space and making mass opinion ever more immediate in its impact on government. The "insiders," the members of Congress honored for their legislative craft or personal integrity, are still around in some numbers (I think, for example, of such public servants as Representative Henry Hyde and Senator Robert Byrd), but they are part of an older generation, losing place and prominence to those who play to a mass audience. As for the parties, they hold the affections and loyalty of fewer and fewer of us, and their organizations, attacked by a century of reform, are barely shadow.

I am anything but an admirer of Mr. Gingrich, but his "Contract with America" has done a good deal to reassert accountability and partisan honor, and for that he and his allies deserve credit. They also merit some praise—once their opponents forced them to abandon the dishonorable premise of the balanced budget amendment—for seriously addressing the problem of the deficit. But Gingrich's version of party, like its Democratic rival, is a centralized organization whose power is money, one not rooted in local, deliberative communities (characteristics contemporary parties share with more and more political associations). In fact, money has become so dominant a consideration in our politics *because* the electorate is so massified. Consequently, Mr. Gingrich has been pursuing decentralized *government* through the medium of a centralized *politics,* a prescription of doubtful efficacy.

All of this means that the general public is less and less challenged as the source of political honor. But the public, uncertain about its own dignities, is not overly disposed to honor others. Tocqueville saw work as a pillar of democratic honor, and in this he echoed Jefferson, who had been concerned to establish that ordinary Americans had sufficient economic autonomy to be capable of honorable citizenship.[15] Jefferson's reliance on farm proprietors is less important, for us, than his later observation that American wage laborers were confident of their ability to obtain a "satisfactory situation"—work at wages high enough to provide for their families and their old age.[16] *Confidence* in the availability of honorable work is crucial: without it, workers will feel dependent on their employers, a dependence that grows greater the more affluently they are paid.[17]

Jefferson may have exaggerated the availability of honorable work, but he was accurately describing a cultural norm and expectation. Today, on the other hand, vast numbers of us are anxious about jobs and uncertain whether we are or may become superfluous, especially given the rising inequality that seems to be dividing us into the exempt and the trapped. And beyond economics, more and more of us are alone, without the support and assurance of stable families and communities. Americans are not nuts, for the most part, but too many people are in a "paranoid position," moved by forces they half understand, and affect even less.[18]

For too many of us, our leaders are no longer a reflection of our hopes, but a sign of our dependence. We admire leaders who seem strong and masterful and have the gift of success (and heaven help leaders who appear to lack these qualities, as recent presidents have all learned, in their different ways). But we fear to commit ourselves too far. Leaders must not ask us for very much; even Mr. Gingrich feels compelled to assure us, for example, that budget cuts will not "substantially" affect Medicare. This hesitancy indicates that we prefer leaders whose moral ascendancy is not overawing and that we feel free to despise. Never far below the surface, we envy and resent those we raise to honor, a fact of which the media, obviously, are only too aware.

Democratic politics, in fact, is becoming less able to educate us in the standards of democratic honor. Even the fraction of us who count as active citizens are moving away from genuinely public life and toward dangerously plural systems of honor. Social fragmentation and new technologies are allied in encouraging political groupings of the like-minded that—whether we are referring to talk radio, the Internet, or cocktail parties on the West Side of Manhattan—develop internal ideas of what is honorable that are sometimes admirable but include some very nasty forms of self-righteousness. These circles can be at least as narrow as any traditional small community, especially since they lack its stability, its foundation in interpersonal relations, or its reach across roles. At its worst, local communities pointed *toward* a public in a way that more specialized and ideological groups do not.

This privatization of honor is related to the long-term tendency to substitute dignity for honor, to move to a standard that is personal and inward, not bound up with conventions and forms. From the beginning, as Tocqueville taught, democracy has been inclined to deprecate the artificialities of aristocratic honor, aiming to base its order of rank on natural principles, rights, which are available to everyone and prior to institutions. Even in these terms, dignity was still in a vital respect political and a version of honor: it presumed that one's rights were priceless and worthy of great sacrifice, a demand that in practice all but requires the support and upholding of friends and society.[19]

But liberal democracy also embraces change, "the pursuit of happiness," and seen in the light of that commitment, codes and principles and forms of honor are apt to seem rigid and antiquated, so many barriers to opportunity. In "constant motion," as Tocqueville saw, Americans catch only "glimpses" of honor from their Celestial Railroad.[20] Even natural rights, as we all know, are now likely to be regarded as no more than claims to hegemony by white, male members of the eighteenth-century bourgeoisie. Honor has been assailed by the relentless relativism of the market; Jim Fisk's saying, "Nothing is lost save honor" epitomizes capitalism's teaching on the subject.[21] And it has suffered at least as much from historicism. Back when we thought we knew where history was going, there was a kind of honor in defending the leading class or party. It was honorable to crack eggs because we were sure about the omelette. Now, we are not so confident, and a great many Americans are inclined to identify honor—much diminished—with change itself, so that it is regarded as vaguely dishonorable to be "maladapted" or not "with it." That standard is evidently contentless, and it is just as dangerous, since it suggests that cracking eggs is acceptable, if not honorable, whenever it seems like the thing to do at the time.

As Tocqueville foresaw, it comes to seem altogether imprudent or wrong to identify honor with anything outward; it retreats inward, to "character" or "sincerity" or any of the versions of an authentic self.[22] Honor, in a word, becomes deinstitutionalized. The self secedes, and institutions—laws, parties, churches, families, even language—"cease to be the 'home' of the self and instead become oppressive realities."[23] More and more, dignity seems to be identified with standing for one's "rights" against public (or any) authority. Pap Finn's defense of his rights against the "govment" could easily be given, I think, by any number of contemporary Republicans.[24] And separated from institutions and forms and authorities, honor and dignity are exposed to the temptations and dangers that are inherent when human beings are judges in their own cases.

Of course, there is ambition in American politics, but, as in Tocqueville's day, it is not particularly lofty. The most advanced views (following the lead of the Tofflers) seek to remake America in the image of "third-wave" technology, a kind of postmodernism applied to society and a further threat to forms and institutions, including constitutional government. And no one should be deceived: technological innovation may unsettle old elites, but it does not democratize. It puts power into the hands of those who command the latest in a constantly changing series of new techniques.[25]

It is a higher ambition, I think, to encourage the recognition that the first step in public policy is determining what is good, not what is likely. That understanding would lead us to the attempt to defend or refurbish our representative institutions, including local party organizations. (I have a number of utopian proposals that I will be happy to furnish on request.) It would also prompt *serious* efforts to shore up the family which—posturing aside—will cost money and require government. And any republican vision worth having should move us to uphold the sense of self-worth among citizens, a goal that entails the expectation that every citizen make a contribution to the commonweal and the corresponding public guarantee of the opportunity to do so. All of us owe a debt of honor to our country, and yes, a debt of shame, for the old offenses are also part of the republic's grand history.

Notes

This essay was originally presented as "Honor in Contemporary American Politics" to the John Olin Center Conference on Democratic Honor, University of Chicago, May 20, 1995.

1. Benjamin Barber, *An Aristocracy of Everyone* (New York: Ballantine, 1992).

2. Here, and throughout this essay, I draw on Hans Speier, "Honor and Social Structure," in *Social Order and the Risks of War* (New York: George Stewart, 1952), 36–52.

3. Similarly, in *On the Waterfront*, Terry's complaint that "I coulda been somebody" turns on the distinction between being somebody—to say nothing of being a contender—and being a bum.

4. Alexis de Tocqueville, *Democracy in America* (New York: Knopf, 1980), 2:232.

5. Mark Twain, *The Adventures of Tom Sawyer* (Berkeley and Los Angeles: University of California Press, 1982), 1.

6. Ibid., 33, 162, 173.

7. Ibid., 69.

8. *Democracy in America*, 2:230n1.

9. *Crito*, 46B–C.

10. *Democracy in America*, 2:240.

11. *Gorgias*, 481E.

12. *Democracy in America*, 1:264.

13. Ibid., 1:43.

14. *The Federalist*, #63.

15. *Democracy in America*, 2:237.

16. Thomas Jefferson, letter to John Adams, October 28, 1813, in *The Life and Selected Writings of Thomas Jefferson*, ed. Adrienne Koch and William Peden (New York: Modern Library, 1944), 633.

17. What makes the longshoremen in *On the Waterfront* so comparatively servile is the doubt that they can obtain better (or adequate) work elsewhere.

18. Michael Rogin, "JFK: The Movie," *American Historical Review* 97 (1992): 502, 505.

19. Harvey C. Mansfield Jr., *America's Constitutional Soul* (Baltimore: Johns Hopkins University Press, 1991), 82, 218.

20. *Democracy in America*, 2:239.

21. Cited in Vernon L. Parrington, *Main Currents in American Thought* (New York: Harcourt Brace, 1930), 3:13.

22. *Democracy in America*, 2:99.

23. Peter Berger, "On the Obsolescence of the Concept of Honor," *European Journal of Sociology* 11 (1970): 345.

24. Mark Twain, *The Adventures of Huckleberry Finn* (Berkeley and Los Angeles: University of California Press, 1985), 33–34.

25. Jacques Ellul, *The Technological Society* (New York: Vintage, 1964), 208–18.

Part 4

Democracy as a
Moral Enterprise

Democracy as Means and End

Americans these days are uneasy patriots, their celebration of the country's laws and liberties balanced by a long list of discontents. They value democracy and tend to identify it with the American Constitution, but great numbers of them do not vote and—despite the surge of support that followed September 11—they have a good many doubts that government can be trusted to do what is right or that it cares about people like them. Yet while this level of disenchantment is relatively high, the ambivalence it reflects is anything but new: from the beginning, American political life and culture have embraced two very different versions of the nature and office of democracy.

Democracy as a Means

It is no secret that the American Constitution is not the last word in democracy or that it embodies many features that have to be called undemocratic.[1] Nevertheless, if we ask Americans to define democracy, the first things that come to mind are likely to be free elections, majority rule, and individual rights, and by those measures—the standards the framers set for themselves—the Constitution does deserve to be called democratic.

The framers said critical or snobbish things about democracy from time to time, and they addressed an electorate composed of white men, but they followed John Locke in regarding majority rule as the natural basis of political authority.[2] James Madison was particularly emphatic, never wavering in his devotion to that "republican principle." Even when, in *The Federalist*, #10, Madison spoke of the danger of majority faction, he did not argue against majoritarianism: quite the contrary, he claimed that a large and diverse republic would make majority rule safe—little threat to the rights of the minority or the "permanent and aggregate interests" of political society as a whole. In such a regime, Madison observed, any majority would necessarily be a complex coalition resting on more or less delicate compromises, unable to agree about very much or for very long. And toward the end of his life, Madison argued forcefully for majority rule against the thesis that states or regions should have the right to veto or nullify federal law.[3] As Alexis de Tocqueville indicated in *Democracy in America,* the American Constitution *limits* majorities, but it denies that public authority can derive from any other source.[4]

Despite this majoritarianism, however, the American framers did not regard democracy as a political end. The Declaration of Independence teaches that *any* form of government is legitimate if it secures natural rights, and in his more explicitly republican version of that spirit, Madison proclaimed in *The Federalist,* #10 that the preservation of the "diversity in the faculties of men" is the "first object of government." The American Constitution frames a *liberal* democracy, a regime which aims at preserving and enhancing individual liberty: democracy is a political means, but not an end.

The Constitution's version of democracy is government conducted by representatives for whom we vote, but Aristotle classified voting as an aristocratic institution, since we are presumably seeking those who are the best at rule (although one would be hard-pressed to know that based on our recent choices). Democracy, Aristotle argued, promised more than a choice of rulers: it offered citizens a share in rule, not so much through holding office, but in having a voice, a say in the shaping of policy.[5] In Aristotle's view, democracy seeks to bring citizens *to* public life; the American framers were more concerned to protect individuals *from* it—and, for that matter, to give government considerable insulation against the public's short-term enthusiasms and passions.

Government by representatives was no new discovery, Madison conceded: what was new in America's republics was government that was entirely representative, one that rested on the "total exclusion of the people in their collective capacity" from any share in governing beyond choosing their rulers and holding them accountable.[6] Under the Constitution, government is distant and difficult to comprehend—"intricate and perplexed," the Anti-Federalist "Cato" wrote, "and too misterious for you to understand, and observe."[7] It calls for specialized knowledge and talents— for professionals who we engage to represent our interests, like attorneys hired to speak for us. The scale of America's "big democracy" makes Madison's representative regime necessary because, given the limits of time and attention, only a tiny minority of us will ever be able to speak in a national forum.[8] And the framers expected that most of us would accept this shift from voice to vote because, limiting our political involvement, it leaves us free to pursue our private interests and to take advantage of the resources and opportunities offered by a large and complex republic.

However, even if we agree with the framers' theorizing, we will have to concede that it lowers the standard for—and the standing of—democratic political life. In their school, democracy is a valuable convenience; it has only a conditional claim to rule.

Democracy as an End

From the beginning, however, there has been a second voice in American political culture, urging public life in a less contingently democratic direction, regarding self-government as a reason *for* rights rather than a means *to* rights and emphasizing our individual differences less than our common nature. Lincoln appealed to that understanding at Gettysburg, reinterpreting the American founding: the Declaration of Independence asserts that we are created equal and that government exists to secure rights; Lincoln argued that the Union, conceived in liberty, is *dedicated* to equality.[9] In that understanding, in other words, democracy is the end of America as a political society, its standard for aspiration.

Aristotle held that, in the last analysis, the character of a political society is discerned less in the form of its laws than in its prevailing idea of justice, its scale of political goods. For an oligarchy, wealth is the ranking public good and the greatest contribution to civic life. Consequently, in the oligarchic view, those who most contribute to the wealth of a regime deserve the most from it: it follows, as in President Bush's argument, that the rich deserve a bigger tax cut because they pay the most taxes, just as it makes sense to take a hard line on welfare recipients while being more accommodating to corporations.

Democracy, by contrast, measures contribution by the quality of human devotion; it sees the greatest gift to the public in a free life, freely given. And since all citizens have a life to give, democratic justice is relatively equal.[10] And where democracy as a means emphasizes the value of rights, democracy as an end points to the benefits of the opportunity to serve, ideally including the chance to make a difference. Accordingly, egalitarian justice does not necessarily imply equal treatment: it reserves special honor for those who sacrifice themselves for the common good—soldiers and firefighters and police officers, of course, and all those, known and unknown, who devote their lives to the struggle for equality. Similarly, it holds that citizens have an equal right and duty to contribute what they can, so that all of us are subject to taxation, but taxes are properly assessed according to the ability to pay.

In these terms, as Aristotle was careful to indicate, although we ordinarily think of democracy as rule by the many and oligarchy as the rule of the few, it is possible for a regime to be oligarchic even if it rests on majority rule: All that it takes is for the majority to be informed by an oligarchic idea of justice, as when a relatively well-off majority is indifferent to its less fortunate fellows. It would not be difficult, of course, to make a case that just such conditions obtained in the Reagan years or, for that matter, that they do in most subsequent administrations. Institutions matter, not least because they affect our ways of thinking and living: no one should discount the importance of majority rule in democratic life. But institutions, as Aristotle indicated, are not the whole of the democratic story.

Tocqueville argued that America's egalitarian "habits of the heart"—largely rooted in the "spirit of religion"—were more important than the Constitution and the laws in accounting for democracy in America. But Tocqueville also recognized that if laws do not support and sustain habits, those mores will tend to erode over the long term.[11]

Americans, Tocqueville observed, justified almost all their actions by reference to the principle of "self-interest rightly understood," even though they often acted in ways that were altruistic or public-spirited. "They are more anxious," Tocqueville argued, "to do honor to their philosophy than to themselves."[12] In other words, the doctrine that human beings are at bottom self-interested individuals—the public philosophy enshrined in the laws—was coming to dominate public speech. And if Tocqueville recommended clinging to the idea of "self-interest rightly understood," it was as a defense against the more radical individualism he feared might be on the horizon. The tendency of the Constitution and the laws, in other words, is to mute America's second voice, and with it, the idea of democracy as an end.

Democracy in Contemporary Politics

There is abundant evidence for that proposition in contemporary America. In politics, arguments for democracy as an end are hard-pressed when they are heard at all, and any public discussion of morality is likely to be conducted in the various languages of individualism.[13] Comparing America to other democracies, Robert Dahl finds that the United States ranks high, among what Dahl takes to be indices of democratic performance, only in its relatively strong economic growth. In unemployment, budget deficits, and inflation America can claim to be mediocre, but by a range of standards—voter turnout, social expenditure, economic inequality, the percentage of citizens in prisons, energy efficiency, women in the legislature, and foreign aid—the United States ranks at or near the bottom of the list.[14] Probably the great majority of Americans would share Dahl's judgment that low rates of voting and high rates of incarceration are something to worry about. However, a very large number of us—and possibly most of us—would not be alarmed that the United States ranks low in social expenditures or economic equality, to say nothing of foreign aid or the number of women representatives. Almost all of our fellow citizens, on the other hand, take comfort from the American record of economic growth and are eager to see it resume. At any rate, the terms of political debate are increasingly defined by the assumption that the people who count in American politics see democracy as a means for protecting individual and private rights and for pursuing what can only be called oligarchic ends.

At the same time, there is abundant discontent with that sort of politics, even if it lacks an effective public voice.[15] Americans have rights: what they need are realistic opportunities to exercise those rights, a kind of political aerobics suited to redevelop the habits of the democratic heart. Tocqueville's greatest worry about democracy more or less discounted formal rights. He was concerned that the weight of opinion in mass democracies would be so overwhelming that citizens—feeling their rights useless—would simply adapt themselves to the prevailing current while retreating psychologically into ever smaller private circles, a regime defined by a soft "tyranny of the majority" on one hand and an impenetrable individualism on the other.[16] Democratic liberty, Tocqueville argued, requires a politics based on associations in which citizens have voices and faces, linking common purpose with personal dignity.[17]

As Robert Putnam argues, the art and experience of association is declining in contemporary America.[18] This is most evident in politics, where parties and political groups are increasingly fund-raising bureaucracies, while primaries and elections seem to be so many contests of media and money.

Democracy as a goal calls for every effort to rebuild, as far as possible, a politics of association. And high on that agenda must be the effort to undo the Supreme Court's decision in *Buckley v. Valeo* that contributions of money are speech, protected by the First Amendment and beyond any effective limitation by Congress.[19] *Buckley* lays down the essentially oligarchic doctrine that greater wealth deserves a stronger voice; in fact, if money is speech, isn't bribery logically entitled to the First Amendment's guarantees?[20] Democratic principle, by contrast, requires us to aim at equal access to public forums; the recent, much-trumpeted campaign reform law is no more than a step in that direction, even if it survives challenges in the courts.[21]

Moreover, we need to attend to an even more fundamental aspect of democratic citizenship. Historically, it was always recognized that citizens need economic autonomy to be fully free persons: "In the general course of human nature," Hamilton wrote, "a power over a man's subsistence amounts to a power over his will."[22] Hence Jefferson's vision of a republic of yeoman farmers, each living, more or less, on the product of his own land. But Jefferson came to be reconciled to increasing numbers of wage earners: in America, Jefferson argued, workers could be confident of a "satisfactory situation," assured of their ability to earn enough to provide for themselves and for their old age.[23] The worker's assurance of socially adequate work, as Jefferson saw it, made him independent of any *particular* job, affording him autonomy against his employer as well as a measure of dignity, the bases of civic freedom. It was the sense of security that mattered, not economic equality and certainly not affluence: well-paid but insecure employment, as Jefferson knew, breeds courtiers and lickspittles rather than citizens. Of course, this was a very rosy picture of America, even in Jefferson's time, especially since it took no notice of slaves. Still, Jefferson's argument captures a vital dimension of historic American experience, and more important, it speaks truly to and about the democratic ideal.

The lack of confidence in socially adequate employment—for the middle class as well as the poor—is an evident condition of contemporary economic life. Under the discipline of globalization and technological change, one observer writes, the workplace may have become "leaner," but it is definitely "meaner," more competitive and less secure.[24] And as Jefferson would warn us, that insecurity undermines the psychological foundations of democratic citizenship. In that sense, full employment and living-wage policies can be defended, whatever their economic effects, as bulwarks of civic freedom.

With democracy "on trial," Americans have every reason to try to strengthen the political and economic habits of democratic hearts, insisting on the right and duty of every citizen to make an appropriate contribution to the common life.[25] But that program will depend on intellectuals and activists capable, against a formidable array of enemies, of articulating and advancing democracy as a political goal, the measure of public philosophy and life.

Notes

This essay derives from an unpublished manuscript dated 2002.

1. Robert Dahl, *How Democratic Is the American Constitution?* (New Haven: Yale University Press, 2001).

2. John Locke, *Second Treatise on Civil Government,* sec. 96.

3. For example, see Dahl, *How Democratic Is the American Constitution?* 31–37.

4. Alexis de Tocqueville, *Democracy in America* (New York: Knopf, 1980), 1:173, 254–80.

5. Aristotle, *Politics,* 1294b.

6. *The Federalist,* #63.

7. Herbert Storing, ed., *The Complete Anti-Federalist* (Chicago: University of Chicago Press, 1981), 2:111.

8. Bertrand de Jouvenel, "The Chairman's Problem," *American Political Science Review* 55 (1961): 368–72; the phrase "big democracy" is taken from Paul Appleby, *Big Democracy* (New York: Knopf, 1949).

9. Garry Wills, *Lincoln at Gettysburg* (New York: Simon and Schuster, 1992).

10. Aristotle, *Politics,* 1279a11–1281a11.

11. *Democracy in America,* 1:43, 299; Similarly, in John Locke's very different theorizing, the moderately social state of nature will gradually slide into a state of war without a judge to interpret and enforce natural law. *Second Treatise,* secs. 4–21.

12. *Democracy in America,* 2:122.

13. Robert Bellah et al., *The Habits of the Heart* (Berkeley and Los Angeles: University of California Press, 1985); Alan Wolfe, *One Nation After All* (New York: Viking, 1998).

14. Dahl, *How Democratic Is the American Constitution?* 117, 169.

15. Michael Sandel, *Democracy's Discontent* (Cambridge, Mass.: Harvard University Press, 1996).

16. *Democracy in America,* 1:263–64; 2:98–99, 215–16.

17. Ibid., 1:191–95, 248–53; 2:102–11.

18. Robert Putnam, *Bowling Alone* (New York: Simon and Schuster, 2000).

19. *Buckley v. Valeo,* 424 U.S. 1 (1976); see also Dahl, *How Democratic Is the American Constitution?* 150–51.

20. Bribery, after all, might effect a modest redistribution of wealth.

21. [Editors' note:] Of course, restrictions on corporate speech in the act in question were deemed unconstitutional in the subsequent case *Citizens United v. Federal Election Committee,* decided January 21, 2010.

22. *The Federalist,* #79.

23. Letter to John Adams, October 28, 1813, in *Letters and Selected Writings of Thomas Jefferson,* ed. Adrienne Koch and William Peden (New York: Modern Library, 1944), 633.

24. Kristin Downey Grimsley, "Leaner—and Definitely Meaner," *Washington Post National Weekly,* July 20–27, 1998, 21; see also Theodore Lowi, "Think Globally, Lose Locally," *Boston Review,* April/May 1998, 4–10.

25. Jean Bethke Elshtain, *Democracy on Trial* (New York: Basic Books, 1995).

The Search for a
Public Philosophy

At the beginning of a new millennium, the American republic is prosperous and unrivaled, its material power matching the New Rome of the founders' imagining, but its public life marked by "discontents," or even a "lost soul."[1] The century's last year began with the president impeached before the bar of the Senate, but behind the headlines, it is American democracy that stands "on trial."[2]

Americans seem increasingly apt to regard government with suspicion, begrudging its authority. Policy makers, fearing to offend, walk on tiptoes. By contrast, party conflicts have grown bitter, but Theodore Lowi is right to call the parties "brain dead," lacking any public vision capable of calling for broad civic commitment or sacrifice.[3] And generally, in our political practice, we attach more and more limitations and qualifications to democratic institutions' moral title to rule.

Neither side in the abortion debate, for example, is willing to entrust the issue to majorities; the contenders volley salvos of competing "rights talk," each asserting that its position should be constitutionally protected against democratic politics.[4] "Identity politics"—which includes the demands of religious groups as well as those claiming to represent women, gays and lesbians, and racial or ethnic minorities—is not so much a claim to be *part* of the public as to be *separate* within it. Similarly, the major initiatives in education, following the example of a number of areas of public policy, appear to focus on lending public support to private or quasi-private institutions. Public authority, in part being "devolved" to states and localities, in a much more fundamental sense is being *dismantled*.[5]

The heart of American public philosophy has always been the quest for self-government.[6] Today, however, many Americans wonder whether self-government is really possible, or more precisely, whether it is worth the price. A considerable majority of us worry, too, that the American public is a "phantom," just as Walter Lippmann said more than seventy years ago.[7] Many see a fraying of the moral fabric of American life; to others, contemporary conflicts only reveal differences long suppressed or slighted. In fact, Americans have a remarkably common morality, but one defined in terms of essentially *private* decencies; their major public principle is a tolerance that reflects their despair of any public standards by which values and virtues may be evaluated.[8] In that sense, Americans have common values: what they are losing, as Todd Gitlin writes, is common dreams.[9] In our politics, public philosophy is increasingly reduced to whispers; the strong voice belongs to private philosophy expressed in and through public institutions. Yet this is also a familiar problem: the scales of our politics, delicately poised, have always tended to tip in a private direction, chronically needing—as they do today—statecraft and citizenship to right the balance.

For the American founders, public philosophy began with the teaching that human beings are naturally free, separate individuals who construct government to better fulfill their private purposes, primarily their desires for safety and well-being: the "first object" of government, Madison wrote, lies in protecting individual liberty and diversity. In this view, government exists to overcome the threats and obstacles posed by nature and by other humans; its positive aim is mastery, and hence the acquisition of power. But clearly, government so conceived can be dangerous to its creators, and the framers' political science aims to check and channel government's dynamic in ways that make the "power house" compatible with individual variety and liberty.[10]

The goal of the public philosophy underlying the Constitution, then, is the effort to maximize both individual liberty and aggregate power. Government is measured by its utility in advancing our private interests, but also by two crucial public standards: (1) the goal of securing the rights of its citizens; and (2) the principle that just authority derives from the "consent of the governed," a doctrine that at least points in the direction of democratic politics.

So conceived, government also was understood to rely on certain virtues beyond the calculations of interest. In the first place, the framers recognized a need for honor, at least to the extent of keeping one's word, even when doing so no longer seems in one's interest, because "promises, covenants, and oaths," in their theorizing, are the fundamental "bonds of human society."[11] The success of political society, they reasoned, makes citizens ever more prone to forget the harsh necessity that drove human beings under governance. We are all tempted to believe that we are clever enough to evade some laws without being detected, or that others will not imitate our lawlessness, or at least that the potential gains outweigh the risks. That danger is especially great among the poor, the obscure, and the oppressed—or private persons generally—who may easily feel that what they do will go unnoticed, or that they have little to lose. With reason, the "obligation of contracts" has special status as the only duty mentioned in the Constitution, saving the oaths of high officials, and the founding generation hoped that Americans would see promise keeping as a sacred duty.[12]

Second, the American founders relied on the readiness of citizens to defend their rights even at the price of comfort or safety, including their willingness to risk or sacrifice their lives to preserve the rightful freedom of others. They never doubted, in other words, that republican citizenship calls for at least some ability to subordinate the body and its goods to what the soul loves and regards as worthy.[13]

Third, the founding generation expected and desired citizens to be influenced by generosity of spirit, especially in caring for the helpless and dependent. Locke took it as a vital argument for revealed religion that reason and interest had not persuaded even the most civilized ancients that it is criminal to kill one's children by exposing them.[14] Most of the framers would have agreed, and all of them would have insisted on a morality that recognizes the claims of humanity.[15]

Finally, they looked to economic life to provide the material bases of civic morality and freedom. In Jefferson's well-known thesis, abundant land peopled by small proprietors meant a public capable of avoiding the economic dependence that can easily lead to political servility.[16] More important, Jefferson later observed that, given labor scarcity, even those who worked for wages could expect a "satisfactory situation," so that they enjoyed a citizen's portion of independence. In this argument, income is not the critical factor, although a socially adequate wage is clearly a part of what Jefferson had in mind: by itself, relative affluence can make workers even more dependent on their employers. Political independence turns, rather, on the security of employment, the worker's confidence that adequate employment will be available, so that no particular employer is essential to his or her livelihood.[17] Economic inequality, under these conditions, is roughly compatible with political equality, but that coexistence is always uneasy and a matter for public concern.

The framers' design, consequently, relied on civil society—on families, churches, communities, and economic life—to provide the moral and psychological basis for republican citizenship. Preoccupation with "mere life," Aristotle argued, is essentially a private philosophy, not genuinely free because driven by the body and its desires. Public life grows naturally out of the human yearning for a "good life" beyond material satisfactions, and especially out of the desire for a voice in shaping the conditions and directions of life, self-government's freedom beyond price.[18] The framers trusted that civil society would provide the crucial intermediate step, the ability to think and feel beyond the limits of self-interest that is the precondition of public spirit and public philosophy alike.

But although they relied on civil society to provide the characterological foundations of citizenship, the framers gave it no explicit recognition. The Constitution speaks only of states and individuals; it is silent about civil institutions, taking them more or less for granted. If anything, the framers were concerned about *limiting* the authority of states and localities in the service of individual freedom. The highest laws, and hence the highest forms of public speech, acknowledge individual liberty as a public principle, but not the claims of families, churches, and communities.[19] The longer-term problem of this imbalance seemed clear to Tocqueville: allied with the authority of the laws, the "spirit of liberty" would play an increasingly strong role in shaping the "habits of the heart." Americans, Tocqueville wrote, tended to justify their actions in terms of "self-interest rightly understood" as the all-but-universal language of public morality. Tocqueville acknowledged the advantages of this way of speaking, but he noted that it was misleading: in fact, Americans often acted from motives that were more generous and public spirited but seemed embarrassed to admit it: "They are more anxious to do honor to their philosophy than to themselves." That American public philosophy—the doctrine that all human beings act from interest—was preempting public speech meant that the ideal of self-sacrifice and civic spirit would become increasingly voiceless, locked in the private silences of the soul.[20]

Today, Tocqueville's prophecies are mirrored in American public life. Culturally and morally, we are considerably more diverse than we were in the past, and what once could be taken for granted now inspires dissent. At the same time, it is important to remember that America was *always* diverse, and a good deal more various than appearances suggested, since the expression of that diversity was constrained by public opinion and authority. Now, as we have observed, the majority of Americans incline to regard morality, even when beliefs are widely shared, as an essentially private matter. They are apt to say that morality is "relative," and that we should not "judge" or "impose on" the sincerely held convictions of others. At least in public speech, a gentle individualism is sweeping the field.[21] Reflecting a broad unwillingness to hurt others, this persuasion also shows little inclination to *help* them. Conceived in these terms, the public plays a weak hand in any contest with private interests, falling short even of the limited standard of civic spirit the framers set for republican government.

More than words is involved: all our institutions, civil and political, are being unsettled, their powers reduced, their authority questioned.[22] New technologies and new forms of economic life—most obviously "globalization" and the "information revolution"—are shaking or shattering old relationships and the order of communities and nationalities. Old forms and organizations seem increasingly outdated and irrelevant.[23] Yet while the past grows more distant from our experience, the future becomes unimaginable: Americans find it prudent to go cautiously, limiting—if not avoiding—their commitments to place, relationships, or moralities.[24]

But while these developments privatize us psychologically, they also make us more interdependent. Private life, John Dewey argued, is defined by matters that are our "own business," having few if any consequences beyond the individuals immediately concerned; public affairs includes acts that have important consequences for relatively distant others.[25] In these terms, as more and more of our lives become integrated by economics and technology, the less there is that can be called purely private or local: my business is too deeply affected by yours, and by the great, seemingly impersonal processes of communication and the market.[26] These intrusions of the public sphere, however, emphasize our weakness and vulnerability, and make us more eager for the consolation of those private spaces that remain. Tocqueville saw the principle clearly enough: an expanding public pushes us, psychologically, in the direction of an ever more isolated individualism.[27]

It only accentuates matters, of course, that "domestic insecurity"—the term is Theodore Lowi's—is the ordering principle of so much of social and economic life.[28] Jefferson's confidence in a democratizing economy does not match our experience. For a quarter century, real wages for hourly workers have tended to fall, and working families have kept up only by having more family members work, by taking extra jobs, or by working longer hours.[29] Worse, work itself has become increasingly unreliable: "downsizing" layoffs and the increase in part-time and temporary employment have created an anxious workplace notable for a decline in loyalty between employees and employers.[30] A rising concern for money and for private interest, as W. Lance Bennett observes, is "a realistic response to an unpredictable economy defined by job and career instability."[31] As Jefferson would have warned, the price of insecure employment and inadequate wages is a decline in "social capital" and public spirit that threatens even basic civility.[32] The comparative well-being of the last few years only heightens worries about the future: the electorate's unwillingness to rock the boat, so evident in recent campaigns, testifies less to a complacent moderation than to a desperate sense that things could easily be worse.

In recent elections, in fact, America's growing economic inequality has been a suppressed issue, treated like an improper story in polite company. Yet the disparity among Americans, already the greatest among industrial countries, is becoming still greater, threatening to create a two-tier market and a two-tier society.[33] Even people like Mickey Kaus, who regards fairly extreme inequality of income as inevitable and acceptable, recognize that it undermines the sense of being one people with a common destiny.[34]

Like the economy, upper-income Americans are increasingly international, with weaker ties to place and to particular communities. The "underclass," by contrast, is minutely local, trapped in relatively confined neighborhoods by a lack of jobs, skills, and resources. And between these peoples, the middle sectors have been losing ground.[35] Middle-class Americans prefer, understandably enough, to see their fortunes as linked to those of the well-to-do, a disposition that helped fuel the right-leaning politics of the eighties, with its emphasis on opportunity. That tendency has been reinforced by the recent escalation of the stock market, which touches—disproportionately—so many Americans. But this feeling of prosperity, present or prospective, is evidently uneasy. In movie theaters and on Broadway, Americans in the millions have been engrossed by the story of the *Titanic,* seeing in that old disaster, I think, a cautionary tale of our time: the great ship was characterized by radical inequality; in its abortive voyage, humanity was sacrificed to the goals of speed and profit; its technological wonders were entrusted to very imperfect humans. And it is also suggestive that the *Titanic,* shadowed by nemesis, sank in 1912, in the heyday of the Progressive Era.

In fact, in the embattlement of the contemporary middle class, E. J.

Dionne sees the basis for a new progressivism.[36] There are stirrings that support his view, more a matter of motion than an organized movement, but capable of great power: consider the assault on smoking and the tobacco industry so reminiscent of the temperance movement a century ago, or the political weight of environmentalism and the concern for historic preservation, which parallel the old Progressive zeal for conservation. On both the right and the left, moreover, legions of Americans seek to invoke government's support for what they take to be a just order of domesticity and social life, a goal which was the leitmotif of the Progressive movement.[37] In a stumbling, half-articulate way, great numbers of Americans are looking to politics to shore up or reconstruct the foundations of civic life.

Across the political spectrum, Americans have very little trust in government. Many citizens see government—massive and impersonal—as only another of the overwhelming powers that are shaping their lives, dimly comprehended and presumptively malign. More Americans, probably, regard government as proverbially bumbling and inefficient, and millions hold both views in an uneasy synthesis.

Even those who think of government more positively are bound to suspect that it matters less, that it possesses only a shrinking ability to rule. Capital and jobs, technology and information—and with them, plagues and terrorists—cross and recross national borders in ways that seem increasingly beyond government's control. In the nineteenth century, international capital—through institutions like banks and the gold standard—called the tune in much of national economic policy making, but today the effects of globalization are more pervasive, reaching even into once-inviolate areas of life.[38] In this much at least, Marx and Engels look to have been right: the dynamics of capitalism have "drawn from under the feet of industry the national ground on which it stood."[39]

In critical areas, government itself appears to agree: American antitrust policy, for example, has grown more tolerant of megamergers, based on the argument that competition must be seen in terms of the international market, in which such combinations are necessary to permit American corporations to hold their own against giant foreign and quasi-foreign rivals. Even if accurate, however, this analysis is limited to the *economic* effects of consolidation: it ignores the consequences of concentrated economic power for democratic politics, probably because policy makers are assuming that politics must adapt itself to the logic of the market. It is no wonder, then, that so many Americans, as Bennett notes, see government as "at worst, responsible for the economic conditions that dominate their private lives and, at best, of little use for remedying them."[40]

Loyalty to large-scale institutions, however, depends decisively on their ability to act effectively. Nations and mass parties are inevitably somewhat impersonal, complex collectivities in which public policy depends on compromise: their moral claims have always lacked luster when compared to those of more intimate and more coherent communities. It is not surprising, then, that identification with nations and parties has been declining in Europe and the United States.[41]

Challenges to elites and authorities—refusals to "work within the system"—have become a feature of contemporary politics, more routine than remarkable.[42] That style fits a society in which rapid technological transformations unsettle *old* elites, but immediately create *new* ones, endowed with power—for the moment, until the next round of change—but without institutional or moral ties to most citizens.[43]

Political allegiances, consequently, show signs of fragmenting. Political fashion features "identity politics," which—by emphasizing different experiences and unique perspectives—points first to groups (most insistently, genders, races, and sexual orientations), but ultimately to individuals. Organized group membership, accordingly, is declining in favor of "networks" and volunteering, styles of participation—fluid, informal, often intense, but relatively episodic—in which civic involvement is shaped to the mood and convenience of individuals.[44] And, as Gilles Lipovetsky saw in the French student movement of 1968, this sort of individualized, designer politics, even in its radical versions, is essentially reactive in its rhythms: outbursts of activity in response to events succeeded by periods of withdrawal. It lacks the sense of obligation, the persistent devotion to an idea of the public good, that is at least possible in unions, parties, and formal political organizations generally.[45] Once again, Lance Bennett is on the mark: a great deal of what currently passes for political activity is largely driven by "socially dislocated individuals seeking social recognition and credible representation for their personal concerns," a defensible goal but one that falls short of genuinely public life.[46]

We continue, however, to have a vital stake in public policies, and the more we depend on or care about particular public programs, the less willing we are to let majorities decide their fate. The importance of *government* becomes an argument against democratic *politics;* public policy argues against public life. Citizens are less inclined to rely on electoral politics, which demands the aggregation of money and mass support.[47] Instead, they seek to have their favored policies defined as "rights" protected by courts and administrative agencies, tribunals where it is possible to wage one's *own* politics with comparatively little help from others. In this kind of politics, lawyers and accountants are probably needed as champions, but these are people we *hire,* and their fees, however high, are not apt to come close to the cost of an electoral campaign.[48] It is also a remedial and negative politics, aimed at protecting one's interests and damaging one's enemies; as the Paula Jones case shows, litigation can do that even without winning—to the extent, in that instance, of unsettling the verdict of an election. And in general, to the degree that political issues are decided elsewhere, democratic politics is reduced—at best—to entertainment, something between a sitcom and a soap opera.

Certainly, that describes politics in 1998, dominated as it was by the president's "inappropriate relationship" with Monica Lewinsky. Majority opinion, which consistently supported President Clinton, was relatively sensible, but its very immunity to the scandal emphasizes the privatization of public life.[49] Most Americans find the president's conduct reprehensible; they do not trust him or respect him as a person. Nevertheless, they are persuaded that he is doing a "good job" because the country is prosperous and at peace, making few demands on our considerable comforts. They see the president as like an attorney, a technician engaged to further our private ends, someone whose skill matters but whose moral character is largely irrelevant. (In fact, too much rectitude might put the president at a disadvantage in any contest with rogues.) Great *public* goals, however, call on citizens to change habits and make sacrifices, running risks and enduring discomforts that presume trust, not only in the craft of leaders, but in their moral direction. That Bill Clinton is not evaluated in those terms indicates how little we expect from public life.

There is, however, another side to American opinion. Baffled and battered by colossal forces, most of us yearn for some greater degree of human control over human artifacts, especially since it is once again becoming clear that the market, left to itself, goes to extremes, undermining its social roots and threatening an economic "meltdown."[50] Millions of us want, at least, someone to blame or hold responsible for the course of events, which helps account for the extraordinary range and popularity of conspiracy theories: notably, worries about a "New World Order" and its supposed covert masters.[51] That impulse easily slides into an eagerness for someone to "take charge," as in the movie *Independence Day,* a temptation that sits uncomfortably with constitutional rule. But at the bottom of all these responses is the very desire to be treated with dignity and to have a say, the itch for self-government that—given the manifold weaknesses of individuals—can only be satisfied in politics.

Through most of the last two decades, political memories have been dominated by events that testify to the limits of politics—Vietnam and Watergate, the disappointments of the Great Society, and the collapse of Soviet communism—and opinion, here and abroad, has tended to disparage and turn away from government. Jimmy Carter was as much a part of that move toward privatization as Ronald Reagan, but its master spirit was Margaret Thatcher, with her iron willingness to let the market shatter society, embracing inequality in the confidence that economic dynamism would eventually build a new and better order.

In the nineties, however, the wind changed. Electorates turned more doubtful about the direction of things and tiptoed, with many fits and starts, toward government as a defender of families, civil society, and values "beyond the dreams of avarice."[52] In Europe, electorates leaned to the left, but in India, a similar—though more threatening—impulse brought the Hindu nationalists to power. In Benjamin Barber's terms, if the result was not always "jihad," there was no mistaking the uneasiness with "McWorld."[53]

In America, the mood has been ever more uncertain and ambivalent, but the signs are clear: no fire, but plenty of political smoke. Social conservatism has been a portent, although a muddled one. Detesting sixties liberalism, social conservatives have allied themselves with the opponents of "big government," but they also despise media culture and are at least half aware that the moral teaching of the market, on its own terms, is a self-seeking relativism. At least at the local and state level, conservatism champions an extended view of government's office as a defender of moral order, an attitude that conservatives often—even regularly—extend into national politics.[54] And on the other side of the spectrum, Bill Clinton's promise of a "New Covenant" appealed to fairly ambitious hopes—vaguely, to be sure, and in his usual soft tones—before the failures of his early presidency led him to settle for "third-way" politics, mild humanitarianism linked to enthusiasm for technology and international trade.[55] Still, the policy of substituting work for welfare—even in the harsh form passed by Congress and signed by the president—reflects the conviction that government should support the moral discipline and civic dignity of labor. A gentler inclination toward the rehabilitation of government, moreover, is evident in the strengthening of the electorate's long-standing sympathy for public programs like education, health care, and the environment. That disposition—and the perception that the Republican Congress was obsessed to the point of inaction by the scandal surrounding the president—contributed to the surprising result of the 1998 elections. And among public intellectuals, more and stronger voices are acknowledging the perennial human need for political community.[56]

So far, however, these developments are not much more than offstage murmurs; in the theater of American politics, the high drama is the danger to democratic life. Aristotle warned that in defining a regime, the *form* of rules may be deceptive: its real character lies in its implicit public philosophy, its evaluation of the *claims to and obligations of citizenship.* The heart of democracy, he held, is not "rule by the many"—although that is clearly an element of democratic governance—so much as the belief that the contribution to public life that matters is a freely given life. What deserves to rule, in democratic teaching, is love of country, the willingness, if need be, to sacrifice everything to preserve its self-government, a gift the poor can offer as well as any. Government by majority, by contrast, can also be *oligarchic* if political society presumes that the highest public good is material prosperity, so that wealth deserves a stronger voice, and special consideration, in public councils.[57]

All commercial societies have at least some tendency toward that oligarchic public philosophy; these days, in the United States, the tilt is all too visible. In the absence of serious campaign reform, public office is increasingly limited to the wealthy or those who can enlist their support. Money is not a sufficient claim to rule—Californians, for example, defeated both Michael Huffington and Al Cecchi—but it is virtually a necessary one, and fund-raising consumes more and more of the time and attention of public servants. And it is part of the same current that prosperity and well-being have so high a rank in American lives, and in our judgment of goods and presidents.

Democratic public philosophy points to the need to redress the political balance, strengthening the links between citizens and their government in order to make self-government seem less a matter of form and more an everyday possibility. That agenda requires rebuilding confidence that democratic institutions are more than shams: a first item, obviously, is policy effectively reducing the power of money in elections (a goal that probably necessitates a Supreme Court willing to reverse its insistence, in *Buckley v. Valeo,* on the free speech rights of wealth against the government's right to protect relatively equal access to public forums).[58] It also calls for expanding the opportunities for effective participation, encouraging local party organizations, political associations, and the skills and habits of democratic deliberation.[59]

Beyond laws and structures, however, democratic citizenship and politics rely heavily on democratic souls, on the moral qualities Tocqueville described as "habits of the heart."[60] In the contemporary quest for a public philosophy, this is a matter of controversy: many pluralists— and democratic theorists of other schools—argue that it is unnecessary and undesirable, as well as impossible, for Americans to expect common first principles or foundations. Such "nonfoundational" thinkers argue that we should accept the fact of diversity and different perspectives as a starting point, looking for public principles and policies to *emerge* from democratic debate and discussion, as the endpoints of a political process, subject to continuing challenge and reformulation rather than limiting preconditions.[61]

Yet theorists of this persuasion characteristically presume that politics will be inclusive, making room for all voices, and that speech will be civil, respecting (and possibly celebrating) the differences of others. Inclusive civility, however, is hardly a given in human affairs, and "nonfoundationalist" doctrines, on their own terms, provide no basis for regarding it as normative, beyond the very uncertain calculations of utility. In fact, "nonfoundational" ideas of deliberation *rely* on certain foundations and fundamentals, norms of inclusion and respect that derive from religious precepts like the Golden Rule (or, at least, their Kantian equivalents). Similarly, democratic institutions rest on a hard teaching: the egalitarian convention by which the minority, however wise or strong, agrees to be governed by the majority's vote. These convictions and conventions can never be taken for granted, and certainly not in our time.[62]

Samuel Bowles and Herbert Gintis point to a humanly natural basis for public philosophy, a disposition to cooperate and to be generous with one's fellows, a "strong reciprocity" that leads individuals to make sacrifices and to act against self-interest, narrowly defined, in the service of community. Bowles and Gintis emphasize that this is not altruism: human beings expect their fellows to make appropriate contributions to the common good. Recognizing that self-interest is *always* a temptation, and that it is sure to be the ruling principle of at least a minority, most people are acutely aware of the risk that "free riders"—both those who take too much and those who give too little, the "welfare cheat" and the tax-evading elite—will undermine public spirit. Liberals, at least in recent years, have underrated the extent to which an insistence on punishing free riders—on seeing contribution as a *duty*—is a vital element of civic generosity.[63]

But conservatives have their own purblindness. On the right, public intellectuals have been prone to argue that, if government would get out of the way, civil society would be revitalized and would be able to remoralize society in general. But the institutions of civil society, battered by social change, need to be helped, not left on their own. As Bowles and Gintis point out, greater social distance among people—and hence, any increase in the scale, diversity, or inequality of political society—makes it difficult for them to assert or protect common values, since they are dealing with others they don't know, and who cannot be controlled effectively by informal sanctions and rewards. In large and diverse societies, consequently, civil society cannot defend its own commonalities: it needs the formal sanctions and authority of government.[64] In its pursuit of justice, public philosophy necessarily involves a debate— the centerpiece of democratic contestation—about which contributions are most deserving. Its premise, however, is the duty and right of every citizen to make an appropriate contribution to the common life, a goal that includes the attempt to make good the shortcomings of the economy and society. It is the task of public philosophy, consequently, to assure and demand—for and from all of us in contemporary America—dignified work, a fair share of taxes, and the opportunity to serve. (Transforming Bill Clinton's rather anemic Americorps into a universal program of national service might be a place to begin.)[65]

Human beings are not born free, but indebted; their identities are more defined by what they owe that by what they own.[66] In that sense, the possibilities of human liberty—and the first principles of public philosophy—turn on our right to reduce that debt.

Notes

This essay was originally published as "The Search for a Public Philosophy," in *The Politics of Ideas: Intellectual Challenges Facing the American Political Parties*, ed. John Kenneth White and John Clifford Green (New York: State University of New York Press, 2001).

1. Michael Sandel, *Democracy's Discontents: America in Search of a Public Philosophy* (Cambridge, Mass.: Harvard University Press, 1996); John P. Diggins,

The Lost Soul of American Politics (Chicago: University of Chicago Press, 1986). The imagery of a New Rome among the American founders is described in James S. Young, *The Washington Community, 1800–1828* (New York: Columbia University Press, 1986).

2. Jean Bethke Elshtain, *Democracy on Trial* (New York: Basic Books, 1995).

3. Theodore J. Lowi, "Toward a Responsible Three-Party System," in Theodore J. Lowi and Joseph Romance, *A Republic of Parties: Debating the Two-Party System* (Lanham: Rowman and Littlefield, 1998), 3.

4. Mary Ann Glendon, *Rights Talk: The Impoverishment of Political Discourse* (New York: Basic Books, 1991).

5. Theodore J. Lowi, "Think Globally, Lose Locally," *Boston Review*, April/May 1998, 4–10.

6. Michael Sandel, "America's Search for a New Public Philosophy," *Atlantic Monthly*, March 1996, 58.

7. Walter Lippman, *The Phantom Republic* (New York: Macmillan, 1925).

8. Alan Wolfe, *One Nation After All* (New York: Viking, 1998).

9. Todd Gitlin, *The Twilight of Common Dreams* (New York: Henry Holt, 1995).

10. Madison's comments are made in *The Federalist*, #10. The reference to the "power house" is from Henry Adams, *The Education of Henry Adams* (Boston: Houghton Mifflin, 1961), 421.

11. John Locke, *A Letter concerning Toleration* (Indianapolis: Bobbs-Merrill, 1955), 52.

12. Art. 1, sec. 10; on the general point, see Wilson C. McWilliams, "In Good Faith: On the Foundations of American Politics," *Humanities in Society* 6 (1983): 32–35.

13. As Harvey Mansfield writes, "It can easily be in one's interest to accept satisfaction at the cost of one's freedom" whenever that freedom is "costly or irksome or dangerous." *America's Constitutional Soul* (Baltimore: Johns Hopkins University Press, 1991), 82.

14. John Locke, *The Reasonableness of Christianity*, ed. I. T. Ramsey (Stanford: Stanford University Press, 1958), 64.

15. Many of the founders, of course, believed in a "moral sense" or instinct, more or less inherent in the body. See Jefferson's letter to Peter Carr, August 10, 1787, and his letter to Thomas Law, June 13, 1814, in *Life and Selected Political Writings of Thomas Jefferson*, ed. Adrienne Koch and William Peden (New York: Modern Library, 1944), 430–31, 638–39.

16. *Notes on Virginia* and letter to John Jay, August 23, 1785, in *Life and Selected Writings of Thomas Jefferson*, 280, 377.

17. Letter to John Adams, October 28, 1813, in *Life and Selected Writings of Thomas Jefferson*, 633.

18. Aristotle, *Politics*, 1252b8–1253a3.

19. Strikingly, the Preamble to the Constitution refers to "posterity," but not to *family*.

20. Alexis de Tocqueville, *Democracy in America* (New York: Knopf, 1980), 2:121–25.

21. Wolfe, *One Nation After All;* Robert Bellah et al., *Habits of the Heart* (Berkeley and Los Angeles: University of California Press), 1985.

22. Hannah Arendt, *Crises of the Republic* (New York: Knopf, 1969), 69.

23. Ithiel deSola Pool, *Technologies without Boundaries* (Cambridge, Mass.: Harvard University Press, 1990); fixed forms and relations are visibly undermined; Marx and Engels wrote: "All that is solid melts into air." *The Communist Manifesto* (London: Penguin, 1985), 83.

24. Robert Putnam, "Bowling Alone: America's Declining Social Capital," *Journal of Democracy* 6 (1995): 65–78; Tocqueville, *Democracy in America,* 2:98–99.

25. John Dewey, *The Public and Its Problems* (New York: Holt, 1927).

26. Consider the Court's argument in *Wickard v. Filburn,* 317 U.S. 111 (1942).

27. Tocqueville, *Democracy in America,* 2:215–16.

28. Lowi, "Think Globally, Lose Locally," 10.

29. Barry Bluestone and Stephen Rose, "Overworked and Underemployed," *American Prospect,* March/April 1997, 59, 60, 67.

30. Kristin Downey Grimsley, "Leaner—and Definitely Meaner," *Washington Post National Weekly,* July 20–27, 1998, 21; W. Lance Bennett, "The UnCivic Culture: Communication, Identity and the Rise of Lifestyle Politics," *PS* 31 (1998): 750–53.

31. Bennett, "UnCivic Culture," 751.

32. Putnam, "Bowling Alone," 69; Bluestone and Rose, "Overworked and Underemployed," 69.

33. Jeff Gates, "The Ownership Solution," *Boston Review,* December 1998/January 1999, 32–33.

34. Mickey Kaus, *The End of Equality* (New York: Basic Books, 1992).

35. Gates, "The Ownership Solution," 33.

36. E. J. Dionne Jr., *They Only Look Dead: Why Progressives Will Dominate the Next Political Era* (New York: Simon and Schuster, 1996).

37. Robert Wiebe, *The Search for Order, 1877–1920* (New York: Hill and Wang, 1966).

38. Karl Polanyi, *The Great Transformation* (Boston: Beacon, 1957).

39. *The Communist Manifesto,* 83.

40. Bennett, "UnCivic Culture," 758.

41. Ronald Inglehart, *Modernization and Postmodernization* (Princeton: Princeton University Press, 1997) 304–5, 311.

42. Ibid., 295–96, 298–305, 307–23.

43. Jacques Ellul, *The Technological Society* (New York: Vintage, 1964), 208–18; James Lardner recently pointed out that radio, too, was acclaimed as a "flattener of hierarchy" that would provide "unprecedented access to information" and end isolation. "Ask Radio Historians about the Internet," *U.S. News and World Report,* January 25, 1999, 48.

44. Bennett, "UnCivic Culture," 745–47.

45. Gilles Lipovetsky, "May '68; or, The Rise of Transpolitical Individualism," trans. L. Maguire, in *New French Thought,* ed. Mark Lilla (Princeton: Princeton University Press, 1994), 214, 218.

46. Bennett, "UnCivic Culture," 755.

47. Benjamin Ginsberg and Martin Shefter, *Politics by Other Means* (New York: Basic Books, 1990).

48. Marc K. Landy and Martin A. Levin, eds., *The New Politics of Public Policy* (Baltimore: Johns Hopkins University Press, 1995).

49. John Zaller, "Monica Lewinsky's Contribution to Political Science," *PS* 31 (1998): 182–89.

50. The phrase is Theodore Lowi's. "Think Globally, Lose Locally," 8.

51. Pat Robertson, *The New World Order* (Dallas: Word, 1991). This helps explain the peculiar excess of right-wing reactionaries to Bill Clinton, raising that weak man to demonic stature.

52. The phrase is taken from Russell Kirk, *Beyond the Dreams of Avarice* (Chicago: Regnery, 1956).

53. Benjamin R. Barber, *Jihad vs. McWorld: How Globalism and Tribalism Are Reshaping the World* (New York: Ballantine, 1996). On European developments, see Roger Cohen, "A Matter of Trust for Europe," *New York Times,* January 31, 1999, WK1 (one of a pair of articles under the headline "Voters All Over Take the Wheel from Conservatives").

54. Lowi, "Think Globally, Lose Locally." Conservative recognition of the moral defects of the market is especially marked among the students of Leo Strauss.

55. Stephen Skowronek, "The Risks of 'Third-Way' Politics," *Society,* September/October 1996, 32–36. On American developments generally, see Richard L. Berke, "An Identity Crisis in the U.S.," *New York Times,* January 31, 1999, WK1 (the second of the paired articles mentioned in n. 53).

56. Rogers Smith, *Civic Ideals* (New Haven: Yale University Press, 1997); Amitai Etzioni, *The New Golden Rule: Community and Morality in Democratic Society* (New York: Basic Books, 1996).

57. Aristotle, *Politics,* 1279a11–1281a11.

58. *Buckley v. Valeo,* 424 U.S. 1 (1976); Scott Turow, "The Supreme Court's Twenty-Year-Old Mistake," *New York Times,* October 12, 1997, WK15.

59. For example, Amy Gutmann and Dennis Thompson, *Democracy and Disagreement* (Cambridge, Mass.: Harvard University Press, 1996).

60. Tocqueville, *Democracy in America,* 1:299.

61. Iris Marion Young, *Justice and the Politics of Difference* (Princeton: Princeton University Press, 1990), 227–28, 238–40.

62. Ibid., 191, 236; Smith, *Civic Ideals,* 486; Nancy Rosenblum, *Membership and Morals: The Personal Uses of Pluralism in America* (Princeton: Princeton University Press, 1998), 35.

63. Samuel Bowles and Herbert Gintis, "Is Equality Passé?" *Boston Review,*

December 1998/January 1999, 4–7; Stanley C. Brubaker, "Can Liberals Punish?" *American Political Science Review* 82 (1988): 821–36.

64. Bowles and Gintis, "Is Equality Passé?" 7–8.

65. For example, see Edmund Phelps, *Reworking Work* (Cambridge, Mass.: Harvard University Press, 1997).

66. Bertrand de Jouvenel, *Sovereignty,* trans. J. F. Huntington (Indianapolis: Liberty Fund, 1997), 316–17.

Toward Genuine Self-Government

It is no secret that Americans are wretchedly informed about public affairs. The New Millennium Project of the National Association of Secretaries of State found that only 25 percent of young citizens (ages eighteen to twenty-four) could correctly answer all three of the following questions: Who is the vice president of the United States? Who is the governor of your state? How long is the term for a member of the House of Representatives? And at the beginning of a recent American government class at my university, only 9 percent of students could name the chief justice of the Supreme Court; 54 percent, however, knew the president's pet.

But civic education is not primarily a matter of information. It is easy to imagine a master spy or a Professor Moriarty who would be wonderfully informed without satisfying the canons of good citizenship.

The problem of civic education, in the first instance, is affective and moral, and in that sense, it is less alarming that young Americans—and their elders—know relatively little about American public life than that they do not appear to care very much about it. In 1998, only a little over a quarter of college freshmen (26.7 percent) held that "keeping up to date with political affairs" was an important goal; in 1966, that figure was more than twice as high (57.8 percent).[1] At that, college students probably care more about government and public life than Americans in general.[2] Asked to identify the qualities of a good citizen, a substantial majority of Americans in a Public Agenda poll listed virtues that have little or no specific relation to the American regime—working for a living, being tolerant, speaking English or trying to learn it, and rising when the national anthem is played. Just over half indicated that a good citizen votes and accepts jury duty, at least some of the time. But *less* than half (48 percent) said that taking "no interest" in important public issues makes one a bad citizen, and not much more than a third (36 percent) felt that only a bad citizen "knows virtually nothing about America's history or founding fathers."[3] So understood, citizenship is primarily a private excellence, a virtue of subjects who obey and rely on law rather than of public persons who share in self-government.[4]

Any number of recent events have contributed to this disaffection—Vietnam, government's perceived domestic failures, the series of scandals around the presidency, globalization—all prompting the growing suspicion that government is either irrelevant or malign.[5] More fundamentally, however, it is only the latest chapter in a grander story, the struggle to maintain the balance Tocqueville saw in American culture between the "spirit of liberty" and the sense of obligation rooted in the "spirit of religion."[6]

From our earliest days, that struggle for America's political soul has been unusually dependent on texts and teaching. In the large and complicated republic of the framers' designing, national civic education has always necessarily been largely a matter of what we read or are told, rather than something learned through what we do or observe at first hand.[7]

It was a concern for teaching, after all, that overcame Madison's doubts about a Bill of Rights—that such "parchment barriers," virtually irrelevant to "real power," are ineffective precisely when they are most needed, when confronting a factional majority—in favor of the view that such provisions might "acquire by degrees the character of fundamental maxims of free government, and as they become incorporated with the National sentiment, counteract the impulses of interest and passion."[8]

Anti-Federalist writers had their own reasons for agreeing. A Bill of Rights, one wrote, could help young citizens "sustain the dignity of their being," even in a vast and perplexing republic.[9] (Both Madison and his sometime opponent were surely right: if there is one thing Americans know about our public life, it is that they have rights, even if they are only imperfectly aware of what those rights are.) The laws, in other words, are a textbook crucial in the training of our political sensibilities.

Any number of voices in the founding generation, however, thought such pedagogy was not enough. The Virginia Anti-Federalist "Denatus," for example, argued that the "first or second article" of the Constitution ought to have provided for the establishment of academies aimed to educate citizens "in the principles of morality, religion, jurisprudence and the art of war." The laws, in this view, needed to be supplemented by schools for the fuller shaping of civic spirit.[10]

Those who agreed with Denatus (they included a considerable number of Federalists) had at least an inkling of the process Tocqueville detected later on, the tendency of the "spirit of liberty," entrenched in the laws, to gain at the expense of the "spirit of religion" in shaping the "habits of the heart."[11]

Americans, Tocqueville noted, justified "almost all their actions" by reference to the principle of "self-interest rightly understood." In fact, they were often moved by generous impulses or public spirit, but they were "more anxious to do honor to their philosophy than to themselves." The philosophy underlying the laws, the doctrine that all human conduct springs from motives that are interested or self-regarding, was displacing the older teaching, silencing it in public language and perhaps in self-understanding. Tocqueville advised his readers to cherish the principle of self-interest rightly understood as an alternative to more radical forms of self-concern, fearing that the logic of mass democracy would ultimately confine Americans—in speech and in spirit—to the prison of the self.[12]

Preserving or rearticulating the second voice of American democracy, as Denatus realized, depends on the schools, and in those terms, teaching is a high and essential public office.

Today, however, it would be hard to argue that the schools acknowledge, let alone teach, the "principles of morality, religion, and jurisprudence," to say nothing of "the art of war." The moral language of higher education is largely confined to variations on individualism, from postmodernism on the left to libertarianism on the right. And correspondingly, an extraordinary amount of academic discussion takes it as given that laws and forms are the constructs of power, utilitarian at best and impositions at worst, so that citizenship and civic duty are not much more than a pose and a sham. There was remarkably little stir when Richard Cheney explained his lack of military service—even though he had no moral objection to any of America's involvements—by the fact that he had "other priorities" at the time. Right and left, the academic consensus apparently holds that it is normal, if not admirable, to minimize one's obligations; the natural course of things is to go your own way.[13]

Citizenship, by contrast, is at odds with individualism and with any view that sees values and virtues as only so many particularities and preferences. In civic education, as the ancients understood, learning how to be ruled comes before learning how to rule, among other reasons, because both involve constraint. Citizens are asked to see themselves as parts of a whole, defined not simply by their individual particularities or partisan loyalties—although both are inevitable and always part of the story—but by their larger relationship. And this requires the restraint of powerful, immediate impulses and feelings.[14]

In a higher sense, politics is natural to us, just as Aristotle said, but political conversation is certainly not spontaneous.[15] It includes people of differing ages and trades and educations, different ethnicities and genders and levels of beauty. It is, in other words, a discussion that almost certainly would never start—and certainly would not be sustained—without constraint and form.[16]

Even in small constituencies like those Tocqueville and the Anti-Federalists admired, democratic deliberation is an irksome discipline, literally a de-liberation. Among other things, it demands civility, attending to the sensibilities of the other at least as much as to those of the self. Even when, obeying an outraged inner nature, one rises in solitary protest, in the civic dimension of the act what matters is not what one says, but what the others *hear*.

Shrewdly, Aristotle compared politics to exercise, since the pains are certain and up front, and the gains are prospective and contingent.[17] That observation has a special truth in democracies. In the first place, democracy requires us to listen to many voices, so that democratic discussion is dead slow; in mastering Tocqueville's "art of association," a brilliant mind is less important than a durable derrière. Second, since democracy treats all voices as entitled to a hearing, it demands that we spend a good deal of time listening to fools. (Even the wrongheaded, in my experience, are easier to take than people who cannot follow the parliamentary situation: the third repetition of the question "What are we voting on now?" inspires thoughts of justifiable homicide.) In mass politics, of course, most of us cannot do anything *but* listen; our only alternative is to tune out altogether, which to many seems the only dignified course. To make matters worse, even in very local matters, politics involves technical issues and stupefying detail; a debate on the kinds and diameters of sewer pipe required to carry a given volume of effluent loses me even faster than Al Gore discussing the Dingell-Norwood Bill. And in the final affront, having suffered all the pains and frustrations of democratic politics, you are very likely to lose, and the more you care, the more it hurts. Even victories ordinarily require compromises and setbacks, and not always petty ones, so that triumph—especially in a great and diverse republic like ours—leaves a slightly bitter taste. Democratic politics, in other words, subjects us to fools, makes us feel foolish, and reminds us of our limited power and our very great vulnerability; the practice of citizenship offers mortal offense to amour propre.

Tocqueville's Americans, so caught up in public affairs, had few competing diversions other than religion. Yet even so, Tocqueville argued that, at first, they were driven into associations and collectivities by necessity, the risk of being ruled by worse people or of being left out of decisions touching some vital concern. Once in associations they found more positive satisfactions—political friendship, along with a measure of dignity and self-rule and a link to the higher levels of government. But it was only in those later stages that citizenship became a habit and a choice; it began, like most great disciplines, with constraint.[18]

By contrast, we swim in a rich stew of delights—television, year-round sports, gambling, rock concerts, even academic conferences—compared to which politics seems a drag. And localities—and for that matter, the national government—have only a diminished power to drive us into public forums.[19] We don't conscript any more: we ask for volunteers, appealing to impulses which are decent, but which are largely episodic, effective when they suit personal convenience. Americans are protected, or so they feel, by rights and by mobility, able to immunize themselves against public life or to escape from it into some private space or virtual reality.

Of course, this is largely an illusion, a kind of autoanesthesia. The private sphere contracts, Tocqueville taught us, precisely because the public sphere expands: genuine privacy is retreating before the intrusions of economic and technological interdependency.[20] But these are chains we do not see. Practice, especially in relatively good times, can't be relied on to drive many of us into citizenship; we will need to be drawn.

Americans, after all, are capable of considerable self-restraint when they feel the goal is worth it: millions of us are at least attempting to observe a regimen of diet and exercise, many for reasons of health, but legions because they admire strength and beauty and hope to acquire or preserve a measure of both. That aspiration is paralleled in politics: one need not agree with John F. Kennedy or admire him as a person to recognize that he brought magnetism and grace to the presidency, captivating a good part of a generation with the charms of public life.

Heroes are pretty thin on the contemporary political stage, but the yearning for them is there: witness the extraordinary response to the television program *West Wing*. For that matter, viewers, especially young Americans, were fascinated with the real but much less grand politics of *Survivor*, where the action emphasized factions and persuasions, each episode culminating in a vote and always confined by forms and rituals. The drama, however contrived, was a politics for important stakes in which the citizens knew they mattered.[21]

In both cases, the theme of the story is the art of rule, with all its possibilities and limitations, a craft we need to appreciate, if not to know firsthand. Few of us will ever be rulers, in the ordinary sense of the term. Only a fraction of us will ever hold public office, and most of those will be confined to duties that are administrative or petty. But for citizens, it isn't enough to be law-abiding: we are required to *evaluate* laws and rulers, and in voting—that moment's breath of rule—we stand outside the law, judging its adequacy.

Our experience offers only deficient preparation for that task. We tend to see and judge leaders in terms of the concerns and temptations that dominate our largely private lives, primarily the control of avarice and sexual desire. When we say that a public official is "corrupt," we are almost always referring to some fiscal impropriety, just as, when we accuse a leader of "immorality," we are probably speaking of sexual misconduct. Obviously, these things happen, and in very high places. But public life has temptations that private life barely knows: the pride of office, for example, or that yearning for popularity that prompts the most common failing of democratic leaders, telling us the falsehood we want to hear in place of the uncomfortable truth.

The media, the greatest rival of the schools, only exaggerate this problem. They speak to us, on the whole, in private settings where private issues are uppermost, and, accordingly, in private terms. Throughout the Lewinsky scandal, sizeable majorities consistently told pollsters that they wanted less coverage of the affair, convinced that the story was damaging our institutions. But that was the citizenry speaking as *public* persons; the media knew that as private persons, we would not be able to resist that tawdry saga, with all its salacious details. And the result was pretty much what the public had feared.[22]

The schools, in contrast to the media, have this great advantage as civic educators: that the classroom is to some extent a public place where our private voices—still strong—speak a little more softly. Contemporary social science, of course, is all too apt to forego that opportunity. "Rational choice" theorizing in political science, for example, cannot explain, on its own terms, why citizens bother to vote; framed by methodological individualism, it slights or ignores civic affiliation and obligation. Even more of my colleagues, moreover, are caught up in the effort to predict political events, and while such studies are useful, they speak to citizens essentially in their roles as subjects or spectators, not to the side of citizenship that involves rule. If you are a voter or a juror—to say nothing of a legislator or a judge—being able to predict how you are *likely* to vote does not necessarily help in deciding how you *ought* to vote. At best, like being aware of your prejudices, it clears some obstacles from the path to judgment. Citizenship in the high sense has to come from somewhere else.

Fortunately, however, teachers can bring their students to great texts that address the burdens and glories of rule from the inside, whether written by people who had experienced command—Sophocles, for example, or Xenophon or Augustine—or legislators like Burke and Madison, or people who moved familiarly in ruling circles, Shakespeare, or Plato, that descendant of kings, or Aristotle, who taught Alexander. All of them speak to the political animal in our souls, and the civic task of contemporary education is to give that animal the words and speech appropriate to a citizen.

Notes

This essay was originally published as "Toward Genuine Self-Government," *Academic Questions: A Publication of the National Association of Scholars* 15, no. 1 (2001/2002).

1. Ethan Bronner, "College Freshman Aiming for High Marks in Income," *New York Times*, January 12, 1998, A14.

2. Adam Clymer, "College Students Not Drawn to Voting or Politics, Poll Shows," *New York Times*, January 12, 2000, A14.

3. Richard Morin, "What Makes a 'Bad' American," *Washington Post National Weekly*, November 30, 1998, 35.

4. This view has been articulated in high places: consider the Supreme Court's opinion in *Wisconsin v. Yoder*, 402 U.S. 205 (1972).

5. W. Lance Bennett, "The UnCivic Culture: Communication, Identity and the Rise of Lifestyle Politics," *PS* 31 (1998): 750–53; see also my *The Politics of Disappointment* (New York: Chatham House, 1995).

6. Alexis de Tocqueville, *Democracy in America* (New York: Knopf, 1980), 1:43.

7. *The Federalist*, #63; Tocqueville stressed the educational role of local democratic practice, but he commented that "instruction powerfully contributes to the support of the democratic republic." *Democracy in America*, 1:317–18.

8. Letter to Thomas Jefferson, October 17, 1788, in *The Writings of James Madison*, ed. Gaillard Hunt (New York: Putnam's, 1900–1910), 5:271–75.

9. "Letter from a Delegate Who Has Catched Cold to the *Virginia Independent Chronicle*," June 25, 1788, in *The Complete Anti-Federalist*, ed. Herbert J. Storing (Chicago: University of Chicago Press, 1981), 5:273.

10. "Address by Denatus," *Virginia Independent Chronicle*, June 11, 1788, in Storing, *The Complete Anti-Federalist*, 5:264.

11. *Democracy in America,* 1:246; Americans, Tocqueville observed, "transport the habits of public life into their manners in private." Ibid., 1:318; the phrase "habits of the heart" is taken from 1:299.

12. Ibid., 2:122, 99.

13. Bending with the wind, the army's latest recruitment slogan retreats from self-interest rightly understood ("Be all that you can be") to the starkly individualistic "An Army of One." But as Lucian Truscott points out, the motive for joining the army rarely has much to do with individualism or money: much more commonly, it is "a desire to serve your country" and the attractions of being part of a corps. "Marketing an Army of Individuals," *New York Times,* January 13, 2001, A23. (Compare, by contrast, the Marines' offer of an elite fraternity—"the few, the proud, the Marines.")

14. Pairing in the family, Aristotle comments, reflects an "earlier and more necessary" aspect of human nature than politics, though naturally subsidiary to it. *Ethics,* VIII.12.

15. Aristotle, *Politics,* 1253a2; *Ethics,* IX.9.

16. Our greatest political conversation, in Plato's *Republic,* is possible only because Socrates is compelled, by a playful threat of force—and, much more, by his own sense of obligation—to attend a dinner party at the house of Cephalus. Once he's there, of course, the charm of the conversation is such—here our higher nature comes into play—that the young men forget all about the vaguely orgiastic parade in tribute to the goddess Bendis that was a good part of the reason for the party in the first place.

17. *Politics,* 1288b10–40. Aristotle hints that political science is more theoretical and less authoritative than gymnastics, since both the best regime and regimes that impose some limiting assumption or condition rank higher among its concerns.

18. *Democracy in America,* 2:105. Leon Panetta, whose Panetta Institute promotes student involvement in public life, recently echoed Tocqueville: "Someone has to push them on stage before they learn to enjoy it." Clymer, "College Students Not Drawn to Voting or Politics."

19. School curricula are sometimes an exception: any rumor that *Catcher in the Rye* is about to be added to—or removed from—the required reading list still seems to have the power to increase public attendance at school board meetings; creationism is probably even more reliable.

20. *Democracy in America,* 2:215–16.

21. By contrast, *Big Brother,* which attracted viewers overseas, did badly in the United States: decisions on that show were made by an anonymous, call-in public, a mass politics in which citizenship was largely effaced.

22. John R. Zaller, "Monica Lewinsky's Contribution to Political Science," *PS* 31 (1998): 182–89.

Democratic Multiculturalism

Historically, multiculturalism has often not been associated with democracy; more often, it has been the practice of empires and hegemonies, the condition of a policy of divide and rule.[1] In fact, multiculturalism is not easily compatible with democracy: Yugoslavia managed, more or less, as a one-party autocracy, but it proved unable to survive democratization, and it would be easy to add other painful examples.

Nor is this surprising: a grand tradition of political theory holds that democracy requires a high level of trust in one's fellow citizens, or at least a broad sphere of the taken-for-granted in civil life. As in the New England of Tocqueville's describing, an *open* politics presumes a more or less closed *society*.[2]

The Federalist's argument for a large and diverse republic, of course, reverses this order of things. It prescribes social openness of a fairly radical sort, making it a first principle to protect the differences in our faculties and opinions. The new order of the American republic, consequently, is not defined by usages and habits but by forms and laws.[3] The framers' tolerance did have limits: they assumed and relied on a people who observed the decencies and for whom a word was a bond. At bottom, however, they afforded us a relatively open society on the basis of a *politics* that is closed in critical respects. The Constitution's constraints and barriers only follow the even stricter teaching of the Declaration of Independence, according to which we are allowed to calculate our interests and to bargain them away, but our rights are inalienable, immune to the discountings of interest or culture.[4]

It is worth remembering that there were serious conflicts of culture in eighteenth-century America, most evident in the problem of slavery—for slavery, as Anne Norton reminds us, did create a culture, and a tenacious one—but also simmering in the relations between Europeans and aboriginal peoples, in the conflict between religion and secularism, and in the largely forgotten animosities among sects.[5] From the beginning, multiculturality has tested the Constitution and the laws, raising the question of whether conflicts between cultures can be subordinated to and confined within democratic forms or whether "culture wars" will be fought with weapons other than words and votes.[6]

Slavery, of course, proved too much for democratic politics, and Tocqueville, who feared as much, was also too close to the mark in his pessimism about race. But Tocqueville was impressed by the American entente with religion, especially because the republic seemed on the way to an accommodation with Roman Catholicism; and his argument has a good deal to say about the conditions of successful multiculturality.

Tocqueville observed that any religious doctrine (and, he might have added, any culture) has a political tendency that will assert itself if unchecked. Circumstances, however, can alter the *effects* of belief, its expression in day-to-day life. Thus, despite its aristocratic structure and historic affinities, Roman Catholicism in America had some sympathy for republican government, just as most Catholics supported the Democratic Party, if only because, en masse, American Catholics were poor.[7]

Confrontation with new circumstances unsettles authority and forces a belief or culture to abandon the habitual for the more or less conscious and chosen, separating those things that seem essential—that must be remembered, and retained—from those that can be safely left behind.[8] The new world of Tocqueville's discerning, of course, challenges all ways and faiths to accommodate themselves to democratic principles. Prudence dictates that the majority not be opposed except in vital matters, and even then, with the foreknowledge that defeat is likely: "In ages of equality, kings may often command obedience, but the majority always commands belief."[9] That counsel is even more urgent in a country like the United States, where democracy has shaped the laws. Religions and cultures are fortunate, consequently, if their tenets are at least compatible with democratic doctrine. Without that consonance, they face political society on an implicit field of battle; and even those, like Tocqueville, who are confident that they can predict the winner may regret the war.

In Tocqueville's view, Catholics were among the lucky, because America imposed only a kind of purification on a faith already egalitarian at root. As Tocqueville explained it, amid the unequal societies of the feudal era, responding to a world of nations, castes, and classes, the church—while clinging to the universal sovereignty of God—had "improperly enhanced" the importance of "divine agents."[10] America, Tocqueville claimed, had allowed and compelled the church to return to first things, and especially to an emphasis on human unity. (By contrast, Tocqueville thought that any relation between democracy and Islam would be more troubled, because so much traditional legal and political teaching is included in the Koran, at the heart of the creed; and there is very little, so far, to suggest that he was not right.)[11]

Moreover, among Catholics, American laws were nurturing new political beliefs. Catholics had accepted a religiously neutral government partly from necessity and partly to protect themselves against old animosities, but Tocqueville found them increasingly positive in their support for a separation of church and state. Even the zealous Father Mullon told Tocqueville and Beaumont that state support for religion was harmful; and, startlingly, the vicar-general claimed that "enlightenment" was favorable to the "religious spirit."[12]

As Catholicism was "modified" in a democratic and republican direction, Tocqueville contended, there was a reciprocal growth of tolerance between Catholics and non-Catholics, a softening of the boundaries between communions. Not that Catholicism had dissolved into indistinction: its rites and beliefs still seemed bizarre to the Protestant majority. But, as Tocqueville saw it, the church was winning a respected place in American political life, with more promise for the future.[13]

Uncharacteristically, Tocqueville was overoptimistic: memories of the Reformation remained a fault line in American party politics at least until 1960, along with the even more tenacious legacy of slavery and the Civil War.[14] Yet partisan conflicts, as George Washington Plunkitt reminded us, mark democracy's ascendancy over cultures; and in the long term, Tocqueville seems to have been right in thinking that he had discerned a successful story in the American politics of culture.[15]

What his argument shows us, however, is stern as well as sunny. Economic and social circumstances, especially well-being, can combine with cultural compatibility to make matters much less painful; but in the end, democracy can accommodate a culture only to the extent it accepts the sovereignty of democratic laws, and hence the certainty of at least some cultural attenuation. In America, all cultures and faiths—the established as well as the excluded—are caught up in an ongoing redefinition in relation to the laws and to each other, a process of learning, forgetting, and selectively remembering that lays down both the boundaries of community and the civil meaning of the term "American."[16]

Since, as a rule, the Constitution insists on an individual's right to leave faith or community behind, the hold of such cultures depends on persuasion and social sanctions, and especially on an early education capable of armoring the soul against the power of majority opinion. In critical respects, consequently, a multicultural politics is always a politics of schooling. As institutions, the schools are a proving ground, for there, if not before, the public can make itself heard. (These days, of course, the media insert their "hidden curriculum" much earlier and more pervasively.)[17] In the dialogue between the public and the cultures, an element of multiculturalism is only good manners, an acknowledgement of one's audience that schools commonly have tried to practice. But contemporary multiculturalism goes farther: up to a point, it seeks to enlist public authority on the side of the cultures—though not, significantly, on the side of faith.

For most of its contemporary defenders, multiculturalism is only a means in the service of a generous, democratic end: their real goal is inclusion, the hope of drawing new groups and cultures into a respected place in a strengthened civic life. As multiculturalists observe, there are cracks in some of the old pillars of American civic education. In lean economic times, there are no guarantees of the assurance of work at socially adequate wages that Jefferson saw as the right bower in the game of civic dignity.[18] And multiculturalists are even moved by the fact that the economy and the media are fragmenting communities and cultures, muting the second voice of America's grand dialogue in favor of an increasingly radical individualism on the one hand and tyranny of the majority on the other.[19] Multiculturalism, in this view, is an attempt to check disintegration and to promote a political pluralism in the image of Randolph Bourne's celebrated essay "Trans-National America."[20]

Notice at the outset, however, that this sort of multiculturalism regards a broadly democratic politics not as one culture among many, but as a superior standard entitled to rule. That assumption is reflected in the common tendency to slide over or suppress the nondemocratic aspects of the cultures being recognized, implicitly rejecting whatever is incompatible with a democratic life and creed. (I will have more to say about this later on.) And, of course, commitment to multiculturalism is ordinarily accompanied by the insistence that racism, sexism, homophobia, and the like are thoroughly unacceptable. Multiculturalism aspires to substitute a salad bowl for the melting pot, but—as the metaphor indicates—it still looks for a politics enclosed by a democratic orthodoxy.

Yet in their thinking about democracy, multiculturalists incline to focus on the social and the cultural, and to slight democratic *institutions*—a tendency that is especially unfortunate given the close relationship between the Constitution and the very idea of a multicultural republic. In fact, the multicultural persuasion is apt to stress the presence of slavery and the absence of women in the Constitution, or to argue that even the proclamation of natural equality in the Declaration of Independence refers only to "men," and implicitly only to white men, and to conclude that the Declaration and the Constitution reflect only the culture and interests of European males in the then-dominant class.

A good deal of this is simply silly. There is ample evidence, for example, that the Declaration of Independence's affirmation of equality was understood to refer to all races, and that the accommodation with slavery—made necessary, paradoxically, by the multicultural goal of including the South in the Union—was regarded as a violation of natural right. Consider the exchange in South Carolina, when one legislator asked that stock-in-trade Anti-Federalist question, "Why was not this Constitution ushered in with a bill of rights?" Charles Cotesworth Pinckney answered that, among other reasons, "Such bills generally begin with declaring that all men are by nature born free. Now, we should make the declaration with very bad grace, when a large part of our property consists in men who are actually born slaves."[21]

Even where the multiculturalist critique tells us something important about the Constitution, as it does by pointing to oppressions based on race and gender, it underrates the importance of constitutional forms. The norm of equality makes violations of that rule anomalous, things that have to be euphemized or explained. The exceptions are constantly criticized by the rule, which by setting a direction can become, as Harvey Mansfield observes, "the cause of going if not getting there."[22]

Democracy, moreover, is a hard school, and the culture of democracy depends on forms, especially in a large republic. Its cornerstone, majority rule, depends on the form by which every vote is treated as equal; similarly, the vast majority of us can have a voice in public councils only through the form of representation, determined in districts and by election. Even our efforts to acquire a more substantial voice through participation requires the "art of association," and hence the discipline of Roberts' Rules or some other form of order.[23] At best, our politics involves frustrations and indignities, and rapid economic change and the resulting disorder of society weaken the compensations of private life. Americans are eager for a kind of strong government, but their support for democratic institutions is dangerously thin.[24] Multiculturalists, the champions of minorities, have good reason to give more—and more serious—attention to the institutional frame of American democratic life.

It is a far more serious problem, however, that democratic multiculturalists are tempted to adopt, as a weapon of convenience against established America, the doctrine of the *equality of cultures,* forgetting that the enemy of my enemy is not necessarily my friend.[25] This philosophic multiculturalism holds that cultures are incommensurable, "separate realities" or "stories," so that there can be no ranking of cultures or the comparative excellence of their parts. And for democratic multiculturalists, that teaching involves at least two towering problems.

In the first place, it disdains cultures themselves, for on their own terms, cultures engage in just this sort of comparison and ranking. When Marc Swartz studied Truk, early in his distinguished career, he expected the islanders to be ethnocentric, proclaiming their ways superior to all others. He found, however, that Trukese often expressed admiration for American technology and deprecated their own crafts. At the same time, the Trukese to whom Swartz talked were shocked by his accounts of family life in America, and especially by the fact that he was not expected, periodically, to work for his brother-in-law, reasoning their own ways were more likely to unify families (a conclusion that seems tenable, to say the least.) The Trukese, in other words, did not see cultures as monads, each locked into the island of its own uniqueness, but as more or less effective answers to human problems.[26] In the same way, Michael Herzfeld observes that the Cretan villagers he studied understand the world on the basis of a "folk theory," which includes ideas of what it means to be a good man (or, to be more exact, to be good at *being* a man). The superiority of one's self, one's village, or one's nation, in these terms, is inseparable from excellence in fulfilling norms that are asserted as universals.[27] Even a culture that maintains that "our blood is superior to yours" thinks we can be measured by the same rule. Great cultures instruct and challenge us precisely because they ask, and offer compelling answers, to the questions "What is human? And what is the best life?" To take cultures seriously is to recognize that such encounters lead to arguments and point toward philosophy, just as diversity is only humanity in masquerade.

Second, a belief in the equality of *cultures* is at odds with the principle of *equality.* Plenty of cultures, after all, include a hierarchy of castes or classes or teach a hankering after dominion, to say nothing of racism and sexism. To support democratic equality is to maintain that, in this respect, some creeds and cultures are better and others worse: even the secular spirits among the framers, for example, were inclined to find good words for Christianity—whatever their quarrels with it—because of its devotion to egalitarian teaching in the realm of the spirit.[28] On its own terms, equality is a ruling standard, entitled to judge the cultures, weighing their customs in the scales of nature.

As I have observed, because most multiculturalists are democrats at bottom, they are tempted or disposed to discount any antidemocratic aspects they meet in a culture. But the fostering of illusions aside, such "playful multiculturalism"—the term is David Carlin's—loses precisely what is best in a confrontation with a profound and unfamiliar teaching: its capacity to shake our complacency, to force us to articulate our first principles, and in general to make us think more seriously about political things. Fuzzing the debate also obscures the likelihood that American citizenship is incompatible with at least some aspects of any ethnic tradition, with the consequence that such citizenship requires that a great deal of any heritage be left behind—a hard truth, but a necessary one for democratic life, and not only in such obvious cases as the Irish and the South Slavs.[29] G. K. Chesterton put democratic multiculturalism in perspective when, not altogether playfully, he likened the United States to the Spanish Inquisition, because while America is not entitled to exclude per se a Catholic or a Muslim, a Japanese or a Zulu, it has both a right and a duty to reject any challenge to equality as the ruling principle of public life.[30]

And while, unlike the inquisitors, we are not allowed to burn the heterodox—the self-immolation of the Branch Davidians constrains me to add "at least not on purpose"—it is incumbent on us to recognize that the "equality of cultures" is a rival principle, one that asserts its superiority over democracy, which it reduces to one culture among many. In fact, it regards *all* cultures as decisively inferior to the enlightened perspective that sees them as no more than a kind of entertaining storytelling. In the view of those Carlin calls "grave multiculturalists," the real title to rule rests with nihilists, happy or otherwise, who recognize that true ranking of human understanding.[31]

It is a troubled time for the republic, and we have every reason to draw on what is best in all our cultures and traditions—including, if it needs to be said, voices from the underside and from new or neglected corners of human life. (Among many possibilities, I am thinking of Maxine Hong Kingston's *The Woman Warrior* and Carlos Bulosan's remarkable *America Is in the Heart*.)[32] But when economic circumstances are not cheering and the compatibility of cultures is imperfect, even more than usual the possibilities of multicultural democracy depend on the framing strength of the Constitution and the laws. For democratic multiculturalists, no imperative is greater than the need to rebuild the institutions that connect citizens with their government, and with them, a politics guided by the proposition that all human beings are created equal.[33]

Notes

This essay was originally published as "Democratic Multiculturalism," in *Multiculturalism and American Democracy* (Lawrence: University Press of Kansas, 1998).

1. Among modern examples, British India comes to mind, especially because the British so often justified their rule as essential to multicultural peace. Ironically, those who are attracted to the language of "Hegemon" and "Other" tend to pass lightly over these connections between multiculturalism and elite rule, although, as I will be arguing, there is a sense in which it is not ironic after all.

2. Alexis de Tocqueville, *Democracy in America*, trans. Henry Reeve (New York: Knopf, 1980), 1:43. See also Joshua Miller, *The Rise and Fall of Democracy in Early America, 1630–1789* (University Park: Pennsylvania State University Press, 1991), 21–49.

3. Despite anxieties about immigrants, which found expression in the early naturalization laws, the Constitution's requirements for habituation are extremely modest. The debate in the Convention is instructive. See James Madison, *Notes of Debates in the Federal Convention of 1787* (Athens: Ohio University Press, 1966), 409–11.

4. Harvey C. Mansfield Jr., *America's Constitutional Soul* (Baltimore: Johns Hopkins University Press, 1991), 82.

5. Anne Norton, *Alternative America: A Reading of Antebellum Political Culture* (Chicago: University of Chicago Press, 1986).

6. Part of the contemporary version of this test is discussed in James D. Hunter, *Culture Wars: The Struggle to Define America* (New York: Basic Books, 1991).

7. Alexis de Tocqueville, *Journey to America*, ed. J. P. Mayer (New Haven: Yale University Press, 1962), 150.

8. Tocqueville, *Democracy in America*, 2:25–26. Tocqueville noticed a tendency among Catholic clergy to emphasize the "spirit" rather than the "letter" of the law. Ibid., 2:27.

9. Ibid., 2:26.

10. Ibid., 2:23–24.

11. Ibid., 2:23. While Christianity includes political teachings, John Hallowell wrote, it "is not itself a political philosophy or an economic program." *Main Currents in Modern Political Thought* (New York: Holt, Rinehart, and Winston, 1950), 692.

12. Tocqueville, *Journey to America*, 33, 206, 257.

13. Ibid., 59–60, 236–37; and Tocqueville, *Democracy in America*, 2:29–30.

14. Samuel P. Hays, "Political Parties and the Community-Society Contin-

uum," in *The New American Party System,* ed. William N. Chambers and Walter D. Burnham (New York: Oxford University Press, 1967), 152–81; V. O. Key, "The Future of the Democratic Party," *Virginia Quarterly* 28 (1952): 161–75; and John H. Schaar and Wilson C. McWilliams, "Uncle Sam Vanishes," *New University Thought* 1 (1961): 61–68.

15. William Riordon, *Plunkitt of Tammany Hall* (New York: Dutton, 1963), 13.

16. For example, in 1993, the Ancient Order of Hibernians won the right to exclude Irish gays and lesbians from the St. Patrick's Day parade in New York, arguing that the holiday is distinctively Catholic. Yet only a few Americans remember the conflict of Green and Orange, and to most of those who do, it seems curmudgeonly to wear Protestant colors—as do I—on March 17.

17. Uri Bronfenbrenner, "Contexts of Child Rearing," *American Psychologist* 34 (1979): 844–50. Of course, communities can create their own schools as supplements to public education or as alternatives to it. But the requirement of accreditation means that public doctrine cannot be altogether excluded.

18. Letter to John Adams, October 28, 1813, in *Life and Selected Writings of Jefferson,* ed. Adrienne Koch and William Peden (New York: Modern Library, 1944), 633.

19. Robert Bellah et al., *Habits of the Heart: Individualism and Commitment in American Life* (Berkeley and Los Angeles: University of California Press, 1985).

20. Randolph Bourne, "Trans-National America," *Atlantic Monthly,* July 1916, 86–97.

21. Cited in Robert M. Weir, "South Carolina: Slavery and the Structure of the Union," in *Ratifying the Constitution,* ed. Michael Allen Gillespie and Michael Lienesch (Lawrence: University Press of Kansas, 1989), 222.

22. Mansfield, *America's Constitutional Soul,* 12.

23. Tocqueville, *Democracy in America,* 2:102–5, 109–10.

24. See my essay "The Meaning of the Election," in Gerald M. Pomper et al., *The Election of 1992* (Chatham: Chatham House, 1993), 194–97.

25. This is an old temptation to which—as Eric Goldman observed—the American reform tradition is particularly subject. *Rendezvous with Destiny* (New York: Knopf, 1952). It is, of course, not confined to reformers or to America: "Are you secretly, then," an anguished Demea asks belatedly, "a more dangerous enemy than Cleanthes himself?" David Hume, *Dialogues concerning Natural Religion,* in *Hume: Selections,* ed. Charles W. Hendel (New York: Scribner's, 1927), 382.

26. Marc Swartz, "Negative Ethnocentrism," *Journal of Conflict Resolution* 5 (1961): 79.

27. Michael Herzfeld, *The Poetics of Manhood* (Princeton: Princeton University Press, 1985).

28. For example, Jefferson's letter to Benjamin Rush, April 21, 1803, in *Life and Selected Writings of Jefferson,* 566–70.

29. Compare Tocqueville's description in *Democracy in America,* 1:7.

30. G. K. Chesterton, *What I Saw in America* (London: Hodder and Stoughton, 1922), 7.

31. David Carlin, "Let Them Eat Cake: A Love Letter to Multiculturalists," *Commonweal,* April 23, 1993, 9–10.

32. Maxine Hong Kingston, *The Woman Warrior* (New York: Vintage, 1975); Carlos Bulosan's *America Is in the Heart,* originally published in 1943, was reprinted by the University of Washington Press in 1973.

33. For some suggestions, see my essay "Tocqueville and Responsible Parties: Individualism, Partisanship, and Citizenship in America," in *Challenges to Party Government,* ed. John K. White and Jerome Mileur (Carbondale: Southern Illinois University Press, 1992), 190–211.

Critical Rebound

Why America Needs a Catholic Recovery

Begin with the Augustinian truth: the Catholic Church, like its rivals, aspires to speak of and for the City of God, but it must speak in and to the City of Man. The transcendent is its reason for living, but it must live in order to fulfill that reason. Compelled to adapt to the temporalities, religion must also be watchful lest it become simply a function of time and place.[1] If a church accommodates too much to society, it loses its distinctive character, and along with it any strong sense of community or claim on the identity of its members. But if it makes the social cost of membership too high, a church risks shrinking to the dimensions of a sect.[2] At least implicitly, religion bargains with society, distinguishing between the first principles that are the perennial heart of its faith and the teachings and disciplines that it can de-emphasize or abandon in response to new circumstances.[3]

The current clergy sex abuse scandals represent the most severe crisis in the history of the American Catholic Church, calling, in some measure, its bargains with society and with its own membership into question.[4] American Catholics must hope for a season of atonement, knowing that this will bring turbulence and pain. Yet all Americans have a stake in the outcome: the church's future in this red-dawning century is inseparable from that of the republic.

Alexis de Tocqueville once observed that, despite Catholicism's aristocratic structure and affinities, the American Catholic Church had embraced political democracy, and American Catholics were "the most republican and the most democratic class in the United States."[5] In part, this was attributable to interest: a minority, and the object of suspicion and ancient animosity, Catholics took refuge in laws protecting religious liberty and separating church and state.[6] Similarly, since most Catholics were at the low end of the income scale, they were natural democratic partisans. But Tocqueville also discerned a more fundamental compatibility between Catholicism and democracy.[7]

Every faith, Tocqueville argued, has an inner logic deriving from its first principles that will make itself felt even when it is overborne by circumstance. During the Middle Ages, he contended, the church was impelled to shape its institutions for a world of classes and castes, so that it "improperly enhanced" the authority of its "divine agents."[8] However, the church never wholly lost the egalitarian core of Christian teaching.[9] America's insistent democracy allowed and compelled Catholicism to return to first things, a pattern Tocqueville discerned in the early half of the nineteenth century in the tendency among the American clergy to stress the spirit and not the letter of faith and law.[10] As Tocqueville saw it, in other words, American democracy was liberating the church from its historical distortions and returning Catholicism to its original vision—and in the process, gaining patriots and citizens.[11]

None of this implied any formal democratization of the church or a lessening of episcopal authority, and Tocqueville had no notion of the possibility of a married clergy or the ordination of women or any of the similar reforms under discussion today. Rather, he spoke of Catholics as "submissive and sincere," devoted to a faith that disposed them to obedience, but not to inequality. And he also detected a change in the church's tone and ways.[12] The "habits of public life," Tocqueville noted in another context, tend to be introduced into private manners.[13] That dynamic promised a disposition, however hesitantly applied, to attend to lay opinion and the societies of the faithful that have been a feature of American Catholic history.

Tocqueville carried his argument to a vision of Catholics moving soon into the mainstream of American civic life. About that he was uncharacteristically overoptimistic.[14] Immigration heightened anxieties about Catholic intentions and power, and Catholics, in turn, became more protective of their communities and communions.[15] Catholicism remained a fault line in American party politics at least until 1960, but even during difficult times Tocqueville's main argument held: Catholics were steady champions of democracy and American institutions.[16]

Contemporary America, moreover, realizes Tocqueville's vision. Catholicism is increasingly audible as a "public religion," offering a cultural option in American political life.[17] It is probably the most articulate communitarian voice in our politics, upholding claims of a "consistent ethic of life" in a moral community.[18] Moreover, Catholics are grand advocates for equality, the republic's moral foundation, at a time when it needs defenders. Despite the obvious advances in equalizing races and genders, equality today as a human, universal given remains desperately embattled.[19] Meanwhile, in the academy, the relativists and postmodernists reign and are engrossed with contexts and, hence, the differences of history, culture, and perspective. And in the practice of politics, equality confronts titanic and growing inequalities of wealth and power. Democracy, Aristotle observed, sees a life freely devoted to the common good as the greatest contribution to community.[20] September 11, 2001, taught us that democratic lesson: community is a fact, and the heroes are not those who lost the most money, but those who gave their lives. No magistracy in America offers better instruction on that point than American Catholicism.

It is a mark of the authenticity of Catholic social and political teaching that it is uncomfortable with the country's major parties and all ideologies. "Being a Catholic liberal or a Catholic conservative," columnist E. J. Dionne wrote during the 2000 campaign, "inevitably means having a bad conscience about something."[21] That ambiguity points to the crucial role Catholics are playing in our politics: As Dionne may have anticipated, Catholics were divided just about fifty-fifty in the election of 2000, and even marginal success in the competition for Catholic allegiances is likely to tip the balance of electoral power in the immediate future.

Yet the "mainstreaming" of American Catholicism comes with two very American price tags, both of which are evident in the church's present travail. In the first place, Catholicism can no longer count on the defensive solidarity associated with an embattled subculture. The differences among Catholics—always an element of Catholic history in the United States—can be expected to become sharper, reflecting the "culture wars" that are dividing all the great American confessions. The church can expect changes in its ethnic composition, increasing differences in the education and class of its membership, and widening variations in the extent to which communicants will follow this or that teaching. At the same time, globalization means a more immediate relation to the dazzling plurality of the church's international communion. All of these developments underline the hierarchy's responsibility in preserving, and if necessary reweaving, the fabric of unity.[22]

But the second cost of full inclusion in American civic culture has been a decline in the automatic deference that clerical leaders once received. Tocqueville saw American Catholics as "submissive believers," but a great number of today's communicants look positively feisty—including, paradoxically, those who regard themselves as conservatives and the special defenders of churchly authority.[23] An increase in the practical influence of the laity is in the cards: the only questions are what form this will take and how far it will extend.[24]

Nevertheless, the hierarchy, duly chastened, is indispensable to a high Catholic mission in the spiritual life of American democracy.[25] Famously, Tocqueville traced the character of American civilization to a balance between the "spirit of liberty" and the "spirit of religion."[26] But much as he admired that equilibrium, he expected that, with law and the marketplace in support, liberty would gain at the expense of religion in the habits of American hearts.

Tocqueville held religion to be "the most precious bequest of aristocratic ages," a fragile inheritance that teaches democracy the language of true nobility.[27] Hence his warning about introducing new religions into America, where lacking the ballast of habit and tradition they would be caught up by the current of individualism. And he was concerned for the old faiths as well, noting that the Protestant reliance on individual conscience would work in combination with the law's "spirit of liberty" to undermine religious education generally, leaving Americans without serious spiritual discipline.[28]

Americans, he observed, on the one hand were prone to secular individualism, afflicted by restlessness and "strange melancholy," often drawn to hazy pantheism; on the other hand, they sometimes leaned toward an excessive and fanatical spirituality that was likely to go beyond proper bounds into "religious insanity."[29] The description has not lost force over the years.

The Catholic Church offers an alternative precisely because it retains an institutional link to "aristocratic ages." Tocqueville's description of American Catholics—"the most submissive believers and the most independent citizens"—strikingly parallels the qualities he had earlier assigned to Puritans: a "passive though . . . voluntary obedience" in the spiritual and moral sphere and "an independence scornful of experience and jealous of all authority" in politics.[30] Tocqueville was suggesting that while Catholics could not have created free institutions in America, they are more suited to maintain them, since the church's authoritative institutions are relatively less exposed to individualism and spiritual indiscipline, the rising dangers of his time and ours.[31]

Tocqueville could still assume, as had the framers, that religion was a source of moral unity for Americans.[32] In contemporary America, by contrast, the definition of religion has become very expansive indeed; citizens tell pollsters that they believe in God, but about an eighth of these self-proclaimed believers declare their faith to be in a "life force or spirit" that speaks to them through astrology or various extraterrestrial presences.[33] (We are not alone: in Britain, nearly four hundred thousand people list their religion as "Jedi," outnumbering Jews, Sikhs, and Buddhists.)[34]

Americans retain considerable agreement about morals, but they are inclined to see their convictions as so many private preferences, and a sizeable majority say that "we should be more tolerant of people who choose to live according to their own moral standards, even if we think they are wrong."[35] In a recent survey, for example, Catholic students at Catholic colleges expressed relatively traditional judgments on casual premarital sex but far more liberal opinions on the right of homosexuals to marry. The first instance dealt with personal morality; the second primarily tested their tolerance.[36] Boston College political scientist Alan Wolfe is right: the current in religious America runs in the direction of a "new autonomy" in which individuals decide what God suits their temperament, what family structure fulfills their needs, and what laws merit respect.[37]

Still, Americans are restive, just as Tocqueville would have expected. Great numbers of us are troubled by emptiness, aware perhaps of the moral ambiguities of our own conduct, worried about the moral direction of the country. Many are looking to faith now, not as a code of rules but as a source of goodness, seeking the meta-moral in our leaders and ourselves.[38] This was evident in the campaign of 2000, when candidates regularly proclaimed their faiths, not in support of this or that policy but as a kind of personal testimony, scratching the electorate's itch for leadership with a moral center.[39]

The quality of this latest spiritual pursuit will depend on the public's ear for the authentic pitch of profound faith, and hence on the character of religious education.[40] Here, the news is not good. Given the competing temptations of the time, the great majority of American religions are unusually prone to follow the path of consumer preference.[41] This is not improved by a general disposition toward an ecumenicalism that smoothes away the sharper tastes of faith in favor of a kind of religious Jell-O, sweet and vaguely sticky, but with little character and less subtlety.[42] The conversation skirts deeper fears and yearnings and allows for all sorts of spiritual dottiness: almost a third of Americans, a few years ago, reported their conviction that the government was covering up its contacts with space aliens.[43]

Catholicism is not immune to fads and fashions, but, as Tocqueville suggested, the church still finds it easier to be magisterial, and it could set a standard for debate over first principles among the great confessions, faiths disciplined as well by text and tradition.[44] God wills religious unity, the Jesuit theologian John Courtney Murray used to argue, but pluralism is the human condition, and that tension suggests that human beings, and their faiths, are at their best when they are engaged in civil argument about the things that matter.[45]

Of course, this prescription is dangerous. Murray called for pluralism with blood in it, and no one needs to be told that religious argument has often turned bloody and could do so again. But Americans, on the whole, have been well trained in religious tolerance. And religion, even with its abiding rivalries, rests on at least one elementary affirmation: the conviction that there is something to argue about, that the world ultimately makes sense, and that truth is more than personal interpretation and appearance. Faith, John Paul II wrote in *Fides et Ratio*, serves as reason's "convinced and convincing advocate," stirring reason to overcome its fears.[46]

The great faiths also share a recognition that a preoccupation with survival, well-being, and individual independence is enslaving, that human dignity and moral agency are linked to the realization that rights are given to us on terms, and that love carries us beyond the control of earthly powers. It was precisely the "transpolitical" nature of Christian transcendence, Boston College's late great theologian Ernest Fortin argued, that "enable[d] Christianity to be effective in the midst of the changing configurations and innumerable contingencies of human existence." Catholicism, uneasy in this as in any political present, may for that reason hold keys to the American political future.[47]

Notes

This essay was originally published as "Critical Rebound: Why America Needs a Catholic Recovery," *Boston College Magazine* 63, no. 3 (2003).

1. Alexis de Tocqueville, *Democracy in America* (New York: Knopf, 1980), 2:25–26; Ernest Fortin, *Human Rights, Virtue and the Common Good,* ed. J. Brian Benestad (Lanham: Rowman and Littlefield, 1996), 63–64; see also Fortin's excellent discussion of *Rerum Novarum and Centesiumus Annus,* 191–229.

2. Lawrence Iannaccone, "Why Strict Churches Are Strong," *American Journal of Sociology* 99 (1994): 1180–1212.

3. James Davison Hunter, *American Evangelicalism* (New Brunswick: Rutgers University Press, 1983). Not so many decades ago, for example, evangelical Protestants characteristically held (following Matthew 5:32 and 19:8, among

other texts) that divorced persons could not rightly remarry; by the 1980s—witness evangelical enthusiasm for Ronald Reagan—that doctrine no longer received much attention.

4. David O'Brien observes that Jay Dolan, the Notre Dame historian, made this argument more than a decade ago. "How to Solve the Church Crisis," *Commonweal*, February 14, 2003, 10.

5. *Democracy in America*, 1:300.

6. Ibid., 1:301, 308.

7. Alexis de Tocqueville, *Journey to America*, ed. J. P. Mayer (New Haven: Yale University Press, 1962), 150.

8. *Democracy in America*, 2:23–24.

9. For example, see François Guizot, *History of Civilization* (London: George Bell and Sons, 1894), 94–100.

10. *Democracy in America*, 1:301, 2:27.

11. Even the militant Father Mullon, for example, told Tocqueville and Beaumont that state support for religion is harmful, and the vicar-general found kind words to say about "enlightenment." *Journey to America*, 33, 206, 257.

12. For example, he detected in the American church a decreased taste for "minute individual observances" and for "extraordinary or peculiar means of salvation." *Democracy in America*, 2:27.

13. Ibid., 1:318.

14. Ibid., 2:29–30; *Journey to America*, 59–60, 236–37.

15. See David O'Brien's discussion of "immigrant religion" in *Public Catholicism* (New York: Macmillan, 1989). Depending on the time and issue, Catholics and Catholic power were a target for both the Right and the Left: my liberal-left family for example, admired Paul Blanshard's *Communism, Democracy and Catholic Power* (Boston: Beacon, 1951).

16. V. O. Key, "The Future of the Democratic Party," *Virginia Quarterly* 28 (1952): 161–75; John H. Schaar and Wilson C. McWilliams, "Uncle Sam Vanishes," *New University Thought* 1 (1961): 61–68. Most famous was Al Smith's notable assertion that not only had he "never known" a conflict between his religion and his official duties, "no such conflict could exist" ("Catholic and Patriot," *Atlantic Monthly*, May 1927, 722). This stance was complicated, of course, by the necessity, before the era of Vatican II, to maintain that, in principle, a state should establish Catholicism, a position defended even by so progressive—and pragmatically pluralistic—a thinker as Monsignor John Ryan (John A. Ryan and Moorhouse Millar, *The State and the Church* [New York: Macmillan, 1922], 34–38). Ryan never changed this view (Martin Marty, *Modern American Religion* [Chicago: University of Chicago Press, 1986], 2:369). Patriotism—and especially anticommunist patriotism—involved fewer ambiguities.

17. Hugh Heclo, "An Introduction to Religion and Politics," in *Religion Returns to the Public Square*, ed. Hugh Heclo and Wilfred McClay (Baltimore: Johns Hopkins University Press, 2003), 15; see also José Casanova, "What Is a Public Religion?" in Heclo and McClay, *Religion Returns to the Public Square*, 130–31.

18. John Coleman, "Neither Liberal nor Socialist," in *One Hundred Years of Catholic Social Thought,* ed. John Coleman (Maryknoll: Orbis, 1991), 25–42, and "A Common Good Primer," *Dialog* 34 (1995): 249–54; Joseph Cardinal Bernadin, *Consistent Ethic of Life* (Kansas City: Sheed and Ward, 1988).

19. The evidence of our senses, Chesterton observed, suggests that equality is a "crude fairy tale about all men being equally tall or equally tricky." *What I Saw in America* (New York: Dodd, Mead, 1922), 17.

20. Aristotle, *Politics,* 1279b–1280a.

21. E. J. Dionne, "Courting the 'Catholic Vote,'" *Washington Post National Weekly,* June 26, 2000, 22.

22. José Casanova, "Religion, the New Millennium and Globalization," *Sociology of Religion* 60 (2001): 415–41.

23. *Democracy in America,* 1:302.

24. James Reichley, "Faith in Politics," in Heclo and McClay, *Religion Returns to the Public Square,* 179, 184. During his speech to the U.S. Conference of Catholic Bishops in November 2002, Bishop Wilton Gregory, while emphasizing the need to purify but uphold traditional structures within the Church, included a carefully phrased call for laity to "assist" bishops in various councils. Laurie Goldstein, "Tradition as Healer," *New York Times,* November 16, 2002, A13.

25. "Ours remains an apostolic and hierarchical church," Margaret O'Brien Steinfels writes, "and bishops are key to its proper ordering," although that "fundamental understanding" calls for "better bishops." "Continuing the Conversation," *Commonweal,* March 14, 2003, 7.

26. *Democracy in America,* 1:43–44; Booth Fowler, *Unconventional Partners: Religion and Liberal Culture in the United States* (Grand Rapids: Eerdmans, 1989).

27. *Democracy in America,* 2:145.

28. Ibid., 1:314–17, 2:135.

29. Ibid., 2:134, 138–39.

30. Ibid., 1:44, 302, 305.

31. Francis McMahon made a similar argument in *A Catholic Looks at the World* (New York: Vanguard, 1945), 147, 151, arguing for a kind of religious check and balance: Protestantism, with its tendency to fragmentation, set against Catholicism, with its temptation to authoritarianism (184). The contention that Catholicism could not have created the republic, of course, was a theme of traditional Protestant criticism, as in Charles Clayton Morrison's argument against Al Smith's candidacy: Catholicism is "a culture sharply alien to the culture which produced American institutions" ("The Religious Issues," *Christian Century,* October 18, 1928, 1252).

32. *Democracy in America,* 1:303.

33. Richard Morin, "Can We Believe in Polls about God?" *Washington Post National Weekly,* June 1, 1998, 30.

34. *New York Times,* February 14, 2003, A8.

35. Richard Morin and David Broder, "Worried about Morals but Reluctant to Judge," *Washington Post National Weekly,* September 21, 1998, 10–11.

36. Tamar Lewin, "Catholics Adopt More Liberal Attitudes during Their Years in College, a Survey Finds," *New York Times*, March 5, 2003, B8. Entering college in 1997, 27.5 percent of these students endorsed the propriety of casual sex, 37.9 percent thought abortion should be legal, and 52.4 percent supported same-sex marriage. At the time of the students' graduation in 2001, these figures had risen to 48 percent, 51 percent, and 69 percent respectively.

37. Alan Wolfe, "The Pursuit of Autonomy," *New York Times Magazine*, May 7, 2000, 54.

38. David Leege, "Divining the Electorate," *Commonweal*, August 20, 2000, 19.

39. Gustav Niebuhr, "God, Man and the Presidency," *New York Times*, December 19, 1999, WK 7. See also Laurie Goldstein, "White House Seekers Wear Faith on Sleeve and Stump," *New York Times*, August 31, 1999, A1, and "The Religion Issue," *New York Times*, August 6, 2000, 20.

40. Fortin, *Human Rights, Virtue and the Common Good*, 29–47.

41. Ibid., 14–17; Peter L. Berger, *The Sacred Canopy* (Garden City: Doubleday, 1969), 145–46.

42. Avery Dulles, *The Challenge of the Catechism* (New York: Fordham University Press, 1994), 20–21; Randall Balmer, "United We Fall," *New York Times*, August 28, 1999, A13.

43. Michael Paul Rogin, "JFK: The Movie," *American Historical Review* 97 (1992): 503–5; Frank McConnell, "Expecting Visitors?" *Commonweal*, November 22, 1996, 20–21. A compelling argument on the point can be found in Paul Cantor's *Gilligan Unbound* (Lanham: Rowman and Littlefield, 2001).

44. José Casanova, *Public Religion in the Modern World* (Chicago: University of Chicago Press, 1994), 234; Avery Dulles, *Religion and the Transformation of Politics* (New York: Fordham University Press, 1992), 16.

45. John Courtney Murray, *We Hold These Truths: Catholic Reflections on the American Proposition* (New York: Sheed and Ward, 1960), 22–23, 74–76.

46. Pope John Paul II, *Fides et Ratio* (Boston: Pauline Books and Media, 1998).

47. Fortin, *Human Rights, Virtue and the Common Good*, 55.

Religion, Morality,
and Public Life

Like quarrelsome kindred forced to live under the same roof, faith and morals—and with them, religion and political society—are often pressed to stay on speaking terms.

Evidently, religion can offer society invaluable support, adding divine sanctions to law and identifying society's fundamental orders—the distinctions of gender, age, family, and property—with the sacred or natural. In political society, where ways and rules are at least partly departures from custom, religion can veil the extent to which the laws are conventions, products of speech and hence open to question and contradiction. It can make government into a kind of sacrament, hearing the echoes of divinity even in the cacophonies of democracy.[1] And of course, this contribution is appreciated even by—or especially by—those for whom religion is simply a way to take advantage of the credulity of the many.[2]

But religion also involves, and edges human beings toward, an encounter with the divine, the transcendent Other beyond appearances. In that aspect, it provokes or reflects the recognition that our ways are contingent and our knowing confined to signs and artifacts, that we see "through a glass, darkly," disordering and shaking the world it otherwise maintains.[3] It may insist that our institutions are useful, even the best we are capable of achieving in practice, but it will also deny that they deserve our highest allegiance or are entitled to more than a conditional obedience. "There is neither Jew nor Greek, bond or free, male or female, for all are one in Christ Jesus," Paul wrote, denying ontological status to distinctions of nation, class, and gender.[4] Christianity, John Winthrop told his Puritans, requires believers to surpass even the laws of nature—to love their enemies, for example, and to give to their brethren *beyond* their ability, naturally understood.[5] Religion in this high sense is clearly dangerous, at least in theory—and often more than that—a challenge to civil order.[6] It may *lend* sanctity to the laws, but it insists on retaining *ownership,* and such uncertain tenure is bound to be uncomfortable for civil authority.[7]

For the American framers, a "solution to the religious problem" was a precondition of free and stable government, and they held that, separated from the state, religion could be *both* supportive of morality and subordinated to the laws.[8] Their design, successful for much of American history, has nevertheless tended to weaken the civil role the framers themselves envisioned for religion. I argue, in fact, that in contemporary America, at least part of the framers' thinking needs to be reoriented if not reversed: in our times, religion is frequently, even regularly, at odds with the dominant ideas of morality, and hence a source of conflict and controversy as much as of civil order. And I will be contending that the greatest contribution religion can make to American life lies in theory rather than practice, through the affirmation of the transcendent bases of faith and reason.

God was not in the Pledge of Allegiance when the Supreme Court decided that states could not compel students to recite it against their convictions.[9] He was added later on, in the years after World War II. But while the amended Pledge, referring to "one Nation, under God," acknowledges divine supremacy, it asks us to vow allegiance to the *republic*, and to God only through this political connection. To believers, it would make more sense to say, "I pledge allegiance, *under God*, to the flag of the United States of America."[10] The Pledge, by contrast, is an exercise in civil religion, an effort to attach God to the cause of the nation, rather than the reverse. And that—although the amended pledge would have made Madison itchy—is pretty much the way the framers would have wanted it.

Any effort to control or dictate to the soul they regarded as a violation of natural, unalienable right: liberty, Madison declared in *The Federalist*, #10, is "essential to political life" of any legitimate sort, not merely—if we take Madison at his word—to republican politics.[11] Attempts to remove the "causes of faction" by shaping the soul are either utopian or constraining, ineffective or a violation of freedom, and in practice, likely to lead to *both* oppression and disorder.[12]

The Constitution, accordingly, confines itself to what human beings and governments do: it is silent on religion, but *also* on natural right, the basis of America's civil creed. And in relation to action, the reliable principle— morality in the natural sense—is premised on self-preservation and self-interest.[13] Human beings may behave well when they are convinced they will be seen and given credit, and the "noblest minds" are drawn by the love of fame, but the rule in public life is that the great majority will be guided by their immediate interests and passions.[14] The framers, consequently, set out to minimize reliance on the virtue of statesmen or citizens, preferring to rely on the "silent operation of the laws"—the rivalry of interests in a large and diverse republic—to undermine attachments, moderate political passions, and promote a circumspect and ordered liberty.[15]

However, the framers also recognized that a morality based simply on calculations of personal interest would prove inadequate for republican politics, and they had no doubt of "the advantage of a religious Character among private Persons" in shoring up the characterological foundations of civic life.[16]

In the first place, they regarded religion as a surety for contracts, and hence for civil society itself. Reason and interest make an unanswerable case for agreeing to whatever promises are needed to escape the insecurities of the state of nature, but once society is established, the argument for keeping those pledges seems less compelling. I have an interest in the existence of law and order, but my interests tempt me to consult only my own convenience. There is, of course, the risk that I will be caught and punished if I break the rules, and if I escape detection, my successful villainy may undermine trust and inspire imitation, pushing society back toward its precivil disorder. Calculations of this sort may deter those who are likely to be seen and who have much to lose, but for great stakes, the risks may seem worth running, and as President Clinton's strayings indicated, the most public of persons can be reckless in the pursuit of very trivial goals. Private people, especially the poor, the obscure, and the oppressed, may easily feel they have little to lose. Locke thought "promises, covenants and oaths" would be hopelessly insecure without religion, rejecting toleration for atheists: "The taking away of God, though but even in thought, dissolves all."[17] The American founders did not go so far, but they shared the view that it is important for citizens to see contracts as "sacred things," and even Jefferson was moved to declare that the belief that liberties are the gift of God is the only secure basis of freedom.[18]

For the founding generation, it was virtually axiomatic that the morality appropriate to a modern republic—civility in the truest and highest sense—requires a benevolence and a humanity most readily nurtured by religion. Even in the "civilized parts" of the ancient world, Locke observed, reason had not been sufficient to establish that it is criminal to kill one's children by exposing them. By forbidding infanticide, revealed religion is consistent with reason, which shows us that we have some responsibility for what we have begotten, but fortifies that duty and greatly extends it.[19] It is the "peculiar superiority of the system of Jesus," Jefferson wrote, that it inculcates "universal philanthropy," gathering "all mankind into one family."[20]

Finally, the framers knew that rights can be lost in practice, lacking a "vigilant and manly spirit" determined to defend them.[21] Not many agreed with Nathaniel Niles's late Puritan theorizing, but as a practical matter, most would have sympathized with Niles's contention that civil liberty without spiritual liberty "is but a body without a soul."[22] Self-government presumes citizens who are willing to endure discomfort and unpopularity, who stand prepared to sacrifice their interests and even their lives to preserve the liberty of others.[23] Civic duty, in other words, defies ordinary calculations of utility: it demands the conviction that if "it is great, it is glorious to espouse a good cause, . . . it is still more great and glorious in such a cause to stand alone," a nobility most easily translated into republican idiom through the mediation of religion.[24]

The most enduring voices of the founding generation, however, associated religion with credulousness, indoctrination, and unreason, at best a kind of primer in moral education: the belief in a "particular Providence," Franklin said, was suited only for "weak and ignorant Men and Women, and . . . inexperienced and inconsiderate Youth of both Sexes."[25] On those terms, religion did not rise to the dignity of a public life dedicated to freedom and reasoned consent.

In fact, the framers were very likely to reduce theology and specifically religious argument—and virtually all the transcendent dimension of faith, saving the presumptively useful belief in an afterlife—to folly or priestcraft. Franklin expressed regret for the time he had wasted reading his father's books of "polemic Divinity," and he disdained sermons which seemed aimed "to make us Presbyterians rather than good Citizens."[26] Traditional Christian doctrines Jefferson called "artificial systems" deserving of "euthanasia," and in his celebrated letter to James Smith, he proclaimed the number of gods in whom a citizen believes to be a matter of civic indifference, so long as the religions in question "make honest men."[27] Seeing a need for Christian *morals*—or at least, so much of that morality as supports a liberal regime—the framers rejected the public claims of Christian *faith*.[28]

Hoping to domesticate religion, the Constitution relies politically on America's plurality of sects and confessions, which—in the familiar logic of *The Federalist*, #10—makes it unlikely that any persuasion can acquire strength enough to suppress the others.[29] And intellectually, religious plurality guarantees that any doctrine will be contested and subjected to challenge. Evidently, moreover, the Constitution—the highest secular authority—is prohibited from attempting to resolve such quarrels, implicitly because there is no answer or argument sufficiently conclusive to be compelling in a public forum. The laws, in other words, cast their vote for incertitude, as far as religious doctrine is concerned, or, at the very least, for open-mindedness. In this sense, the Constitution relies on, but also hopes to promote, a public opinion that works to moderate religious claims, rejecting or ridiculing enthusiasm, and controlling faith without the intervention of the state.[30]

At the same time, the framers looked to the institutions of civil society—families, churches, and local communities—to nurture and discipline moral character. And they expected public authority to recognize those institutions and to give them considerable active support. In the first place, although the leading spirits at Philadelphia would have been happy to place greater limits on state authority, as a practical necessity the Constitution left the states with a relatively free hand in matters of morals and religion. They could establish churches, until the Fourteenth Amendment was held to apply the First to the states, and while formal state establishments disappeared in the nineteenth century, states were certainly empowered to foster religious education (through practices like Bible reading and prayer in schools), to aid the secular functions of religious institutions, to recognize religious symbols, and to provide civil advantages (tax breaks, for example, or the authority to solemnize marriage) to churches and clergy.[31] And generally, the framers held the Lockean position that it is proper for government to regulate *conduct*, even if associated with religious observances, so long as it acts through general laws applicable to all citizens.[32] Historically, this has meant governmental support for the moral code of the religio-civil mainstream, and efforts to limit or forbid any religious practices thought to threaten the order of civil society, as in the case of Mormonism and polygamy.[33] Where public policy has offended the convictions of any substantial body of opinion, government has often given ground, and minority religions—even very small ones—have frequently found support at and in law.[34] But in such instances, religion wins by making its case on civil terms: the constitutional rule is the subordination of religion to the laws.[35]

Over the years, the relationship between religion and the republic has been at least civil, a little watchful but ordinarily warm, with many expressions of mutual respect.[36] Yet Tocqueville, admiring the accommodation, expected the "spirit of liberty," entrenched in the laws, to gain ground at the expense of the "spirit of religion."[37] Emphasizing the "habits of the heart" over the laws, Tocqueville followed Guizot's teaching that political institutions, in the first instance, are an "effect," the products of society. But Guizot had also argued that institutions, once established, become a "cause," changing ways of living and feeling.[38] A religion's first principles always remain as the tendency of its teaching, Tocqueville observed, but it must adapt its practice to circumstance and the demands of civil society.[39] In America, religious freedom made churches dependent on the active commitment of believers—on the whole an advantage, Tocqueville thought—but it also emphasized the need of churches to persuade, and hence their temptation to play down demands that are exacting or disabling in civil life.[40]

Tocqueville saw the increasing ascendancy of liberty in American speech. Even though Americans sometimes acted from generous or public-spirited motives, he observed, they explained themselves by reference to the principle of "self-interest rightly understood," readier "to do honor to their philosophy than to themselves."[41] The doctrine that human beings act from essentially private and interested motives, in other words, was preempting public speech and affecting self-understanding.[42] And since change was shaking or shattering instinctive or customary virtues, religion was in danger of losing both its habits and its voice. That forecast seems all too prescient in our time.[43]

In part, religious discourse was bound to become less coherent as American religion became more pluralistic, with a country once described as "Protestant" becoming first "Christian" and then "Judeo-Christian" and, increasingly, simply "religious."[44] In contemporary America, however, pluralism has become more radical, in fact and mood. Within the biblical religions, of course, there are sharp theological arguments about which texts to read and how to read them, but that sort of contestation is relatively familiar: in the controversy over slavery, Southern whites clung to the Bible's explicit acceptance of slavery as an endurable element of the human condition, while the opponents of slavery read the text in the spirit of Exodus, as a promise of liberation. And the confrontation between Darrow and Bryan in the "monkey trial," back in the twenties, has become part of American folklore. Our current disagreements, however, are more apt to focus on moral codes and social institutions, "problematizing" the foundations of civil life.[45]

Too, more and more of American religiosity stands outside the biblical tradition, wholly or in part. Islam "at least springs from the Bible," Pat Robertson reminded his readers, but the same cannot be said of Hindus and Buddhists, not to mention pagan revivals and New Age doctrines.[46] During a recent election in Massachusetts, then-governor Paul Cellucci had to apologize for a remark offensive to witches, probably causing tremors in Puritan graveyards.[47] The polls indicate that the vast majority of Americans continue to express a belief in God, but these numbers conceal the thinning of religious agreement: for some 12 percent of Americans, these professions reflect a belief in a "life force or spirit"—including extraterrestrial presences and astrology—rather than a personal Deity.[48]

The extent of such diversity, however, is less significant than the broad acceptance of that multiformity by the general public. A majority of Americans still adhere to more or less traditional moral precepts, but they regard those principles essentially as personal choices or preferences: the prevailing public ethic and language of morals is individualism, utilitarian, or expressive.[49] Fulfilling Tocqueville's prediction, this also echoes the long, inward-turning, Emersonian ramble of intellectual America: John Dewey's celebration of the transformation of morality from code to conscience, for example, or Reinhold Niebuhr's emphasis on the ethic of love.[50] But Dewey and Niebuhr, for all their differences, were more than a little confident about what conscientiousness or love demands of us, and of public policy. Contemporary thinking, by contrast, combines uncertainties about texts and traditions with a kind of moral complacency, willing to rest with differing "communities of interpretation."[51]

Social and political discourse, especially among younger Americans, is notable for what Harvey Mansfield has called "creeping . . . libertarianism," a moral stance that is willing to condemn violence, psychological abuse, or intrusions on privacy out of respect for the other as an autonomous subject, but otherwise is content to leave individuals free to do as they please.[52] "Imposing" your convictions on others is more and more held to be beyond the pale. A majority of Americans, in a recent *Washington Post* poll, worried about the country's moral direction and the decline of values, but 70 percent agreed that we should be "more tolerant of people who choose to live according to their own moral standards, even if we think they are wrong."[53]

"Judge not, that ye be not judged," Americans of this persuasion are apt to say, almost the only instance in which they spontaneously cite Scripture. Unfortunately, they misread the teaching of that text. Jesus is asserting that we ought not to judge others by any standard we are unwilling to have applied to ourselves, but his doctrine is not a tolerant indifference: he does not tell us to leave a speck in our brother's eye; he commands us to remove our own *first*.[54]

In contemporary practice, the moral picture is not entirely bleak. Despite much uneasiness and more posturing, there have been gains in the relations between the races and the genders, and many old abuses are now subject to sanction. And religion, if it needs saying, provides support for the decencies and for some sense of obligation. But the temple, if standing, is in need of repair, especially since so many of the institutional pillars of the framers' moral design have been unsettled or pulled down.

That states and local governments are now held to the essentially secular standards of national law would inspire some sympathy among the framers, although the Supreme Court's insistence on the "wall of separation"—rendered almost labyrinthine by the Court's opinions—goes far beyond the understanding and practice of the founding generation.[55]

It is a matter for greater concern that the institutions of civil society have been so thoroughly penetrated and reshaped—and often shattered—by economics, technology, and the "hidden curriculum" of the media.[56] In the new order of things, indignity is commonplace: the media confront us with superstars, just as the market disproportionately rewards elites; by comparison, the intermediate dignities offered by local communities seem tawdry.[57] This perception is strengthened by the fact that localities—and with them, a good many personal relationships—increasingly are exposed to mobility and change, transient connections to which we are apt to limit our liability.[58]

Despite general prosperity, economics adds desperations, weakening our already slender resources of trust and moral community. Inequality is escalating, with the middle class recently losing ground to both rich and poor.[59] The vogue of "outsourcing" and "downsizing" makes jobs feel insecure, even in good times.[60] Responding in kind, Kristin Downey Grimsley reports, employees are becoming less loyal to the firm or to their fellows, resulting in a workplace that may be "leaner," but is surely "meaner."[61]

It is hardly surprising, consequently, that so many Americans are hesitant or halfhearted about commitments, or that they seek solace in immediate or short-term gratifications, inclinations evident even in the seats of power. It is also understandable that we are tempted to treat market forces as if they were autonomous and irresistible, partly because doing so saves us from the burden of responsibility, allowing us a more or less guiltless pursuit of interests and enjoyments.[62] But conceding sovereignty to the market leaves us only the consumer's passive freedom to make choices, rather than having a say in defining what is choiceworthy.[63] All of these retreats from society, politics, and faith diminish us, so that more and more Americans seem to be looking, sometimes furiously and sometimes wistfully, for what is missing.[64]

Regarded hopefully, America is in transition, seeking new and better forms of social and moral order. It may be so. What is unmistakable, however, is the cataract of change.

Elderly Americans, for example, are thought to be due a measure of kindness, but certainly not honor: increasingly isolated, they are treated—with some guilt, a small grace—as irrelevant or even ludicrous, on the model of Grandpa Simpson. Age and experience, in a society undergoing and celebrating transformation, is less a source of wisdom than a fatal attachment to a vanishing order of things. The mastery of technique, the key to the present as well as the future, belongs to the young. Until recently, Mark Gauvreau Judge observes, young people aspired to be adults, but today, adult culture has almost disappeared; in the prevailing view, there are relatively few challenges to the perennial desire to be or seem youthful.[65]

The foundations of civility that the framers expected religion to safeguard are embattled or in question. We retain enough of Locke's "reasonable" religion to forbid infanticide, but a considerable—and so far, decisive—minority supports the right to choose a partial-birth abortion, which surely comes close, and with the growing support for assisted suicide, there are grounds to worry about a "culture of death." As for contracts, marriage—our most common sacred promise—is treated with remarkable casualness, and as we have abundant reason to know, a substantial majority of Americans think it proper to lie or mislead, even under oath, to preserve one's privacy, especially in sexual matters.[66] And of course, the idea of human equality is subject to a fashionable critique from partisans of the "politics of difference."[67]

In the moral discourse of American civil society, religion finds itself an increasingly critical voice, less likely to uphold the prevailing pattern than to confront it prophetically, exposing its superficial pieties and its indifference masked as toleration. In different ways and with different objects, this is pretty much true across the religious spectrum. "Mainstream" religion, relatively sympathetic to social and moral change, offers some of the strongest censures of consumerism and its associated fantasies.[68] Conservative religious teachers—mostly deep-dyed patriots, who are feeling almost dispossessed—are even less sparing. A symposium in *First Things,* in November 1996, discussed the proprieties of resistance to political iniquity; William Bennett proclaims that moral outrage has died; Paul Weyrich writes that he no longer believes in a "moral majority," and that the culture war is lost, at least for the moment.[69] And the subtlest among them are at least beginning to suspect that their alliance with capitalism's dynamism and the relentless relativism of the market is undermining the virtues and convictions they cherish.[70]

Eager to exploit social trends, the media recognize and amplify the adversarial aspect of religion's relation to civil society. In dramas and news programming, the clergy and serious believers are regularly presented as hypocritical or mad (and sometimes both). In this context, Robert Duvall's portrayal, in *The Apostle,* of a deeply troubled evangelist, guilty of homicide but sincere and no respecter of racial distinctions, is generally counted as benign. Advertising appropriates at least some of the theme; in a recent ad for beyond.com, the residents at a "Spirituality Center" are depicted partly as well-meaning cranks eating unappetizing food, but also as hypocrites: facing her computer screen, one young woman remarks, "My tech fund just scored. I am *so* out of here." And on TV news, with very few exceptions—most notably Jesse Jackson, obviously a peculiar case, and Billy Graham—there are almost no appearances by clergy from mainstream denominations. Religion is represented by leaders like Louis Farrakhan, Pat Robertson, or Al Sharpton, all identified with social extremism if not disruption.

Religion's increasingly contentious role in relation to moral life has its dangers, but also its own civic value. Contemporary America has every need for voices defending the proposition that human life is not trivial and that human conduct matters, especially if they are loving critics, informed by the teaching that God cares for all cities and peoples, even for those who are fools.

Religion's best gift to the republic, in these times, will be its transcendent, theoretical dimension, especially faith that is disciplined by text and tradition and, above all, by humility. Tocqueville worried that secular society, caught up with the "interests of the world," would be blind to the needs of the soul and would neglect its education. Yet since the demands of the soul are "constituent principles of human nature," they will make themselves felt, sometimes with great force. If the soul is both frustrated and untrained, Tocqueville noted, when it does assert itself it is likely to be "unrestrained, beyond the bounds of common sense."[71]

Tocqueville's argument is easily confirmed in contemporary America. Religious education, the victim of a long decline, is socially marginal at best. Consider a famous incident: in 1976, in his ill-advised interview with *Playboy,* Jimmy Carter—seeking to reassure Americans, and especially liberals, that he was not hopelessly self-righteous—said that he lusted after women in his heart. Prevailing opinion took this to mean that Carter was, well, Bill Clinton, or something close to it: not many recognized that Carter was referring to Matthew 5:28, suggesting that, informed by Christian teaching, he did not think his own decent conduct made him utterly distinct from or spiritually superior to sinners. Whatever their Scriptural knowledge, Carter's successors have learned to keep their references simple.

Evidence of what Tocqueville called "religious insanity" is just as easily come by, and not just in marginal cults. More and more Americans find themselves in a position which is essentially paranoid, subject to overwhelming and baffling forces, sensing invisible dominations and powers.[72] Conspiracy theory waxes in political fiction, but also in a remarkable amount of nominally nonfiction argument, right and left. *The X-Files* reflects a very broad mood: almost half of Americans, *Newsweek* reports, believe in UFOs and that the government is covering up the evidence, while nearly a third think that the government has contact with extraterrestrials.[73]

It makes matters worse that Americans have little trust in the direction of change: one *X-Files* epigraph urges us to "Fight the Future." On stage and screen, Americans have been drawn to the story of the *Titanic,* a metaphor for our ship of state, divided by towering inequalities, its course and especially its too-great speed moved by competition and the desire for profit, its powerful technology entrusted to imperfect humans.

Most of all, we worry that no one is in charge. Trust in democratic institutions is low and falling, and not only because our leaders are so apt to be knaves and psychological teenagers. We worry that government—or republican government—may be largely irrelevant, more and more an epiphenomenon, forced to shape itself in the image of global forces. At the same time, in its dealings with us as individuals, we fear government's strength, suspecting that it may be the creature of great and hostile interests. Yet we also know how much we depend on public institutions: in *The X-Files,* the government is honeycombed with conspirators, but the heroes are also government agents. And there are many signs in popular culture that we are attracted by a government or leaders who take control of things, even if that mastery comes at great cost.

Faith offers, by way of therapy, its working hypothesis (after all, faith is exposed to doubt and can be lost) that the world is a creation that, whatever its anguish and mystery, will ultimately prove to make sense and reflect glory. It knows our yearning for a truth more fundamental than images and interpretations, just as it recognizes that the very comprehensibility of the universe is radically incomprehensible.[74] "It is faith," John Paul II reminds us, "which stirs reason to move beyond all isolation and willingly to run risks," acting as reason's "convinced and convincing advocate."[75] That faiths differ is an occasion for argument; faith itself assures them that they have something to argue *about*. American laws deserve thanks for having helped teach the great faiths to conduct those debates civilly; in return, they have something to teach the republic about civil life.

In the first place, faith does not forget that humans are dependent and subject to the limits of nature. For example, religion recognizes the complex claims and moral dimensions of the body. It knows sin and shortcoming, but it also knows the power of sensory experience and of the erotic and their potential dignity, as in the Christian mystery in which the body is deemed worthy to receive the divine. Secular teaching these days is inclined to reduce sexuality to one more "choice," one desire among many.[76] Similarly, it is tempted to believe that community can, through technology, be indefinitely extended. Yet history aside, experience with "virtual reality" suggests that its version of community is at best inadequate and tends to result in an "overall decline in feelings of connection."[77] Faith understands, by contrast, that in this world—short of grace—communion is a matter of body and blood as well as spirit. And it counsels us not to expect from the framers' republic a warmer fraternity than it can afford.

At the same time, the great traditions remind us that preoccupation with gratification and survival is at bottom enslaving, making us the captives of whoever or whatever can credibly threaten our comfort and safety. Individual independence is a trap as well as an illusion: it is having obligations, being willing to sacrifice estate or life or even liberty, as ordinarily understood, that sets us free from the earth's powers and our own weaknesses.[78] Over time, by contrast, the American pursuit of self-government has yielded to the desire for personal fulfillment.[79] Even in our contemporary discordances, however, religion—that old ally of the art of association—can hear our hope for dignity, and by affirming that in secular life, human beings are capable of moral agency, it speaks to the possibility of citizenship and self-rule.[80]

Faith offers, as a foundation, its own form of dignity: humility, a quality as paradoxical as knowledge of ignorance and not really distinct from it, a soul confronted with its own unworthiness by the intimation of divinity that lifts it above despair. Benjamin Franklin saw the paradox: after a few days of practicing that excellence, Franklin said, he became proud of his humility.[81] But even Franklin valued the freedom from vanity, and religion's humility carries a dignity without pride, confident in its knowledge that the proud will fall. In a world littered with Ozymandias heads, that is wisdom worth having. In this perishing century, as Chesterton remarked, "the secularists have not wrecked divine things; but the secularists have wrecked secular things, if that is any comfort to them. The Titans did not scale heaven; but they laid waste the world."[82]

Notes

This essay derives from a 1999 manuscript, portions of which were published in "Faith and Morals: Religion in American Democracy," *The Good Society: A PEGS Journal* 10, no. 1 (2001).

1. Peter L. Berger, *The Sacred Canopy* (Garden City: Doubleday, 1969), 24–27, 34; Marcel Gauchet, *The Disenchantment of the World: A Political History of Religion,* trans. Oscar Burge (Princeton: Princeton University Press, 1997).

2. In Mary Renault's *The Last of the Wine* (New York: Pantheon, 1956), Kritias finds fault with Alkibiades' too visible impiety as endangering the "strongest ally" of rule. "Long ago," Kritias explains, "there lived a wise old tyrant. We do not know his name or city, but we can infer him. His guards were sufficient to protect his person, perhaps, but not to rule with. So out of the stuff of his mind he created twelve great guardians and servants of his will: all-knowing, far-shooting, earthshaking, givers of corn and wine and love. He did not make them all terrible, because he was a poet, and because he was wise; but even to the beautiful ones he gave terrible angers. 'You may think yourselves alone,' he said to the people, 'when I am in my castle. But they see you and are not deceived.' So he sent out the Twelve, with a thunderbolt in one hand and a cup of poppy juice in the other, and they have been excellent servants ever since" (32).

3. 1 Cor. 13:12; Berger, *Sacred Canopy,* 100; Eric Voegelin, *Israel and Revelation* (Baton Rouge: Louisiana State University Press, 1956).

4. Gal. 3:28; the Dionysia, Nietzsche argued, momentarily shattered "all the hostile, rigid walls which either necessity or despotism has erected between men," so that "the slave emerges as a freeman." *The Birth of Tragedy and the Genealogy of Morals,* trans. Francis Golffing (Garden City: Doubleday, 1956), 23.

5. "A Model of Christian Charity," in *Puritan Political Ideas*, ed. Edmund S. Morgan (Indianapolis: Bobbs-Merrill, 1965), 77–78.

6. Herbert L. Schneidau, *Sacred Discontent* (Berkeley and Los Angeles: University of California Press, 1977); Peter L. Berger, *The Precarious Vision* (Garden City: Doubleday, 1961).

7. H. Richard Niebuhr, *Christ and Culture* (New York: Harper and Row, 1951), 8.

8. Walter Berns, "Religion and the Founding Principle," in *Moral Foundations of the American Republic*, 3rd ed., ed. Robert H. Horwitz (Charlottesville: University Press of Virginia, 1977), 223.

9. *Minersville School District v. Gobitis*, 310 U.S. 586 (1940); *West Virginia State Board of Education v. Barnette*, 319 U.S. 624 (1943). Had God been referred to in the Pledge, the Court's opinion would probably have been more emphatic.

10. Presuming, of course, that the believers—unlike the Jehovah's Witnesses in *Gobitis* and *Barnette*—did not object to the implicit idolatry of swearing allegiance to a flag.

11. *The Federalist*, ed. Jacob Cooke (Middletown: Wesleyan University Press, 1961), 58. See also Thomas Jefferson's letter to Benjamin Rush, April 21, 1803, in *The Life and Selected Writings of Thomas Jefferson*, ed. Adrienne Koch and William Peden (New York: Modern Library, 1944), 567.

12. The effort to produce religious unity, Madison wrote, had spilled "torrents of blood." *The Writings of James Madison*, ed. Gaillard Hunt (New York: Putnam, 1900–1910), 2:189; their only effect, Jefferson claimed in *Notes on Virginia*, was to "make one half of the world fools, and the other half hypocrites." *Life and Selected Writings*, 276.

13. Madison, *Writings*, 4:387; when our interests and our duties seem to be at variance, Jefferson wrote, "we ought to suspect some fallacy in our reasonings." February 1, 1804, *Life and Selected Writings*, 575.

14. *The Federalist*, #55, 72, ed. Cooke, 374, 488.

15. Madison, *Writings*, 6:86; *The Federalist*, #51, ed. Cooke, 349.

16. Benjamin Franklin, *Benjamin Franklin: Writings*, ed. J. A. Lemay (New York: Library of America, 1987), 336.

17. John Locke, *A Letter concerning Toleration* (Indianapolis: Bobbs-Merrill, 1955), 52. Locke also rejected toleration for Catholics because the church taught that faith need not be kept with heretics.

18. Jefferson, *Life and Selected Writings*, 278. The reference to the sanctity of contracts is taken from Nathaniel Niles, *Two Discourses on Liberty* (1774), in *American Political Writing during the Founding Era*, ed. Charles Hyneman and Donald Lutz (Indianapolis: Liberty Press, 1983), 1:267–68n. Pointedly, Niles links "*truce breakers and traitors*" (his italics) to persons who are self-loving, covetous, and unholy, adoring pleasures more than God (2 Tim. 3:1–4), suggesting that secular individualists are inherently a threat to contracts. Even Jefferson had moments in which he questioned whether an atheist's testimony was reliable

enough to be received at law. *Notes on the State of Virginia,* ed. William Peden (Chapel Hill: University of North Carolina Press, 1955), 159.

19. John Locke, *The Reasonableness of Christianity,* ed. I. T. Ramsey (Stanford: Stanford University Press, 1958), 64.

20. Letter to Benjamin Rush, April 21, 1803, in *Life and Selected Writings,* 570.

21. *The Federalist,* #57, ed. Cooke, 387.

22. *Two Discourses on Liberty,* 1:258.

23. The highest duty of the citizen, Jefferson argued, is not obedience to written law, but to the commands of "necessity, of self-preservation, of saving our country when in danger" (letter to J. B. Colvin, September 20, 1810, in *Life and Selected Writings,* 606–7). In this Lockean formulation, it should be noticed that *collective* self-preservation rivals or takes preference over *personal* self-preservation, which presumes at least the subordination of the body to extended ideas of self.

24. Niles, *Two Discourses on Liberty,* 1:274. Heroism, John Witherspoon declared, is "not open to every man," but Christian magnanimity is a virtue accessible to the "very lowest stations." *The Works of Reverend John Witherspoon* (Philadelphia: Woodward, 1802), 3:98–99.

25. Benjamin Franklin, *Writings,* 748.

26. Benjamin Franklin, *The Autobiography of Benjamin Franklin and Other Writings,* ed. Kenneth Silverman (New York: Penguin, 1986), 13, 90. See also Jefferson's letter to John Adams, October 13, 1813. On the subject of Presbyterians, Jefferson was more vehement than Franklin (letter to Thomas Cooper, March 13, 1820). *Life and Selected Writings,* 632, 697.

27. Letter to William Short, October 31, 1819; letter to James Smith, December 8, 1822, in *Letters and Selected Writings,* 694, 704. It is worth noting that, as a private matter, Jefferson was not at all indifferent about the question, telling Smith with misplaced confidence that he expected Unitarianism to become the "general religion of the United States" within the "present generation."

28. Wilfred McClay, "Mr. Emerson's Tombstone," *First Things,* May 1998, 16–22; to that extent, Isaac Kramnick and R. Lawrence Moore are right to call the Constitution "godless." *The Godless Constitution* (New York: Norton, 1996).

29. See Madison's letter to Jefferson, August 20, 1785. Late in life, Madison found good words to say about national religious associations, because—themselves too divided to pose a problem for the nation—they were a strong political weight against state establishments that disadvantaged their members. Letter to an unidentified person, March 1836, in *Writings of James Madison,* 2:163–64, 9:610.

30. Jefferson, *Notes on the State of Virginia,* in *Life and Selected Writings,* 275; see also Jean Yarbrough, *American Virtues: Thomas Jefferson on the Character of a Free People* (Lawrence: University Press of Kansas, 1998), 190.

31. In fact, until *Pierce v. Society of Sisters* (268 U.S. 510 [1925]), it was not clear that states could not *require* public education. Similarly, the "child benefit" test was applied pretty generally to aid to the secular functions of schools until the late forties. (*Cochran v. Louisiana State Board of Education,* 281 U.S. 370

[1930]; *McCollum v. Board of Education,* 333 U.S. 203 [1948]). Theodore J. Lowi, sharply critical of this aspect of American constitutionalism, indicates its historic force in his *The End of the Republican Era* (Norman: University of Oklahoma Press, 1995), 28–30, 175–82; such practices at least troubled Jefferson and Madison. Yarbrough, *American Virtues,* 189.

32. Thomas Jefferson, "Notes on Locke and Shaftesbury," in *The Papers of Thomas Jefferson,* ed. Julian Boyd (Princeton: Princeton University Press, 1954), 1:544–48; Locke, *Letter concerning Toleration,* 17. See *Employment Division, Department of Human Resources v. Smith,* 494 U.S. 872 (1990); and *City of Boerne v. Flores,* 117 S.C. 2157 (1997). When the Court struck down a local ordinance forbidding animal sacrifice, it did so because the law specifically targeted religious practices. *Church of Lakumi Babalu v. City of Hialeah,* 113 S.C. 2217 (1993).

33. *U.S. v. Reynolds,* 98 U.S. 145 (1879); *Cleveland v. U.S.,* 323 U.S. 14 (1946).

34. John West, *The Politics of Revelation and Reason* (Lawrence: University Press of Kansas, 1996); *Wisconsin v. Yoder,* 406 U.S. 205 (1972).

35. Walter Berns, *The First Amendment and the Future of American Democracy* (New York: Basic Books, 1976), 26. For example, the Amish won exemption from compulsory school attendance in *Yoder,* and by statute they were exempted from Social Security taxes, but the Court held that they were required to pay Social Security and other taxes demanded of them as employers, their religious convictions to the contrary. *U.S. v. Lee,* 455 U.S. 252 (1982).

36. Robert Booth Fowler, *Unconventional Partners: Religion and Liberal Culture in the United States* (Grand Rapids: Eerdmans, 1989).

37. Alexis de Tocqueville, *Democracy in America,* trans. Henry Reeve (New York: Knopf, 1980), 1:43; Sanford Kessler, *Tocqueville's Civil Religion* (Albany: State University of New York Press, 1994).

38. I cite Guizot's *Essays on the History of France* from Larry Siedentop, *Tocqueville* (New York: Oxford University Press, 1994), 23; for Tocqueville's appeal to the "habits of the heart," see *Democracy in America,* 1:299, 304–5.

39. *Democracy in America,* 2:23–24.

40. American religion, Berger notes, tends to follow the "dynamics of consumer preference," limited by a certain "product loyalty." *Sacred Canopy,* 145–46.

41. *Democracy in America,* 2:122.

42. In 1861, the theologian John Williamson Nevin contended that American spirituality was only "sublimated utilitarianism," an "attenuated sensuousness" that still turned on calculations of profit and loss. Richard Wentz, *John Williamson Nevin: American Theologian* (New York: Oxford University Press, 1997), 56.

43. Jacques Ellul, *The Humiliation of the Word,* trans. Joyce Main Hanks (Grand Rapids: Eerdmans, 1985).

44. Berger, *Sacred Canopy,* 137.

45. James Davison Hunter, *Culture Wars* (New York: Basic Books, 1991).

46. Pat Robertson, *The New Millennium* (Dallas: Word, 1991), 86.

47. Gustav Niebuhr, "Salem Journal: Witches Appeal to a Political Spirit," *New York Times,* October 31, 1998, A8.

48. Richard Morin, "Can We Believe in Polls about God?" *Washington Post National Weekly,* June 1, 1998, 30.

49. Alan Wolfe, *One Nation After All* (New York: Viking, 1998); Robert Bellah et al., *The Habits of the Heart* (Berkeley and Los Angeles: University of California Press, 1985).

50. John Dewey and James Tufts, *Ethics* (New York: Henry Holt, 1908), 419, 422; Reinhold Niebuhr, *An Interpretation of Christian Ethics* (New York: Scribner's, 1935), 39.

51. Ellen Charry, "Literature as Scripture: Privileged Reading in Current Religious Reflection," *Soundings* 74 (1991): 64–65.

52. Harvey C. Mansfield, "Change and Bill Clinton," *TLS,* November 13, 1992, 14.

53. Richard Morin and David Broder, "Worried about Morals, but Reluctant to Judge," *Washington Post National Weekly,* September 21, 1998, 10–11.

54. Matt. 7:1–5.

55. Michael Malbin, *Religion and Politics: The Intentions of the Authors of the First Amendment* (Washington, D.C.: American Enterprise Institute, 1978); on the Court's doctrine, see Jeffrey Rosen, "Lemon Law," *New Republic,* March 29, 1993, 17.

56. Allan Hertzke, *Echoes of Discontent* (Washington, D.C.: CQ Press, 1993); Urie Bronfenbrenner, "Contexts of Child Rearing," *American Psychologist* 34 (1979): 844–50; Robert Putnam, "Tuning In, Tuning Out: The Strange Disappearance of Social Capital in America," *PS* 28 (1995): 671–81.

57. Robert H. Frank and Philip J. Cook, *The Winner-Take-All Society* (New York: Basic Books, 1995).

58. Robert Putnam, "The Strange Death of Civic America," *American Prospect,* Winter 1996, 34–38.

59. Clay Chandler, "A Market Tide That Isn't Lifting Everybody," *Washington Post National Weekly,* April 13, 1998, 18.

60. Theodore Lowi refers to "domestic insecurity" as virtually a way of life. "Think Globally, Lose Locally," *Boston Review,* April/May 1998, 10.

61. Kristin Downey Grimsley, "Leaner—and Definitely Meaner," *Washington Post National Weekly,* July 20–27, 1998, 21.

62. Louis Uchitelle, "The Economics of Intervention," *New York Times,* May 31, 1998, BU1; William Finneran, "Prosperous Times, Except for the Young," *New York Times,* June 12, 1998, A21.

63. Colin Campbell, "Consuming Goods and the Good of Consuming," *Critical Review* 8 (1994): 503–20; Harry Frankfurt, "Freedom of the Will and the Concept of a Person," *Journal of Philosophy* 68 (1971): 6–7.

64. Tocqueville, *Democracy in America,* 2:98–99, 136–39.

65. Mark Gauvreau Judge, "All Grown Up and No Place to Go," *Washington Post National Weekly,* April 13, 1998, 23.

66. Janny Scott, "Bright, Shining or Dark: The American Way of Lying," *New York Times*, August 16, 1998, WK3; John R. Zaller, "Monica Lewinsky's Contribution to Political Science," *PS* 31 (1998): 182–89.

67. Iris M. Young, *Justice and the Politics of Difference* (Princeton: Princeton University Press, 1990); see Rogers Smith's sympathetic criticism in *Civic Ideals* (New Haven: Yale University Press, 1997), 485–86. On the general point, see Sheldon S. Wolin, "Democracy in the Discourse of Postmodernism," *Social Research* 57 (1990): 5–30.

68. Laurence Moore, *Selling God: American Religion in the Marketplace of Culture* (New York: Oxford, 1994).

69. Gustav Niebuhr and Richard L. Berke, "Unity Is Elusive as Religious Right Ponders 2000 Vote," *New York Times*, March 7, 1999, 11; William J. Bennett, *The Death of Outrage: Bill Clinton and the Assault on American Ideals* (New York: Free Press, 1998).

70. Francis Fukuyama, *Trust: The Social Virtues and the Creation of Prosperity* (New York: Free Press, 1995); I am reminded of Demea's belated discovery of the danger of joining forces with Philo (David Hume, *Dialogues*).

71. Tocqueville, *Democracy in America*, 1:310; 2:20–22, 25–26, 134–35, 148.

72. Michael Paul Rogin, "JFK: The Movie," *American Historical Review* 97 (1992): 503–5.

73. *Newsweek*, July 8 1996; Frank McConnell, "Expecting Visitors?" *Commonweal*, November 22, 1996, 21–22.

74. Dennis Overbye, "Did God Have a Choice?" *New York Times Magazine*, April 18, 1999, 180; "Postmodernists enjoy skating on the surface," Todd Gitlin writes, but when something important is involved, it becomes clear that "they, we, are still probing for bedrock truth." "On Being Sound-Bitten," *Boston Review*, December 1991, 17.

75. John Paul II, *Fides et Ratio*, excerpted in the *New York Times*, October 16, 1998, A10.

76. Peter Steinfels, "Beliefs," *New York Times*, August 22, 1998, A11.

77. Amy Harmon, "Sad, Lonely World Discovered in Cyberspace," *New York Times*, August 30, 1998, 1.

78. Bertrand de Jouvenel, *Sovereignty: An Inquiry into the Political Good* (Indianapolis: Liberty Fund, 1997), 316–17.

79. Robert Wiebe, *Self-Rule: A History of American Democracy* (Chicago: University of Chicago Press, 1995).

80. Peter Berkowitz, "The Art of Association," *New Republic*, June 24, 1996, 44–49.

81. *The Autobiography of Benjamin Franklin and Other Writings*, 103.

82. G. K. Chesterton, *Orthodoxy* (New York: Dodd, Mead, 1936), 260.

Index

abolitionism, 100, 105, 115n19
abortion debate, 219, 336, 379n36, 388
absenteeism, 7
achievement, discrimination based on, 296
Acts, Book of, 85n29
Adams, Henry, 4, 102, 104, 199–200, 201, 206n43
Adams, John, 217, 225n68
Adams, Samuel, 46, 57, 80, 96
Addison, Joseph, 77
advertising, 389
affirmative action, 295, 296
AFL-CIO, 184, 189n12
African Americans, 35, 253, 256
afterlife, 79
age, 388
Age of Reason, The (Paine)
  as antireligious polemic, 62, 70
  Christianity as religion of feeling in, 70–76, 87n64, 89n98, 89nn104–5
  civil religion critiqued in, 63–66
  framers critiqued in, 67
  French Revolution as background for, 62–63
  historicism critiqued in, 67–68
  Locke critiqued in, 64, 67
  natural religion in, 76–80
  the "new man" in, 69–70
  premises of, 68
  religion vs. rationalism in, 62
  revolutionary praxis critiqued in, 68–70
  scriptural references in, 73
agrarianism, 135
Agrippa (Anti-Federalist), 93

Alexander the Great, 359
alienation, 272
alimony, 297
American Catholic Church, 371, 373–74, 377n12
American culture, 141, 178
Americanism, 120
American Political Science Association, 3, 14, 262n6
American Revolution, 56
"America's Second Voice," 4–5, 13, 52, 198, 201, 331, 332, 355
Americorps, 348
Amherst College, 114n6
Amish, 395n35
anarchy, 40n17, 100, 151, 277
Ancient Order of Hibernians, 369n16
Animal Farm (Orwell), 137
anticommunism, 133
Anti-Federalists, 92–97
  Bill of Rights as viewed by, 96–97, 354–55, 365
  Covenant doctrine as influence on, 92–93
  diversity as viewed by, 165–66
  on representation, 35, 53n10, 96, 330
  as "second voice," 4
  significance of, 92
  small state as ideal for, 93–96, 356
  social contract rhetoric of, 93
antigovernment sentiments, 342–44
antiquity, censorship during, 286–87, 292n8
antirationalism, 141–42
antismoking campaigns, 342

antiwar movement, 13
apathy, 353
Apostle, The (film; 1997), 389
Arabella (ship), 12
Aristotelianism, 182, 199
Aristotle, 303
  on completeness, 124
  on democracy, 330, 373
  on democracy vs. oligarchy, 331–32
  democratic liberty as defined by, 8,
    28–29
  on equality, 26, 295
  family relationships as viewed by,
    302–3, 316–17n47, 317n48
  natural limits as viewed by, 22
  Niebuhr's view of, 157
  on political nature, 208, 356
  on political society, 11, 93, 125, 157,
    331
  on public philosophy, 346
  on public vs. private life, 339
  virtue as defined by, 40n23
Arkes, Hadley, 114n6
arms, right to keep and bear, 175n26
Arnold, Thurman, 193
Articles of Confederation, 96
assembly freedoms, 97
association, arts of, 172, 333, 356
association rights, 36
AT&T, 309
atheism, 50, 66, 83n20, 156, 215,
  223n30, 382, 393–94n18
Atwater, Jeremiah, 56
Augustine, Saint, 144, 149, 233, 238,
  359, 371
authoritarian regimes, 120, 123, 126,
  257
autonomy, 23–24, 60
  See also self-rule

Bacon, Francis, 216, 229
Baldwin, James, 4
Barber, Benjamin, 345

Baron, Salo, 204n11
Barron v. Baltimore, 96–97
Bascom, John, 102–3
Basler, Roy, 203–4n9
Beauharnais v. Illinois, 299
Beecher, Henry Ward, 104
behavioralism, 206n41
belief, and illegitimacy, 259–61
Bellah, Robert, 52
Bellamy, Edward, 108
Beneš, Edvard, 191n54
benevolence, 70, 78–79, 87n71
Bennett, William, 389
Bennett, W. Lance, 341, 343
Benson, Thomas Hart, 320
Bentham, Jeremy, 221n2
Bentley, Arthur, 110
Berger, Peter L., 395n40
Berns, Walter, 286–87, 288, 289–90,
  291n
Beyond the Politics of Disappointment
  (McWilliams), 3
Bible
  New Testament, 74
  Paine's critique of, 64–65, 71–72,
    88–89n91–92, 90nn117–18,
    90n127
  Progressive view of, 105
  prophecy in, 68–69, 76
  reading of, in schools, 384
  slavery accepted in, 385
  women in, 71–72, 76, 89nn104–5
  See also specific book
biblical tradition, 10–12, 44, 52, 56–
  57, 124, 163–64
  See also Christianity; Judaism
Big Brother (TV series), 360n21
Bill of Rights, 96–97, 166, 171, 354,
  365
Bismarck, Otto von, 102
Blackstone, William, 288
Blanshard, Paul, 377n15
Bloom, Allan, 13, 192, 193, 203n2

Boorstin, Daniel, 193
bourgeoisie, 217
Bourne, Randolph, 162
Bowles, Samuel, 347–48
Branch Davidians, 367
Brandeis, Louis, 263n32
Brennan, William J., Jr., 37
Bretall, Robert W., 159n28
British Empire, 152, 368n1
Brooklyn College, 3
Brotherhood of Man, 154–56
Brown v. Board, 37, 256
"Brutus" (Anti-Federalist), 53n10
Bryan, Samuel, 95
Bryan, William Jennings, 104, 385
Bryce, James, 277
Buckley, William F., Jr., 2
Buckley v. Valeo, 173, 186–87, 333, 347
Buddhism, 386
Buenker, John, 114n5
Bulosan, Carlos, 367
Burger Court, 296–97
Burgess, John W., 268
Burke, Edmund, 148, 195, 197–98,
    281n11, 359
Bush, George H. W., 331
Byrd, Robert, 322

Calvinism, 11
campaign finance reform, 173, 333–
    34, 346–47
Campbell, Angus, 283–84n41
Campbell, Tim, 252
capitalism
    American political thought and, 193
    conservative alliance with, 389
    family vs., 310
    globalization and, 342
    as individualistic, 135
    limitations on, 127
    Orwell's view of, 133, 134
    Protestantism and, 199
    relativism caused by, 324

religion and, 395n42
success of, and power, 185
See also economic inequality;
    globalization
Carlin, David, 367
Carter, Jimmy, 345, 390
castes, 366
Catcher in the Rye, The (Salinger),
    360n19
Catholicism, 215, 362, 363
    democracy and, 371–72
    equality and, 372–73
    Locke's intolerance of, 393n17
    "mainstreaming" of, in U.S., 373–
        74, 378nn24–25
    morality and, 375, 379n36
    pluralism and, 376, 378n31
    as political target, 372, 377n15
    as public religion, 372
Catholic rationalism, 145
Cato (Anti-Federalist), 330
Cavell, Stanley, 176n46
Cecchi, Al, 346
celebrity worship, 387
Cellucci, Paul, 386
censorship
    Berns's case for, 286–87, 288, 289–
        90, 291n
    critic and, 289
    disappearance of, 287–88
    modern dangers of, 288–89
    of self, 290–91
Central Intelligence Agency (CIA),
    279
"centrifugalism," 220
"Chairman's Problem, The"
    (Jouvenel), 187
Chamfort, Nicolas, 156
change, 34, 112, 156, 236, 268, 274
Chaunt v. U.S., 283n29
Cheney, Richard, 355
Chesterton, G. K., 32, 135, 163, 221,
    367, 378n19, 392

Chicago (IL), civil disobedience in, 270

children
  in ancient Greek families, 303
  consent of, lacking, 303–4
  custody of, 297
  education of, 70, 211, 303
  Paine's view of, 71, 72, 79
  women as trustees for, 297
  women's power exercised through, 71

China, 120

Christianity
  "amphibious" qualities of, 71, 89n98
  citizenship in, 47, 82n11
  as civil religion, 60
  as effeminate, 71–72
  egalitarian core of, 372
  framers' accommodation with, 50–51, 59–62, 366–67, 383
  French Revolution and, 63
  grace doctrine in, 47
  liberty in, 47
  morality of, 383
  natural limits as viewed in, 22
  Paine's attacks on, 62, 66, 70, 71–72, 87n64, 88n80, 89n98
  political society and, 45–46
  political teachings of, 60, 368n11
  Providence in, 150
  redemption doctrine in, 44–45, 47, 57, 83n15
  as religion of feeling, 70–76
  sacrifice in, 74
  U.S. descended from, 120, 124
  See also Catholicism; Protestantism

Christian Sparta, Adams's idea of, 46, 57, 80, 96

Christian universalism, 50–51, 60

1 Chronicles, Book of, 75, 90nn117–18

church
  as association form, 36

  as constitutional agency, 267
  educational role of, 384
  feminization of, 111
  honor in, 321
  individualism and fragmentation of, 127
  permanent obligation in, 209
  public support of, 36–37
  public virtue and, 83n14
  republican citizenship and, 338–39
  state establishment of, 166, 384
  tax breaks for, 384, 395n35

church/state separation, 36–37, 381

Cincinnatus (Anti-Federalist), 96

citizen, development of, 275–77

citizenship
  Christian idea of, 47, 82n11
  constitutional vision of, 16n9
  democratic, 347
  dignity as first principle of, 296
  economic insecurity and, 334
  education as foundation of, 37
  equality and, 295
  ethnic traditions and, 367
  friendship and, 4, 26–27
  individualism vs., 355
  legal status of, 276
  local forums as common schools of, 172
  national, 166
  political society and, 315n9
  private realm and, 275–76, 353–54
  republican, 338–39
  voting as prerogative of, 294

city-state, 125–26

civic education, 353–55
  Anti-Federalist view of, 94
  Christian ideas of, 46
  liberty and, 29
  media and, 358
  multiculturalism and, 364
  political parties and, 38
  religious means for, 37

schools and, 358
texts recommended for, 359
civic morality, 286
civil disobedience
constitutionalism and, 265, 274–80, 280
good citizen and, 276–77
judicial authorization of, 269
legitimacy and, 278–79
Locke's view of, 267, 273
to private governments, 278
punishments for, 277, 279–80
rule of law and, 265, 267
civilization, 103
civil religion, 37
American popular hopes for, 56–57
Christian doctrine and, 57–58
elitism of, 66
framers' intent regarding, 58–62
idolatry in, 86n34
liberalism and, 80–81
liberal theory and, 58–59
Paine's critique of, 63–66
Pledge of Allegiance and, 381
religion vs., 199
See also *Age of Reason, The* (Paine)
civil rights movement, 217
civil society
democracy and, 220–21
democratic, institutions of, 173
Etzioni's view of, 168, 173–74
framers and, 338–39
in liberal theory, 49, 59
Locke's view of, 49–50, 58, 83n16, 209–10, 214
Paine's view of, 67
reconciliation doctrine and, 83n16
religion and, 49–51, 61, 381–84, 393n12
republican citizenship and, 338–39
Rousseau's view of, 23
Wolin's view of, 217
See also church; community; family

civil speech, 172, 299–300, 347, 385
Civil War, 101–4, 217
Clark, Tom C., 283n29
class, social, 17n17, 366
class struggle, 102, 233
clergy sex abuse scandals, 371
Clinton, Bill, 336, 344, 345–46, 348, 351n51, 382, 390
Clinton, George, 96
Coffin, William Sloane, 266
Cold War, 118n82, 133
colonialism, 250
Coming Up for Air (Orwell), 134
commerce
Anti-Federalist view of, 95
community and, 169–70
Paine's critique of, 67
relativist influence of, 6–7, 12
supremacy of, in America, 38, 320
commercialism, 217
Committee of the Surety General, 63
Committee on Public Safety, 86n45
common good, 9
Anti-Federalist view of, 95–96
democracy and, 373
economic growth as, 120
freedom and, 143, 146–48
government as actor for, 31
in modern political philosophy, 24
national service and, 171
politics as means to, 14–15
private realm as subordinate to, 5
public philosophy and, 347–48
sacrifice for, 331
common law, 96
Common Sense (Paine), 62, 65–66, 224–25n52
Commonweal (journal), 3
communism, 13, 263n32
See also Marxism; Marxism-Leninism
Communist Manifesto (Marx and Engels), 213
communitarianism, 11, 163–64, 166

community
    Anti-Federalist view of, 97
    coercion in, 175n22
    "of communities," Etzioni's idea of,
        162–63, 166–67, 171–74
    constitutional ambivalence toward,
        165
    constraining effects of, 170–71
    democratic, 172
    education and, 172–73, 369n17
    electronic, 172
    ethnic, 117n60
    federal authority and, 169–70
    government support for, 170
    honor in, 321
    identity/meaning found in, 33
    justice and, 253–54
    liberty vs., 163
    local, decline of, 38–39, 43n80, 219
    media and, 168–69
    national, 171
    Niebuhr's view of, 148, 154–56
    nonliberal assumptions behind, 4
    private/semipublic entities as
        training ground of, 10
    Progressive view of, 107–9, 117n60
    republican citizenship and, 338–39
    in small vs. large states, 29–31
    subcommunities, 167
    U.S. institutions and exit from,
        167–68
    vulnerability of, in modern
        America, 33–34, 127
    world, 154
competition, 135, 300, 342
Complete Anti-Federalist, The (ed.
    Storing), 92
Comte, August, 106
confidence, 268–69
conflict
    cultural, 361–62
    Hobbes's view of, 159–60n35
    ideological, of 1930s, 230

illegitimacy and, 261
institutionalization of, 149–50
Locke's view of, 210
Niebuhr's view of, 147–48, 160n48
See also war, state of
conscience, 100, 101, 104–6, 109–10,
    210, 276–77
conscription, 258, 357
consent, principle of, 66, 245–46, 247–
    48, 303–4, 337
conservativism/conservatives
    antigovernment ethic of, 308
    capitalism and, 389
    Catholic, 373–74
    Cold War end and, 118n82
    equal opportunity and, 33
    "family values" rhetoric of, 311
    as McWilliams's friends, 13–14
    McWilliams's criticism of, 12
    Niebuhr and, 141
    social, 100, 345
conspiracy theories, 344–45, 351n51,
    390–91
Constant, Benjamin, 221n2
Constitution
    ambivalence toward community,
        165, 166, 167
    American "creed" and, 120
    "America's Second Voice" muted in,
        332
    Anti-Federalists and, 92
    citizenship as envisioned in, 16n9
    civil institutions not mentioned in,
        339
    congressional duties assigned by,
        122
    contractual duty mentioned in, 338
    as democratic, 329
    Eighteenth Amendment, 258
    First Amendment, 173, 384
    Fourteenth Amendment, 166, 171,
        293, 384
    habituation requirements in, 368n3

majority rule limited in, 330
multiculturalism and, 361–62, 365
Nineteenth Amendment, 294
plurality of factions in, 383–84
political parties and, 10
public philosophy underlying,
    337–39
religion unmentioned in, 381
Second Amendment, 175n26
separation of powers in, 180–81
Thirteenth Amendment, 28
undemocratic features in, 329
war powers in, 250–51, 269
See also framers
Constitutional Convention, 94–95,
    216
constitutional dictatorships, 268
*Constitutional Government in the
    United States* (Wilson), 282n16
constitutionalism
    challenges facing, 184
    civil disobedience and, 265, 274–80,
        280
    crisis of, 272–74
    liberal, Jouvenel's view of, 182, 183,
        184
    public/private distinction and,
        270–74
    public vs. private realms and,
        189–90n24
    rule of law and, 265
    traditional principles of, 266–70,
        281n11, 284n50
consumerism, 200, 213, 388–89,
    395n40
Cook, Joseph, 104
Cooley, Charles Herbert, 98–99, 107
Corinthians 1, Book of, 84–85n29
corruption, 186, 190n48, 358
Cotton, John, 83n14
Court of Chauncery, 248
creationism, 360n19
"credibility gap," 271

Crick, Bernard, 136
Croly, Herbert, 106
Cropsey, Joseph, 193, 196, 203n4
Crunden, Robert, 114n5
cultural conflict, 361–62, 373, 389
cultures, equality of, 366–67
Czechoslovakia, 191n54

Dahl, Robert, 332–33
Daniel, Book of, 65
Darrow, Clarence, 385
Darwin, Charles, 102
Darwinism, 102–3, 204n12
Davies, James, 260
decentralization, 219, 322
Declaration of Independence, 87n63,
    120, 195, 330, 331, 361, 365
Declaration of the Rights of Man,
    189n11
Dedlock, Leicester, 248
Deism, 50, 63, 76, 79, 86n42, 87n71
democracy, 151
    American, character of, 127, 168
    bourgeois origins of, 145
    campaign financing and, 173
    in contemporary politics, 332–34
    economic insecurity and, 334
    as end, 331–32
    equality in, 277, 331
    fact/value distinction and, 200
    family and, 308, 313–14
    fugitive, and politics of limits,
        218–21
    groups in, 224n45
    ideals of, 238–39
    illegitimacy and, 244, 257
    individualism in, 30–32, 127, 307–8
    institutions of, distrust in, 390–91
    liberty and, 8
    majority rule in, 27–29, 30–31
    mass, 31, 320–21, 355
    as means, 329–31
    multiculturalism and, 364–68

democracy *(cont.)*
  oligarchic, 331, 332, 346
  open politics of, 165
  political institutions in, 89n93
  Progressive quest for, 99
  public/private distinction and, 272, 307
  reform of, needed, 39
  religion and, 198–200, 362–63
  science and, 213–14
  in Soviet Union, 155
  technology vs., 190n42
  values of, 200
Democracy (H. Adams), 199–200
Democracy in America (Tocqueville), 330
democratic culture, 163
democratic economy, 219
Democratic Party, 13, 321, 322
democratic politics, 163, 342–44, 356
democratic speech, 21
democratization, 66
Denatus (Anti-Federalist), 354–55
Deneen, Patrick, 213
Dennis, Jack, 271
despotism, 303
devolution, 170
Dewey, John
  on community autonomy, 168
  on democratic political institutions, 89n93
  education of, 98
  on end in secular history, 107
  experimentalism of, 201, 212, 213–14
  liberalism as redefined by, 213–14
  on locality and community, 108, 172
  morality as viewed by, 386
  on nation-state, 109
  natural law rejected by, 201
  Niebuhr criticism of, 141, 142
  as optimist, 194

  political engagement of, 218
  on private life, 340
  on progress as social ideal, 104
  Strauss criticism of, 201
  on technique, 110
dialectic, 231, 234
dictatorships, 123, 126, 128, 235, 268
Dionne, E. J., 14, 341–42, 373
diplomacy, 153
discrimination, and equality, 294–97
dissent, 244
distrust, 256–57
diversity
  equality and, 163, 181
  framers' view of, 165, 197, 330
  increase of, in U.S., 171, 339
  religion as "bulwark" of, 199
  religious, 374–75, 385–86
  See also multiculturalism; pluralism
divorce, 310–11, 377n3
Does Civilization Need Religion? (Niebuhr), 143
Dolan, Jay, 377n4
domesticity, 312, 314, 342
Douglas, William O., 36, 311
downsizing, 341, 387
DuBois, W. E. B., 111, 112–13
Durham (NC), 36
duty, 9
Duvall, Robert, 389

economic discriminations, 296–97
economic growth
  American scorn for "materialism" vs., 120
  as common good, 120
  democracy and, 219
  family and, 309–10, 311
  liberalism and, 200
  mobility and, 309–10
  political society and, 164
  power and, 185
  private governments and, 270

republican citizenship and, 338–39
Republican social conservatism and, 128
Strauss's view of, 200
economic inequality, 332–33, 338, 341, 345, 387, 396n60
See also poverty/the poor
ecumenicalism, 375
education
of children, 70, 211, 303
citizenship and, 37
community and, 172–73, 369n17
democratic ideal reanimated through, 201
liberal, 200
"masculine," for women, 312–13
multiculturalism and, 363–64
politics and, 10–12, 38
public, 394–95n31
relativism in, 373
relativist influence on, 373
religious, 375, 384, 390
secular, 63, 394–95n31
of the soul, 112
See also civic education; moral education
egoism, 147
Einstein, Albert, 291
Eisenach, Eldon, 109
Eisenstadt v. Baird, 36, 311
elections (1996), 346
elections (2000), 373, 375
elites, 343, 368n1, 387
elitism, 238
Ellison, Ralph, 4
Ely, Richard, 103, 107
Emerson, Ralph Waldo, 104–5, 106, 164, 195, 217–18
empire, 152–53, 155, 361
empiricism, 61, 67
employment, 334, 338, 341, 387, 396n60
energy efficiency, 332–33

Engels, Friedrich, 213, 250, 342
Enlightenment, 120, 127, 151, 194
environmental degradation, 8, 16n11, 134
environmentalism, 342
E pluribus unum, 162
equality, 378n19
American valuing of, 21
Catholicism and, 372–73
as characteristic of friendship, 26, 28
children's education and, 70
Christianity and, 372
citizenship and, 295
civic, 38, 39, 300
classical ideas of, 26–27
community and, 43n80, 163–64, 171
in democracy, 277, 331
democratic ideals and, 239
discrimination compatible with, 294–97
diversity and, 163
as end, 25, 295
equality of cultures and, 366–67
equal treatment vs., 27, 39
fact/value distinction and, 200
human fraternity and, 154
in liberal tradition, 294–95
Locke's view of, 214
majority rule and, 27–29, 30–31
meaning of, 293–94
modern ideas of, 24–25
multiculturalism and, 365–67, 369n16
"of conditions," 24–25
of opportunity, 32–33
political, 34–37
private, 31
weighted representation and, 35
equality of cultures, 366–67
equal rights, 214, 298–99, 301
Equal Rights Amendment (ERA), 293, 298

equal rights movement, 311
  opponents of, 299, 301
Essays on the Scientific Study of Politics
  (Strauss), 200
Esther, Book of, 72
ethics, 147
ethnicity, 17n17, 35, 253, 296, 299–
  300, 336
ethnic slurs, 287
ethnocentricity, 366
Etzioni, Amitai
  on civil order and community, 170
  on "community of communities,"
    162–63
  as critic, 162
  inclusiveness stressed by, 169
  on local authority, 166–67
  "megalogues" of, 163, 167
  on national community, 171
  significance of, 162
  on Supreme Court and community,
    167
Euclid, 64
evangelism, 80, 104–5, 377n3
evolutionary theory, conflict over,
  385
executive power, 182–83, 284n49
extremism, 389
Ezekiel, Book of, 65
Ezra, Book of, 90n117

factions, 187, 305
faith, benefits of, 391–92
Falwell, Jerry, 134
family
  ancient Greek, 302–3
  antiliberal values of, 305–7
  capitalism and, 310
  as constitutional agency, 267
  democracy and, 308, 313–14
  educational role of, 304–5, 384
  external threats to, 307–10
  framers' view of, 303–5

government support for needed,
  311, 325
  honor in, 321
  identity/meaning found in, 33
  internal crisis in, 310–11
  nonliberal assumptions behind, 4, 9
  parental authority in, 303–4,
    316–17n47
  as political model, 209
  political society and, 301–2
  public realm and, 305–7
  rights of, 311
  sacrifice and, 209
  socialization in, 168–69
  Supreme Court cases involving, 36
  vulnerability of, in modern
    America, 33–34
  working, 340
"family values," 311
fanaticism, 66
Fanon, Fritz, 251
Farrakhan, Louis, 389
fascism, 135
"fast track" legislation, 189n22
Federalist, The
  on diversity, 330
  on "great and extraordinary
    moments," 97
  large/diverse republic promoted in,
    361
  on majority rule, 329
  on plurality of factions, 305, 381,
    383
  on public vs. private realms, 16n9
  on small vs. large states, 196, 211–
    12, 223n33, 305
  Strauss's manipulation of quotes
    from, 187
Federalist, The, #10, 187, 329, 330, 381,
  383
Federalist, The, #49, 16n9, 97
Federalist, The, #63, 359n7
Federalists, 93

feminism, 116n32, 117–18n68, 293, 298, 310
Fides et Ratio (John Paul II), 376
First Things (symposium; 1996), 389
First Treatise (Locke), 209
Fisk, Jim, 324
Flemington (NJ), 4
Foner, Philip, 86n42
Fordham University, 3
foreign aid, 333
foreign policy, 135
Fortas, Abe, 266, 275, 277
Fortin, Ernest, 376
fragmentation, 171
framers
  Anti-Federalists vs., 97
  Burke and, 197–98
  Christianity and, 50–51, 59–62, 83n15, 366–67
  church/state separation as viewed by, 36–37
  civil religion prescribed by, 58–62
  commercial republic as ideal of, 48–49, 51–52
  community as envisioned by, 165–66, 175n26
  family as viewed by, 303–5
  gentlemanly code of, 44, 56
  honor and, 337–38
  individualistic philosophy of, 121, 300
  laws and, 60–62
  liberty as viewed by, 31, 34, 121
  Locke's influence on, 60–61, 196–98, 303, 329
  morality as viewed by, 349n15
  Paine's critique of, 67
  political parties and, 10
  political society as viewed by, 122
  public philosophy of, 337–39
  religious role as envisioned by, 381–84
  "science of politics," 31
  shameless thinking of, 44, 52n1
  undemocratic statements of, 329
  See also Constitution; Hamilton, Alexander; Jefferson, Thomas; Madison, James; *specific person*
Franklin, Benjamin, 79–80, 91n138, 383
fraternity, 154–56
freedom
  at birth, 208, 222n5
  common good and, 143, 146–48
  economic autonomy and, 334
  equality and, 28–29
  ethics and, 147
  human fraternity and, 154
  international politics and, 153
  inward, 66–67
  as lack of constraint, 7, 28–29
  law and, 123
  liberal politics and, 208–12
  in liberal theory, 7, 142–43
  in modern political philosophy, 23
  morality vs., 128
  natural, 48, 208–12
  politics of, 187–88
  power needed for, 147–48
  See also assembly freedoms; liberty; press freedoms; religious freedoms; speech freedoms
"free riders," 348
French Revolution
  Age of Reason publishing history and, 62–63
  Paine's critique of, 66, 68, 71
  price controls during, 87n71
  revolutionary foundings and, 66
  rhetoric of, 86n34
  Strauss's view of, 196
French student movement, 343
Friedrich, Carl J., 274, 284n50
friendship, 4, 26–27, 28
Frontiero v. Richardson, 297
frugality, 46, 82n9, 95

Fulbright, J. William, 284n49
fundamental rights, doctrine of, 295–96, 315n9

Galbraith, John Kenneth, 33
Galston, William, 192
Gandhi, Mohandas, 139
gay marriage, 375, 379n36
gays, 336, 369n16
Gellhorn, Walter, 269
gender distinctions, 297–99, 387
generosity, 338
Genesis, Book of, 52n1, 90n127
Germany, Progressives educated in, 102
Gettysburg Address (1863), 21, 105, 331
Gilman, Charlotte Perkins, 116n32, 117n60, 117–18n68, 118n77
Gingrich, Newt, 322, 323
Gintis, Herbert, 347–48
Gitlin, Todd, 337, 397n74
Gitlow v. N.Y., 255, 263n32
G. K.'s Weekly, 135
Gladden, Washington, 106–7
Glaucon, 25
Glendon, Mary Ann, 311
globalization, 168, 184, 219, 334, 342, 354
Golden Rule, 174, 261n1, 347
Goldman, Eric, 104, 204n12, 369n25
government
    Anti-Federalist view of, 330
    community as foundation of, 154
    decentralization of, 322
    democratic politics and, 343–44
    distrust in, 329, 342–44, 354, 390–91
    as impersonal, 342
    legitimacy of, 245, 249, 262n8
    market economy and, 12
    moral mission of, 100–101
    parliamentary model of, 179–80
    private, 270–71, 278
    rehabilitation of, 344–48

representative, 96, 253, 267–68, 330, 365
    role of, 12–13, 31, 48, 165, 188, 197, 330, 337
    size of, 33, 46, 128
    as violation of natural rights, 246
    violent overthrow of, 263n32
grace, 47, 48, 52, 57–58, 66
graft, 186, 190n48
Graham, Billy, 389
Grant, Ruth, 222n5
Great Society, 345
Greeks, ancient, 10–11, 124, 238, 302–3, 317n49
Gregory, Wilton, 378n24
Grimsley, Kristin Downey, 387
Griswold v. Connecticut, 36, 311
growth, 25, 32
Guizot, François, 385

Haas, Ernst, 237
Hall, G. Stanley, 106
Hallowell, John, 368n11
Hamilton, Alexander, 5, 223n34
    Caesar as hero of, 224n51
    on city-states, 49, 216
    democracy as viewed by, 151
    on economic autonomy and freedom, 334
    on government, choice of, 101–2
Hammermill Paper Corporation, 278
Handlin, Oscar, 204n15
Hartz, Louis, 120–21, 141–42, 193
Harvard University, 3
Haven, Joseph, 100
Haverford College, 3
Hawthorne, Nathaniel, 4, 251
Hayek, Friedrich von, 185
Hebrews, Book of, 76
Hebrew Scriptures, 105, 198
hedonism, 134
Hedrick, Earle Raymond (grandfather), 1

Hedrick family (mother's family), 1
Hegel, G. W. F., 23, 150, 221n2, 231, 234, 237
Hendin, Herbert, 34
Henry, Patrick, 96, 216–17
heroes, 357, 373
Herzen, Alexander, 24
Herzfeld, Michael, 366
Hinds County (MS), 35
Hinduism, 386
Hindu nationalism, 345
Hirschman, Albert, 167
historical materialism, 235–36
historicism, 204n20
    framers and, 198
    honor and, 324
    liberal education infected with, 200
    in modern political philosophy, 192, 193
    Orwell's view of, 136
    Paine's skepticism about, 67
    Strauss and, 203n5
history
    Marxist, 233–36
    modern creed of, 229–30
    nemesis in, 233
    philosophy of, 204n20, 266
    progress in, 143, 145–46, 147, 150–52
    sacred, 233, 235, 236
    secular, 234, 235
    traditional, 232
    See also time and history
History of Political Philosophy, The (ed. Strauss and Cropsey), 193, 196, 203n4
History of Political Theory (Sabine), 193, 203n4
Hitler, Adolf, 138, 230
Hobbes, Thomas, 5, 53n17, 196
    conflict as viewed by, 147–48, 159–60n35
    on humans and nature, 48
    on illegitimacy, 240, 261n1
    liberalism of, 4
    liberty as defined by, 22
    modern political thought and, 24
    natural state in, 208–9
    as secular "realist," 144
Hofstadter, Richard, 193
Holmes, Oliver Wendell, 93, 142, 249, 263n32, 300
Holmes, Oliver Wendell, Sr., 290
home, crisis of, 301
    See also children; family
Home Guard, 137
homophobia, 364
honor
    bestowal of, 319–21
    deinstitutionalization of, 324
    democratic, 319, 321–23
    dignity vs., 323–24
    framers and, 337–38
    inequality of, 319
    partisan, 322
    sacrifice and, 331
    sources of, 321
    technology and, 321–22, 324–25
    undermining of, 320, 324–25
Hopkins, Mark, 106
housing, open, 39
Huffington, Michael, 346
human rights, 121, 128
Hume, David, 67–68
humility, 392
Hunterdon County (NJ) Democratic Committee, 4
Hunterdon County (NJ) Historical Society, 4
Huxley, Aldous, 134
Hyde, Henry, 322

idealism, 147, 149
Idea of Fraternity in America, The (McWilliams), 3
identity politics, 169, 171, 336, 343

ideology, 133, 138, 231
Ideology and Utopia (Mannheim), 231
idolatry, 86n34
illegitimacy, political
    arbitrariness and, 258–59
    bad faith and, 256–57
    belief and, 259–61
    civil disobedience and, 278–79
    constitutional procedure and,
        248–50
    crisis of, 240, 247
    criteria of, 252–59
    impersonality and, 252–54
    internal standards of, 247–52
    political bankruptcy and, 254–56
    progress and, 250–52
    reason and, 247–48
    use of term, 243, 244–45
immigration, 13, 368n3, 372
imperialism, 95, 152, 201
impersonality, 10, 252–54, 342–43
incarceration rates, 332–33
income tax, 295
Independence Day (film; 1996), 171,
    345
India, 345, 368n1
Indiana Senate, 35
individualism
    Americans and, 52, 120, 127–29
    bourgeois, 185
    capitalism and, 135
    citizen proneness to, 30
    citizenship vs., 355
    in democracies, 31–32, 307–8
    distrust strengthened by, 107
    DuBois's view of, 113
    liberal, 300–301
    liberalism and, 209
    military recruiting and, 360n13
    modern idea of liberty and, 23
    modernity "first wave" vs., 192
    morality and, 386
    policy proposals and, 8

public realm infected with, 34
secular, 374, 393–94n18
individual rights, 10, 58, 167, 178, 179,
    213
    defense of, 338
industrial society, 282n16, 287, 288–89
industry, 46, 82n9, 104, 124
infantilism, 71, 74
instinct, 67
insulation effect, 256
intellectuality, Orwell's critique of,
    137–38, 139
interest groups, 187
intermarriage taboos, 171
international capital, 342
international politics, 152–54, 268
international trade, 345
Internet, 214
Iraq, U.S. invasion of, 210
Isaiah, Book of, 72
Islam, 362–63, 386
Israel, 258

Jackson, Andrew, 5
Jackson, Jesse, 389
Jackson, Robert H., 269
Jacobinism, 75, 156
Jacobson, Norman, 2–3
Jaffa, Harry V., 203–4n9
James, William, 103
Jefferson, Thomas
    Christianity as viewed by, 70, 88n73,
        383
    on democracy, 220, 225n68
    on economic autonomy and
        freedom, 334, 338, 340, 341, 364
    honorable work as viewed by,
        322–23
    intellectuality of, 186
    Paine and, 80
    philosophical liberalism and, 120
    "protective imperialism" policy of,
        152

on religion and civil society, 393n12, 394n27
religion as viewed by, 50, 83n20, 84n22, 223n30, 382
as "second voice," 4
on self-preservation, 394n23
Jensen, Arthur Robert, 287
Jeremiah, Book of, 72
Jesus, 70–71, 77, 84n23, 87n58, 105, 111, 115n19
Job, Book of, 65, 74, 78
John, Gospel of, 81n6, 87n64
John Paul II, Pope, 376, 391
Johnson, Lyndon B., 5, 253
Jones, Jesse Henry, 104
Jones, Paula, 344
Joshua, Book of, 75
Jouvenel, Bertrand de, 9, 224n37
    American power as viewed by, 178–79, 189n22
    Beneš and, 191n54
    on Declaration of the Rights of Man, 189n11
    economic power as viewed by, 185–86
    legitimacy as viewed by, 246–47, 254
    liberty and power as viewed by, 179–80
    as "pessimistic evolutionist," 179
    political liberty as viewed by, 187–88
    political parties as viewed by, 186–87
    political science redefined by, 182–85
    on rule of law, 181–83
    social contract theory as viewed by, 209
Judaism, 22, 60, 70, 71, 120, 124, 205n33
Judge, Mark Gauvreau, 388
Judges, Book of, 73, 76
judicial review, 180–81

judiciary, 269, 281n12
    See also United States Supreme Court
jury, 183, 254, 300, 358–59
justice, 149, 214, 215, 243, 252, 253–54, 331, 348

Kammen, Michael, 205n28
Kant, Immanuel, 147, 150, 155, 221n2
Kateb, George, 217–18
Kaus, Mickey, 341
Keep the Aspidistra Flying (Orwell), 137
Kegley, Charles W., 159n28
Keniston, Kenneth, 237
Kennedy, John F., 357
Kent State massacre (1970), 250
Key, V. O., 272
Kings 1, Book of, 90n117, 198
Kingston, Maxine Hong, 367
Kipling, Rudyard, 108, 135
Kirk, Russell, 221–22n4
Koran, 363
Korea, South, 120, 123
Kristol, William, 192

Lafayette College, 3
laissez-faire economics, 185
Landers, Ann, 305–6
Lapham, Lewis, 168
Lardner, James, 350n43
Lasch, Christopher, 9
Last of the Wine, The (Renault), 392n2
Lathrop, Joseph, 45
law
    American, 31–32
    "America's Second Voice" muted by, 332
    Christian theory and, 45
    civil religion and, 60–62, 67
    of "common decency," 287–88
    community and, 167
    consent given in, 66

law (cont.)
  as divinely founded, 199
  equality before, 26
  evaluation of, 358
  framers' trust in workings of, 60–62
  judicial review of, 180–81
  jury as interpreter of, 183
  in liberal theory, 6
  liberty as public principle in, 339
  limitations of, 293
  moral, 102, 106
  multiculturalism and, 361–62
  natural, 136
  negative stating of, 267
  political society and, 122, 126
  religion and, 380, 393–94n18
  rule of, 122–24, 128, 180, 181–83,
    216–17, 265, 277–78
  self-interest and, 6
  statute, 268
Lawrence, D. H., 224n49
layoffs, 341, 387
Lee, Richard Henry, 93–94
legislature, and constitutionalism,
    267–69, 281–82n16
legitimacy, political
  consent and, 245–46
  defined, 240, 241, 244, 262n4
  expectation and, 254–56
  moral content of, 241–43, 246–47,
    262n6
  use of term, 240–45
  See also illegitimacy, political
lesbians, 336, 369n16
Letters concerning Toleration (Locke),
    51, 224n46
Leviathan (Hobbes), 148, 208, 261n1
Lewinsky, Monica, 344, 358
Lewis, Anthony, 285n66
liberal education, 200
liberal individualism, 300–301
liberalism
  American "creed" and, 120

  as "amphibious," 80
  Anglo-American, 207, 221n2
  argumentative style of, 143
  central doctrines of, 143
  civil society and, 49
  constitutionalism of, 182,
    189–90n24
  equality and, 294–95
  family and, 305–7
  fears of, 273–74
  fraternity and, 154
  freedom as viewed by, 142–43
  groups favored in, 16–17n15
  individualism and, 8, 209
  "interest group," 187
  "irrational Lockeanism" of, 142
  legitimacy and, 246–47
  liberty as viewed by, 216
  market economy and, 6–7
  as nemesis, 207
  Niebuhr as critic/exemplar of, 141–
    43, 150–51, 153–54
  Paine's critique of, 75–76, 80–81
  philosophic, 120–21, 122, 123
  preliberal inheritance behind, 4, 124
  progress and, 122, 290–91
  as rationalistic, 207
  reason and, 200, 211, 221–22n4
  relativism of, 6
  religion and, 143
  rightist defenses of, 13
  science and, 213–14
  self-rule and, 124–25
  Superpower doctrine and, 207
  totalitarian logic of, 212–15, 218
  universalism of, 154, 156
liberal politics, 208–12, 215–18
liberal spirits, 215–18
liberal theory, 11
  civil religion and, 58–59
  ends vs. means in, 5–6
  freedom in, 7
  illegitimacy in, 247–52

mastery in, 216
nation-state in, 10
public as subordinate to private in, 5, 7
war vs. peace in, 123–24
liberal utopianism, 142
liberation, 113
libertarianism, 188, 355, 386
liberty
American valuing of, 21, 33, 34, 385
Anti-Federalist view of, 95
Christian idea of, 47
community vs., 163
current threats to, 171
democratic, 8, 28–29
as end, 80
fragmentation as result of, 37–38
framers' view of, 121
as lack of constraint, 7–8, 24
liberalism and, 216
modern ideas of, 23–24, 25
moral foundations of, 189n11
negative vs. positive, 22
Paine's view of, 80
political, 187–88
power and, 22, 159n28, 179–80
as public principle, 339
public vs. private, 28
religion and, 381
rethinking role of, 39
security and, 224n46
"spirit of," 354–55
spiritual, 22
traditional ideas of, 22–23, 39
See also freedom
limits, 22, 145, 218–21
Lincoln, Abraham, 21, 105, 166, 188, 195, 203–4n9, 331
Lipovetsky, Gilles, 343
Lippmann, Walter, 336
Lipset, Seymour M., 240, 241, 244, 285n56
Lipsitz, Lewis, 36, 275

Livy, 292n8
lobbies, 94
localism, 220
localities, 166, 339
Lochner v. New York, 270
Locke, John, 5, 76, 83n20, 205n25
Catholicism as viewed by, 393n17
childhood education idea of, 211, 223n30
civil disobedience as viewed by, 267, 273
conflict as viewed by, 148, 210, 335n11
as empiricist, 61
equal rights as viewed by, 214
family as viewed by, 209
framers influenced by, 60–61, 196–98, 303, 329
freedom as viewed by, 23, 148
on humans and nature, 48
individualism promoted by, 196
on law, strict interpretation of, 267
legitimacy as viewed by, 249, 250
liberalism of, 4, 216
on natural reason, 54n24, 83n16
natural rights idea of, 205n25
natural state in, 208, 208–11, 335n11
Paine's critique of, 64
politics, origin of, 47
on progress, 250
property idea of, 196, 198, 223n24
on reason and consent, 247
on religion and civil society, 49–50, 51, 58, 59, 223n30, 382–83
"reserved rights" doctrine of, 179
Rousseau's critique of, 205n25
scriptural references in, 223n24
Strauss's linking of Madison to, 196–97, 205n25
theology of, 51, 54nn30, 32, 60, 70, 78, 84–85n29, 85n31, 87nn58–59, 388
toleration of, 215

Lockeanism, 142, 179–80, 267
Longfellow, Samuel Wadsworth, 47,
105
love, 120
among citizens, 4
ethic of, 386
grace and, 57–58
identity/meaning found in, 33
justice and, 149
mutual, 83n12
private, 33–34
Progressive view of, 107
as self-sacrifice, 146–47
vulnerability of, in modern
America, 33–34
women's power in, 71
Lovejoy, Elijah, 204n9
Lowell, James Russell, 101
Lowenstein, Allard, 256
Lowi, Theodore, 249, 336, 340,
395n31, 396n60
Löwith, Karl, 206n43
Luke, Gospel of, 54n32, 71, 85n31
Lyall, Charles, 102

Machiavelli, Niccolò, 5, 144, 156,
159n28, 196, 199, 229, 232
MacLeish, Archibald, 194–95, 204n12
Madison, James, 5, 16n9, 88n78
on Bill of Rights, 354
civic education and, 359
democracy as viewed by, 151,
220–21
diversity as ruling principle of, 48,
197
fears of, 273
on government, role of, 165, 197,
337
on "great and extraordinary
moments," 97
liberty as viewed by, 216, 381
majority rule as viewed by, 329–30
natural rights as viewed by, 197

property as viewed by, 198
on reason, unreliability of, 211
on religion and civil society, 393n12,
394n29
on self-government, 175n20
on small vs. large states, 94
on Socrates's moral tone, 50, 83n19
Strauss's linking of Locke to, 196–
97, 205n25
on war and legitimacy, 251
majority rule
community and, 171–72
as equality, 27–29
force and, 220
framers' arguments for, 329–30
oligarchy and, 346
restrictions on, 274, 330, 365
rightness vs., 47
as tyranny, 30–31, 162, 197
Mamercus, 292n8
man
brotherhood of, 154–56
imperfections of, 157
perfectibility of, 143–46, 147
Mannheim, Karl, 138, 231
Mansfield, Harvey C., 14, 166, 216,
365, 386
Marcuse, Herbert, 136, 289
marijuana, 258
Mark, Gospel of, 54n30, 85n29
market economy, 345, 387–88
See also capitalism
marriage, 36, 303, 310–11, 388
Marshall, John, 96–97
Marx, Karl, 13, 218, 221n2
on consumerism, 213
freedom as viewed by, 23
globalization predicted by, 342
history and, 231
legitimacy and, 250
Niebuhr compared to, 150
Marxism, 124, 156, 232, 233–36
Marxism-Leninism, 113, 145, 168

mass communications, 110
mastery
  equality and, 25
  of history, 230
  of humanity, 212
  in liberal theory, 216
  quest for, 129, 135, 200
  technical, Progressive view of, 103–4
  of technique, 388
  See also nature, human mastery of
materialism, 8, 107, 120, 235–36
Matthew, Gospel of, 81n6, 390
McCarthy, Joseph, 270
McClosky, Herbert, 271
McConnell, Grant, 270
McCosh, James, 100, 112
McMahon, Francis, 378n31
McWilliams, Carey (father), 1–2
McWilliams, Dorothy Hedrick
  (mother), 1
McWilliams, Nancy Riley (wife), 3–4
McWilliams, Wilson Carey
  awards received by, 3, 14–15
  birth of, 1
  childhood of, 1–2
  community life of, 3–4
  death of, 3, 14
  educational background, 2–3, 207
  as leftist, 13–14, 292n6
  political philosophy of, 4–15
  publication record of, 3
  teaching career of, 3
media
  celebrity worship in, 387
  civic education and, 358
  as controlling instrument, 214
  electronic, campaign expenditures
    on, 173
  local community weakened by, 172
  new, 172
  news manipulated by, 257
  as private government, 270
  public dependence on, 270–71

  public/representative distance
    eliminated through, 322, 350n43
  religion/civil society relations as
    portrayed in, 389
  socialization through, 168–69
media culture, 345
Medicare, 323
medievalism, 149, 150
megamergers, 342
Melville, Herman, 4
Merced (CA), 2
Merriam, Charles, 98, 194
Meyer, D. H., 99, 100
middle class, 136–37, 334, 341–42
military, 7–8
  conscription, 258
  politics vs., 123–24
  rule by, 124, 126–27, 128
militia, obligation to serve in, 175n26
Mill, John Stuart, 221n2, 250
Miller, Perry, 81n4
Mills, C. Wright, 255
Milton, John, 89n109
Minersville School District v. Gobitis,
    393n9
minority rights, 27–28
miracles, 64, 87n59, 88n91
mobility
  culture of, 2, 7, 38–39, 168, 309–10,
    357
  upward, 32
"Model of Christian Charity, A"
    (Winthrop), 12
modernity
  defects of, need to address, 201
  "first wave" vs. historicists/
    individualists, 192, 196–98, 202
  intellectuals as voice of, 138
  liberty and, 23–24
  Niebuhr's view of, 141
  Orwell's view of, 133, 138
  time/history relations and, 239
monarchy, 24, 165

monotheism, 70
Montesquieu, 180, 182, 196, 221n2
Moore, J. Howard, 102, 103, 107, 108
moral education
  Berns's view of, 291n
  democracy and, 291n
  through family, 304–5
  framers' view of, 167, 304–5, 383
  human need for, 9
  Paine's view of, 79
  through private institutions, 9, 167,
    384
  Progressivism and, 109–10
  religion and, 383
  schools inadequate for, 355
  Tocqueville's view of, 314
  women and, 312, 314
morality
  American, 337
  Catholicism and, 375, 379n36
  Christian, 70, 383
  civic, 286
  commerce and, 56
  community and, 171
  democratic liberty and, 189n11
  Etzioni's view of, 171, 173–74
  framers and, 349n15
  individualism and, 386
  legitimacy and, 241–43, 246–47,
    262n6
  natural, 68
  Orwell's view of, 135–36
  Paine's view of, 67–68, 70, 73–74,
    77–78
  political science and, 182–83
  political society and, 126
  privatization of, 339–40
  Progressive view of, 106
  religion and, 374–75, 381, 386–89
  sexual, 288
  sexual conduct and, 358
  socialism and, 136
moral law, 102, 106, 115n19

Moral Man and Immoral Society
  (Niebuhr), 141
Moral Science, 99–101, 104–5, 112
Moral Science (Wayland), 105, 115n14
Moral State, 100–101
Mormonism, 384
Morris, Gouverneur, 48, 216, 224n46
Morrison, Charles Clayton, 378n31
Moses, 74–75, 105
multiculturalism
  Constitution and, 361–62, 365
  contemporary, 162, 364
  democracy and, 364–68
  education and, 363–64
  elite rule and, 368n1
  equality and, 365–67, 369n16
  McWilliams and, 9
  religion and, 362–63
Mumford, Lewis, 234
Murdoch, Rupert, 134
Murray, John Courtney, 376

Napier, John, 290
Nation (magazine), 2
National Association of Secretaries of
  State, 353
National Endowment for the
  Humanities, 3
National Historical Society, 3
nationalism, 71, 107, 109, 152
national service, 171, 348
nation-state, 10, 109, 152, 155
natural law, 136, 145, 152, 201, 380
natural man, 144, 148
natural morality, 68
natural religion, 76–80
Natural Right and History (Strauss),
  195, 196, 197, 198
natural rights
  Anti-Federalist view of, 96
  classical vs. modern ideas of, 22–23,
    47–48
  constitutional mentions of, 381

framers' view of, 47–48, 61, 121, 197, 205n25, 330
government as violation of, 246
law and, 123
in liberal theory, 246
Niebuhr's view of, 145
Paine's view of, 62
Sabine's view of, 193
Strauss's view of, 201
natural selection, 155
nature
abundance of, 210–11
conflict in, 210
framers and, 198
liberty and, 22–23
limits set by, 22, 45, 67
man's imperfections and, 157
as moral government, 100
obedience to, 129, 229
perfectibility of man and, 143–44
Progressive view of, 103
self-rule and, 124–25
nature, human mastery of
Christian redemption doctrine and, 44–45
framers' view of, 48–49, 121–22
as goal of modern political philosophy, 133, 164, 198, 229
in liberal theory, 6, 156, 200, 212, 250
Niebuhr's view of, 156
Orwell's view of, 133, 138
progress as, 250
Strauss's view of, 200
Wolin's view of, 212
nature, state of
anarchy and, 40n17
Anti-Federalist view of, 93
equality and, 31
escaping, in liberal thought, 6, 49, 58–59, 216, 246
family and, 306–7
framers' view of, 31, 306–7, 382
illegitimacy of, 246

liberal society and, 123
Locke's view of, 208–11, 214, 220, 335n11
majority rule and, 220
Niebuhr's placement of, in Eden, 148
political society vs., 93
rediscovery of, Wolin's view of, 208, 211
Nazi Germany, 138, 244–45, 260, 291
Nevin, John Williamson, 395n42
New Age religion, 386
New Deal, 114n5, 178, 181, 185–86
New Golden Rule, 170
New Jersey Committee for the Humanities, 14–15
New Jersey Supreme Court, 43n80
New Left, 244, 292n6
"new man," the, 69–70
New Millennium Project, 353
Newsday (journal), 3
Newton, Isaac, 216
"New World Order," 344–45
Niebuhr, Reinhold
bankruptcy of ideas of, 157
community as viewed by, 154–56
Dewey criticized by, 141, 142
freedom as social good in, 146–48
historical progress as viewed by, 150–52, 160n48
as idealist, 147, 149
international politics as viewed by, 152–54
liberalism critiqued/exemplified by, 141–43, 150–51, 153–54
morality as viewed by, 386
on patriotism, 109
perfectibility of man as viewed by, 143–46, 147
as "realist," 143, 147, 150–51
significance of, 141, 142
social contract theory and, 148–50
stylistic faults of, 158n2
utopianism and, 156–57

Nietzsche, Friedrich, 195, 217–18, 392n4
nihilism, 23, 110, 248
Niles, Nathaniel, 45, 47, 82nn7, 11, 93, 383, 393n18
1984 (Orwell), 133–34, 135, 137, 139
Nixon, Richard M., 241, 243
noblesse oblige, 24
Noll, Mark, 106
Norton, Anne, 361
Numbers, Book of, 74–75

Oberlin College, 3, 108
O'Brien, David, 377n4
obscenity, censorship of, 286
Ohio Supreme Court, 37
oikos, polis as servant of the, 7
oligarchy, 331, 332, 333, 346–47
On Power (Jouvenel), 178–79, 186
On the Waterfront (film; 1954), 325n3, 326n17
opportunity, equality of, 32–33
optimism, 32
Organization of Petroleum Exporting Countries (OPEC), 95
original sin, 84–85n29, 104
Orwell, George
  ideology and, 133, 138
  intellectuality critiqued by, 137–38, 139
  political society as viewed by, 134–35
  significance of, 139–40
  as socialist, 136–37
  on truth and freedom, 139
outsourcing, 387

paganism, 60, 86n34, 386
Paine, Thomas
  ideas of, as unoriginal, 86n42
  imprisonment of, during French Revolution, 62, 86n45
  market economy and, 87n71

political praxis of, 88n82
  Reagan's quoting of, 12
  on "the happy something," 224–25n52
  writing style of, 65, 195
  See also *Age of Reason, The*
Panetta, Leon, 360n18
Pangle, Thomas, 195, 204n15
parochialism, 169
Parsons, Talcott, 262n4
patriarchalism, 303
patriotism, 9, 50, 59, 109, 126, 329, 360n13, 377n16
Paul, Saint, 69, 76, 111, 380
peace, 153, 154, 250–51
Pearson, David, 175n22
perfectibility, 143–46, 147
Persecution and the Art of Writing (Strauss), 194
perspectivism, 206n41
philanthropy, 164, 383
philosopher-kings, 285n57
philosophy, 14–15, 199
  of history, 204n20, 266
  See also public philosophy, American
Pierce v. Society of Sisters, 394–95n31
Pinckney, Charles Cotesworth, 365
Plato, 14
  civic education and, 359
  equality in, 25
  on family and politics, 314
  law as viewed by, 266
  natural limits as viewed by, 22
  Niebuhr's view of, 157
  on political friendship, 26–27
  on political society, 11, 125, 157
  See also *Republic*
Player Piano (Vonnegut), 137
Pledge of Allegiance, 381, 393nn9–10
Plunkitt, George Washington, 363
pluralism, 224n45
  Catholicism and, 376, 378n31

common first principles and, 347
framers' view of, 305, 381, 383–84
new media and, 172
Niebuhr's advocacy of, 152
religion and, 385
plutocracy, 184, 225n61
polis
Anti-Federalist view of, 96
liberty and, 26, 39
political friendship and, 26–27
as prior to the individual, 93
as servant of the *oikos*, 7
political bankruptcy, 254–56
political imagination, 231
Political Liberalism (Rawls), 215
political movements, 253
political participation, decline of, 7
political parties
centralization of, 322
community and, 173
dangers of, 186
decline of, 38, 186–87, 271–72, 284n41
honor in, 322
as links between individuals and
government, 10
local organizations, 325
mass, 343
in parliamentary government
model, 179–80
as private governments, 271
Progressive criticism of, 98
political philosophy, American
goal of, 221
liberalism and decline of, 207
religion and, 198–200
stature of, 193–94
Strauss and, 192–93, 194
theory vs. practice in, 195–98
writing in, 194–95, 204n11
political science
Jouvenel's redefinition of, 182–85
"legitimacy" as buzzword in, 240
new, need for, 182

relevant debate in, 202
Strauss's view of, 203n2
political society
Anti-Federalist view of, 93–97
as bargain, 216
citizenship and, 315n9
contractual creation of, 211
family and, 301–2
founding of, on opinion, 286
framers' view of, 122
harmony in, 148–49
individualism and, 127
military and, 126–27
Niebuhr's view of, 148–50
Orwell's view of, 134–35
power and, 212
private components of, 301
rule of law and, 181
self-rule and, 124–25
small state ideal for, 125–26
youth and, 202
politics
campaign financing in, 173
classical vs. modern views of, 5–6
decadence of, 290
educational role of, 10–12, 45
equality and, 26
as exercise, 356, 360n17
of freedom, 187–88
of limits, 218–21
limits of, 345
as means, 14–15
military vs., 123–24
open, 361
radical solutions needed for, 8–9
religion and, 362–63
religion as support for, 49–51, 58
"science of," 31, 151
"third-way," 345
Politics and Vision (Wolin), 207,
221n2
Politics of Disappointment, The
(McWilliams), 3

Pollak, Otto, 317n58
Polsby, Nelson, 282n18
polygamy, 384
polytheism, 71
Popper, Karl, 214, 221n2
populism, 9
positivism, 200
postmodernism, 162, 219, 220,
    225n64, 355, 373, 397n74
poverty/the poor
  discrimination based on, 296–97
  equality of opportunity and, 32
  framers and, 49, 50
  Jesus as tied to, 77
  Supreme Court cases involving,
    35–36, 38–39
  See also economic inequality
power
  American, 178–79
  balance of, 152–53
  division of, 149, 180–81, 211–12,
    223n33, 267–70
  economic, 185–86
  as end, 126
  executive, 182–83
  expansion of, 7–8, 190n39, 212–15
  in family relationships, 303–4
  federal, and community, 169–70
  freedom and, 147–48
  inequality of, 34, 225n61
  legitimacy and, 247
  liberty and, 7–8, 22, 159n28, 179–80
  mastery of nature and, 6
  natural history of, 224n37
  political society and, 212
  quest for, 147–48
  restraints on, 184–85, 189n11
  rule of law and, 181–83
  Superpower doctrine, 212–15
  war, 250–51, 269
pragmatism, 101, 110, 135
prediction, 231, 237
press freedoms, 263n32

primaries, direct, 10, 173
privacy rights, 13, 36
private governments, 270–71, 278
private realm
  American retreat into, 33–34, 169,
    386
  citizenship and, 275–76, 339,
    353–54
  community and, 169
  in liberal theory, 5
  pre-/nonliberal sources of, 9
  religion and, 50, 58
private rights, 93
privatization, 171, 344
progress
  equality and, 32–33
  framers' view of, 198
  industrial, 124, 136
  intellectual, 88n80
  legitimacy and, 250–52
  liberalism and, 143, 290–91
  material, 56, 101, 122
  as measure of political good, 122
  modern ideologies of, 13
  moral, 101, 107
  Niebuhr's view of, 142, 145–46, 147,
    150–52
  Paine's view of, 68, 88n80
  Progressive view of, 101, 104, 106,
    107–8, 112, 112–13, 201
  rationalist faith in, 67–68
  scientific, 200
  Strauss's view of, 203n5
Progressive Era, 341
Progressivism
  community as end in, 107–9
  ethnic communities and, 117n60
  exceptions to, 111–13
  moral education and, 109–10
  Moral Science background of,
    99–101
  movement characteristics, 98–99,
    101

post–Civil War cultural crisis and, 101–4

"reform Darwinism" and, 204n12

relativism in argumentation of, 104–6, 110, 204n12

significance of, 99, 109

study of, in American political thought, 193

urban/ethnic dimensions of, 114n5

progressivism, new, 342

Prohibition, 287–88

proletariat, 136, 234–35

property, 196, 197, 223n24

prophecy, 68–69, 76, 88n91

Protestantism, 44, 57, 98–99, 376–77n3, 378n31

Proverbs, Book of, 73–74

Providence, 150

Psalms, Book of, 77

public office, right to seek/hold, 295–96

public philosophy, American

antigovernment sentiments, 342–44

decline of, 336–37

democratic, 346–47

of framers, 337–39

goal of, 337

government, rehabilitation of, 344–48

oligarchic, 346–47

private philosophy vs., 337

public life vs., 339–42

self-government as focus of, 336

self-interest and, 339

public realm

churches and, 83n14

citizenship and, 339

expectations of, 344

family and, 305–7

indignity of, in modern America, 33–34

law and, 167

in liberal theory, 5

limitations of, 34

political excluded from, in tyranny, 274–75

private realm as subordinate to, 5

privatization of, 344

in republics, 47

temptations in, 358

women in, 312–13

public spirit, 47, 82n8

Puritanism, 134

Puritans, 4, 12, 46, 100, 165, 199, 204n15, 383

Putnam, Robert, 333

Qur'an, 363

race, 108, 111, 112–13, 296, 387

racial minorities, 17n17, 35, 166, 170, 253, 299–300, 336

racial segregation, 219

racism, 107, 260, 287, 364, 366

radio, 168–69, 350n43

rationalism, 44, 67, 120, 145, 150, 198

liberalism as rooted in, 207

Rauschenbusch, Walter, 109, 111–12

Rawls, John, 214–15, 221n2, 224n45

Raynal, Abbé, 67, 68

Reagan, Ronald, 12, 80, 311, 345, 377n3

realism, 143, 144–45, 157, 193

reason

consent and, 247–48

French Revolution as proof of insufficiency of, 63

liberalism and, 200, 221–22n4

natural, 54n24, 83n16

religion and, 59–60, 382–83

unreliability of, 210, 211

reconciliation, 89n109

Reconstruction, 166

redemption, Christian doctrine of, 44–45, 47, 52, 73–74, 83n15

Reformation, 88n80, 363

regionalism, 155
Reich, Robert, 169
Reid, Thomas, 99–100
relativism
  "comparative world culture" courses
    and, 169
  in contemporary education, 373
  framers and, 205n28
  historical, 145, 234, 236
  honor and, 324
  influence of, at universities, 373
  liberalism and, 6
  market economy and, 345, 389
  Marx's view of, 234, 236
  Niebuhr's view of, 145
  Orwell's view of, 136, 138
  perspectivism and, 206n41
  in Progressive argument, 104–6,
    110, 204n12
  youth and, 109
religion
  in American cultural dialogue,
    198–99
  capitalism and, 395n42
  civil religion vs., 199
  civil role of, 381–84, 393n12
  constitutional mentions of, 381
  cultural conflict over, 361–62
  democracy and, 362–63
  individualism limited by, 32
  liberalism and, 143
  "mainstream," 388–89
  morality and, 374–75, 381, 386–89
  natural, 76–80
  need for, in modern U.S., 389–92
  philosophy vs., 199
  pluralistic, 385
  political society and, 380–81
  politics and, 14–15, 49–51, 362–63
  popular culture and, 56–57
  reason and, 59–60, 382–83
  republics and, 82n9
  revealed, 71, 338, 382–83

science vs., 88n80, 101
  "spirit of," 354, 355
  state support for, 377nn11, 16
  theory vs. practice and, 199
  See also Christianity; civil religion
religious education, 375, 384, 390
religious freedoms, 37, 81n5, 385
religious organizations, 336
religious tests, 51, 81n5
religious wars/persecutions, 58
Renault, Mary, 392n2
Reno (NV), 2
representative government, 96, 253,
    330, 365
repression, 166, 171
republic
  Christian grace doctrine in, 58
  citizenship in, 338–39
  civic virtue in, 94–96
  civil disobedience within, 273
  commercial, as framers' ideal, 48–
    49, 51–52
  large, 48–49, 50, 53n10, 82n9, 92, 94
  public spirit in, 47, 82n8
  small, 46, 49
Republic (Plato)
  criminality as invisible in, 123
  on family and politics, 316n41
  on legitimacy, 243
  on military, 127
  political conversation in, 360n16
  on rule of the strong, 302
  on shamelessness and political
    founding, 52n1
  on women in public realm, 317n48
republicanism, 196, 199
Republican Party, 128, 322, 324, 346
  "reserved rights," 179
revolution, 234, 255, 263n32
  See also French Revolution
revolutionary praxis, 68–70
Reynolds v. Sims, 35
rhetoric, 172

"rights of man," 293–94
right-wing reactionaries, 351n51
Road to Wigan Pier, The (Orwell), 136
Robertson, Pat, 386, 389
Robert's Rules of Order, 172
Robespierre, Maximilien François, 63
Robinson Crusoe (Defoe), 205n32
Rogin, Michael Paul, 270
Romans, Book of, 84n29
Roosevelt, Franklin D., 5, 178, 185
Roosevelt, Theodore, 99, 114n6, 184,
   185, 217
rootedness, 2
Rorty, Richard, 217
Rousseau, Jean-Jacques, 23, 156, 179,
   186, 196, 205n25, 273
Rove, Karl, 14
Royce, Josiah, 162, 163
rule, art of, 357–58
Rush, Benjamin, 45, 52, 62, 63, 80,
   82n8, 83n12
Russell, Bertrand, 231
Rutgers University, 3
Ruth, Book of, 72, 89nn104–5
Ryan, John, 114n5, 377n16

Sabine, George, 193, 203n4, 204n11
sacrifice, 211, 339
  Anti-Federalist view of, 95–96
  Christian ethic of, 74
  family and, 209
  honor and, 331
  love and, 146–47
1 Samuel, Book of, 69, 90n118
2 Samuel, Book of, 75, 198
Santa Monica (CA), 1
Santería, 166
scandals, 354
Schaar, John, 2–3, 5, 189–90n24, 202
Schelling, Friedrich Wilhelm Joseph
   von, 23
Schenck v. U.S., 249, 263n32
Schlesinger, Arthur, Jr., 189n22

schools
  civic education and, 355
  community education in, 172
  as constitutional agency, 267
  curricula of, 360n19
  denominational, 37, 38, 98
  multiculturalism and, 364
  neighborhood, 38
  prayer in, 36, 384
  private, 369n17
science, 7–8
  liberalism and, 213–14
  progress of, 200
  religion vs., 88n80, 101
scientific method, 109–10
Second Reich, 102
Second Treatise (Locke), 209, 224n46
secularism,
  biblical religion vs., 44
  civic virtue, 57
  civil religion and, 58
  education, 63
  history and time in, 234–35, 236
  individualism and, 374, 393–94n18
  realism and, 144
  religion and, 391–92
security, 231, 279
Selective Service System, 258
self-determination, 191n54
self-government, 336, 345, 353–55,
   383, 391
self-interest
  American valuing of, 164–65, 332,
   385
  civil society and, 49, 59, 339
  community and, 347–48
  equality and, 31
  individualism and, 52
  law and, 6
  liberalism and, 81
  military recruiting and, 360n13
  morality based on, 381–82
  Niebuhr's view of, 147, 153, 155

self-interest *(cont.)*
  Progressive view of, 100, 103
  religion and, 50, 59–60
  Strauss's view of, 192
  Tocqueville and, 5, 332
  virtue needed with, 167
self-preservation, 217, 381, 394n23
self-righteousness, 243–44, 323
self-rule, 23–24, 92, 124–25, 175n20
sensualism, 134
separation of powers, 180, 248, 267–
    70, 281–82n16, 284n49
September 11 (2001) terrorist attacks,
    329, 373
sexism, 299, 364, 366
sex roles, traditional, 312
sexual harassment, 300–301
sexuality, 117–18n68, 209, 288,
    379n36, 391
Shakespeare, William, 359
Sharpton, Al, 389
Shelley v. Kraemer, 278
Sherman, Roger, 94–95
Sherman Anti-Trust Act, 300
Shklar, Judith, 193–94
Shotwell, James T., 204n11
Sidney, Algernon, 281n12
Simkhovitch, Mary K., 98
SLATE, 292n6
slavery
  biblical acceptance of, 385
  conflict over, in U.S., 361–62, 385
  constitutional accommodation of,
    166
  family relationships confounded
    with, 302–3
  framers and, 49
  freedom defined against, 28
  inner freedom and, 66–67
  Jefferson and, 50, 84n22, 334
  Progressive view of, 100, 101, 105
  as violation of natural rights, 50,
    84n22

Smilie, John, 165–66, 167
Smith, Al, 114n5, 377n16, 378n31
Smith, James, 383, 394n27
Smith, Melancton, 96
Snow, C. P., 237
social capital, 177n56, 184, 341
social conservatism, 100, 345
social contract theory
  Anti-Federalists and, 93
  framers' view of, 48, 122
  historicity of, 148
  Jeffersonian version of, 115n14
  Jouvenel's view of, 209
  in liberal theory, 59
  Locke's view of, 47
  Niebuhr's view of, 143, 148–50
  political society and, 47, 122, 211
  Progressive view of, 115n14
  public realm and, 82n7
social Darwinism, 152
social fragmentation, 323
Social Gospel, 99, 111
social injustice, 77
socialism, 102, 107, 133, 134–37, 141
socialization, 168–69
social rights, 185
social sciences, 103–4, 242, 243–44
Social Security, 32, 395n35
Socrates, 29, 50, 83n19, 275
Sophocles, 359
Souls of Black Folk, The (DuBois),
    112
*Southern Burlington County (NJ)
    NAACP v. Township of Mount
    Laurel,* 43n80
Sovereignty (Jouvenel), 182
Soviet Union, 136, 138, 155, 258
Spanish Inquisition, 367
speech freedoms, 10, 66–67, 97, 173,
    263n32, 347
Spinoza, Baruch, 196, 205n34
spirituality, 374, 375, 395n42
Stalin, Joseph, 230

state
American distrust of, 168
church/state separation, 36–37, 381
as human contrivance, 148
large, 165, 305
small, 154, 157, 289
states, 339
states' rights, 190n39
State University of New York
(Buffalo), 3
statute law, 268
Steinfels, Margaret O'Brien, 378n25
Stone, Harlan F., 315n9
Storing, Herbert, 92
Strauss, Leo
on American political writing, 194–
95, 204n11
as elitist, 201
on Greek historical sense, 238
legacy of, 202
political project of, 201–2
on political theory vs. practice, 195–98
progress as viewed by, 203n5
on religion and American
democracy, 198–200
scriptural references of, 198
significance of, 192, 194
students of, 192–93, 204n15
Weber and, 205n32
strike, right to, 278–79
student movement, 13, 225n62, 253
suburbanization, 169
Sumner, William Graham, 103, 104,
194, 209, 225n61
Superpower doctrine, 207, 212–15
Survivor (reality TV show), 357–58
Swartz, Marc, 366

Taft, William Howard, 5
Tarbell, Ida, 98
taxes, 92, 93, 170, 295, 331, 384, 395n35
technique, 6, 8, 110, 201, 283n29, 388
technocratic ethos, 200

technological state, 135
technology
community and, 168, 172, 340
control over, needed, 219, 237
dehumanization through, 133
democracy and, 325
economic insecurity and, 334, 387
elites created/displaced by, 343
family and, 321–22
human adjustment to, 237
ideology and, 138
labor displaced by, 137
legitimacy and, 250
liberty and, 7–8
mobility and, 309
Niebuhr's view of, 151, 153
Orwell's view of, 133, 134, 135, 136,
137
political participation and, 7
Progressive view of, 101, 107
socialism and, 136
"third-wave," 324–25
"third-way" politics and, 345
as ungovernable, 171, 190n42
Wolin's view of, 219
television, 10, 169, 173
Tennent, Gilbert, 45, 53n9, 83n12
terror, 154–55, 156
Thatcher, Margaret, 345
Third Reich, 244–45
"third-way" politics, 345
Thoreau, Henry David, 195, 208, 276
Thucydides, 206n43, 233, 238
Tillich, Paul, 158n2
time and history
democratic ideals and, 238–39
distinction between, 229
Marxist history, 233–36
modern creed and, 229–30
modern idea of time, 237–38
prediction, 231
sacred history, 233, 235, 236
traditional history, 232–33

Timothy, Epistles to, 54n32, 85n31, 223n24
Titanic (film; 1997), 341, 390
tobacco industry, 342
Tocqueville, Alexis de, 221n2, 284–85n55
  America's founding date as viewed by, 11–12
  "America's Second Voice" in, 5
  on "art of associations," 136, 221
  on Catholicism, 368n3, 371–72, 374, 376, 377n12
  on democracy, 21, 163, 244, 333, 355
  on equality, 24–25, 277
  on "habits of the heart," 347, 355, 385
  on honor, 319, 320, 321, 322, 324
  on humility, 280
  on individualism, 127, 164–65
  on law, 167, 368n3
  legitimacy and, 244
  on liberty and religion, 354–55
  on majority rule, 330
  on private institutions, 9
  on public vs. private life, 307, 357
  on religion and politics, 362–63
  on self-interest, 355
  on small vs. large states, 29–31, 356
  on women in public realm, 312–13
Tom Sawyer (Twain), 319–20, 324
Torah, 74
totalitarianism
  communitarianism and resistance to, 168
  factions as counterpoint to, 187
  hedonism and, 134
  intellectuals' affinity with, 138
  Jouvenel's view of, 187
  liberalism and, 212–15, 218
  Orwell's view of, 134, 135, 138
  as pragmatism, 135
  state terror as central to, 94
  U.S. as bulwark against, 178

trade, international, 345
travel, right to, 38–39
Truman, David, 224n45
Truman, Harry S., 182–83, 321
Truscott, Lucian, 360n13
Tufts, James H., 104, 106, 109
Tussman, Joseph, 275
Twain, Mark, 4, 290, 319–20
tyrannicide, 274
tyranny
  civil disobedience against, 274–75
  classical political tradition and, 126
  as freedom of the highest man, 218
  as ideal life, 122
  liberty as similar to, 24, 29, 122
  majority rule as, 30–31, 162, 197
  modern political thought and, 198
  social contract and, 47
  socially invisible criminality and, 123
  technology and, 135

UFOs, belief in, 390
underclass, 341
Unitarianism, 394n27
United Arab Republic, 258
United States, 386
  anticommunitarian elements in, 163
  biblical religion in, 52, 56–57, 82n9, 198–99
  change in, 34
  civic morality in, 286
  civil religion in, 60–61
  classical vs. modern cultures in, 127–29, 195–98
  communitarian thought in, 11, 163–64
  as "contract society," 32
  culture of mobility in, 2
  current doubts about, 21, 32–33
  democratic performance of, 332–34
  diversity in, 171
  foreign policy of, 128
  founding of, 12, 44, 195–98, 204n20, 331

future political thought in, 21–22
honor in, 320–21
"idealism" of, 32
individualism in, 164–65
institutions of, and exit from
     community, 167–68
law in, 31–32, 60–62
massive organizations controlling, 33
morality in, 127–29, 386
political participation decline in, 7
political parties in, 186–87
power in, 178–79
public vs. private institutions in,
     33–34
relations with authoritarian
     regimes, 120, 123
religion vs. rationalism in, 44, 56, 120
religious diversity in, 374–75, 385–
     86, 395n40
rule of law in, 181–83
"trans-national," Bourne's hope for, 162
United States Army, 360n13
     Eleventh Airborne Division, 2
United States Conference of Catholic
     Bishops, 378n24
United States Congress, 96, 122, 182,
     189n22, 284n49, 322, 345–46
United States Internal Revenue
     Service (IRS), 92
United States Supreme Court, 28
     community undermined by, 38–39
     constitutional procedure and, 266
     demeaning speech cases before,
        299–300
     discrimination permitted by, 295–97
     gender discrimination cases before,
        297–99
     historic role of, 269
     individual rights focus of, 167
     New Deal and, 181
     packing of, 181
     Pledge of Allegiance rulings, 381,
        393n9

political equality as viewed by,
     34–37
the poor and, 35–36
reason and consent in, 247–48
Warren Court, 34
See also individual court cases
universalism
     Christian, 50–51, 60
     framers and, 50–51, 60, 121,
        205n28
     human rights and, 121
     liberalism and, 154
     nationalism and, 109
     Niebuhr's view of, 154–55
     postmodern suspicions of, 162
     Progressive, 108, 109
     social Darwinism and, 152
University of California (Berkeley),
     2, 3, 13
University of California (Los Angeles),
     1, 3
urban poor, 87n71
U.S. v. Seeger, 37
utilitarianism, 100, 201, 214, 395n42
utopianism, 142, 144, 156–57, 230

Van Buren, Martin, 4–5
Vatican II, 377n16
Vietnam War, 13, 243, 268, 345, 354
violence, 254, 261, 263n32
virtue, 146
Volstead Act, 258
volunteer military, 357
Vonnegut, Kurt, 4, 137
voters, 358–59
voter turnout, 332–33
voting rights, 294, 295–96

Wada, George, 260
wages, falling, 340
Walden (Thoreau), 195
Wallace, Henry, 133
Walzer, Michael, 255

war
  declarations of, 268
  legitimacy and, 250–51
  powers, 250–51, 269
war, state of, 122–24, 147–48, 154–55,
    159–60n35, 209, 335n11
Warren, Earl, 34, 37
Warren, Mercy Otis, 95
Warren Court, 295–96, 315n9
Washington Post, 386
Watergate scandal, 345
Wayland, Francis, 100, 105, 115n14
wealth
  as end, 126
  inequality of, 32, 33, 34, 35–36,
    225n61
  limits on, Christian ideas of, 46
  political influence of, 173, 333–34,
    346–47
weapons of mass destruction, 219
Weber, Max, 143, 199, 205n32
Wecter, Dixon, 80
welfare, 32, 35–36, 38, 331
welfare reform, 345–46
Wells, H. G., 135
Welsh, Elliott, 37
Wertheimer, Alan, 262n6
West, Cornel, 14
West, Thomas G., 205n25
*West Virginia State Board of Education
    v. Barnette*, 393n9
West Wing (TV series), 357–58
Weyrich, Paul, 389
White, Morton, 109, 156
Whitlock, Brand, 98
Whittaker, Charles Evans, 265, 266, 278
Wiebe, Robert, 99
Wilson, Woodrow, 98, 112, 141,
    281–82n16
Winthrop, John, 12, 27, 46, 93, 380
Wisconsin v. Yoder, 37, 175n26, 395n35
Wise, John, 81n4
witchcraft, 386

Witherspoon, John, 60, 394n24
Wolfe, Alan, 375
Wolfson, Harry Austryn, 204n11
Wolin, Sheldon, 2–3, 202
  on democracy and politics of limits,
    218–21
  on liberal politics and natural
    freedom, 208–12
  on liberal politics vs. liberal spirits,
    215–18
  significance of, 207–8
  on Superpower doctrine, 212–15
women
  educational role of, 314
  employment of, 299, 308–9
  equal treatment of, 35, 293–94
  framers' accommodation with
    Christianity and, 50
  identity politics of, 336
  as legislators, 332–33
  liberal reformers and, 17n17
  "masculine" education of, 312–13
  maturity age of, 297–98
  Paine's view of, 69–70, 71–72, 74–
    75, 76
  sexual harassment of, 300–301
  values of, 303, 312
women's movement, 253, 298
women's rights, 106, 293, 298, 310–11
work, 340–41
working families, 340
world community, 154
world cultures, respect for, 169
World War I, 109, 141
World War II, 137, 144, 230, 257

Xenophon, 359
X-Files, The (TV series), 390–91

Yale University, 3
youth, 17n17, 32–33, 201–2, 251–52,
    256, 353
Yugoslavia, 162, 361